Thinking Machines and the Philosophy of Computer Science:
Concepts and Principles

Jordi Vallverdú
Universitat Autònoma de Barcelona, Spain

INFORMATION SCIENCE REFERENCE

Hershey · New York

Director of Editorial Content:	Kristin Klinger
Director of Book Publications:	Julia Mosemann
Acquisitions Editor:	Lindsay Johnston
Development Editor:	Christine Bufton
Publishing Assistant:	Casey Conapitski, Natalie Pronio
Typesetter:	Travis Gundrum
Production Editor:	Jamie Snavely
Cover Design:	Lisa Tosheff
Printed at:	Yurchak Printing Inc.

Published in the United States of America by
Information Science Reference (an imprint of IGI Global)
701 E. Chocolate Avenue
Hershey PA 17033
Tel: 717-533-8845
Fax: 717-533-8661
E-mail: cust@igi-global.com
Web site: http://www.igi-global.com

Library of Congress Cataloging-in-Publication Data

Thinking machines and the philosophy of computer science : concepts and principles / Jordi Vallverdu, editor.
        p. cm.
    Includes bibliographical references and index.
    Summary: "This book offers a high interdisciplinary exchange of ideas pertaining to the philosophy of computer science, from philosophical and mathematical logic to epistemology, engineering, ethics or neuroscience experts and outlines new problems that arise with new tools"--Provided by publisher.
    ISBN 978-1-61692-014-2 (hardcover) -- ISBN 978-1-61692-015-9 (ebook) 1. Computer science--Philosophy. 2. Computers--Moral and ethical aspects. 3. Artificial intelligence. I. Vallverdz, Jordi.
    QA76.167.T485 2010
    004--dc22
                                2009052666

British Cataloguing in Publication Data
A Cataloguing in Publication record for this book is available from the British Library.

All work contributed to this book is new, previously-unpublished material. The views expressed in this book are those of the authors, but not necessarily of the publisher.

Editorial Advisory Board

Table of Contents

Section 1
Philosophy of Information

Chapter 1

    Luciano Floridi, University of Hertfordshire, UK & University of Oxford, UK

Chapter 2

    Hilmi Demir, Bilkent University, Turkey

Chapter 3

    Gordana Dodig Crnkovic, Mälardalen University, Sweden

Chapter 4

    Walter Riofrio, University Ricardo Palma, Lima-Peru & Complex Systems Institute (ISC-PIF),
    Paris-France

Section 2
Philosophy of Computer Science

Chapter 5

    Ray Turner, University of Essex, UK

Section 3
Computer and Information Ethics

Detailed Table of Contents

Section 1
Philosophy of Information

Chapter 1
How to Account for Information...1
Luciano Floridi, University of Hertfordshire, UK & University of Oxford, UK

In Floridi (2005), I argued that a definition of semantic information in terms of alethically-neutral content – that is, strings of well-formed and meaningful data that can be additionally qualified as true or untrue (false, for the classicists among us), depending on supervening evaluations – provides only necessary but insufficient conditions: if some content is to qualify as semantic information, it must also be true. One speaks of false information in the same way as one qualifies someone as a false friend, i.e. not a friend at all. According to it, semantic information is, strictly speaking, inherently truth-constituted and not a contingent truth-bearer, exactly like knowledge but unlike propositions or beliefs, for example, which are what they are independently of their truth values and then, because of their truth-aptness, may be further qualified alethically.

Chapter 2
The Fundamental Properties of Information-Carrying Relations 16
Hilmi Demir, Bilkent University, Turkey

Philosophers have used information theoretic concepts and theorems for philosophical purposes since the publication of Shannon's seminal work, "*The Mathematical Theory of Communication*". The efforts of different philosophers led to the formation of Philosophy of Information as a subfield of philosophy in the late 1990s (Floridi, in press). Although a significant part of those efforts was devoted to the mathematical formalism of information and communication theory, a thorough analysis of the fundamental mathematical properties of information-carrying relations has not yet been done. The point here is that a thorough analysis of the fundamental properties of information-carrying relations will shed light on some important controversies. The overall aim of this chapter is to begin this process of elucidation. It therefore includes a detailed examination of three semantic theories of information: Dretske's entropy-based framework, Harms' theory of mutual information and Cohen and Meskin's counterfactual theory. These three theories are selected because they represent all lines of reasoning available in the literature in regard to the relevance of Shannon's mathematical theory of information for philosophical purposes. Thus, the immediate goal is to cover the entire landscape of the literature with respect to this criterion. Moreover, this chapter offers a novel analysis of the transitivity of information-carrying relations.

Chapter 3
Gordana Dodig Crnkovic, Mälardalen University, Sweden

The dynamics of natural systems, and particularly organic systems, specialized in self-organization and complexity management, presents a vast source of ideas for new approaches to computing, such as natural computing and its special case organic computing. Based on paninformationalism (understanding of all physical structures as informational) and pancomputationalism or natural computationalism (understanding of the dynamics of physical structures as computation) a new approach of info-computational naturalism emerges as a result of their synthesis. This includes naturalistic view of mind and hence naturalized epistemology based on evolution from inanimate to biological systems through the increase in complexity of informational structures by natural computation. Learning on the info-computational level about structures and processes in nature and especially those in intelligent and autonomous biological agents enables the development of advanced autonomous adaptive intelligent artifacts and makes possible connection (both theoretical and practical) between organic and inorganic systems.

Chapter 4
Walter Riofrio, University Ricardo Palma, Lima-Peru & Complex Systems Institute (ISC-PIF), Paris-France

We will focus this chapter on studying the set of special characteristics molecular networks which constitute living systems might have. In order to do that, we will study them from the perspective which allows us to visualize the most basic element constituting that which is living. This approach should lead us to uncover the essential properties which form any dynamic entity that could be called a living system. It will furthermore permit us to understand the intrinsic relationship produced between the handling of biological information and the start-up of something completely new that is revealed in the set of aspects which bear natural computations within living systems.

Section 2
Philosophy of Computer Science

Chapter 5

Ray Turner, University of Essex, UK

That computer science is somehow a mathematical activity was a view held by many of the pioneers of the subject, especially those who were concerned with its foundations. At face value it might mean that the actual activity of programming is a mathematical one. Indeed, at least in some form, this has been held. But here we explore a different gloss on it. We explore the claim that programming languages are (semantically) mathematical theories. This will force us to discuss the normative nature of semantics, the nature of mathematical theories, the role of theoretical computer science and the relationship between semantic theory and language design.

Chapter 6

Selmer Bringsjord, Rensselaer AI & Reasoning (RAIR) Lab & Rensselaer Polytechnic Institute (RPI), USA

I'm a dualist; in fact, a substance dualist. Why? Myriad arguments compel me to believe as I do, some going back to Descartes. But some sound arguments for substance dualism are recent; and one of these, a new argument so far as I know, is given herein | one that exploits both the contemporary computational scene, and a long-established continuum of increasingly powerful computation, ranging from varieties \beneath. Turing machines to varieties well beyond them. This argument shows that the hypercomputational nature of human cognition implies that Descartes was right all along. Encapsulated, the implication runs as follows: If human persons are physical, then they are their brains (plus, perhaps, other central-nervous-system machinery; denote the composite object by 'brains+'). But brains+, as most in AI and related _elds correctly maintain, are information processors no more powerful than Turing machines. Since human persons hypercompute (i.e., they process information in ways beyond the reach of Turing machines), it follows that they aren't physical, i.e., that substance dualism holds. Needless to say, objections to this argument are considered and rebutted.

Chapter 7

Matteo Casu, Università degli Studi di Genova, Italy
Luca Albergante, Università degli Studi di Milano, Italy

The notion of identity has been discussed extensively in the past. Leibniz was the first to present this notion in a logically coherent way, using a formulation generally recognized as "Leibniz's Law". Although some authors criticized this formulation, Leibniz's Law is generally accepted as the definition of identity. This work interprets Leibniz's Law as a limit notion: perfectly reasonable in a God's eye view of reality, but very difficult to use in the real world because of the limitedness of finite agents. To illustrate our approach we use "description logics" to describe the properties of objects, and present an approach to relativize Leibniz's Law. This relativization is further developed in a semantic web context, where the utility of our approach is suggested.

    Timothy Colburn, University of Minnesota, USA
    Gary Shute, University of Minnesota, USA

Among empirical disciplines, computer science and the engineering fields share the distinction of creating their own subject matter, raising questions about the kinds of knowledge they engender. We argue that knowledge acquisition in computer science fits models as diverse as those proposed by Piaget and Lakatos. However, contrary to natural science, the knowledge acquired by computer science is not knowledge of objective truth, but of values.

    David J. Saab, Penn State University, USA
    Uwe V. Riss, SAP AG, CEC Karlsruhe, Germany

In this chapter we will investigate the nature of abstraction in detail, its entwinement with logical thinking, and the general role it plays for the mind. We find that non-logical capabilities are not only important for input processing, but also for output processing. Human beings jointly use analytic and embodied capacities for thinking and acting, where analytic thinking mirrors reflection and logic, and where abstraction is the form in which embodied thinking is revealed to us. We will follow the philosophical analyses of Heidegger and Polanyi to elaborate the fundamental difference between abstraction and logics and how they come together in the mind. If computational approaches to mind are to be successful, they must be able to recognize meaningful and salient elements of a context and engage in abstraction. Computational minds must be able to imagine and volitionally blend abstractions as a way of recognizing gestalt contexts. And it must be able to discern the validity of these blendings in ways that, in humans, arise from a sensus communis.

    Alison Pease, University of Edinburgh, UK
    Andrew Ireland, Heriot-Watt University, UK
    Simon Colton, Imperial College London, UK
    Ramin Ramezani, Imperial College London, UK
    Alan Smaill, University of Edinburgh, UK
    Maria Teresa Llano, Heriot-Watt University, UK
    Gudmund Grov, University of Edinburgh, UK
    Markus Guhe, University of Edinburgh, UK

One current direction in AI research is to focus on combining different reasoning styles such as deduction, induction, abduction, analogical reasoning, non-monotonic reasoning, vague and uncertain reasoning. The philosopher Imre Lakatos produced one such theory of how people with different reasoning styles collaborate to develop mathematical ideas. Lakatos argued that mathematics is a quasi-empirical, flexible, fallible, human endeavour, involving negotiations, mistakes, vague concept definitions and disagreements, and he outlined a heuristic approach towards the subject. In this chapter we apply these heuristics to the AI domains of evolving requirement specifications, planning and constraint satisfaction problems. In drawing analogies between Lakatos's theory and these three domains we identify areas of work which correspond to each heuristic, and suggest extensions and further ways in which Lakatos's philosophy can inform AI problem solving. Thus, we show how we might begin to produce a philosophically-inspired AI theory of combined reasoning.

Section 3
Computer and Information Ethics

Chapter 11

Doris Allhutter, Austrian Academy of Sciences, Austria
Roswitha Hofmann, WU Vienna, Austria

This chapter presents a critical approach to software development that implements reflective competences in software engineering teams. It is grounded within qualitative research on software engineering and critical design practice and presents conceptual work in progress. Software development is a socio-technological process of negotiation that requires mediation of different approaches. Research on the co-construction of society and technology and on the social shaping of technological artefacts and processes has highlighted social dimensions such as gender and diversity discourses that implicitly inform development practices. To help design teams implement reflective competences in this area, we introduce 'deconstructive design'—a critical-design approach that uses deconstruction as a tool to disclose collective processes of meaning construction. For this purpose, the idea of value-sensitive design is linked to approaches of practice-based, situated and context-sensitive learning and to the concepts of 'trading zones' and 'boundary objects'.

Chapter 12

Luc Schneider, Institut Jean Nicod (CNRS, EHESS, ENS), Paris, France & Institute for Formal Ontology and Medical Information Science, Saarbrücken, Germany

This contribution tries to assess how the Web is changing the ways in which scientific knowledge is produced, distributed and evaluated, in particular how it is transforming the conventional conception of scientific authorship. After having properly introduced the notions of copyright, public domain and (e-)commons, I will critically assess James Boyle's (2003, 2008) thesis that copyright and scientific (e-)commons are antagonistic, but I will mostly agree with the related claim by Stevan Harnad (2001a,b, 2008) that copyright has become an obstacle to the accessibility of scientific works. I will even go further and argue that Open Access schemes not only solve the problem of the availability of scientific literature, but may also help to tackle the uncontrolled multiplication of scientific publications, since these publishing schemes are based on free public licenses allowing for (acknowledged) re-use of texts. However, the scientific community does not seem to be prepared yet to move towards an Open Source model of authorship, probably due to concerns related to attributing credit and responsability for the expressed hypotheses and results. Some strategies and tools that may encourage a change of academic mentality in favour of a conception of scientific authorship modelled on the Open Source paradigm are discussed.

Chapter 13
    Jutta Weber, University of Uppsala, Sweden

In the 21st century, militaries are no competing for military dominance through specific superior weapon systems but through networking these systems via information and communication technologies. The 'Revolution in Military Affairs' (RMA) relies on network centric warfare, 'precision' weaponry and 'intelligent' systems such as uninhabited, modular, globally connected robot systems. While some Western forces (and the U.S. Central Intelligence Service C.I.A.) claim that robots help to avoid the death of one's soldiers (respectively agents), NGOs point out the increase of killed civilians. In my chapter, I discuss the deployment of uninhabited combat aerial vehicles (UCAV) in Western 'wars on terror' and their political and techno-ethical consequences. The question arises whether the new military philosophy, network centric (armchair) warfare, targeted assassinations and robot technology work towards the weakening of international humanitarian law.

Chapter 14
    Pak-Hang Wong, University of Twente, The Netherlands

In Information and Computer Ethics (ICE), and, in fact, in the normative and evaluative research of Information Technology (IT) in general, analyses of the prudential values of IT are often neglected by the researchers. Yet, these analyses contain important insights for answering normative questions about people's well-being. In this chapter, I urge researchers in ICE to take these analyses of IT seriously. A serious study of these analyses will broaden the scope of ICE. But, what are these analyses? I will distinguish the analyses of the prudential values of IT from other types of normative and evaluative analysis of IT by noting their unique guiding ideal, i.e. the Well-being. Then, I will explain why these analyses are not taken seriously by researchers in ICE, and argue why they should not be neglected. After that, I will outline a framework to analyse and evaluate these analyses, and I will apply the framework to analyse and evaluate an actual prudential analysis, i.e. Nicholas Carr's "Is Google Making Us Stupid". Finally, I will briefly conclude this chapter by outlining the limits of the framework proposed in this chapter, and then to identify the further research that that to be done.

The conjunction of the disciplines of computing and philosophy implies that discussion of computational models and approaches should include explicit statements of their underlying worldview, given the fact that reality includes both computational and non-computational domains. As outlined at ECAP08, both domains of reality can be characterized by the different logics applicable to them. A new "Logic in Reality" (LIR) was proposed as best describing the dynamics of real, non-computable processes. The LIR process view of the real macroscopic world is compared here with recent computational and information-theoretic models. Proposals that the universe can be described as a mathematical structure equivalent to a computer or by simple cellular automata are deflated. A new interpretation of quantum superposition as supporting a concept of paraconsistent parallelism in quantum computing and an appropriate ontological commitment for computational modeling are discussed.

We start this chapter by introducing an ultimate limit of knowledge: as observers that are part of the universe we have no access on information concerning the fundamental nature of the elementary entities (particles) composing the universe but only on information concerning their behaviour. Then, we use this limit to develop a vision of the universe in which the behaviour of particles is the result of a computation-like process (not in the restricted sense of Turing machine) performed by meta-objects and in which space and time are also engendered by this computation. In this vision, the structure of space-time (e.g. Galilean, Lorentzian, …) is determined by the form of the laws of interactions, important philosophical questions related with the space-time structure of special relativity are resolved, the contradiction between the non-locality of quantum systems and the reversal of the temporal order of events (encountered in special relativity when we change inertial frames) is conciliated, and the "paradoxes" related with the "strange" behaviour of quantum systems (non-determinism, quantum superposition, non-locality) are resolved.

From recent debates about the paper of scientific instruments and human vision, we can conclude that we don't see through our instruments, but we see with them. All our observations, perceptions and scientific data are biologically, socially, and cognitively mediated. So, there is not 'pure vision', nor 'pure objective data'. At a certain level, we can say that we have an extended epistemology, which embraces human and instrumental entities. We can make better science because we can deal better with scientific data. But at the same time, the point is not that be 'see' better, but that we only can see because we design those cognitive interfaces. Computational simulations are the middleware of our mindware, acting as mediators between our instruments, brains, the worlds and our minds. We are contemporary Thomas, who believe what we can see.

Chapter 18

This work is meant to revisit Francesco Guala's paper Models, simulations, and experiments. The main intention is to rise some reasonable doubts on the conception of 'ontological account' described in his work. Accordingly, I develop my arguments in three (plus one) steps: firstly, I show that his conception of 'experiment' is too narrow, suggesting a more accurate version instead. Secondly, I object to his notion of 'simulation' and, following Trenholme, I make a further distinction between 'analogical' and 'digital' simulations. This distinction will also be an enrichment of the concept of 'experiment'. In addition, I suggest that his notion of 'computer simulation' is too narrow as well. All these arguments have the advantage of moving the 'ontological account' into a new ontological map, but not getting rid of it. Hence, as a third step I discuss cellular automata as a potential solution of this new problem. Finally, I object to his conception of 'hybrid simulations' as another way of misrepresenting computational activity.

Section 5
Intersections

It is now possible to grow a biological brain within a robot body. As an outsider it is exciting to consider what the brain is thinking about, when it is interacting with the world at large, and what issues cause it to ponder on its break times. As a result it appears that it will not be too long before we actually find out what it would really be like to be a robot. Here we look at the technology involved and investigate the possibilities on offer. Fancy the idea of being a robot yourself? Then read on!

Considerable progress is being made in AI and Robotics to produce an android with human-like abilities. The work currently being done in mainstream laboratories cannot, unfortunately, succeed in making a machine that can interact meaningfully with people. This is because that work does not take seriously the fact that an intelligent agent receives most of the information he or she needs to be a productive member of society by accepting other people's assertions. AI and Robotics are not alone in marginalising the study of testimony; this happens in science generally and also in philosophy. After explaining the main reason for this and surveying some of what has been done in AI and philosophy on understanding testimony, by people working outside the mainstream, I present a theory of testimony and investigate its implementability.

Chapter 21

David Casacuberta, Universitat Autònoma de Barcelona, Catalonia-Spain
Saray Ayala, Universitat Autònoma de Barcelona, Catalonia-Spain
Jordi Vallverdú, Universitat Autònoma de Barcelona, Catalonia-Spain

After several decades of success in different areas and numerous effective applications, algorithmic Artificial Intelligence has revealed its limitations. If in our quest for artificial intelligence we want to understand natural forms of intelligence, we need to shift/move from platform-free algorithms to embodied and embedded agents. Under the embodied perspective, intelligence is not so much a matter of algorithms, but of the continuous interactions of an embodied agent with the real world. In this chapter we adhere to a specific reading of the embodied view usually known as enactivism, to argue that (1) It is a more reasonable model of how the mind really works; (2) It has both theoretical and empirical benefits for Artificial Intelligence and (3) Can be easily implemented in simple robotic sets like Lego Mindstorms (TM). In particular, we will explore the computational role that morphology can play in artificial systems. We will illustrate our ideas presenting several Lego Mindstorms robots where morphology is critical for the robot's behaviour.

Chapter 22

Klaus Mainzer, Technical University Munich, Germany

After an introduction (1) the article analyzes complex systems and the evolution of the embodied mind (2), complex systems and the innovation of embodied robotics (3), and finally discusses challenges of handling a world with increasing complexity: Large-scale networks have the same universal properties in evolution and technology (4). Considering the evolution of the embodied mind (2), we start with an introduction of complex systems and nonlinear dynamics (2.1), apply this approach to neural self-organization (2.2), distinguish degrees of complexity of the brain (2.3), explain the emergence of cognitive states by complex systems dynamics (2.4), and discuss criteria for modeling the brain as complex nonlinear system (2.5). The innovation of embodied robotics (3) is a challenge of complex systems and future technology. We start with the distinction of symbolic and embodied AI (3.1). Embodied robotics is inspired by the evolution of life. Modern systems biology integrates the molecular, organic, human, and ecological levels of life with computational models of complex systems (3.2). Embodied robots are explained as dynamical systems (3.3). Self-organization of complex systems needs self-control of technical systems (3.4). Cellular neural networks (CNN) are an example of self-organizing complex systems offering new avenues for neurobionics (3.5). In general, technical neural networks support different kinds of learning robots (3.6). Embodied robotics aims at the development of cognitive and conscious robots (3.7).

Foreword

Philosophy is an evolving, open and critic research field. For these reasons, the philosophy of 21st Century is involved into some of the most fascinating investigations of the whole history of philosophical thinking, that is, computer sciences. This book covers the broad range of philosophical topics on computer sciences, from ethics, to epistemology, AI, information theories, robotics or computational logic, just to quote some fields.

From Thursday 2 to Saturday 4 July 2009 the 7th European Conference on Computing and Philosophy (ECAP09) was held at the Universitat Autònoma de Barcelona, Catalonia. E-CAP is the European affiliate of the International Association for Computing and Philosophy (IACAP, president: Luciano Floridi).

There we were, researchers from all around the world, coming from 20 different countries (United Kingdom, USA, Italy, the Netherlands, Brazil, Canada, Finland, Catalonia, Japan, Kuwait, Turkey, Germany, the Russian Federation, Austria, Spain, Sweden, Finland, Greece, Belgium, Norway, Switzerland, Hungary, France …), young and old, women and men ready for the philosophical analysis of computer science. With an extraordinary call for papers response and an excellent Program Committee, we selected the best research papers from the conference and also included the superb researches of the invited keynotes.

In this book you'll find the last and meaningful results on the philosophical debates of computer science, but not only theoretical debates, but also empirical and interdisciplinary researches.

The present and future of our societies and knowledge are completely determined by computer science. We create machines and programs to investigate into the deep space, to improve our knowledge of the remote areas of our planet, to manage our economies, to make life fun (with games) and easy (domestic robots), to make the war and maintain peace, to keep us on a good health, to communicate between themselves (mobile phones, the Internet,…)… Computer science is around us all throughout our lives and at any situation. Even as an indirect aspect of our day-to-day live, they can affect us (remember the Y2K!).

Technology does not mean the end of philosophy, as many authors all throughout the history have claimed for, especially in recent times. From my humble point of view is completely the opposite situation: we can simulate things with computers (like the cosmological big bang, complex molecular dynamics, artificial evolution…and so on with a large list) that otherwise could not be thought with our brains. Thanks to magnetic techniques (like fMRI, NMR,…) we can look inside the minds and change our ideas about its functioning and the relations between body, mind and environment. Robotics makes possible experimental philosophy. Computer programming allows us to create and verify very complex mathematical proofs. Computer resources are the natural allies of philosophers. In fact, these machines are the result of the own history of philosophy (look at Llull, Leibniz, Boole, Frege, Turing, …). For all these reasons, Philosophy of Computer Science, with all the possible different sub-fields, is perhaps the only and true philosophy of our days. Western and Eastern philosophers reached some centuries ago the limits of classic thinking and showed that there not so much possibilities when we talk about the world and all its entities. Philosophy of Computer Science is the next step of the adventure of Knowledge. It is the present and the future of the most genuine characteristic of human species: curiosity. Nothing is better than feel the emotion of the discovery of new knowledge. Obviously, we'll assist to mistakes, dead-ends and errors during this process, but these are the essence scientific spirit: to learn from mistakes and be able to look bravely at the limits of our knowledge. We know that we not know but that we will know.

All the authors of this book are at the front line of research in science, technology and human studies. Unexplored and misty territories often lie ahead of us, but we are confident that we'll find enough light to show us the path to shaping a new future and a new knowledge. As Hilbert promised: *Wir müssen wissen. Wir werden wissen (We must know. We will know).*

I hope you learn so much as I've learnt from all these exciting researchers. The future is now in your hands.

Jordi Vallverdú
Universitat Autònoma de Barcelona, Spain

Preface

Philosophy of computer science is a very young, healthy and productive research field, as we can infer from the great number of academic events and publications held every year all around the world. Besides, it offers a high interdisciplinary exchange of ideas: from philosophical and mathematical logic to epistemology, engineering, ethics or neuroscience experts. New problems are faced with new tools, instrumental as well as theoretical.

For all the previous and next reasons this volume is a very special work: first of all, because it includes the ideas of some of the world leading experts on the field; secondly, because all these experts are not only the established knowledge in the field but also the leading and ongoing research force, they are working in the future of the Philosophy of Computer Science (this is not contemporary scholastics!); third, because young and new researchers shape new directions into the current investigations; fourth, because it includes some brave attempts to change our ideas about human and non-human relationships with the environment.

The book is divided into five sections that cover the principal topics in the field, from the richness of the idea of information (Section 1) to its philosophical analysis (Section 2), the posterior ethical debate about it (Section 3), the specific nature of computer simulations (Section 4) and a final space for the crossroads between robotics, artificial intelligence, cognitive theories and philosophy (Section 5).

Section 1. Philosophy of Information

This initial section is devoted to the basic material of computer science: information. In fact, the idea of information is central to the sciences of 20th as well as of 21st Century, from Biology (the DNA code), to Chemistry, Physics, Mathematics or Philosophy. The analysis of the idea of information from several perspectives offers us the best possible introduction to the field.

In "*How to Account for Information*", Luciano Floridi develops a next step into the philosophy of information studies, from which he is a seminal and leading expert. Prof. Floridi affirms that semantic information is, strictly speaking, inherently truth-constituted and not a contingent truth-bearer, exactly like knowledge but unlike propositions or beliefs, for example, which are what they are independently of their truth values and then, because of their truth-aptness, may be further qualified alethically.

On the other side, "*Information Carrying Relations: Transitive or Non-Transitive*", of Hilmi Demir, analyzes the fact that a thorough analysis of the fundamental mathematical properties of information-carrying relations has not yet been done. The point here is that a thorough analysis of the fundamental properties of information-carrying relations will shed light on some important controversies. The overall aim of this chapter is to begin this process of elucidation.

The third chapter, *"Biological Information as Natural Computation"*, written by Gordana Dodig Crnkovic, proposes a new approach of info-computational naturalism, emerged as a result of the synthesis of paninformationalism (understanding of all physical structures as informational) and pancomputationalism or natural computationalism (understanding of the dynamics of physical structures as computation).

This section ends with another chapter about biological information (one of the key ideas of 21st Century Biology): *"On Biological Computing, Information and Molecular Networks"*, by Walter Riofrio. Studying the set of special characteristics molecular networks which constitute living systems might have. It will furthermore permit us to understand the intrinsic relationship produced between the handling of biological information and the start-up of something completely new that is revealed in the set of aspects which bear natural computations within living systems

Section 2. Philosophy of Computer Science

Second section contains different chapters situated at the core of Philosophy of Computer Science: the construction of meaning and identity with computational tools, which include references to mathematics, logic programming and philosophical analysis.

First chapter of this section is written by Ray Turner, *"Programming Languages as Mathematical Theories"*. He explores the claim that programming languages are (semantically) mathematical theories. This will force him to discuss the normative nature of semantics, the nature of mathematical theories, the role of theoretical computer science and the relationship between semantic theory and language design.

After this deep analysis of the nature of programming languages, Selmer Bringsjord, *"The Hypercomputational Argument for Substance Dualism"*, considers (hyper)computational aspects of human cognition and makes a clear written and argued debate on the dualism. Since human persons hypercompute (i.e., they process information in ways beyond the reach of Turing machines), it follows that they aren't physical, i.e., that substance dualism holds. Needless to say, objections to this argument are considered and rebutted.

"Identity in the Real World", written by Matteo Casu and Luca Albergante discuss the notion of identity and propose to use "description logics" to describe the properties of objects, and present an approach to relativize Leibniz's Law. This relativization is further developed in a semantic web context, where the utility of their approach is suggested.

Timothy Colburn and Gary Shute are the authors of the next chapter *"Knowledge, Truth, and Values in Computer Science"*, in which they argue that knowledge acquisition in computer science fits models as diverse as those proposed by Piaget and Lakatos. However, contrary to natural science, the knowledge acquired by computer science is not knowledge of objective truth, but of values.

After this analysis of values in computer Science, David J. Saab and Uwe V. Riss sign *"Logic and Abstraction as Capabilities of the Mind: Reconceptualizations of Computational Approaches to the Mind"*. They investigate the nature of abstraction in detail, its entwinement with logical thinking, and the general role it plays for the mind, concluding that Computational minds must be able to imagine and volitionally blend abstractions as a way of recognizing gestalt contexts. And it must be able to discern the validity of these blendings in ways that, in humans, arise from a sensus communis.

Finally, an extended number of co-researchers (Alison Pease, Andrew Ireland, Simon Colton, Ramin Ramezani, Alan Smaill, Maria Teresa Llano and Gudmund Grov), explains us how to *"Applying Lakatos-Style Reasoning to AI Domains"*. In drawing analogies between Lakatos's theory and these three domains they identify areas of work which correspond to each heuristic, and suggest extensions and further ways in which Lakatos's philosophy can inform AI problem solving. Thus, they show how we might begin to produce a philosophically-inspired AI theory of combined reasoning.

Section 3. Computer and Information Ethics

This third section offers us a different approach to the Computer Science and Information analysis: the ethical one. After discussing in previous sections about the essence of information and its computational meaning, now we must face with the ethical dimensions of the field.

"*Deconstructive Design as an Approach for Opening Trading Zones*", by Doris Allhutter and Roswitha Hofmann, presents a critical approach to software development that implements reflective competences in software engineering teams. Software development is a socio-technological process of negotiation that requires mediation of different approaches. Research on the co-construction of society and technology and on the social shaping of technological artefacts and processes has highlighted social dimensions such as gender and diversity discourses that implicitly inform development practices. They introduce 'deconstructive design'—a critical-design approach that uses deconstruction as a tool to disclose collective processes of meaning construction. For this purpose, the idea of value-sensitive design is linked to approaches of practice-based, situated and context-sensitive learning and to the concepts of 'trading zones' and 'boundary objects'.

Next author, Luc Schneider, talk us about "*Scientific Authorship and E-Commons*". This contribution tries to assess how the Web is changing the ways in which scientific knowledge is produced, distributed and evaluated, in particular how it is transforming the conventional conception of scientific authorship Some strategies and tools that may encourage a change of academic mentality in favour of a conception of scientific authorship modelled on the Open Source paradigm are discussed.

"*Armchair Warfare 'on Terrorism'*. On Robots, Targeted Assassinations and Strategic Violations of International Law" is the interesting contribution of Jutta Weber. In the 21st century, militaries are no competing for military dominance through specific superior weapon systems but through networking these systems via information and communication technologies. The 'Revolution in Military Affairs' (RMA) relies on network centric warfare, 'precision' weaponry and 'intelligent' systems such as uninhabited, modular, globally connected robot systems. The question arises whether the new military philosophy, network centric (armchair) warfare, targeted assassinations and robot technology work towards the weakening of international humanitarian law.

Closing this section, Pak-Hang Wong develops an study on "*Information Technology, the Good and Modernity*". According to him, in Information and Computer Ethics (ICE), and, in fact, in the normative and evaluative research of Information Technology (IT) in general, analyses of the prudential values of IT are often neglected by the researchers. I will explain why these analyses are not taken seriously by researchers in ICE, and argue why they should not be neglected. After that, he will outline a framework to analyse and evaluate these analyses, and he will apply the framework to analyse and evaluate an actual prudential analysis, i.e. Nicholas Carr's "Is Google Making Us Stupid". Finally, he will briefly conclude this chapter by outlining the limits of the framework proposed in this chapter, and then to identify the further research that that to be done.

Section 4. Simulating Reality?

After the previous sections arises a hot topic in Computer Science studies: the nature and epistemic value of scientific computer simulations. In certain areas of Theoretical Physics, for example, the only way to check some hypothesis is to use computer simulations.

With "*Computing, Philosophy and Reality: A Novel Logical Approach*", Joseph Brenner considers that discussion of computational models and approaches should include explicit statements of their underlying worldview, given the fact that reality includes both computational and non-computational domains. A new "Logic in Reality" (LIR) was proposed as best describing the dynamics of real, non-computable processes. A new interpretation of quantum superposition as supporting a concept of paraconsistent parallelism in quantum computing and an appropriate ontological commitment for computational modeling are discussed.

Michael Nicolaidis, propose a computational vision of the Universe with his chapter "*Computational Space, Time and Quantum Mechanics*". The debate between reality, computation, information and quantum systems continues the debate started with Brenner's chapter, opening an inner debate for the reader about the limits of physical entities (real as well as simulated).

From a cognitive point of view, Jordi Vallverdú, "*Seeing for Knowing: The Thomas Effect and Computational Science*" makes a study of computer visualization processes, especially about simulations. We don't see through our instruments, but we see with them. We have an extended epistemology, which embraces human and instrumental entities. We can make better science because we can deal better with scientific data. But at the same time, the point is not that be 'see' better, but that we only can see because we design those cognitive interfaces. Computational simulations are the middleware of our mindware, acting as mediators between our instruments, brains, the worlds and our minds.

The last chapter of this section is devoted to the ontological debate about computer simulations. "*Computer Simulations and Traditional Experimentation: From a Material Point of View*", written by Juan Manuel Durán, is meant to revisit Francesco Guala's chapter Models, simulations, and experiments. The main intention is to arise some reasonable doubts on the conception of 'ontological account' described in his work.

Section 5. Intersections

This last section includes interdisciplinary researches and also theoretical approaches with are made from several perspectives. These chapters are at the same time a meeting point for specialists of different disciplines as well as a starting point to focus in a new manner our own (field) beliefs.

Always provocative and able to translate philosophical ideas to surprising technological realities, Kevin Warwick ask us "*What is it like to be a Robot?*". It is now possible to grow a biological brain within a robot body. As an outsider it is exciting to consider what the brain is thinking about, when it is interacting with the world at large, and what issues cause it to ponder on its break times. As a result it appears that it will not be too long before we actually find out what it would really be like to be a robot. Here we look at the technology involved and investigate the possibilities on offer.

Antoni Diller makes a different approach to the analysis of Robotics and AI, explaining "*Why AI and Robotics are Going Nowhere Fast*". Considerable progress is being made in AI and Robotics to produce an android with human-like abilities. The work currently being done in mainstream laboratories cannot, unfortunately, succeed in making a machine that can interact meaningfully with people. This is because that work does not take seriously the fact that an intelligent agent receives most of the information he or she needs to be a productive member of society by accepting other people's assertions After explaining the main reason for this and surveying some of what has been done in AI and philosophy on understanding testimony, by people working outside the mainstream, he presents a theory of testimony and investigate its implementability.

Next chapter represents the essence of interdisciplinary studies in Computer Science: from cognition, to philosophy of mind, logics and robotics, David Casacuberta, Saray Ayala and Jordi Vallverdú explains us how to *"Embodying Cognition: A Morphological Perspective"*. After several decades of success in different areas and numerous effective applications, algorithmic Artificial Intelligence has revealed its limitations. They need to shift/move from platform-free algorithms to embodied and embedded agents. In this chapter they adhere to a specific reading of the embodied view usually known as enactivism. In particular, they explore the computational role that morphology can play in artificial systems and illustrate their ideas presenting several Lego Mindstorms robots where morphology is critical for the robot's behaviour.

And last but not least, Klaus Mainzer (*"Challenges of Complex Systems in Cognitive and Complex Systems"*). The chapter analyzes complex systems and the evolution of the embodied mind, complex systems and the innovation of embodied robotics, and finally discusses challenges of handling a world with increasing complexity: Large-scale networks have the same universal properties in evolution and technology. Embodied robots are explained as dynamical systems. Embodied robotics aims at the development of cognitive and conscious robots.

Jordi Vallverdú
Universitat Autònoma de Barcelona, Spain

Acknowledgment

I wish to thank many people have helped me to complete this book. IGI Global had confidence in my project of editing a book of Philosophy of Computer Science. I also thanks to the E-CAP Steering Committee for their trust in my decision and support for the organization of the ECAP09 International Conference. I thank to Luciano Floridi for being at the origin of this project. My thanks go also for all ECAP09 Track Chairs for their hard work, selecting the best among the best.

To my research group, TECNOCOG (UAB), who are working on Cognition and Technological Environments, [FFI2008-01559/FISO], for all their advice and management support. To the members of my own research group SETE (Synthetic Emotions in Technological Environments), for offering me new paths for thinking.

To the Philosophy Department of my university, Universitat Autònoma de Barcelona, my deep grateful desires for their trust into my quality as teacher and researcher. I must also show my gratitude for the several facilities they have provided to me for the management of this book.

Finally, to my family, Francina and Sujan for being so patient with me, so much time closed into my office, sit in front of my laptop for long, long hours. I'm completely fed by their growing love.

Jordi Vallverdú
Universitat Autònoma de Barcelona, Spain

Section 1
Philosophy of Information

Chapter 1
How to Account for Information

Luciano Floridi
University of Hertfordshire, UK & University of Oxford, UK

INTRODUCTION

In Floridi (2005), I argued that a definition of semantic information in terms of alethically-neutral content–that is, strings of well-formed and meaningful data that can be additionally qualified as true or untrue (false, for the classicists among us), depending on supervening evaluations–provides only necessary but insufficient conditions: if some content is to qualify as semantic information, it must also be *true*. One speaks of false information in the same way as one qualifies someone as a false friend, (i.e. not a friend at all). This leads to a refinement of the initial definition into:

[DEF]: *p* qualifies as semantic information if and only if *p* is (constituted by) *well-formed, meaningful* and *veridical data*.

[DEF] captures the general consensus reached by the debate and mentioned at the outset of this section. According to it, semantic information is, strictly speaking, inherently *truth-constituted* and not a contingent *truth-bearer*, exactly like knowledge but unlike propositions or beliefs, for example, which are what they are independently of their truth values and then, because of their truth-aptness, may be further qualified alethically.

DOI: 10.4018/978-1-61692-014-2.ch001

THE NATURE OF THE UPGRADING PROBLEM: MUTUAL INDEPENDENCE

[DEF] nests semantic information into knowledge so tightly that one is naturally led to wonder whether anything else might be missing, in order to upgrade from the weaker to the stronger phenomenon, and hence between their corresponding concepts. Indeed, the threshold can be so fine that one may often overlook it, and thus fail to distinguish between the two propositional attitudes, treating "Mary *is informed that* the water in the electric kettle is boiling" and "Mary *knows that* the water in the electric kettle is boiling" as if they were always interchangeable without loss. In everyday life, this might be the norm and the conflation is usually harmless: it can hardly matter whether the bus driver is informed or knows that the traffic light is red. Philosophically, however, the distinction captures an important difference, and hence it is important to be more accurate. It takes only a moment of reflection to see that one may be informed (hold the information) that p without actually knowing that p. Not only because holding the information that p does not have to be a *reflective* state (although it is not necessarily the case that $I_a p \rightarrow II_a p$, one may also object that $K_a p \rightarrow KK_a p$ is notoriously controversial as well) but also because, even when it is, it might still arguably be *opaque* and certainly *aleatoric* (epistemic luck), whereas knowledge cannot.

Consider *opaqueness* first. It is open to reasonable debate whether a messenger carrying (in her memory, in her hand on in a pocket, it does not matter) an encrypted message p that she does not understand–even if she is informed that she carries p–may be said to hold the information that p. On the one hand, one may argue that she is not genuinely informed that p. On the other hand, one may retort that, if she can deliver the information that p (and we are assuming that she can) then she can legitimately be said to be informed that p or hold that information. The interesting point here is not to solve the dispute, but to note that the dispute itself is reasonable, whereas, if the same messenger knows that p, there can be no doubt that she must also understand the information carried by p. It might be open to debate whether holding the information that p is necessarily a non-opaque state, but such a dispute would be pointless in the case of knowing that p.

Next, consider *epistemic luck*. When asking how semantic information may be upgraded to knowledge, we are not asking what further axioms may need to be satisfied by **K**. For even if we were to upgrade **K** all the way up to **S5**, as we are perfectly and indeed easily able to do, we would still be left with the problem of the non-aleatoric nature of knowledge. Now, raising the issue of epistemic luck serves two purposes. It further strengthens the conclusion that there is a clear difference between (holding) the semantic information that p and (having) the knowledge that p. And it points in the direction of what might be missing for semantic information to upgrade to knowledge.

Regarding the first purpose, epistemic luck affects negatively only knowledge but not semantic information. To see why, one may use a classic Russellian example: if one checks a watch at time t and the watch is broken but stopped working exactly twelve hours before ($t-12$) and therefore happens to indicate the right time $t-12$ at t, one is still informed that the time is t, although one can no longer be said to know the time. The same applies to a more Platonic example in which a student memorises, but fails to grasp, the proof of a geometrical theorem: she is informed (holds the information) that the proof is so and so, but does not really know that the proof is so and so. Generalising, Russell- Plato- or Gettier-type counterexamples may succeed in degrading "knowing" to merely "being informed" ("holding the information that"), but then "being informed" is exactly what is left after the application of such counterexamples and what remains resilient to further subjunctive conditionalization.

Regarding the second purpose, epistemic luck, if properly diagnosed, should be understood as a symptom of the disease to be cured, rather than the disease itself, and therefore as providing an indication of the sort of possible treatment that might be required. To explain how, let me introduce the following thought experiment.

Imagine a memoryless Oracle, who can toss a magic coin to answer Boolean questions. The coin is magic because it unfailingly lands heads whenever the correct answer to the Boolean question is yes, and tails whenever it is no. The Oracle has two alternatives. Either she remains silent and does not answer the Boolean question at all. This happens whenever the question cannot be answered uncontroversially and unambiguously either yes or no. Examples include "is the answer to this question 'no'?", "do colourless green ideas sleep furiously?", or "will there be a naval battle tomorrow?" Or she can toss the coin and thereby give the correct answer by reading the result aloud. Let us assume that there is no significant time lag between question and answer: if no answer is provided within a few seconds, it means that the Oracle will provide no answer at all (recall that she has no memory). It seems clear that the Oracle is the ultimate reliable source of information, but that she has no propositional knowledge. Imagine now a Scribe. He knows that heads means yes and tails means no. He asks answerable Boolean questions of the Oracle and methodically records her correct answers in his scroll, thus acting as an external memory. The entries in the scroll are ordered pairs that look like this:

[...]

<Q: "Is Berlin the capital of France?" A: "no">

<Q: "Is Berlin in Germany?" A: "yes">

<Q: "Is Berlin the capital of Germany?" A: "yes">

<Q: "Has Berlin always been the capital of Germany?" A: "no">

<Q: "Did Berlin become the capital of reunified Germany in 1990?" A: "yes">

<Q: "Is Berlin the largest city in Europe?" A: "no">

<Q: "Is Germany in Europe?" A: "yes">

[...]

The scroll will soon resemble a universal Book of Facts, with each entry (each ordered pair) as an information packet. Now, it has been customary, at least since Plato, to argue that the scroll contains at most information but not knowledge, and that the Scribe may at best be informed (even counterfactually so: if *p* were not the case, the Oracle would not have given the answer she has given), but does not know, that for example, "Germany is in Europe", because knowledge cannot be aleatoric. This much seems uncontroversial. What is less clear is the exact nature of the problem. By seeking to uncover it, we enter into the second half of this section: understanding what the difference is between semantic information and knowledge.

It might be tempting to argue that epistemic luck is the actual problem because, if we were to depend on it for our knowledge of reality, sooner or later we would run into trouble. We cannot be lucky in all circumstances, and, even in the same circumstances, we might have been unlucky, so other epistemic agents might easily disagree with us, for they might enjoy different degrees of epistemic luck, which means that further coin-tossing would hardly help and that interactions with the world and other agents embedded in ti might be utterly haphazard. Yet giving in to this temptation would be short-sighted. Semantic information is impervious to epistemic luck whereas knowledge is not, but epistemic luck is only a criterion that helps us to differentiate between the two, a device used to cast light on the real difficulty. This is why the Oracle-Scribe example ensures that we see that the erratic and unreliable nature of epistemic luck plays no role. By definition, the Oracle is infallible in the sense that she always provides the correct answer, and the Scribe is fully reliable, in the sense that he is perfectly able to record and later access the right piece of information. Moreover, if a second Scribe were to consult the Oracle, he would obtain the same piece of information (ordered pairs). Indeed, the Oracle would be the ultimate Salomonic judge of any Boolean dispute. Nevertheless, we are facing a case of information at most, not of knowledge. If the problem with epistemic luck were that we may never have it, or that we might not have had it, or that we may never have enough of it, or that different epistemic agents may have different degrees of it, then surely the argument should be that hoping or trusting to be always (by oneself) and consistently (with respect to others) lucky cannot be a successful epistemic strategy even in the short term, rather than, when one is actually lucky, that one still fails to win the epistemic game. But this is exactly what we are asserting above, and rightly so. There is indeed something epistemically unsatisfactory with answering questions by tossing a coin, yet the aleatoric nature of the process is not the fundamental difficulty, it is only the superficial symptom, and that is why taking care of the features that are most obviously problematic by using a magic coin clarifies that we are still failing to tackle the real issue.

At this point, one may concede that, yes, epistemic luck is only evidence of a more profound failure, but then conclude that this failure might be related to truth-conductivity, subjective justification or a combination of both. Yet this too would be a mistake. By hypothesis, the procedure of asking Boolean questions of the Oracle and recording her answers is as truth-conducive as anyone may wish it to be. Likewise, the Scribe holding the information contained in the scroll is perfectly justified in doing so, and his attitude is indeed very rational: given the circumstances and the availability of the Oracle, he ought to consult her, and rely on her answers both in order to obtain information and in order to justify and manage (increase, refine, upgrade etc.) his own information states (set of beliefs, in the doxastic vocabulary). He is not prey to some wishful thinking, but sensibly constrained by his source of information. So, epistemic luck is indeed a warning sign but neither of some alethic ineffectiveness on the side of the epistemic process nor of some rational laxity on the side of the knowing subject.

The problem lies elsewhere: the aleatorization of information (i.e., the randomization of the ordered pairs or scroll entries in the lucky sense seen above) dissolves the bonds that hold it together coherently (its consilience), like salt in water. If one analyses each entry in the scroll, there is clearly nothing epistemically wrong either with it or with the subject holding it. What the aleatoric procedure achieves is the transformation of each piece of information into a standalone, mutually independent item, entirely and only dependent on an external and unrelated event, namely, the tossing of the magic coin. The problem is therefore systemic: aleatorization tears information items away from the fabric of their inter-relations, thus depriving each resulting information packet of its potential role as evidence and of its potential value for prediction or retrodiction, inferential processes and explanation.

Consider our thought experiment once again. This time, in order to explain mutual independence, let us assume that the Oracle uses an ordinary coin and that we have no reassurance about the truth or falsity of each ordered pair so obtained.

Each $<Q_x, A_x>$ will now have a probability value P independent of any other ordered pair $<Q_y, A_y>$ (for x ≠ y), that is, $P(< Q_X, A_X > \cap < Q_y, A_y >) = P(< Q_X, A_X >)P(< Q_y, A_y >)$ More generally, the scroll will contain only mutually independent entries, in the precise sense that any finite subset $S_1,..., S_n$ of ordered pairs listed in the scroll will satisfy the multiplication rule: $P(\bigcap_{i=1}^n S_i) = \prod_{i=1}^n P(S_i)$. This feature is somewhat hidden when the coin is magic, since, in that case, each ordered pair and any finite subset of them in the scroll has probability 1. But consider what happens in the process of making an ordinary coin increasingly better at providing the correct answer (i.e. more and more "magic"): all the difficulties concerning chance and unreliability, truth-conductivity and subjective justification gradually disappear, until, with a perfectly magic coin, total epistemic luck indicates no other problem but the semantic lack (if we are trying to upgrade semantic information to knowledge) or removal (if we are trying to downgrade knowledge to semantic information) of any structural pattern stitching the various pieces of information together.

Such mutual independence is not yet a difficulty *per se* yet, but it finally points towards the problem that we need to solve. As Dummett (2004) nicely puts it "We do not merely react piecemeal to what other people say to us: we use the information we acquire, by our own observation and inferences and by what we are told, in speech and writing, by others, to build an integrated picture of the world" (p. 29). Yet, by definition, mutually independent pieces of information cannot yield this integrated picture of the world because they cannot *account* for each other, that is, they cannot answer the question *how come* that $<Q_x, A_x>$. Both italicised expressions require clarification.

Plato famously discusses the importance of embedding truths (our packets of semantic information) into the right network of conceptual interrelations that can "provide reason" (*logon*

didonai) for them in order to gain knowledge of them. Plato seems to have meant several different things with "provide reason", as this could refer to giving a definition, a logical proof, some reasonable support (e.g. dialectically), an explanation (e.g., causally) or some clarification (e.g., through an analogy), depending on the context. We shall see that this range of meanings is worth preserving. It is roughly retained in English by "giving a reasoned account" or simply "accounting", hence the use of the term above.

Aristotle, not less famously, discusses the range of questions that an account may be expected to answer. For our purposes, we may organise them into teleological (future-oriented why, or what for, or for what goal or purpose), genealogical (past-oriented why, or where from, or through which process or steps) and functional questions (present-oriented why, or in what way, or according to which mechanism). Again, in English "how come" captures these different meanings without too much semantic stretching. If we apply this clarification to our examples, when someone asks today "how come that Berlin is the capital of Germany?" one may be asking what future purposes this might serve (teleological question), or which events in the nineties led to the transfer of the capital from Bonn to Berlin (genealogical question), or (admittedly less obviously in this example) how Berlin works as the re-established capital of a re-unified Germany (functional question). "How come" questions (henceforth HC-questions) may therefore receive different answers. "How come that the water in the electric kettle is boiling?" may receive as an answer "because Mary would like some tea" (teleological account), or "because Mary filled it with water and turned it on" (genealogical account), or "because electricity is still flowing through the element inside the kettle, resistance to the electric flow is causing heat, and the steam has not yet heated up the bimetallic strip that breaks the circuit" (functional account).

In the next section, we shall see that the wide semantic scope of both expressions ("account" and

"HC-questions) is an important feature essential to develop a sufficiently abstract theory that can show how information can be upgraded to knowledge. At the moment, the previous clarifications suffice to formulate more precisely our problem (P) and working hypothesis (H) to solve it, thus:

P) (a packet of) semantic information does not qualify yet as (an instance of) knowledge because it raises HC-questions that it cannot answer;

H) (a packet of) semantic information can be upgraded to (become an instance of) knowledge by having the HC-questions it raises answered by an account.

What is an account then, and how does it work?

SOLVING THE UPGRADING PROBLEM: THE NETWORK THEORY OF ACCOUNT

Each piece of semantic information is an answer to a question, which, as a whole, poses further questions about itself that require the right sort of information flow in order to be answered correctly, through an appropriate network of relations with some informational source. Until recently, it would have been difficult to transform this general intuition about the nature of epistemic account into a detailed model, which could then be carefully examined and assessed. Fortunately, new developments in an area of applied mathematics and computational algorithms known as *network theory* (Ahuja et al. (1993), Newman et al. (2006)) has provided all the technical and conceptual resources needed for our task.

The task is fairly simple: we need to construct a network through which the right sort of information flows from a source *s*, to a sink target *t*. In this network, *t* poses the relevant questions and *s* accounts *for t* if an only if *s* provides the correct answers. If the biconditional holds, we shall say

that the whole network yields an account *of t*. Let us see the details.

We start by modelling the network as a finite directed graph *G*, representing the pattern of relations (a set *E* of *edges*) linking *s* and *t*. The edges work like communication channels: they have a set capacity *c* (e.g., how much information they can possibly convey) and implement an actual flow *f* (e.g., the amount of information they actually convey), which can be, at most, as high as their capacity. The path from *s* to *t* is usually mediated, so we shall assume the presence of a set (*V*) of other nodes (called *vertices*) between *s* and *t* that relay the information. Figure 1 provides an illustration.

More precisely, the system just sketched qualifies as a flow network if and only it satisfies the following conditions (where *u* and *v* are any two vertices generating an edge):

1. $G = (V, E)$ is a finite directed graph in which each edge $(u, v) \in E$ has a capacity $c(u, v) \geq 0$. Although we shall assume that *c* could be real-valued, for our purposes we may deal only with non-negative, natural values;

2. In *G* there are two special vertices: a source *s*, and a sink *t*;

3. Every vertex lies on some path from *s* to *t*;

4. Any (u, v) that is not an edge is disregarded by setting its capacity to zero;

5. A flow is a real-valued function on pairs of vertices $f: V \times V \rightarrow R$, which satisfies the following three properties:

    i. Capacity Constraint: $\forall v, u \in V, f(u, v) \leq c(u, v)$, that is, the flow along an edge can be at most as high as the capacity of that edge;

    ii. Skew Symmetry: $\forall v, u \in V, f(u, v) = -f(v, u)$, that is, the net flow forward is the opposite of the net flow backwards;

    iii. Flow Conservation: $\forall v, u \in V$ and u $\neq s$ and u $\neq t$, $\sum_{W \in V} f(u, w) = 0$, that is, the net flow to a vertex is zero,

Figure 1. Example of a flow network

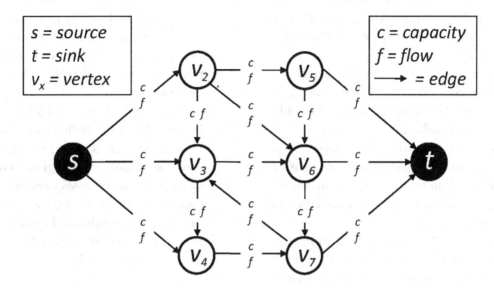

except for s, which generates flow, and t, which consumes flow. Given (b), this is equivalent to flow-in = flow-out.

The next step is to transform the flow network into an *information* flow network A, which can successfully model the process through which some semantic information is accounted for.

Since A is a flow network, it satisfies all the previous five conditions. In order to obtain a rather idealised but still realistic model of informational accounting, A needs to satisfy the following additional conditions:

a) *Single commodity.* This is a standard simplification in network theory. In A there is only one good (information as answers to questions) that flows through the network, with no constraint on which vertex gets which part of the flow. In real life, it usually matters how the flow is distributed through which vertices, but this feature would only increase the complexity of A with no heuristic added-value for our present purpose. Multi-commodity flow problems turn out to be NP-complete even for natural-valued

flows and only two commodities. This is a good reminder that A is meant to be an abstract, conceptual model of the process of accounting, not a blueprint for some algorithmic application.

b) *Single source.* This is another standard assumption in network theory since, even if there were more than one source s_n, we could always add a special supersource S of information linking it to all the other s_n with edges with infinite capacity. By pushing the maximum flow from S to t we would actually produce the maximum flow from all the s_n to t.

c) *Redundancy* $= 0$. Intuitively, we assume that each packet of information is sent only once. More precisely, the vertices between s and t are not real secondary sources but rather ideal witnesses, constructed by means of a partition of the set of Boolean answers possible within the network (capacity) and actually required by t (flow). This because, contrary to ordinary physical flow networks (e.g. water through pipes, automobile traffic through a road network and so forth), in A, s could send the same piece of information repeatedly through different channels without any loss, and this would make it more difficult to quantify it. It is possible to revise (c) by applying linear logic constraints to network theory that safeguard a realistic deployment of packets of information (interpreted as truths) as resources, but it would not be philosophically useful here.

d) *Fidelity* = 1. Following information theory, we assume a completely accurate transfer of information from s to t. This means no noise and no equivocation, as specified in (e) and (f);

e) *Noise* = 0. Recall that, in information theory, noise is defined as any information received but not sent. In A, this means that any vertex different from s adds nothing to the information provided by s. Again, it is possible, but not philosophically useful, to model more complex scenarios, known as networks with gains, in which at least some vertices have a real-valued gain $g \geq 0$ such that, if an amount of information x flows into v then an amount gx flows out of v.

f) *Equivocation* = 0. In information theory, this is information sent but never received.

g) *Processing* = 0. This follows from conditions 5.i-iii and (e)-(f): every vertex between s and t merely retransmits the information it receives, without elaborating it, coding it or even reinforcing it (as repeaters do). Recent research on network information flow (Ahlswede et al. (2000), Yeung (2008)) has proved that, in real circumstances, information can be multicast at a higher rate by using network coding, in which a receiver obtains as input a mix of information packets and elaborates which of them are meant to reach a sink. Yet this refinement is not essential for our purposes.

h) *Memory* = 0. As in (g), every vertex between s and t does not register the information flow, it merely multicasts it (see (j) below).

i) *Cost* = 0. Again, following information theory, we shall disregard any cost involved in the transmission of information from one vertex to another. Network theory does provide the technical tools to handle this problem, by assigning to each edge $(u, v) \in E$ a given cost $k(u, v)$ and then obtaining the overall cost of sending some flow $f(u, v)$ across an edge as $f(u, v) \times k(u, v)$. This would be crucial in any logistic context in which transmission costs need to be minimised, but it can be disregarded here.

j) *Routing scheme*: multicast. Realism requires that s may deliver its information to many vertices simultaneously.

The information flow network A that we obtain from conditions (1)-(5) and (a)-(j) is a standard idealization, which contains all the elements required for our theoretical purposes but does not abstract from any feature that would be relevant. It merely simplifies our task, which is now that of showing how A models the process of accounting for some semantic information.

We have seen that epistemic luck dismantles the machinery of knowledge into its constitutive components, leaving them in perfect epistemic condition but piled up in a heap, unable to account properly for each other. This mutual independence is the semantic loss that needs to be tackled in order to upgrade semantic information to knowledge. We need to restore the epistemic fabric within which each piece of information is a thread. This is what (an implementation of) the information flow network A achieves, in the following way.

The semantic information to be accounted for is the sink t. Using our toy example, let us set t = "the water in the electric kettle is boiling". The sink t poses a number of HC-questions. For the sake of simplicity, we shall disregard the important fact that such questions will be formulated for a particular purpose, within a context and at some level of abstraction. Further simplifying, we transform each HC-question into a Boolean ques-

Figure 2. An information flow network with capacities and cut

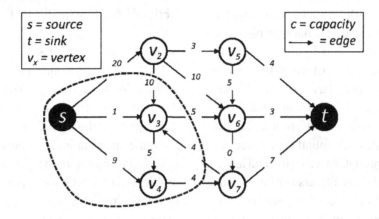

tion. For example: "how come that the water in the electric kettle is boiling?" may become "Is the water in the electric kettle boiling because Mary wants some tea?" So, *t* comes with an information deficit, which is quantifiable by the number of Boolean answers required to satisfy it. In our example, let us assume that *t* requires 10 Boolean answers. Accounting for *t* means answering *t*'s HC-questions correctly, that is, providing the necessary flow of information that can satisfy *t*'s Boolean deficit satisfactorily. The required answers come from the source *s*, but the connection between *s* and *t* is usually indirect, being mediated by some relay systems: a document, a witness, a database, an experiment, some news from the mass media,

may all be vertices in the information flow, with the proviso that they are constituted by their capacity and flow values according to condition (c) above. Following standard practice, and again for the sake of illustration only, let us assume the presence of six intermediate vertices. Each vertex v_x and the source *s* can provide a maximum number of Boolean answers. This is the capacity *c*. An edge is now a vector with direction, indicating where the answers come from, and magnitude, indicating how many answers the starting point could provide in theory. In Figure 2, the edge (v_5, t), for example, can convey up to 4 Boolean answers, while the total capacity of the selected area (known as a *cut*) is 20 + 5 + 4 = 29.

Figure 3. An information flow network with capacities and flow

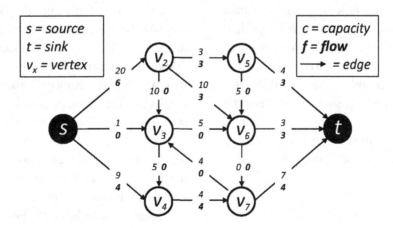

The next task is to identify the flow of information, that is, the set of Boolean answers actually required by t. Information percolates through the network but, ultimately, it is assumed to come from a single source s. In most cases, the source and the layers of vertices have a much higher informational capacity c. This because s and any v_x may be a very rich source of information, like a complex experiment, a perceptual experience, an encyclopaedia, a large database, a universal law, a whole possible world, the universe or indeed our Oracle with a magic coin (recall the Supersource in (b) above). Clearly, s and the vertices between s and t can answer many more questions than the ones posed by t. Figure 3 shows a possible flow of information, given our example. The vectors (edges) now have a magnitude constituted by the numeric values for c (first value) and f (second value, in bold).

If all the HC-questions posed by t are correctly answered by s through A, then s accounts for t and A is an account of t. If the answers are incorrect or insufficient in number, then t remains unaccounted for, A is insufficient and may need to be improved or replaced. Before exploring some of the features of the model just proposed, let us take stock of the results obtained so far.

There is a difference between semantic information and knowledge, which can be highlighted by epistemic luck. The difference is that semantic information lacks the necessary structure of relations that allow different packets of information to account for each other. It follows that, for semantic information to be upgraded to knowledge, it is necessary to embed it in a network of relevant questions and corresponding correct answers. An information flow network of type A fulfils such a requirement, by making sure that the erotetic deficit, which the target semantic information t has by default, is satisfied by the flow of correct answers, provided by an adequate informational source s.

TESTING THE NETWORK THEORY OF ACCOUNT

So far, I have argued that (an interpreted) A provides the *necessary* condition to upgrade semantic information to knowledge. The time has come to deal with a difficult question: does (an interpreted) A also provide the *sufficient* condition to upgrade semantic information to knowledge? The alert reader may spot here the ghost of a Gettier-type problem, with which we may as well deal openly by rephrasing the problem thus: is the analysis of knowledge as accounted semantic information Gettierisable? The short answer is no, the long answer requires some toil.

To begin with, it is important to clarify that Gettier-type problems are logically unsolvable because they are a sub-class of the more general "coordinated attack" problem, which is demonstrably insolvable in epistemic logic (Floridi [2004b]). The difficulty at the root of this mess is that the tripartite definition presupposes the possibility of coordinating two resources, the objective truth of p and the subjective justification of the knowing subject S, which, by hypothesis, can always be de-coupled. There is a *potential lack of successful coordination*, between the truth of p and the reasons that justify S in holding that p, that is inherently inerasable. So a Gettier-type counterexample can always arise because the truth and the justification of p happen to be not only mutually independent (as they should be, since we are dealing with fallibilist knowledge) but may also be opaquely unrelated, that is, they may happen to fail to converge or to agree on the same propositional content p in a relevant and significant way, without S realising it (Gettierization). All this entails that the tripartite definition of knowledge is not merely inadequate as it stands, as proved by Gettier-type counterexamples, but demonstrably irreparable in principle because of the constraints it set ups, so that efforts to improve it can never succeed. With an analogy, the problem is not that one cannot square the circle, but that squaring the circle with algebraic means (straight-edge and compass) is impossible.

Given such a disheartening conclusion, one is entitled to interpret Gettier-type problems as symptoms of a bankrupt approach. The assumption remains, however, that we in many cases we do enjoy epistemic propositional states: Mary knows that the kettle is boiling. So the constructive strategy consists in breaking away from the constraints that make the problem unsolvable: we no longer try to define knowledge doxastically and by relying on a logic of subjective justification, but informationally, and by using a logic of objective accounting. Of course, the new tools require shaping and sharpening, but that was exactly the task of the previous sections. So we are now ready to reap the fruit of our labour: some semantic information t (which is constitutively true), if correctly accounted by an information flow network A, is rigidly coordinated to the source s that correctly accounts for it, and cannot be de-coupled from it without making A an incorrect account, so it follows that Gettier-type counterexamples cannot arise. In epistemic logic, this is equivalent to saying that the Byzantine Generals (in our case the two resources s and t) do not try to coordinate their attack infallibly, which is impossible (Fagin et al. (1995)), but rather join forces first, and then attack, which is perfectly feasible.

Let us now consider what happens to our Scribe. So far we have employed an extensional approach: packets of semantic information have been treated as conceptual artefacts or, more figuratively, as items in the Scribe's scroll. We can now translate them intentionally, in the following way: a knowing subject (e.g., the Scribe) S knows that t if and only if:

i) t qualifies as semantic information;
ii) A accounts for t, that is, $A(A, t)$;
iii) S is informed that t; and
iv) S is informed that $A(A, t)$.

This informational definition of knowledge faces at least one major objection, but, before discussing it, a few essential clarifications are in order.

The first two clauses (i) and (ii) seem to require no further comments, but the third clause is meant to satisfy at least the information logic based on **B**, if not some higher epistemic logic, and this leads to a first clarification. Depending on whether we assume S's informational states in (iii) and (iv) to be non-opaque–that is, depending on whether S not only holds the information, but also understands that t and that $A(A, t)$–we may be able (or fail) to include current artificial agents among the class of epistemic subjects. Since at least 2005 (First International Symposium on Explanation-aware Computing), there has been increasing interest in so-called explanation-aware computing (ExaCt) and more results have become available in recent years. However, it is important to stress that the sort of explanatory processes in question in ExaCt are not the ones that have been discussed here. The goal is to develop ways in which artificial expert systems may interact more profitably with human users, and hence increase their rate of success at solving problems collaboratively by "explaining" their operations and making their procedures and results more accessible. So we should be rather cautious: extensionally, knowledge is accounted information, and this is why we say that a scientific textbook or a website like Wikipedia, for example, contains knowledge, not just information. However, intentionally it seems that knowing requires understanding, or at least that the two are mutually related, and hence that current artificial agents cannot qualify as knowing subjects. They may hold knowledge extensionally, but they cannot know intentionally. This of course says nothing about futuristic artefacts that, should AI ever become possible, would be welcome to join us.

A second, apparent restriction comes with the more or less explicit holding not just of an informational content *t*, but also of a satisfactory account for it. It seems clear that animals do not hold explicit accounts for their information, so it follows that even the smartest dog can at most be informed that the neighbour's cat is a nasty beast, and yet not know it. However, animals do not hold justifications for their believes either, but when we acknowledge the old, doxastic, tripartite definition to be more inclusive, we mean that, as observers, it allows us to attribute to animals justificatory grounds supporting their believes implicitly. But if this is the case, then the same stance can be adopted in the case of holding an account. The dog knows that the neighbour's cat is a nasty beast because we may attribute to it the (at least implicit) memory of the historical account, for example, of the events that led to such belief. Animals do not hold *explicit accounts for* their information but it seems unproblematic to attribute to them both reasonable levels of understanding (contrary to engineered artefacts) and *implicit accounts of* their information, and therefore knowledge.

A third restriction concerns human knowing subjects. It is an advantage of the informational analysis of knowledge over the doxastic one that the former but not the latter allows for a graded evaluation of epistemic states. This is an important requirement. The doxastic approach is binary: either the Scribe knows that *t* or he does not, and if he does, his knowledge would be as good as that of an omniscient subject. This is simplistic and the informational approach redresses the situation by making the acknowledgement of expertise possible: the Scribe might know that *p* better than his dog does because he can provide an account for it, not just hold an implicit account of it. However, a scientist or an historian, for example, might know that *p* better than the Scribe. This because it is possible to agree on a minimal range of HC-questions that need to be answered correctly in order to qualify as a knowing subject–this is what we ordinarily do in educational and training contexts–but of course there is a vast number of further HC-questions

that only an expert will be able to answer. Mary may know that her TV is not working properly because she is well informed about it and what accounts for it, but only the expert will have the right level of advanced knowledge to answer further HC-questions. Knowledge comes in degrees, and insipience as well as omniscience are not only a matter of scope–as we have seen above when discussing the possibility of not upgradeable information–but also of depth.

The profile of a knowing subject that emerges from the informational analysis of knowledge is, unsurprisingly, rather Greek. One important difference, however, is that the analysis links propositional knowledge to practical knowledge (know-that to know-how) in a way that Plato and Aristotle might have found less congenial, but might have pleased Bacon and Kant for being closer to their constructionist approach to knowledge. For it seems clear that knowing that *t* relies on knowing how to build, articulate and defend a correct account for *t*. Yet this is often acknowledged in Greek epistemology only partly and somewhat reluctantly, not in terms of ability to manufacture the required conceptual artefact, but merely in terms of ability to convey its properties. In Plato, it is the user that is considered to know something better than the artisan that has produced it. The informational analysis of knowledge is more engineer-friendly: according to it, the production of knowledge that *t* relies, ultimately, on the intelligent mastery of the practical expertise (including modelling or, more mundanely, story-telling) required to produce not only *t* but also its correct account *A*.

The last comment concerns the potential objection anticipated above, to which we can now finally turn. One may contend that the informational analysis of knowledge merely shifts the de-coupling problem. In the doxastic analysis, this affects the relation between the truth of *t* and *S*' justification for believing in it. In the informational analysis–the objection continues–the problem merely resurfaces by affecting the relation between the correct account of *t* and the possibility that *S* may hold it.

This objection deserves to be taken seriously, not because it represents anything close to a refutation, but because it does highlight a significant difficulty, which is different from what the objection seems to imply, and that can be turned into an advantage. Let me explain.

The objection suggests that we did not really get rid of Gettier-type counterexamples but only moved them out of sight. This is mistaken. The task was to show how semantic information can be upgraded to knowledge and the previous analysis provides the necessary and sufficient conditions to achieve this. The problem left unsolved is not the potential Gettierisation of the informational analysis because–once the logic of accounting replaces that of justification–the condition of possibility of Gettier-type counterexamples (i.e., de-coupling) is removed. Nonetheless, the objection is correct in raising the more generic suspicion that something has been left unsolved. For the trouble is that the informational analysis converts Gettier-type problems into sceptical ones. How can *S* be certain that *A* is the correct account of *t*? This is not among the questions answered by any account of *t*. Indeed, it must be acknowledged that nothing has been said in this article that goes towards tackling this sceptical question. But then, nothing should, because this is not the challenge we had set out to address. Of course, one may find this unsatisfactory: we are jumping out of Gettier's frying pan only to land into the sceptic's fire. Yet such dissatisfaction would be ungenerous. The sceptical challenge concerns the truth of *t* and, broadly speaking, the correctness of an account *A* of *t* (or of the answers offered with respect to the HC-questions posed by *t*) and *S*' possibility of not being mistaken about holding *A*. But such a challenge was always going to affect any analysis of knowledge, including the doxastic one. So, by converting Gettier problems into sceptical problems we have made progress, because the latter problems are not made any more serious by such

conversion and we now need to take care of only one set of difficulties instead of two. Fighting on only one front is always preferable and it is an improvement. Von Clausewitz *docet*.

REFERENCES

Achinstein, P. (1983). *The Nature of Explanation.* New York: Oxford University Press.

Ahlswede, R., Cai, N., Li, S.-Y. R., & Wai-Ho Yeung, R. (2000). Network Information Flow. *IEEE Transactions on Information Theory, 46*(4), 1204–1216. doi:10.1109/18.850663

Ahuja, R. K., Magnanti, T. L., & Orlin, J. B. (1993). *Network Flows: Theory, Algorithms, and Applications.* Englewood Cliffs, NJ: Prentice Hall.

Bar-Hillel, Y., & Carnap, R. (1953). An Outline of a Theory of Semantic Information, repr. in Bar-Hillel [1964], (pp. 221-74).

BonJour. L. (1985). The Structure of Empirical Knowledge. Cambridge, MA: Harvard University Press.

Burgin, M., & Kuznetsov, V. (1994). Scientific Problems and Questions from a Logical Point of View. *Synthese, 100*(1), 1–28. doi:10.1007/BF01063918

Chellas, B. F. (1980). *Modal Logic: An Introduction.* Cambridge, UK: Cambridge University Press.

Chen, W.-K. (2003). *Net Theory and Its Applications: Flows in Networks.* London: Imperial College Press.

Colburn, T. R. (2000a). Information, Thought, and Knowledge. In *Proceedings of the World Multiconference on Systemics, Cybernetics and Informatics,* (pp. 467-471).

Colburn, T. R. (2000b). *Philosophy and Computer Science.* Armonk, NY: M.E. Sharpe.

Cormen, T. H., Leiserson, C. E., Rivest, R. L., & Stein, C. (2001). *Introduction to Algorithms* (2nd ed.). Cambridge, MA: MIT Press.

Devlin, K. J. (1991). *Logic and Information*. Cambridge, UK: Cambridge University Press.

Dodig-Crnkovic, G. (2005). System Modeling and Information Semantics. In J. Bubenko, O. Eriksson, H. Fernlund, & M. Lind, (Eds.), *Proceedings of the Fifth Promote IT Conference*, Borlänge, Sweden. Lund, Sweden: Studentlitteratur.

Dretske, F. I. (1981). *Knowledge and the Flow of Information*. Oxford: Blackwell.

Dretske, F. I. (1988). *Explaining Behavior: Reasons in a World of Causes*. Cambridge, MA: MIT Press.

Dummett, M. A. E. (2004). *Truth and the Past*. New York: Columbia University Press.

Elias, P., Feinstein, A., & Shannon, C. E. (1956). Note on Maximum Flow through a Network. *I.R.E. Transactions on Information Theory*, (IT-2), 117–119. doi:10.1109/TIT.1956.1056816

Fagin, R., Halpern, J. Y., Moses, Y., & Vardi, M. Y. (1995). *Reasoning About Knowledge*. Cambridge, MA: MIT Press.

Fetzer, J. H. (2004). Information, Misinformation, and Disinformation. *Minds and Machines*, *14*(2), 223–229. doi:10.1023/B:MIND.0000021682.61365.56

Floridi, L. (2004a). Information . In Floridi, L. (Ed.), *The Blackwell Guide to the Philosophy of Computing and Information* (pp. 40–61). Oxford, UK: Blackwell. doi:10.1002/9780470757017

Floridi, L. (2004b). Open Problems in the Philosophy of Information. *Metaphilosophy*, *35*(4), 554–582. doi:10.1111/j.1467-9973.2004.00336.x

Floridi, L. (2005). Is Information Meaningful Data? *Philosophy and Phenomenological Research*, *70*(2), 351–370. doi:10.1111/j.1933-1592.2005.tb00531.x

Floridi, L. (2006). The Logic of Being Informed. *Logique et Analyse*, *49*(196), 433–460.

Floridi, L. (2007). In Defence of the Veridical Nature of Semantic Information. *The European Journal of Analytic Philosophy*, *3*(1), 1–18.

Floridi, L. (2008a). Data . In Darity, W. A. (Ed.), *International Encyclopedia of the Social Sciences*. Detroit, MI: Macmillan.

Floridi, L. (2008b). Understanding Epistemic Relevance. *Erkenntnis*, *69*(1), 69–92. doi:10.1007/s10670-007-9087-5

Floridi, L. (in press). *Semantic Information and the Correctness Theory of Truth*.

Ford, L. R., & Fulkerson, D. R. (1956). Maximal Flow through a Network. *Canadian Journal of Mathematics*, *8*, 399–404.

Grice, H. P. (1989). *Studies in the Way of Words*. Cambridge, MA: Harvard University Press.

Jungnickel, D. (1999). *Graphs, Networks, and Algorithms*. Berlin: Springer.

Mayr, E. (1961). Cause and Effect in Biology. *Science*, *134*, 1501–1506. doi:10.1126/science.134.3489.1501

Newman, M. E. J., Barabási, A.-L., & Watts, D. J. (Eds.). (2006). *The Structure and Dynamics of Networks*. Princeton, NJ: Princeton University Press.

Sequoiah-Grayson, S. (2007). The Metaphilosophy of Information. *Minds and Machines*, *17*(3), 331–344. doi:10.1007/s11023-007-9072-4

Stering, R. (2008). *Police Officer's Handbook: An Analytical and Administrative Guide*. Sudbury, MA: Jones and Bartlett Publishers.

Taylor, C. C. W. (1967). Plato and the Mathematicians: An Examination of Professor Hare's Views. *The Philosophical Quarterly*, *17*(68), 193–203. doi:10.2307/2218154

Taylor, C. C. W. (2008). Plato's Epistemology . In Fine, G. (Ed.), *The Oxford Handbook of Plato* (pp. 165–190). New York: Oxford University Press. doi:10.1093/oxfordhb/9780195182903.003.0007

Van Fraassen, B. C. (1980). *The Scientific Image*. Oxford, UK: Clarendon Press. doi:10.1093/0198244274.001.0001

Walton, D. (2007). Dialogical Models of Explanation. In Explanation-Aware Computing: Papers from the 2007 Aaai Workshop, Association for the Advancement of Artificial Intelligence, (pp. 1-9). Menlo Park, CA: AAAI Press.

Whaley, B. B., & Samter, W. (Eds.). (2006). *Explaining Communication: Contemporary Theories and Exemplars*. London: Routledge.

Yeung, R. W. (2008). *Information Theory and Network Coding*. New York: Springer.

Chapter 2
The Fundamental Properties of Information–Carrying Relations

Hilmi Demir
Bilkent University, Turkey

ABSTRACT

Philosophers have used information theoretic concepts and theorems for philosophical purposes since the publication of Shannon's seminal work, "The Mathematical Theory of Communication". The efforts of different philosophers led to the formation of Philosophy of Information as a subfield of philosophy in the late 1990s (Floridi, in press). Although a significant part of those efforts was devoted to the mathematical formalism of information and communication theory, a thorough analysis of the fundamental mathematical properties of information-carrying relations has not yet been done. The point here is that a thorough analysis of the fundamental properties of information-carrying relations will shed light on some important controversies. The overall aim of this chapter is to begin this process of elucidation. It therefore includes a detailed examination of three semantic theories of information: Dretske's entropy-based framework, Harms' theory of mutual information and Cohen and Meskin's counterfactual theory. These three theories are selected because they represent all lines of reasoning available in the literature in regard to the relevance of Shannon's mathematical theory of information for philosophical purposes. Thus, the immediate goal is to cover the entire landscape of the literature with respect to this criterion. Moreover, this chapter offers a novel analysis of the transitivity of information-carrying relations.

INTRODUCTION

Philosophers have used information theoretic concepts and theorems for philosophical purposes since the publication of Shannon's seminal work,

"The Mathematical Theory of Communication". The efforts of different philosophers led to the formation of Philosophy of Information as a subfield of philosophy in the late 1990s (Floridi, in press). Although a significant part of those efforts was devoted to the mathematical formalism of information and communication theory, a thor-

DOI: 10.4018/978-1-61692-014-2.ch002

ough analysis of the fundamental mathematical properties of information-carrying relations has not yet been done. This is an important gap in the literature because fundamental properties such as reflexivity, symmetry and transitivity are not only important for mathematical purposes, but also for philosophical purposes. For example, in almost all attempts to use information theoretic concepts for philosophical purposes, information-carrying relations are assumed to be transitive. This assumption fits our intuitive understanding of information. On the other hand, the transitivity assumption has some controversial consequences. For information theoretic concepts to be useful for philosophical purposes, the semantic informational content of a signal needs to be uniquely identified. In standard accounts, the informational content of a signal is defined by conditional probabilities. However, conditional probabilities obey transitivity only if when they are 1, and thus the informational content of a signal is fixed in an absolute manner. This leads to the denial of partial information and misinformation, which sounds implausible at first glance (Lehrer & Cohen 1983; Usher 2001). Some have preferred to accept the dichotomy and live with the ensuing seemingly implausible consequence (Dretske 1981). Others have tried to avoid the implausible consequence by using some other notions from the stock of mathematical theory of communication, such as mutual information (Usher 2001; Harms 1998). The point here is that a thorough analysis of the fundamental properties of information-carrying relations will shed light on some important controversies. The overall aim of this chapter is to begin this process of elucidation. It therefore includes a detailed examination of three semantic theories of information: Dretske's entropy-based framework, Harms' theory of mutual information and Cohen and Meskin's counterfactual theory. These three theories are selected because they represent all lines of reasoning available in the literature in regard to the relevance of Shannon's mathematical theory of information[1] for

philosophical purposes. Thus, the immediate goal is to cover the entire landscape of the literature with respect to this criterion. Moreover, this chapter offers a novel analysis of the transitivity of information-carrying relations. Until recently, transitivity has been assumed without question. Cohen and Meskin's work (2006) is the first in the literature that challenges this assumption. They claim that information-carrying relations need not be transitive; there are cases where this assumption fails. They state this claim, however, without giving any argument; they simply assert it, which is understandable given the scope of their article. This chapter provides a novel argument in support of their claim. The argument is based on the Data Processing Inequality theorem of the mathematical theory of information.

Given this framework, the chapter is organized as follows. Section 1 is a basic introduction to equivalence relations and may be bypassed by those who are already familiar with this topic. Section 2 is a brief historical survey of the literature. Section 3 analyzes the three semantic theories mentioned in the previous paragraph, in chronological order. Section 4 answers the following question: What are the desired properties of information-carrying relations for philosophical purposes? Lastly, Section 5 concludes the chapter with some suggestions for future research. There is also a short glossary of technical terms at the end.

EQUIVALENCE RELATIONS: A PRELIMINARY INTRODUCTION

A relation could have any number of arguments: one, two, three, four and so on. For example, a 'being in between' relation requires three arguments, that a is in between b and c, and therefore is a 3-place relation. Similarly, 'being the father of' is an example of a 2-place relation with two arguments: the father and the child. These 2-place relations are also called binary relations. Our main focus in this chapter is binary relations, since an

Figure 1. Domain Set

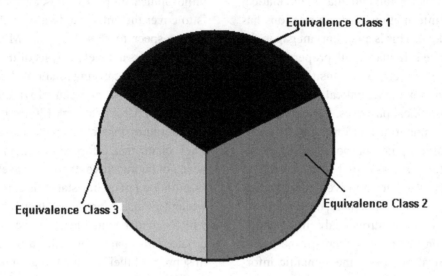

equivalence relation is a binary relation with some specific properties.

A binary relation is a collection of ordered pairs. The first member of the pair comes from the domain; the second member is a member of a set called the co-domain. The collection of ordered pairs is a subset of the Cartesian product of the domain and the co-domain. For example, *A x A* is the Cartesian product of *A* with itself, and any subset of this product is a binary relation. In formal notation, let *X* (domain) and *Y* (co-domain) be sets; then any *R* that satisfies the following condition is a binary relation.

R ⊆ X x Y or equivalently, R = {<a,b> |a ∈ X and b ∈ Y }

When a pair forms a relation, the first member of the pair is related to the second member of the pair. In other words, if *<a,b>* ∈ R, then we write *aRb*. One of the first questions that mathematicians ask about a binary relation is whether or not it is an equivalence relation. Equivalence relations split up their domain into disjoint (mutually exclusive) subsets; they partition their domain. Each of these disjoint subsets is called an equivalence class. Members of an equivalence class are equivalent

under the terms of the relation. Any member of the domain is a member of one and only one equivalence class. This is a desirable feature because it neatly organizes the domain and avoids any ambiguity in terms of class membership. Figure 1 is a visual example of how an equivalence relation may divide up the domain set into mutually exclusive subsets.

For a binary relation to be an equivalence relation, it has to have three properties: reflexivity, symmetry and transitivity. Reflexivity simply means that every member of the relation has to enter into relation with itself. Symmetry, which may also be called mirroring, implies that for every pair (*<a,b>*) that falls under the relation, the mirror image of the pair, (*<b,a>*), is also a member of the relation. As the name suggests, transitivity requires that if *a* is related to *b* and *b* is related to *c*, then *a* must be related to *c*. It may be helpful to state these properties in mathematical notation and explain some of their features.

Reflexivity

A relation is reflexive if and only if

∀ a∈X, aRa

An example of a reflexive relation is 'being divisible by itself'. The opposite of reflexivity is anti-reflexivity. Anti-reflexivity is not simply a failure of reflexivity; rather, it is a stronger condition. A relation is anti-reflexive if and only if no member of the domain enters into relation with itself.

A relation is anti-reflexive if and only if

$$\forall\ a \in X,\ \sim aRa$$

'Being the father of' is such a relation, because no human being is the father of himself. Since anti-reflexivity is stronger than the mere failure of reflexivity, we have some relations that are neither reflexive nor anti-reflexive. For such relations, both the reflexivity and anti-reflexivity conditions fail. An example of such a relation is 'liking himself'. Since some people do not like themselves, this relation is not reflexive. Likewise, since some people do like themselves, it is not anti-reflexive. Like reflexivity, both symmetry and transitivity also have a middle category which neither has the property nor has the opposite of the property. As will be explained in the following sections, this middle category turns out to be very important for the philosophy of information.

Symmetry

A relation is symmetric if and only if

$$\forall\ a,b \in X,\ aRb \Rightarrow bRa$$

An example of a symmetric relation is 'being a relative of'. If a is a relative of b, then b is also a relative of a. Similar to reflexivity, the opposite of symmetry (anti-symmetry) is not simply a failure of the original condition.

A relation is anti-symmetric if and only if

$$\forall\ a,b \in X,\ (aRb \wedge a \neq b) \Rightarrow\ \sim bRa$$

As the condition states, anti-symmetry requires that for no pair of the relation is its mirror image a member of the relation, unless the members of the pair are identical to each other. An example of an anti-symmetric relation is 'being greater than' as defined in the domain of numbers. If a is greater than b, then there is no way for b to be greater than a. As in the case of reflexivity, there are some relations that are neither symmetric nor anti-symmetric. 'Being fond of someone' is such a relation. If a is fond of b, b is also fond of a in some cases, but in other cases this may not be true. Thus, both symmetry and anti-symmetry conditions fail.

Transitivity

A relation is transitive if and only if

$$\forall\ a,b \in X,\ (aRb \wedge bRc) \Rightarrow aRc$$

A simple example of a transitive relation is identity. If a is identical to b and b is identical to c, then a has to be identical to c. As in the case of reflexivity and symmetry, the opposite of transitivity, which is called anti-transitivity, is not simply the failure of the transitivity condition. It states that the transitivity condition must not hold for any member of the relation. More formally:

A relation is anti-transitive if and only if

$$\forall\ a,b \in X,\ (aRb \wedge bRc) \Rightarrow\ \sim aRc$$

Although the common name for this characteristic is anti-transitivity, in order to be consistent with the philosophy of information literature, we shall refer to it here as intransitivity. An example of an intransitive relation is 'being the mother of'. The transitivity condition fails for all pairs that fall under this relation. Whether or not there is a third category in which both transitivity and intransitivity fail is an important question. Some claim that preference relations (*a* is preferred over *b*) are such an example. If *a* is preferred over *b*, and *b* is preferred over *c*, then *a* may be preferred over *c* in some cases and not in some others. One of the main claims of this chapter is that information-carrying relations are neither transitive nor intransitive.

Now we have completed our basic introduction to equivalence relations. In the following section, we will examine some selective proposals for identifying the content of information-carrying relations and then analyze those proposals in terms of the basic properties covered in this section.

INFORMATION-CARRYING RELATIONS: A BRIEF HISTORICAL SURVEY

When we say 'information-carrying relations,' what we intuitively mean by this is that some entity carries information about some other entity. This intuitive idea definitely points to a relation, but it is neither precise nor formal enough to be used in a theoretical framework. Step by step, it needs to be clarified and formalized. Let's start with a simple information-carrying claim.

A carries information that B.

There are two important questions that need to be answered for clarifying this claim. First, what are A and B? In other words, what is the domain over which the relation is defined? The domain could be just propositions or it could also include natural signs. Let's call this 'the domain question.' The second question is about the content of the 'information-carrying relation.' What does it mean to carry information about something else? To put it differently, how could we formalize the content of the relation? It is natural to call this 'the content question.'

The Domain Question

Although Shannon's mathematical work may be considered the starting point of the philosophy of information, his work was mainly for engineering purposes. He clearly stated that his mathematical formalism does not deal with philosophical questions. When philosophers began using Shannon's work for their own purposes, they labeled their efforts as 'semantic theories of information' in order to emphasize their interest in philosophical questions. For example, Bar-Hillel and Carnap (19520, in the earliest attempt of using information theoretic concepts in philosophy, called their theory 'An Outline of a Theory of Semantic Information'. More or less, this trend has continued since then, and Floridi's theory (2004), 'A Strongly Semantic Theory of Information,' is one of the most recent examples of this trend. Use of the qualifier 'semantic' is not just for emphasizing an interest in philosophical questions; it also gives us pointers as to the answer of the domain question. The word 'semantic' tells us that the members of the domain over which the information-carrying relations are defined must have an identifiable semantic content. Thus, the domain consists of propositions. Although restricting the domain to propositions is perfectly acceptable for some philosophical purposes, such a domain does not encompass all possible entities that may carry information. For example, natural signs such as smoke or dark clouds also carry information (Grice 1989). If that is the case, then the domain must include these signs, as well. Natural signs are not the only category that is an example of non-propositional information bearers. Some non-natural signs may also carry information. As Floridi puts it, "when you turned the ignition key, the red light of the low battery indicator flashed. This signal too can be interpreted as an instance of environmental information" (Floridi, in press). Although the red light is not a natural sign, it does still carry information. Floridi calls this type of information 'environmental information.' He accepts the legitimacy of such information but claims that it can be reduced to 'semantic information', which is necessarily propositional. Whether or not Floridi is right in his reductive claim is controversial, but to pursue this question would take us too far away from the general framework of this chapter. Suffice it to mention that the jury is still out on Floridi's claim.

Dretske also focuses on propositional information in his theory of semantic information. He chooses all of his examples from propositions with identifiable content. However, he also acknowledges the possibility of information-bearers without an identifiable content, i.e., non-propositional information bearers. In his own words,

Up to this point examples have been carefully chosen so as to always yield an identifiable content. Not all signals, however, have informational content that lends itself so neatly and economically to propositional expressions. (Dretske 1981, p. 68)

Similar to Dretske and Floridi, Cohen and Meskin, in their exploration of a counterfactual theory of information, also use the set of propositions as the domain for information-carrying relations. Here is how they define information-carrying relations: "x's being F carries information about y's being G if the counterfactual conditional 'if y were not G, then x would not have been F' is non-vacuously true" (Cohen & Meskin 2006, p. 335). In this definition, the entities that may bear information clearly are propositions. However, this does not mean that Cohen and Meskin do not accept the possibility of non-propositional entities as information bearers; they only restrict their counterfactual analysis to propositions.

After this brief survey, we may conclude that almost all theories of semantic information identify the domain as the set of propositions. However, non-propositional entities such as natural signs also need to be taken into account while identifying the proper domain for information-carrying relations. Thus, the conclusion is that the fundamental properties of information-carrying relations must be analyzed for two different possible domains: one that includes only propositions and another

that includes non-propositional signals as well as propositions.

The Content Question

To identify the domain of a relation is the first order of business, but it is not the whole story. The content of a relation also needs to be unambiguously determined. For most relations, this task is straightforward. For example, 'the greater than' relation for numbers is clear and unambiguous, and so is the 'being the father of' relation. Any controversy about whether this relation holds between two human beings can be resolved with a DNA test. In the case of information-carrying relations, however, the situation is rather messy because the concept of information is prevalently used in many different senses (Floridi, in press; Allo 2007; Scarantino and Piccinini, in press). In fact, whether or not there could be a common denominator for all different uses of information is also not clear. Shannon himself pointed out this wide usage of information and also stated his suspicion about the existence of a common denominator.

The word 'information' has been given different meanings by various writers in the general field of information theory. It is likely that at least a number of these will prove to be useful in certain applications to deserve further study and permanent recognition. It is hardly to be expected that a single concept of information would satisfactorily account for the numerous possible applications of the general field. (1950, p. 80)

Given this prevalent and ambiguous usage of the notion of information, philosophers who need to identify the content of such relations can only proceed by providing a formalism for the meaning of 'information' that they use. There have been several attempts to do so. A brief historical survey, starting with Shannon's formalism, is useful for understanding the evolution of these endeavors. Before we start our historical survey, though, a disclaimer is in order. This is by no means a complete historical survey; rather, I included four representative theories. Bar-Hillel and Carnap's theory is included because it is the first example of a semantic theory of information. Dretske's theory is covered because of its scope and influence. Harms' and Cohen and Meskin's theories are surveyed because they represent different attitudes toward the relevance of Shannon's mathematical theory of information. There are several important philosophical theories of information that had to be left out due to the space constraints of this chapter. Some examples are Sayre (1976), Devlin (1991), Barwise and Seligmann (1997) and Floridi (2004). Needless to say, exclusion from this chapter does not represent any judgment about the quality of those semantic theories of information.

Since the first edition of Shannon's seminal article, "The Mathematical Theory of Communication", both philosophers and psychologists began adopting the notions that Shannon develops for their own purposes. They realized the potential value of notions such as information, entropy and channels for solving philosophical and psychological problems. After all, the relation between the human mind and the external world is one of communication, and Shannon's formalism has proven to have a high explanatory power for the notions of communication channels and information transmission. After that initial enthusiastic reaction, however, philosophers realized that there are fundamental differences between Shannon's information and the notion that they need for their own philosophical purposes. Shannon's goal was to formalize the best method for coding and encoding messages for communication purposes. Given these engineering purposes, he had to work at an abstract level at which the content of a signal did not matter. After all, he needed a theory that could be applied to any content that might be communicated.

Shannon's main question was the following: given a set of possible states, what is the expected surprisal value of a particular state that belongs to the set of all possible states? More formally, he strove to determine the expected value of a random r_i where r_i is a member of S={ r_1, r_2, r_3 ... r_n}. He started out with three basic intuitions:

i.   The expected value should depend only on the probability of r_i, not on the content of r_i;

ii. The expected surprise should be a kind of expected value;

iii. The expected surprisal value of an r_i should increase as the r_i s become more equiprobable.

The last intuition is similar to the case of a fair and unfair coin. The result of a toss of a fair coin is less anticipated than that of an unfair coin. Surprisingly enough, the only set of functions that satisfy these three intuitions is the set of entropy functions of thermodynamics.[2] The very first of Shannon's three basic intuitions implies that his theory is not about the content of a signal, but rather it is about the amount of information that a signal or a probability distribution for a set of states has. Shannon clearly stated this fact in their seminal work: "These semantic aspects of communication are irrelevant to the engineering problem" (Shannon 1948, p. 382). In a similar vein, Colin Cherry, another communication engineer, emphasized this aspect of the mathematical theory of communication: "It is important to emphasize, at the start, that we are not concerned with the [content] or the truth of messages; semantics lies outside of the scope of mathematical information theory" (Cherry 1951). This statement about the mathematical theory of information shows the point where Shannon's and the philosophers' interests diverge. Philosophers are interested in identifying the content of a signal, whereby the signal may be a linguistic or mental entity. This divergence led philosophers to search for a more suitable notion of information. Bar-Hillel and Carnap's theory of semantic information was the earliest such attempt. Their theory is based on Carnap's logical analysis of probability (Carnap 1950). Accordingly, the content of an informational signal can be defined negatively by the set of all possible state descriptions that are excluded by the signal (Floridi, in press, p. 141). Although this was a step toward identifying the content of an informational signal consistent with the requirements of Shannon's mathematical theory of information, Bar-Hillel and Carnap's theory had a serious shortcoming that leads to a paradoxical situation. In their formalization, contradictions carry an infinite amount of information (Bar-Hillel & Carnap 1952, p. 21).[3] This feature of their theory, to say the least, is implausible.

Dretske, in his 1980 book *Knowledge and the Flow of Information*, also tried to provide a semantic theory of information consistent with the mathematical theory of information. Dretske's framework deserves attention for three main reasons. First, Dretske attempted to explain perceptual content, belief and knowledge in terms of informational content. In that respect, his framework encompasses a wide range of philosophical issues. Second, his theory is the earliest example of one of the relational properties of information carrying, (i.e., transitivity, playing a central role). Despite its importance, however, transitivity also leads to a controversial feature of the theory. For Dretske, information necessarily implies truth. In other words, propositions that are not true do not carry information. Third, according to Dretske, Shannon's mathematical theory of information is not very useful for epistemology or philosophy of mind because it is about the average information that a set of messages contains, whereas epistemology and philosophy of mind are concerned about whether a person knows or acquires a particular fact on the basis of a particular signal. In other words, philosophical issues hinge on the specific content of information, not just the amount of

information that a signal carries. Despite these diverging interests, Dretske believes that some notions of Shannon's theory could be a starting point for solving philosophical problems. He borrows the notion of entropy of a signal from Shannon and develops his semantic theory of information.

Several philosophers, however, questioned some of Dretske's claims. The first targeted claim was the inseparable connection between information and truth. Some found truth encapsulation, i.e., that if a signal carries information about *p*, then *p* has to be true, to be too demanding. The second target was Dretske's claim about the lack of usefulness of Shannon's mathematical theory. Contrary to Dretske, several philosophers claimed that Shannon's theory could be more useful for philosophical purposes. For example, Grandy (1987) provided an information theoretic approach based on Shannon's mutual information, and claimed that a proper use of mutual information could serve as a basis for an ecological and naturalized epistemology. Similarly, Harms (1998) claimed that mutual information provides an appropriate measure of tracking efficiency for the naturalistic epistemologist, and that this measure of epistemic success is independent of semantic maps and payoff structures. Usher (2001) proposed a naturalistic schema of primitive conceptual representations using the statistical measure of mutual information. In order to see how the notion of mutual information develops in regard to philosophical problems, it is useful to examine this line of reasoning, but because of current lack of space, it is not possible to thoroughly cover these three attempts. We shall therefore pick Harms' framework as the representative of this line of reasoning and examine it in detail in the next section.

Finally, there is one more theory that needs to be included in our historical survey and analysis: Cohen and Meskin's counterfactual theory of information. The importance of the counterfactual theory of information lies in the fact that it does not borrow any notions from Shannon's mathematical theory of information. In fact, Cohen and Meskin claim that using Shannon's insight about entropy and uncertainty reduction, as in Dretske's framework, leads to a doxastic theory of information and not an objective one (Cohen & Meskin 2006, p. 340). Moreover, their theory is the first in the literature in which the transitivity of information-carrying relations is questioned. Thus, in terms of their take on Shannon's theory and transitivity, they represent a line of reasoning different from both Dretske's and Harms'.

To review, in this section we have surveyed three suggestions for answering the 'content question.' Dretske identifies the content of information-carrying relations in terms of entropy and conditional probabilities. In that respect, his framework utilizes some conceptual tools of Shannon's mathematical theory of information, leading to an independent semantic theory in which perceptual content, belief and knowledge are accounted for in terms of informational content. Contrary to Dretske, Harms thinks that Shannon's framework is much more in line with semantic purposes of philosophers, and he develops a theory based on the notion of mutual information. Cohen and Meskin think that the fundamental insights and concepts of Shannon's mathematical theory are not good candidates for clarifying semantic issues; instead, they suggest a counterfactual account. Thus, an analysis of these three theories in terms of relational properties (reflexivity, symmetry and transitivity) will cover the landscape of the literature of philosophy of information to a satisfactory extent. Doing so is the main task of the next section.

THREE DEFINITIONS OF SEMANTIC CONTENT

In this section, we will analyze Dretske's, Harms' and Cohen and Meskin's theories in more detail and also evaluate their suggestions for identifying

informational content in terms of the fundamental relational properties.

Dretske

Dretske bases his theory on the notion of informational content. By using this notion, together with the tools of Shannon's theory, Dretske aims to give an account of mental content, perception, belief and knowledge. Dretske defines the notion of informational content as follows:

Informational Content: *A signal r carries the information that s is F = the conditional probability of s's being F, given r (and k), is 1 (but, given k alone, less than 1) [k refers to background knowledge]. (Dretske 1981, p. 65)*

As a result of assigning unity to the conditional probability, Dretske rejects the possibility of partial information and misinformation. He says that ""information is certain; if not, it is not information at all." Although this claim, dubbed the 'Veridicality Thesis' by Floridi, is useful for some philosophical purposes (e.g., semantic analysis of true propositions; Floridi 2007), for some other purposes (e.g., accounting for mental representation; Demir 2006) it turns out to be counter-productive. Before making any judgment about this issue, it is important to understand Dretske's rationale for insisting on this claim about information-carrying relations. His main rationale is to distinguish genuine information-carrying relations from coincidental correlations. If your room and my room have the same temperature at a given moment, the thermometers in both rooms will show the same temperature, yet it would be wrong to say that the thermometer in your room carries information about my room's temperature. For an information-carrying relation, there needs to be some lawful dependency between the number that the thermometer shows and the temperature of the room. This dependency holds between the thermometer in my room and my room's temperature. There is no such dependency between my room's temperature and the thermometer in your room. The nomic dependency requirement does not directly appear in Dretske's informational content definition. However, assigning unity to the conditional probability in the definition is a direct result of nomic dependencies.

In saying that the conditional probability (given r) of s's being F is 1, I mean to be saying that there is a nomic (lawful) regularity between these event types, a regularity which nomically precludes r's occurrence when s is not F. (Dretske 1981, p. 245, emphasis original)

Besides this rationale, Dretske presents three arguments for claiming that the value of conditional probability in his definition of informational content must be 1, nothing less. Although many scholars have questioned the legitimacy of assigning unity to conditional probabilities, Dretske says that no one has attempted to reject his arguments (Dretske 1983, p. 84-85).[4]. What Dretske says is true. There is no comprehensive attempt to reject his arguments. In this chapter, we will be focusing only on one of them, the argument from transitivity, and will only briefly mention the other two.

Dretske's first argument rests on the transitivity of information-carrying relations. He claims that information flow is possible only if the flow is transitive, (i.e., if a signal *A* carries the information *B*, and if *B* carries the information *C*, then *A* must also carry the information *C)*. He calls this property of transitivity the Xerox Principle. The name is straightforward. The photocopy of a photocopy of a document has the same printed information as the original. The only way of accommodating this principle within his conditional probability framework is to assign unity, because it is a simple mathematical fact that conditional probabilities are not transitive unless they are equal to 1. Hence, in order to satisfy the transitivity property, (i.e., the Xerox Principle), conditional probabilities must be 1.

Secondly, Dretske says that "there is no arbitrary place to put the threshold that will retain the intimate tie we all intuitively feel between knowledge and information." If the information of 's's being F' can be acquired from a signal which makes the conditional probability of this situation happening something less than 1–say, for example 0.95–then "information loses its cognitive punch" (Dretske 1981, p. 63).

The principle that he uses for his third argument is a close relative of the Xerox Principle, and he calls it the Conjunction Principle. If a signal carries the information that *B* has a probability of p_1 and the information that *C* has a probability of p_2, the probability of carrying the information that *B* and *C* must not be less than the lowest of p_1 and p_2. However, again it is a simple mathematical fact that this could not happen with conditional probabilities if they are less than 1.

Dretske's arguments become more intuitive once thought of as a result of a learning metaphor. For Dretske, information-carrying relations are very similar to, if not identical to, 'learning' relations. If I can learn *B* from *A* and *C* from *B,* then I should be able to learn *C* from *A*. This intuitive claim is nothing but the Xerox Principle, i.e., transitivity. 'Learning *B* from *A*' is identical to '*A* carries the information that *B*.' Likewise, 'learning *C* from *B*' means '*B* carries the information that *C*.' These two together imply that 'I can learn *C* from *A*,' i.e., *A* carries the information that *C*. A similar reasoning applies to the Conjunction Principle. For the Arbitrary Threshold Thesis, since the metaphor is to learn, we ideally want to learn the truth, not an approximation of truth. In short, Dretske's intuitive motivation for his arguments is the metaphor of learning.

After this brief exposition, we are now in a position to evaluate the fundamental properties of Dretske's informational content. His definition is reflexive because the conditional property of a signal's content (*s is F*), given the same signal (*s is F*), is 1:

Table 1.

	Reflexive	Anti-Reflexive	Symmetric	Anti-Symmetric	Transitive	Intransitive
Dretske's Theory	√	X	X	X	√	X

Pr ('s is F' | 's is F') = 1

Since the definition is reflexive, we automatically know that it is not anti-reflexive. Dretske's definition is neither symmetric nor anti-symmetric. For symmetry to hold, for any signal, such as '*s is F*,' if it carries information that '*t is G*,' then '*t is G*' must also carry the information that '*s is F*.' The antecedent of this conditional implies the following equation:

Pr ('s is F' | 't is G') = 1

This equation, however, does not guarantee that the conditional probability of '*t is G*' given '*s is F*' is 1, which is required for the truth of the consequent of the symmetry conditional. In some cases, *Pr ('t is G' | 's is F')* will be less than 1; in others, it might be exactly 1. Thus, Dretske's definition is neither symmetric nor anti-symmetric.

Lastly, it is obvious that Dretske's definition is transitive. He builds his very framework on the basis of transitivity. We can summarize these findings with a simple table (see Table 1)

Harms

Harms (1998), in "The Use of Information Theory in Epistemology," undertakes an ambitious task which has two main components:

i. To identify the relevant measure of information for tracking efficiency of organisms;
ii. To flesh out the relationship between the information measure and payoff structures.

For the first part of his task, he offers mutual information as the right tracking efficiency measure. For the second part, he shows that mutual information is independent of payoff structures. Although both of these tasks are philosophically important, for our immediate purposes we shall focus only on the first one.

For identifying the relevant measure of efficiency tracking, Harms looks to Shannon's mathematical theory of information because he thinks that the gap between Shannon's theory and philosophically relevant aspects of information is not as large as Dretske and some others think. As previously mentioned, Shannon's theory focuses on measuring the amount of information that a signal carries, whereas philosophers are interested in the content of the signal, not just the amount. As a result, some philosophers think of Shannon's theory as not very relevant to philosophical questions. Harms disagrees:

It is one thing to calculate the accuracy of sending and receiving signals; it is another thing entirely to say what those messages are about, or what it means to understand them. Consequently, one might think that since the notion is not semantic, it must be syntactic or structural. The dichotomy is false, however. What communication theory offers is a concept of information founded on a probabilistic measure of uncertainty. However, even respecting that information theory does not presume to quantify or explain meaning, there remains the possibility that the information theoretic notion of information can be applied to semantic problems. (Harms 1998, p. 481)

The notion of mutual information, which Harms offers as a good candidate for philosophical purposes, is simply a similarity measure between two variables. It has properties that are useful for defining semantic content of informational signals or messages. In Shannon's formalism, the mutual information between two variables, $I(s,r)$, is defined as follows. Lower case letters without subscripts are random variables and lower case letters with subscripts are the values of random variables (please see the glossary for the definition of random variables).

(Mutual Information) $I(s,r) = - \sum Pr(s_i) \log Pr(s_i) + \sum Pr(s_i \mid r_j) \log Pr(s_i \mid r_j)$

Since the probability values range between 0 and 1, the logarithm of a probability is always negative, and as a result, the second term in the above equation is negative. But the first term, because of the minus sign, is positive. Thus, the highest value of the mutual information between two variables is the same as the value of the first term. The first term is nothing other than the entropy of the first variable (again, please see the glossary). Hence, the amount of mutual information ranges between zero and the entropy of the first variable. This leads to an interesting result for information-carrying relations: whether or not A carries the information that B is not a "yes" or "no" issue anymore. In Dretske's framework, two signals either enter into an information-carrying relation or they do not; there is no gradation between these two options. The situation is different in Harms' theory; information-carrying relations lie on a continuum in his framework.

This brief exposition of Harms' theory provides enough ground for evaluating his definition's properties. For reflexivity, we need to calculate the amount of mutual information of a signal with itself.

(Reflexivity) $I(s,s) = - \sum Pr(s_i) \log Pr(s_i) + \sum Pr(s_i \mid s_i) \log Pr(s_i \mid s_i)$

Since $Pr(s_i \mid s_j)$ is 1 and the logarithm of 1 is 0, the second term is 0. $I(s,s)$ ends up being equal to the first term of the equation, which is the entropy of the variable s. As stated above, this is the highest possible value of mutual information. In other words, a signal has the highest amount of mutual information with itself. Thus, mutual information is reflexive.

For symmetry to hold, the following two equations need to return the same value.

(Symmetry 1) $I(s,r) = - \sum Pr(s_i) \log Pr(s_i) + \sum Pr(s_i \mid r_j) \log Pr(s_i \mid r_j)$

(Symmetry 2) $I(r,s) = - \sum Pr(r_j) \log Pr(r_j) + \sum Pr(r_j \mid s_i) \log Pr(r_j \mid s_i)$

Since it only takes basic knowledge of algebra and probability to show that these equations are equal to each other, we leave the proof to the interested reader and conclude that mutual information is a symmetric notion.

Whether or not mutual information is transitive is a bit more complicated than determining symmetry and reflexivity. Under special circumstances, it turns out to be transitive. But in most cases, it is not transitive. This fact is a corollary of the Data Processing Inequality theorem of the mathematical theory of communication.

Data Processing Inequality Theorem: If there is an information flow from A to C through B, then the mutual information between A and B is greater than or equal to the mutual information between A and C. More formally:

If $A \rightarrow B \rightarrow C$ then $I(A,B) \geq I(A,C)$. (Cover 1991, p. 32)[5]

For transitivity to hold for mutual information, if A carries information that B, and B carries information that C, then A has to carry information that C. In other words, the mutual information between A and B needs to be equal to the mutual information between A and C. As the theorem

Table 2.

	Reflexive	Anti-Reflexive	Symmetric	Anti-Symmetric	Transitive	Intransitive
Dretske's Theory	√	X	X	X	√	X
Harms' Theory	√	X	√	X	X	X

suggests, equality happens only in some cases; in other cases, *I(A, C)* turns out to be smaller than *I(A, B)*. Thus, mutual information is transitive only in some cases, but not in others.

Now, let's expand our summary table (see Table 2) from the previous section with our new findings.

Cohen and Meskin

Cohen and Meskin, in their 2006 article, "An Objective Counterfactual Theory of Information," explore an alternative route for defining informational content. Their motivation for seeking an alternative is to avoid using the notion of conditional probabilities. As we saw in the previous sections, both Dretske and Harms appeal to conditional probabilities in their definitions of informational content. In fact, this has been the standard approach since Shannon. Appeals to conditional probabilities, however, come with many problems related to the notion of probability and its interpretations.[6] Cohen and Meskin suggest a radically different alternative that appeals to counterfactuals instead of probabilities.

In their paper, Cohen and Meskin begin with a crude version of their counterfactual theory, and then revise it by adding a non-vacuousness clause to avoid some difficulties concerning necessary truths. For both the crude and revised accounts, they present one weak and one strong version. The weak versions take the counterfactual criterion as only a sufficient condition for information-carrying relations, whereas the strong versions take it as both necessary and sufficient. The difference between their strong and weak versions

is irrelevant for our purposes. Hence, for the sake of simplicity, we shall state only the weak version of their claim:

x's being F carries information about y's being G if the counterfactual conditional 'if y were not G, then x would not have been F' is non-vacuously true. (Cohen & Meskin 2006, p. 335)

The non-vacuousness clause excludes assigning the information-carrying relation to cases where *y's being G* is necessarily true. If *y's being G* is necessarily true, then the counterfactual will prove to be true no matter what; hence, the counterfactual will be vacuously true. Following the generally accepted intuition that necessary truths carry no information at all,[7] Cohen and Meskin aim to exclude necessary truths from the set of information-carrying signals by adding the non-vacuousness clause. Cohen and Meskin argue that the counterfactual theory of information may be preferable to the standard approaches. Leaving aside the issue of whether or not their claim is true, we shall proceed to analyze the properties of their counterfactual definition.

Since the information-carrying relation is determined by a conditional in Cohen and Meskin's framework, the relation automatically becomes reflexive. Any conditional, for which the antecedent and the consequent are the same propositions, is always true.

For symmetry, we have to assume that one signal, say, *x's being F*, carries information about another signal, say, *y's being G*. This assumption leads to the truth of the following counterfactual:

(Counterfactual 1) 'If y were not G, then x would not have been F' is non-vacuously true.'

If this conditional implies its converse, then symmetry holds for Cohen and Meskin's counterfactual definition; otherwise, it does not. The converse claim is the following:

(Counterfactual 2) 'If x were not F, then y would not have been G' is non-vacuously true.'

The standard semantics for evaluating the truth condition of counterfactuals is Lewis' possible worlds (Lewis 1973; also see the Glossary). In Lewis' semantics, the first counterfactual is true if and only if in the closest world where *y is not G*, *x is not F*. Let's call this world w_1. For the second counterfactual to be true, in the closest world where *x is not F*, *y must be not G*. Let's call this world w_2. The truth condition of the first counterfactual does not guarantee the truth condition of the second counterfactual, because there could be a world closer than w_2 where *x is not F* and yet *y is G*. In some cases, by coincidence, w_2 might turn out to be the closest to the actual world, but this is not necessarily the case. Thus, the counterfactual definition is neither symmetric nor anti-symmetric.

It is a well-established fact that counterfactual conditionals are not transitive.[8] The simplest way of seeing this fact is to evaluate the validity of the following inference schema:

- A counterfactually implies B.
- B counterfactually implies C.

Therefore,

- A counterfactually implies C.

This inference is NOT valid because the closest possible A-world may not be a C-world, given that the closest possible A-world is a B-world and the closest possible B-world is a C-world. So even if the conclusion follows from the premises in some cases, there could be other cases in which it does not. Thus, the counterfactual definition of information-carrying relations is neither transitive nor intransitive. In Cohen and Meskin's own words,

[The counterfactual] account implies that the information-carrying relation is non-transitive, it does not imply that the information-carrying relation is intransitive. Our account denies that information-carrying is transitive tout court, but it allows that in many (but not all) cases information may flow from one event to another along a chain of communication. (Cohen & Meskin 2006, p. 340)

We could complete our summary table (see Table 3) by adding the results of the analysis of Cohen and Meskin's counterfactual theory.

As the above table suggests, there is a consensus about reflexivity. This is only to be expected because, after all, a signal, if it has some informational content, will carry information about its own content. The disagreement, however, arises in the cases of symmetry and transitivity. The next section focuses on this disagreement.

Table 3.

	Reflexive	Anti-Reflexive	Symmetric	Anti-Symmetric	Transitive	Intransitive
Dretske's Theory	√	X	X	X	√	X
Harms' Theory	√	X	√	X	X	X
C & M's Theory	√	X	X	X	X	X

INFORMATION-CARRYING RELATIONS: A GENERAL ANALYSIS

Among the three theories analyzed above, only Harms' theory is symmetric. Symmetry, although it provides neat mathematical features, may not be a desirable feature for some philosophical purposes. One of the long-standing projects in philosophy of mind is to give a naturalistic account of mental representation. The notion of information seems to be a promising candidate for the foundation of such a naturalistic account,[9] because, after all, a mental state acquires information from a state of affairs in the world, and thus carries information about that state of affairs. If this simple intuition is right, however, the required information-carrying relation needs to be not symmetric. My mental state that represents a dog carries information about the dog in my yard, but the dog in my yard does not carry information about my mental state. Of course, the dog in the yard causes my mental state, but it would be wrong to claim that it carries information about my mental state. In other words, information-carrying relations are different than causal relations. For the goal at hand, i.e., to account for mental representation, any symmetric notion of informational content fails to do the job. A similar story could easily be told for linguistic representation as well. Thus, ideally, we want a non-symmetric conceptualization of information-carrying relations, especially for explaining mental and linguistic representation.

After this short analysis, one may conclude that Harms' claim about the relevance of Shannon's theory for philosophical purposes is wrong (please see the quotation in Section 3.2.). However, this would be too quick of a judgment, because there may be some other notions within the rich repertoire of the mathematical theory of information that may serve better for Harms' theory. In fact, there is a very good candidate that has all the desired features of mutual information without being symmetric: it is the Kullback-Leibler divergence

measure. Further research is needed for evaluating the plausibility of this measure.

For assessing whether or not transitivity is a desired feature for information-carrying relations, the Data Processing Inequality theorem, as stated in Section 3.2., is crucial. For the ease of readers, let us state the theorem once again:

Data Processing Inequality Theorem: *If $A \rightarrow B \rightarrow C$ then $I(A,B) \geq I(A,C)$*

Transitivity holds only for the equality condition in the greater than or equal to relation between $I(A, B)$ and $I(A, C)$. For other cases, transitivity fails. The equality condition occurs only if the chain formed by the information from A to C through B ($A \rightarrow B \rightarrow C$) is a Markov chain[10]. A Markov chain occurs when the conditional distribution of C depends only on B and is independent of A. Obviously, this is a very strict constraint, and it is rarely true in real life information channels. If this constraint is not fulfilled, then the probability of having equality becomes lower and lower as the chain of information flow becomes longer. Hence, transitivity is valid only in idealized cases. Once again, it should be noted that transitivity corresponds to the equality between $I(A,B)$ and $I(A,C)$ in the data processing equality theorem, not the greater than relation.

Markov chains, i.e., informational chains where only the two subsequent members of the chain conditionally depend on each other, are not strong enough to exploit the statistical regularities that may exist in an informational source. Shannon, in his seminal article, "The Mathematical Theory of Communication", showed the importance of longer conditional dependencies in a sequence for exploiting the statistical regularities in an informational source (Shannon 1948, p.413-416). The informational source that he chose was English. As it is known, some letters are more frequent than others in English. This is the main reason for assigning the highest point value to the letter

Table 4. Improvement index

	Meaningful Sequences (MS)	Length of MS	Total Length	Success Index	% Increase
1ˢᵗ Order	-	0	72	0	NA
2ⁿᵈ Order	ON, ARE, BE, AT, ANDY	13	118	0.11	NA
3ʳᵈ Order	IN, NO, IN NO, WHEY, OF, OF, THE, OF THE, IS OF	30	108	0.28	154%

Q in Scrabble; it is the least frequently used letter in the English language. This is an important statistical regularity of English, but not the only one. There are also patterns depending on the previous letters that occur in a sequence. For example, the probability of having an 'S' after an 'I' is different than the probability of having a 'C' after an 'I.' Similarly, the probability of having a 'U' after the sequence 'YO' is different than the probability of having an 'R.' Shannon used these statistical patterns in sequence in order to produce intelligible sequences in English without feeding any extra rule to the sequence-producing mechanism. For all sequences, he assumed a 27-symbol alphabet, the 26 letters and a blank. In the first sequence, he used only the occurrence frequencies of letters; he called this "first-order approximation." The idea behind the process by which he produced the sequence can be thought of in the following way. Imagine a 27-sided die upon which each side is biased according to its occurrence frequency. Then, by simply rolling the die at each step, one decides the symbol that should appear for that step. The output of his first sequence where only letter frequencies are used is the following:

- First-Order Approximation

    OCRO HLI RGWR NMIELWIS EU LL NBNESEBYA TH EEI ALHENHTTPA OOBTTVA NAH BRL.

For the second sequence, the frequencies that he used were the frequency of a letter given the letter that comes just before E. That is to say, instead of using the simple occurrence frequency of the letter E, he used the conditional frequency of E given the previous letter. For example, if the previous letter were K, then he used the occurrence frequency of E given K. This is his second-order approximation.

- Second-Order Approximation

    ON IE ANTSOUTINYS ARE T INCTORE ST BE S DEAMY ACHIN D ILONASIVE TUCOOWE AT TEASONARE FUSO TIZIN ANDY TOBE SEACE CTISBE.

In the third-order approximation, he used the occurrence frequencies of letters given the previous two letters instead of one.

- Third-Order Approximation

    IN NO IST LAT WHEY CRATICT FROURE BIRS GROCID PONDENOME OF DEMONSTURES OF THE REPTAGIN IS REGOACTIONA OF CRE.

There is an improvement from the second-order approximation to the third-order. This improvement may not seem significant at first glance. However, when measured quantitatively, the third-order approximation almost triples the success of the second-order approximation. Unfortunately, Shannon did not provide such a quantitative success index, because for his purposes the improvement was noticeable enough. A simple success index that can be used is the ratio of the length of the meaningful sequence to the

Table 5.

	Reflexive	Anti-Reflexive	Symmetric	Anti-Symmetric	Transitive	Intransitive
Dretske's Theory	√	X	X	X	√	X
Harms' Theory	√	X	√	X	X	X
C & M's Theory	√	X	X	X	X	X
Ideal Expectation	√	X	X	X	X	X

length of the entire sequence. The success index values calculated accordingly are shown in Table 4. The index value of the third-order approximation is equal to 2 ½ times the index value of the second-order approximation. That is to say, there is a significant improvement from the second to the third order, and the level of improvement increases exponentially when one moves to higher order approximations such as the fourth-order, the fifth-order and so on.

In short, the sequence of English letters becomes much more meaningful when one increases the length of the dependencies in conditional probabilities. In other words, a successful use of statistical regularities requires longer informational chains in which the conditional probability of an entity depends not just on the previously occurring one, but on several others that come before that entity. Shannon's second-order approximation, conditional probabilities given just the previous letter, corresponds to the idea of Markov chains as mentioned above. Dretske's insistence on transitivity presumes a Markov chain and hence stops at the second-order approximation level. However, the amount of information that one can exploit from an informational source by a Markov chain is very limited, as shown in Shannon's second-order approximation. Most of the informational sources (for example, natural languages and the external world) are much richer, and to exploit such richness one needs to extend dependencies beyond the limits of a Markov chain. As Table 4 shows, even going one order level up from a strict Markov chain significantly increases the ability

to exploit regularities in an informational source. Hence, transitivity is not a desirable feature for such purposes.

In this section, we have concluded that a non-symmetric and non-transitive approach to identifying the content of information-carrying relations will serve better for some philosophical purposes. This means that an information-carrying relation is not an equivalence relation. Although equivalence is needed for a neatly organized domain of informational entities, it turns out that reality is much messier than we would like it to be. Let's add these findings into our summary table (see Table) for a complete visual depiction.

CONCLUSION

In this chapter, we have completed a comprehensive analysis of information-carrying relations in terms of fundamental mathematical properties: reflexivity, symmetry and transitivity. As Table 5 above depicts, a reflexive, non-symmetric and non-transitive content definition is better suited for philosophical purposes. Given this, it looks as though Cohen and Meskin's counterfactual theory of semantic information is the best available candidate for the philosopher's ideal expectation. This result, however, needs to be taken with a grain of salt, because Cohen and Meskin's theory completely avoids Shannon's formalism. Shannon's mathematical theory of information has proven to have a high explanatory power for the technical features of information flow. The main motivation for using information-theoretic notions for solving philosophical problems was to exploit this explanatory power. Cohen and Meskin's counterfactual theory does not have this benefit because it avoids Shannon's formalism. Whether or not this is a price worth paying is an important question that requires further research.

Although the chapter provides a thorough analysis of the issue at hand, it does, by necessity, leave some questions unanswered. Attempting to answer these questions will be an essential part of the future trends in the literature. For now, let us state three of these questions as suggestions for future research:

i.   What is the role of non-propositional information bearers for the philosophically relevant analysis of information flow?

ii. Is there a non-symmetric notion within the repertoires of the mathematical theory of information that successfully accounts for information measure and payoff structures, as Harms' theory does? As suggested above, the Kullback-Leibler divergence measure seems to be a good candidate for this purpose and it needs to be analyzed from this perspective.

iii. Is it possible to provide a probabilistic version of Dretske's informational content? A probabilistic version of Dretske's definition would carry the exact definition without assigning unity to conditional probabilities. In this way, some of the seemingly implausible consequences of assigning unity would be avoided.

'If A had been the case, C would have been the case' is true (at a world w) iff (1) there are no possible A-worlds (in which case it is vacuous), or (2) some A-world where C holds is closer (to w) than is any A-world C does not hold (Lewis 1973, p. 560).

REFERENCES

Allo, P. (2007). Logical pluralism and semantic information. *Journal of Philosophical Logic, 36*(4), 659–694. doi:10.1007/s10992-007-9054-2

Bar-Hillel, Y., & Carnap, R. (1952). *An outline of a theory semantic information* (Tech. Rep. No. 247). Cambridge, MA: Massachusetts Institute of Technology, Research Laboratory of Electronics.

Barwise, J., & Seligman, J. (1997). *Information Flow: The Logic of Distributed Systems.* Cambridge, UK: Cambridge University Press.

Bremer, M. E. (2003). Do Logical Truths Carry Information? *Minds and Machines, 13,* 567–575. doi:10.1023/A:1026256918837

Brogaard, B., & Salerno, J. (2008). Counterfactuals and context. *Analysis, 68,* 39–45. doi:10.1093/analys/68.1.39

Carnap, R. (1950). *Logical Foundations of Probability.* Chicago, IL: University of Chicago Press.

Cherry, C. E. (1951). A History of the Theory of Information. In *Proceedings of the Instiute of Electrical Engineers, 98.*

Cohen, J., & Meskin, A. (2006). An Objective Counterfactual Theory of Information. *Australasian Journal of Philosophy, 84,* 333–352. doi:10.1080/00048400600895821

Demir, H. (2006). *Error Comes with Imagination: A Probabilistic Theory of Mental Content.* Unpublished doctoral dissertation, Indiana University, Bloomington, Indiana.

Demir, H. (2008). Counterfactuals vs. conditional probabilities: A critical analysis of the counterfactual theory of information. *Australasian Journal of Philosophy, 86*(1), 45–60. doi:10.1080/00048400701846541

Devlin, K. J. (1991). *Logic and Information.* Cambridge, UK: Cambridge University Press.

Dietrich, E. (2007). Representation . In Thagard, P. (Ed.), *Handbook of Philosophy of Science: Philosophy of Psychology and Cognitive Science* (pp. 1–30). Amsterdam: Elsevier. doi:10.1016/B978-044451540-7/50018-9

Dretske, F. (1981). *Knowledge and the flow of information*. Cambridge, MA: MIT Press.

Dretske, F. (1983). Precis of Knowledge and the flow of the information. *The Behavioral and Brain Sciences*, 6, 55–63. doi:10.1017/S0140525X00014631

Floridi, L. (2004). Outline of a theory of strongly semantic information. *Minds and Machines*, 14(2), 197–222. doi:10.1023/B:MIND.0000021684.50925.c9

Floridi, L. (in press). *The Philosophy of Information*. Oxford, UK: Oxford University Press.

Grandy, R. E. (1987). Information-based epistemology, ecological epistemology and epistemology naturalized. *Synthese*, 70, 191–203. doi:10.1007/BF00413935

Grice, P. (1989). *Studies in the Way of Words*. Cambridge, MA: Harvard University Press.

Harms, W. F. (1998). The use of information theory in epistemology. *Philosophy of Science*, 65, 472–501. doi:10.1086/392657

Hintikka, J. (1970). Surface information and depth information . In Hintikka, J., & Suppes, P. (Eds.), *Information and Inference* (pp. 263–297). Dordrecht, The Netherlands: Reidel.

Kyburg, H. E. (1983). Knowledge and the absolute. *The Behavioral and Brain Sciences*, 6, 72–73. doi:10.1017/S0140525X00014758

Lehrer, K., & Cohen, S. (1983). Dretske on Knowledge. *The Behavioral and Brain Sciences*, 6, 73–74. doi:10.1017/S0140525X0001476X

Lewis, D. (1973). *Counterfactuals*. Oxford: Blackwell.

Loewer, B. (1983). Information and belief. *The Behavioral and Brain Sciences*, 6, 75–76. doi:10.1017/S0140525X00014783

Sayre, K. M. (1976). *Cybernetics and the Philosophy of Mind*. London: Routledge & Kegan Paul.

Scarantino, A., & Piccinini, G. (in press). Information without Truth. *Metaphilosophy*.

Shannon, C. (1948). A Mathematical Theory of Communication. *The Bell System Technical Journal, 27*, 379-423 & 623-656.

Shannon, C. E. (1993). The Lattice Theory of Information . In Sloane, N. J. A., & Wyner, A. D. (Eds.), *Collected Papers*. Los Alamos, CA: IEEE Computer Society Press.

Usher, M. (2001). A statistical referential theory of content: Using information theory to account for misrepresentation. *Mind & Language*, 16, 311–334. doi:10.1111/1468-0017.00172

KEY TERMS AND DEFINITIONS

Counterfactuals: A counterfactual is a conditional where the antecedent is a non-factual statement. For material conditionals, when the antecedent is false, then the conditional is automatically true. However, this is not the case for counterfactual conditionals as can be seen from the following example: If Oswaldo had not shot the Kennedy, someone else would have.

Entropy: In Shannon's theory, entropy is the measure of the uncertainty of a message. This concept, which is originated from Thermodynamics, is prevalently used in different fields and in different senses. Shannon's entropy is the sense that is being used in this chapter.

Kullback – Leibler Divergence Measure: This information-theoretic concept is a measure of the divergence between the probability distributions of random variables. If we assume that p and q are the probability distributions of two random variables, then the Kullback-Leibler Divergence, $D(p\|q)$, is calculated with the following formula: $\sum p_i \cdot log\ (p_i/q_i)$

Markov Chains: A Markov chain is a stochastic process with the Markov property: A process has the Markov property if the conditional probability distribution of the future states of the process depends upon only the present state and a specific (say m) number of past states. The number m determines the order of the Markov chain. For example, Markov chains of order 0 are called memoryless systems because the future states depend only on the present state. In this chapter, we use the term Markov chain as a shortcut for Markov chains of order 1.

Possible Worlds Semantics: As stated in the counterfactuals entry above, the truth condition for counterfactuals is different than the truth condition for material conditionals. Possible worlds semantics developed for specifying the truth condition for counterfactuals by Lewis and Stalnaker. Lewis defines the truth condition as following:

Random Variable: Random variables are used in probability theory. They assign numerical values to the outcomes of an experiment. Usually, they are represented by capital letters such as X, Y.

ENDNOTES

1   In the title of his article, Shannon intentionally used the word 'communication' to avoid philosophical ambiguities of 'information'. Despite this, the common practice in the literature is to call his theory 'the mathematical theory of information'. This common practice is adapted in this chapter for consistency with the literature.

2   Several people claimed that this connection between the entropy of thermodynamics and the measure for the expected surprisal value (information) points out some deep metaphysical connections (Wiener 1961, Wheeler 1994, Chalmers 1996, Brooks & Wiley 1988].

3   For an analysis of and a suggested solution for this paradox, please see Floridi (2004) and Floridi's forthcoming book, *The Philosophy of Information*.

4   Dretske's BBS open commentary article (1983) and the special issue of *Synthese* on Dretske's theory (1987) together give us a valuable collection of these criticisms.

5   The theorem is rephrased for the sake of simplicity.

6   For details regarding these problems, please see Demir's dissertation (2006), which is available at http://scholarworks.iu.edu.

7   It is important to note that some philosophers disagree with this claim. Bar-Hillel (1952), Hintikka (1970) and Bremer (2003) are useful sources for a balanced presentation of this debate.

8   Brogaard and Salerno (2008) claim that when the contextual features of an argument are taken into account, counterfactuals satisfy transitivity. It needs to be stated that their claim is based on a misunderstanding of Lewis' possible worlds semantics. The details of their misunderstanding will need to be explained some other time.

9   Dietrich (2007) has a concise review of such attempts.

10   For the sake of simplicity, I use 'Markov chains' for 'Markov chains of order 1'. Markov chains can have any number of order. For details, please see the Glossary.

Chapter 3
Biological Information and Natural Computation

Gordana Dodig Crnkovic
Mälardalen University, Sweden

ABSTRACT

The dynamics of natural systems, and particularly organic systems, specialized in self-organization and complexity management, presents a vast source of ideas for new approaches to computing, such as natural computing and its special case organic computing. Based on paninformationalism (understanding of all physical structures as informational) and pancomputationalism or natural computationalism (understanding of the dynamics of physical structures as computation) a new approach of info-computational naturalism emerges as a result of their synthesis. This includes naturalistic view of mind and hence naturalized epistemology based on evolution from inanimate to biological systems through the increase in complexity of informational structures by natural computation. Learning on the info-computational level about structures and processes in nature and especially those in intelligent and autonomous biological agents enables the development of advanced autonomous adaptive intelligent artifacts and makes possible connection (both theoretical and practical) between organic and inorganic systems.

INTRODUCTION

Information has become a conceptual tool above others and it is found everywhere across research disciplines and in everyday use. Physics may be founded on informational grounds, and so other sciences involving physical objects (*paninformational stance, informational structural realism,*

Floridi). *Pancomputationalism (natural computationalism)* at the same time views the physical universe as a computational system. According to *pancomputationalists* (Zuse (1967), Fredkin (2009), Wolfram (2002), Chaitin (2007), Lloyd (2006) and others) the dynamics of the universe is a computational process; universe on the fundamental level may be conceived of as a computer which from the current state, following physical laws computes its own next state. The computa-

DOI: 10.4018/978-1-61692-014-2.ch003

tion that pancomputationalism presupposes is *natural computation*, defined by MacLennan as "computation occurring in nature or inspired by that in nature", where the structure of the universe may be assumed as both discrete and continuous at different levels of abstraction. Our present day computing machinery is a proper subset of natural computing.

Combining informational structures as the fabric of the universe and natural computation as its dynamics leads to the idea of *info-computationalism (info-computationalist naturalism),* the framework which builds on two fundamental concepts: information as a structure and computation as its dynamics.

As both physical structures and processes can be expressed in terms of info-computationalism, a new means arise of smoothly connecting two traditionally disparate spheres: bodies and their minds, and so naturalizing epistemology. The unified framework presents the epistemological feed-back loop between theoretical model–simulation–experimental tests–data analysis–theory. It opens the possibility to integrate the human as natural being with the rest of the physical world into the common framework by integrating current knowledge from neurosciences, biology, physics, complexity etc.

For complex systems such as biological ones, both the analysis of experiments and theory is increasingly done by computer simulations. Life itself on a fundamental level may be viewed as a process of computation, where hardware at the same time is the software (such as DNA). Our studying of life as information processes leads to production of simulations able to mimic relevant characteristics and behaviors of living biological systems: dynamic and recursive behavior, morphogenetic patterns, emergency phenomena etc. A good example of computer simulation aimed at reverse-engineering of the brain is a Blue Brain project which will be described later on.

This paper will highlight current developments and trends within the field of natural computing in the framework of info-computational naturalism.

Interesting to observe is epistemic productiveness of natural computing as it leads to a significantly bidirectional research (Rozenberg & Kari, 2008); while natural sciences are rapidly absorbing ideas of information processing, field of computing concurrently assimilates ideas from natural sciences. There is thus an interesting synergy gain in the relating of human designed computing with the computing going on in nature.

FUNDAMENTAL QUESTIONS

Promises of info-computational programme rely on learning from nature using predictability of its physical processes and structures as a means to improve our understanding of computation and its counterpart information.

The following questions are of interest:

- Learning from natural computation, is non-algorithmic computation possible?
- Is there a universal model (for which the TM model is a special case) underlying all Natural computation?
- What can be learned about intelligence, cognition and our epistemological and ontological premises within info-computational naturalism?
- What computational problems can our understanding of natural self-organization and management of complexity help to solve?
- If our brains and nervous systems are info-computational networks, what can we say about mind?
- How to develop artifactually intelligent autonomous systems based on insights from organic computing?

Those questions are best approached on the inter-disciplinary/trans-disciplinary ground as a study of the foundational issues of computing and information at the intersection of computing and philosophy, a present-day Natural Philosophy.

WHAT IS COMPUTATION?

Computation is in general defined as any kind of information processing. It includes processes such as human cognition, cell metabolism as well as calculations performed by computing devices. For a process to be a computation a model must exist such as algorithm, network topology, physical process or in general any mechanism which ensures predictability of its behavior.

The three-dimensional characterization of computing can be made by classification into orthogonal types: digital/analog, interactive/batch and sequential/parallel computation.

Nowadays digital computers are used to simulate all sorts of natural processes, including those that in physics are described as continuous. In this case, it is important to distinguish between the mechanism of computation and the simulation model.

Computation as a Physical Process

According to physics of computation (the branch of theoretical physics), computation can be seen as a physical phenomenon occurring inside physical systems (digital computers, quantum computers, DNA computers, molecular computers, analog computers, organic computers, etc).

Mathematical Models of Computation

In the theory of computation, a diversity of mathematical models of computers has been developed, among others state models such as Turing Machine, functional models such as lambda calculus and concurrent models such as process calculi.

TURING MACHINE MODEL AND COMPUTING BEYOND TURING MACHINE

The rapid development of the computing field in the past half a century was based on the classical understanding of computation as symbol manipulation performed by a Turing Machine. Ever since Turing proposed his model which identifies computation with the execution of an algorithm, there have been questions about how widely the model is applicable. Church-Turing Thesis after establishing the equivalence between a Turing Machine and an algorithm claims that all of computation must be algorithmic. However, with the advent of computer networks, the model of a computer in isolation, represented by a Turing Machine, has become insufficient[1].

A number of contemporary philosophers and scientists have noticed the necessity of considering computation beyond currently governing Turing machine model. New research results from computer science, physics, logics, bioinformatics, neurosciences, biology, chemistry and related research fields provide strong and increasing support for this claim.

Generalization of Turing model of computation is addressed in essentially two ways:

1. Generalization of *the physical realization* of computation process (Copeland, Lloyd, MacLennan, Cooper, Hogarth).
2. Generalization of *the model*, such as extending the idea of algorithm to a non-halting process (Wegner, Burgin, Rice).

The two above are necessarily linked. As soon as a new kind of physical process is identified as computation we will need an adequate theoretical model. Likewise, a new model will necessarily be linked with its implementations.

In search for a new generalized model of computation, interactive computation is proposed by (Wegner, 1998), (Goldin, Smolka, & Wegner,

2006) which unlike Turing machine implies communication of the computing process with the external world during the ongoing process of computation.

The search for new physical computation processes aims at enrichment of the conventional computing repertoire. Present-day computers have developed from the tools for mechanizing calculations into adaptive devices interacting with the physical world, which itself may be conceived of as a computer. In that sense natural computing represents the extension of the domain of physical phenomena which are understood as computational processes and it goes beyond Turing model of computation.

TURING MACHINE AS MECHANISTIC IDEALIZATION

The mechanistic world view is based on the following principles, Dodig Crnkovic and Müller in Dodig Crnkovic and Burgin (2010):

- (M1) The ontologically fundamental entities of the physical reality are [*space-time & matter* (mass-energy)] defining physical structures and *motion* (or change of physical structures).
- (M2) All the properties of any complex physical system can be derived from the properties of its components.
- (M3) Change of physical structures is governed by laws.

Mechanistic models assume that the system is closed, i.e. isolated from the environment, which has for the consequence that laws of conservation (energy, mass, momentum, etc.) hold. Environment (if modelled at all) is treated as a perturbation for the steady state of the system. Implicitly it is assumed that the observer is outside of the system observed. Organic systems pose insurmountable problems for mechanistic/reductionist modelling because of their inherent complexity.

Turing model as it consists of an isolated computing device operating over an input of atomic symbols represents a typical mechanistic idealisation.

COMPLEXITY, COMPUTING, ALGORITHMS AND HYPERCOMPUTATION

In order to not only understand, but also to be able to interact in real time with the physical world, computation must match its environment, which, according to Ashby (1964) means to correspond to the complexity of the environment. Ashby's Law of requisite variety states namely, that to control a state, the variety of system responses must at least match the variety of disturbances. This amounts to the claim that in order for a computer to achieve adequate control of a complex system, the complexity of the repertoire of its responses must correspond to the complexity of the environment.

If we compare Turing machines with the physical world (including biological organisms) the latter exhibit a much higher degree of complexity. That would imply that we need more powerful machines than what is represented by Turing model in order to be able to control by computers the real world phenomena on those levels of organization.

A NEW PARADIGM OF COMPUTATION: NATURAL COMPUTING

In these times brimming with excitement, our task is nothing less than to discover a new, broader, notion of computation, and to understand the world around us in terms of information processing. Rozenberg and Kari (2008)

Computing beyond Turing limit or hypercomputing, Copeland (2002), seen as the possibility of carrying on infinitely many (computational) steps in a finite time is a question of our idea of the infinity and our understanding of the nature of the world (continuous, discrete). The problem of hypercomputation can be seen as the problem of induction. *Inductive Turing machines* described Burgin (2005) always give results after a finite number of steps, do not use infinite objects such as real numbers and are more powerful than Turing machines.

In general the approach the question of computing beyond the Turing model goes under different names and has different content: natural computing, unconventional computing, analog computing, organic computing, sub-symbolic computing, etc. (for an introduction see http://en.wikipedia.org/wiki/Natural_Computing) Common strategy of this approach is Simon's *satisficing* (Simon 1978), that focus on *adequacy*, rather than searches an *optimal* solution.

Natural computing is a new paradigm of computing (MacLennan, Rozenberg, Calude, Bäck, Bath, Müller-Schloer, de Castro, Paun) which includes the following:

1. *Theoretical* computational methods *inspired by nature* (such as artificial neural networks, computing on continuous data, evolutionary algorithms, swarm intelligence, artificial immune systems). This includes computer simulations used to functionally synthesize natural phenomena (artificial life, engineering of semi-synthetic organisms)
2. *Physical computing methods* based on new *natural materials* besides present-day electronic hardware (such as organic/biological computing, DNA computing and quantum computing)

The above computational approaches are abstracted from the range of natural phenomena - characteristics of living organisms such as the defining properties of life forms, cell membranes, and morphogenesis, self-replication, self-defense, self-configuration and self-repair; the information processing mechanisms of the brain, evolution, autonomy and automatic coordination of group behavior, self-explaining and context-awareness. Processes like self-assembly, developmental processes, gene regulation networks, protein-protein interaction networks, biological transport networks, and gene assembly in unicellular organisms are at present studied as information processing. Understanding of biological organisms as information processing systems is a part of understanding of the universe as a whole as an information processing computational structure.

Natural computing has different criteria for success of a computation. Unlike Turing model, the halting problem is not a central issue[2], but instead the adequacy of the computational response. Organic computing system adapts dynamically to the current conditions of its environment by self-organization, self-configuration, self-optimization, self-healing, self-protection and context-awareness. In many areas, we have to computationally model emergence not being algorithmic, Sloman and Cooper in (Dodig Crnkovic & Burgin, 2010), which makes it interesting to investigate computational characteristics of non-algorithmic natural computation (sub-symbolic, analogue).

The research in theoretical foundations of natural computing aims at improving our understanding on the fundamental level of *computation* as *information processing* which underlie all of computing in nature. Importantly, Solutions are being sought in natural systems with evolutionary developed strategies for handling complexity in order to improve complex networks of massively parallel autonomous engineered computational systems.

Natural computational models are most relevant in applications that resemble natural systems, as for example real-time control systems, autonomous robots, and distributed intelligent systems in general.

If computation is to be able to match the observable natural phenomena, such as: adequacy, generality and flexibility of real-time response, adaptability and robustness, relevant characteristics in natural computation should be incorporated in new models of computation. Maclennan (2004).

ILLUSTRATIVE EXAMPLES OF RESEARCH PROJECTS INSPIRED BY NATURAL COMPUTING

BIO-ICT

New perspectives in ICT exploit the understanding of information processing in biological systems that have demonstrable advantages in terms of functionality, operating conditions, resilience or adaptability or lead to systems that can be naturally combined with biological systems. BIO-ICT Projects integrate some of the following topics: Novel computing paradigms, derived from the information representation and processing capabilities of biological systems (networks of neurons or other cells), or from the computational interpretation of biological processes (molecular signaling, metabolism) and with measurable advantages over current approaches to difficult problems in information processing. Biomimetic artefacts: ad hoc hardware implementations of bio-inspired systems in areas where standard devices do not provide the required performance. This may use analogue and digital circuits, evolvable hardware, artificial cells, neuro-morphic chips or sensors for achieving life-like functionality or properties such as self organisation, robustness or growth. Bidirectional interfaces between electronic or electro-mechanical systems and living entities, at or close to the cellular level, with adequate control and/or signal processing algorithms, enabling direct interfacing to the nervous system or to other types of cells. Biohybrid artefacts, involving tightly coupled ICT and biological entities (e.g.

neural or other types of biological tissue) for new forms of computation, sensing, communication or physical actuation or adaptation http://www.bio-ict.org

IBM Autonomic Computing

Over the past forty years (…) the focus has been on raw processing power and the individual components that allow ever smaller and greater capacity to store, process and move data. And while scientists and researchers have met this demand with astonishing regularity, we have missed an opportunity to look at the evolution of computing from a more holistic perspective.

There are a number of immediate needs that require us to adjust our thinking and reinterpret our approach to computing in general, and specifically to the interaction between computer hardware, software and networks. The current strain on I/T services demands that we turn our best minds to developing computer systems to be more automated and less reliant on human intervention. http://www.research.ibm.com/autonomic/research/

The above examples show that the research within natural computing is already going on and we can expect in the near future a substantial paradigm shift from present day Turing machine-centric view of computing towards natural computing, both in terms of new models of computation and in terms of new computational devices.

NATURAL COMPUTATIONALISM (PANCOMPUTATIONALISM): THE UNIVERSE IS A COMPUTER

Pancomputationalism (Pan-computationalism, Natural computationalism) is a view that the universe is a huge computational machine or rather a network of computational processes which following fundamental physical laws compute (dynamically develop) its own next state from the current one. In this approach the stuff of the universe is:

- Essentially informational
- Both digital and analog: depending on the level of abstraction

Pancomputationalism claims that all physical processes can be understood as computational processes. In principle, there seems to be no ontological hindrance to our including the system or process we try to compute among the models we use. We then get what I take to be the fundamental idea of pancomputationalism: The function governing a process is calculated by the process itself[3]. The following remark by Richard Feynman explains lucidly the idea and our hopes about natural computing:

It always bothers me that according to the laws as we understand them today, it takes a computing machine an infinite number of logical operations to figure out what goes on in no matter how tiny a region of space and no matter how tiny a region of time ... I have often made the hypothesis that ultimately physics will not require a mathematical statement, that in the end the machinery will be revealed and the laws will turn out to be simple. Richard P. Feynman, The Character of Physical Law (1965), 57.[4]

Digital vs. Analog and Continuum vs. Discrete

Georg Leopold Kronecker believed that, while everything else was made by man, the natural numbers were given by God. For the logicists the natural numbers were sufficient for deriving of all of mathematics. We can see this subject resurface in Chaitin's question about the existence of real numbers, see Chaitin *How real are real numbers,* Chaitin (2007) 276. For Chaitin real numbers are chimeras of our own minds, they just simply do not exist!

Even though pragmatic minded people would say that discrete set can always be made dense enough to mimic continuum for all practical purposes, on purely principal grounds we cannot dispense with only one part in a dyadic pair for continuum and discrete are mutually defining.[5]

Discrete–continuum problem lies in the underpinning of calculus and Bishop George Berkeley in his book "The analyst: or a discourse addressed to an infidel mathematician" argued that, although calculus led to correct results, its foundations were logically problematic. Of derivatives (which Newton called fluxions) Berkley wrote:

And what are these fluxions? The velocities of evanescent increments. And what are these same evanescent increments? They are neither finite quantities, nor quantities infinitely small, nor yet nothing. May we not call them ghosts of departed quantities?[6]

Philosophical problems closely attached to the idea of infinity in mathematics are classical ones. From physics on the other hand, there are persistent voices, such as (Lesne 2007) witnessing for the necessity of continuum in physical modeling of the world. Here is the summary:

This paper presents a sample of the deep and multiple interplay between discrete and continuous behaviours and the corresponding modellings in physics. The aim is to show that discrete and continuous features coexist in any natural phenomenon, depending on the scales of observation. Accordingly, different models, either discrete or continuous in time, space, phase space or conjugate space can be considered. Lesne (2007)

The question of continuum vs. discrete nature of the world is ages old and it is not limited to the existing technology. Digital philosophy as well as Turing machine has been epistemologically remarkably productive (see Stephen Wolframs work, e.g. (Wolfram 2002) along with Ed Fredkin and number of people who focused on the digital aspects of the world). Digital is undoubtedly one of the levels we can use for the description, but from physics it seems to be necessary to be able to handle continuum too (as we do in Quantum Mechanics). For a very good account, see Lloyd (2006).

Finally it should be remembered (as already pointed out) that both digital and analog systems can be discrete or continuous, depending on the level of description/level of description or organization.

PANINFORMATIONALISM: INFORMATIONAL STRUCTURAL REALISM

According to Floridi (2008) the ultimate nature of reality is an informational structure, a view called informational realism. Using the methodology of the levels of abstractions Floridi shows that, within the debate about structural realism, epistemic and ontic structural realism are reconcilable.

Floridi (2009) goes a step further arguing that digital ontology (the ultimate nature of reality is digital, and the universe is a computational system equivalent to a Turing Machine) should be carefully distinguished from informational ontology (the ultimate nature of reality is informational). His conclusion is that digital ontology does not cover all aspects of physical reality while informational ontology does:

Digital vs. analogue is a Boolean dichotomy typical of our computational paradigm, but digital and analogue are only "modes of presentation" of Being (to paraphrase (...) Kant), that is, ways in which reality is experienced or conceptualized by an epistemic agent at a given level of abstraction. A preferable alternative is provided by an informational approach to structural realism,

according to which knowledge of the world is knowledge of its structures. The most reasonable ontological commitment turns out to be in favor of an interpretation of reality as the totality of structures dynamically interacting with each other. Floridi (2009)

This dynamic interaction of informational structures is what is called natural computation. *Pancomputationalism does not automatically imply digital (discrete) computing.* As the whole of the universe computes, both sorts of computing are part of natural computation, discrete and continuous. As Seth Lloyd points out, on the basic quantum-mechanical level both discrete and analogue, digital and continuous computing is going on. See more about the question of digital/analog universe in Dodig Crnkovic (2006).

INFO-COMPUTATIONAL NATURALISM

Info-computational naturalism unifies pancomputationalism with paninformationalism, the view that the fabric of the universe is informational. Its claim is that while the structure of the universe is informational, its dynamics (change) is computation i.e. information processing, see Dodig Crnkovic (2006) and Dodig Crnkovic (2008). This computation process is natural computing, see MacLennan in Dodig Crnkovic and Burgin (2010). Burgin's article, *Information Dynamics in a Categorical Setting*, in the same volume, offers a common framework for information and computation, building a mathematical stratum of the general theory of information based on category theory.

The main feature of info-computationalist naturalism is that it makes possible unification of nonliving and living physical world within the same framework, thus even providing clues to mental (information processing) capacities in humans and animals. Of all grand unifications or *système du monde* as Greg Chaitin says in his *Epistemology as Information Theory: From Leibniz to Ω,* Chaitin (2007), this is the first one holding promise to be able to explain and simulate not only non-living universe but also the structure and behavior of living organisms including the human mind.

Complexity is an essential characteristic of life, the domain in which info-computational approach best shows its explanatory power. Living organisms are complex, goal-oriented autonomous information-processing systems with ability of self-organization, self-reproduction (based on genetic information) and adaptation. They evolved through pre-biotic and biological evolution from inanimate matter. Understanding of basic info-computational features of living beings has consequences for many fields, especially information sciences, cognitive science, neuroscience, theory of computing, artificial intelligence and robotics but also biology, sociology, economics and other fields where informational complexity is essential.

The info-computational idea is based on the following principles:

- (IC1) The ontologically fundamental entities of the physical reality are *information* (structure) and *computation* (change).
- (IC2) Properties of a complex physical system cannot be derived solely from the properties of its components. Emergent properties must be taken into account.
- (IC3) In general, the observer is a part of the system observed.

Info-computational models include *open systems* in communication with the environment. Environment is a constitutive element for an open complex info-computational system. *Network* of interconnected parts is a typical configuration, where understanding is sought on the meta-level with respect to constituent parts. Info-computational models include mechanistic ones as a special case when the internal interaction between the parts of the system and the interaction of the system with the environment may be neglected.

EPISTEMOLOGICAL CONSEQUENCES OF INFO-COMPUTATIONAL NATURALISM

One might suspect that the computationalist idea is vacuous, and if everything is info-computational, then it says nothing about the world. The computationalist claim however should be understood as similar to the claim that universe is made of atoms. Atom is a very useful concept which helps understanding the world in many fields. So is the info-computational approach. Universe is NOT "nothing but atoms", but on some view (level of organization, level of abstraction) may be seen as atoms.

As already emphasized, physical reality can be addressed at many different levels of organization. Life and intelligence are the phenomena especially characterized by info-computational structures and processes. Living systems have the ability to act autonomously and store information, retrieve information (remember), anticipate future behavior in the environment with help of information stored (learn) and adapt to the environment in order to survive. In Epistemology Naturalized, Dodig Crnkovic (2007), I present a model which connects mechanisms of information processing and knowledge generation in an organism. Thinking of us and the universe as a network of computational structures and processes allows easier approaching of the question about boundaries between living and non-living beings.

Info-computationalism views our bodies as advanced computational machines in constant interaction with the environmental computational processes and structures. Our brains are informational architectures undergoing computational processes on many levels of organization. On the levels of basic physical laws there is a computation going on. All which physics can conceptualize, describe, calculate, simulate and predict can be expressed in info-computationalist terms. On the level of molecules (with atoms and elementary particles as structural elements) there are computational processes going on. The nerve cell level can be understood as the next level of relevance in our understanding of the computational nature of the brain processes. Neurons are organized in networks, and with neurons as building blocks new computational phenomena appear on the level of neural network. The intricate architecture of informational structures in the brain, implementing different levels of control mechanisms are not unlike virtual machines on higher level running on the structure below, Sloman and Chrisley (2003). What we call "informational architecture" is fluid and interactive, not so much crystal-lattice-type rigid construction but more like networks of agents, Minsky's society of minds, Minsky (1988).

The development is going on into two directions: analyzing living organisms as info-computational systems/agents, and implementing natural computation strategies (organic computing, bio computing) into artifacts. Lessons learned from the design and implementation of our understanding of living natural computational agents through iterative process of improvements will lead to artifacts that in increasingly higher degree will be capable of simulating characteristics of living organisms.

Naturalist Understanding of Cognition

According to Maturana and Varela (1980) even the simplest organisms possess cognition and their meaning-production apparatus is contained in their metabolism. Of course, there are also non-metabolic interactions with the environment, such as locomotion, that also generates meaning for an organism by changing its environment and providing new input data.

Maturana's and Varelas' understanding of cognition is most suitable as the basis for a com-

putationalist account of the naturalized evolutionary epistemology. A great conceptual advantage of cognition as a central focus of study is that all living organisms possess some cognition, in some degree.

THEORETICAL ADVANCES IN LEARNING FROM NATURE THROUGH INFO-COMPUTATION

In what follows examples are given of the research where we learn through info-computational approaches about cognition and functions of the brain.

EPISTEMOLOGY NATURALIZED

Naturalized epistemology (Feldman, Kornblith, Stich) is, in general, an idea that knowledge may be studied as a natural phenomenon; that the subject matter of epistemology is not our concept of knowledge, but the knowledge itself, knowledge in the world.

The stimulation of his sensory receptors is all the evidence anybody has had to go on, ultimately, in arriving at his picture of the world. Why not just see how this construction really proceeds? Why not settle for psychology? Quine (1985)

Why not settle for info-computational naturalism?

Indeed, cognitive ethologists find the only way to make sense of the cognitive equipment in animals is to treat it as an information processing system, including equipment for perception, as well as the storage and integration of information; that is, after all, the point of calling it cognitive equipment. That equipment which can play such a role confers selective advantage over animals lacking such equipment no longer requires any argument. Kornblith (2003)

Evolutionary Development

One cannot account for the functional architecture, reliability, and goals of a nervous system without understanding its adaptive history. Consequently, a successful science of knowledge must include standard techniques for modeling the interaction between evolution and learning. Harms (2004)

A central question is thus what the mechanism is of the evolutionary development of cognitive abilities in organisms. Critics of the evolutionary approach mention the impossibility of "blind chance" to produce such highly complex structures as intelligent living organisms. Proverbial monkeys typing Shakespeare are often used as an illustration; an interesting account is given by Gell-Mann (1994). However, (Lloyd, 2006) mentions a very good counterargument, originally due to Chaitin and Bennet. The "typing monkeys" argument does not take into account physical laws of the universe, which dramatically limit what can be typed. Moreover, the universe is not a typewriter, but a computer, so a monkey types random input into a computer. The computer interprets the strings as programs.

Quantum mechanics supplies the universe with "monkeys" in the form of random fluctuations, such as those that seeded the locations of galaxies. The computer into which they type is the universe itself. From a simple initial state, obeying simple physical laws, the universe has systematically processed and amplified the bits of information embodied in those quantum fluctuations. The result of this information processing is the diverse, information-packed universe we see around us: programmed by quanta, physics give rise first to chemistry and then to life; programmed by mutation and recombination, life gave rise to Shakespeare; programmed by experience and imagination, Shakespeare gave rise to Hamlet. You might say that the difference between a monkey at a typewriter and a monkey at a computer is all the difference in the world. Lloyd (2006)

The universe/computer on which a monkey types is at the same time the hardware and the program, in a way similar to the Turing machine. An example from biological computing is the DNA where the hardware (the molecule) is at the same time the software (the program, the code). In general, each new input restructures the computational universe and changes the preconditions for the future inputs. Those processes are interactive and self-organizing. That makes the essential speed-up for the process of getting more and more complex structures.

Based on natural phenomena understood as info-computational, computing in general is conceived on an open interactive system (digital or analogue; discrete or continuous) in communication with the environment. The classical Turing machine is seen as a subset of a more general interactive/adaptive/self-organizing universal natural computer. A "living system" is defined as an "open, coherent, space-time structure maintained far from thermodynamic equilibrium by a flow of energy through it" Chaisson (2001). On a computationalist view, organisms are constituted by computational processes, implementing computation in vivo. In the open system of living cells an info-computational process takes place using DNA, exchanging information, matter, and energy with the environment.

All cognizing beings are in constant interaction with their environment. The essential feature of living organisms is their ability to manage complexity and to handle diverse environmental conditions with a variety of responses that are results of adaptation, variation, selection, learning, and/or reasoning. As a consequence of evolution, increasingly complex living organisms arise. They are able to register inputs (data) from the environment, to structure those into information and, in more developed organisms, into knowledge. The evolutionary advantage of using structured, component-based approaches (data–information–knowledge) is improving response time and the computational efficiency of cognitive processes.

The main reason for choosing info-computationalist view for naturalizing epistemology is that it provides a unifying framework that makes it possible for different research fields such as philosophy, computer science, neuroscience, cognitive science, biology, and a number of others to communicate, exchange their results, and to build a common knowledge.

It also provides the natural solution to the old problem of the role of representation in explaining and producing information, a discussion about two seemingly incompatible views: a symbolic, explicit, and static notion of representation versus an implicit and dynamic (interactive) one. Within the info-computational framework, those classical (Turing-machine type) and connectionist views are reconciled and used to describe different aspects of cognition.

The info-computationalist project of naturalizing epistemology by defining cognition as an information-processing phenomenon is based on the development of multilevel dynamical computational models and simulations of intelligent systems and has important consequences for the development of artificial intelligence and artificial life, the subject of the next chapter.

INTELLIGENCE, CHESS, COMPUTING AND AI FROM DEEP BLUE TO BLUE BRAIN

Chess Relevance for AI and Deep Blue

Many people would even today agree with the following claim made in 1958:

If one could devise a successful chess machine, one would seem to have penetrated to the core of human intellectual endeavor. Newell, Shaw, and Simon (1958)

Chess play is by Ross (2006) even called "the Drosophila of Cognitive Science" for its frequent use in cognitive experiments, Charness (1992). The story of IBM's Chess supercomputer Deep Blue winning in 1997 the match against the world chess champion Gary Kasparov is therefore a very instructive one. The computer was programmed by a computer scientists assisted by a chess grandmaster. They developed the evaluation function to assess every given position. The method may be described as combinatorial "brute force".

It turned out that what was believed to be "at the core of human intellectual endeavour" could be better performed by a programmed machine applying basically simple strategy. This was the beginning of a development of machines dedicated to mimic what would be considered to be intelligent behaviour.

Descendant of Deep Blue, Blue Gene an Engine of Scientific Discovery

The methods devised in Deep Blue project were employed as a foundation of Blue Gene supercomputer and used among others for protein folding, genetic and brain research. The project was exceptionally fruitful.[7] Searching for the optimum configurations of systems consisting of simple elements is typical of not only chess play but also of a range of other scientific problems. Solving this category of problems brings us closer to constructing intelligent computers and facilitates scientific progress in general.

Blue Brain Project

In 2005 EPFL and IBM initiated a research project analogous in scope to the Genome Project, with the aim to create a biologically accurate model of the brain using Blue Gene supercomputer. This project has already delivered important results with biologically accurate computational neurons made on the basis of experimental data. These neurons are automatically connected in a network by positioning around 30 million synapses in exact

3D locations. Such networks have been used to simulate the basic functional unit of the brain, the neocortical column, http://news.bbc.co.uk/2/hi/science/nature/8012496.stm.

This development from Deep Blue via Deep Gene to the Blue Brain demonstrates how scientific progress can be made through learning by construction. There is a clear paradigm shift in computing as a scientific discipline with respect to classical scientific fields, Dodig Crnkovic (2003). Understanding neocortical information processing by reverse-engineering the mammalian brain makes foundation for simulation of the whole brain and is an essential step in our understanding of brain functions including intelligence in info-computational terms, Dodig Crnkovic (2008).

PROMISES OF THE INFO-COMPUTATIONAL NATURALIST RESEARCH PROGRAMME

The central question is how *epistemologically productive* this paradigm is, as info-computational naturalism really is a *research programme* whose role is to mobilize researchers to work in the same direction, within the same global framework. The majority of natural sciences, formal sciences, technical sciences and engineering are already based on computational thinking, computational tools and computational modelling, Wing (2008).

So the time has come for paradigm change in computing. Following are some of the promises of info-computationalism:

The synthesis of (presently disconnected) knowledge from different fields within the common info-computational framework which will enrich our understanding of the world as a whole. Present day narrow specialization into different isolated research fields has gradually led into impoverishment of the common world view.

Integration of scientific understanding of the phenomena of life (structures, processes) with the rest of natural world helping to achieve "the unreasonable effectiveness of mathematics" such as in physics (Wigner) even for complex phenomena like biology that today lack mathematical effectiveness (Gelfand)[8]. In this case, mathematical effectiveness will be replaced by computational effectiveness.

Understanding of the semantics of information as a part of data-information-knowledge-wisdom sequence, in which more and more complex relational structures are created by computational processing of information. An evolutionary naturalist view of semantics of information in living organisms is given based on interaction (information exchange) of an organism with its environment.

A unified picture of fundamental dual-aspect information/computation phenomenon applicable in natural sciences, information science, cognitive science, philosophy and number of others.

Relating phenomena of information and computation understood in interactive paradigm makes it possible for investigations in logical pluralism of information produced as a result of interactive computation.[9] Of special interest are open systems in communication with the environment and related logical pluralism including paraconsistent logic. Japaridze (2003)

Advancement of our computing methods beyond the Turing-Church paradigm, computation in the next step of development becoming able to handle complex phenomena such as living organisms and processes of life, knowledge, social dynamics, communication and control of large interacting networks (as addressed in *organic computing* and other kinds of *unconventional computing*), etc.

Of all manifestations of life, mind seems to be information-theoretically and philosophically the most interesting one. Info-computationalism (pancomputationalism + paninformationalism) has a potential to support (by means of models and simulations) our effort in learning about mind. On the practical side, understanding and learning to simulate and control functions and structures of living organisms will bring completely new medical treatments for all sorts of diseases including mental ones which to this day are poorly understood. Understanding of our information-processing features of human brain will bring new insights into such fields as education, media, entertainment, cognition etc.

CONCLUSION

Today's software-intensive and intelligent computer systems have become large, consisting of massive numbers of autonomous and parallel elements across multiple scales. At the nano-scale they approach programmable matter; at the macro scale, multitude of cores compute in clusters, grids or clouds, while at the planetary scale, sensor networks connect environmental data to track climate and other global-scale phenomena. The common for these modern computing systems is that they are *ensemble-like* (as they form one whole in which the parts act in concert to achieve a common goal like an organism that is an ensemble of its cells) and *physical* (as ensembles act in the physical world and interact with their environment through sensors and actuators).

Info-computationalism will help us answering the focal research questions and understanding the potential and the limits of the emerging computational paradigm which will have significant impact on the research in both computing and sciences. It has high relevance for the development of future computing theories and technologies as well as for the improvement of computational models of natural and phenomena. Applications such as BIO-ICT and Autonomic computing show possible domains of practical use.

REFERENCES

Ashby, W. (1964). *An introduction to Cybernetics*. London: Methuen.

Burgin, M. (2005). *Super-recursive Algorithms*. Berlin: Springer Monographs in Computer Science.

Chaisson, E. (2001). *Cosmic Evolution. the Rise of Complexity in Nature*. Cambridge, MA: Harvard University Press.

Chaitin, G. (2007). Epistemology as information theory: From Leibniz to Ω. In Dodig Crnkovic and Stuart (Ed.), Computation, information, cognition: the nexus and the liminal (pp. 27-51). Newcastle, UK: Cambridge Scholars Publishing.

Chaitin, G. (2007). *Thinking about Gödel and Turing: Essays on Complexity, 1970-2007*. Singapore: World Scientific. doi:10.1142/9789812708977

Charness, N. (1992). The Impact of Chess Research on Cognitive Science. *Psychological Research, 54*, 4–9. doi:10.1007/BF01359217

Copeland, J. (2002). Hypercomputation. *Minds and Machines, 12*, 461–502. doi:10.1023/A:1021105915386

Dodig Crnkovic, G. (2003). Shifting the Paradigm of the Philosophy of Science: the Philosophy of Information and a New Renaissance. *Minds and Machines: Special Issue on the Philosophy of Information, 13*(4).

Dodig Crnkovic, G. (2006). *Investigations into information semantics and ethics of computing*. Västerås: Mälardalen University Press. Retrieved from http://www.diva-portal.org/mdh/theses/abstract.xsql?dbid=153

Dodig Crnkovic, G. (2007). Epistemology Naturalized: the Info-Computationalist Approach. *APA Newsletter on Philosophy and Computers, 6*(2). Retrieved from http://www.apaonline.org/publications/newsletters/computers.aspx

Dodig Crnkovic, G. (2008). Semantics of Information as Interactive Computation. In M. Moeller, W. Neuser & T. Roth-Berghofer (Ed.), *Fifth international workshop on philosophy and informatics*. Berlin: Springer. Retrieved from http://sunsite.informatik.rwth-aachen.de/Publications/CEUR-W

Dodig Crnkovic, G., & Burgin, M. (Eds.). (2010). *Information and Computation*. Singapore: World Scientific.

Endnotes

Floridi, L. (2008). Defence of Informational Structural Realism. *Synthese, 161*(2), 219–253. doi:10.1007/s11229-007-9163-z

Floridi, L. (2009). Against Digital Ontology. *Synthese, 168*(1), 151–178. doi:10.1007/s11229-008-9334-6

Fredkin, E. (n.d.). *Digital Philosophy*. Retrieved October 4, 2009, from http://www.digitalphilosophy.org

Gell-Man, M. (1994). *The Quark and the Jaguar: Adventures in the Simple and the Complex*. New York: Freeman.

Goldin, D., Smolka, S., & Wegner, P. (2006). *Interactive Computation: the New Paradigm*. New York: Springer-Verlag.

Goldin, D., & Wegner, P. (2002). Paraconsistency of Interactive Computation. In *Workshop on Paraconsistent Computational Logic*. Denmark

Harms, W. (2004). *Information and Meaning in Evolutionary Processes*. Cambridge, UK: Cambridge University Press. doi:10.1017/CBO9780511498473

Japaridze, G. (2003). Introduction to Computability Logic. *Annals of Pure and Applied Logic, 123*, 1–99. doi:10.1016/S0168-0072(03)00023-X

Kornblith, H. (2003). *Knowledge and its Place in Nature*. Oxford, UK: Oxford University Press.

Lesne, A. (2007). The Discrete Versus Continuous Controversy in Physics. *Mathematical Structures in Computer Science, 17*, 185–223. doi:10.1017/S0960129507005944

Lloyd, S. (2006). *Programming the Universe: A Quantum Computer Scientist Takes on the Cosmos*. New York: Alfred A Knopf.

Maclennan, B. (2004). Natural Computation and Non-Turing Models Of Computation. *Theoretical Computer Science, 317*, 115–145. doi:10.1016/j.tcs.2003.12.008

Maturana, H., & Varela, F. (1980). *Autopoiesis and Cognition: the Realization of the Living*. Boston: Reidel.

Minsky, M. (1988). *The Society of Mind*. New York: Simon and Schuster.

Newell, A., Shaw, C., & Simon, H. (1958). Chess-playing Programs and the Problem of Complexity. *IBM Journal of Research and Development, 2*, 320–325. doi:10.1147/rd.24.0320

Quine, W. (1985). Epistemology Naturalized . In Kornblith, H. (Ed.), *Naturalizing Epistemology (reprint from in 'Ontological Relativity and other Essays'; Columbia University Press, 1969)*.

Ross, P. (2006). The Expert Mind. *Scientific American*, (August): 64–71. doi:10.1038/scientificamerican0806-64

Rozenberg, G., & Kari, L. (2008). The Many Facets of Natural Computing. *Communications of the ACM*, 51.

Sloman, A., & Chrisley, R. (2003). Virtual Machines and Consciousness. *Journal of Consciousness Studies, 10*(4-5), 133–172.

Wegner, P. (1998). Interactive Foundations of Computing. *Theoretical Computer Science, 192*, 315. doi:10.1016/S0304-3975(97)00154-0

Wing, J. (2008). Five deep Questions in Computing. *CACM, 51*(1), 58–60.

Wolfram, S. (2002). *New Kind of Science*. Retrieved from http://www.wolframscience.com/nksonline/toc.html

Zuse, K. (1967). Rechnender Raum. *Elektronische Datenverarbeitung*, 8, 336–344.

KEY TERMS AND DEFINITIONS

Pancomputationalism (Pan-computationalism, Natural computationalism): is a view that the universe is a huge computational machine or rather a network of computational processes which following fundamental physical laws compute (dynamically develop) its own next state from the current one. In this approach the stuff of the universe is essentially informational and both digital and analog – depending on the level of abstraction.

Paninformationalism (Informational structural realism): According to this view, the ultimate nature of reality is an informational structure.

Info-Computational Naturalism (Info-computationalism): unifies pancomputationalism with paninformationalism. Within this framework the structure of the universe is informational while its dynamics (change) is computation i.e. information processing

Computation: is in general defined as any kind of information processing. It includes processes such as human cognition, cell metabolism as well as calculations performed by computing devices. For a process to be a computation a model must exist such as algorithm, network topology, physical process or in general any mechanism which ensures predictability of its behavior.

Natural Computation (Natural computing): includes theoretical computational methods inspired by nature and physical computing methods based on new natural materials besides present-day electronic hardware.

Organic Computing: is an emerging science which is developing the basis for understanding of the organic structure of life on different levels of organization, ranging from molecular up to societal levels, and developing an organically inspired ICT.

Digital Physics: is a set of theoretical perspectives that the universe is computable. It can be conceived as either the output of some computer program or as being some sort of vast *digital* computation device.

Hypercomputation: refers to computation beyond Turing model, capable of computing non-Turing-computable functions, following super-recursive algorithms. It also includes other forms of computation interactive computation. The term was first introduced Jack Copeland.

Naturalized Epistemology: is, in general, an idea that knowledge may be studied as a natural phenomenon; that the subject matter of epistemology is not our concept of knowledge, but the knowledge itself, knowledge in the world.

ENDNOTES

[1] By now there is a vast literature on computing beyond Turing limit, hypercomputation and superrecursive algorithms.

[2] In the Turing model a computation must halt when execution of an algorithm has finished.

[3] For this formulation I thank KB Hansen.

[4] Used as the motto for the 2008 Midwest NKS Conference, http://www.cs.indiana.edu/~dgerman/2008midwestNKSconference/index.html

[5] This dyadic function seems to come from our cognitive apparatus which makes the difference in perception of discrete and continuous. It is indirectly given by the world, in a sense that we as a species being alive in the world have developed those dyadic/binary systems for discrete (number) and continuous (magnitude) phenomena as the most effective way to relate to that physical world.

[6]   Berkeley talks about *the relationship between the model and the world*, not about the inner structure of the model itself. Worth noticing is KB Hansen's remark that "problems observed by Berkeley have been solved by Bolzano, Cauchy, Riemann, Weierstrass, and Robinson. Modern mathematical analysis rests on solid foundations."

[7]   For comparison, Deep Blue had 32 processors and could process about 200 million chess moves per second in its match against Kasparov. Today Blue Gene uses 131000 processors to perform 280 trillion operations per second. http://www-03.ibm.com/servers/deepcomputing/bluegene.html

[8]   See Chaitin, Mathematics, Biology and Metabiology (Foils, July 2009)

[9]   This logical pluralism is closely related to phenomena of consistency and truth; see also de Vey Mestdagh & Hoepman in Dodig Crnkovic and Burgin (2010).

Chapter 4
On Biological Computing, Information and Molecular Networks

Walter Riofrio
University Ricardo Palma, Lima-Peru & Complex Systems Institute (ISC-PIF), Paris-France

ABSTRACT

The author will focus this chapter on studying the set of special characteristics molecular networks which constitute living systems might have. In order to do that, he will study them from the perspective which allows us to visualize the most basic element constituting that which is living. This approach should lead us to uncover the essential properties which form any dynamic entity that could be called a living system. It will furthermore permit us to understand the intrinsic relationship produced between the handling of biological information and the start-up of something completely new that is revealed in the set of aspects which bear natural computations within living systems.

1. INTRODUCTION

The term biological computing is also called natural computing, and we employ these two terms to refer to a sort of computation that nature carries out.

On the other hand, we also use them to refer to nature-inspired computational models.

For example, evolutionary algorithms and neural network-based algorithms are being implemented on conventional computers.

Thus, it is not possible to disregard contributions coming from the field of computer science since it has revealed that complex natural processes can be seen as computational processes.

The same can be stated concerning biology when we observe the fact it has pushed forward the understanding of processes within its field, with ongoing assistance from applications created through information science that have coalesced into more sophisticated programs and advanced computers.

However, there is one branch of research that possesses a long list of questions investigators have

DOI: 10.4018/978-1-61692-014-2.ch004

yet to pose on account of newly found data, and that is research into the question on whether certain forms, which we could call "computations", are spontaneously produced in nature.

The following discussion will form our attempt to shine some light on this electrifying topic.

Our chapter is structured the following way. In the section *"Origin of Biological Information"*, we shall briefly go over different alternatives that could be used for biological information and their possible relationship to signs.

In the section *"Looking at Biological Networks"*, we shall begin presenting our proposals in relation to the topics, moving backwards in time to the pre-biotic world. Here, we contend the pre-biotic era ushered in a protocell that contained very new properties.

In our last section, *"Insights into Biological Computing"*, we shall provide an examination of the consequences that are derived from the previous sections.

Once concluded, we should have our first glimpse of what our protocell may have generated: the appearance or emergence of a primary capacity of what we shall call biological computation.

2. ORIGIN OF BIOLOGICAL INFORMATION

The first issue which strongly calls our attention is the fact there is no clear acceptance of the term biological information. Moreover, many times that term is even considered equivalent to the term "genetic information". This is perhaps owing to the very fact that the notion of information in biology is deeply connected to the birth of molecular biology. The first time we read about the notion of information forming part of a biological study's explanation is in Watson and Crick's second work in 1953:

"...It follows that in a long molecule many different permutations are possible, and it therefore seems
likely that the precise sequence of the bases is the code which carries the genetical information..." (Watson & Crick, 1953, p. 965).

Later in (Crick, 1958; Crick, 1970), we can see what he called the "central dogma of molecular biology" characterized as follows:

"...Because these were all the possible transfers from protein, the central dogma could be stated in the form 'once (sequential) information has passed into protein it cannot get out again'..." (Crick, 1970, p. 562).

Here, we must point out that the crux of this chapter is not an exploration of the different uses of the notion of information in the history of molecular biology (if the reader is so interested, please consult the following: Darden, 2006; Kay, 1993; Kay, 2000; Watson et al., 1988).

Nevertheless, what we are definitely interested in underscoring is that different researchers have begun to use the notion of information, codes, signs, and similar ideas to discuss other aspects that make up the biological dynamic and that are not necessarily related to genetic information (Jablonka, 2002; Jablonka & Lamb, 2005; Kauffman et al., 2008; Maynard, 2000).

On the other hand, we do want to stress that our approach to the notion of information, signs, and the like is set within the perspective of evolution.

For us, this implies we draw upon no assumptions, characteristics, or properties coming from humans or the world of human products. In truth, we hold that the notions we are studying need to be clarified from a naturalist point of view.

In other words, we need to avoid extrapolations coming from the human world, like ascriptional interpretations or epiphenomenal ones.

In agreement with Bickhard's (2004) proposals, we are confident that normative emergence is necessary for any naturalistic account of biology.

An interesting spin upon research carried out on the nature of the living and its difference to that of the non-living is found in the set of implications derived from the following statement made by Pattee: "life is distinguished from the nonliving world by its dependence on signs." (Pattee, 2005, p. 299).

In order to have some means of differentiating between the world of the living and the world of the nonliving, we first must be able to distinguish if what we have characterized as a living system depends upon signs.

This leads us to ask what the implications are for something to be dependent upon signs. Would it be possible to measure that dependency? Moreover, how can we detect if there is dependency at all?

Thus, our conceptual quest conclusively brings us to ask these questions: What is a sign? What its nature may be?

What is the nature of a sign? There are many challenges that we must surmount in order to develop an account of the nature of signs that could be seen from a naturalized perspective (Hoffmeyer, 1996; Pattee, 1995; Sebeok, 1991; Sebeok, 1994).

In order to do so, we will study this problem within a process metaphysics, and our guiding principles shall be (1) natural existence is best understood in terms of 'processes' rather than 'things' and (2) time and change are among the fundamental features of our physical reality.

Consequently, we accept neither the existence of something like 'signs as things' nor the existence of signs in and of themselves.

If there are such things as signs in reality, then they would have much to do with the existence of certain processes; they would be connected with natural relationships developed inside certain spatial–temporal dynamic interactions; such a proposal is very similar to the approach of Peirce (1868).

It seems appropriate, in a naturalistic approach, to connect the matter–energy variations with the possible emergence of signs. If a sign is not a thing but a product of certain relationships, then its nature will depend on the type of relationship in which it is involved. In other words, signs will be

formed—will emerge, so to speak—when certain relationships take place.

We propose, therefore, that the emergence of signs is linked to the emergence of a kind of phenomenon which has, within itself, an interconnected network of molecular processes that are mainly made up of chemical compounds. We wish to say that signs, signals, and codes essentially belong to the world of the living, not only to the world of the human.

We need to point out here that our proposal views signs as phenomena that appear in the physical world from a very special and specific relationship.

Therefore, the concept of a sign turns out to be a relational notion, and the relation we are referring to is produced when matter-energy variations exert an influence on a dynamic entity of the universe made up of a network of molecular processes which contain properties we believe are fundamentally possessed by every living system (more on these topics in *Looking at Biological Networks*).

Our line of reasoning follows from the fact that whatever kind of energy variation may occur in biological system, it will only turn into a (it will become *'potential information'* for the system) when the system has the capability to react accordingly. And this happens when the energy variation impacts something in the system and is incorporated into the system—as a variation—with capacity of becoming part of the system's processes.

If an energy variation does not have the capacity to be incorporated in the form of a variation (any kind of variation) in the system, then it is not a sign for the system, and, as a consequence, the system cannot develop a response. This is the form in which signs emerge from physical reality.

In consequence, our proposal concerning conditions in which it is possible for biological information to emerge finds its roots in the dynamic transmission of matter-energy variations.

Later on, after these variations are incorporated into a dynamic entity that can detect them (it turn into a signs for the system) and that also contains the ability to form some type of response in tune with them, the signs then becomes *completely meaningful information* for that dynamic entity (biological system or, in our case, prebiotic system).

We propose the following: information emerges in the biological world as 'information with meaning' or 'meaningful information'. To be exact, it emerges as information with biological meaning or what we like to call *'bio-meaning'*.

Like signs, information is also a relational notion, and as such it will depend on processes, specifically biological processes. Information will always be meaningful information for biological systems.

In other words, the physical substrata that allow for the emergence of biological information are found within our universe. Whenever we observe reality, we will always find matter-energy variations: changes in chemical compound concentrations, pH changes, different conformations of macromolecules, physical and chemical process changes, electrical potential changes, etc.

From this last statement, we realize that a matter-energy variation on its own is nothing more and nothing less than a matter-energy variation. Yet, under certain circumstances, that same matter-energy variation is subject to becoming a sign.

What we are stating, then, is that given the circumstances, which we will discuss further on, any type of matter-energy variation will "become a sign" when it can incorporate itself as "a variation" into the interior of a complex adaptive system upon drawing near it.

And, incorporating itself into the interior of these systems as a variation implies this determined matter-energy variation is capable of interacting with certain process components these types of systems possess.

As a result of this interaction, the matter-energy variation, which exerted an influence on the system, turns into another type of variation that, later on, may be transmitted–as a "variation"–through

the set of processes characterizing that complex adaptive system.

Resuming, we can say:

"...Our proposal is an evolutionary theory of semantics where meaning first emerged in the form of bio-meaning. We claim that signs in biological systems (and in pre-biotic systems as well) are related to matter–energy transformations as they are incorporated into the system as 'variations'. In turn, these variations become biological information—always with bio-meaning— ... [which] is followed by a response from the specific type of biotic or pre-biotic system. From its initial emergence in the physical world, we can hypothesize that bio- meaning has the ability of increasing its levels of complexity and sophistication all the way up to the human world. Meaning and biological information were connected at their very beginning, and this bond conditioned the evolution of both notions well into the abstract levels of human culture..." (Riofrio, 2008, p. 375).

3. LOOKING AT BIOLOGICAL NETWORKS

Our approach to biological information through an evolutionary perspective need not be related to any specific ontology which involves design or intentional notions (e.g., Jablonka, 2002; Maynard, 2000) or to any kind of interpretive sub-system inside the receiver system (Jablonka, 2002, p. 602).

We are interested in the basic properties of life and the way they initially emerged, generating the conditions that allow a kind of dynamic self-organization—those that contain simple chemical components, as well as a minimal set of processes that is sufficiently robust to suggest that it could be the direct ancestor of biological systems.

In the last paragraph, we attempted to summarize our principal assumption from which we will infer the conclusions of our arguments.

The task we are left with, then, is to specify the type of molecular network that may have triggered the dawning of the prebiotic world, the emergence of which placed a special interconnection and interdependence of molecular processes, which was probably already present on Earth during that remote time period, on the pathway towards becoming a living system.

Nevertheless, we need to set the record straight that before the appearance of this class of protocell, the terrestrial environment consisted entirely of inert phenomena and properties, that is, phenomena related solely to physics, chemistry, and physical chemistry.

When these protocells made their appearance–from these complex adaptive systems–we can infer that, along with the abovementioned phenomena and properties, other, newer types also came into existence.

In other words, we can verify the emergence of what we are calling signs, biological information, biological functions, prebiotic evolutionary phenomena related to autonomous agent behaviors of these protocells, etc., starting from the dawn of the prebiotic world.

The above corresponds to the origin of the prebiotic world, one that possessed a great evolutionary dynamic and, in the end, brought about Darwinian or vertical evolution, although today we see that horizontal evolution is not uncommon among bacteria and archaea (Woese, 2002).

We also believe that the origin of pre-biotic systems already carry with them a certain level of complexity in their dynamic organization. Put in different terms, to understand the conditions that make the appearance of living forms possible is to understand that their most basic properties were present at the origin of the pre-biotic world.

We place our theoretical proposals in the distant past, and this era tell us that the types of chemical constituents we might find available on the

Earth would be incredibly simple chemical compounds, mainly inorganic, yet perhaps a very small amount of organic ones.

Taking into account the current understanding about what the conditions of primitive Earth could

have been like and meteor impacts during this time period, it is possible to theorize the feasibility of the existence of amino acids and carboxylic acids. Furthermore, the fact of massive volcanic activity makes it possible to theorize the existence of sulfhydryl [Bada et al., 1995; Cooper et al., 2001; Bernstein et al., 2002; Monnard et al., 2002].

We additionally hold that the dawning of the prebiotic world implied formation of a self-organizing dynamic that, in reality, was a determined type of protocell. It emerged in the remote past, thanks to the correlation produced among three very different types of molecular processes.

What is interesting here is that each process, left by itself, has no evolutionary potential. Yet, when they are interrelated, they trigger the appearance of an entity, what we are calling the Informational Dynamic System, which contains a certain level of interaction with its surroundings, that is, it behaves as an autonomous agent (Kauffman, 2000).

This provides it the capacity to adapt to its environment–it is a complex adaptive system–and, hence, it would have the ability to evolve (while this trait would have been minimal at its start up).

In addition, the informational dynamic system contains properties that would not have been found within the process types that form it if those were separated one from another.

This discovery should make us consider the appearance of these new properties in the universe was an outcome of a special interconnection between the processes. Truth be told, we now realize this interconnection generated an interdependence among the processes at the same time.

This interdependence to which we are alluding has to do with the three process types that interact amongst each other so as to become a self-sustaining and self-maintaining molecular network of processes vis-à-vis an ever changing environment.

And, moreover, we know that two of the three processes act as system constraints.

These constraints are neither what were normally produced in the prevailing conditions of the young Earth's hydrosphere nor what could be produced in physics, chemistry, and physical chemistry.

Rather, prior to the formation of the Informational Dynamic System protocell, the constraints we are talking about were molecular processes with precise molecular mechanisms inside each chemical reaction and, taken as a whole, were a particular course of chemical reactions intended to achieve a result, one marked by gradual changes through a series of molecular states.

With the passage of time and the emergence of the Informational Dynamic System, two of the processes forming part of its structure began to interact in coordination with each other since they contain similar molecular reactions.

What process types are we referring to? Let's take a look at what they consist of.

This way, the first class of processes:

"... [It] is fundamental for providing the system a certain degree of independence with respect to its environment since it generates the conditions for being in non-equilibrium state. This is the endergonic-exergonic cycle capable of producing–in each cycle–quantities of free energy to the system that are appropriate to generate work (of a type fundamentally chemical). This cycle is, in its own right, the one providing the system with the far from equilibrium characteristic since it forms a component part of its dynamic organization. To be a system in the non-equilibrium state is a priority intrinsic to the system; because of that, it is the most basic fundamental of informational dynamic systems..." (Riofrio, 2007, p. 238).

And in case of the second process group:

"... [It] would form another important part of the dynamic organization of these systems. This is the one that makes up the protoplasmic membrane. First, this component permits a separation, a physical barrier between the system and its environment, causing from there a different distribution of compounds, a different dynamic,

and a different interaction among the processes. It also permits certain properties of chemistry to have a focal point of action to generate possible problematic circumstances which in turn produce the conditioning situations for exploring different solution strategies for the system in the future... It is the part of the system that regulates the interaction with its environment as well as providing the necessary constituents (matter and energy) so that the internal system processes continue producing their mechanisms in conditions compatible to their survival... This part of the system organization is one that is a complete agent since it allows for the resolution of the osmotic problems, the adequate concentration of components in the internal system processes, the management of electrochemical gradients, the reduction of chances for the entrance of foreign elements into its organization, etc..." (Riofrio, 2007, pp. 238-239)."

As for the third process group:

"... [It] is a network of reactions that would perform the organizational dynamic's reparation, maintenance, and reproduction processes of the informational dynamic system..." (Riofrio, 2007, p. 239).

An Informational Dynamic System is therefore organized by the interdependence of the above three sets of processes, and we know that a correlation among processes is to be expected whenever a system is in a far from thermodynamic equilibrium state (Kosztin & Schulten, 2004; Levine, 2005).

It is reasonable to postulate that the compounds encountered during the pre-biotic era would have mostly been very simple in nature, and might have been immersed in the natural dynamic of the physical world and in phenomena of self-organization. Therefore, it is quite possible that they would have formed a relationship among the three types of processes that we have proposed.

Moreover, our proposal rests upon the naturalistic supposition that the Informational Dynamic

System is different from other self-organizing systems because it is able to develop and maintain a capacity for remaining in, or even for increasing, the far from thermodynamic equilibrium state, an essential condition for its existence.

We contend that Informational Dynamic Systems already have in their organization those basic properties that are present in all living systems and are expressed at increasing levels of complexity as we move forward in evolution.

Thus, since we propose that information emerges simultaneously with function in an integrated and interrelated network of molecular processes, we now have a related mechanism that enables us to detect information flow:

"...Briefly, we think that both information and function emerge at the same time, in unison, in the informational dynamic systems and that the physical emergence of both notions happens in an interrelational way: information-function... Both ideas of information and function are directed towards the network of interrelations among the processes. It is in the processes and the relationships among them that both capacities emerge for the first time in the physical world in such a way that through the function pole ("informational function"), we observe that the contribution of the processes among each other for their appropriate performance in the integral logic of the system's organization causes the system to maintain itself far from thermodynamic equilibrium. Through the information pole ("functional information"), we observe that the meaning for the system of some signal or sign (that is the physical means of transporting some matter-energy variation) will be expressed in agreement with maintaining the system in the far from equilibrium state. However, it can also be that it was in opposition to maintaining the far from equilibrium state..." (Riofrio, 2007, pp. 241-242).

It must be made clear that our Informational Dynamic System is made up of simple molecular compounds related to each other by interconnected processes. The relationships between them produce dynamic processes of transformation and maintenance, given that they are interdependent. If cohesion is a concept that integrates the totality of these processes and their interrelationships, then there is no reason against adopting this notion to address the underlying causes that characterize the identity of the Informational Dynamic System.

And with respect to the connection between biological information and biological function:

"...We can see that both information and function are strongly connected by their definition with the idea of far from thermodynamic equilibrium. And this is precisely what we propose. Because of this, it is possible to consider, through a naturalist perspective, the far from thermodynamic equilibrium state as a basic norm that the system imposes on itself for continuing to be the system that it is..." (Riofrio, 2007, p. 242).

We now see how signs turn into meaningful information (bio-meaning). If a matter-energy variation becomes incorporated in the form of a variation somewhere inside the system, then it will turn into a sign for the system. Once inside the system, if this sign has an effect on its cohesion, in one way or another, then it will become meaningful information for the system. Cohesion is the idea that gives the Informational Dynamic System its identity in all its transformations through time (Collier, 1986; Collier, 2004).

Also, we could claim that 'something is a function' when a certain group of molecular actions manage to maintain the most basic state of the Informational Dynamic System, i.e., the far from thermodynamic equilibrium state. If this does not happen and there is a reduction of the far-from-equilibrium state, then we can consistently affirm that that 'something' is dysfunctional. As we can see, the normative nature of functions is a relational concept because the collection of actions produced by a process "is a function" only when these actions have their *raison d'être* in the concert of interdependent connections that make up the system.

4. INSIGHTS INTO THE BIOLOGICAL COMPUTING

One could say that research into trying to discover the basis of what can be called "biological computation" is strongly related to studies into theoretical biology (Noble, 2002).

In effect, we cannot overwhelmingly confirm the existence of any aspects in theoretical biology that broach biological phenomena from a general study framework. Instead, what we have right now is:

"...instead we apply the basic theories of chemistry and physics to biology... Moreover, we have not resolved fundamental questions in the central theory of biology, that of evolution. Is it dependent on contingent events—such as weather change or meteorite impacts—with no overall trend, or are there features that would inevitably emerge in any evolutionary process?... if there were to be some general principles (what some would call the 'logic of life'), then these—in their formulations as equations—would eventually become the basis of a fully theoretical biology..." (Noble, 2002, pp. 462-463).

Therefore, we can assume that research purposed to elucidate the core components that may encompass the type and nature of natural computations in biological systems is not just important, but has also become central and completely applicable to our modern times, if viewed as an attempt to contribute to the development of theoretical biology.

To clarify, when we mention natural computation, we are usually citing the following three types of methods: (1) nature-inspired, related to developing novel problem solving techniques,

(2) those that are based on the use of computers to synthesize natural phenomena, and (3) natural substance-applied (e.g. molecules), related to computing.

Nonetheless, here we want to point out a fourth possibility, one that is beginning to gain acceptance and is at the heart of our chapter's thesis: natural computation in biological systems is real. Consequently, our strategy relies on the quest for methods that blaze trails to our uncovering its nature.

Our thesis will take us down a path of investigation that is still in its infancy, i.e. we will put forth all the necessary investigative effort to begin discovering the implications behind the very nature of computation and its connections with other related concepts.

Some of what we are talking about here is related to the notion of mechanisms, the nature of signs and symbols, possible meanings behind digitality, non-deterministic computation, implications of absolute computability, relationship between information processing and computation, and many others.

We are firmly convinced that new research lines will begin appearing in the next few years, and perhaps, during the 21st century, we will witness a huge revolution with respect to the foundations of biological science.

So, in an effort towards that end, we shall try to sketch out our modest contribution in the following paragraphs.

Since our protocell paints the picture of the dawning of the pre-biotic world and given the emergence of biological information and the existence of the internal constraint which secures a far from thermodynamic equilibrium state for the Informational Dynamic System, we find ourselves in a place where we can conclude the system will, through decentralized processes, behave in ways that may be related to different externally and internally generated signs.

This bio-meaning (generator of protocell behavior, i.e. type of response) is the result of the transmission of a "variation"–originating from a matter-energy variation that affected the system–that travels across the Informational Dynamic System's processing network and that ends up producing a consequence that will increase, maintain, or decrease the far from thermodynamic equilibrium state.

We might be able to assign to this matter-energy variation, transmitted across the molecular mechanisms involved in the system's processes, a relationship or link to what could be ***the way in which the biological world "computes"***.

We now grasp that the Informational Dynamic System's interdependent processing network has produced an interesting phenomena; since, fundamentally, its two self-constraints are especially interconnected, the matter-energy variation (regardless of which process kick started the transmission) will inexorably conclude as a micro-cycle formed by endergonic–exergonic processes.

As we know all too well, this self-constraint causes a change in the system's free energy ($\Delta Gsys$), (i.e. a trend towards negative values).

Hence, there are three possible outcomes the matter-energy variation may have on that trend: none, positive, or negative. One implication from this line of reasoning we can come up with is that the self-constraint has, for the entire range of action produced within the Informational Dynamic System, turned into an unavoidable checkpoint along the pathway of creating a future set of responses that are generated in another part of the interconnected and interdependent processing network.

So, when faced with some sort of variation in its surrounding or internal environment and when that variation reaches this unavoidable checkpoint (the self-constraint), it is as if the Informational Dynamic System has a short conversation with itself:

"...since I detect this particular variation to have (1) no effect whatsoever or (2) an increasing effect or (3) a decreasing effect on my far from thermodynamic equilibrium state, then I will (1) continue with what I am doing or (2) take advantage of it to

improve my dynamic order or (3) take necessary action to counteract and expel it from the system... now, as for this other variation that just arrived, I detect it to have..."

This tentative explanation might lead us to the question of how small world structures spontaneously emerged in the biological realm, containing, among other elements, scale-free characteristics and evolutionary capacities (Watts & Strogatz, 1998; Kleinberg, 2000; Bork et al., 2004; Gong & van Leeuwen, 2004).

In addition, it may provide us the necessary tools to begin looking at the related question of how a sort of "relative reference point" that enabled the development of "something to be greedy about" on the routing paths of the biological small-world could have emerged.

Perhaps the self constraint, that impetus for the change in the system's free energy, might be seen as the "relative reference point" that first time appeared in the physical world in this integrated, interconnected, and interdependent network that is the Informational Dynamic System.

5. CONCLUDING REMARKS

Thus far we have presented a concept that might provide the implications resulting from the existence of intrinsic relationships between biological information and biological function.

Defending a fundamentally informational and functional dynamic organization in biological systems led us directly to their origins in pre-biotic systems, ones that also featured additional and interesting traits.

From the dawning of the pre-biotic world, one of those traits the primordial protocell had was the capacity to compute.

Additionally, this incredibly distant period in time may be when we can see the appearance of the first small world structures as core characteristics to the way in which the biological realm computes.

REFERENCES

Bada, J. L., Miller, S. L., & Zhao, M. (1995). The stability of amino acids at submarine hydrothermal vent temperatures. *Origins of Life and Evolution of the Biosphere, 25*, 111–118. doi:10.1007/BF01581577

Bernstein, M. P., Dworkin, J. P., Sandford, S. A., Cooper, G. W., & Allamandola, L. J. (2002). Racemic amino acids from the ultraviolet photolysis of interstellar ice analogues. *Nature, 416*, 401–403. doi:10.1038/416401a

Bickhard, M. H. (2004). Part II: applications of process-based theories: process and emergence: normative function and representation. *Axiomathes—An International Journal in Ontology and Cognitive Systems, 14*(1), 121– 155.

Bork, P., Jensen, L. J., von Mering, C., Ramani, A. K., Lee, I., & Marcotte, E. M. (2004). Protein interaction networks from yeast to human. *Current Opinion in Structural Biology, 14*, 292–299. doi:10.1016/j.sbi.2004.05.003

Collier, J. (1986). Entropy in evolution. *Biology and Philosophy, 1*, 5–24. doi:10.1007/BF00127087

Collier, J. (2000). Autonomy and process closure as the basis for functionality. In J. L. R. Chandler & G. van de Vijver (Eds.), Closure: Emergent organizations and their dynamics (pp. 280–290). Annals of the New York Academy of Science, 901.

Cooper, G., Kimish, N., Belisle, W., Sarinana, J., Brabham, K., & Garrel, L. (2001). Carbonaceous meteorites as a source of sugar-related organic compounds for the early Earth. *Nature, 414*, 879–883. doi:10.1038/414879a

Crick, F. H. C. (1958). On Protein Synthesis. *Symposia of the Society for Experimental Biology, The Biological Replication of Macromolecules, XII*, 138-163.

Crick, F. H. C. (1970). Central Dogma of Molecular Biology. *Nature, 227*, 561–563. doi:10.1038/227561a0

Darden, L. (2006). Flow of Information in Molecular Biological Mechanisms. *Biological Theory, 1*, 280–287. doi:10.1162/biot.2006.1.3.280

Gong, P., & van Leeuwen, C. (2004). Evolution to a small-world network with chaotic units. *Europhysics Letters, 67*(2), 328–333. doi:10.1209/epl/i2003-10287-7

Hoffmeyer, J. (1996). *Signs of meaning in the universe*. Bloomington, IN: Indiana University Press.

Jablonka, E. (2002). Information: its interpretation, its inheritance, and its sharing. *Philosophy of Science, 69*, 578–605. doi:10.1086/344621

Jablonka, E., & Lamb, M. (2005). *Evolution in Four Dimensions*. Cambridge, MA: MIT Press.

Kauffman, S. (2000). *Investigations*. New York: Oxford University Press.

Kauffman, S., Logan, R. K., Este, R., Goebel, R., Hobill, D., & Shmulevich, I. (2008). Propagating organization: an enquiry. *Biology and Philosophy, 23*(1), 27–45. doi:10.1007/s10539-007-9066-x

Kay, L. E. (1993). *The Molecular Vision of Life: Caltech, The Rockefeller Foundation, and The Rise of the New Biology*. Oxford, UK: Oxford University Press.

Kay, L. E. (2000). *Who Wrote the Book of Life? A History of the Genetic Code*. Stanford, CA: Stanford University Press.

Kleinberg, J. M. (2000). Navigation in a small world. *Nature, 406*, 845. doi:10.1038/35022643

Kosztin, I., & Schulten, K. (2004). Fluctuation-driven molecular transport through an asymmetric membrane channel. *Physical Review Letters, 93*, 238102. doi:10.1103/PhysRevLett.93.238102

Levine, R. D. (2005). *Molecular reaction dynamics*. Cambridge, UK: Cambridge University Press. doi:10.1017/CBO9780511614125

Maynard Smith, J. (2000). The concept of information in biology. *Philosophy of Science*, *67*, 177–194. doi:10.1086/392768

Monnard, P. A., Apel, C. L., Kanavarioti, A., & Deamer, D. W. (2002). Influence of ionic inorganic solutes on self-assembly and polymerization processes related to early forms of life-implications for a prebiotic aqueous medium. *Astrobiology*, *2*, 139–152. doi:10.1089/15311070260192237

Noble, D. (2002). The rise of computational biology. *Nature Reviews. Molecular Cell Biology*, *3*(6), 459–463. doi:10.1038/nrm810

Pattee, H. H. (1995). Evolving self-reference: matter, symbols, and semantic closure. *Communication and Cognition–Artificial Intelligence*, *12*(1–2), 9–28.

Peirce, C. S. (1868). On a new list of categories. [Eprint: http://www.cspeirce.com/menu/library/bycsp/newlist/nl-frame.htm]. *Proceedings of the American Academy of Arts and Sciences*, *7*, 287–298.

Riofrio, W. (2007). Informational Dynamic Systems: Autonomy, information, function . In Gershenson, C., Aerts, D., & Edmonds, B. (Eds.), *Worldviews, science, and us: Philosophy and complexity* (pp. 232–249). Singapore: World Scientific.

Riofrio, W. (2008). Understanding the Emergence of Cellular Organization. *Biosemiotics*, *1*(3), 361–377. doi:10.1007/s12304-008-9027-z

Sebeok, T. A. (1991). *A sign is just a sign*. Bloomington, IN: Indiana University Press.

Sebeok, T. A. (1994). *Signs: An introduction to semiotics*. Toronto, Canada: University of Toronto Press.

Watson, J. D., & Crick, F. H. C. (1953). Genetical Implications of the Structure of Deoxyribonucleic Acid. *Nature*, *171*, 964–967. doi:10.1038/171964b0

Watson, J. D., Hopkins, N. H., Roberts, J. W., Steitz, J. A., & Weiner, A. M. (1988). *Molecular Biology of the Gene* (4th ed.). Menlo Park, CA: Benjamin/Cummings.

Watts, D. J., & Strogatz, S. H. (1998). Collective dynamics of 'small-world' networks. *Nature*, *393*, 440–442. doi:10.1038/30918

Woese, C. R. (2002). On the evolution of cells. *Proceedings of the National Academy of Sciences of the United States of America*, *99*(13), 8742–8747. doi:10.1073/pnas.132266999

KEY TERMS AND DEFINITIONS

Biological Information: It is any matter-energy variation that is incorporated into pre-biotic or biological systems and that generates a response in accordance with that variation. It is, furthermore, meaningful information, or better said, "information with biological meaning". It can also be called "bio-meaning".

Informational Dynamic Systems: (IDS): In our thesis, it is a theoretical construct denoting a type of protocells that probably emerged at the dawn of the pre-biotic world. We furthermore hold it possessed the most basic properties of living systems: biological information, autonomy, and biological function. Hence, its self-organizing dynamic is Informational and Functional.

Self-Constraints: These are possibly generated through the spontaneous and dynamic relationship of certain process types that form part of an Adaptive Dynamic System.

Biological Computing: It is the way in which the biological realm computes, yet its nature is unknown. It seems to be connected to matter-energy variations that travel across molecular mechanisms produced in response to the execution of a specific biological function and found in the Adaptive Dynamic System's processes.

Pre-Biotic World: It is the time in which protocell structures existed and is different from the inert world because its phenomena do not just line up with the laws of physics, chemistry, and physical chemistry. It is a very important time period since that is when molecular processes were redirected toward the future appearance of living systems and because some of the most important properties living beings possess arrived on the scene.

Darwinian or Vertical Evolution: In this evolutionary form, genetic information is transmitted from parent to child cells and is the device used in natural selection.

Horizontal Evolution: It is also another form for genetic information transmission, most likely in existence before the Darwinian kind and very commonly found in living systems from the Archaea and Bacteria domains. It is quite possible an evolutionary form similar to this one was produced during the pre-biotic era.

Section 2
Philosophy of Computer Science

Chapter 5
Programming Languages as Mathematical Theories

Raymond Turner
University of Essex, UK

ABSTRACT

That computer science is somehow a mathematical activity was a view held by many of the pioneers of the subject, especially those who were concerned with its foundations. At face value it might mean that the actual activity of programming is a mathematical one. Indeed, at least in some form, this has been held. But here we explore a different gloss on it. We explore the claim that programming languages are (semantically) mathematical theories. This will force us to discuss the normative nature of semantics, the nature of mathematical theories, the role of theoretical computer science and the relationship between semantic theory and language design.

INTRODUCTION

The design and semantic definition of programming languages has occupied computer scientists for almost half a century. Design questions centre upon the style or paradigm of the language, (e.g. functional, logic, imperative or object oriented). More detailed issues concern the nature and content of its type system, its model of storage and its underlying control mechanisms. Semantic questions relate to the form and nature of programming language semantics (Tennent, 1981; Stoy, 1977;

Milne, 1976; Fernandez, 2004). For instance, how is the semantic content of a language determined and how is it expressed?

Presumably, one cannot entirely divorce the design of a language from its semantic content; one is not just designing a language in order to construct meaningless strings of symbols. A programming language is a vehicle for the expression of ideas and for the articulation of solutions to problems; and surely issues of meaning are central to this. But should semantic considerations enter the picture very early on in the process of design, or should they come as an afterthought; i.e. should

DOI: 10.4018/978-1-61692-014-2.ch005

we first design the language and then proceed to supply it with a semantic definition?

An influential perspective on this issue is to be found in one the most important early papers on the semantics of programming languages (Strachey C., 2000).

I am not only temperamentally a Platonist and prone to talking about abstracts if I think they throw light on a discussion, but I also regard syntactical problems as essentially irrelevant to programming languages at their present state of development. In a rough and ready sort of way, it seems to be fair to think of the semantics as being what we want to say and the syntax as how to say it. In these terms the urgent task in programming languages is to explore the field of semantic possibilities....When we have discovered the main outlines and the principal peaks we can go about describing a suitable neat and satisfactory notation for them. But first we must try to get a better understanding of the processes of computing and their description in programming languages. In computing we have what I believe to be a new field of mathematics which is at least as important as that opened up by the discovery (or should it be invention) of the calculus.

Apparently, *the field of semantic possibilities* must be laid out prior to the design of any actual language i.e., its syntax. More explicitly, the things that we may refer to and manipulate, and the processes we may call upon to control them, needs to be settled before any actual syntax is defined. We shall call this the *Semantics First* (**SF**) principle. According to it, one does not design a language and then proceed to its semantic definition as a post-hoc endeavour; semantics must come first.

This leads to the second part of Strachey's advice. In the last sentence of the quote he takes computing to be a new branch of mathematics. At face value this might be taken to mean that the activity of programming is somehow a mathematical one. This has certainly been suggested

elsewhere (Hoare, 1969) and criticized by several authors e.g. (Colburn T. R., 2000; Fetzer, 1988; Colburn T., 2007). But, whatever its merits, this does not seem to be what Strachey is concerned with. The early part of the quote suggests that he is referring to programming languages and their underlying structures. And his remark seems best interpreted to mean that (semantically) programming languages are, in some way, mathematical structures. Indeed, this is in line with other publications (Strachey C., 1965) where the underlying ontology of a language is taken to consist of mathematical objects. This particular perspective found its more exact formulation in denotational semantics (Stoy, 1977; Milne, 1976), where the theory of complete lattices supplied the background mathematical framework. This has since been expanded to other frameworks including category theory (Oles, 1982; Crole, 1993).

However, we shall interpret this more broadly i.e., in a way that is neutral with respect to the host theory of mathematical structures (e.g. set theory, category theory, or something else). We shall take it to mean that programming languages are, via their provided semantics, mathematical theories in their own right. We shall refer to this principle as the Mathematical Thesis (**MT**).

Exactly what **MT** and **SF** amount to, whether they are true, how they are connected, and what follows from them, will form the main focus of this paper. But before we embark on any consideration of these, we need to clarify what we understand by the terms *mathematical theory* and *semantics*.

MATHEMATICAL THEORIES

The nature of mathematical theories is one of the central concerns of the philosophy of mathematics (Shapiro, 2004), and it is not one that we can sensibly address here. But we do need to say something; otherwise our claim is left hanging in the air. Roughly, we shall be concerned with theories that are axiomatic in the logical sense.

While we shall make a few general remarks about the nature of these theories, we shall largely confine ourselves to illustrating matters and drawing out significant points by reference to some common examples.

Geometry began with the informal ideas of lines, planes and points; notions that were employed in measuring and surveying. Gradually, these were massaged into Euclidean geometry: a *mathematical theory* of these notions. Euclid's geometry was axiomatic but not formal in the sense of being expressed in a formal language, and this distinction will be important later. Euclidean geometry reached its modern rigorous formulation in the 20th century with Hilbert's axiomatisation.

A second, and much later example, is Peano arithmetic. Again, this consists of a group of axioms, informally expressed, but now about natural numbers. Of course, people counted before Peano arithmetic was formulated. Indeed, it was intended to be a theory of our intuitive notion of number, including the basis of counting. In its modern guises it is formulated in various versions of formal arithmetic. These theories are distinguished in terms of the power of quantification and the strength of the included induction principles.

ZF set theory (Jech, 1971) began with the informal notion of set that was operating in 19th century mathematics. It was developed into a standalone mathematical theory by Cantor who introduced the idea of an infinite set given in extension. It had some of the characteristics of the modern notion, but it was still not presented as an axiomatic theory. This emerged only in 20th century with the work of Zermelo and Fraenkel. The modern picture that drives the axioms of ZF is that of the cumulative hierarchy of sets: sets arranged in layers where each layer is generated by forming sets made of the elements of previous layers.

These axiomatic theories began with some informal concepts that are present in everyday applications and mathematical practice. In many cases, the initial pre-axiomatic notions were quite loose, and most often the process of theory construction added substance and precision to the informal one. This feature is explicitly commented upon by Gödel in regard to Turing's analysis of *finite procedure or mechanical computability* (Turing, 1937). In the words of Wang (Wang, 1974.), Gödel saw the problem of defining computability as: *an excellent example of a concept which did not appear sharp to us but has become so as a result of a careful reflection.* The pre-theoretic analogues of such theories are not always sharp and decisive, and the informal picture is often far from complete. In this respect, the process of theory construction resembles the creation of a novel. And, as with the notion of *truth in the novel,* some things are determined (John did kill Mary) but not everything is (it is left open whether he killed Mary's dog). The mathematical process itself brings these theories into existence. They are in this sense, *definitional* theories.

Although all this is still quite vague, it captures something about what is demanded of an axiomatic theory for it to be considered mathematical. Arbitrary sets of rules and axioms will not do: to be mathematically worthy an axiomatic theory must capture some pre-theoretical intuitive notions in an elegant, useful and mathematically tractable manner. And this is roughly the notion of mathematical theory that we have in mind in the proposition that programming languages are mathematical theories (**MT**).

With this much ground cleared, we may now turn to the function and nature of *semantics*. This will take a few sections to unravel.

NORMATIVE SEMANTICS

Syntax is given via a grammar of some sort e.g., context free, BNF, inference rules or syntax diagrams. But a grammar only pins down what the legal strings of the language are. It does not determine what they mean; this is the job of the semantics. We shall illustrate some issues with the following toy programming language.

$P ::= x := E \mid skip \mid P; P \mid if \ B \ then \ P \ else \ P \mid while \ B \ do P \mid$
$E ::= x \mid 0 \mid 1 \mid E + E \mid E * E \mid$
$B ::= x \mid true \mid false \mid E < E \mid \neg B \mid B \wedge B \mid$

The expressions (E) are constructed from variables (x), 0 and 1 by addition and multiplication. The Boolean expressions (B) are constructed from variables; **true**, **false**, the ordering relation ($<$) on numbers, negation and conjunction. Finally, the programs of the language (P) are built from a simple assignment statement ($x: = E$) via sequencing ($P; Q$), conditional programs (**if** B **then** P **else** Q) and while loops (**while** B **do** P). According to the grammar, with parenthesis added, the following program is legitimate, where n is an input variable.

$x := 0; y := 1;$
$while \ x < n \ do \ (x := x + 1; y := x * y)$

But in order to construct or understand this program, one needs to know more than the syntax of its host language; one must possess some semantic information about the language (Turner R., 2007). Most importantly, in general, a semantic account of a language of any kind must tell us when we are using an expression correctly, and when we are not.

The fact that the expression means something implies that there is a whole set of normative truths about my behavior with that expression; namely, that my use of it is correct in application to certain objects and not in application to others. .... The normativity of meaning turns out to be, in other words, simply a new name for the familiar fact that, regardless of whether one thinks of meaning in truth-theoretic or assertion-theoretic terms, meaningful expressions possess conditions of correct use. Kripke's insight was to realize that

this observation may be converted into a condition of adequacy on theories of the determination of meaning: any proposed candidate for the property in virtue of which an expression has meaning, must be such as to ground the 'normativity' of meaning-it ought to be possible to read off from any alleged meaning constituting property of a word, what is the correct use of that word. (Boghossian, 1989)

A semantic account must provide us with an account of what constitutes correct use. It seems generally recognized (Gluer, 2008) that this requirement on a theory of meaning has two components: a criterion of correctness and an obligation to do what is correct. We shall only be concerned with the first. Although aimed at theories of meaning for ordinary language, it is not hard to see that any semantic account of a programming language must equally distinguish *correct* from *incorrect* uses of program constructs. Indeed, in the case of programming languages, there are several central applications of semantic definitions that involve notions of *correctness*.

A semantic account must guide a compiler writer in implementing the language. It must enable a distinction to be drawn between the correct and incorrect implementation of a construct. In other words, it must facilitate a specification of compiler correctness. The compiler must correctly translate the source code into the target code, and correctness demands that the semantic definitions of the two languages must somehow agree under the translation.

From the user perspective, a semantic account must enable a distinction to be drawn between correct and incorrect use of programming constructs - not just syntactically, but in the sense of meeting their intended specifications (formal or otherwise). For instance, assume the specification is a specification of the factorial function. Then a semantic account must determine whether or not the following program meets it. Syntax alone cannot do this.

$$x := 0; y := 1;$$
$$while \; x < n \; do \, (x := x + 1; y := x * y)$$

More generally, a semantic account must enable a distinction to be drawn between software that is intended for different ends (i.e., meet different user requirements). For example, it must enable a distinction to be drawn between software intended to act as a web browser and software intended to aid in asset management of power generation. Presumably, a programmer who supplies one rather than the other will get told off.

Given these normative demands, how is a semantic definition of a language to be given? One not obviously implausible suggestion is via an interpretation into another programming language (or a subset of the source one). This is little more than a demand that a compiler provides the semantics. But a little reflection should be sufficient to convince the reader that such an approach does not satisfy our normative demands. Unless the semantics of the target language is given, and thus grounded, the semantics of the source language is not grounded: it just passes the burden of normativity from one language to another. We also need to have some semantic account of the language in which the translation is written. So, by itself, a translation cannot guide the implementer; it is an implementation, not an independent guide to one[1].

THE ROLE OF MACHINES

One way in which this picture might be grounded is in terms of a machine of some sort. This may be achieved stage by stage, one language getting its interpretation in the next, until a machine provides the final and actual mechanism of semantic interpretation. For instance, for our toy language, we require a machine with an underlying state whose role is to store numerical values in locations. Pictorially, this might take the shape of Table 1.

Table 1.

x	y	z	w....
5	7	9	7......

The semantics of assignment is then unpacked by its impact on it. But what is the nature of this store? Is it physical or abstract? One common sense view is that, in order to block the potentially infinite regress of languages, it must be a physical device that grounds the meaning in the physical world. More explicitly, the intended meaning of the language is to be given by the actual effect on the state of a physical machine.

In particular, consider the following assignment instruction.

$$x := E$$

How is its semantics to be given on a physical machine? Apparently, the machine does what it does when the program is run - and what it does determines the meaning of assignment. But there are dissenters to such a view.

Actual machines can malfunction: through melting wires or slipping gears they may give the wrong answer. How is it determined when a malfunction occurs? By reference to the program of the machine, as intended by its designer, not simply by reference to the machine itself. Depending on the intent of the designer, any particular phenomenon may or may not count as a machine malfunction. A programmer with suitable intentions might even have intended to make use of the fact that wires melt or gears slip, so that a machine that is malfunctioning for me is behaving perfectly for him. Whether a machine ever malfunctions and, if so, when, is not a property of the machine itself as a physical object, but is well defined only in terms of its program, stipulated by its designer. Given the program, once again, the physical object is superfluous for the purpose of determining what function is meant. (Kripke, 1982)

There is no appeal to an independent specification; meaning is completely determined by what the machine does. It follows that there is no notion of malfunction, and no notion of correctness. So there is no sense to be made of the demand that the machine behave correctly. For this, some machine independent account is needed. This may be expressed in the following way.

When the state is updated by placing v in location x, and then the contents of x is retrieved, v will be returned. For any other location, the contents remain unchanged.

Where **Update** changes the value in a given location and **Lookup** returns the value at a given location, we may rewrite this more symbolically as follows.

- **Lookup** (**Update** $(s,x,v),x) = v$
- **Lookup** (**Update** $(s,x,v),y) = $ **Lookup** (s,y)
  where $x \neq y$

But these simple equations determine an operation on an abstract machine. And it is this that supplies the specification of the physical one, and makes the latter (semantically) superfluous. If the command $x{:}{=}10$ places 28 in location y, this is not correct.

It would seem that any normative semantic account of our toy language must be given in terms of its impact upon such an abstract machine. Physical operations may conform to the specification given by the abstract ones, but they cannot provide a semantic correlate for a program.

INFORMAL SEMANTICS

But the nature of the machine is only part of the story. We still need to say how a whole programming language is to be interpreted. The most common approach employs natural language, where such accounts most often take the form of a reference manual for the language. And they can be big: the one for Java Language is almost 600 pages. The following is taken from The Java Language Specification, Third Edition - TOC

A while statement is executed by first evaluating the expression. If the result is of type Boolean, it is subject to unboxing conversion (§5.1.8). If execution of the expression or the subsequent unboxing conversion (if any) completes abruptly for some reason, the while statement completes abruptly for the same reason. Otherwise, execution continues by making a choice based on the resulting value: If the value is true, then the contained statement is executed. Then there is a choice: If execution of the statement completes normally, then the entire while statement is executed again, beginning by re-evaluating the expression. If execution of the statement completes abruptly, see §14.12.1 below. If the (possibly unboxed) value of the expression is false, no further action is taken and the while statement completes normally. If the (possibly unboxed) value of the expression is false the first time it is evaluated, then the statement is not executed.

This is the standard semantics of the *while* statement within the Java language. However, there are several complications that pertain to the special character of this language. For the time being, we shall ignore most of these and concentrate on the central issues. For this purpose we shall illustrate the semantic process with our toy language. Later we shall consider some of the complexities that arise with real languages.

As with the semantic conception of truth, our abstract notion of *execution* emerges from a recursive semantic description of the whole language.

1. If the execution of E in the state s returns the value v, then the execution of $x:=E$ in a state s, returns the state that is the same as s except that the value v replaces the current value in location x i.e., ***Update**(s,x,v)*.
2. The execution of **skip** in a state s, returns s.
3. If the execution of P in s yields the state s' and the execution of Q in s' returns the state s'', then the execution of $P;Q$ in s, returns the state s''
4. If the execution of B in s returns **true** and the execution of P in s returns s', then the execution of **if** B **then** P **else** Q in s, evaluates to s'. If on the other hand, the execution of B in s returns **false** and the execution of Q in s returns s', then the execution of **if** B **then** P else Q in s, evaluates to s'.
5. If the execution of B in s returns **true**, the execution of P in s returns s', and the execution of **while** B **do** P in s' yields s'', then the execution of **while** B **do** P in s, returns s''. If the execution B in s returns false, then the execution of **while** B **do** P in s, return s.
6. The execution of a variable in state s returns the value obtained by looking it up in s.
7. If the execution of E in state s returns v and the execution of E' returns v' then the execution of the addition of E and E', returns the addition of v and v'. We proceed similarly for multiplication.

This provides a natural language semantic account for our toy language. But being based upon an underlying abstract machine, it is an abstract account i.e., the semantics is given in terms of relations on the abstract machine.

Such an approach works well with simple languages, but with real ones matters are less clear. It is difficult to express essentially technical notions in natural language. For one thing, it does not always facilitate being clear about what we are talking about. Furthermore, the consequences of

design decisions, articulated in natural language, may not be as sharp as they could be.

In particular, Java has integrated multithreading to a far greater extent than most programming languages. It is also one of the only languages that specifies and requires safety guarantees for improperly synchronized programs. It turns out that understanding these issues is far more subtle and difficult than was previously thought. The existing specification makes guarantees that prohibit standard and proposed compiler optimizations; it also omits guarantees that are necessary for safe execution of much existing code (Pugh, 2000)

This indicates that there are deeper problems than ambiguity, the normal source of problems with natural language definitions. Lack of clarity cuts deeper than scope distinctions. In particular, there is a lack of semantic clarity over the basic notions such as *threading* and *synchronization*. It is not a reformulation in a more formal language that is required, but a better conceptual understanding of these fundamental notions. Nor can we glean what they are supposed to do by running experiments on a machine. What they are supposed to do must be fixed by an abstract normative account.

Furthermore, even the simple consequences of the semantics are not easy to articulate. For example, to ensure that it is coherent, we shall need to establish that expression execution does not change the state. This much we have assumed in our informal semantic account. Similarly, a compiler writer will need to argue, with some degree of precision, that the compiler is correct. This will involve an inductive argument that must take place during the construction not after it. Such arguments are not optional; at some level, and with some degree of precision, one cannot construct a compiler without undertaking such reasoning.

So despite its prevalence, there are non-trivial problems with natural language accounts.

OPERATIONAL SEMANTICS

However, a little notation will help with some of them. More specifically, we shall write

$$< P, s > \Downarrow s'$$

to indicate that evaluating P in state s terminates in s'. With this notation we can rewrite the whole semantic account of our simple language. It will be little more than a rewrite of the informal account with this notation replacing the words execute/execution.

1. Assignment

$$\frac{< E, s > \Downarrow v}{< x := E, s > \Downarrow Update(s, x, v)}$$

2. Skip

$$< skip, s > \Downarrow s$$

3. Sequencing

$$\frac{< P, s > \Downarrow s' \quad < Q, s' > \Downarrow s''}{< P; Q, s > \Downarrow s''}$$

4. Conditionals

$$\frac{< B, s > \Downarrow true \quad < P, s > \Downarrow s'}{< If \ B \ do \ Pelse \ Q, s > \Downarrow s'}$$
$$\frac{< B, s > \Downarrow false \quad < Q, s > \Downarrow s'}{< If \ B \ doP \ else \ Q, s > \Downarrow s'}$$

5. While

$$\frac{< B, s > \Downarrow true \quad < P, s > \Downarrow s' \quad < while \ B \ do \ P, s' > \Downarrow s''}{< while \ B \ do \ P, s > \Downarrow s''}$$
$$\frac{< B, s > \Downarrow false}{< while \ B \ do \ P, s > \Downarrow s}$$

6. Variables

$$< x, s > \Downarrow < Lookup(x, s), s >$$

7. Addition and Multiplication

$$\frac{< E, s > \Downarrow < v, s' > \quad < E, s' > \Downarrow < v', s'' >}{< E + E', s > \Downarrow < v + v', s'' >}$$

In addition to the use of our simple notation, we have replaced the conditional form of the informal semantics by rules. In particular, the antecedents of the informal rules e.g.

If the execution of B in s returns **true** and the execution of P in s returns s', then... are represented as the premises of the formal ones e.g.

$$< B, s > \Downarrow true < P, s > \Downarrow s'$$

So, apart from the fact that the inferential structure of the rules is now made explicit, these are minor changes.

But with this version of the semantics in place, we can more explicitly state a result that guarantees that the evaluation of expressions has no side effects.

For all expressions E and states s

if $< E, s > \Downarrow < v, s' >$ *then* $s = s$

The actual proof proceeds by induction on the expressions using the rules for the respective cases: we argue, by induction, that the execution of expressions does not yield side effects. For the base case, we observe that the execution of variables does not change the state. For the induction step, on the (inductive) assumption that the execution of E and E' do not, i.e.,

$$< E, s > \Downarrow < v, s > < E', s > \Downarrow < v', s >$$

it is clear that the execution of $E+E'$ does not i.e.,

$$<E+E', s> \Downarrow <v+v', s>;$$

And the same result hold for multiplication.

Such arguments ensure that the informal semantics is *safe*. Without them, the semantic account for the execution of programs needs to be adjusted in order to take account of state change during expression execution.

So our simple notation enables a more transparent formulation of the results about the theory. It is not that far removed from the informal account, but it is more wholesome.

A THEORY OF PROGRAMS

But it is not just a semantic account; looked at more abstractly, our semantics constitutes *a theory of programs*. More exactly, we can read the above semantic account as a theory of operations determined by their evaluation rules. Here the relation $\Downarrow$ is taken to be sui-generis in the proposed theory and axiomatised by the rules.

To emphasize this mathematical nature, we shall mathematically explore matters a little. For example, we may define

$$<P, s> \Downarrow \triangleq \exists s' \cdot <P, s> \Downarrow s'$$

This provides a notion of *terminating* program. We may also define a notion of equivalence for programs.

$$P \simeq Q \triangleq \forall s \cdot \forall s' \cdot <P,s> \Downarrow s' \leftrightarrow <Q,s> \Downarrow s'$$

i.e., we cannot tell them apart in terms of their extensional behaviour. Technically, this is an equivalence relation. Moreover, we have the provability of the following three propositions that govern the partial equality of our programming constructs.

1. **If true then** P **else** $Q \simeq P$
2. **If false then** P **else** $Q \simeq Q$
3. **While** B **do** $P \simeq$ **if** B **then** (P; **while** B **do** P) **else skip**

So we have the beginnings of a theory of programs. It certainly captures ones intuitions about the evaluation mechanism that is implicit in the standard informal understanding of these constructs. While not a deep and exciting one, it is still a mathematical theory. Consequently, it would appear that a programming language (i.e., the bundle that is its syntax and semantics) is a mathematical theory (i.e., we appear to have arrived at **MT**).

Unfortunately, this claim may be challenged at every step.

EMPIRICAL SEMANTICS

We can attempt to block matters at the outset i.e., we may attack the practical necessity for any kind of semantics, even of the informal variety, i.e., one might claim that semantics is irrelevant in practice. Whatever, the intention of the original designer, it is how the language functions in the working environment that determines the activity of programming. And for this, any pre-determined normative semantic description is largely irrelevant. This would block **SF**; indeed it seems to deny any role for semantics. So is it plausible? Here is one set of considerations in its favour.

A programmer attempting to learn a programming language does not study the manual, the semantic definition. Instead, she explores the implementation on a particular machine. She carries out some experimentation, runs test programs, compiles fragments etc. until she figures out what the constructs of the language do. Learning a language in this way is a practical affair. Moreover, this what programmers require in practice. Indeed, in order to program a user needs to know what will actually happen on a given physical machine. And this is exactly what such a practical investigation yields.

In other words, a programming language is treated as an artefact that is subject to experimental investigation. The programmer still needs to construct her own theories about the semantic content of the language. But presumably, through testing and experimentation, together with her previous knowledge of programming languages and their constructs, she could systematically uncover the evaluation mechanism of the language. Indeed, she might be able to piece together something like our operational semantics[2]. But such theories are constructed as scientific theories about the language and its implementation, and as such they are subject to falsification. On this scenario, it is this experimental method that enables us to discover the actual meaning of the language. This is a very different methodological picture to that supplied by the normative one.

Of course, we might doubt whether such theory construction is practically feasible: can one from scratch unpack matters to the point where one has enough information to use the language? But even assuming that we find such methodology persuasive, and that we can write down the evaluation mechanism, there is a more significant problem with this empirical approach. Empirical theories are subject to falsification and so, by their very nature, cannot be normative. So it would seem to follow that the advocate of this empirical picture must believe that no normative account is necessary, and that matters are always up for revision. But, this cannot be right. As we originally argued, without some normative account, there can be no criterion of correctness and malfunction, and no standard by which to measure progress. Programming involves reasoning, and this requires a distinction between the correct and incorrect use of expressions of the language. And this can only take place against a semantic account of the language that fixes the correct use of its constructs. Although the activity of programming will almost

always involve some form of experimentation and testing, this must take place against the backdrop of some normative account.

To square this demand with the present empirical picture we might amend matters slightly in order to make room for a normative role for the extracted theory. We might begin with the empirical approach. But what may have been first formulated as a scientific theory of the language, in the activity of programming, must assume normative status i.e., once formulated, this initial scientific theory of the language must act as (a reverse engineered) semantic specification of the language.

However, there are serious objections to even this picture. In particular, there must still be an initial normative account that underpinned the original compiler. Even the compiler writer, who just happens also to be the language designer, has semantic intentions. So this experimental picture cannot gain any purchase without some initial normative foundation. Moreover, assuming a normative status for any empirically derived theory faces the very same problem that made the construction of the scientific theory seem necessary in the first place: in the future, the whole system may malfunction in new ways not predicted by the theory. In this empirical setting, the user requirement that initiated the scientific perspective (i.e., the user needs to know what actually happens) will lead to the development of a new theory. And so on. Indeed, it would seem that this user requirement is unobtainable: continual revision is required to feed this desire to know what actually happens. This is not to say that some experimentation of the sort described, may not occur in practice. All sorts of things may occur in practice. But it is to say that one cannot dispense with a normative role for theories of the language, however they are come by.

Indeed, this whole approach to the semantics of a language seems confused. There is a clear difference between what the language is taken to mean and how we discover its meaning. Any attempt to discover the meaning of the language by testing and experimentation, presupposes that there is some pre-determined notion of meaning to discover.

So there seems little possibility of undermining **MT** by this route i.e., arguing away the need for a normative semantics. However, we might challenge the second step i.e., the move from the informal to the formal semantics.

INFORMAL MATHEMATICS

Have we not assumed the conclusion of **MT** in moving from the informal to the formal account i.e., by providing a rule based account using the more formal notation, have we not pre-judged the issue? Indeed, the objector might agree that the formal account is mathematical, but argue that we do not need it for practice, thereby undermining **MT**.

The arguments given for the formal account were essentially pragmatic in nature; they insist that precise accounts enable us to more carefully articulate the ontology and express and prove the properties of the language. But such arguments are not arguments that show the necessity of such a formal semantics. The informal ones, carefully formulated, might still be sufficient to define and explore the language.

However, even if we doubt the need for the more formal account, it is not clear that we need to give up **MT**: if we stick to informal semantics and informal argumentation, does it follow that we lose mathematical status for our theories? Not obviously. Actually, it seems that not much hangs on the formalization step.

In our brief account of the nature of mathematical theories we alluded to the distinction between being *formal* and being *mathematical*. Although formal logic and set theory have influenced the style and presentation of proofs, ordinary mathematical proofs are not articulated in any formal language. Most mathematicians do not work inside formal theories expressed in some variant of predicate logic; most mathematics is articulated in ordinary language with a sprinkling of notation to pick out the underlying concepts. Moreover, the use of the formal notation does not transform a non-mathematical account into a mathematical one. The mathematical status of the theory does not depend upon such formal presentation: its mathematical nature is not brought into existence by it. In fact, the move from the informal to the formal is common place in mathematics. Informal theories often get rigorously axiomatised later e.g., Hilbert's Geometry. But the informal accounts are still mathematical. Euclid's geometry, despite its informality, is still taken to be a mathematical theory. It did not suddenly get mathematical status in the 20th century with Hilbert's axiomatisation.

In the case of our toy language, apart from the fact that one is expressed in English and the other with some abbreviational notation, and in the formal version the rule based structure has been made explicit, there is a no difference between the two versions of the semantics. Surely such cosmetic changes cannot have such a significant conceptual consequence.

Consequently, the argument that semantic accounts are mathematical does not depend upon the semantics and underlying theory being formally articulated. And this is consistent with the standard development of axiomatic mathematical theories. In our case, there seems to be an underlying theory of operations that forms part of the thing that is a programming language. Consequently, at this point, at least for our toy language, we have no compelling reason to give up **MT** in its present form. In particular, the thing that is our programming language is a theory of programs, formally presented or not.

CONSERVATIVE EXTENSIONS

However, although we might allow that simple theories such as our theory of programs are worthy of mathematical status, we might still insist that this is not so for actual programming languages; what might hold for simple toy languages does not scale up. In particular, theories acceptable to the mathematical community must have some aesthetic qualities: they must have qualities such as elegance and ease of application in their intended domain of application. Moreover, part of being elegant involves the ability to be mathematically explored. If they cannot, for whatever reason (e.g. their complexity), they will not be given the mathematical communities stamp of approval. And while it is possible to provide semantic definitions of the kind given for our toy language for large fragments, and even whole languages (for example, (Wikibooks, 2009) provides a semantic definition of Haskell), in general, such definitions are not tractable theories. They are hard, if not impossible, to mathematically explore. They are often a complex mixture of notions and ideas that do not form any kind of tractable mathematical entity. Consequently, when provided, such semantic definitions are often complicated and unwieldy, and therefore of limited mathematical value. Often, the best one can do with some of these is to marvel at the persistence and ingenuity of the person who has written the semantic description. Given this, it is harder to argue that actual programming languages are genuine mathematical theories.

However, there is an observation that, on the face of it, might be taken to soften this objection. And this involves the logical idea of a *conservative extension*. Suppose that we have constructed a theory T_1 of a language L_1. Suppose also that, in the sense of mathematical logic, we have shown that T_1 is a conservative extension of a smaller theory T_2, a theory of a language L_2, a subset of L_1. Further suppose that T_2 meets our criteria for being a mathematical theory. Can we then claim that T_2 is also a mathematically acceptable theory? In other words, is a theory that is a conservative extension of a mathematical theory, also a mathematical theory? A positive answer fits mathematical practice where mathematical exploration results in the construction of conservative extensions. Indeed, the construction of these extensions is itself part of the exploration process of the core theory.

Programming languages admit of a similar distinction. While the whole language/theory may not have sufficient simplicity and elegance to be mathematically explored, it may nevertheless possess a conceptual core that may be. Such a core should support the whole language in the sense that the theory of the latter is a conservative extension of the theory of its core. This offers a slightly different interpretation of **MT**. But it is one in line with mathematical practice.

Unfortunately, there are further problems to overcome. No doubt there are some simple economies of syntax and theory that may be made for almost all languages. But it will generally be a non-trivial task to locate such mathematically acceptable cores for existing languages. Many languages have been designed with a meagre amount of mathematical input, and it would be somewhat miraculous if such languages/theories could post-hoc be transformed into elegant cores.

MT AND SF

But there is another route. And one that brings **SF** back to the fore. The nature of existing languages does not dictate how new languages might be designed. It does not logically prevent elegant computational theories from being used as an aid to the design of new languages; languages that come closer to achieving mathematical status.

And this brings in the role of theoretical computer science. One of its goals has been to isolate pure computational theories of various kinds. Some of these notions were already embedded in actual programming languages, and, in many cases, formed the source of the underlying intuitions that were sharpened and moulded into an axiomatic theory. Mostly they have not been devised to be used, but to provide careful axiomatic articulations of informal, yet significant, computational concepts. Such theories include axiomatic theories of the following notions.

- Operations
- Types and Polymorphism
- Concurrency and Interaction
- Objects and Classes

Theories of operations mostly emanate from the Lambda Calculus (Church, 1941). This was invented as a formalism to provide a formal account of computability. But from a computer science perspective (Landin P., 1965; Landin P., 1964), it provides a mathematical account that underlies the notions of *function/procedure definition* and *function/procedure call* as they occur in actual programming languages. Landin (Landin P., 1966) actually advocated that the calculus be used as the design core for future languages. Other variations on the calculus take seriously the fact that expressions in the language of the lambda calculus may fail to terminate under the standard rules of reduction. This leads to the Partial Lambda Calculus (Moggi.A., 1988).

However, most programming languages admit some notion of *type*, and so these pure untyped theories of operations do not reflect the operational content of existing languages. Consequently, logicians and theoretical computer scientists have developed variations on the calculus that incorporate types (Barandregt, 1992). While the elementary theories have *monomorphic* type systems, most languages now admit some notion of *polymorphism*. Theories of the impredicative notion (e.g. System **F**) were invented independently by the logician Girard (Girard, 1989) and the theoretical computer scientist Reynolds

(Reynolds, 1974). This is an impredicative theory in that the polymorphic types are included in the range of the type variables. Less powerful theories, in particular predicative ones restrict the range to exclude these types from the range. Others carve out various subsets of the type system and restrict the range to these. These theories and their mathematically established properties provide us with hard information for the activity of design.

The π-calculus (Milner R., 2006) belongs to the family of *process* calculi: mathematical formalisms for describing and analyzing properties of *concurrent computation* and *interaction*. It was originally developed as a continuation of the Calculus of Communicating Systems. Whereas the λ-calculus is a pure theory of operations, the π-calculus is a pure theory of processes. It is itself Turing complete, but is has also inspired a rich source of extensions that get closer to being useable programming languages e.g. (Barnes, 2006).

Our final example concerns *objects*, *classes* and *inheritance*. (Abadi, 1996) contains an extensive source for such calculi (e.g. ς–*calculus*), including some with type structure. The authors also consider the interaction of such theories with other notions such as polymorphism.

One would be hard pushed to argue that such theories are not mathematical ones. They not only reflect clear computational intuitions, often derived from existing languages, but they are capable of being mathematically explored. Indeed, the pure lambda calculus is now a branch of mathematical logic/theoretical computer science with its own literature and mathematical goals (Barendregt, 1984).

The design and exploration of such theories might well be used, as one tool among many, to aid the process of language design. Actual programming languages might then be designed around such cores with actual implemented programming languages and their theories as conservative extensions. Some languages have been designed using this broad strategy. For example, *the logic of computable functions* of (Scott, 1993) is an extension of the simple typed lambda calculus that includes a fixpoint/recursion operator. A predicative polymorphic version of this (with type variables ranging over types with decidable equality) forms the logical spine of ML (Milner R. T., 1999). But one would need to do a fair amount of work to even articulate the theory of the whole language, let alone investigate whether or not it is a conservative extension of this core. Still, it is within the spirit of the present proposal.

Moreover, programming languages are rarely based upon a single core notion. In reality we require languages that support quite complex mixtures of such. For example, we might form a theory made up from the π–*calculus*, the ς–*calculus* and some predicative version of system **F**. This should enable us to explore combinations of polymorphism, concurrency and objects (i.e., we may subject such a theory to mathematical analysis). We might for example show that type membership is decidable. This informs the language design process. Indeed, we would be able to investigate and prove *safety guarantees for improperly synchronized programs* (Pugh, 2000). While putting such theories together in coherent ways is no easy task, there are theoretical frameworks that support such merging activity (Goguen, 1992; Turner R., 2009).

Strachey's plan was that such fundamental notions should be first clarified and languages designed with this knowledge to hand. This idea has actually furnished a whole industry of language design. More specifically, the last forty years have seen the employment of denotational and operational semantics as tools in programming language design (Tennent, 1977; Schmidt, 1986).

Our approach is slightly different but still in line with the **SF** principle. In our case it is our core theories that supply the material from which actual languages may be constructed. Of course, Strachey never put it in these terms; such theories were largely not around at the time of his pronouncement. His original idea alluded to some

underlying structures that were left unspecified. The interpretation that resulted in denotational semantics came later. Nevertheless, the spirit of what we are suggesting is much the same. It is a version of Strachey's idea with his informal ideas being fleshed out with foundational axiomatic theories.

This is a very clean picture, but it must represent the ideal situation. In practice, there is more to design than devising and exploring such core theories and their combinations. One also needs also to take pragmatic issues, into account. Central here are issues of programming practice and implementation (Wirth, 1974). Indeed, the whole enterprise of language design is a two-way street with theory and practice informing each other. In order to build pure computational theories, one must have some practice to reflect upon. Practice plus some theory leads to actual languages, which in turn generates new theories that feed back into language design. The various activities bootstrap each other. This finds the appropriate place for theory: it advocates a *theory first principle,* for each new generation of programming languages. This endorses both a more realistic interpretation of the semantics first principle, and increases the chances that the resulting theory will be mathematically kosher.

CONCLUSION

This is just one topic in the conceptual analysis of the nature of programming languages. Such work should form a significant part of a philosophy of computer science. In particular, the status of programming languages, as mathematical theories, raises issues that impinge upon some of the central and contemporary questions in the philosophies of language, mathematics, science and engineering. In particular, in examining Strachey's claims, we are as much engaged in clarifying the nature of mathematical theories as we are in examining the nature of programming languages.

REFERENCES

Abadi, M. a. (1996). *A Theory of Objects*. New York: Springer-Verlag, Monographs in Computer Science.

Abramsky, S. D. M. (1992). Handbook of Logic in Computer Science. Vol 2. Oxford: Oxford University Press.

Barandregt, H. (1992). Lambda Calculi with Types. In Abramsky, D. M. S. (Ed.), *Handbook of Logic for Computer Science* (*Vol. 2*, pp. 117–309). Oxfrod, UK: Oxford University Press.

Barendregt, H. P. (1984). The Lambda Calculus: Its Syntax and Semantics (Vols. Studies in Logic and the Foundations of Mathematics, 103 (Revised edition ed.). Amsterdam: North Holland.

Barnes, F. a. (2006). Retrieved from Occam-pi: blending the best of CSP and the Pi-calculus: http://www.cs.kent.ac.uk/projects/ofa/kroc/

Boghossian, P. (1989). The Rule-following Considerations. *Mind*, 507–549. doi:10.1093/mind/XCVIII.392.507

Church, A. (1941). The Calculi of Lambda Conversion. Prineton: Princeton University Press.

Colburn, T. (2007). Methodology of Computer Science. In L. Floridi, The Blackwell Guide to the Philosophy of Computing and Information (pp. 318--326). Blakwell, Oxford.

Colburn, T. R. (2000). *Philosophy and Computer Science*. New York: Explorations in Philosophy. Series. M.E. Sharpe.

Crole, R. (1993). *Categories for Types*. Cambridge: Cambridge University Press.

Davidson, D. (1984). Radiical Interpretation . In Davidson, D. (Ed.), *Inquiries into Truth and Interpretation* (pp. 125–140). Oxford: Oxford University Press.

Fernandez, M. (2004). *Programming Languages and Operational Semantics: An Introduction*. London: King's College Publications.

Fetzer, J. (1988). Program Verification: The Very Idea. *Communications of the ACM, 31*(9), 1048–1063. doi:10.1145/48529.48530

Girard, L. a. (1989). *Proofs and Types*. Cambridge: Cambridge University Press.

Gluer, K. W. (2008). *The Normativity of Meaning and Content*. Retrieved from Stanford Encyclopedia of Philosophy: http://plato.stanford.edu/entries/meaning-normativity/

Goguen, J. a. (1992). Institutions: Abstract Model Theory for Specification and Programming. *Journal of the ACM, 39*(1), 95–146. doi:10.1145/147508.147524

Hoare, A. (1969). An Axiomatic Basis For Computer Programming. *Communications of the ACM, Volume 12 / Number 10*, 576-583.

Jech, T. (1971). *Lecture Notes in Set Theory*. New York: Springer.

Kripke, S. (1982). *Wittgenstein on Rules and Private Language*. Boston: Harvard University Press.

Landin, P. (1964). The Mechanical Evaluation of Expressions. *The Computer Journal, 6*(4), 308–320.

Landin, P. (1965). A Correspondence Between ALGOL 60 and Church's Lambda-Notation. *Communications of the ACM, 8*(2), 89–101. doi:10.1145/363744.363749

Landin, P. (1966). The next 700 Programming Languages. *Communications of the ACM*, 157–166. doi:10.1145/365230.365257

Milne, R. a. (1976). *A Theory of Programming Language Semantics*. Chapman and Hall.

Milner, R. (2006). *The Polyadic π-Calculus*. Berlin: Springer.

Milner, R. T. (1999). *The Definition of Standard ML*. MIT Press.

Moggi.A. (1988). http://www.lfcs.inf.ed.ac.uk/reports/88/ECS-LFCS-88-63/.

Oles, F. J. (1982). *A category-theoretic approach to the semantics of programming languages*. Syracuse, NY, US: Syracuse University.

Plotkin, G. (2004). A structural approach to operational semantics. *Journal of Logic and Algebraic Programming, 60-61*, 17–139. doi:10.1016/j.jlap.2004.03.009

Pugh, W. (2000). The Java Memory Model is Fatally Flawed. *Concurrency (Chichester, England), 12*(6), 445–455. doi:10.1002/1096-9128(200005)12:6<445::AID-CPE484>3.0.CO;2-A

Quine. (1960). *Word and Object*. . Cambridge, Mass: MIT Press.

Rapaport, W. (2004). Implementation is Semantic Interpretation. *The Monist, 82*, 109–130.

Reynolds, J. (1974). Towards a theory of type structure . In *Lecture Notes in Computer Science* (pp. 408–425). Berlin: Springer.

Schmidt, D. (1986). *Denotational Semantics: A Methodology for Language Development*. Boston: Allyn and Bacon.

Scott, D. (1993). A type-theoretical alternative to ISWIM, CUCH, OWHY. *Theoretical Computer Science*, 411–440. doi:10.1016/0304-3975(93)90095-B

Shapiro, S. (2004). *Philosophy of Mathematics: Structure and Ontology*. Oxford: Oxford University Press.

Stoy, J. (1977). *The Scott-Strachey Approach to Programming Language Semantics*. Boston: MIT Press.

Strachey, C. (1965). Towards a formal semantics . In Steel, T. B. (Ed.), *Formal Language Description Languages for Computer Programming*. Amsterdam: North Holland.

Strachey, C. (2000). Fundamental Concepts in Programming Languages. *Higher-Order and Symbolic Computation.*, 11-49.

Tennent, R. (1977). Language design methods based on semantic principles. *Acta Informatica, 8*, 97–112. doi:10.1007/BF00289243

Tennent, R. (1981). *Principles of Programming Languages*. Oxford: Prentice-Hall International.

Turing, A. (1937). On Computable Numbers, with an Application to the Entscheidungsproblem. *Proceedings of the London Mathematical Society, 2 42.*, 230--65.

Turner, R. (2007). Understanding Programming Languages. *Minds and Machines, 17*(2), 129–133. doi:10.1007/s11023-007-9059-1

Turner, R. (2009). *Computable Models*. New York: Springer. doi:10.1007/978-1-84882-052-4

Wang, H. (1974). *From Mathematics to Philosophy. London*. London: Routledge & Kegan Paul.

Wikibooks. (2009). *Haskell/Denotational Semantics*. Retrieved from Wikibooks: http://en.wikibooks.org/wiki/Haskell/Denotational_semantics

Wirth, N. (1974). On the Design of Programming Languages. *IEEE Transactions on Software Engineering*, 386–393.

KEY TERMS AND DEFINITIONS

Axiomatic Theories: Theories constituted by groups of axioms/rules. These are not necessarily cast within a formal language i.e., they may be informally presented.

Computational Theories: Theories that are axiomatisations of computational notions. Examples include the λ and π calculi.

Informal Mathematics: Mathematics as practised; not as formalised in standard formal systems.

Operational Semantics: A method of defining programming languages in terms of their underlying abstract machines.

Mathematical Theories: In this paper these are interpreted as axiomatic theories in the logical sense.

Theoretical Computer Science: the mathematical theory of computer science. In particular, it includes the development and study of mathematical theories of computational notions.

ENDNOTES

[1] But see (Rapaport, 2004).

[2] This might be seen as similar in spirit to Quine's field linguist engaged in what he refers to as *radical translation* (Quine, 1960). In so far as a user could by some form of experimentation fix the interpretation of the language, it is. However, this form of empirical uncovering of semantics is not an argument against its normative function. It is merely a route to finding out what it means. Once the translation manual has been constructed, it provides a means of fixing correct use. Indeed, this provision is built into Davidson's' perspective (Davidson, 1984) where the role of the field linguist is radical interpretation not translation. Here the goal is the construction of a *theory of meaning* that is compositional. But these issues require more careful analysis than is possible here.

Chapter 6
The Hypercomputational Case for Substance Dualism

Selmer Bringsjord
Rensselaer AI & Reasoning (RAIR) Lab & Rensselaer Polytechnic Institute (RPI), USA

ABSTRACT

I'm a dualist; in fact, a substance dualist. Why? Myriad arguments compel me to believe as I do, some going back to Descartes. But some sound arguments for substance dualism are recent; and one of these, a new argument so far as I know, is given herein: one that exploits both the contemporary computational scene, and a long-established continuum of increasingly powerful computation, ranging from varieties "beneath" Turing machines to varieties well beyond them. This argument shows that the hypercomputational nature of human cognition implies that Descartes was right all along. Encapsulated, the implication runs as follows: If human persons are physical, then they are their brains (plus, perhaps, other central-nervous-system machinery; denote the composite object by 'brains$^+$'). But brains$^+$, as most in AI and related fields correctly maintain, are information processors no more powerful than Turing machines. Since human persons hypercompute (i.e., they process information in ways beyond the reach of Turing machines), it follows that they aren't physical, (i.e., that substance dualism holds). Needless to say, objections to this argument are considered and rebutted.

INTRODUCTION

I'm a dualist; in fact, a *substance* dualist. As you probably know, this places me within a rather small minority, at least among academics, and certainly among professional philosophers.[1] There are of course a number of *property* dualists about

(e.g. Jjacquette 1994, Clarmers 1996),[2] but those of my ilk are rather hard to find. Why then do I believe what I believe? Well, myriad arguments compel me to believe as I do, some going back to Descartes. (The vast majority of these arguments are elegantly and crisply canvassed by Meixner 2004). But one of these arguments is a new one that I articulate herein; this argument exploits the contemporary computational scene, as well as a

DOI: 10.4018/978-1-61692-014-2.ch006

long-established logico-mathematical continuum of increasingly powerful information processing, ranging from the processing that devices below Turing machines can muster, to what Turing machines can do, to what "hypercomputing" machines can do.

As I soon explain, it's the hypercomputational nature of human cognition which entails that Descartes (with a Chisholmian slant[3] was right all along. Encapsulated, the entailment can be charted as follows: If human persons are physical, then they are their brains (plus, perhaps, other central nervous system machinery; denote the composite object by `brains+`). But brains+, as most in AI and related fields correctly maintain, are information processors no more powerful than Turing machines. Since human persons hypercompute (i.e., they process information in ways beyond the reach of Turing machines), it follows that they aren't physical, that is, substance dualism holds.

The plan for the paper is as follows. After some remarks on the niceties of defining dualism (§ 2), I give (§ 3) enough background from relative computability theory to understand my argument, and then, in section 4, I give a more explicit version of it that can be effortlessly certified as deductively valid. Each premise in the argument is then separately defended (in some cases against objections), with the majority of attention paid to premise (4), which says that human persons hypercompute. In the penultimate section (5), I consider some additional objections, and emphasize that my objective in the present paper is only to present a *formidable* argument for substance dualism. The fully developed case for substance dualism that the present paper points to includes many previously published arguments for the proposition that human persons hypercompute; and these publications include answers to numerous objections. I thus claim herein not that the main argument expressed in the present paper is conclusive, but rather that, again, it's quite formidable: put another way, that it provides enough ammunition to make being a substance dualist, in

our day, perfectly rational. That said, the content herein, *plus* supporting argumentation published elsewhere (cited below), *does* by my lights constitute a *conclusive* case for substance dualism. I end the paper with a brief conclusion (§ 6).

WHAT IS SUBSTANCE DUALISM?

In the first chapter of his *The Two Sides of Being*, Meixner (2004) considers a series of propositions that express versions of dualism (and physicalism). What he there calls "mind-body" dualism consists of a set of propositions that are essentially a superset of the one I here take to express substance dualism.[4] I say 'essentially' because while Meixner is content to refer to minds and/or mental entities, following Chisholm (see note 4), I think it imprudently multiplies entities to countenance a framework in which we have in play human bodies, human persons, and human minds. We simply don't need the third category; it's dispensable. All substantive natural-language sentences making reference to human minds can be (usually wisely, I submit) translated into sentences making reference to only persons instead. For example, the sentence "Jones has a sharp mind," can be replaced with "Jones is sharp." Additional examples are easy enough to come by.[5] In addition, while I happily concede that substance dualism (or mind-body dualism) is traditionally taken to include (or outright deductively entail) property dualism, since the focus in the present paper is on the class of human persons as objects, rather than on properties, I rest content with identifying substance dualism with one proposition.[6]

So, what is the one proposition that sums things up for me? The doctrine of substance dualism consists for me in this proposition:

D Human persons are not physical.

Of course, since you and I are human persons, it follows immediately from *D* that we aren't physical.

BACKGROUND

Turing Machines

Turing machines will be familiar to many readers, as they are often introduced in elementary and/or intermediate logic (e.g., see Boolos & Jeffrey 1989), in philosophy of mind, and sometimes in introductory philosophy courses (if based, e.g., on books like Glymour 1992). TMs customarily include a two-way infinite tape divided into squares, a read/write head for writing and erasing symbols (from some finite, fixed alphabet; let's assume here that it's $\{0, 1\}$) on and off this tape, a finite control unit which at any step in a computation is in one particular state from among a finite number of possible states, and a set of **instructions** (= a program) telling the machine what to do, depending upon what state it's in and what (if anything) is written on the square currently scanned by its head. Of course, there are varying definitions of Turing machines. The formalism I prefer is the quadruple-transition, implicit-halt-state one. In this scheme, each transition consists of four things: the state the machine is in, the symbol it's scanning, the action it is to perform (move right or left, or write a symbol), and the new state it is to enter.[7]

A sample Turing machine, dubbed "Gordon's 19 in 186," is shown in flow-graph form in (Figure 1); it's designed to start on a 0-filled infinite tape and produce, after 186 steps, 19 contiguous 1s, halting in the required position once done. The reader can easily read off the quadruples I refer to in the previous paragraph, from this flow-graph. For example, focus on the arcs running from the node labeled with 0 to the node labeled with 1. Each node represents a state. There are thus two quadruples involved in this fragment of the flow-graph; they are:

$$0* \Rightarrow 1$$
$$0- \Rightarrow 5$$

This Turing machine was discovered long ago by Gordon Greene, and marks an interesting sub-chapter in the attempt, on the part of many researchers, to divine the productivity of ever-larger machines with respect to the "busy beaver," or Σ, function.[8]

The Σ function is a mapping from $\mathbf{N}$ (the natural numbers) to $\mathbf{N}$ such that: $\Sigma(n)$ is the largest number of contiguous 1's that an n-state Turing machine with alphabet $\{0, 1\}$ can write on its initially blank tape, just before halting with its read/write head on the leftmost 1, where a sequence

$$\overset{m \quad times}{11...11}$$

is regarded simply as m.[9] rado proved this function to be Turing-*un*computable long ago; a nice contemporary version of the proof (which is by the way not based on diagonalization) is given in (Boolos & Jeffrey 1989). Nonetheless, the busy beaver problem is the challenge of determining $\Sigma(n)$ for ever larger values of n.

As you can see, to speak of a Turing machine M computing some function f from tne natural numbers ($\mathbf{N}$) to the natural numbers, we let the machine start with $n \in \mathbf{N}$ encoded on its tape (e.g., 1 1 1 1, with each 1 on one square, can encode 4), and the output is what the machine M leaves as an unbroken sequence of filled-in squares, its read/write head resting on the leftmost symbol in the sequence. Given this scheme, readers can easily convince themselves that Gordon's machine works as advertised, and (e.g.) that arithmetic functions (addition, multiplication, etc.) are Turing-computable, by specifying a TM that would get the job done in each case.[10]

As many readers will know, the original Turing-uncomputable problem is not the Σ function, but rather the halting problem; the proof goes back to Turing turing.1936 himself. For every Turing machine M there is a corresponding natural number n^M (the Gödel number of M); and M_i, where $i \in$

*Figure 1. Gordon's 19 in 186, shown in Turing's World Flow-Graph Form. Note that instead of the alphabet {0, 1} we use {--, * }. Movement to the left and right is indicated by arrows.*

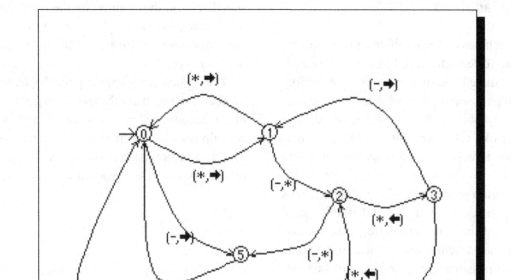

N, is the *i*th Turing machine. (It's easy to establish an enumeration $M_1, M_2, M_3, \ldots$ of all Turing machines.) The following function, which should be easy enough to understand from the present context, is not Turing-computable.

$$h(n^M, m) = \begin{cases} 1 & if \ M : m \ \rightarrow \ halt \\ 0 & if \ M : m \rightarrow \infty, \end{cases}$$

The so-called *Turing Limit* can be defined by either or both of the two Turing-uncomputable functions we have just visited.[11] An information processor that can compute these two functions (and equivalent ones, and more difficult ones) is capable of hypercomputation, or is simply a hypercomputer. I now discuss these powerful machines.

Hypercomputation

We now understand well that there *are* information-processing machines that can exceed the Turing Limit (e.g., they can solve the halting problem, etc.); such machines just aren't standard TMs and the like. There are in fact now many such machines. Indeed, just as there are an infinite number of mathematical devices equivalent to Turing machines (first-order theorem provers, Register machines, the λ-calculus, abaci, Kolmogorov-Uspenskii machines, ...; many of these are discussed in the context of an attempt to define standard computation in Bringsjord brings.beneath), there are an infinite number of devices beyond the Turing Limit. For example, there are *trial-and-error machines* (Burgin 2001, Kugel 1986, Putnam 1965, Gold 1965), *inductive*

TMs (Burgin 2001), *infinite time TMs* (ITTMs) (Hamkins & Lewis 2000), *analog chaotic neural nets* (Siegelmann & Sontag 1994), *dial machines* (Bringsjord 2001), *analog chaotic neural nets* (Siegelmann & Sontag 1994), *dial machines* (Bringsjord 2001), *accelerated Turing machines* (Copeland 1998) *"time-bending" machines* (Etesi & Nemeti 2002), and so on. Furthermore, as you might imagine, such devices can be placed within a hierarchy, because while they are all more powerful that TMs, some hypercomputers are more powerful than others.

For the present paper, it is sufficient to save time and space by referring not to one or more specific kind of hypercomputer, but only to intuitive supertask machines called *Zeus machines* (ZMs) by Boolos & Jefrey (1989). Zeus machines are based on the character Zeus, described by Boolos & Jefrey (1989). Zeus is a superhuman creature who can enumerate **N** *in a finite amount of time*, in one second, in fact. He pulls this off by giving the first entry, 0, in $\frac{1}{2}$ second, the second entry, 1, in $\frac{1}{4}$ second, the third entry in $\frac{1}{8}$ second, the fourth in $\frac{1}{16}$ second, ..., so that, indeed, when a second is done he has completely enumerated the natural numbers. Obviously, it's easy to adapt this scheme so as to produce a Zeus machine that can solve the halting problem (recall the function *h* introduced above): just imagine a machine which, when simulating an arbitrary Turing machine *M* operating on input *u*, does each step faster and faster. (There are countably many Turing machines, and those that don't halt are trapped in an unending sequence of the same cardinality as **N**.) If, during this simulation, the Zeus machine finds that *M* halts on *u*, a 1 is returned; otherwise 0 is given.

Please note that ZMs are really quite intuitive, despite the fact that their computational power is extreme. For example, see Figure 2, which is taken from page 268 of ((Eicholz, O'Daffer, Charles, Young, Barnett, Clemens, Gilmer, Reeves, Renfro, Thompson & Thornton 1995)). Children can be asked to determine the "percent pattern" of the outer square consumed by the ever-decreasing shaded squares. The pattern, obviously, starts at $\frac{1}{4}$, and then continues as $\frac{1}{16}, \frac{1}{64}, \frac{1}{256}, \ldots$. When asked what percent "in the limit" the shaded square consumes of the original square, young math students are expected to say "Zero": but of course the notion of a limit is understandably a bit tricky for them. When asked what percentage the shaded square would "get down to" if someone could work faster and faster, and smaller and smaller, at drawing the up-down and left-right lines that make each quartet of smaller squares, many school-children will indeed say "Zero." The bottom line is that the nature of Zeus machines is not that mysterious.

THE ARGUMENT

At this point, we are in command of sufficient background to consider my new argument for a Cartesian/Chisholmian view of persons. The argument consists first of a top-level argument, and then level-two arguments for the key premises in the top-level argument. Only premise (4) in the top-level argument [from among three premises, viz., (2), (3), and (4)] will be the explicit conclusion of a step-by-step level-two argument. Here, without further ado, is the top-level argument (Table 1):

The Top-Level Argument

I have left this argument enthymematic to preserve readability. But it's easy enough to formalize it completely. For example, using an obvious symbol set, (1) and (2), respectively, could be

$$\{\forall x((Hx \wedge Px) \to x = b(x)), \forall x((Hx \wedge Px) \to L^{\leq}b(x))\}$$

Figure 2. Picture of supertask from seventh grade math text

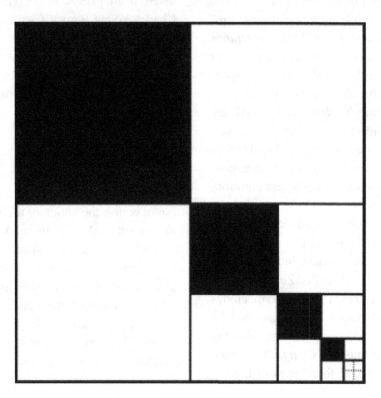

from which (3), (i.e., $\forall x((Hx \wedge Px) \to L^{\leq}x)$), can be easily derived in Fitch-style natural deduction by assuming $Ha \wedge Pa$ and finishing that sub-derivation with $L^{\leq}a$. Conditional introduction and universal introduction complete the proof.

Are the Premises in the Top-Level Argument True?

Note that propositions (3), (5), and (7) are intermediate conclusions. Premise (6) is unassailable, since, as is indicated in the justification column for it, this proposition is true by definition. The only vulnerable spots are premises (1), (2), and (4), and I turn now to a brief defense of each of these propositions.

Defending Premise (1): If Physical, Persons = Brains

This premise is unexceptionable. No one will dispute the claim that *if* human persons are physical things, then they must be their brains[+]. What would the other candidates be? If I'm a physical thing, I'm certainly not that rock over there, or that ashtray, or that elevator. Of course, as noted at the outset (see § 2), I presuppose that persons are not logical constructions; 'person' is not a *facon de parlor*. Those who assume that persons are fictions, and not real things, are not likely to be moved by my argument.[12]

It's important to note that my argument for substance dualism makes no use of a premise to the effect that all physical processes can be captured by the activity of a Turing machine. (This proposition would be a reasonable version of a *physicalized* version of the Church-Turing Thesis.)

Table 1.

	(1)	Human persons, if physical, are identical to their brains⁺.		
	(2)	Human brains⁺ are information processors at or below the Turing Limit.	see separate, level-two arguments below	
∴	(3)	Human persons, if physical, are information processors at or below the Turing Limit.	(1), (2)	
	(4)	Human persons are information processors *above* the Turing Limit.	see separate, level-two arguments below	
∴	(5)	Human persons aren't physical.	(3), (4); *reductio*	
	(6)	If human persons aren't physical, substance dualism is true.	*D*	
∴	(7)	Substance dualism is true.	(5), (6); *modus ponens*	

I have no idea if such a claim is true, and certainly for present purposes I have no interest in what the truth-value of this proposition is.

Defending Premise (2): Brains are Fundamentally Standard Computers

Premise (2) is affirmed by the vast majority of philosophers and scientists who think seriously about the nature of the brain and central nervous system. I could cite literally hundreds of them to make the point. I now proceed to present part of this list:

- At the dawn of AI, Turing (1950) himself got the ball rolling in the direction of (2), courtesy of his famous "Computing Machinery and Intelligence."[13] Turing therein introduces what he calls the 'imitation game' (now known as the 'Turing Test'), in which a computer and a woman are each sequestered from a judge who converses with them. The judge's challenge is to try to ascertain which interlocutor is the woman (machine). If the judge can do no better than chance, the machine has passed, and, according to Turing, ought to be considered capable of "thinking". It's clear from this paper that Turing regards

the challenge of building a machine to prevail in the Turing Test to consist in building a machine that is at roughly on par with our brains. For example:

As I have explained, the problem is mainly one of programming. Advances in engineering will have to be made too, but it seems unlikely that these will not be adequate for the requirements. Estimates of the storage capacity of the brain vary from 10^{10} to 10^{15} binary digits. I incline to the lower values and believe that only a very small fraction is used for the higher types of thinking. Most of it is probably used for the retention of visual impressions, I should be surprised if more than 10^9 was required for satisfactory playing of the imitation game.

- The roboticist Hans Moravec (1999).robot follows Turing: He explicitly compares the increasingly greater processing speed and capacity of modern-day digital computers with the human brain. For Moravec, once artificial computers reach the processing power of the human brain, true artificial intelligence will be achieved.
- Kosslyn (1996) has detailed his search for the neural networks in our brains that correspond to the information processors

responsible for enabling our powers of mental imagery. He is utterly convinced that standard artificial neural networks are quite up to the task of capturing the information processing behind mental imagery. (As is well-known, standard artificial neural networks are equivalent in power to Turing machines. See (Bringsjord 1991.))

- The field of *computational cognitive modeling* is devoted to capturing all of human cognition in one comprehensive computer program: a so-called *cognitive architecture*.[14] Arguably the leading scientist in the CCM field is John Anderson; he has recently made it abundantly clear (e.g., in Anderson & Lebiere 2003) that he is as optimistic as ever that his research program, which consists in programming a standard digital computer, and giving it sensors and effectors, will capture all of human cognition. By moving CCM to a study of the brain, and specifically to the attempt to verify the accuracy of models by comparing their performance to data obtained by inspection of the brain, Anderson makes his affirmation of (2) plain.

- The affirmation of brain implants often signals the acceptance of premise (2). For example, the philosopher of mind Paul Churchland has said[15] that malfunctioning brain matter will soon enough be "cured" by replacing it with machine workalikes. Motivated readers will be able to confirm the plausibility of Churchland's prediction by searching the Web for a short while, because the fact of the matter is that direct machine-brain hookups have arrived on the scene. These hookups link small computing devices with brain matter that is likewise treated as a computer.

- ⋮ By the vertical ellipsis here I indicate that this list could be continued indefinitely. For example, it seems that the recent surge of interest in evolutionary psychology is in no small part driven by the conviction that human persons, qua brains[+], are not only the product of Darwinian evolution, but are specifically, as for example Pinker (1997) puts it, "evolved *computers*".

Lest it be thought that premise (2) is only affirmed by "thinkers and that in "real life" no one affirms the proposition in question, I point out that large sums of money are being spent on the basis of a commitment to the premise. For instance, consider the so-called "Blue Brain" Project, summed up by IBM at the launch of the project[16] as follows.

IBM and The Ecole Polytechnique Fédérale de Lausanne (EPFL) are today announcing a major joint research initiative–nicknamed the Blue Brain Project–to take brain research to a new level. Over the next two years scientists from both organizations will work together using the huge computational capacity of IBM's eServer Blue Gene supercomputer to create a detailed model of the circuitry in the neocortex: the largest and complex part of the human brain. By expanding the project to model other areas of the brain, scientists hope to eventually build an accurate, computer-based model of the entire brain.

Of course, it doesn't follow from the fact that (2) is presupposed by computational neuroscience, cognitive neuroscience, cognitive psychology, and cognitive science, that this proposition is *true*. It follows only that my argument will not be attacked at this point (which is something I'm not unhappy about). But, as a matter of fact, I think those who affirm (2) are dead-on correct; and it's even clear why they are. The basic argument in favor of (2) has been around quite a while. It's based on the brute fact that, at the cellular level, the brain appears to be an automaton. Specifically, we seem able now to be able to capture a significant amount of brain circuitry in the form of traditional "building block" algorithms; that is, in the form of Turing-level computation. The person whose work best expresses the relevant approach and results is Richard Granger (Granger 2004a, 2004b, forthcoming), and readers are directed to his work for details.[17]

The Level-Two Argument for Premise (4): Persons Hypercompute

Are there arguments in the literature for the view that we are (or encompass) Zeus machines and the like? Indeed there are. For example: After presenting the relevant mathematical landscape, Kugel (1986) argues that human persons are trial-and-error machines. Bringsjord (1992)[18] gives a sustained argument for the view that human persons are Zeus machines, and has also argued (1997) specifically that logicians who work with infinitary systems routinely and genuinely hypercompute (when, e.g., using the ω-rule; see the use of the rule in Bringsjord & van Heuveln 2003). New, technical arguments for (4) are given in (Bringsjord & Arkoudas 2004) and–in a paper that is based on the aforementioned Σ functions– (Bringsjord et al 2006). Unfortunately, these arguments are too long and technical to reproduce here in their entirety. I'm able only to give an encapsulated version of one of them. However, I do present some new evidence for the soundness of this particular argument.

But before I do so, allow me to say that I suspect the best place to find hypercomputation at work in human cognition is in the kind of thinking required to formalize and map out hypercomputation itself. It would be very surprising if human persons could discover the ins and outs of information processing above the Turing Limit, mathematically specify and grasp that terrain, but could not themselves hypercompute. It strikes me that, in general, if a person s can formalize and chart ϕ-ing, than s can herself ϕ, at least in principle. I have no doubt that AI will manage to formalize and chart mere animal cognition, top to bottom. I thus have little

doubt that, in principle, human persons can, for example, match the reasoning power of a canine: or a parrot or horse, and so on.

Of course, human persons currently only fly in ways rather less subtle than those employed by birds. Nonetheless, at least sooner or later, we will no doubt have completely mathematized the ins and outs of avian flight. Given this, it may be said against my intuition that we will not *ourselves* be able to fly in accordance with the formalization. But notice that I spoke immediately above about what can be done *in principle*. This is crucial. Surely once we have a complete formal specification of avian flight, we know that it's logically possible that we fly in the specified manner. I've shown elsewhere (in "The Modal Argument for Hypercomputing Minds", Bringsjord & Arkoudas 2004) that since human persons are such that it's logically possible that they hypercompute, whereas it's logically necessary that a Turing machine *fail* to hypercompute, it follows that human persons hypercompute. This argument presupposes that human persons are (or include) information processors of *some* kind, but this proposition is pretty much universally assumed.[19]

Now let me give the promised encapsulated argument for human hypercomputational thought, that is, for (4).

To begin, note that the operation of a standard Turing machine is equivalent to inference in appropriately configured first-order logic (FOL).[20] Let's denote this logical system by L_I.[21]

Just as Turing machines have their limtations, L_I does as well. In fact, most mathematical concepts cannot be expressed in L_I. (For a list of some ordinary mathematical concepts beyond the reach of L_I, see Keisler keisler.) One such concept is that of a "finite world (model)".

In order to understand that it's not possible to capture the ordinary notion of finitude in FOL, it's helpful to see, first, that capturing the ordinary notion of *in*finitude *is* possible, indeed downright easy, in L_I. To see that infinitude is within reach, begin by considering the L_I-sentence

$$\psi_{\geq 2} = \exists x \exists y \; x \neq y.$$

Any interpretation on which $\psi_{\geq 2}$ is true must have a domain that contains at least two elements, since $\psi_{\geq 2}$ says that there exist two distinct things x and y. Put in terms of the standard notation for expressing that a model satisfies a formula (or set of formulas), this becomes $\mathcal{I} \vDash \psi_{\geq 2}$ if and only if $\mathcal{I}$'s domain contains at least two elements. The technique here can be generalized. The sentence

$$\psi_{\geq 3} = \exists x \exists y \exists z \, (x \neq y \wedge x \neq z \wedge y \neq z)$$

can only be true in a world with an at-least-three-element domain, etc. Now suppose that we collect together the set of all such formulas, with n getting larger and larger forever. Formally, this set–call it 'Ω'–is $\{\psi_{\geq n} : n \geq 2\}$. Since any interpretation on which all of the members of Ω is true must be an interpretation with at least 2 members, 3 members, 4 members, *ad infinitum*, it follows that such an interpretation must be infinite. In addition, it's obvious that any infinite interpretation will satisfy Ω. So we have assembled a recipe for expressing, in FOL, the notion of infinitude. However, and this is the present point, *there is no set of first-order formulas that can express the concept of finitude*. (Formally, there is no set of first-order formulas such that an interpretation models this set if and only if it's finite.)

How can this be demonstrated? Space precludes providing a full, rigorous answer. But a pedagogical trick I sometimes deploy can perhaps provide some insight: Most readers will be familiar with the characterization of infinitude due to Dedekind; in short, it's that a set X is infinite just in case there is a bijective (= one-to-one) function f from X to some proper subset thereof. (There is

e.g. an obvious bijective function from **N** to the set of even numbers, viz., *f(n)=2n*.) If we now had a wff ϕ*(X)* of L_I that that ascribed Dedekind-infinity to the set *X*, a free variable in ϕ, our challenge would be met, for we could express finitude via $\neg\phi(X)$. But after reflection it becomes apparent that if confined to L_I one cannot build ϕ*(X)*, because this formula would have to allow quantification over *sets* in the domain, and not merely over particular objects in the domain.[22]

Because on the one hand L_I is so limited, and on the other humans are adept at reasoning in infinitary fashion about infinite objects (as we just seen while we have ourselves considered finitude and infinitude!), logicians have studied infinitary logics like $L_{\omega_1\omega}$, which we now proceed to define. As we shall see, it turns out that the limit on FOL we just noted can be handled easily by $L_{\omega_1\omega}$.

The basic idea behind $L_{\omega_1\omega}$ is straightforward. This logical system allows for infinite disjunctions and conjunctions,[23] where these disjunctions and conjunctions are no longer than the size of the set of natural numbers (let's use ω to denote the size of the set of natural numbers).[24] This fundamental idea is effortlessly regimented: First we simply add to the customary alphabet for first-order logic the symbols $\bigvee$ and $\bigwedge$. To the ordinary formation rules for building grammatically correct first-order formulas, we add

- If $\boldsymbol{\Phi}$ is a set of wffs $\{\phi_1, \phi_2, \ldots\}$ no larger than $\boldsymbol{\omega}$, then $\bigvee\Phi (\bigwedge\Phi)$ is also a well-formed formula, viz., the disjunction (conjunction) of the formulas in $\boldsymbol{\Phi}$.

The condition under which an infinite formula is true is fixed by extending the notion of truth in ordinary first-order logic:

- A possibly infinite disjunction, $\bigvee\Phi$, is true on an interpretation I (written $I \vDash \bigvee\Phi$) if and only if there is a formula ϕ in $\boldsymbol{\Phi}$ which is true on $\boldsymbol{I}$.

- A possibly infinite conjunction, $\bigwedge \Phi$, is true on an interpretation $\boldsymbol{I}$ (written $\boldsymbol{I} \vDash \bigwedge \Phi$) if and only if every formula ϕ in $\boldsymbol{\Phi}$ is true on $\boldsymbol{I}$.

Proofs (= derivations) in $\boldsymbol{L}_{\omega 1 \omega}$ can, as the relevant literature states, be "infinitely long" (Ebbinghaus et al. 1984). This is because in addition to classical cornerstones like *modus ponens*,

from $\phi \rightarrow \psi$ and ϕ infer to ψ,

$\boldsymbol{L}_{\omega 1 \omega}$ allows rules of inference like

from $\phi \rightarrow \psi$ *for all* $\psi \in \Phi$, *infer to* $\phi \rightarrow \bigwedge \Psi$.

This rule says that if in a derivation you have an infinite list of if-thens (i.e., formulas of the form $\phi \rightarrow \psi$) where each consequent (ψ) in each if-then is an element of some infinite set $\boldsymbol{\Phi}$, then you can infer to an if-then whose consequent is the infinite conjunction obtained by conjoining all the elements of $\boldsymbol{\Phi}$.

It may be worth pausing a bit to create a picture of the sort of derivation which is here permitted: Suppose that $\boldsymbol{\Gamma}$ is an infinite set of the same size as $\mathbf{N}$, the natural numbers. So $\boldsymbol{\Gamma}$ is $\{\gamma_1, \gamma_2, \ldots, \gamma_n, \gamma_{n+1}, \gamma_{n+2}, \ldots\}$. Then here is one possible picture of an infinite derivation:

$$\phi \rightarrow \gamma_1$$
$$\phi \rightarrow \gamma_2$$
$$\phi \rightarrow \gamma_3$$
$$\vdots$$
$$\phi \rightarrow \gamma_n$$
$$\phi \rightarrow \gamma_{n+1}$$
$$\vdots$$
$$\phi \rightarrow \gamma_1 \wedge \gamma_2 \wedge \ldots \wedge \gamma_n \wedge \gamma_{n+1} \wedge \gamma_{n+2} \cdots$$

It should be clear from this that derivations in $\boldsymbol{L}_{\omega 1 \omega}$ can indeed be infinitely long.

Now, let's return to the limitation we saw in the case of $\boldsymbol{L}_1$ in order to see how $\boldsymbol{L}_{\omega 1 \omega}$ surmounts them. The limitation was that the concept of finitude couldn't be captured by any set of $\boldsymbol{L}_1$ formulas, let alone by one such formula. But here is one simple formula in $\boldsymbol{L}_{\omega 1 \omega}$ which is such that every interpretation that satisfies it is finite, and every finite interpretation satisfies it:

$$\bigvee_{n < \omega} \exists x_1 \ldots \exists x_n \forall y (y = x_1 \vee \ldots \vee y = x_n).$$

I think it's worth making sure we understand this formula (and thereby understand some of the power of $\boldsymbol{L}_{\omega 1 \omega}$). This formula is an infinite disjunction; each disjunct has a different value for $\boldsymbol{n}$. One such disjunct is

$$\exists x_1 \exists x_2 \forall y (y = x_1 \vee y = x_2),$$

which says, put informally, there exist at most two things $\boldsymbol{x_1}$ and $\boldsymbol{x_2}$ with which everything in the domain is identical, or there are at most two things in the domain. Obviously, any interpretation which satisfies this formula is finite, since it can at most have a two-element domain. Another disjunct in the infinite disjunction is the one generated by setting $\boldsymbol{n}$ to 4, i.e.,

Table 2. Argument for Premise (4)

	(8)	All human reasoning is Turing-computable.	supp. for contradiction
∴	(9)	For every case of human reasoning R there exists a Turing machine (or other equivalent machine) M such that some computation C of M is such that $R=C$.	from (8)
	(10)	For every computation C of every TM M there is an equivalent deduction D in some instantiation of the first-order system L_I.	separate theorems, as noted
∴	(11)	For every case of human reasoning R there exists a deduction D in some instantiation of the first-order system L_I such that $R=D$.	from (9), (10); universal elimination, hypothetical syllogism, universal introduction
	(12)	There exists a case of human reasoning R^* --- viz., reasoning with $L_{\omega 1 \omega}$ --- which is such that for every deduction D in some instantiation of the first-order system L_I, $R^* \neq D$.	see immediately below
∴	(13)	It's not the case that all human reasoning is Turing-computable.	*reductio ad absurdum*; (11), (12) contradictory
	(14)	All human reasoning is information processing of some sort.	as noted elswhere in paper; affirmed by modern cognitive sciences
∴	(15)	Some human reasoning is hypercomputation.	from (13), (14)

$\exists x_1 \exists x_2 \exists x_3 \exists x_4 \forall y (y = x_1 \lor y = x_2 \lor y = x_3 \lor y = x_4)$,

which says that there are at most four things. Here again, any interpretation which satisfies this formula is finite. But how do we go in the other direction? How do we ensure that any interpretation which is finite satisfies the selected formula? [25] This is where the infinite disjunction does its job. For notice that every finite domain will have a certain size k, where k is some natural number. This domain will make true the disjunct in the infinite disjunction where $n=k$; and since a disjunction, no matter how big, is true if but one of its disjuncts is true, this k-sized domain will make the entire infinite disjunction true.

We are now in position to consider an explicit argument for premise (4) (Table 2)

Clearly, this argument could be completely formalized; there thus seems to be no question that it's formally valid. We noted earlier that premise (14) is unproblematic. But what about proposition (12)? Well, clearly, reasoning in $L_{\omega 1 \omega}$ cannot be recast as reasoning concerning ordinary first-order logic: The ratiocination in question,

as we've just witnessed, includes representing the finitude of interpretations in $L_{\omega 1 \omega}$. So, if this reasoning *could* be recast in FOL, it would follow that the limitation on FOL we noted above would not in fact be a limitation, for the recasting of the reasoning here would constitute a rendering in FOL of precisely that which we know, on the basis of separate proofs, to be beyond the reach of FOL.

Sedulous readers who desire to assimilate the full case for substance dualism to which this paper points are directed to the full presentation of the argument I've just given (Bringsjord 1997, Bringsjord & Zenzen 2003), and to the other arguments for premise (4) cited above. However, I complete this section by presenting what I regard to be serious evidence in support of premise (12). This is evidence that I haven't presented elsewhere.

Isaacson's Conjecture and Irrepressible Infinitary Reasoning

Someone might object as follows: "Your argument for premise (4) fails completely. $\mathcal{L}_I$ is inexpressive when conceived as a pure logic, (i.e., as, in your terms (Bringsjord 2008) a logical system. But a logical system doesn't have axioms. The axioms for set theory can be formulated in $\mathcal{L}_I$,

and the reasoning about finiteness and infinity which is enabled by these axioms is itself entirely finitary and representable by computation on a Turing machine".

This objection fails completely, for n reasons. First, while the systematization of mathematics provided by many decades of formal exposition in books authored by Bourbaki[26] shows, formally speaking, that much discovery and confirmation in mathematics consists, fundamentally, in the derivation and use of theorems all extractable from the Zermelo-Fraenkel axioms for set theory (ZF), ZF is itself infinitary in nature, since it includes the concept of an axiom-*schema*.

Second, I am concerned with the actual practice of professional logic and mathematics, and the actual cognition bound up therewith. In this practice, the brute fact is that all sufficiently difficult theorems have been established by infinitary reasoning that is apparently not reducible to finitary reasoning. What do I mean by ``sufficiently difficult''? This question can be answered by appeal to aspects of the continuum that undergirds section 3, when this continuum is viewed propositionally rather than through the lens of increasingly powerful computing machines. Let me explain.

As is well-known, Gödel established that certain axiomatic theories are incomplete, where a theory $\mathcal{T}$ has this property iff there is a well-formed formula γ in the underlying formal language $\mathcal{L}$ such that it can't be proved from $\mathcal{T}$ (customarily symbolized by $\mathcal{T} \nvdash \gamma$), nor can't its negation ($\mathcal{T} \nvdash \neg\gamma$): and yet it's the case that γ is true on the standard interpretation $\mathcal{I}$ in question ($\mathcal{I} \vDash \gamma$). For example, where $\mathcal{T}$ is a theory of arithmetic, such as Peano Arithmetic (PA), there are truths of arithmetic, expressed in the language $\mathcal{L}_A$, beyond PA: but nonetheless true

on the standard interpretation $\mathcal{I}_A$ of arithmetic. Elegant and economical coverage of all of this is provided, for example, in (Ebbinghaus, Flum & Thomas 1994).

Now, there are a number of truths of arithmetic beyond PA which have nonetheless *been proved by human beings*. One example is Goodstein's Theorem (GT); a nice summary is provided in (Smith 2007). So, while it's true that

$$PA \nvdash GT \quad and \quad PA \nvdash \neg GT$$

GT has nonetheless been proved. There are other examples (e.g., König's Lemma) as well. And as intro_godel_theorems_smith observes, the demonstrations of such results, "use conceptual resources which go beyond those which are required for understanding the basic arithmetic of finite natural numbers" (p. 204). In fact, Smith, by drawing on (Isacson n.d.), presents the following speculative conjecture ("Isaacson's Conjecture", as he calls it).[27]

Isaacson's Conjecture: If we are to give a rationally compelling proof of *any* true sentence of $\mathcal{L}_A$ [= the language of arithmetic] which is independent of PA, then we will need to appeal to ideas that go beyond those which are constitutive of our understanding of basic arithmetic.

I take no stand on this conjecture, but I present a related one that, for reasons to be momentarily shared, advances my case, to wit:

In order to produce a rationally compelling proof of any true sentence of $\mathcal{L}_A$, but independent of PA, it's necessary in the human case to deploy concepts and structures of a infinitary nature.[28]

This conjecture, if true, would establish premise (12). In light of this, evidence in support of my conjecture is ipso facto evidence in support of (12). Is there evidence in support of my conjecture? Indeed there is. For example, while Smith notes that Isaacson's Conjecture seems to run afoul of PA-independent sentences that don't relate to Gödel's incompleteness results (e.g. see the footnote on p. 205 of Smith 2007), he concedes that while the *content* of some PA-independent theorems can apparently be entirely finitary, in all present cases the *proofs* of such theorems do involve infinitary concepts. I am in fact not aware of any evidence against my conjecture, and it thus provides some additional evidence in support of premise (12).

The upshot is that premise (4) should at the very least be considered extremely plausible.

TWO ADDITIONAL OBJECTIONS

A full dialectic is beyond the scope of this paper. My objective, again, is to put on the table a formidable argument for substance dualism: in front of contemporary thinkers the vast majority of whom are at best (worst?) property dualists and indeed almost certainly thoroughgoing materialists when it comes to the mind. Nonetheless, I do consider two additional objections, another one against the level-two argument given for premise (4), and one aimed directly at this premise.

Objection: "It's just Manipulation of Finite Strings"

The first additional objection runs as follows: "Clearly, humans cannot actually manipulate an infinite expression, so to carry out 'infinitary reasoning' with $L_{\omega 1 \omega}$ must mean to reason with the manipulation of finite strings used to represent hypothesized infinite expressions. For example, look at the formula which you made so much of above, viz.,

$$\bigvee_{n < \omega} \exists x_1 \ldots \exists x_n \forall y (y = x_1 \vee \ldots \vee y = x_n).$$

You will notice that this formula is a finite string: it fits nicely on one line of this paper. But of course we all know that Turing machines (and the

like) have no trouble manipulating finite strings; that, after all, is the essence of what they do, as your own earlier exposition confirms".

It seems to me that this objection reflects an attitude exactly analogous to at least one behind Hilbert's Gödel-killed finitistic program for mathematics. Hilbert observed that mathematical proofs were invariably presented as finite strings on finite pieces of paper, and he hit upon an idea: proofs were to be entirely mechanical, step-by-step *finite* strings; and all problems in mathematics could be solved by such finitary methods. Demonstrations of consistency were to involve only finite procedures making reference to but a finite number of properties possessed by formulas, and procedures that employed only a finite number of operations over these formulas.

But as we all know by now, Gödel obliterated Hilbert's program. He proved that human mathematical reasoning is *not* always limited to Hilbertian reasoning: some form of infinitistic reasoning must be employed for some proofs of formulas about **N**: formulas which expert mathematicians and logicians can see to be true. A bit more specifically, Gödel found a sentence of the form $\forall x \phi(x)$ about the natural numbers (i.e., a formula that says that every natural number has a certain property ϕ) which couldn't be proved by finite means, even though each of $\phi(0), \phi(1), \phi(2), \ldots \phi(n), \ldots, \phi(n+1), \ldots$ (where each of these formulas says that a particular natural number has the property ϕ) *is* provable by a finite proof from the first-order version of the axioms characterizing the natural numbers. Gödel found a formula which expressed a truth about the natural numbers that couldn't be proved by finite means.

What was the reaction? Interestingly enough, many suggested that first-order formalizations of arithmetic be replaced by formalizations in $L_{\omega 1 \omega}$.[29]

But the heart of the objection under consideration would seem to be a denial that human mathematicians and logicians are *using* $L_{\omega 1 \omega}$. It is a claim accompanied by a concession that it's quite possible for a human expert mathematician or logician to use some finite mental representation to reason *about* $L_{\omega1\omega}$. But the skeptic is insisting that humans can't be reasoning *with* $L_{\omega1\omega}$: it can't be a proper description of their language of thought.

In response, I readily admit that sometimes mathematicians and logicians (and, for that matter, non-mathematicians) merely reason *with* a *finite* representation and reasoning system. (I suppose the paradigmatic case of this would be the carrying out of derivations in some natural deduction system for L_I.) But it doesn't follow from this fact that my argument founders on the distinction between reasoning with and reasoning in. The key is that I've selected $L_{\omega1\omega}$ for good reason: some of the reasoning *about* this logical system is clearly reasoning *with* a representation and reasoning system having *at least* the infinitary grade of $L_{\omega1\omega}$. In order to see this we have but to look a bit at what goes on when a relevant theorem about $L_{\omega1\omega}$ is pondered and proved. Take, for example, the following simple theorem, which I have often asked students learning about $L_{\omega1\omega}$ to prove:

Scott's Isomorphism Theorem: Let I be an interpretation for L_I. Then there is a sentence φ of $L_{\omega1\omega}$ such that for all countable interpretations I^* for L_I, $I^* \vDash \phi$ iff I^* is isomorphic to I.

Intuitively, this theorem says that a single infinitary sentence can perfectly characterize a countable interpretation for L_I. The customary proof involves (among other things) constructing infinitely long conjunctions (*outside of* $L_{\omega1\omega}$), each conjunct of which is an atomic formula capturing a truth about the elements in the domain of I. For example, if the domain of I is **N**, and I includes > (ordinary greater than), then the following are elements of >: (3,2), (4,3), (5,4), ... Hence, if we are to capture I, there must be an atomic formula corresponding to each such fact, and the conjunction of these formulas (which is still only a part of the construction at the heart of Scott's Theorem) becomes (with the relation symbol G interpreted as >, and c_i as constants):

$$Gc_3c_2 \wedge Gc_4c_3 \wedge Gc_5c_4 \wedge \ldots,$$

or, in the notation for infinitely long conjunctions in $L_{\omega1\omega}$,

$$\bigwedge \{Gc_ic_j : c_i, c_j \text{ are constants } \& \quad I \vDash Gc_ic_j\}.$$

The point is that, *contra* my critic, the sort of mathematical reasoning needed for carrying out such proofs requires that one reason *with* a "language of thought" that parallels $L_{\omega1\omega}$ itself.[30]

Objection: "But Turing-Uncomputable Problems Stump Us

The objection is expressed as follows: "Enough beating around the bush. If human persons are capable of hypercomputation, then they should be able to present the answer to Turing-uncomputable problems, period. You began by introducing two such problems: the Σ and halting problems. If you're right, then human persons should simply be able to produce the correct output for input we submit to them. For example, human persons should be able to figure out the productivity of an *n*-state Turing machine, for all *n*. But you have produced no such person".

There are three reasons why this objection fails.

First, I have not maintained that the hyper-computational part of our cognition is *consciously harnessable* across the range of inputs for some particular problem. When we hypercompute, we may well do so unconsciously, and then suddenly the solution may pop into consciousness, as a result of mechanisms beyond our control. This may only happen for some cases. This issue is discussed at length in (Bringsjord & Zenzen 2002).

Second, it's not at all clear that what the skeptic here demands isn't happening before our eyes. To make this point, I first report the following. Quite a few years ago, a referee offered an objection against the view, defended in a preliminary version of (Bringsjord 1992) that humans can in principle solve the halting problem; this objection was rather similar to the one we're presently considering. He (or she) pointed out that there exists a Turing machine *M* and input *u* such that *M:u→halt* iff Fermat's Last Theorem (FLT) is true, and *M:u→∞* otherwise.[31] He then said that if I was correct about the power of the human mind, we should be able to crack the FLT puzzle. I responded by cheerfully conceding that such a machine/input pair clearly existed: but I pointed out that, given that there is a fact of the matter with respect to the truth-value of FLT, and given the power of the human mind, the issue might well be settled soon enough; who knows? This exchange came well before Wiles did in fact settle the issue (Wiles 1995, Wiles & Taylor 1995). Now we know that FLT was not beyond the reach of human persons. For all we know, it seems to me, the situation is the same with respect to various Turing-uncomputable puzzles that humanity is currently attacking.[32]

CONCLUSION

Let me sum up: Descartes, understood in Chisholmian fashion,[33] held that we are non-physical (thinking) things. Since the two explicit arguments presented herein are formally valid; and since, for me, the premises are true in both cases, this pair constitutes by my lights an outright proof that Descartes and Chisholm and Göde[34] are right. Some readers, of course, will resist: they will specifically persist in rejecting (since this is really their only alternative) premise (4): even after reading the now-extensive body of work aimed at substantiating this proposition. Nonetheless, it seems to me that all readers must admit that before them now stands at least a formidable case for substance dualism. If so, this doctrine may continue to be unfashionable, but non-starter it is not; not in the least.

ACKNOWLEDGMENT

I'm indebted to Roderick Chisholm for unabashedly maintaining, day in, day out at Brown during my stay there, that we ought go where common-sense and logic lead, however unfashionable their destination may be.

REFERENCES

Ashcraft, M. (1994). *Human Memory and Cognition*. New York: HarperCollins.

Baron, R., & Kalsher, M. (2001). *Psychology* (5th ed.). Boston: Allyn and Bacon.

Barwise, J., & Etchemendy, J. (1993). *Turing's World 3.0*. Stanford, CA: CSLI.

Boolos, G. S., & Jeffrey, R. C. (1989). *Computability and Logic*. Cambridge, UK: Cambridge University Press.

Bourbaki, N. (2004). *Elements of Mathematics: Theory of Sets*. New York: Springer Verlag.

Bringsjord, S. (1992). *What Robots Can and Can't Be*. Dordrecht, The Netherlands: Kluwer.

Bringsjord, S. (1997). An Argument for the Uncomputability of Infinitary Mathematical Expertise. In Feltovich, P., Ford, K., & Hayes, P. (Eds.), *Expertise in Context* (pp. 475–497). Menlo Park: CA AAAI Press.

Bringsjord, S. (2001). In Computation, Parallel is Nothing, Physical Everything. *Minds and Machines, 11*, 95–99. doi:10.1023/A:1011257022242

Bringsjord, S. (2008). Declarative/Logic-Based Cognitive Modeling. In Sun, R. (Ed.), *The Handbook of Computational Psychology* (pp. 127–169). Cambridge, UK: Cambridge University Press.

Bringsjord, S., & Arkoudas, K. (2004). The Modal Argument for Hypercomputing Minds. *Theoretical Computer Science, 317*, 167–190. doi:10.1016/j.tcs.2003.12.010

Bringsjord, S., Kellett, O., Shilliday, A., Taylor, J., van Heuveln, B., & Yang, Y. (2006). A New Gödelian Argument for Hypercomputing Minds Based on the Busy Beaver Problem. *Applied Mathematics and Computation, 176*, 516–530. doi:10.1016/j.amc.2005.09.071

Bringsjord, S., & Zenzen, M. (2002). Toward a Formal Philosophy of Hypercomputation. *Minds and Machines, 12*, 241–258. doi:10.1023/A:1015651216328

Bringsjord, S., & Zenzen, M. (2003). *Superminds: People Harness Hypercomputation, and More*. Dordrecht, The Netherlands: Kluwer Academic Publishers.

Burgin, M. (2001). How We Know What Technology Can Do. *Communications of the ACM, 44*(11), 83–88. doi:10.1145/384150.384166

Chisholm, R. (1978). Is There a Mind-Body Problem? *Philosophic Exchange, 2*, 25–32.

Chisholm, R. (1989). Bolzano on the Simplicity of the Soul . In Gombocz, W. L., Rutte, H., & Sauer, W. (Eds.), *Traditionen und Perspektiven der Analytischen Philosophie*. Vienna, Austria: Holder-Pichler-Tempsky.

Chisholm, R. (1991). On the Simplicity of the Soul . In Tomberlin, J. (Ed.), *Philosophical Perspectives 5: Philosophy of Religion*. Atascadero, CA: Ridgeview.

Copeland, B. J. (1998). Even Turing Machines Can Compute Uncomputable Functions . In Casti, J. (Ed.), *Unconventional Models of Computation* (pp. 150–164). London: Springer-Verlag.

Dickmann, M. A. (1975). *Large Infinitary Languages*. Amsterdam, The Netherlands: North-Holland.

Ebbinghaus, H. D., Flum, J., & Thomas, W. (1984). *Mathematical Logic*. New York: Springer-Verlag.

Ebbinghaus, H. D., Flum, J., & Thomas, W. (1994). *Mathematical Logic* (2nd ed.). New York, NY: Springer-Verlag.

Eicholz, R. E., O'Daffer, P. G., Charles, R. I., Young, S. I., Barnett, C. S., & Clemens, S. R. (1995). *Grade 7 Addison-Wesley Mathematics*. Reading, MA: Addison-Wesley.

Etesi, G., & Nemeti, I. (2002). Non-Turing Computability via Malament-Hogarth Space-Times. *International Journal of Theoretical Physics, 41*(2), 341–370. doi:10.1023/A:1014019225365

Goldstein, E. B. (2005). *Cognitive Psychology: Connecting Mind, Research, and Everyday Experience*. Belmont, CA: Wadsworth.

Granger, R. (2004). Brain circuit implementation: High-precision computation from low-precision components . In Berger, T., & Glanzman, D. (Eds.), *Toward Replacement Parts for the Brain* (pp. 277–294). Cambridge, MA: MIT Press.

Granger, R. (2004). Derivation and analysis of basic computational operations of thalamocortical circuits. *Journal of Cognitive Neuroscience, 16*, 856–877. doi:10.1162/089892904970690

Granger, R. (in press). Engines of the Brain: The computational instruction set of human cognition. *AI Magazine*.

Hamkins, J. D., & Lewis, A. (2000). Infinite Time Turing Machines. *Journal of Symbolic Logic, 65*(2), 567–604. doi:10.2307/2586556

Isaacson, D. (1985). Arithmetical Truths and Hidden Higher-Order Concepts. In The Paris Logic Group, (Ed.), Logic Colloquium. Amsterdam: North-Holland.

Newell, A. (1973). You Can't Play 20 Questions With Nature and Win: Projective Comments on the Papers of This Symposium. In W. Chase, (Ed.), *Visual Information Processing*, (pp. 283-308). New York: Academic Press.

Siegelmann, H., & Sontag, E. D. (1994). Analog Computation Via Neural Nets. *Theoretical Computer Science, 131*, 331–360. doi:10.1016/0304-3975(94)90178-3

Smith, P. (2007). *An Introduction to Gödel's Theorems*. Cambridge, UK: Cambridge University Press.

Stillings, N., Weisler, S., Chase, C., Feinstein, M., Garfield, J., & Rissland, E. (1995). *Cognitive Science*. Cambridge, MA: MIT Press.

Wang, H. (1995). On Computabilism' and Physicalism: Some Sub-problems . In Cornwell, J. (Ed.), *Nature's Imagination: The Frontiers of Scientific Vision* (pp. 161–189). Oxford, UK: Oxford University Press.

Wiles, A. (1995). Modular Elliptic Curves and Fermat's Last Theorem. *The Annals of Mathematics, 141*(3), 443–551. doi:10.2307/2118559

Wiles, A., & Taylor, R. (1995). Ring-Theoretic Properties of Certain Hecke Algebras. *The Annals of Mathematics, 141*(3), 553–572. doi:10.2307/2118560

KEY TERMS AND DEFINITIONS

Dualism: Dualism denotes a state of two parts. The word's origin is the Latin *duo*, "two". The term 'dualism' was originally coined to denote co-eternal binary opposition, ameaning that is preserved in metaphysical and philosophical duality discourse but has been diluted in general or common usages.

Substance Dualism: A generally well-known version of dualism is attributed to René Descartes (1641), which holds that the mind is a nonphysical substance. Descartes was the first to clearly identify the *mind* with consciousness and self-awareness and to distinguish this from the brain, which was the seat of intelligence. Hence, he was the first to formulate the mind-body problem in the form in which it exists today. Dualism is contrasted with various kinds of monism, including physicalism and phenomenalism. Substance dualism is contrasted with all forms of materialism, but property dualism may be considered a form of emergent materialism and thus would only be contrasted with non-emergent materialism

Mind-Body Dualism: In philosophy of mind, dualism is any of a narrow variety of views about the relationship between mind and matter, which claims that mind and matter are two ontologically separate categories. In particular, mind-body dualism claims that neither the mind nor matter can be reduced to each other in any way, and thus is opposed to materialism in general, and reductive materialism in particular. Mind-body dualism can exist as substance dualism which claims that the mind and the body are composed of a distinct substance, and as property dualism which claims that there may not be a distinction in substance, but that mental and physical properties are still categorically distinct, and not reducible to each other. This type of dualism is sometimes referred to as "*mind and body*" and stands in contrast to philosophical monism, which views mind and matter as being ultimately the same kind of thing. See also Cartesian dualism, substance dualism, and epiphenomenalism.

Hypercomputation: refers to non-Turing computation. This includes various hypothetical methods for the computation of non-Turing-computable functions, following super-recursive algorithms (see also supertask). It also includes other forms of computation, such as interactive computation. The term was first introduced in 1999 by Jack Copeland and Diane Proudfoot[. A similar term is super-Turing computation. Hypercomputation may have the additional connotation of entertaining the possibility that such a device could be physically realizable. Some models have been proposed.

Infinitary Reasoning: mathematical reasoning that seems to be explicitly and irreducibly infinitary. The best example of such reasoning that we are aware of is found in *infinitary* mathematical logic. The key idea is to find mathematical cognition that is provably *beyond* computation. Such cognition seems to be exhibited by logicians and mathematicians who prove things in and about *infinitary* logics (which of course arose in no small part as a way to "surmount" Godel).

ENDNOTES

1   The group includes, e.g., Meixner (2004), Swinbrune (1997) and Chisholm (1991).

2   Meixner (2004) interestingly counts Searle's searlecra "Chinese Room Argument" as a recent argument for property dualism. This is somewhat surprising, as most people familiar with CRA don't regard it to be an argument for dualism. I'm not at all sure that Searle himself embraces property dualism. But at any rate I certainly do regard the argument, when suitably modified, to be sound missing.thought.experiment (for such a sound argument, see Bringsjord & Noel 2002).

3   Chisholm maintained that it was inaccurate and misleading to speak of a mind-body problem. He claimed the issue was whether *persons* are extended entities, and preferred to speak of the *person*-body problem. Moreover, Chisholm maintained that persons were indeed immaterial objects. Relevant papers include: (Chisholm 1978, 1989 and 1991). This paper marks my allegiance not only to Descartes and Chisholm, but to Gödel as well, since he was quite convinced of two things, viz., that the human brain is a digital computer dressed up in biological clothes,

and that the human mind exceeds such information processing. For a nice summary, see (Wang 1995).

4   The set recommended as an expression of mind-body dualism by Meixner (meixner_two_sides, 43) is composed of these five theses:
MBDua0 At least one actually existing *mental* entity is not physical.
MBDua1 At least one actually existing *mental* substantial individual is not physical.
MBDua2 At least one actually existing *mental* property is not physical.
MBDua3 At least one actually existing *mental* event is not physical.
MBDua4 At least one actually existing *mental* state of affairs is not physical.

5   "Jones has lost his mind." → "Jones is insane." "Jones has a fine mind." → "Jones is smart." "My mind isn't a physical thing." → "I'm not a physical thing." And so on.

6   Note that Meixner's (2004) analysis of dualism and physicalism yields niceties that haven't been attended to by proponents of dualism. This can be seen by studying Meixner's (2004) own analysis of such proponents in his book.

7   For teaching this variety of TMs to philosophy students, a particularly nice system is Barwise and Etchemendy's *Turing's World* software (Barwise & Etchemendy 1993). Using this software, one can build (simple) TMs with point-and-click ease.

8   In short, at the time, Gordon's machine was the most productive known five-state Turing machine in the quadruple framework.

9   There are a number of variations in the exact format for the function. For example, one can drop the conditions that the output 1's be contiguous.

10 A nice specification of a Turing-machine multiplier can be found in (Boolos & Jeffrey 1989).

11 It can obviously be defined by any equally difficult function. One that might resonate with some readers is the function that takes a well-formed formula (a wff) ϕ in classical first-order logic as input, and outputs 1 if ϕ is a theorem and 0 otherwise.

12 I don't have the space to take on arguments for the view that persons are fictions, and that we are all massively self-deceived, since if we believe anything, we believe that we really and truly exist. Following Chisholm, it seems to me that we ought to base our philosophizing on propositions that are common-sensical and epistemically innocent: until perhaps these propositions are overturned by separate, watertight argumentation.

13 The paper is available online. Just search for the title; and once you find it, search for 'brain' through the paper. One location of the paper, at present, is http://www.loebner.net/Prizef/TuringArticle.htmlhttp://www.loebner.net/Prizef/TuringArticle.html

14 CCM can be traced back to Alan Newell. See his (Newell 1973).

15 In an interview ("Thinking About Thinking") in *Wired***4.12**. The archives for *Wired* are available online. Here's the specific entry in these archives for the Churchland interview: http://www.wired.com/wired/archive/4.12/churchland.htmlhttp://www.wired.com/wired/archive/4.12/churchland.html

16 See http://domino.research.ibm.com/comm/pr.nsf/pages/rsc.bluegene_cognitive.html-http://domino.research.ibm.com/comm/pr.nsf/pages/rsc.bluegene_cognitive.html

17 Granger's lab, the Brain Engineering Laboratory, is on the Web: http://www.dartmouth.edu/ rhghttp://www.dartmouth.edu/:rhg

18 Before the concept of hypercomputation, let alone the concept of hypercomputing minds.

19 Contemporary cognitive psychology, cognitive science, and cognitive neuroscience: all are predicated on the view that the human mind is an embodied information processor. For a nice survey that brings this point across clearly, see (Goldstein 2005). In addition, see: (Ashcraft 1994, Baron & Kalsher 2001, Stillings, Weisler, Chase, Feinstein, Gar_eld & Rissland 1995).

20 A nice formalization and proof is provided by boolos.jeffrey. By 'appropriately configured' is meant nothing more than that a particular set of predicate letters and functors must be selected to model the operation of a TM.

21 This follows a standard notation for referring to logical systems, as they are featured in Lindström's results. See (Ebbinghaus, Flum & Thomas 1984).

22 The formula $\phi(X)$ can be easily built in *second*-order logic, L_{II}.

23 Of course, even finitary logics have underlying alphabets that are infinite in size (the propositional calculus comes with an infinite supply of propositional variables). $L_{\omega_1\omega}$, however, allows for *formulas* of infinite length: and hence allows for infinitely long derivations. More about such derivations in a moment.

24 This paper is aimed at an audience assumed to have familiarity with but elementary classical logic. So this isn't the place to baptize readers into the world of cardinal numbers. Hence we leave the size implications of the subscripts in $L_{\omega_1\omega}$, and other related niceties, such as the precise meaning of ω, to the side. For a comprehensive array of the possibilities arising from varying the subscripts, see [19].

25 Note that there are *first*-order formulas such that any interpretation that satisfies them must be infinite. The converse is the rub.

26 A group allonym for the mathematicians who authored a collection of eight painstak-

ingly rigorous, detailed books apparently showing that all the publishable results of classical mathematics can in fact be expressed as derivations from axiomatic set theory using $\mathcal{L}_I$. The starting place in the Bourbaki oeuvre is (Bourbaki 2004).

27 (Isaacson n.d.) writes the truths independent of PA "are such that there is no way that their truth can be perceived in purely arithmetical terms" (p. 203).

28 A defense of the conjecture would obviously require a standalone paper, at least. But two quick remarks are seemingly in order here: One, notice that I say *in the human case*. It may well be possible for beings outside the class of our own (human persons) to produce a rationally compelling proof in ways utterly different than the ones we follow. Second, I don't say that the concepts and structures in question are of an *irreducibly* infinitary nature. Human chess grandmasters don't play chess the way computing machines do, and yet machines in general reach similar levels of performance. I don't say here that there are finitary routes to the same end of proving PA-independent sentences.

29 A nice treatment of the issues here can be found in Smullyan's (1992) recent book on Gödel's incompleteness results. Many philosophers have a general notion of Gödel's first incompleteness theorem, but few know that Gödel showed that there is

a formula $\phi(y)$, with one free variable y, such that $\phi(1), \phi(2), \phi(3), \ldots \phi(n), \ldots$ are all provable PA, while the sentence $\forall y \phi(y)$ *isn't*. This phenomenon–called ω- incompleteness by Tarski–can be remedied by invoking the system PA$^+$, which contains the ω-rule (sometimes also called Tarski's rule or Carnap's rule) allowing one to infer $\forall y \phi(y)$ from the infinitely many premises $\phi(1), \phi(2), \phi(3), \ldots \phi(n), \ldots$

30 Please note that my rebuttal doesn't in the least conflate object theory with metatheory. I am in fact invoking this very distinction: but I'm pointing out that the metatheory in question (unsurprisingly) deploys some of the very same infinitary constructions as seen *in* $L_{\omega 1 \omega}$. This seems utterly undeniable: and so much the worse for those (e.g., Ebbinghaus et al. 1984)., who believe that ``background" logic/mathematics is fundamentally first-order.

31 Goldbach's Conjecture might make for a better example, actually. Such TMs aren't hard to specify.

32 It's interesting to note that specifically in the case of the busy beaver problem, considerable effort is being expended to divine every larger $\Sigma(n)$ values, and progress is being made. See [13].

33 Recall note 1.

34 Once again, note note 1.

Chapter 7
Identity in the Real World

Matteo Casu
Università degli Studi di Genova, Italy

Luca Albergante
Università degli Studi di Milano, Italy

ABSTRACT

The notion of identity has been discussed extensively in the past. Leibniz was the first to present this notion in a logically coherent way, using a formulation generally recognized as "Leibniz's Law". Although some authors criticized this formulation, Leibniz's Law is generally accepted as the definition of identity. This chapter interprets Leibniz's Law as a limit notion: perfectly reasonable in a God's eye view of reality, but very difficult to use in the real world because of the limitedness of finite agents. To illustrate our approach we use "description logics" to describe the properties of objects, and present an approach to relitivize Leibniz's Law. This relativization is further developed in a semantic web context, where the utility of our approach is suggested.

INTRODUCTION

While the notion of identity is commonly used in the scientific field, its formal definition is not so straightforward. In the past many philosophers proposed a range of techniques to define and deal with it. However we have to wait until the so called "Leibniz's Law" (LL), to achieve a definition that undercovered its intimate connection with logic and ontology.

One of the main aspects of LL is its dependence on the notion of property. Second-order logic is required to characterize properties, and therefore to formulate LL. While generally accepted, some philosopher criticized the characterization of identity proposed by LL. Moreover even if accepted as a definition, the logical formalization of LL poses some problems. There is no complete calculus for second-order logic, and LL requires second-order logic for its formulation. Additionally, second-order quantification commits to the existence

DOI: 10.4018/978-1-61692-014-2.ch007

of properties. This fact is sometimes considered problematic by philosophers and logicians.

To prevent some of these problems, we use description logics (DLs). DLs provide us a mean to deal with properties in a first-order logic environment, and allow us to make quantification over properties less problematic. The use of DLs is justified by the consideration that finite agents are able to access only a restricted set of properties. Moreover, DLs are decidable. This is compatible with the idea of construction of software agents using DLs and deciding identity between two objects.

A paradigmatic environment in which it is reasonable to consider software agents using DLs and dealing with objects is semantic web. An applicative example is presented and discussed in order to illustrate the usefulness of our idea.

The work is organized as follows: Section 2 presents the required philosophical and logical preliminaries, Section 3 presents our idea, and Section 4 draws some conclusions and suggests additional researches. More precisely, Section 2 presents an historical and philosophical overview of some attempts to characterize identity (2.1, 2.2, 2.3, 2.4) and discusses some foundational issues about identity (2.4, 2.5). The final subsections of Section 2 present some basics of DLs and our motivations for using them (2.7, 2.6). Section 3 presents a relativization of identity with respect to agents (3.1, 3.2) and discusses an example of application of the idea (3.3).

BACKGROUND

Logic and Metaphysics

"To say that things are identical is to say that they are the same." (Noonan 2008). This is the notion of *numerical* (or *absolute*) *identity*, which the tradition distinguished from, for example, *qualitative* identity, i.e. when two objects share some prop-erties. For the scope of this work with "identity" we will mean numerical identity. Moreover we will deal with *contemporary* characterizations of identity.

It is only with Frege and Peano (late XIX century) that we achieved the conceptual framework we use today in logic and in philosophy of language (see their fundamental works (Frege 1879) and (Peano 1889)). For example, Peano distinguished between different forms of predication: the difference between "Cats are feline" (inclusion between classes) and "Mark is human" (membership of an element to a class) was not clearly formulable before the XIX century.

Identity is generally considered a binary relation. However this poses a problem: is identity a relation between objects or between names for objects? The question is not as naïve as it seems: Frege, founder of modern logic, in (Frege 1884), accepted one of Leibniz's characterizations of identity as his definition of equality:

Eadem sunt quorum unum potest substitui alteri salva veritate[1]

This sentence hides a confusion between use and mention, as observed by (Church 1956, p. 300), that corrects:

(S) "Things are identical if the name of one can be substituted for that of the other without loss of truth."

We have to add the clause that the substitution must occur in *referential* contexts, because in *opaque* (or intensional) contexts names for the same thing could not be substituted *salva veritate*[2].

This characterization of identity is of linguistical flavour: it deals with substitutions of names denoting objects, and is pre-theoretical. In fact, (S) is a formulation of what is generally called the substituting principle.

There are other ways of thinking about the same notion. Identity can also be thought in one of the following alternative ways:

- as the relation everything has to itself and to nothing else
- as the smallest equivalence relation
- as the identity relation: $\Delta = \{(x,x) | x \in D\}$ over a domain of discourse D.

We will now see how to embed the notion of identity in a formal system.

Defining Identity

First Order Logic (FOL)

In propositional logic we do not have any notion of identity: the objects of propositional logic are propositional formulae, such as $A \rightarrow (B \vee \neg C)$, which is logically *equivalent* to $A \vee C \rightarrow B$, but the formula $A=B$ would be ill-formed.

In first order logic (from now on FOL) we *do* have a notion of identity. The standard way to obtain first order logic with identity (FOL$^=$) is by adding to FOL a binary predicative constant "=" and the following two axioms:

(Ref) $\forall x(x=x)$
(L) $\forall x \forall y (x=y \rightarrow (A(x) \rightarrow A(y)))$

where (L) holds for all firs-order formulas A with one free variable. The value of "=" is true in an interpretation I and a domain D if and only if I assign to the individual constants t_1 and t_2 the same elements in D:

$I \vDash t_1 = t_2$ if and only if $I(t_1)=I(t_2)$
or (equivalently)
$I(=) = \Delta$
where Δ is the identity relation over D.

(Ref) is the reflexive property of identity, while (L) is an axiom schema of the indiscernibility of identicals[3]. From these axioms it can be derived that identity is a congruence relation.

Identity is not first-order definable, and we have at least three ways to present this fact:

1. (Ref) and (L) do not constrain the interpretation of "=" to be the identity relation $\Delta = \{(x,x) | x \in D\}$ over the domain D[4]. Interpretations in which this happens are called *normal*. This limitation can be overcome taking, for every non-normal interpretation, $D/_{I(=)}$ as the domain[5]. But this means that our system is not able to distinguish between individuals and equivalence classes.

2. (L) is in fact a schema, not a single axiom. It must hold for every predicate A. But suppose to have a countably infinite domain D. In the standard set-theoretic semantics of FOL 1-place properties are interpreted in subsets over the domain. By Cantor's theorem, the properties over D would be more than numerable. However predicates in a language cannot be more than numerable, therefore we could have $A(a) \leftrightarrow A(b)$ even if $a \neq b$ for some a and b.

3. The principle of indiscernibility of identicals does not hold in FOL$^=$. Consider an interpretation in which all predicates are interpreted in the empty set, and the domain contains at least two objects. Then the two objects would be indiscernible but still different.

Therefore first-order languages are not strong enough to characterize identity. This is not surprising: identity can be thought as "the smallest equivalence relation", which requires quantifying over relations.

Second Order Logic (SOL)

In second order logic (from now on SOL) it is possible to define identity, taking (Ref) and the Leibniz's Law

(LL) $x = y \equiv_{def} \forall F (F(x) \leftrightarrow F(y))$

It is worth noticing that, if we assume the property "being identical to x" in the range of F, the conditional on the right side of the definition do not need to be a biconditional, because the biconditional derives from (LL).

A reason not to admit "being identical to x" as a legitimate property is that this would turn (LL) into an *impredicative* definition (i.e., a definition that depends on a set of entities, at least one of which is the entity being defined).

Other problems with (LL) come from the logical (and philosophical) properties of SOL. In particular, if interpreted in its standard semantics, SOL is committed with set theory, and with the existence of particular sets. Hence someone considers SOL not a genuine logic, for logic is supposed to be neutral with respect to the existence of anything[6]. Moreover, SOL quantifies over predicates, committing to a heavy ontology, that some philosophers, like Quine, do not accept.

Relative Identity

In (Geach 1967) and (Geach 1967), Geach claimed that every sentence about identity of two objects hides a predicate under which the two objects fall, and this predicate must be clear from the context. Let *a* and *b* be objects and *P* and *Q* be predicates. E.g.

"a is identical to b"
must be read as:
(G) "a is the same P of b"

Hence two things can be the same P and yet not the same Q[7]. Two things can be the same apple, the same book, the same man, but not *the same*. Geach rejects absolute identity and defends *relative identity*. Note that according to Geach the translation of (G) is not

"a is a P, b is a P and a=b"

for this sentence uses the absolute notion of identity. Objects *a* and *b* could be, for example, the same piece of metal but not the same armor.

What Geach also suggests in his works is that identity is language-relative: two objects could be indiscernible in a language L_1 but discernible in a richer language L_2. This happens if we treat identity not as a logical notion, but as a predicate whose interpretation is forced by (Ref) and (L) to be the identity relation[8].

In particular, Geach calls a predicate that satisfies (Ref) and (L) in a theory an *I-predicate* for that theory (for example an I-predicate could be "having the same height as"). It is always possible that an I-predicate in a theory would not be an I-predicate for a richer theory. Hence no predicate in a theory can be the absolute identity.

Geach entered in a dispute with Quine, who suggested that moving to the quotient structure can always turn our I-predicates into absolute identity: take a domain whose elements are equivalence classes of men having the same heights. Geach replies that applying Quine's method would lead us to a Meinongian universe of discourse, and this would be incoherent with Quine's principles of ontological sobriety[9].

We will not go further in this discussion. It is enough to say that Geach's (and Quine's) problems are of little interest if one turns to SOL. SOL has its problems too, as we have seen, but we will propose an approach for identity that can prevent them. However we presented Geach's ideas for they have somehow inspired our approach.

Identity and Objects

The observations about Frege in this section broadly rely on (Cozzo 1997).

In §62 of (Frege 1884), Frege formulates his criterion of identity for objects: if the sign *a* wants to designate an object then we must have a criterion that, at least in principle, permits us to know if another object *b* is the same as *a* or not. This principle has been largely adopted in philosophy: Quine's slogan "no entity without identity" stems from it.

The principle has generally been applied to abstract objects, or equivalently, to sortal terms[10]: e.g. to know what a set is, is to know when two sets are the same set[11]. In general to know what it means to be an object is to know when two objects of that kind are the same.

The criterion of identity, together with the observation that an object is always given to us in a certain way (or by a certain description), can easily lead to the idea that identity is *constitutive* of our knowledge of objects.

What we claim is not that objects are always given through a description or through a certain *mode of presentation* (a Fregean *sinn*). From God's viewpoint this is not necessary true. Our claim is that this happens for objects when considered by rational agents with finite cognitive power, such as humans or software agents.

It is by following this line of thinking that we believe it is possible to consider the question:

(Q) "When are two objects the same?"

Paradoxical Questions?

This section presents the philosophical foundations of our approach. We do not aim at giving a theory of objects or a theory of identity, but we simply want to show that (Q) can be seriously considered.

Question (Q) might seem paradoxical, or even contradictory: if the problem is to decide when *two* objects are the same, we might get stuck at the beginning. One possible and quite straight objection to the sensibleness of (Q) is the observation that if there are *two* objects they cannot be the same. But let's consider the following example. In the famous novel *Flatland* by E. A. Abbott the main character is a square living in a flat world and thus perceiving only 2D objects. Imagine that this square meets two similar square objects. From his point of view these objects are different, however from a 3D point of view these two similar squares could be two sections of the same horseshoe. In this case the limited capability of perception of

the square prevents him from understanding that he is actually seeing two parts of the same object.

A possible objection is that this is not a case of two objects being the same object, but of two objects being two (different) part of the same object. However in our framework, as we have discussed in the previous section, from the point of view of finite agents, there is no perception of objects without a mode of presentation of them. Therefore, without referring to a context of evaluation, we cannot enumerate the objects in the world until we are able to recognize them. From the point of view of the square, the other two squared objects are different objects. Consider this more radical example: assume we have one particle that travels through time. Travelling back and forward in time, the particle could be more than once in the same time. In this situation we could see, or interact with, many particles that are actually just one. So, how many particles we see? We would say many. But that "many" are one. While someone could intuitively say that we have one object of a particular nature, others may say that we have many objects that are one. Both points of view seem reasonable.

If we do not know that the many particles are in fact one, we would just say that they are many. Are we *wrong*? This could depend on our theory of knowledge, on the presence of someone who knows the truth about that particle, on our notion of truth, and so on. In the case in which we know that the many particles are one, would we deny that those objects seem different objects but in fact they are not? And if so, would we continue to say it if those object could harm us? We do not have an answer, but we think that these examples show the intrinsic difficulty of the problem.

With regard to the last example, we can consider the many particles as one if we know the laws of physics involved in the phenomenon. Hence we distinguish objects using Leibniz's Law and our knowledge about the world. The particular restriction of Leibniz's Law that we present in section 3.1 is conceived to being used in a linguistic environment, where properties are given in the form of linguistic descriptions.

At this point, the task of deciding if some objects are the same or not begins to sound more sensible. The fact is that, *prima facie*, in the situations we depicted there is no way to decide if the objects we see (they are objects in any usual interpretation of the word) are a unique object or not. One could object that what we see are different representations of the same object. However we are not talking of "shadows" of an object: to make another (and less exotic) example, in our actual world we recognize as the same object ourselves at different ages, even if a child at 8 is an object and the same child at 10 is another one.

This situation is described in contemporary philosophy approximately in the following way: philosophers who think that the 8 years old child and the same child at 10 are different objects are called tridimensionalist. They think the identity of an object is given at a specific time. Their world is populated by ordinary, solid, tridimensional things, like persons, tables and so on. Other philosophers, so-called quadridimensionalist, think that objects whose existence persists through time must be described as quadridimensional objects. Their world is populated by persons in four dimensions, i.e. a person is a sort of "temporal worm", and at any time we can see just a piece of it.

Our vision is different: in order to give a sense to (Q) we think that a person, considered as a temporal worm, as a tridimensional object in the present, and as tridimensional object at 8, are the same object. In a sense, we are redefining the notion of object. This notion seems to collapse in the notion of representation, and hence it is clearly different from the classical notion of object as "objective thing". The reason why we are adopting such a notion is that we have to deal with agents for which the objects in their domains are not given in advance. In the following section, we will continue the discussion about (Q).

Classical Identity

Leibniz's Law

So when are two objects the same? The only real answer we inherited from logic is "when they share the same properties". This answer corresponds to the second-order definition of identity, or Leibniz's Law

$$(LL) \ x = y \equiv_{def} \forall F \ (F(x) \leftrightarrow F(y))$$

The tradition has often treated (LL) as an axiom instead of a definition, and distinguished between the two sides of the biconditional

$$(L_1) \ \forall F \ \forall x \ \forall y \ (x = y \rightarrow F(x) \leftrightarrow F(y))$$
$$(L_2) \ \forall F \ \forall x \ \forall y \ (F(x) \leftrightarrow F(y) \rightarrow x = y)$$

(L_1) is known as the "indiscernibility of identicals", (L_2) as the "identity of indiscernibles".

While (L_1) is generally accepted (it is an axiom in FOL⁻), (L_2) has been questioned, between others, by (Black 1952): his argument runs as follows. Imagine a perfectly symmetrical universe, in which we have two indiscernible spheres. We cannot find a property holding for one sphere but not for the other. In his article Black considers a lot of objections, and replies to them. One of the most representative is that sphere A will have the property of being different from sphere B, while B will not[12]. Black replies that the property is not legitimate and that even giving names to the spheres would be problematic in its universe. Here we do not want to take part in this discussion. Our approach is inspired by Black as well as by Geach, but takes a completely different direction. While Black contests the identity of indiscernibles, we take Leibniz's Law as a base definition.

(LL) is a second-order formula, and quantifies over properties: this is one of the reasons why some philosophers are not in tune with SOL. From our point of view second-order quantification is not a problem *per se*: from a logical standpoint the set over which the second order quantifiers range is the power set of the domain of discourse. Problems arise when we consider Leibniz's Law as a criterion to be used by finite agents.

The Power Set

We will assume that agents have to recognize and classify objects given via some mode of presentation or description. The only way to decide whether two objects are identical is by using Leibniz's Law, but two problems arise:

1. the domain of discourse is not characterized *a priori*, and hence its power set is not characterized either;
2. even if we could consider the collection of all individuals in our world, the power set may be simply too large, and, if the domain is countably infinite, by Cantor's theorem, the power set is uncountably infinite (i.e. it has the cardinality of the set of real numbers)

Moreover, from a constructivist point of view, the power set is a quite obscure construction. An axiomatization known as "Constructive Set Theory" has been proposed in (Aczel 1978) and subsequent works. In this type of proposals the power set construction is restricted in various ways.

From a pragmatic point of view, our approach moves from the consideration that, given a way to name properties, we could limit the set of properties to be numerable[13]. This restriction is compatible with the assumption that real world agents have access to a limited set of properties. A very straightforward way to name properties and deal with them is by using *description logics*.

Description Logics

Description logics (DLs) are a family of logical formalisms used to represent knowledge that captures an application domain[14]. DL formulas are mappable to first-order formulas with one free variable; therefore they represent properties under a standard set-theoretic semantics. The aim of DLs is to construct complex formulas (and hence complex properties) out of simple primitive predicates (unary and binary, denoting properties and binary relations) using so called "constructors", i.e. boolean connectives and quantifiers.

For example, assume we have primitive predicates "P" and "F" intuitively standing for penguins and flying objects respectively[15]. In a DL the formula

$$P \sqcap F$$

denotes flying penguins. Imagine now to also have binary predicates and other constructors, such as negation, disjunction and quantifiers. Using these constructors we can build complex properties. Quantifiers are used to construct properties binding a variable in a binary predicate. In the following we present the language *ALC* (attributive language with complement), a simple example of DL.

Syntax

The syntax of *ALC* is given by the following Backus-Naur form, where C and D are complex formulas, A is a primitive unary predicate and R is a primitive binary predicate. In DLs primitive unary and binary predicates are called *concepts* and *roles* respectively.

$$C, D ::= A \mid \top \mid \bot \mid \neg C \mid C \sqcap D \mid C \sqcup D \mid \forall R.C$$

A sublanguage of *ALC* is *AL*, where the constructor "¬" is only applicable to atomic concepts.

Semantics

Let Δ^I be a domain of objects. The interpretation I of a DL is given by a couple $(\Delta^I, \cdot^I)$ where I is a function. Assume also a set **I** of names for individuals, a set **C** of names for atomic concepts and a set

R of names for atomic roles (binary predicates).

The interpretation function maps elements of **I** to elements of the domain, elements of **C** to subsets of the domain and elements of **R** to binary relations over the domain. With respect to the constructors, the interpretation acts in the following way

$$\top^I = \Delta^I$$
$$\bot^I = \emptyset$$
$$(\neg C)^I = \Delta^I \setminus C^I$$
$$(C \sqcap D)^I = C^I \cap D^I$$
$$(\forall R.C)^I = \{\, a \in \Delta^I \mid \forall b \,.\, (a, b) \in R^I \rightarrow b \in C^I \,\}$$

Then we define:

$$C \sqcup D =_{def} \neg(\neg C \sqcap \neg D)$$

and

$$\exists R.C =_{def} \neg\forall R.\neg C$$

Note that in *AL* the last definition is not suitable, for in *AL* the negation is only applicable to atomic concepts.

Knowledge Bases

Given the above definitions, we are now able to denote properties, that is to say, to describe sets of individuals, as "the flying penguins that are cousins of at least one two-legged penguin" or "the penguins whose children are all female penguins". Moreover DLs were also designed to make *assertions* over an application domain. Therefore we now present *knowledge bases*[16].

A knowledge base *K* is a couple *K = (T, A)* where *T* is a T-Box and *A* is an A-Box.

A T-Box *T* is a set, possibly empty, of logical axioms called "concept inclusions" (CI) of the form:

$$C \sqsubseteq D$$

or of the form:

$$C \equiv D$$

where C and D are DL formulas. Given an interpretation *I* the semantics of "⊑" is the following:

$C \sqsubseteq D$ if and only if $C^I \subseteq D^I$
$C \equiv D$ is defined as the conjunction
$C \sqsubseteq D$ and $D \sqsubseteq C$.

Note that a CI as $C \sqsubseteq D$ is equivalent to the FOL formula $\forall x\ (C^* \rightarrow D^*)$ where C* e D* are the first-order translation of C and D.

Examples of CI are definitions or partial definitions describing the domain of application, as:

Bachelor ≡ ¬Married ⊓ Man (a bachelor is exactly a man who's not married)
Penguins ⊑ Animals (a penguin is an animal)

An ABox *A* is a set, possibly empty, of logical axioms, called *ABox assertions*, of the form:

a:C
or
(a,b):R

where a, b ∈ **I**, C ∈ **C**, R ∈ **R**. The semantics is:
a:C if and only if $a^I \in C^I$

and
(a,b): R if and only if $(a^I, b^I) \in R^I$.

ABox assertions deal with particular objects, for example:

john:Penguin
or
(john, maria): in_love

Suppose we have a knowledge base K=(T,A) with:

T={Penguin ⊑ ∀ in_love.Penguin}
A={john:Penguin, (john, maria): in_love}

The CI in the Tbox says that penguins only love penguins. The ABox says that john is a penguin and loves maria. Therefore maria too is a penguin.

Reasoning on *ALC* is decidable and PSPACE-complete.

MAIN FOCUS

Our Model

According to our view, in the world there are agents and objects (agents are assumed to be active entities while objects are assumed to be passive). Agents recognize and classify objects using properties, whose logical counterparts are predicates. Objects are defined by asserted properties that are accessible to agents. Our world will be characterized by a variable set of agents and a variable set of objects: both new agents and new objects can enter the world. Properties of the objects are characterized by DL formulas.

Formulas are built from n-ary predicates (with $n \in N \setminus \{0\}$) and constructors. We denote 1-ary predicates with P1, P2, … and n-ary ($n > 1$) predicates with R1, R2, …). The agents can also use a collection of symbols a, b, …, that stand for the objects that the agents encounter.

Every agent is characterized by:

- a BNF for a DL-language
- a set of primitive predicates
- a knowledge base, possibly empty
- its computational resources
  ◦ We assume that agents are able to:
- identify an object[17]
- verify if an object satisfies a predicate P
- verify if a 2-uple of objects (a, b) satisfies a relation

To every agent is associated what we call its *space of properties*, that is, the set of properties it can access. For each agent A is given a set of properties Σ_A that is the language generated by the grammar of A. Each formula in Σ_A denotes a set, possibly empty, of objects.

As an example, for agent *i* formulas C and D in Σ_i are defined by the following BNF:

$$C, D ::= P \mid \top \mid \bot \mid \neg C \mid C \sqcap D \mid C \sqcup D \mid \forall R.C \mid \exists R.C$$

where P is a 1-ary predicate from Si, C, D $\in \Sigma_i$, R is a binary relation in S_i.

It is possible to consider different agents. For example, consider an agent with *AL* as language:

$$C, D ::= P \mid \top \mid \bot \mid \neg P \mid C \sqcap D \mid \forall R.C \mid \exists R.\top$$

Automated reasoning in *AL* is easier than in *ALC*. However the agent will not be able to consider properties such as

$$\exists R.(C \sqcap \neg D)$$

This formula could denote objects that have at least one cousin that is male and not married. On the contrary, there is no problem with

$$\forall R.(C \sqcap \neg P)$$

provided P is a primitive property.

In specific applications (as the applicative example discussed in section 3.3) the classical semantics of DLs, as defined before, could be not applicable. For example, in a relational database all information that is not declared is generally assumed to be false. This is known as the *closed world assumption*. In classical semantics this assumption does not hold, and we have *open world assumption*: this is also the case of DLs. We will not go into details: the "right" semantics to use depends on the particular purposes of the application[18].

Relativized Leibniz's Law

We can relativize Leibniz's Law with respect to agent *i* as:

$$x =_i y \equiv_{def} \forall C \in \Sigma_i \, (C(x) \leftrightarrow C(y))$$

This means that different agents will have a possibly different set of primitive predicates (different Σ_i) and a mean of constructing new properties from old ones in their knowledge domain.

Every agent has its space of accessible properties, and is able to reason about flying penguins only if he possesses the concepts of Flying objects, of Penguin and the ability to intersect their associated sets. The problem of identity of two objects can be considered for different agents A1 and A2. For example, if $\Sigma_{A1} \subset \Sigma_{A2}$ it is possible that A1 will identify two objects while A2 will not.

A Semantic Web Example

In our view, a document is a mean to describe knowledge. However this knowledge depends heavily on the agent that analyzes the document. Specifically on the ability of the agent to recognize and understand the document. To clarify this idea, consider a document written in English, an agent that does not know English will probably gain very little knowledge from reading if (of better by starring at it). Similarly the "sensorial power" of the agents is very important. That is, a blind agent will not be able to read a standard book.

To use a terminology comparable to (Goldreich 2007), while the information that a document bears is fixed, the knowledge that various agents can derive from this information depends on the agent.

As a consequence of this, two documents bearing the same information can be different from the point of view of the knowledge conveyed. In the following we will restrict our attention to software agents, that is, agents that can be coded on a computer. Specifically agents build with the only goal of determining if two documents are indeed the same.

The documents that these agents analyze are characterized by its content and by the set of associated properties. Note that, with the term "document", we mean not only text files, but also more complex binary files, like for example video or audio file. All agents are able to read the contents, while the list of readable properties can vary from agent to agent.

Given this setup, how can we determine, if documents are the same? A simple solution would be to check that the content of the two documents is the same. This solution, while reasonable, presents a number of problems. For example, if we create a webpage, and modify it by adding a new space between two words, this new webpage should be the considered identical to the old one, by most reasonable agents. This is a very important problem in the context of digital rights. For example images can be watermarked, that is digitally signed in such a way that it is possible to determine the author of the image. However, many techniques exist to circumvent these algorithms, and images that should be recognized as the same, are not.

Given this setup, how can we verify the identity of two documents? In the classical internet structure, this task can be very difficult, as the only option we have is to compare the contents of the two documents, and, as we saw, this can be tricky.

However, semantic web allows documents to be described by properties. Intuitively one could think that identical documents will have the same value for all the properties. Unfortunately this is not always the case. For example, the property "Last modified" is likely to be different even if two documents have exactly the same content. Moreover we might want to consider agents that posses a "broad" definition of identify and consider equal two webpages with the biography of the same person.

While the properties of the documents can be represented using a number of formalisms, in the following we will describe these properties using DLs. DLs provide a logical underpinning to semantic web languages such as the Ontology Web language (OWL)[19]. OWL is a W3C recommendation[20], therefore DLs seems adequate candidates for the purposes of semantic web, as they are expressive and yet decidable logical languages.

We describe a toy-example that is compliant to the constraints of a semantic web environment[21]. Specifically each document is associated with a list of properties that depends on its nature and type. For example, the properties of a video file will differ from the properties of a text document; moreover, even between different text documents we expect the properties of a biography of a philosopher to be different from the properties of a computer science article.

Since different agents check different properties and possess different knowledge, it is possible that their notion of identity varies. How can this be an advantage? To begin with, checking complex set of properties can require a lot of time, moreover, as described previously, different users, may have different concepts of identity, and they probably expect the software agents to reflect this idea. Having different types of agents—and hence different strategies in checking identity—allow the users to benchmark them, and select the ones that better suits a specific user, for a specific need.

Moreover, while this aspect will not be discussed in the present work due to space constraints, agents can be evolved and combined using for example evolutionary algorithms, to improve the quality of results.

As described above, each agent is characterized by a set of properties: its accessible properties. These properties are classified by file type and topic. This allows for a certain flexibility of the agent. For example, if we are comparing text documents describing music composers we might expect the property "music genre", but not the property "power consumption".

When agent A is asked to determine if documents P1 and P2 on topic T are identical, it proceeds as follow:

1. A selects a subset of its accessible properties with respect to topic T
2. A match the selected properties for P1 and P2
3. If at least one property is different, the P1 and P2 are different

Note that the selection of the set of properties can be performed in different ways. The simplest solution is random selection, but we can think of ranking of properties, and even evolution of this ranking.

To determine if two properties match we use the following conventions:

1. If the two descriptions are empty and the theory is empty, the properties match
2. If the two descriptions are singletons and the theory is empty, then perform string matching
3. If one of the two descriptions is empty, then the two properties do not match (this step introduces non-monotonicity)
4. Otherwise, use agent-dependent policies

We will now present a simple example to illustrate the working of the mechanism described above.

Assume we have the three documents D1, D2, and D3 describing the biography of Einstein. D2 is text file containing an autobiography written by Einstein himself, D1 is a picture of the pages of a book containing the same content as D2, and D3 is a text file containing a chapter of a book on biographies of physicists. A subset of the properties of the documents is described in (Table 1). We assumed a DL with the constructors "<", ">", and enumeration: "{}". The enumerator permits to build a concept enumerating it elements, while ">60000" and "<80000" denote the set of integer

Table 1.

	File type	Writer	Title	Subject	# of Words
D1	∃has_type.{JPEG}	∃has_author.{Einstein} ⊓ ∀has_author.{Einstein}	∃has_title.{"Auto-biography"}	∃has_subject.{Einstein, Relativity}	N/A
D2	∃has_type.{TXT}	∃has_author.{Einstein} ⊓ ∀∀has_author.{Einstein}	∃has_title.{"Auto-biography"}	∃has_subject.{Einstein, General Relativity}	∃has_words.(>60000 ⊓ <80000)
D3	∃has_type.{TXT}	∃has_author.{Segrè}	∃has_title.{"Great physicists"}	∃has_subject. {Einstein,Physicists, World War II}	∃has_words.{160000}

less than 60000 and the set of integers greater than 80000 respectively. For space constraints we will not present the details.

- D1 is a jpeg files, the writer is Einstein, the title is "Autobiography", the subjects are Einstein and Relativity, and the properties "number of words" is not applicable
- D2 is a text files, the writer is Einstein, the title is "Autobiography", the subjects are Einstein and Relativity, and the number of words is between 60000 and 80000
- D3 is a text files, the writer is Segrè, the title is "Great physicists", the subjects are Einstein, Physicists and World War II, and the number of words is exactly 160000

As we can see the properties are DL formulas. As we can see, some properties are more informative than others. For example, we are not sure about the exact number of words of D2, but we know exactly the number of words of D3. We now have the following two agents: A1, and A2. Both agents are able to recognize unary and binary predicates used to describe properties in Table 1, and are characterized by the same BNF.

- A1 checks the properties "writer", "title" and "subject", and considers two non contradictory descriptions corresponding to a property as equal.
- A1 checks the properties "file type", "writer", "title" and "subject" and "# of word",

and uses logical equivalence to check descriptions corresponding to properties.

Agent A1, recognizes D1 and D2 as the same. Specifically,

- ∃has_author.{Einstein} ⊓ ∀∀has_author. {Einstein} ⊓ ∃∃has_author.{Einstein} ⊓ ∀has_author.{Einstein}
- ∃∃has_title.{"Autobiography"} ⊓ ∃∃has_title.{"Autobiography"}
- ∃has_subject.{Einstein, Relativity} is compatible with ∃∃has_subject.{Einstein, Special Relativity}, as the agent, because of its theory, recognizes General Relativity as a special case of Relativity

Agent A1, recognizes D1 and D3 as different. Specifically,

- ∃has_author.{Einstein} ⊓ ∀∀has_author. {Einstein} is not compatible with ∃has_author.{Segrè}

Finally, agent A1 recognizes D2 and D3 as different. Specifically,

- ∃has_author.{Einstein} ⊓ ∀∀has_author. {Einstein} is not compatible with ∃has_author.{Segrè}
- Agent A2, recognizes D1 and D2 as different. Specifically
- ∃has_type.{JPEG} is not equivalent to ∃∃has_type.{TXT}

- Agent A2, recognizes D1 and D3 as different. Specifically
- ∃has_type.{JPEG} is not equivalent to ∃∃has_type.{TXT}
- Agent A2 recognizes D2 and D3 as different. Specifically
- ∃has_author.{Einstein} ⊓ ∀∀has_author.{Einstein} is not equivalent to ∃∃has_author.{Segrè}

As we can see, simple modifications of agents can lead to quite different results, even for a very simple example. We want however to stress that neither the results are right (or wrong) from an absolute point of view. They simple represent different instantiations of a general concept of identity.

CONCLUSION AND FUTURE TRENDS

In this work, the authors presented an approach to the relativization of identity. That is, while the idea of a global notion of identity is very important from a theoretical point of view, when this notion needs to be actually used a number of aspects need to be taken into consideration. Specifically, when the agents willing to evaluate the identity of two objects are limited—and this is true both for humans and for computer programs—they have to restrict the notion of identity to account for their limited knowledge and resources. To better illustrate this idea, a simple example in the context of semantic web has been presented.

This work is not meant to be an exhaustive exposition of the various topics discussed. Of particular relevance for future researches are:

- a more detailed inquiry into the foundational aspects of the notion of identity presented
- connections between our relativization of identity and mathematical theories such as Constructive Set Theory
- a discussion of some semantic issues of DLs when used in specific applications, for example the differences between open world and closed world assumptions
- the extension of the presented framework to other branches of computer science such as robotics (a robot may need to determine the identity of two objects for learning or geo-localization purposes)

REFERENCES

Abbott, E. A. (1963). *Flatland: A Romance of Many Dimensions*. New York: Dover Publications Inc.

Aczel, P. (1978). The type theoretic interpretation of constructive set theory . In MacIntyre, A., Pacholski, L., & Paris, J. (Eds.), *Logic Colloquium '77* (pp. 55–66). Amsterdam: North Holland. doi:10.1016/S0049-237X(08)71989-X

Baader, F., Horrocks, I., & Sattler, U. (2005). Description Logics as Ontology Languages for the Semantic Web. In D. Hutter & W. Stephan (Eds.), Mechanizing Mathematical Reasoning: Essays in Honor of Jörg Siekmann on the Occasion of His 60th Birthday. (LNAI 2605, pp. 228-248). Berlin: Springer.

Baader, F., McGuinness, D., Nardi, D., & Patel-Schneider, P. (Eds.). (2003). *The Description Logic Handbook*. Cambridge, UK: Cambridge University Press.

Black, M. (1952). The identity of indiscernibles. *Mind*, •••, 61.

Boolos, G. (1984). To be is to be the value of a variable (or to be some values of some variables). *The Journal of Philosophy, 81*, 430–449. doi:10.2307/2026308

Church, A. (1956). *Introduction to Mathematical Logic (Vol. 1)*. Princetonm, NJ: Princeton University Press.

Cozzo, C. (1997). Identità: logica e ontologia. *Almanacchi Nuovi, 2*, 96.

Ferrara, A., Lorusso, D., & Montanelli, S. (2008). Automatic Identity Recognition in the semantic web. In P. Bouquet, H. Halpin, H. Stoermer, & G. Tummarello (Eds.), IRSV (Vol. 422). Retrieved from CEUR-WS.ORG

Frege, G. (1879). Begriffsschrift . In Heijenoort, J. (Ed.), *From Frege to Gödel: A Source Book in Mathematical Logic, (1879-1931)*. Cambridge, MA: Harvard University Press.

Frege, G. (1884). *Grundlagen der Arithmetik*. Breslau, Poland: Wilhelm Koebner.

Geach, P. (1962). *Reference and Generality*. Ithaca, NY: Cornell University Press.

Geach, P. (1968). Identity. *The Review of Metaphysics, 22*, 3.

Goldreich, O. (2007). *Foundations of Cryptography: Basic Tools*. Cambridge, UK: Cambridge University Press.

Leibniz, G. W. (1931). *Die Philosophische Schriften*. Leipzig, Germany: Lorenz.

Motik, B., Horrocks, I., & Sattler, U. (2009). Bridging the Gap Between OWL and Relational Databases. *Journal of Web Semantics, 7*(2), 74–89. doi:10.1016/j.websem.2009.02.001

Noonan, H. (2008). *Identity*. Retrieved September 1, 2009, from *The Stanford Encyclopedia of Philosophy*, http://plato.stanford.edu/archives/fall2008/entries/identity/

Peano, G. (1889). *Arithmetices Principia, nova methodo exposita*. Torino, Italy: Fratres Bocca.

KEY TERMS AND DEFINITIONS

Description Logics (DLs): DLs are family of decidable logical formalisms used in knowledge representation to describe a domain of interest and assertions on it

Identity: Identity, or sameness, is the relation everything has to itself and to nothing else Leibniz's Law. Leibniz's Law is the leibnizian definition of identity and is formulable in Second Order Logic. Some authors use this term to refer to the principle of identity of indiscernibles. **Identity of Indiscernibles:** The principle of Identity of indiscernibles states that if two objects share the same properties, than they are identical (i.e. the same object)

Semantic Web: Semantic web, sometimes referred to as WEB 3.0, will probably be the next great step in web technologies after WEB 2.0. In semantic web content on the web should be machine-readable, in order to exchange information in a more effective way. Some technologies used for semantic web are computational logic, ontologies and natural language processing.

First Order Logic (FOL): FOL is a formal logic allowing quantification over individuals. FOL can be seen as an enrichment of propositional logic. FOL is semi-decidable: there are calculi to derive all valid formulas.

Second-Order Logic (SOL): SOL can be seen as an enrichment of First Order Logic, which allows to quantify over predicates. Under standard semantics, there are no complete calculi for SOL.

ENDNOTES

[1] "Those things are identical of which one can be substituted for the other without loss of truth.". The original quote is from (Leibniz 1931, p. 219).

[2] In philosophy of language, intensional contexts are exactly those for which substituding co-referent expressions in a sentence can alter the truth-value of the sentence. Typical examples come from doxastic, epistemic, and modal logic.

3   Some authors call the indiscernibility of identicals "Leibniz's Law". Following another widely accepted convention, we reserve the name "Leibniz's Law" to the second-order definition of identity.

4   In modular arithmetic there can be relations that satisfy (Ref) and (L) but that are not the identity over the domain.

5   This is a form of passage to the quotient.

6   George Boolos has been a champion of plural quantification, an alternative way of extending FOL providing the power of (monadic) SOL but without ontological commitments. See for example (Boolos 1984).

7   This thesis is interesting only if we assume that the two objects fall under both P and Q; otherwise consider two objects a and b being P but not Q: we would have that a and b are the same P but (trivially) not the same Q.

8   The problem of the logicality of notions was discussed in Tarski 1986. In the philosophical community there is an ongoing discussion on the question if identity is to be considered as a logical notion or not.

9   Alexius Meinong (1853 - 1920) proposed an original theory of objects. He is often cited as archetype of ultra-realist philosopher, where we mean the platonic acceptation of realism.

10   Sortal terms are terms denoting properties.

11   In set theory, the *axiom of extensionality* is the answer: two sets are the same if they contain the same elements.

12   This property is usually not admitted for it would make impredicative the principle.

13   This is a classical result of formal language theory.

14   A good introduction to description logics is (Baader, McGuinness, Nardi, & Patel-Schneider 2003).

15   In FOL we would write $P(x)$ and $F(x)$ respectively. DLs intentionally do not show free variables.

16   For a detailed description see for example (Baader, McGuinness, Nardi, & Patel-Schneider 2003).

17   Here for "object" we mean what appears as object to the agent. See section 2.5.

18   A good exposition of the relations between DLs and relational databases is (Motik, Horrocks, & Sattler 2009).

19   See (Baader, Horrocks, & Suttler 2005) for a gentle introduction to DLs as semantic web languages.

20   See http://www.w3.org/2004/OWL/

21   A similar approach has been discussed in (Ferrara, Lorusso, & Montanelli 2008)

Chapter 8
Knowledge, Truth, and Values in Computer Science

Timothy Colburn
University of Minnesota, USA

Gary Shute
University of Minnesota, USA

ABSTRACT

Among empirical disciplines, computer science and the engineering fields share the distinction of creating their own subject matter, raising questions about the kinds of knowledge they engender. The authors argue that knowledge acquisition in computer science fits models as diverse as those proposed by Piaget and Lakatos. However, contrary to natural science, the knowledge acquired by computer science is not knowledge of objective truth, but of values.

INTRODUCTION

Computer science, insofar as it is concerned with the creation of software, shares with mathematics the distinction of creating its own subject matter in the guise of formal abstractions. We have argued (Colburn & Shute, 2007), however, that the nature of computer science abstraction lies in the modeling of interaction patterns, while the nature of mathematical abstraction lies in the modeling of inference structures. In this regard, computer science shares as much with empirical science as it does with mathematics.

But computer science and mathematics are not alone among disciplines that create their own subject matter; the engineering disciplines share this feature as well. For example, although the process of creating road bridges is certainly supported by activities involving mathematical and software modeling, the subject matter of the civil engineer is primarily the bridges themselves, and secondarily the abstractions they use to think about them.

Engineers are also concerned, as are computer scientists, with interaction patterns among aspects of the objects they study. The bridge engineer studies the interaction of forces at work on bridge

DOI: 10.4018/978-1-61692-014-2.ch008

superstructure. The automotive engineer studies the interaction of motions inside a motor. But the interaction patterns studied by the engineer take place in a physical environment, while those studied by the software-oriented computer scientist take place in a world of computational abstractions. Near the machine level, these interactions involve registers, memory locations, and subroutines. At a slightly higher level, these interactions involve variables, functions, and pointers. By grouping these entities into arrays, records, and structures, the interactions created can be more complex and can model real world, passive data objects like phone books, dictionaries, and file cabinets. At a higher level still, the interactions can involve objects that actively communicate with one another and are as various as menus, shopping carts, and chat rooms.

So computer science shares with mathematics a concern for formal abstractions, but it parts with mathematics in being more concerned with interaction patterns and less concerned with inference structures. And computer science shares with engineering a concern for studying interaction patterns, but it parts with engineering in that the interaction patterns studied are not physical. Left out of these comparisons is the obvious one suggested by computer science's very name: What does computer science share with empirical *science*? In this chapter we will investigate this question, along with the related question: What is the nature of computer science knowledge?

METAPHOR AND LAW

We were led to these questions, interestingly, when, in our study of abstraction in computer science, we found ourselves considering the role of *metaphor* in computer science (Colburn & Shute, 2008). Computer science abounds in physical metaphors, particularly those centering around *flow* and *motion*. Talk of flow and motion in computer science is largely metaphorical,

since when you look inside of a running computer the only things moving are the cooling fan and disk drives (which are probably on the verge of becoming quaint anachronisms). Still, although bits of information do not "flow" in the way that continuous fluids do, it helps immeasurably to "pretend" as though they do, because it allows network scientists to formulate precise mathematical conditions on information throughput and to design programs and devices that exploit them. The flow metaphor is pervasive and finds its way into systems programming, as programmers find and plug "memory leaks" and fastidiously "flush" data buffers. But the flow metaphor is itself a special case of a more general metaphor of "motion" that is even more pervasive in computer science. Descriptions of the abstract worlds of computer scientists are replete with references to motion, from program jumps and exits, to exception throws and catches, to memory stores and retrievals, to control loops and branches. This is to be expected, of course, since the subject matter of computer science is *interaction* patterns.

The ubiquitous presence of motion metaphors in computer science prompted us to consider whether there is an analogue in computer science to the concern in natural science with the discovery of natural laws. I.e., if computer science is concerned with motion, albeit in a metaphorical sense, are there laws of computational motion, just as there are laws of physical motion? We concluded (Colburn & Shute, 2010) that there are, but they are laws of programmers' own making, and therefore prescriptive, rather than descriptive in the case of natural science. These prescriptive laws are the programming invariants that programmers must first identify and then enforce in order to bring about and control computational processes so that they are predictable and correct for their purposes. The fact that these laws prescribe computational reality rather than describe natural reality is in keeping with computer science's special status, that it shares with mathematics and engineering, as creating the subject matter that it studies. This seems well and good, but it begs an obvious question: aside from the metaphors and analogies, what does computer science really have in common with science as ordinarily conceived by philosophy?

We contend that the similarity relationship between computer science and natural science is deeper than mere metaphorical language would suggest. To make the case, we consider as background two approaches at opposite ends of a continuum of models of knowledge acquisition. At one end is the acquisition of concepts in children as studied by J. Piaget (1963; 2000). At the other end is the general philosophy of science as elaborated by I. Lakatos (1978a; 1978b).

MODELS OF KNOWLEDGE ACQUISITION

Piaget's work is of interest to us because he attributed the development of intelligence in children to layers of concepts embodying structural relationships, much like the arrangement of various objects in the abstraction layers employed by software designers and programmers. Piaget studied the development of concepts like number, movement, speed, causality, chance, and space. He was particularly interested in how children's primitive concepts become more sophisticated as more experience is brought to bear on them. In his words,

... [T]he input, the stimulus, is filtered through a structure that consists of the action-schemes (or, at a higher level, the operations of thought), which in turn are modified and enriched when the subject's behavioral repertoire is accomodated to the demands of reality. The filtering or modification of the input is called *assimilation*; the modification of internal schemes to fit reality is called *accomodation*. (Piaget, 2000, p. 6)

The modification of internal schemes to accomodate new demands of reality can be seen to model how software designers and programmers work, as we discuss below.

At the other end of the spectrum of knowledge acquisition models are the various general philosophies of science. Consider the philosophy of Lakatos regarding what he calls "research programs", which are temporal progressions of theories and models within a science. For example, the Newtonian research program is that culminating in Newton's three laws of motion. For Lakatos, a research program contains methodological rules that both inhibit and encourage various lines of research. He calls these rules the "negative heuristic" and "positive heuristic", respectively:

This research policy, or order of research, is set out—in more or less detail—in the *positive heuristic* of the research programme. The negative heuristic specifies the 'hard core' of the programme which is 'irrefutable' by the methodological decision of its proponents; the positive heuristic consists of a partially articulated set of suggestions or hints on how to change, develop the 'refutable variants' of the research programme, how to modify, sophisticate, the 'refutable' protective belt. (Lakatos, 1978a, p. 50)

As noted by B. Indurkhya (1992), Lakatos' philosophy of science can be understood in terms of Piaget's assimilation and accomodation. The negative heuristic of a research program can be viewed as assimilative because it refuses to change a hardcore theory to fit new demands. An example within the Newtonian research program is Newton's laws of motion. The positive heuristic, on the other hand, is accomodative, allowing an adjustment of the research program's protective belt. This description of research programs is strikingly similar to Piaget's schemes ("schema" in his earlier writing (Piaget, 1963, pp. 407--417)).

ACCOMODATION IN COMPUTER SCIENCE

Indurkhya has pointed out the role of accomodation in the acquisition of knowledge through metaphor, and we have highlighted the importance

Figure 1.

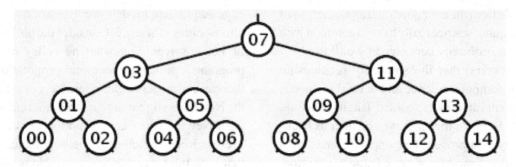

of metaphor in computer science. But beyond that, the creation, refinement, and evolution of software structures and designs can be seen to fit both Piaget's and Lakatos' views of knowledge acquisition.

For an example, consider a data structure known as a *binary search tree* (BST). BSTs facilitate looking up data using a key. Their functionality is similar to telephone directories, where the keys are people's names and the data are addresses and telephone numbers. Here is a BST whose keys are simple strings (for simplicity, the data associated with the keys are not shown):

In order to preserve order among a BST's data items, a programmer must maintain the following invariant: for any node in the BST, all keys in its left subtree must be less than its key, and all keys in its right subtree must be greater than its key. When a new node is added to a BST, the follow-

ing algorithm is followed: First, the node's key is compared with the key of the tree's root (the top-most node). If it is less, the new node will be placed in the left subtree, otherwise the right. The appropriate subtree is recursively searched until an available space is found on one of the tree's leaves (bottom-most nodes). Here is the example tree after the node with key **09a** is added:

This arrangement facilitates data retrieval by key, since a key can be located in time proportional to the height of the tree. If a tree is balanced, as in the one above, a key can be located efficiently even if the number of nodes is large. For example, a balanced tree of one million nodes has a height of about 20.

Unfortunately, the structure of a BST is determined by the order in which nodes are added to it, so nothing guarantees that a BST will be balanced. Here is a BST in which nodes with keys

Figure 2.

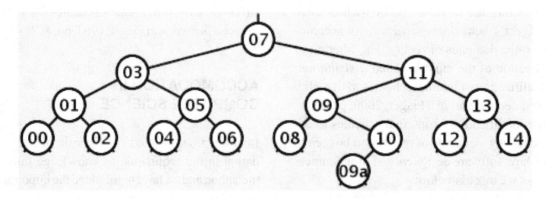

Figure 3.

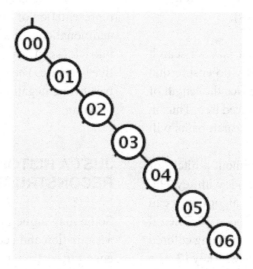

00, **01**, **02**, **03**, **04**, **05**, and **06** have been added in that order:

Although this structure satisfies the order invariant for BSTs, it cannot be efficiently searched since it is not balanced. If one million nodes are added to a BST in key order, finding nodes with higher numbered keys will take time proportional to its height, which is one million (compared to 20 in a balanced BST of a million nodes).

To solve this problem, computer scientists have devised a kind of self-balancing BST known as a *red-black tree* (RBT). In addition to the ordering invariant imposed on BSTs, RBTs introduce the concept of a node's *color*, requiring every node to be either red or black with the following additional constraints:

1. All downward paths from the top (root) of the tree to the bottom (leaves) must contain the same number of black nodes, and
2. The parent of a red node, if it exists, is black.

Figure 4.

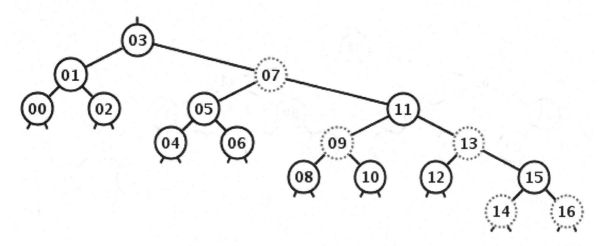

Here is a BST that is also a RBT (red nodes are also shown as dashed circles):

The RBT constraints do not make a search tree perfectly balanced, but they do ensure that no search path is longer than twice the length of search paths in a perfectly balanced tree. Thus in a tree with one million nodes, search paths will be no longer than 40.

This arrangement works without a hitch for some cases. Consider adding a node with key **09a**. Using the standard BST adding algorithm it can be added as the left subtree of node **10**. Then it can satisfy the RBT constraints by being colored red. Now consider adding a node with key **17**. The BST adding algorithm would put it as the right subtree of node **16**. However, coloring it black would violate RBT constraint 1, while coloring it red would violate RBT constraint 2.

However, research into the behavior of RBTs revealed that by tweaking them in various ways (through structural changes known as rotations and certain recolorings) they can be nudged into satisfying both RBT constraints:

This is a paradigm example in computer science of structure being modified to accomodate the demands of reality. Similarly, the inviolability of the basic BST structure and its ordering invariant can be viewed as the negative heuristic in the "research program" of studying the computational representation of ordered lists of data, while the additional constraints imposed by turning BSTs into RBTs can be viewed as arising from the positive heuristic. These constraints can then become part of the negative heuristic of a new research program.

JUST A HISTORICAL RECONSTRUCTION?

Some may argue that the preceding example of assimilation and accomodation in computer science suffers from the problem that we have very little evidence to support the claim that BST data structure researchers actually went through the accomodative thought processes as described. After all, researchers typically devote minimal time in their writing explaining the motivations behind the algorithms, and we can only offer *plausible* explanations of their motivating logic (the invariants). The account we have just given, therefore, is just a historical reconstruction.

But historical reconstructions have their place. Lakatos, in addition to dealing with philosophy of science, addresses issues in meta-philosophy of science, specifically criteria that can be used to assess methodology in the philosophy of science.

Figure 5.

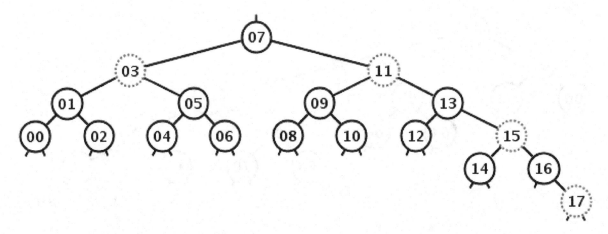

He views historical reconstructions of science as an important part of that methodology:

[T]he historiography of science should learn from the philosophy of science and vice versa. It will be argued that (a) philosophy of science provides normative methodologies in terms of which the historian reconstructs `internal history' and thereby provides a rational explanation of the growth of objective knowledge; (b) two competing methodologies can be evaluated with the help of (normatively interpreted) history; (c) any rational reconstruction of history needs to be supplemented by an empirical (socio-psychological) 'external history'. (Lakatos, 1978a, p. 102)

Lakatos gives concise, but controversial, criteria for assessing research programs in philosophy of science. These criteria capture the heart of a naturalistic philosophy of science. "Thus progress in the theory of scientific rationality is marked by discoveries of novel historical facts, by the reconstruction of a growing bulk of value-impregnated history as rational." (p. 133) In other words, we accept that scientists for the most part know what they are doing, though perhaps only intuitively, and we expect that they often will not be able to explain what they are doing. A naturalistic philosopher of science assumes that there is usually a rationality behind that intuition. For Lakatos, the task of philosophy of science is to uncover that rationality, much like the truth is uncovered by the judgments of juries in court cases. (p. 137)

Although Lakatos does not mention it, biology and paleontology, when investigating the evolution of species, are necessarily involved in historical reconstruction. Evolutionary science starts with the knowledge that traits are passed on --- imperfectly --- from one generation to the next. It is also known that traits that lead to higher fecundity (roughly, the number of offspring per individual) will eventually become dominant in a biological population. Fecundity is partly accounted for by success at survival and partly by success at reproduction. However, neither survival nor reproductive success can be explained in context-free terms. Traits that are successful for one species may be detrimental in another. Bigger horns or antlers may contribute to fecundity in one species but not in another. Traits interact in complex ways and in most cases must be considered in a complex context. When looking at the development of traits in a single sequence of species the evidence is often ambiguous. Evolutionary scientists just do not know enough about the lives of individual species to make convincing arguments. They can only make plausible historical reconstructions of the past. The justification for evolutionary theory lies not in individual reconstructions, but the enormous body of plausible arguments covering many different species.

Apart from the necessary historical reconstruction involved in evolution studies, some may argue that historical reconstruction in other disciplines borders on our notion of rationalization in its worst sense. But this is mitigated when we consider the importance of historical reconstruction for science and engineering education. When Lakatos looks at scientific progress, to a large extent he treats research programs as single organic wholes. But in fact, they consist of individuals who must be educated before they can participate. This gives rise to a pedagogical role for historical reconstruction. We, as scientists rather than as philosophers (or perhaps as philosopher-scientists working within the discipline), must reconstruct the developments in our science, bring out their underlying rationality, so that new generations of scientists can be "brought up to speed" more rapidly. This is even more important in a rapidly developing discipline such as computer science.

Progress in scientific disciplines (including engineering disciplines) requires that new generations "stand on the shoulders of giants"—their predecessors. But successive generations must climb higher to get to those shoulders. And they must do it in roughly the same amount of time that their predecessors took to climb to earlier shoulders. Laws are an important part of making the climb easier, even if laws as such did not govern the thinking of the earlier giants.

Consider civil engineering for example. Looking back in history it seems obvious that Minoans, Egyptians, Greeks, and Romans had a substantial body of knowledge about building roads, bridges, pyramids, aqueducts, and waste disposal systems. Much of that knowledge was probably an ill-organized body of rules for dealing with particular problems. This kind of knowledge can only be acquired through long experience. Good laws, the laws of physics for example, capture more information in a condensed form that is more readily picked up by a new generation.

We have been arguing that in computer science these laws amount to programming or software design invariants. But it is often asked rhetorically, "Why do most programmers just hammer away at the code until it works, then deal with invariants as an afterthought, if at all?" in an effort to de-emphasize the role of invariants in computer science. The answer to this question is simple: coming up with laws (or invariants) is difficult. History provides ample evidence of that. Consider the short history of civil engineering given above for example. It took two millenia to work out the laws of physics that consolidated (and made computational) the existing knowledge.

There is a stark difference between civil engineering as a discipline whose learning is based on apprenticeship and civil engineering as a discipline whose learning focuses on physical principles. For those who already have the experience, the physical principles may be just an added burden. For the next generation, though, they are a quicker way of acquiring the knowledge necessary to do the job.

With regard to invariants in computer science, it is not surprising that practicing and student software developers often use invariants as an afterthought, if at all. They are often in the position of acquiring experience without the benefit of the laws. Later, invariants are introduced as an

advanced technique of algorithm development. Then students are asked not only to use them to develop and code algorithms, they are also asked to develop the invariants. It would make more sense to first give students invariants, only asking them to use them to develop algorithms, then ask them to develop invariants after they have adequate experience with using them. But this approach places rather significant intellectual demands on students first learning computer science, so some educators prefer not to use it.

DESIGN PATTERNS AS RESEARCH PROGRAMS

Knowledge of structures in computer science finds expression not only in the development of data structures and their algorithms but also in the discipline of object-oriented programming (OOP). OOP, the dominant style of software development today, organizes program objects into abstractions called *classes*. Identifying and relating classes in such a way that they are reusable and modifiable requires that the classes be maximally *cohesive* and minimally *coupled*. That is, objects of different classes must hide as much detail as possible from one another about how they go about implementing the concept they are intended to model. The history of OOP development has taught that software reusability and modifiability lies in decoupling objects of different classes by reducing class *dependencies*, whether those dependencies have their origin in hardware or software platform features, required object operations, required object state, or required algorithms. To the extent that classes have these kinds of dependencies on one another reduced, they need to know fewer details about each other, and they therefore exploit *information hiding*. (See Colburn & Shute (2007) for more about the role of information hiding in computer science.)

How to enforce information hiding in OOP is the objective of an approach to software development taken today through *design patterns* (Gamma et al, 1995). Design patterns first gained an audience in connection with building architecture, but the idea can be applied to software as well. Minimally, a design pattern is composed of a design problem, a context in which the problem is situated, and a design solution. Using a design pattern requires knowing when a problem and context match a given pattern and being able to carry out the given solution. For example, suppose a software developer needs to implement an inventory system for a retailer, so that when a change to the inventory occurs it is reflected immediately in all the displays throughout the store. This general problem, in which an observed subject (the inventory in this instance) needs to notify observing objects (store displays) about changes that occur to it, has been solved often enough that there is a well-known pattern, over time given the name *Observer*, that solves it. Observer accomplishes its solution elegantly by setting up the observed subject and the observing object so that required actions can be triggered in the latter when events are detected in the former without the former needing to know the nature of the actions that it causes. In this way the observer and the observed are effectively decoupled.

A design pattern can be viewed as the culmination of a Lakatosian research program in object-oriented program design, where the negative heuristic includes the list of conditions that must be met before it makes sense to apply the pattern. Design pattern identification and use to promote object decoupling comprises some of the most important aspects of knowledge in software development today.

TRUTH AND VALUES

Despite the similarities that can be found between computer science and the various models of knowledge acquisition—whether at the individual (Piaget) or general scientific (Lakatos) leve—any

philosophy of computer science must account for "the elephant in the room", namely our oft-repeated fact that computer science creates its own subject matter. For it raises an obvious question: if science seeks knowledge about the subject matter it studies through the uncovering of truths concerning that subject matter, and computer science creates its own subject matter, what sort of truth is computer science uncovering?

Recall from the Introduction that computer science shares with engineering the feature of creating its own subject matter. It is therefore instructive to consider this question from the point of view of the engineering disciplines as well. Typically, such disciplines are directed towards large-scale design and manufacture of products through the management of design and production and also through quality control. These objectives, though important, do not exemplify scientific inquiry. Instead, we will consider that part of engineering disciplines that might be called *engineering science*.

Engineering science shares with ordinary natural science a concern for empirical discovery. However, rather than discovering laws that can explain observed events, engineering science attempts to discover *values* that support the design and production of the entity in question. For example, the choice of the type of bridge to build in a given situation depends upon values chosen among beauty, cost, scalability, and ability to withstand load and environmental forces, among others. Different situations require different trade-offs among these values, and so different bridge types have been "discovered" (see for example Matsuo, 1999) that implement these trade-offs. In this regard, bridge types are basic knowledge to bridge builders in the same way that design patterns are basic knowledge to object-oriented programmers. But the knowledge is not about nature in itself, but about how to best situate created artifacts in nature, i.e. knowledge of values.

The discovery of bridge types is science because each type can be viewed as a research program. The general bridge structure defines the negative heuristic. The positive heuristic consists of ongoing accomodations of structural details to support the identified values necessary to enhance strengths and minimize weaknesses, and also take advantage of technological advances and better materials.

Similarly, the discovery of OOP design patterns is science because each pattern can be viewed as a research program. In the case of the Observer design pattern, the general context including an observed subject and an observing object defines the negative heuristic. The positive heuristic consists of the value choices made that require the chosen subject and object classes to be maximally cohesive and minimally coupled.

COMPUTER SCIENCE AND THE ANALYSIS OF KNOWLEDGE

Computer science is science because it can be seen to engage in Lakatosian research programs. But computer science is engineering science because it is about the discovery of values rather than objective truth. This seems to raise a question for the philosophy of computer science, and perhaps the philosophy of any engineering science, because, traditionally, philosophers have defined knowledge as, at least, *justified true belief*, which, on the face of it, does not seem to involve the concept of values. So what kind of knowledge do computer scientists acquire?

Some background in epistemology is in order here. Since Plato, western philosophers have tried to define knowledge. In the *Theaetetus* it is agreed that knowledge is more than mere belief, but neither is knowledge to be equated merely with *true* belief, since one's irrational belief (consider a case of acute paranoia) could be serendipitously true. To count as knowledge, a true belief must have the proper kind of warrant, or justification, that disallows knowledge claims that happen to be true by chance. Such considerations have led to a standard definition of knowledge as necessarily involving *justified* true belief — a tripartite analysis—where it has been assumed that the justification required could be adequately spelled out by a sufficiently robust epistemological theory.

This analysis seems altogether consistent with the kind of knowledge pursued by the natural sciences, which are concerned with uncovering objective truths in the form of descriptive propositions about nature. Such sciences confer the status of knowledge on their beliefs only after they survive the test of justification by being arrived at through the confirmatory process of the venerable scientific method.

But we have just seen that computer science, owing to its status as an engineering science, does not seek to uncover objective truths of nature, but rather values, in the form of prescriptive laws, that aid in the control of computational processes. But knowledge need not always be knowledge of nature, and in computer science we are after knowledge of effective values — values that guide us in the construction of efficient algorithms and data structures, expressive programming languages, reliable and secure operating systems, and well-designed computer architectures. Computer science values, therefore, are not "known" in the traditional sense of scientific discovery, but *adopted* because they work. Of course, the corpus of values making up modern computer science could be regarded as the core "knowledge" of the discipline, but it is knowledge of abstractions and principles that are of computer scientists' own making.

It is interesting, and perhaps not accidental, that the rise of computer science as a discipline has coincided in history with a split in epistemology between philosophers who embrace *internalism*, the view that a subject's knowledge is based on a justificatory relation it has with other beliefs the subject has internally; and those who opt for *externalism*, the view that knowledge can arise through processes of which a subject might not even be directly aware—unconscious cognitive processes for example. Some externalists, for example Dretske (1989), go so far as to jettison the justification condition from the analysis of knowledge altogether.

Philosophers who go this route are sometimes influenced by Gettier's (1963) famous counterexamples showing knowledge cannot be defined as even justified true belief. The basic idea behind the counterexamples is to concoct a situation in which a subject is adequately justified in believing a true proposition, but the proposition happens to be true by serendipity rather than by its relation to the subject's evidence, so the subject does not know the proposition at all. Suppose a dehydrated man in a desert believes there is a water hole in front of him on the basis of a heat mirage. The mirage is very convincing, and looks just like a water hole. Further, just over a hill and out of sight of the man there really is a water hole. So by a stroke of *epistemic luck* the man's belief (that there is a water hole in front of him) is true, but it should not count as knowledge, at least at the time the man made his judgment on the basis of a mirage.

Some externalists believe that Gettier-type counterexamples of this sort cannot be overcome, because thinking of knowledge as internally evidence- or justification-based is wrong-headed. Instead, knowledge can arise from one's situation in the world and from the reliable interaction of one's cognitive processes with that world. Thus, knowledge can arise without internal justification.

Externalism is sometimes associated with *naturalism*, or the general philosophical view that all facts, including true claims to knowledge, are facts about nature. So to check whether a claim to knowledge is true, one studies the world and a subject's place in it, rather than having the subject introspect on his or her internal beliefs to see if they justify what the subject claims to know. A particular variety of philosophical naturalism is ethical naturalism, or the view that moral facts are also facts about nature. An ethical naturalist wants to be able to "locate value, justice, right,

wrong, and so forth in the world in the way that tables, colors, genes, temperatures, and so on can be located in the world." (Harman, 1984, p. 33)

Because of its dependence on prescriptive laws and values, computer science is a normative endeavor in the way that ethics is. In fact, there is a sense in which computer science is a quintessential example of a discipline that embodies naturalism, if "the world" in which we locate facts is the abstract, prescriptive law-abiding world that the computer scientist creates. For these worlds embody the values on which computer science depends. These values, in the form of program and design invariants we have described, do not just guide the computer scientists in their work; they *are* the laws of the world at hand.

CONCLUSION

In this chapter we have tried to give a narrative that leads to a view of computer science knowledge as knowledge about values. This computer science shares with the engineering sciences. But computer science is also unique in that it creates its own subject matter in the abstractions, algorithms, and data structures that are employed to control computational processes. Such processes occur in worlds that need laws, or computational chaos would result. But these laws, being prescriptive, are also dynamic, in that they can be bent and modified in the same way that concepts are assimilated and accommodated in children. Other more stable laws, such as those imposed by design patterns in object-oriented design and programming, can be "uncovered" in ways that are analogous to research programs in the natural sciences.

The laws that computer science creates reflect computer scientists' values as much as the nature of the worlds they govern. These values, in fact, become part of the fabric of the computational reality being studied. So the philosophy of computer science we have been propounding is not only based on values, but it is a naturalist philosophy in the sense that the claims to knowledge in computer science are claims involving values, but those values are embedded in the computational "nature" of computer scientists' own creation.

REFERENCES

Colburn, T. & Shute, G. (2007). Abstraction in computer science. *Minds and machines: journal for artificial intelligence, philosophy, and cognitive science 17*(2), 169--184.

Colburn, T., & Shute, G. (2008). Metaphor in computer science. *Journal of Applied Logic, 6*(4), 526–533. doi:10.1016/j.jal.2008.09.005

Colburn, T. & Shute, G. (2010). Abstraction, law, and freedom in computer science. *Metaphilosophy* (forthcoming in 2010).

Dretske, F. (1989). The need to know . In Clay, M., & Lehrer, K. (Eds.), *Knowledge and skepticism*. Boulder, CO: Westview Press.

Gamma, E., Helm, R., Johnson, R., & Vlissides, J. (1995). *Design patterns: elements of reusable object-oriented software*. Boston: Addison-Wesley.

Gettier, E. (1963). Is justified true belief knowledge? *Analysis, 23*, 121–123. doi:10.2307/3326922

Harman, G. (1984). Is there a single true morality? In Copp, D., & Zimmerman, D. (Eds.), *Morality, reason and truth. New essays on the foundation of ethics* (pp. 27–48). Totowa, NJ: Rowman and Allenheld.

Indurkhya, B. (1992). *Metaphor and cognition*. Dordrecht, The Netherlands: Kluwer Academic Publishers.

Lakatos, I. (1978a). *The methodology of scientific programs*. Cambridge, UK: Cambridge University Press.

Lakatos, I. (1978b). *Mathematics, science, and epistemology*. Cambridge, UK: Cambridge University Press. doi:10.1017/CBO9780511624926

Matsuo Bridge. (1999). Retrieved from http://www.matsuo-bridge.co.jp/english/bridges/index.shtm

Piaget, J. (1963). *The origins of intelligence in children*. New York: W. W. Norton.

Piaget, J. (2000). *The psychology of the child*. New York: Basic Books.

KEY TERMS AND DEFINITIONS

Abstraction: Elimination of inessential detail. In computer science, the hiding of implementation details from a structure's use, where the structure can be a procedure, data object, or machine.

Metaphor: A description of an object or event using concepts that cannot be applied to the object or event in a conventional way.

Prescriptive Law: A law that says what should be the case rather than what is the case. A rule of appropriate behavior, to be distinguished from a descriptive law of natural science.

Invariant: A statement of a condition that holds before and after a particular computational procedure is performed.

Assimilation: In child cognition, the modifying of external stimuli in order to be incorporated into a subject's conceptual structure.

Accommodation: In child cognition, the altering of conceptual structure in order to fit external stimuli to the demands of reality.

Research Program: The temporal progression of theories and models that characterize a science.

Design Pattern: A solution to a problem within a context. In object-oriented programming, the description of communicating objects and classes that is customized to solve a general design problem in a particular context.

Naturalism: A general philosophical view that all facts are facts about nature.

ENDNOTES

[1]   Department of Computer Science, University of Minnesota, Duluth

[2]   Department of Computer Science, University of Minnesota, Duluth

Chapter 9
Logic and Abstraction as Capabilities of the Mind:
Reconceptualizations of Computational Approaches to the Mind

David J. Saab
Penn State University, USA

Uwe V. Riss
SAP AG, CEC Karlsruhe, Germany

ABSTRACT

In this chapter the authors will investigate the nature of abstraction in detail, its entwinement with logical thinking, and the general role it plays for the mind. The authors find that non-logical capabilities are not only important for input processing, but also for output processing. Human beings jointly use analytic and embodied capacities for thinking and acting, where analytic thinking mirrors reflection and logic, and where abstraction is the form in which embodied thinking is revealed to us. The authors will follow the philosophical analyses of Heidegger and Polanyi to elaborate the fundamental difference between abstraction and logics and how they come together in the mind. If computational approaches to mind are to be successful, they must be able to recognize meaningful and salient elements of a context and engage in abstraction. Computational minds must be able to imagine and volitionally blend abstractions as a way of recognizing gestalt contexts. And it must be able to discern the validity of these blendings in ways that, in humans, arise from a sensus communis.

INTRODUCTION

Behind traditional computational approaches to mind we find the idea that we can simulate the mind as we think we might simulate a chess player by computer programs. This approach is assumes that the human mind is based on a symbolic processing model of cognition. Doing so, we overlook that the way a chess player and a computer approach chess playing are fundamentally different. The human player employs not only sequential logic and his

DOI: 10.4018/978-1-61692-014-2.ch009

symbolic processing capabilities, but also other capabilities that are described by a connectionist model of cognition. Rather than work through the numerous logical and sequential permutations of possible moves, the human player will recognize larger (i.e., schematic) patterns among the pieces of the chessboard and make his moves based on experience gained over a lifetime of playing. Human players will 'feel' what is the correct move for maintaining an advantage or overcoming a disadvantage, using their intuitive sense derived from schemas based on their long lasting practice.

Even if the machines built in this way that they show comparable results, it does not prove that the human mind and the symbolic machine work in the same way. Indeed human beings (and not only they) possess one fundamental capability that cannot be reduced to symbolic logic manipulation, i.e., abstraction or the capability to develop and employ schemas or recognize gestalt from concrete objects that they find in their environment. These schemas humans evolve through the repeated exposure to similar stimulus as part of our lived experience. Schemas have a duality about them —they are patterns of strongly connected elements of cognition that activate based on salient elements of a particular context and they serve as auto-completion processors, allowing us to perceive a gestalt. These capabilities become apparent in human abstraction. Although abstraction can be analyzed ex-post in terms of logic, e.g., looking for common features, we cannot reduce it to a formal logical process. Abstraction is fundamentally related to schema theory and gestalt theory.

However, the capability of abstraction even goes beyond what we can describe by schemas. We will illustrate this point by way of some examples and explain why it is nevertheless advantageous to work with such metaphorical images. One of our goals is to show the limitations of such images. To this end we will refer to relevance of embodiment and embeddedness and show the relevance of these concepts for the understanding of abstraction. Regarding the latter point we will discuss the works of Heidegger and Polanyi and their philosophical approaches contribute to this understanding. We will follow their analyses to elaborate the fundamental difference between abstraction and logics and how they come together in the mind. The interplay can also be explicated on the basis of paradoxes such as the heap paradox (Keefe, 2000, p. 56) where the approaches of schematic processing and symbolic processing conflict with each other. There are already approaches that rely on gestalt theory, however, they are mainly applied in robotics and not incorporated in the philosophy of mind or computational approaches to the mind.

We will explore how these fundamental processes of abstraction etc. on the one hand and logical inference on the other work together, referring to insights gained from Heidegger and Polanyi such as the distinction of *present-at-hand* and *ready-to-hand* and *focal* and *subsidiary awareness*, respectively. Each of their philosophical approaches facilitates recognition of context in which the salient element of focus is situated. It is the contextualized focal entity that is essential for and evokes meaning within cognition and, hence, understanding in a way that integrates schematic abstract thinking with sequential logic.

The two paradigms even work together in mathematics where we also find an extensive use of abstraction (in the sense that we use here). One example is the abstraction of topological structures, expressed by topological axioms, gained from the analysis of real numbers and other analytic structures. It was Frege (1882) who pointed out that the usage of symbols opens up particularly new ways of analyzing the developing structures, e.g., by gestalt-oriented abstraction. It is this particular capability to abstract from symbolic structure that make up the core of mathematics and not the application of logical rules to axioms and propositions.

ENACTING A RATIONALIST PARADIGM FOR A COMPUTATIONAL MIND

In the 1960's AI researchers enacted a research program that attempted to enact the rationalist philosophies of 18th and 19th century philosophers: reasoning was calculating (*pace* Hobbes); mental representations are internal to the mind and indicate a separation from body (*pace* Descartes); all knowledge could be expressed by a universally characteristic set of primitives (*pace* Leibniz); concepts are rules (*pace* Kant); concept rules can be formalized (*pace* Frege); and logical atomism (*pace* Russell) is the means to achieve their goal (Dreyfus, 2007). So certain were AI researchers of their progress and success, that Marvin Minsky, leader of the AI lab at MIT, claimed in 1968: "Within a generation we will have intelligent computers like HAL in the film 2001."[1]

AI researchers were critical of philosophers, who they viewed as lacking sufficient understanding of how the mind works despite centuries of philosophical inquiry. After all, if philosophers did have sufficient understanding, wouldn't they have already devised a practical solution to the problem? Those involved in trying to simulate cognition as part of the AI research agenda failed to consider that they were "hard at work turning rationalist philosophy into a research program" (Dreyfus, 2007). Rationality through logic is a core capability of mind, but it is far from sufficient in explaining either the *significance* or *relevance* of what is identified through logic within a particular context, as pointed out by existentialist philosophers such as Heidegger (1927, p. H. 100).

They ran into the problem of context that was taken up by existential philosophers of the 20th century: How can significance and relevance be represented? Heidegger's famous example of the ontological function of a hammer, excluding its defining relationships to nails and other equipment as well as the skills required to use a hammer in favor of a simplified ontological concept of use

for building things, shed light on the complexity of context. For Heidegger, all of these things contributed to the ontology of the hammer. He described the concept of *ready-to-hand* as a way of explaining the complexity of the hammer's *being* and as a way of refuting the 'value characteristics' of an object as its sole definition.

Still, AI researchers, unaware of Heidegger's ontological critique, persisted in their rationalist and reductionist paradigm. If they could only represent a few million facts about objects, the complexity problem might be solved! They had grasped one dimension of context—feature recognition—but failed to see the essential dimensions of *significance* and *relevance* of contextual elements and their associated temporality. When it became clear that their few-million-facts approach was insufficient, they discerned that the problem was a 'frame problem.' For a given context or scenario, there are certain salient elements that take priority over others. If they could describe a scenario (i.e., context) well enough, they could identify essential features that were more relevant and assign them a greater value for computation. Unaware to the AI researchers, Edmund Husserl, who is considered to be the father of phenomenology, had already identified the framing approach (Mingers, 2001). Husserl was also the mentor of Heidegger, who furthered the field of phenomenological inquiry and became one of the most influential philosophers of the 20th century.

Framing, or the use of frames, is both somewhat useful and somewhat problematic. It is useful if one can identify and appropriately value the salient elements of a given context. In fact, the very nature of the frame is intended to do so. However, the frame provides no meta-rules for deciding which frame one should apply to a given context. Which frame is relevant? How does one determine its relevance? The problem of the use of frames for computational approaches to mind is that it sets up a process of infinite regress for "recognizing relevant frames for recognizing relevant facts" (Dreyfus, 2007).

The framing approach lead to an unfruitful path of research, as the boundaries of the framed 'world' became smaller and smaller, ending up as a series of micro-worlds that failed to reflect the real world. After Dreyfus (1972) published *What Computers Still Can't Do*—a heavily Heideggerian critique of the traditional AI of rules, representations, symbols, inferences, and frames--AI researchers began to embrace the Heideggerian problem of embodiment and embeddedness. There were several approaches to the problem, notably Brooks' behaviorist approach, Agre's pragmatist approach, and Freeman's neurodynamic model (Dreyfus, 2007). All three accepted Heidegger's critique of Cartesian internalist representations and embraced the view that cognition is embedded and embodied (Haugeland, 1998).

RATIONALITY AND EMBODIMENT

The traditional computational approach to mind or intelligence conforms to a rationalist perspective. It borrows from the analytical tradition in philosophy embedded in the scientific method of the physical sciences that tends towards reductionism. AI researchers of the 1960's adopted a view of cognition as a physical symbol system in which the neural activations and impulses of our brains became the analog for computation of symbolic bits of data (Newell & Simon, 1988). These computational approaches assume a one-to-one correspondence of concrete objects in our environment and their symbolic representations so that the comprehension of the world, i.e., intelligence, allows us to reduce the workings of the mind to a simple formula:

Input (presented as abstract symbols) + Algorithm (logical inferences) = Output.

This formula is similar to the way in which AI researchers had thought we processed and used language. We have some words (input) and we apply some forms of inferences and rules to the pattern of lexical units (algorithms) from which we create meaning (more algorithms?) and translate that meaning into another set of lexical units (more algorithms?) that take the form of an expression (output) which also serves as the input for someone else's language processing. It is a very reductionist approach, which found its expression in the Communication Theory of Shannon (Shannon, 1948; Shannon & Weaver, 1949).

The simple formulation of *Input + Algorithm = Output* is more complex even than it may originally seem when we apply it to a purely symbolic system such as language. Meaningful communication depends not only on lexicon and syntax, but also semantics and context. It might be appropriate to apply a mathematical reductionist approach to the signal processing of various mechanical sensors, but its application to language is inadequate. Language may be a symbolic system, but the meaningfulness of those symbols depends upon the experiential understanding of the communication participants. Language is part of our embodied and embedded experiences, not simply strings of lexical units that exist in a semiotic relationship with concepts.

What does it mean to be embedded and embodied? To be embedded means that we, as humans, are not separated from the world. In fact we are inseparable from the world. Wherever and whenever we are, we are embedded in a world, a physical universe, from which our physical being can never escape. We cannot experience anything without the world in which we are embedded. Which brings us to the issue of embodiment. Descartes posited a separation of mind from body, a notion that has had powerful influence on Western philosophy and Western thinking. The Heideggerian critique rejects this separation—'we' are not separate from or separable from our bodies. 'We' are not subjective entities inhabiting an objective body. There is no separation between our subjective mind and our objective bodies. We are embodied, just as we are embedded, and can never escape our embodiment. Perhaps Merleau-Ponty said it most succinctly:

In so far as, when I reflect on the essence of subjectivity, I find it bound up with that of the body and that of the world, this is because my existence as subjectivity is merely one with my existence as a body and with the existence of the world, and because the subject that I am, when taken concretely, is inseparable from this body and this world. (Merleau-Ponty, 1962)

These notions of embeddedness and embodiment have important implications for our cognitive models, which have heretofore been based on the idea that our mind holds 'internal representations' of the external world. The internalist notion of representation propelled early AI researchers to reproduce these representations symbolically within machines. The richness of our environments made this representational approach extremely difficult. With the notions of embeddedness and embodiment, however, we came to the realization that humans avoid the problem of internalist representation "because their model of the world is the world itself" (Dreyfus, 2007).

Brooks was one of the researchers who adopted this non-internalist stance (Brooks, 1988) by constructing robots that act with 'swarm intelligence' that emulated insect-level interaction. The problem, as Dreyfus (2007) points out is that Brooks' robots "respond only to fixed isolable features of the environment, not to changing context or significance." From a Heideggerian perspective, *coping*—our way of dealing with the world in which we are embedded via our embodiment—is more than understanding in terms of inferential symbolic representations and more than Skinnerian responses to fixed features of our environment. Our coping entails an *openness* of our being to the world, which allows us to respond to salient features of our environments without having to attend to the non-salient, but which doesn't exclude our ability to organize our world semantically

or express our understanding of it linguistically (Heidegger, 1927, p. H. 163).

Semantic organization includes both the capacity for logical organization and structuring as well as abstraction. Before we continue with our discussion of embodiment, we turn to *abstraction* and show in more detail how abstraction can be understood against the described background.

Abstraction: Transformations from Concrete To Abstract And Back Again

We start with the traditional idea of abstraction and the objects to be abstracted. Abstraction was understood as a psychological process that associates objects, which are part of our experience, with concepts. This association is achieved by attention to those features of the respective concrete object which are common to all objects associated with the respective concept (Honderich, 1995). This notion of abstraction suggests that an abstract object x is defined by a finite set of features $F_x = \{ f_{x,1}, ..., f_{x,n} \}$. In the same assumption a concrete object c is regarded as a (quasi) infinite set of features $F_c = \{ f_{c,1}, f_{c,2}, ... \}$. Consequently this suggests that an abstraction can be understood as subset formation, i.e., the concrete object c is associated to the abstract object x if $F_x \subset F_c$. According to this scheme we can also define generalizations of abstract objects, i.e., an abstract object g is a generalization of an abstract object c if $F_g \subset F_c$. In this way abstraction becomes a process of logical reasoning that can be performed in a sequential manner.

Although this approach is mathematically very convenient the aforementioned counterarguments suggest that it does not describe abstraction in a proper way. In fact, there are several arguments that raise doubts about its suitability. One argument against the described feature notion of abstraction comes from Wittgenstein (1953) and is known under the term *family resemblance*. It says that the concrete objects associated with an abstracted object are united by a *network of overlapping but discontinuous similarities* (Honderich, 1995) and not by a unique set of features. Another argument originates from the observation of concrete abstraction processes. For example, if we ask a person, who stands in front of a table, what the object in front of her is, she might immediately answer that it is a table. If you ask the same person why it is a table she will probably answer that it is obvious. If you insist on an explanation she will perhaps answer that it has a board and four legs. Obviously this is not a collection of necessary features since people are aware of the fact that there exist tables with fewer legs. Such observations do not support the idea that the observer strictly checks features before she associates a concrete object with an abstract concept. Moreover we can exclude the feature approach because of its tendency towards infinite regress—if the abstraction of a table requires the abstraction of the legs and board, the person would have to identify the respective abstraction features for legs and board as well, leading to an infinite regress. A third argument refers to the continuity of processes. Let us assume a thought experiment in which we transform an object, e.g., a table, continuously into another object, e.g., chair. For example, we could do so by removing tiny pieces from one place and add them to another. In this way we obtain a continuous transformation of the table into the chair and vice versa. Tables and chairs, however, should be characterized by different sets of features. This means that there should be specific points in the transformation process at which the respective features as 'switched on' or 'off'. Since the process is continuous this does not seem to be reasonable. This latter argument is closely related to the heap paradox (Keefe, 2000).

Psychology shows that the association with a certain concept depends on the situation you are starting from (Fisher, 1967). Returning to the aforementioned example of the transformation of a table into a chair, observers recognize the appearance of the table or chair at different stages

of transformation depending on what object they start with. When that switch happens is dependent upon the observers' starting points, i.e., whether the transformation begins with the table or the chair. The transformation example indicates that abstraction is a dynamic and context dependent process and not a static mapping of concepts and features. The philosophical conceptualization of abstraction has to take this dynamicism and context dependency into account. This dynamicist perspective encompasses the idea that concepts are learned and that learning is constrained by a capacity to subsume concrete objects within the boundaries of an appropriate concept. The concept of capacity that we refer to here is the same articulated by Aristotle: such capacities become manifest in acts that actualize them (Kern, 2006). For example, a person can actualize her capacity to associate a concrete object with a concept by subsuming such an object under this concept and drawing successful conclusions from the abstract object. This means that the actualization is closely related to concrete acts of the person who possesses this capacity.

If process of learning a new concept starts with an abstract definition, e.g., a table is a board with four legs upon which things are placed. The capacity for this type of abstraction relies on other capacities, i.e., to identify table legs and boards and what it means to deposit things. Over time and through repeated actualization of the association of concrete object with concept, the clustering of associations becomes independent of the respective underlying sub-capacities. The respective composite abstract turns into simple abstract, i.e., the abstract that was initially defined by multiple features becomes a gestalt. Thus, the person possessing the respective capacity is enabled to identify concrete objects as tables even if they have fewer than four legs. The abstraction, which has started with a feature-based definition, has turned into an embodied capacity. Other concepts, which are not frequently actualized, remain dependent on underlying concepts. So, in other words, if we need the features of the abstract to define or recognize it, they will remain as part of the composite abstract, but if we don't need them, the simple abstract becomes more useful and more frequently used.

Intentionality: An Object Is an Object, But Isn't an Object, Per Se

We recognize that non-logical capabilities are essential for input processing (e.g., perception) as well as output processing. In the act of 'thinking' human beings use both abstraction and logics, which appear as analytic and embodied capacities. On the other hand they perform actions according to 'instructions' that are rooted in embodied capacities. These 'instructions' are logical in a strict symbolic sense, but rather embodied capacities that are developed through practice and repeated exposure to the same or similar stimulus. Elite athletes exhibit such embodied capacities as part of their practice. They often first study how to move optimally before they then train for the intended bodily movements by repeated practice. Through this repeated practice they habituate their neural networks to carry out those movements without needing to engage their capacity for logic and rational thinking. When engaged in their athletic activities, they are able to combine their logical and embodied capacities to act (i.e., intentions) strategically and responsively within a competition environment.

In coping with our everyday existence we encounter two basic modes of intentionality according to Heidegger: (1) an objective intentionality corresponding to the *present-at-hand*, and (2) a deictic intentionality responding to the *ready-to-hand* (Agre, 1988). That which is *ready-to-hand* is more appropriately characterized as the holistic affordability for action that surrounds an object rather than discrete characteristics or qualities of an object. What is *ready-to-hand* constrains the temporal paths of possible action one might take based on the salient elements of an object or situation that has become the focus of one's attention as the *presence-at-hand*. We must not mistake, however, the *present-at-hand* or the *ready-to-hand* for objectivity. Our embeddedness and embodiment preclude a state of objectivity, per se.

Computational approaches to mind have difficulty in not-objectifying that which is *ready-to-hand*. What is *ready-to-hand* is by definition context-dependent, but also involves the possible responses to what is *present-at-hand*. Whatever responses or possible actions are afforded within a context require flexibility, simply because no context or situation is ever the same by virtue of its temporality. There is always something different, even if it is only the semantic organization of experience or learning 'within' *Dasein*[2] that has occurred in the interim.

The fundamental dynamic nature of an embedded and embodied coping is described as *coupling* (van Gelder, 1997; Winograd & Flores, 1987). What we normally think of as cognition, flowing as it does from a symbolic processing model, belies the nature of 'the couple'—of coper and the world. Rationalist approaches favor the symbolic processing approach, while the existentialist approaches view the symbolic processing capabilities of cognition as emerging from the 'dynamical substrate' of coupling:

Cognition can, in sophisticated cases, [such as breakdowns, problem solving, and abstract thought] involve representation and sequential processing; but such phenomena are best understood as emerging from a dynamical substrate, rather than as constituting the basic level of cognitive performance. (van Gelder, 1997, pp. 439, 448)

The representational dimensions of symbolic processing "presupposes background coping [and] depends upon a background of holistic, nonrepresentational coping [that] is exactly the Heideggerian project" (Dreyfus, 2007).

THE ENIGMATIC NATURE OF SCHEMAS

In cognitive science, connectionist theory posits the human conceptual system as a network composed of a large number of 'units' joined together in a pattern of connections (Rumelhart & McClelland, 1986). Cognitive anthropologists and educational psychologists refer to these patterns of connections as *schemas* (Anderson, Spiro, & Montague, 1984; D'Andrade, 1995; Davis, 1991; Strauss & Quinn, 1997). Schemas are strongly connected networks of cognitive elements, having a bias in activation through repeated exposure to the same or similar stimulus, but they are not rigid and inflexible. They are adaptable, sometimes resulting in the strengthening of existing schemas, sometimes in their weakening in the face of new experience. D'Andrade (1995) explains in more detail that schemas are "flexible configurations, mirroring the regularities of experience, providing automatic completion of missing components, automatically generalizing from the past, but also continually in modification, continually adapting to reflect the current state of affairs." Describing them as 'flexible, mirrored configurations' implies that schemas are structural entities within cognition that are comprised of several elements. Schemas are not the individual elements rather strongly connected clusters of elements of experience within cognition. Elements of experience are clustered in cognition, in our neural networks, because they are clustered in our lived experiences. Clustering cognitive elements makes them more efficient by reducing the cognitive load associated with processing experience.

Schemas are powerful processors of experience, help with pattern completion, and promote cognitive efficiency. They serve to both inform and constrain our understanding of experience. People recall schematically embedded information more quickly and more accurately (DiMaggio, 1997). In fact, schemas hold such sway in our cognition that people may falsely recall schematically embedded

events that did not occur. They are more likely to recognize information embedded in existing schemas because of repeated activation of the schemas. This repeated activation evokes expectations within cognition and the easy recognition of contradictory or challenging information that does not conform to those expectations formed as part of the existing schemas. Information that is orthogonal to existing schematic structures, that doesn't acquire salience through the repeated activation of schemas and the creation of associated expectations, is much less likely to be noticed or recalled. Because of their functionality in pattern completion, schemas function, in some sense, as flexible filters of experience, enabling us to attend to its salient features while filtering out the non-salient. Schemas allow us to perceive gestalts and help us to limit informational overload.

Schemas don't exist in isolation as objective patterns of neural activation such that they can be plotted on a representational map of a neural network. Schemas are emergent entities that are undergoing subtle changes within a complex network of neural activations that span cortical, limbic and peripheral neural pathways and contribute to our sense of embodiment. Rather than passive receivers of bits of information, our embodiment and embeddedness require us to actively engage the world, to create a *lived experience* (pace Heidegger). The motivational force of some schemas that are activated by salient elements of our environment is what Freeman (1991) refers to as an *attractor landscape*. It is not the particular elements that activate our schemas, but rather their salience—"the significance of the stimulus," (Freeman, 1995). Freeman's research in neurophysiology leads him to the following conclusion:

I conclude that context dependence is an essential property of the cerebral memory system, in which each new experience must change all of the existing store by some small amount, in order that a new entry be incorporated and fully deployed in the existing body of experience. This property contrasts with memory stores in computers…in which each item is positioned by an address or a branch of a search tree. There, each item has a compartment, and new items don't change the old ones. Our data indicate that in brains the store has no boundaries or compartments. …Each new state transition…initiates the construction of a local pattern that impinges on and modifies the whole intentional structure. (Freeman, 1995)

Freeman wants us to imagine a conceptual landscape as if it were a physical landscape with craters. These craters represent concepts, with salient, permeable boundaries that form the rim of the crater. The crater is what Freeman refers to as an *attractor*. And the basin (lowest point) of the crater is a *basin attractor*, which is the conceptual place that it takes minimal energy for our attention to flow.

Now imagine that these craters exist in relation to one another, forming a complex network of basins in the landscape, i.e., an *attractor landscape*. When we view the attractor landscape, we see a vast network of basins, clusters of basins, basins within basins, and basins overlapping basins. Moreover, this landscape of basins lies upon a malleable surface that allows for changes in the landscape based on newly lived experience. Because the entire complex network landscape of craters is interlinked, localized changes arising from experience will have an effect on the structure and strength of the entire network. The attractor landscape metaphor reflects the notion that concepts (i.e., craters) don't exist in isolation but rather as part of the network of schemas we develop through our lived and embodied experiences.

What Freeman postulates is that new conceptual stimuli will impact the attractor landscape and modify its whole structure. Sometimes these conceptual changes obliterate previous topological relationships, resulting in a wholly new localized intentional structure. Sometimes these conceptual

changes are more incremental, resulting in a richer local topology of multiple basins within a crater. What's important is that it is not the stimulus, per se, that modifies the attractor landscape, but rather the class and significance of the stimulus for the subject and its effects on localized networks of craters and the relative depths of their basins brought on by new experience.

Freeman's model instantiates the causal basis of a genuine intentional arc in which there are no linear casual connections between world and brain nor a fixed library of representations, but where, each time a new significance is encountered, the whole perceptual world of the animal changes so that the significance that is directly displayed in the world of the animal is continually enriched. (Dreyfus, 2007)

Schemas and the Dynamical Substrate

Generally schemas are networks of cognitive elements, which we correlate here with abstracts for the sake of simplicity. Henceforth we will use the term schema to describe a flexible representational structure that allows for contextual varieties. What this means is to be explained in the following. Any abstracts we can identify never appear independently. If we imagine a cherry we usually think of a red cherry. Such associations reflect relations between different abstracts that are important for the way we perceive the world. The resulting network of an abstract with other abstracts is considered as a schema. If we consider these relationships we find significant differences in their strength. For example, the relationship between 'cherry' and 'red' is stronger than the relationship between 'cheery' and 'green' while the latter is again stronger than that between 'cherry' and 'purple'.

While schemas represent the wholeness of such relationships, the actual salient representation defined by relevant relationships depends on the particular context in which this schema is expressed. While a schema can include a multitude of possibilities, in a concrete situation only a limited number of relations are relevant (Hagengruber & Riss, 2007). In Heideggerian parlance, this limited set of possible holistic affordances that finds its expression is some of the relevant relations becomes that which is *ready-to-hand*, as we discussed earlier. For example, in the context of art a 'purple apple' might possess some relevance whereas in the context of a supermarket the same relationship would raise astonishment and suspicion whether the respective object is a real apple. Our schemas constrain the *ready-to-hand* possibilities of an apple's color through expectations that become integral to our schemas as part of our patterned experiences.

On the one hand, the schema is compatible with the usual idea of representation of abstract objects by their properties and possible relations to other abstract objects. On the other hand, it is also compatible with Wittgenstein's idea of family resemblance since it allows the same abstract to appear in different relationships to other abstracts depending on the specific context. Relationships are not simply switched on and off but the 'strength' of a relationship can continuously change if the description or experience of the context continuously changes.

The concept of schema helps us to better understand abstraction and the role features actually play in it, i.e., why features can be used to represent abstracts at all and they also explain why a static and context-independent schema is insufficient in explaining abstraction. We start with a fixed model (table = board + 4 legs), and only later through concrete experience realize that it can vary (3 legs). At that point, we draw upon some relevant elements of the schema and blend them with new elements of experience. The blending can vary in significant ways—string from ceiling, single leg, three legs, etc. The schema in this instance is representative of the relationships

of features. On the other hand, schemas can be considered to have inherent variability such that they can be representational structures that express themselves differently depending on the context. The context dependency of a schema represents the independence of the considered abstract (i.e., the table) of the related abstracts (i.e., the legs etc.). In a schema, where the relationships are completely context independent, reduction becomes possible. For example, if we state that 'bachelor' is always identified with 'single male', the former concept can be defined (and replaced) by the latter. In contrast, for other concepts such as 'game' as Wittgenstein has shown such a definition is not generally possible. Thus, the more variable a schema becomes the more difficult it is to introduce analytic definitions.

However, schemas are only auxiliary constructs that allow us to illustrate principle processes in the mind. Due to their context dependency and variability they are not suitable for usage as knowledge representation as we find them in finite relational structures of abstracts and as we use them in analytic mental processing. Conversely, when we introduce new abstracts we start with a finite definition, e.g., that a 'table' is a 'flat board with four legs', in which the table is defined as a rigid and context independent schema. In the course of time other *qualia* of tables and their context dependency comes into play and the schema becomes variable. In this process the analytically defined abstract 'table' becomes a concept that is only loosely related to the original definition. In the next section we describe parallels of this process that we find in Polanyi's philosophy.

The Irreducibility of Tacit Knowledge

Taking such embodied capacities into account, Polanyi (1962) has claimed that human knowledge is mainly tacit. This means that this knowledge cannot be verbally expressed in a way that makes it communicable nor can it be reduced to logical processing. In particular this means that tacit knowledge cannot be formalized or represented in a symbolic way. Consequently tacit knowledge cannot be learned by communication but must be acquired by practice. Tacit knowledge describes a human's particular capacity to perform a specific activity, which is learned by actualizing the capacity as part of an activity. We claim that abstraction is mainly based on tacit knowledge and therefore is not logically specifiable (Polanyi, 1962, p. 56). For example we can recognize a face although we cannot describe which parts of the face determined this recognition. We abstract objects in a way in which we perceive the whole without full awareness of the individual features.

To describe this phenomenon Polanyi introduced the distinction between subsidiary and focal awareness that he explained on the basis of the example of a hammer (Polanyi, 1962). If we use a hammer to drive a nail into the wall our primary or focal awareness is connected to the actual process. Nevertheless we are also aware of the hammer, the hand, the nail, etc. but in another, more hidden or subsidiary way. Every time we focus on a whole, our awareness of the parts is subsidiary. If we turn our focal awareness to the hammer or the nail, the awareness of the process becomes secondary and the execution becomes clumsy and less experienced. This is very close to the idea of gestalt, of which we also lose sight if we concentrate on one of its details. However, these details point to a network of related concepts that can be analyzed but also to aspects 'beyond' the network. For example, the shift of focal awareness, whether volitional or non-volitional, describes a phenomenon that cannot be explained by schemas.

The focus of our awareness is related to the activities in which we are currently involved. For example, if we are busy driving a nail into the wall, we concentrate on this particular activity. If we want to analyze the respective sub-activities, our focus moves from one involved object, hand, hammer, or nail, to the next. We realize that it is our intellectual interest that determines the focus but not our bodily involvement in activi-

ties, i.e., in interactions with the world. In this way we are describing an ex-post analysis of the activity (e.g., 'hammering'). Activity could also encompass everything, including 'thinking.' On the one hand, we have different foci, which are opposed to activity. On the other hand, the activity could be considered a focus. We can decompose an abstract into different elements and can apply this decomposition to activities, where hammering can be a gestalt that can also be deconstructed into several activities. Abstraction in this example is not fundamentally different from what we consider to be primarily bodily activities.

The example of how a single abstract can emerge from the relational structure of several abstracts through repeated actualization, as we described above, reflects how we learn actions. If we use a hammer for the first time to drive a nail into the wall, we will first concentrate on how to deal with the weight of the hammer; we will experience how a blow of the hammer affects the nail, and so on. All these elements are not yet connected. Over time after some practice, however, these individual elements are merged to one action of driving the nail into the wall.

This description also depicts how we perform abstractions. When we see a table we are subsidiarily aware of its features but not in a way that we can directly name them. Moreover, the capacity that is actualized in this abstraction does not depend on a fixed set of features but rather resembles intuition than logical inference. The variable collection of features, which appear in our subsidiary awareness and can be determined ex-post, is expressed in schemas. Here it must be remarked that the features that we call from subsidiary to focal awareness do not form a fixed set but rely on further abstractions. When we try to find out why the object in front of us is a table we must do two things: first, we have to identify those objects that contribute to the tables, and second, we must abstract these parts again.

Polanyi's approach also bears consequences for communication. Thus, Walsham (2005) pointed out that human communication requires sense-giving by the sender of the message, as a process of abstraction, and sense-reading by the recipient. Both processes are based on a shared understanding of what is meant which again is based on embodied capacities. For example, a person can read Einstein's formula $E = mc^2$ but if she does not possess any experience in physics it will remain a meaningless expression. If the respective person possesses some basic knowledge of physics she may at least know the concepts of energy, mass and velocity of light. In this case the person will be able to bring these concepts together in an abstract way, represented by the abstract formula, but does not understand its practical consequences.

Sensus Communis

As beings in the world, we organize our experiences in ways that ensure ease of interaction, coordination of activities, and collaborative interaction. Because we organize our experiences in particular ways, people in the same social environment will indeed experience many of the same typical patterns. In experiencing the same general patterns, people will come to share the same common understandings and exhibit similar emotional and motivational responses and behaviors. However, because we are also individuals, there can be differences in the feelings and motivations evoked by the schemas we hold. "The learner's emotions and consequent motivations can affect how strongly the features of those events become associated in memory" (Strauss & Quinn, 1997, p. 6). Individuals will engage the external world structures and experience the same general patterns. Similar stimuli and experiences will activate similar schemas. It is in that sense we considered them shared schemas. The sharing of schemas does not require people to have the same experiences at the exact same time and place, rather that they experience the same general patterns. It's their quality of sharedness

that makes them a dimension of the cultural and from which we derive our *sensus communis.*[3]

Shared or cultural schemas have other qualities also. Some schemas are durable. Repeated exposure to patterns of behavior strengthens the networks of connections among the cognitive elements. Some schemas show historical durability. They are passed along from one generation to the next. Some schemas show applicability across contexts. We draw upon them to help us make sense of new and unfamiliar experiences. Some schemas exhibit motivational force. Such motivation is imparted through learning, explicitly and implicitly, strengthening the emotional connections among the cognitive elements.

We share the intrapersonal dimensions of culture when we interact with others. In sharing these intrapersonal dimensions, schemas are activated. Activation evokes meanings, interpretations, thoughts, and feelings. We make meaning of our experience. The cultural meaning of a thing, which is distinct from the personal cognitive meaning, is the typical interpretation evoked through life experience, with the acknowledgement that a different interpretation could be evoked in people with different characteristic life experiences. In some cases our experience is intracultural, where we share a similar cultural frame. In other cases our experience is intercultural, where we are sharing different cultural frames. The meanings evoked by one person in relation to a particular extrapersonal structure may not be the same as those evoked in another. In fact, the meanings evoked may not be the same within the same person at different times, for they may experience schema-altering encounters in the interim.

Knowledge Representation and Its Limits

Finally we have to answer the question how we actually come to the idea of abstraction as a feature-based analytical process. This answer is that in reality tables are usually well enough distinguished from chairs, cupboards, etc. Although we can construct transitions between these objects in thought experiments, the transition is insignificant for practical purposes. The few exceptions that we find can be handled in an explicit way. However, this insight does not allow us to reduce abstraction to schema evaluation. It only helps us to rationalize abstractions *ex post* if this is necessary, e.g., if a contradiction has occurred. The contextuality and consequent variability of schemas makes it practically impossible to use them for explicit knowledge representation.

Moreover, there are some natural objects that are not so clearly distinguished, e.g., colors or artworks. Here we find abstracts that depend on the particular society. In particular we find that societies that live in different environment tend to different abstractions. This means they use those abstracts that are most likely to be helpful in this environment. These abstractions cannot be learned solely by direct experience but rather by communication and are based on the *sensus communis*. Since the environment is changing, often by human interference, continuously experienced transitions that did not appear originally come into being so that the concepts become less disjoint. In order to deal with such situations humans have to make a cognitive shift from subsidiary awareness of the respective features to focal awareness and analysis of them. This, of course, requires the insight that the respective abstract no longer adequately describes the altering concrete object. For example, the decrease of a heap by removing grains finally leads to the inadequacy of the concept of heap while the respective process can only be understood by considering the number of grains (as a subsidiary feature).

According to Polanyi the fact that we are actually able to do such analysis of abstracts by transition from subsidiary to focal awareness, reflects an ontological structure, which he calls ontological stratification (Polanyi, 1969). This is not to be understood as synonymous with reducibility. Polanyi uses the example of physics and chemistry to explain the relation. Although chemistry cannot be reduced to physics it is nevertheless possible to explain certain chemical transitions, e.g., chemical reactions, by means of physical consideration.

FUTURE TRENDS

Obviously the traditional proceeding of computational approaches to the mind has to be replaced by other approaches that take the variability of schemas and the embodied embeddedness of the human mind into consideration. The process of abstraction is a perfect example for this requirement. As we have seen fixed schemas can serve as starting point for the formation of a concept but they are not sufficient to deploy the full power of human concepts that are highly adaptive to different concrete situations. The transition from fixed to variable representations results from interaction of humans with their environment. This has to lead to the replacement of static representations by dynamic schemas, which provide capacities that enable the machine to abstract objects that deviate from standard forms.

Moreover even the variability of schemas comes to a limit if we aim at a complete simulation of the human mind. Here we have to take into account that the evolution of abstraction-related capacities is based on structures that even go beyond schemas and reach layers that include more basal bodily systems, such as emotions. Here we hit upon a fundamental problem that consists in the incoherency of bivalent abstracts and continuous processes as they become apparent in the heap paradox. The bivalence of abstracts refers to the fact that we have to associate a concrete object either with an abstract *c* or its negation *not-c* in order to apply logics (otherwise we conflict with the law of the excluded middle) and traditional computational algorithms.

Such an approach requires a certain openness of the machine to new experiences that are not covered by given definitions. In human societies such experience is passed from one individual to another and backed by a *sensus communis*. This means that human beings do not acquires all these capacities on their own but that they learn most of them through communication. This does not mean that knowledge is simply copied from one person to another but it is a complex network of interactions with other persons and the environment that enables the transfer of knowledge, which includes abstraction. This means that it is essential that the system is learning on its own so that the acquired knowledge is compatible to the already existing experience. Simple implementation of predefined knowledge does not meet the requirements in this respect but would only lead to conflicts.

CONCLUSION

If computational approaches to mind are to be successful, they must include the ability to recognize the salience, significance and relevance of elements of a perceptual context that are meaningful. Recognition of symbols is insufficient. The successful computational mind must be able to engage in abstraction and meta-abstraction including self-awareness. It must be able to imagine, to volitionally blend abstractions and elements of abstractions in novel ways that allow it to recognize different gestalts in context rather than a series of distinct symbolic elements. And it must be able to discern the validity of these blendings in ways that, in humans, arise from a *sensus communis*.

We conclude that the mind is an emergent phenomenon that is grounded in the brain and influenced by its functions. Abstraction is an emergent capability of the brain, so that it cannot be reduced to physical functions. The emergent qualities of mind include the qualities of consciousness, as well as the capacities for feeling, imagination and volition as which they become present to the mind as part of the meta-abstraction of self-awareness. We find abstraction and logic

as prominent features of the mind that must be considered in order to move towards a more viable computational comprehension of the human mind.

REFERENCES

Agre, P. E. (1988). *The Dynamic Structure of Everyday Life (MIT AI Technical Report, October 1988, No. 1085)*. Cambridge, MA: MIT.

Anderson, R. C., Spiro, R. J., & Montague, W. E. (Eds.). (1984). *Schooling and the acquisition of knowledge*. Hillsdale, NJ: Lawrence Erlbaum.

Barbiero, D. (2004). Tacit knowledge [Electronic Version]. *Dictionary of Philosophy of Mind*. Retrieved 2009.09.10 from http://philosophy. uwaterloo.ca/MindDict

Brooks, R. A. (1988). Intelligence without Representation . In Haugeland, J. (Ed.), *Mind Design*. Cambridge, MA: The MIT Press.

D'Andrade, R. (1995). *The Development of Cognitive Anthropology*. Cambridge, UK: Cambridge University Press.

Davis, P. M. (1991). Cognition and learning: A review of the literature with reference to ethnolinguistic minorities. Dallas, TX: Summer Institute of Linguistics.

DiMaggio, P. (1997). Culture and cognition. *Annual Review of Sociology*, *23*, 263–288. doi:10.1146/annurev.soc.23.1.263

Dreyfus, H. L. (1972). *What computers can't do: a critique of artificial reason* (1st ed.). New York: Harper & Row.

Dreyfus, H. L. (2007). Why Heideggerian AI failed and how fixing it would require making it more Heideggerian. *Artificial Intelligence*, *171*, 1137–1160. doi:10.1016/j.artint.2007.10.012

Fisher, G. H. (1967). Measuring Ambiguity. *The American Journal of Psychology, 80,* 541–547. doi:10.2307/1421187

Freeman, W. J. (1991). The physiology of perception. *Scientific American,* , 242.

Freeman, W. J. (1995). *Societies of Brains: A study in the neuroscience of love and hate, The Spinoza Lectures, Amsterdam, The Netherlands (Vol. 59).* Hillsdale, NJ: Lawrence Erlbaum Associates.

Gadamer, H.-G. (1975). Truth and Method (2nd Rev. ed. trans. by J. Weinsheimer & D.G. Marshall). New York: Continuum.

Hagengruber, R., & Riss, U. V. (2007). Knowledge in Action . In Dodig-Crnkovic, G. (Ed.), *Computation, Information, Cognition - The Nexus and The Liminal* (pp. 134–146). Cambridge, UK: Cambridge Scholars Publishing.

Haugeland, J. (1998). *Having Thought: Essays in the Metaphysics of Mind.* Cambridge, MA: Harvard University Press.

Heidegger, M. (1962). Being and Time (trans. ed. by J. Macquarrie, & E. Robinson). New York: Harper and Row.

Honderich, T. (1995). *The Oxford Companion to Philosophy.* Oxford, UK: Oxford University Press.

Keefe, R. (2000). *Theories of Vagueness.* Cambridge, UK: Cambridge University Press.

Kern, A. (2006). *Quellen des Wissens.* Frankfurt, Germany: Suhrkamp.

Mai, H. (2009). *Michael Polanyis Fundamentalphilosophie.* Freiburg, Germany: Karl Alber.

Merleau-Ponty, M. (1962). *Phenomenology of Perception.* London: Routledge.

Mingers, J. (2001). Embodying information systems: the contribution of phenomenology. *Information and Organization, 11*(2), 103–128. doi:10.1016/S1471-7727(00)00005-1

Newell, A., & Simon, H. A. (1988). Computer Science as Empirical Inquiry: Symbols and Search . In Haugeland, J. (Ed.), *Mind Design.* Cambridge, MA: MIT Press.

Polanyi, M. (1962). *Personal Knowledge.* Chicago: The University of Chicago Press.

Polanyi, M. (1969). Knowing and Being . In Grene, M. (Ed.), *Knowing and Being: Essays by M. Polanyi.* Chicago: The University of Chicago Press.

Ruben, P. (1978). *Dialektik und Arbeit der Philosophie.* Köln: Pahl-Rugenstein.

Rumelhart, D. E., & McClelland, J. L. (1986). Parallel Distributed Processing: Exploration in the microstructure of cognition, Vols. 1 & 2. In Psychological and Biological Models (Vol. 1 & 2). Cambridge: The MIT Press.

Shannon, C. E. (1948). A Mathematical Theory of Communication. *Bell System Technical Journal, 27,* 379-423 and 623-656.

Shannon, C. E., & Weaver, W. (1949). *The Mathematical Theory of Communication.* Urbana, IL: University of Illinois Press.

Shapiro, S. (2000). Classical Logic [Electronic Version]. *Stanford Encyclopedia of Philosophy.* Retrieved 2009.09.10 from http://plato.stanford.edu/entries/logic-classical/

Strauss, C., & Quinn, N. (1997). *A cognitive theory of cultural meaning.* Cambridge, UK: Cambridge University Press.

van Gelder, T. (1997). Dynamics and cognition. In J. Haugeland (Ed.), Mind Design II (A Bradford Book ed.). Cambridge, MA: The MIT Press.

Walsham, G. (2005). Knowledge Management Systems: Representation and Communication in Context. *Systems . Signs & Action, 1*(1), 6–18.

Winograd, T., & Flores, F. (1987). *Understanding Computers and Cognition: A New Foundation for Design.* Boston: Addison-Wesley.

Wittgenstein, L. (1953). *Philosophical Investigations, (G.E.M. Anscombe 1962 trans* (, Ed.). Oxford: Blackwell.

KEY TERMS AND DEFINITIONS

Abstraction: The transition from the practical or theoretical treatment of different but similar (equivalent) concrete objects (or ensembles of objects) of a given domain to the practical to theoretical treatments of these objects (or ensembles of objects) as representatives of that quality with respect to which the equality has been asserted. Consequently abstraction can be seen as the transition from the consideration of equivalent concrete objects to the consideration of the class to which these objects belong regarding their equivalence (adapted from Ruben, 1978).

Logic: Logic, or better formal logic, is the theory of sound reasoning, governed by well-defined rules. It is expressed in mathematical or algorithmic systems, which derive from the sequential application of the principle rules to symbolic expressions, forming a formal language. These deductive systems capture, codify, or record inferences that are correct within the given formal language. One of the fundamental principles of traditional formal logic is the Law of Bivalence, i.e., that a meaningful proposition formulated in this formal language is either true or false. The limitations of such formal systems appear for example in Gödel's theorem (adapted from Honderich, 1995; Shapiro, 2000).

Capacity: Capacity means an ability or power of a thing or person. It can be innate or acquired and describes a causally effective feature of an object. Examples for capacities are the property of wood to burn or the property of a person to be able to drive a car. To say that an object possesses a capacity does not include that this is true under arbitrary circumstances such as wet wood which might not burn. (adapted from Honderich, 1995).

Embodied: Embodied refers to the integrated nature of cognition with our physical body. It is a recognition of the inseparable nature of 'mind' from 'body' and 'mind' as consisting of more than rational and logical capacities, including emotional, motivational, and experiential capacities.

Embedded: Embedded refers to the relationship between embodied human experience and the world. It is the recognition that immersion in the world is an inescapable fact of human existence, and that the world in which we are embedded consists of not only the physical world but also the cultural and contextualized understanding that we create for it.

Schemas: Schemas are patterns of strongly connected elements of cognition that activate based on salient elements of a particular context and serve as auto-completion processors, allowing us to perceive a gestalt. As strongly connected networks within cognition, they have a bias in activation through repeated exposure to the same or similar stimulus, but they are not rigid and inflexible. They are adaptable, sometimes resulting in the strengthening of existing schemas, sometimes in their weakening in the face of new experience (adapted from D'Andrade, 1995; Strauss & Quinn, 1997).

Tacit Knowledge: Tacit knowledge characterizes a person's capacity to act, to abstract, to make judgments, and so forth without explicit reflection on principles or rules. The person's action is not based on a theory of his or her doing; he or she just performs skillfully without deliberation (adapted from Barbiero, 2004).

Subsidiary awareness: Subsidiary awareness describes that that an object is recognized as part of a gestalt. This means that it is not in the center of the person's attention but on inquiry the respective person is able to identify the particular object as part of the gestalt (adapted from Mai, 2009; Polanyi, 1962).

Focal awareness: Focal awareness describes that an object attracts the attention of a person in contrast to subsidiary awareness. Focal awareness is directed towards the objects of a persons' current interest or activity (adapted from Mai, 2009; Polanyi, 1962).

Ready-to-hand:: *Ready-to-hand* refers to the holistic affordability for action that surrounds an object rather than discrete characteristics or qualities of an object (adapted from Heidegger, 1927).

Present-at-hand:: *Present-at-hand* refers to the salient element, feature or phenomenon that holds the focus of our attention and, because of the temporal nature of our being-in-the-world, is continuously shifting from one thing to another and constrained by *ready-to-hand* possibilities (adapted from Heidegger, 1927).

Sensus communis:: *Sensus communis* is the shared, cultural understanding we create as an essential part of the sense making in which we engage as part of our experience. We use this term in the Gadamerian sense (Gadamer 1975) —the whole set of unstated assumptions, prejudices, and values that are taken for granted; the non-reflective judgments and values learned but not judged.

ENDNOTES

1   1968 MGM Press Release for *2001: A Space Odyssey*.

2   Heidegger coined *Dasein* (literally "there-being") as a way to describe man's way of being in the world. *Dasein's* openness to the experience of being is characterized by *understanding*.

3   *Sensus Communis* is meant here in the Gadamerian sense—the whole set of unstated assumptions, prejudices, and values that are taken for granted; the non-reflective judgments and values learned but not judged.

Chapter 10
Applying Lakatos–Style Reasoning to AI Problems

Alison Pease
University of Edinburgh, UK

Andrew Ireland
Heriot-Watt University, UK

Simon Colton
Imperial College London, UK

Ramin Ramezani
Imperial College London, UK

Alan Smaill
University of Edinburgh, UK

Maria Teresa Llano
Heriot-Watt University, UK

Gudmund Grov
University of Edinburgh, UK

Markus Guhe
University of Edinburgh, UK

ABSTRACT

One current direction in AI research is to combine different reasoning styles such as deduction, induction, abduction, analogical reasoning, non-monotonic reasoning, vague and uncertain reasoning. The philosopher Imre Lakatos produced one such theory of how people with different reasoning styles collaborate to develop mathematical ideas. Lakatos argued that mathematics is a quasi-empirical, flexible, fallible, human endeavour, involving negotiations, mistakes, vague concept definitions and disagreements, and he outlined a heuristic approach towards the subject. In this chapter the authors apply these heuristics to the AI domains of evolving requirements specifications, planning and constraint satisfaction

DOI: 10.4018/978-1-61692-014-2.ch010

problems. In drawing analogies between Lakatos's theory and these three domains they identify areas of work which correspond to each heuristic, and suggest extensions and further ways in which Lakatos's philosophy can inform AI problem solving. Thus, the authors show how they might begin to produce a philosophically-inspired theory of combined reasoning in AI.

INTRODUCTION

The philosophy of mathematics has relatively recently added a new direction, a focus on the history and philosophy of informal mathematical practice, advocated by Lakatos (1976, 1978) Davis & Hersch (1980), Kitcher (1983), Corfield (1997), Tymoczko (1998), and others. This focus challenges the view that Euclidean methodology, in which mathematics is seen as a series of unfolding truths, is the bastion of mathematics. While Euclidean methodology has its place in mathematics, other methods, including abduction, scientific induction, analogical reasoning, visual reasoning, embodiment, and natural language with its associated concepts, metaphors and images play just as important a role and are subject to philosophical analysis. Mathematics is a flexible, fallible, human endeavour, involving negotiations, vague concept definitions, mistakes, disagreements, and so on, and some philosophers of mathematics hold that this actual practice should be reflected in their philosophies. This situation is mirrored in current approaches to AI domains, in which simplifying assumptions are gradually rejected and AI researchers are moving towards a more flexible approach to reasoning, in which concept definitions change, information is dynamic, reasoning is non-monotonic, and different approaches to reasoning are combined.

Lakatos characterised ways in which quasi-empirical mathematical theories undergo conceptual change and various incarnations of proof attempts and mathematical statements appear. We hold that his heuristic approach applies to non-mathematical domains and can be used to explain how other areas evolve: in this chapter we show how Lakatos-style reasoning applies to the AI domains of software requirements specifications, planning and constraint satisfaction problems. The sort of reasoning we discuss includes, for instance, the situation where an architect is given a specification for a house and produces a blueprint, where the client realises that the specification had not captured all of her requirements, or she thinks of new requirements partway through the process, or uses vague concepts like "living area" which the architect interprets differently to the client's intended meaning. This is similar to the sort of reasoning in planning, in which we might plan to get from Edinburgh to London but discover that the airline interpret "London" differently to us and lands in Luton or Oxford, or there may be a strike on and the plan needs to be adapted, or our reason for going to London may disappear and the plan abandoned. Similarly, we might have a constraint satisfaction problem of timetabling exams for a set of students, but find that there is no solution for everyone and want to discover more about the students who are excluded by a suggested solution, or new constraints may be introduced partway through solving the problem. Our argument is that Lakatos's theory of mathematical change is relevant to all of these situations and thus, by drawing analogies between mathematics and these problem-solving domains, we can elaborate on exactly how his heuristic approach may be usefully exploited by AI researchers.

In this chapter we have three objectives:

1. to show how existing tools in requirements specifications software can be augmented

with automatic guidance in Lakatosian style: in particular to show how this style of approaching problems can provide the community with a way of organising heuristics and thinking systematically about the interplay between reasoning and modelling (section 3);

2. to show that Lakatos's theory can extend AI planning systems by suggesting ways in which preconditions, actions, effects and plans may be altered in the face of failure, thus incorporating a more human-like flexibility into planning systems (section 4);

3. to show how Lakatos's theory can be used in constraint satisfaction problems to aid theory exploration of sets of partial solutions, and counterexamples to those solutions, after failed attempts to find a complete solution (section 5).

In each field we outline current problems and approaches and discuss how Lakatos's theory can be profitably applied.

BACKGROUND

Lakatos's Theory

Lakatos analysed two historical examples of mathematical discovery in order to identify various heuristics by which discovery can occur: the proof by Cauchy (1813) of the Descartes-Euler conjecture and the defence by Cauchy (1821) of the principle of continuity. Lakatos has been criticised for overly generalising, since he claimed that his method of proofs and refutations (the key method that he identifies) is "a very general heuristic pattern of mathematical discovery" (Lakatos, 1976, p. 127). For instance, Feferman (1978) argues that these case studies are not sufficient to claim that these methods have a general application. We consider that our arguments in this paper both support and extend Lakatos's claim of generality, by showing

how his theory applies to AI domains. However, while portraying existing AI work in Lakatosian terms is an interesting intellectual exercise, we are more concerned with showing how Lakatos's heuristics can *extend* current AI research. That is, identifying and developing connections between Lakatos's work in the philosophy of mathematics and research in AI could have bidirectional benefits: in the current paper we focus on the contribution towards various AI domains. In this section we describe his heuristics, so that we can show how they can be applied to AI problems in the following sections. We abbreviate the "Lakatos-style reasoning" described here to LSR.

Lakatos's main case study was the development of the Descartes-Euler conjecture and proof. This started with an *initial problem*, to find out whether there is a relationship between the number of edges, vertices and faces on a polyhedron, which is analogous to the relation which holds for polygons: that the number of vertices is equal to the number of edges. The *naïve conjecture* is that for any polyhedron, the number of vertices (V) minus the number of edges (E) plus the number of faces (F) is equal to two. Cauchy's 'proof' of this conjecture (Cauchy, 1813) was a thought experiment in which an arbitrary polyhedron is imagined to be made from rubber, one face removed and the polyhedron then stretched flat upon a blackboard, and then various operations are performed upon the resulting object, leading to the conclusion that for this object $V - E + F = 1$ and hence prior to removing the face, the equation was $V - E + F = 2$. Most of the developments of proof, conjecture and concepts are triggered by counterexamples. Suppose, for instance, that the hollow cube (a cube with a cube shaped hole in it) is proposed as a counterexample to the conjecture that for all polyhedra, $V - E + F = 2$, since in this case $V - E + F = 16 - 24 + 12 = 4$. One reaction is to surrender the conjecture and return to the initial problem to find a different relationship. Alternatively we might modify the conjecture to "for all polyhedra *except those with cavities*, $V - E + F = 2$", thus excluding the counterexample, or to "for all *convex* polyhedra, $V - E + F = 2$" by considering examples which support the conjecture (such as regular polyhedra). Another reaction might be to argue that the hollow cube is *not* a polyhedron and thus does not threaten the conjecture, or to argue that there are different ways of seeing the hollow cube and that one interpretation satisfies the conjecture. Lastly, we might examine the proof to see which step the hollow cube fails, and then modify the proof and conjecture to exclude the problem object.

We outline Lakatos's heuristics below, these are presented in Lakatos (1976) as differing reactions (by different parties in a discussion) to a counterexample to a conjecture, where the outcome is a modification to a particular aspect of a theory. We represent this formally for a conjecture of the form $\forall x(P(x) \rightarrow Q(x))$, supporting examples S such that $\forall s \in S, (P(s) \land Q(s))$ and counterexamples C such that $\forall c \in C, (P(c) \land \neg Q(c))$.

1. *Surrender* the conjecture, and return to the initial problem to find a new naïve conjecture. More formally, abandon the conjecture when the first $c \in C$ is found. The outcome here is a change in focus.

2. Look for general properties which make the counterexample fail the conjecture, and then modify the conjecture by excluding that type of counterexample -- *piecemeal exclusion*, or if there are few counterexamples and no appropriate properties can be found, then exclude the counterexamples individually -- *counterexample barring*. These are types of *exception-barring*. More formally, determine the extension of C, generate an intensional definition $C(x)$ of a concept which

covers exactly those examples in C and then modify the conjecture to $\forall x((P(x) \land \neg C(x)) \rightarrow Q(x))$. The outcome here is to modify the conjecture.

3. Generalise from the positives examples and then limit the conjecture to examples of that type—*strategic withdrawal* (this is the only method for which supporting rather than counterexamples are needed). This is the other type of exception-barring. More formally, determine the extension of S, generate an intensional definition $S(x)$ of a concept which covers exactly those examples in S, and then modify the conjecture to $\forall x((P(x) \land S(x)) \rightarrow Q(x))$. The outcome here is to modify the conjecture.

4. Perform *monster-barring* by excluding the kind of problematic object from the concept definitions within the conjecture: that is, argue that the "counterexample" is irrelevant since the conjecture does not refer to that type of object. More formally, argue that $\forall c \in C$, $\neg P(c)$, either by narrowing an already explicit definition, or by formulating a first explicit definition of P. Each party in the discussion must then accept the new definition of P, and revise their theory accordingly. The outcome here is to modify one or more of the (sub)concepts in the conjecture.

5. Perform *monster-adjusting* by re-interpreting the counterexample as a supporting example. More formally, argue that $\forall c \in C$, $Q(c)$, again formulating and negotiating the definition as for monster-barring. The outcome here is modify one or more of the (sub)concepts in the conjecture.

6. Perform *lemma-incorporation* by using the counterexample to highlight areas of weakness in the proof. A counterexample may be global (violate a conjecture) and/or local

(violate a step in the proof). If it is both global and local then modify the conjecture by incorporating the problematic proof step as a condition. If it is local but not global then modify the problematic proof step but leave the conjecture unchanged. If it is global but not local then look for a hidden assumption in the proof which the counterexample breaks, and make this assumption explicit. The counterexample will then be global and local. More formally, use each $c \in C$ to identify flaws in the proof which can then be rectified. The outcome here is to modify either the proof or the conjecture which it purports to prove. This method evolves into *proofs and refutations*, which is used to find counterexamples by considering how areas of the proof may be violated.

The *problem of content* concerns the situation where a conjecture has been specialised to such an extent that its domain of application is severely reduced. Lakatos (1976, p 57) argues that a proof and theorem should explain *all* of the supporting examples, rather than just exclude the counterexamples. His notion of *concept stretching* provides one solution, where a concept definition is widened to include a certain class of object: this is the opposite of monster-barring.

Computational Accounts of Lakatos's Theory

Our argument that Lakatos's theory applies to particular AI domains will be stronger if we can demonstrate the following. Firstly, we should show that it is possible to provide a computational reading of Lakatos's theory, by interpreting it as a series of algorithms and implementing these algorithms as a computer program. Secondly, we should demonstrate that the theory has already been usefully applied to other AI domains. Lastly, we should draw convincing analogies between mathematics, the domain in which the theory was

developed, and the AI domains for which we claim application. In particular we need to identify parts of the AI domain which correspond to the key notions of mathematical conjecture, proof, concept, supporting example and counterexample. We describe our attempts to support the first two claims below, and draw appropriate analogies between mathematics and requirements specifications, planning and constraint satisfaction problems at the start of each discussion on applying LSR to these domains (sections 3, 4 and 5 respectively).

A Computational Model of Lakatos's Theory

We have developed a computational model of Lakatos's theory, HRL[1], in order to test our hypotheses that *(i)* it is possible to computationally represent Lakatos's theory, and *(ii)* it is useful to do so (Pease *et al.*, 2004; Pease, 2007). HRL is a multiagent dialogue system in which each agent has a copy of the theory formation system HR (Colton, 2002), which can form concepts and make conjectures that hold empirically for the objects of interest supplied. Distributing the objects of interest between agents means that they form different theories, which they communicate to each other. Agents then find counterexamples and use the methods identified by Lakatos to suggest modifications to conjectures, concept definitions and proofs. This system operated in the mathematical domains of number theory and group theory, thus demonstrating that LSR applies to domains other than topology and real analysis, and also with a machine learning data-set from inductive logic programming on animal taxonomy (Pease, 2007, chap. 10).

APPLICATIONS OF LSR TO AI DOMAINS

We have previously built the TM system (Colton and Pease, 2005) which was inspired directly by Lakatos's techniques. TM was built to handle non-theorems in the field of automated theorem proving. Given an open conjecture or non-theorem, TM effectively performed strategic withdrawal and piecemeal exclusion in order to find a specialisation of the problem which could be proved. To do this, it used the MACE model generator (McCune, 2001) to find supporting examples and counterexamples to the conjecture, then employed the HR automated theory formation system (Colton, 2002) to learn concepts which characterised subsets of the supporting examples. The concepts HR produced were used to specialise the conjecture in such a way that the Otter theorem prover (McCune, 1994) could find a proof of the specialised conjecture. We demonstrated the effectiveness of this approach by modifying conjectures and non-theorems taken from the TPTP library of first order theorems. While it may not be surprising that we can apply LSR to theorem proving in AI, since both operate on mathematical domains, the fact that we have both automated and usefully applied LSR supports our argument that it can apply to AI domains.

Colton and Miguel (2001) have already used an indirect form of Lakatosian reasoning to reformulate constraint satisfaction problems (CSPs). They built a system which takes as input a CSP and uses the Choco constraint programming language (Laburthe *et al.*, 2000). to find simple models which satisfy the constraints. These were input to HR, which found implied and induced constraints for the CSPs. A human user interpreted these results and used them to reformulate the CSP to include these additional constraints. As an example, Colton and Miguel ran their system in the domain of quasi groups, *i.e.*, finite algebras where every element appears in every row and column. Given the quasi group axioms and the additional axiom of $(a * b) * (b * a) = a$, which defines QG3, the task was to find example quasi groups of different sizes. Their system found examples up to size 6 and these examples were passed to HR, which found the concept "anti-Abelian", *i.e.*, the con-

straint that no pair of distinct elements commute. It then used Otter to prove that *all* examples of QG3 are anti-Abelian, thus the extension of the examples is the same, although the intension is different. This implied constraint was then added to the CSP, which sufficiently narrowed the search space to enable the system to find examples of size 7 and 8. HR also found the concept "quasi groups with symmetry of left identities", *i.e.*, $\forall a, b(a * b = b \rightarrow b * a = a)$. Since these form a strict subset of QG3, in this case both the extension and the intension are different from the original CSP. When this induced constraint was added, the system found an example of size 9. This can be seen as strategic withdrawal, where the new CSP is a specialisation of the original one. While the CSPs in this example are from a mathematical domain, Colton and Miguel (2001) argue that their system could be applied to other problem classes such as tournament scheduling. The ICARUS system (Charnley et al, 2006) extended the project by Colton and Miguel (2001) by fully automating the process (omitting the human interaction).

We have also developed ideas on applying LSR to work in the AI argumentation field (Pease *et al.*, 2009). In that work we discussed the meta-level argumentation framework described in (Haggith, 1996) in which both arguments and counter-arguments can be represented, and a catalogue of argument structures which give a fine-grained representation of arguments is described. Using Lakatos's case studies, we showed that Haggith's argumentation structures, which were inspired by the need to represent different perspectives in natural resource management, can be usefully applied to mathematical examples. We also showed that combining Lakatos's conjecture-based and Haggith's proposition-based representations can be used to highlight weak areas in a proof, which may be in the relationships between sets of conjectures or in the claims asserted by the conjectures. Applying Lakatos's ideas to Haggith's

Table 1.

Plan:	Flush the QS
Effects:	(1) I will force the player who has the QS to play that card
	(2) I will avoid taking 13 points
Conditions:	(1) I do not hold the QS
	(2) The QS has not yet been played
Actions:	First I win a trick to take the lead, and whenever I lead I play a spade

argumentation structures showed a way of avoiding her black box propositions, thus enabling new areas for flaws to be found and repaired. Lakatos's methods suggested new structures for Haggith (although she made no claim to have identified all structures, adding new examples to the catalogue was a valuable contribution to Haggith's work). Aberdein (2005) also discusses argumentation theory, including references to Lakatos, in the context of mathematics.

Hayes-Roth (1983) describes five heuristics, which are based on Lakatos's methods, for repairing flawed beliefs in the planning domain. He demonstrates these in terms of revising a flawed strategy in a simple card game, Hearts. In Hearts a pack of cards[2] is divided amongst players, one player plays a card and the others must all put down a card in the same suit as the first if they have one, and otherwise play any card. The person who played the highest card in the specified suit wins that trick and starts the next. One point is awarded for each heart won in a trick, and 13 for the queen of spades (QS). The aim of the game is to get either as few points as possible ("go low") or all the points ("shoot the moon"). An example of a justification of a plan (corresponding to a mathematical proof) is "(a) the QS will win the trick, therefore (b) the player holding the QS will get the 13 points, therefore (c) this plan will minimise the number of my points"; an example of an action which is executed according to a plan (corresponding to an entity) is to "play the 9 of spades"; and an example of a concept is "a spade lower than the Queen". Counterexamples

correspond to moves which follow a strategy but which do not have the desired outcome. For instance, a strategy which beginners sometimes employ is to win a trick to take the lead, and then play a spade in order to flush out the QS and avoid the 13 points. Hayes-Roth represents this as shown below (Hayes-Roth, 1983, p.230):

The plan (analogous to a faulty conjecture) may backfire if the beginner starts with the king of spades (KS) and then wins the trick and hence the unwanted points (this situation is a counterexample to the plan). Heuristics provide various ways of revising the plan: we show these in terms of Lakatos's methods below.

In this context, *surrender* is called *retraction*, where the part of the plan which fails is retracted, in this case effect (2). *Piecemeal exclusion* is known as *avoidance*, where situations which can be predicted to fail the plan are ruled out, by adding conditions to exclude them. For example, the condition "I do not win the trick in which the queen of spades is played" might be added, by assessing why the plan failed. A system can further improve its plan by negating the new condition "I win the trick in which the queen of spades is played", using this and its knowledge of the game to infer that it must play the highest card in the specified suit, and then negating the inference to get "I must not play the highest card in the specified suit". This is then incorporated into the action which becomes "First I win a trick to take the lead and whenever I lead, I play a spade which is not the highest spade". *Strategic withdrawal* is known as *assurance*, where the plan is changed so that it only applies to situations which it reliably predicts. In this case the faulty prediction is effect (2) above, and so the system would look for conditions which guarantee it. It does this by negating it, inferring consequents and then negating one of these and incorporating it into the action. For example negating effect (2) gives "I do take 13 points", the game rules state that "the winner of the trick takes the points in the trick" so we can infer that "I win the trick", then use this and the rule that "the person who plays the highest card in the suit led wins the trick" to infer that "I play the highest card in the suit led". Given that "player X plays the QS" we can now infer that "I play a spade higher than the QS" and negate it to get "I play a spade lower than the QS". An alternative heuristic, which also relates to strategic withdrawal is *inclusion*. This differs from assurance in that the situations for which the plan is known to hold are listed rather than a new concept being devised. Therefore, instead of adding "I play a spade lower than the QS" to the action, we add "I play a spade in the set {*2 of spades, 3 of spades, 4 of spades ..., 10 of spades, Jack of spades*}". *Monster-barring:* is called *exclusion*, where the theory is barred from applying to the current situation, by excluding the situation. The condition "I do not play KS" is then added.

We can extend Hayes-Roth's example to include lemma-incorporation, which can be seen as *consider the plan*, where the proof is considered and counterexamples to the following lemmas are sought: *(a)* the QS will win the trick; *(b)* the player holding the QS will get the 13 points; and *(c)* this plan will minimise the number of my points. This plan might suggest the counterexample of the KS which violates *(a)* (and *(b)*). Analysis of the counterexample would show that it is both local and global, and so the first lemma would be incorporated into the conjecture as a further condition. This then becomes: if (1) I do not hold the QS, and (2) The QS has not yet been played,

and (3) The QS wins the trick (is the highest spade in the trick), then (1) I will force the player who has the QS to play that card, and (2) I will avoid taking 13 points.

APPLYING LAKATOS-STYLE REASONING TO EVOLVING REQUIREMENTS SPECIFICATIONS

Lakatos's Methods in Event-B

The process of turning informal customer requirements into precise and unambiguous system specifications is notoriously hard. Customers typically are unclear about their requirements. Clarity comes through an iterative process of development analogous to that of Lakatos's characterisation of mathematical discovery. However, conventional approaches to representing specifications lack the rigour that is required in order to truly support LSR. As a consequence, defects, omissions and inconsistencies may go undetected until late on in the development of a system with obvious economic consequences. In order to embrace Lakatos's ideas fully within software engineering, the use of formal notations and reasoning is required. Adopting the rigour of formal argument, coupled with the Lakatos's methods, holds the potential for real productivity and quality gains in terms of systems development. Below we explore this idea, using Event-B (Abrial, 2009) a formal method that supports the specification and refinement of discrete models of systems. Within the context of Event-B, the methods of Lakatos can be used to reason about the internal coherence of a specification, as well as the correctness of refinements. The formal reasoning is underpinned by the generation of proof obligations (Pos): mathematical conjectures that are discharged by proof.

An Event-B specification is structured into contexts and models. A context describes the static part of a system (*e.g.*, constants and their axioms) while a model describes the dynamic part. Models are themselves composed of three parts: variables, events and invariants. Variables represent the state of the system, events are guarded actions that update the variables and invariants are constraints on the behaviour described by the events. As described in the example below, in a traffic controller system, a traffic-light can be represented as a variable, an event may be responsible for switching a traffic-light to green when another traffic-light is displaying red, and an invariant may constrain the direction of the cars when a particular traffic-light is green. Events can be refined into more concrete events by adding more detailed information about the system. For example, a more concrete version of the events that change the traffic-lights to green could be achieved by adding information about pedestrian crossing signals.

In this domain, Lakatos's terminology can be interpreted in different ways. For instance, an event may be refined to a more concrete event and the refinement verified through the use of invariants. In this case, the abstract event and the invariants can be seen as the concepts while the concrete event can be seen as the conjecture. Furthermore, in order to prove the internal coherence of a model, each invariant must be preserved over all events. In such proofs an invariant can be seen as a concept and an event as the conjecture; or vice versa. A third view is to always see the POs as the conjectures and both the invariants and events as concepts. However, in this scenario a change in the conjecture (PO) is necessarily a change in the concepts, *i.e.*, the invariants and/or events. Animating, or simulating the specification can lead to supporting examples (valid values) and counterexamples (invalid values) being obtained.

If too much detail is introduced within a single step then it may be necessary to backtrack to a more abstract level where a smaller refinement step is introduced. Additionally, within a single step, an invariant, event or variable may be abandoned if it is discovered that it is being represented at the wrong level of abstraction. For example, this

might involve backtracking in order to change an abstraction, or delay the introduction of an event until later within a development. This can be seen as a type of *surrender* in which the naïve conjecture is abandoned, and the initial problem (the overall design) is revisited. However it differs in that it may not be triggered by a counterexample. Another interpretation is *strategic withdrawal*, where withdrawal is to the "safer" domain of the more abstract level.

Piecemeal exclusion involves generalising across a range for which a conjecture is false, then modifying the conjecture to exclude the generalisation. Such exclusion may be achieved by adding guards to the events associated with failed conjectures, or by making invariants conditional. If the generalisation step is omitted then this would be an instance of counterexample barring. *Strategic withdrawal* has a similar effect in the sense that a guard is added, or the invariant is made conditional. However, the process of discovery is different in that it focuses on the supporting examples.

In *monster-barring* we argue that the values leading to a counterexample are not valid. Such values may for example be the input of an event. This type of argument is introduced in a model by adding an additional invariant. Regarding *monster-adjusting*, the counterexamples may be used to modify invariants or events (but without restricting them). An illustration of this case is the introduction of an additional action to an event. Finally, a failure in a proof can be the result of a missing axiom, and lemma-incorporation involves adding an axiom as a result of the counterexample.

An Example in Event-B

We illustrate Lakatos's discovery and justification methods for evolving Event-B specification using Abrial's "Cars on a Bridge" example (Abrial, 2009). (Figure 1) presents the essential details of the example, where the events are identified in bold. We will focus our discussion on a small part

Figure 1. An Event-B example

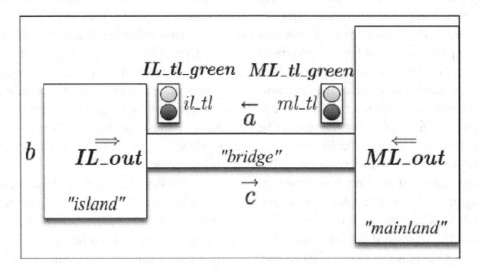

of Abrial's model, which is explained next. The example consists of an island connected to the mainland by a bridge. The bridge has one lane, and the direction of the traffic is controlled by traffic-lights on each side. A maximum number of cars are allowed on the bridge/island, and is denoted by d. Variables a and c denote the numbers of cars travelling towards the island and towards the mainland respectively, while b denotes the number of cars on the island. These variables should be seen as part of the specification of the *environment*, since they are not directly controlled by the system. *ml_tl* and *il_tl* describe the colour of the traffic-lights on the mainland and island respectively, and can be seen as the *system variables*. Events *ML_tl_green* and *IL_tl_green* change the traffic-lights to green, and events *ML_out* and *IL_out* model cars leaving the mainland and the island respectively. We delay to later discussion of how traffic-lights are switched to red. The following invariants state the conditions when the traffic-lights are green.

$$ml\_tl = green \Rightarrow a + b < d \wedge c = 0 \quad (inv1)$$
$$il\_tl = green \Rightarrow 0 < b \wedge a = 0 \qquad (inv2)$$

In Event-B each model must contain an unguarded *Initialisation* event that defines the valid initial state(s). In the example, we require no cars on the bridge/island and the lights set to red, *i.e.*,

$$Initialisation \triangleq Begin\ a, b, c$$
$$:= 0, 0, 0 \,\|\, ml\_tl, il\_tl := red, red\ End$$

This initialisation produces a counterexample with respect to the invariant *inv2*, *i.e.*,

$$red = green \Rightarrow \underline{0 < 0} \wedge 0 = 0$$

Note that the false part is underlined. The counterexample highlights a weakness in the specification, which can be fixed with the *lemma incorporation* method, leading to the introduction of an additional axiom of the form $red \neq green$.

Now consider the following definition of the *ML_out* event, which models a car leaving the mainland:

$$ML\_out \triangleq\ When\ ml\_tl = green\ Then\ a := a + 1\ End$$

Here, $ml\_tl=green$ is the guard of the action which increments a by 1. That is, a car can only leave the mainland when the traffic-light is green. Again, a counterexample with respect to invariant *inv2* is found, *i.e.*,

$$green = green \Rightarrow 0 < 2 \wedge \underline{1 = 0}$$

Using the *piecemeal exclusion* method, the conjecture can be fixed via the counterexample, by restricting either il_tl or a. We prefer not to restrict the environment whenever possible, therefore we use il_tl. The only way to make il_tl $= green$ false is by assigning il_tl the value *red*. *ML_out* is then restricted by this additional guard as follows:

$$ML\_out \;\hat{=}\; When\; ml\_tl = green \wedge \underline{il\_tl = red}$$
$$Then\; a := a + 1\; End$$

Note that the counterexample is used directly; therefore, this is an instance of the *counterexample barring* method. *IL_out* has a similar failure and patch for invariant *inv1*, and becomes:

$$IL\_out \;\hat{=}\; When\; il\_tl = green \wedge \underline{ml\_tl = red}$$
$$Then\; b, c := b - 1, c + 1\; End$$

where the underlined part is added as a result of the counterexample barring method. However, instead of restricting the applicability of events using *piecemeal exclusion*, we can *monster-bar* the counterexample via an invariant. For instance, if we step back and analyse both failures, it becomes clear that the newly introduced guards can be weakened by the existing guards, *e.g.*, within ML_out, $il\_tl = red$ then becomes $ml\_tl = green \Rightarrow il\_tl = red$. In fact, both these failures can be generalised to the same

conjecture, which we monster-bar by adding the following invariant:

$$il\_tl = red \vee ml\_tl = red \quad (inv3)$$

Informally, this invariant is an obvious requirement since it formalises that cars are only allowed on to the bridge in one direction at a given time. Nevertheless, invariant *inv3* is not preserved by the IL_tl_green and ML_tl_green events. We will only discuss the latter:

$$ML\_tl\_green \;\hat{=}\; When\; ml\_tl = red \wedge a + b < d \wedge c = 0$$
$$Then\; ml\_tl := green\; End$$

Here the counterexample arises if il_tl is *green* when the ML_tl_green event is executed. Here, we apply the *monster-adjusting* method and use the counterexample as a supporting example. This results in the introduction of an additional action which eliminates the counterexample. The action sets il_tl to red:

$$ML\_tl\_green \;\hat{=}\; When\; ml\_tl = red \wedge a + b < d \wedge c = 0$$
$$Then\; ml\_tl := green \,\|\, \underline{il\_tl := red}\; End$$

IL_tl_green is monster-adjusted in the same way.

Discussion

The example developed above was supported by the Rodin tool-set (Abrial et al, 2009) and ProB (Leuschel and Butler, 2008). That is, the management of specifications, and the generation of POs, proofs and counterexamples were all automated via the tool-set. In contrast, the high-level Lakatos style analysis was undertaken manually. Our current programme of research is concerned with augmenting the existing tools with automatic guidance in the style of Lakatos. Our approach involves combining heuristic knowledge of proof and modelling, to achieve what we call *reasoned modelling*. Lakatos's methods provides us with a way of organising our heuristics and thinking systematically about the interplay between reasoning and modelling. Moreover, we would like to raise the level of interaction by building upon graphical notations such as UML-B (Snook and Butler, 2008).

APPLYING LAKATOS-STYLE REASONING TO PLANNING

Lakatos's Methods and Planning

The ability to formulate and achieve a goal is a crucial part of intelligence, and planning is one way to tackle this (another way might be situated reflex action, for instance to achieve an implicit goal like survival). The traditional approach to planning in AI involves designing algorithms which take three types of input, all in some formal language: a description of the world and current state, a goal, and a set of possible actions that can be performed. The algorithms then output a plan consisting of a sequence of actions for getting from the initial state to the goal (this is known as batch planning). These work in various ways, for instance by refinement (gradually adding actions and constraints to a plan), retraction (eliminating components from a plan), or a combination of both (transformational planners). Plans can be constructed from scratch (generative planners) or found via some similarity metric from a library of cases (case-based planners). Traditional approaches to planning employ simplifying assumptions such as atomic time (the execution of an action cannot be interrupted or divided), deterministic effects (the same action on the same state of the world will always result in the same effect), an omniscient planning agent, and the assumption

that the rest of the world is static (it only changes via the agent's actions). Weld (1994) describes these characteristics of classical planning in further detail. There are now many variations to the traditional approach which reject some of these simplifying assumptions to get a more sophisticated model, for instance, Donaldson and Cohen (1998). We describe two such approaches in this section and discuss how Lakatos-style reasoning might be used to interpret or extend them.

Different Interpretations of The Analogy

There are strong similarities between the planning domain and a procedural notion of mathematics (as opposed to declarative mathematics). In planning, given certain preconditions, background information about the world and a goal, the aim is to construct a plan which starts from the preconditions and ends with achieving the goal. In mathematics, given an arbitrary object of a certain type and mathematical background knowledge such as axioms and theorems, and the goal of showing that certain properties hold true of the object, the aim is to construct a proof in which mathematical operations are performed on the object and it is demonstrated that the required properties must hold true. (Since it was arbitrary, such a proof would demonstrate that these properties hold for all objects of that type.) Note that the proof may include recursion and case splits, which does not affect our argument. The analogy is particularly clear in Lakatos's Descartes-- Euler case study as Cauchy's proof is procedural: it is represented as a series of actions to be performed on an object which starts as a polyhedron and is transformed via the actions to a two-dimensional object, a triangulated graph, etc. That is, given the input of an arbitrary polyhedron, background mathematical knowledge, and the goal of showing that $V - E + F = 2$ for this polyhedron, Cauchy's proof consists of a set of actions which achieve the goal: *i.e.*, it is a plan. This analogy is strengthened by the "Proofs as processes" perspective presented by Abramsky (1994) in which proofs are seen as concurrent processes (or processes as morphisms) and by Constable's work connecting programs and mathematical proofs, such as Constable and Moczydlowski (2006).

If we accept the analogy between the planning domain and mathematics then we would expect there to be a productive relationship between LSR and planning methods in AI. For instance, LSR should suggest ways in which a rudimentary plan might evolve by being patched or refined in the face of failure; how agents may communicate in social and collaborative planning; how plans can be formed and revised without an omniscient planning agent; when and how beliefs may be revised, or inconsistencies in a plan handled; how a dynamic environment can be used to develop a plan, etc. More specifically, Lakatos's theory and the extended theory in (Pease, 2007) can suggest when a plan should be abandoned (surrendered) and another one formed; how a plan might be modified to exclude cases which are known to fail (piecemeal exclusion), or limited to cases for which the plan is known to work (strategic withdrawal); how cases which fail a plan can be reconstrued such that the plan was not intended to cover them (monster-barring), or examples thought to cause failure reconstrued as supporting example, perhaps by a different interpretation of what it means to achieve a goal (monster-adjusting); how failure can be used to highlight areas of weakness in a plan and then strengthen them (lemma-incorporation), and how examination of steps in a plan could suggest sorts of cases which might fail them (proofs and refutations).

In order to apply LSR to planning we need to have analogical concepts of mathematical conjecture, proof, supporting example and counter-example. There are at least two rival interpretations of mathematical conjecture in the planning domain. Firstly, given a situation s which satisfies certain preconditions, there exists a set of actions such that performing them on s will result in another situation which satisfies certain effects. The second interpretation is that given a set of preconditions, a set of actions to perform on a situation, and a set of effects, if a situation satisfies the preconditions then the result of performing the actions will be another situation which satisfies the effects. In the first interpretation we conjecture that *there exists* a set of actions which will turn one specific situation into another, and in the second interpretation we conjecture that a certain *given* set of actions will turn one specific situation into another. Put formally using the "Result" operator from situation theory, this is:

First interpretation: $\exists A_T$ such that $\forall s \in S_T$, $(P_T(s) \rightarrow E_T(\text{Result}(A_T, s)))$, where A_T is a set of actions in the theory, S_T is the set of possible situations in the theory, $C_T(s)$ means that s satisfies a set of criteria C in the theory (which may be preconditions P_T or effects E_T).

Second interpretation: A_T is a set of actions in the theory such that $\forall s \in S_T$, $(P_T(s) \rightarrow E_T(\text{Result}(A_T, s)))$, where S_T is the set of possible situations in the theory, $C_T(s)$ means that s satisfies a set of criteria C in the theory (which may be preconditions P_T or effects E_T).

In the first interpretation, mathematical proof would correspond to the plan. This fits our notion of a mathematical conjecture in that we can discover and understand it without knowing the proof: for example, Goldbach's conjecture that "every even integer greater than 2 can be expressed as the sum of two primes", which is one of the oldest open conjectures in number theory.

(Polya (1962) suggests how conjectures might arise, without considering proof.) However, the corresponding notions of supporting examples and counterexamples are problematic. There is no notion of a supporting example which is independent of a proof. Similarly, although it may be possible to prove that a situation satisfying certain preconditions cannot be transformed into one which satisfies certain effects, it is difficult to falsify an existential claim. Under this interpretation then, only one of Lakatos's methods, local-only lemma-incorporation (which only involves counterexamples to a step in the proof, in this case to an action), has an obvious analogue.

In the second interpretation, there *is* a notion of supporting and counterexamples: a situation s_1 such that $P_T(s_1) \wedge E_T(\text{Result}(A_T, s_1))$, and a situation s_2 such that $P_T(s_2) \wedge -E_T(\text{Result}(A_T, s_2))$, respectively[3]. Thus, there are analogues to Lakatos's methods. However, the corresponding notion of proof is a justification of a plan, *i.e.*, *why* it would work. Thus, Lakatos's methods would focus on refining the justification rather than the plan: this may be contrary to the desired focus. It may be that the connection between the two interpretations is that of synthesis (the first interpretation) and verification (second interpretation): we can also see the distinction in Lakatosian terms as the initial problem (first interpretation) and naïve conjecture (second interpretation). We may be able to rectify the situation somewhat if we restrict ourselves to a finite domain. Consider, for instance, planning in the context of a game such as chess. A conjecture would take the form "there exists a path from the current state to the goal state" (where the goal state could be a winning state or any other desirable state). Under this analogy, mathematical *axioms* and *inference rules* would map respectively to the start state and the legal moves which each piece can perform. *Theorems* and *lemmas* would correspond to states towards which a path can be shown to exist from the start state[4]. Since we reserve the term "theorem" in mathematics for *interesting* proved statements, we map this to interesting board states, and use the lower status term "lemma" for less interesting board states; intermediate states between the interesting ones. *Entities* correspond to each individual piece, for instance the pawn in square *b2* in the start state is an entity, and *concepts* to types of piece (for instance the concept pawn, which has an extensional definition of all sixteen pawns and an intensional definition of an entity such that it starts in the second and seventh row, advances a single square or two squares (the first time it is moved from its initial position), capture other entities diagonally (one square forward and to the left or right) and may not move backwards). Concepts might be split further into sub-concepts, for instance "pawns" into "white pawn" and "black pawn", just as the concept "number" might be split into "even number" and "odd number". Under this interpretation the notion of supporting and counter examples now makes sense: a *supporting example* for a conjecture would be an entity for which a known path exists from its current state to the goal state. A *counterexample* would be an entity for which it is known that no path exists between its current state and the goal state (for example, if the goal state involves both black bishops on a square of the same colour). This approach more accurately captures the sort of mathematics that Lakatos describes, since it is possible to formulate a conjecture without any supporting or counterexamples, and to find supporting or counterexamples without having a proof.

An Example: Structural and Semantic Misalignment In The Context Of Planning

Developments such as the semantic web and the grid, in which large numbers of agents with different, evolving ontologies interact in a highly dynamic domains without a centralised agent, have raised the need for automated structural and semantic re-alignment. That is, if two interacting agents find that they have different representations or semantics in a given context, then there is a need to able to automatically resolve this on the fly. McNeill and Bundy (2007) have developed an ontology refinement system, ORS, which automatically re-aligns some part of its ontology with that of some part of the world, in the face of a mismatch. This works in the context of planning, and contrasts classical planners. ORS is able to recursively create and execute plans, detect and diagnose failures, repair its ontologies and re-form an executable plan, to avoid a known failure. In this section we discuss this work in the context of LSR.

The main contribution of ORS is the ability to diagnose and repair ontological mismatches discovered during agent communication. The system repairs its ontologies in the face of a mismatch by making changes to its predicates, action rules and individual objects so that the particular problematic representation becomes identical to that of the agent with whom it is communicating.

ORS can change its action rules by adding or removing preconditions or effects. Adding a precondition corresponds to piecemeal exclusion, and removing one is related to Lakatos's problem of content. With regard to mismatches in the effects of an action, ORS is able to explicitly add or remove effects. There is an interesting link to Lakatos's theory here: in his (only) example of local-only lemma-incorporation, in which the preconditions (a triangulated network) are satisfied and the action (removing a triangle) can be performed but the effects (the value of the equation $V - E + F$ is unchanged) are not as predicted (removing an inner triangle *does* change the value of $V - E + F$ by reducing it by 1).

Given the counterexample, or mismatch, one possibility is to add more effects, for instance "either $V - E + F$ is unchanged or it is reduced by 1", or more specifically, "there are now three

possibilities: either remove an edge, in which case one face and one edge disappear; or remove two edges and a vertex, in which case one face, two edges and a vertex disappear; *or* we remove one face, in which case only one face disappears", where the latter effect is the new one to be added. However, this would break the proof. Therefore we want to preserve the effect and make changes elsewhere to compensate. In this example the patch is to change the action to "removing a *boundary* triangle". ORS cannot currently change actions themselves: this idea, in which the original action is replaced by one which is a subtype of it, might be a useful extension.

There is no analogue of strategic withdrawal in ORS: repairs are only made if there is a mismatch. A way of incorporating this method would be to observe that a plan which has worked consistently in a number of examples contains a general predicate, for example the "Paper" predicate, which has only ever been invoked by a subtype of that predicate, such as "PdfPaper", and thus change the general case to the specific. This (unprovoked) refinement might be useful if the goal were to form a fool-proof plan which is known to work (as opposed to the current context of McNeill and Bundy's work, in which a plan is formulated in order to achieve a specific desired goal, and deleted once this has been successfully carried out).

ORS is also able to change the names and types of individual objects, where types may change to a sub or a super-type, one which is semantically related in a different way, or one which is not semantically related. Changing a type to a super-type, such as "Paper" to "Item" is an example of the first aspect of monster barring, in which the type of a problematic object might be changed from "polyhedron" to "three-dimensional object" (note that in monster-barring however, there might not be a replacement type, just the observation that object x is not of type T). The second aspect of monster-barring, in which the focus then turns from an individual object to a concept, or predicate, is represented by the ability of ORS to changing the name, arity, argument type, order of argument and predicate relationships for a predicate mismatch. In particular, when detail is added to a predicate, *i.e.* a refinement is performed, this can be seen as a form of monster-barring. For instance, ORS is able to replace a predicate name by one which is a subtype (*e.g.*, change "Paper" to "PdfPaper") in order to match that of the communicating agent, to avoid failure. This is analogous to changing the predicate "solid whose surface consists of polygonal faces" (which includes the hollow cube) to "surface consisting of a system of polygons" (which excludes the the hollow cube). Conversely, ORS can able to replace a predicate name by one which is a super-predicate (*e.g.*, change "PdfPaper" to "Paper") analogous to Lakatos's concept stretching.

There is no analogue of monster-adjusting in ORS. An example of this might be to change the *value* that an argument takes, rather than its type. (It is possible to do this in ORS by taking away an argument and then adding one, but this requires extra work as there is nothing to link the two types, so the latter type would need to be determined independently.) In Lakatos's example of the star-polyhedron, suppose that a polyhedron is represented as a predicate including arguments of type "natural number" corresponding to the number of faces, edges and vertices: *i.e.* as:

polyhedron

(PolyhedronName, NumberFaces, NumberEdges, NumberVertices, $\vec{x}$)

Then the original interpretation of a star-polyhedron (Lakatos, 1976, p. 16), in which it is raised as a counterexample, would be represented thus:

polyhedron (*star-polyhedron*, 12, 30, 12, $\vec{x}$).

The later interpretation in which it is a supporting example (Lakatos, 1976, p. 31), would be:

polyhedron (*star-polyhedron*, 60, 90, 32, $\vec{x}$).

One can imagine this being useful in the context of McNeill and Bundy's paper example if, for instance, two researchers are collaborating on a paper and the first has made changes to the value (but not type) of any of the arguments "PaperTitle", "WordCount", or "Format" which the second has not recognised: *paper(PaperTitle, WordCount, Format)*. In this case, the second researcher would need to update his or her ontology.

ORS also uses the notion of surprising questions. These are questions asked by a service provider agent to a planning agent, which do not pertain to the planning agent's preconditions of the action to be performed. If a surprising question has been asked directly before a failure, then these are used to locate the source of the problem.

A Further Example: The Slot Machine

McNeill and Bundy illustrate some of their ideas with a hypothetical example of an agent buying something which costs £ 5, from a slot machine. We suggest a set of actions in order to see the example as the following conjecture: "If I have £ 5 (precondition) and I perform the plan (set of actions) then I can obtain the item (effect)", where the plan (which roughly corresponds to a proof idea, with the reservations discussed above) is:

1. insert money into slot
2. select and press button
3. empty the tray.

Suppose that the agent has a £ 5 note and can perform the actions in the plan. McNeill and Bundy suggest modifications that might take place:

• It is discovered that the machine accepts only coins, not notes. While McNeill and Bundy do not elaborate on how this might be discovered, we can imagine that this is a case of *lemma-incorporation* where the counterexample is both global (given the preconditions the goal has not been achieved) and local (the agent cannot carry out step *(1)* since the note will not fit into the slot). The concept "items which satisfy the problem lemma" is then formed, in this case "money in a form which will fit into the slot", *i.e.*, coins and this concept incorporated into the conjecture, in this case into the preconditions. Thus the conjecture becomes "If I have £ 5 in coins then I can obtain the item". Alternatively we could insert an extra action into the the plan *(1a)* convert money into coins, and then change what was previously *(1)* to *(1b)* insert *coins* into slot. This is the same case as the paper format example below.

- The agent then finds that the machine does not take the new 50p coin[5]. We can see this as an example of *hidden lemma-incorporation* since the counterexample is global (given the preconditions the goal has not been achieved) but not local (we seem to be able to perform each step). According to Lakatos's *retransmission of falsity* principle (Lakatos, 1976, p. 47), if there is a problem with the conjecture then there must be a problem with the proof. In this case we examine each of the steps for a hidden assumption, which is marked by a feeling of surprise when it is violated. We might find that when carrying out step *(1)*, while we could insert the coin into the slot it simply dropped down into the tray. To someone who had used slot machine previously this might result in the first notion of surprise that we developed in Pease et al (2009), when an entity does not behave in the expected way, where the "expected way" has been learned from previous examples. In all other cases the inserted money did not fall into the tray (analogous to

the Cauchy example where we expect that having removed a face from a polyhedron and stretched it flat on a blackboard, we are left with a connected network). Therefore, this hidden assumption should now be used to form a new concept which then becomes an explicit condition which is incorporated into the plan and the conjecture. This might result in the new concept "coins which are accepted by the machine", the modified conjecture "If I have £ 5 in coins which are accepted by the machine which then I can obtain the item", and a modified plan, with first step now: " *(1)* insert money into slot so that it does not fall into the tray". Alternatively, we could see this example as exception-barring, where the concept "new fifty pence piece" is found and the conjecture becomes "If I have £ 5 in coins except for the new fifty pence piece, then I can obtain the item".

- The agent finds that some (perhaps old or worn) coins are unexpectedly rejected, and has to further modify the preconditions to exclude these particular coins. This also could be modified in the same way as the *hidden lemma-incorporation* above (and if being carried out chronologically then the concept "coins which are accepted by the machine" would be expanded to exclude the old coin). Alternatively, we could see this as a case of counterexample-barring, where no generalised concept covering the the counterexample is found, and so this specific coin is barred. In that case the conjecture would be modified to: "If I have £ 5 in coins except for this problematic one, then I can obtain the item".

- McNeill and Bundy then discuss the situation when an agent finds that the machine accepts coins which it not designed to accept, such as foreign or toy coins (again, they do not discuss how this may be found). This is a case of concept stretching, in which the problem of content is addressed by widening the domain of application: this has a valuable application since usually the weakest, or most general preconditions are more desirable.

The formulation of new concepts such as " £ 5 in coins", "coins except the new 50 pence piece" "coins except this particular coin", "Sterling coins and these similar foreign coins" and the subsequent modifications to the conjecture are easily describable in Lakatosian terms.

Discussion

McNeill and Bundy's approach has several commonalities with Lakatos's work. They both start from the same point, when a rudimentary proof or plan has been suggested (Lakatos claims that his discussion "starts where Polya stops" (Lakatos, 1976, p. 7), referring to Polya's work on finding a naïve conjecture (Polya, 1945, 1954), and the main thrust of McNeill and Bundy's system starts once a plan has been generated using a classical planner). Both are triggered by counterexamples or failures, and in both cases the aim is not to match the whole mathematical belief system or ontology, but to find local agreement on a particular problem. In both, the notion of surprise is used to guide repair and in particular to suggests *where* two different ontologies may differ. Both approaches are also highly recursive, with the methods being applied as many times as necessary. In Lakatos's case, the methods are repeated until agreement between mathematicians has been reached (which may later be reneged), or until the domain of application has become too narrow -- the "problem of content". In McNeill and Bundy's case ontology refinement is carried out until either the goal has been achieved or it becomes impossible, given the updated ontology, to form a plan to achieve the goal.

Perhaps the most important difference between McNeill and Bundy's approach and Lakatos's work is motivation: Lakatos describes situations in which people want to *understand* something, McNeill and Bundy describe situations in which people want to *achieve* something. McNeill and Bundy's case studies describe a pragmatic approach in which a plan which works well enough to achieve a goal in a specific (possibly one-off) situation is sought: they are not looking for a general, fool-proof plan (we want a slot machine to work, we do not want to understand it). A closer analogy to Lakatos in the planning domain would be someone who wants to write a *generally* usable plan, such as a set of instructions for assembling a piece of flat-pack furniture. Connected to this difference in motivation is a different attitude to counterexamples: Lakatos views them as useful triggers for evolving a theory (proceed by trying to falsify), and McNeill and Bundy view them as obstacles to be overcome (proceed by trying to satisfy a goal).

In developing ORS, McNeill and Bundy made several simplifying assumptions. Further versions of the system could use LSR in order to suggest ways of dealing with more complex situations. Another example is that if it is possible in ORS, then the planning agent will always change its own ontology in the face of a miscommunication. This bypasses issues of trust, status, entrenchment of a belief of representation, and so on. Lakatos indirectly discusses willingness to change one's ontology in order to better fit with that of collaborators.

LSR has a useful application in the planning domain. Consider, for example, the conjecture in the domain of flat packed furniture "given this flat pack kit (preconditions), the item of furniture (goal) can be constructed", where the notion of proof corresponds to the set of instructions (plan). One can imagine using LSR to improve upon a poorly written set of instructions, to find hidden assumptions and make them explicit. Developments in structural and semantic misalignment, in the context of planning as well as other areas, and in particular flexible and dynamic thinking, are of key importance to the semantic web, the grid and other areas. Thus, approaches that may contribute to their development are worth exploring: we hold that LSR is one such approach.

APPLYING LAKATOS-STYLE REASONING TO CONSTRAINT SATISFACTION PROBLEMS

Lakatos's Methods and Constraint Satisfaction Problems

A constraint satisfaction problem (CSP) consists of a set of problem variables, a domain of potential values for each variable, and a set of constraints specifying which combinations of values are acceptable (Tsang, 1993). A solution specifies an assignment of a value to each variable in such a way as to not violate any of the constraints. CSPs are usually represented in a tree-like structure, where a current search path represents a current set of choices of values for variables. CSPs appear in many areas, such as scheduling, combinatorial problems and vision. One example is the classic N-queens problem: given N, the solver is supposed to place N-queens on an $N * N$ chess board in such a way that none of the queens can threaten any other.

A conjecture corresponds to a current search path which is hypothesised to satisfy all the constraints. Supporting examples correspond to constraints which are satisfied by the solution, and counterexamples to constraints which are violated by the solution. We show some correspondences to Lakatos's methods below.

Surrender would entail abandoning a current search path (model) as soon as a single inconsistency is encountered (*i.e.*, a constraint is violated). This is most commonly used for CSPs, and triggers backtracking techniques. Freuder and Wallace (1992) develop techniques for partial constraint satisfaction, which are analogous to retrospective, prospective and ordering techniques for CSPs (a comparable search tree in mathematics might have an initial branching of the different equations under consideration, which of course might be dynamic, *i.e.*, new equations are created in the light of previous ones and added as new branches). These are necessary if there is no complete solution at all (the problem is over-constrained), or we cannot find the complete solution with the resources given (some algorithms are able to report a partial solution while working on improving this solution in the background if and when resources allow), and can be seen as *piecemeal exclusion* and *strategic withdrawal*. Constraints may be weakened by enlarging a variable domain (introduce a new value that a variable might take), enlarging a constraint domain (deciding that two previously constrained values are acceptable), removing a variable (one aspect of the problem is dropped), or removing a constraint (deciding that any combination of two previously constrained variables is acceptable). Of particular interest to us is Freuder *et al.*'s position on alternative problems: "We suggest viewing partial satisfaction of a problem, P, as a search through a space of alternative problems for a solvable problem 'close enough' to P." (Freuder and Wallace, 1992, p. 3). This has a very clear analogue in Lakatosian terms, where 'conjecture' is substituted for 'problem', and 'provable' for 'solvable'. They go on to argue that a full theory of partial satisfaction should consider how the entire solution set of the problem with altered constraints differs from the solution set of the original problem, as opposed to merely considering how a partial solution requires us to violate or vitiate constraints: that is, they compare problems rather than violated constraints.

Monster-barring and *monster-adjusting* would correspond to a claim that the proposed counterexample constraint is not a valid constraint, and formulate properties that a valid constraint must have, or a claim that the model *does* satisfy the problem constraint. Flexible (or soft), as opposed to conventional, CSPs relax the assumption that solutions (or models) must satisfy every constraint (imperative) and that constraints are either completely satisfied or else violated (inflexible). In particular, fuzzy CSP represent constraints as fuzzy relations, where their satisfaction or violation is a continuous function. Ruttakay (1994) discusses the issue of soft constraint satisfaction from a fuzzy set theoretical point of view.

An Example: A Constraint Satisfaction Problem in Scheduling

To explore the possibility of using Lakatos's ideas in constraint solving, we performed a small, hand-crafted experiment. We wrote a simple constraint satisfaction problem which models a scheduling problem (a common problem type for which CSP solvers perform very well). In the problem description there are five people who need to be scheduled for an appointment at a particular time and a particular place. The CSP was designed so that there was in fact no solution. However, if we reduce the number of variables in the CSP, there are indeed solutions. This models the situation with Lakatos, if we consider the variables which we don't solve for as being the counterexamples to the existence proof of a full schedule for the five people. In addition to the CSP, we also randomly generated some data which describes the five people in the scheduling problem. We defined ten predicates of arity one: nurse, pilot, busy, teacher, parent, professional, doctor, live_north_london, and live_south_london. For each person to be scheduled, we randomly chose between 1 and 10 predicates to describe them, for instance, person four was described as a busy parent who is a pilot.

We wrote a wrapper to find all the partial solutions to the CSP, and to determine which variables (people) the solution did not cover. We found that there were 10 schedules which worked for four of the five people, 110 schedules for three people, 170 schedules for two people and 40 schedules for one person. In addition, for each of the partial solu-

tions, we took the list of omitted people and used them as the positive examples in a machine learning classification problem (with the non-omitted people becoming the negatives). In particular, we used the background information about the people (*i.e.*, being a nurse, pilot, etc.), in a session with the Progol inductive logic programming machine learning system (Muggleton, 1995). In each case, we asked Progol to determine a general property of the omitted people. We removed the duplicate cases, *i.e.*, different partial solutions of the CSP which managed to schedule the same subset of people. In total, after this removal, there were 5 cases where four people were scheduled, 10 cases where three people were scheduled, 11 cases where two people were scheduled, and 5 cases where one person was scheduled.

When Progol was run with the machine learning problems, we checked its output for a general solution. That is, if Progol stated that the unscheduled people had a particular set of properties that the scheduled people did not share, we counted this as a success. If, however, Progol had to resort to using the name of one or more people in its solution, we counted this as a failure. We found that Progol was only able to find solutions to 5 of the 31 cases. This is largely due to the very limited amount of data available: in many cases, the compression of the answer was not sufficiently high, so Progol chose not to supply an answer. As an illustrative example, the CSP solver found a schedule for 3 of the 5 people, and Progol highlighted the fact that the two unscheduled people were both pilots (and none of the scheduled people were pilots). Note that we ran the experiment again with different random data for the background of the people to be scheduled, and Progol solved 4 of the 31 problems.

Discussion

Along with our work on TM, work by Colton and Miguel (2001) on HR with CSPs and Charnley *et al.*'s (2006) work on ICARUS, described in section

2.2, this simple experiment hints at the potential for applying Lakatos-inspired methods in constraint solving. The approach contrasts with existing CSP reformulation approaches which tend to change the CSP constraints, rather than the variables. For instance, the CGRASS system applies common patterns in hand-transformed CSPs, in order to improve the CSP model gradually (Frisch et al, 2002). To the best of our knowledge, no CSP reformulation approach appeals to a machine learning system to offer further advice when a solving attempt fails. Note that the TAILOR solver learns parameters for implied constraints (Gent *et al.*, 2009), and the CONACQ system uses version space learning to define a CSP model from scratch given only positive and negative examples of solutions for it (Bessiere *et al.*, 2005). However, these uses of learning in constraint solving are different to our approach.

RELATED WORK

We have given some simple examples of how LSR might be applied to AI problems, and argued that an automation of the type of reasoning that Lakatos describes would be profitable in these domains. Clearly, the examples in this paper are not the only examples of LSR in AI domains, since programs may have implicit aspects of LSR which, while not directly based on LSR, we can link to one of his methods. For example, Skalak and Rissland (1991) indirectly show how LSR might be applied to AI and legal reasoning in their theory of heuristics for making arguments in domains where "A rule may use terms that are not clearly defined, or not defined at all, or the rule may have unspoken exceptions or prerequisites" (Skalak and Rissland, 1991, p 1). In this case, their term *rule* corresponds to the mathematical term *conjecture*, *term* to *concept*, *case* to *entity*, and *argument* to *proof*. In particular, Skalak and Rissland, (1991) are interested in cases where terms within a rule are open to interpretation, and different parties

define the term differently according to their point of view: this corresponds very closely to Lakatos's method of monster-barring. Skalak and Rissland, (1991) discuss argument moves which use cases to determine which interpretation of an ambiguous term in a rule is to be adopted. These moves are implemented within CABARET (Rissland and Skalak, 1991). Winterstein (2004) provides another example. He devised methods for representing and reasoning with diagrams, and argued that his *generalisation method* can be seen as a simple form of Lakatos's method of strategic withdrawal (Winterstein, 2004, p. 69). This method analyses positive examples of a proof, abstracts the key features from these examples, and then restricts the domain of application of the theorem and proof accordingly.

CONCLUSION AND FUTURE WORK

We have described analogies between Lakatos's theory of mathematical evolution and the fields of evolving requirements specifications, planning and constraint satisfaction problems. Showing the relevance of Lakatos's theory to these diverse domains highlights connections between them and suggests ways in which philosophy can inform AI domains. This is a good starting point for a more complete interpretation, and we intend to investigate further the implementation of LSR in each of our three main case study domains. In general, we propose a programme of research in which AI domains are investigated in order to determine: (a) whether there is a useful analogy between them and mathematics, (b) whether we can implement (some of) LSR, (c) how LSR performs: (i) how the methods compare to each other (in mathematics, Lakatos presented them in increasing order of sophistication, but that may not hold in other domains, (ii) whether (and how) LSR enhances the field: how models with LSR compare to models without LSR, according to criteria set by each field.

In order to build the sort of AI which might one day pass the Turing test, whether one views that as strong or weak AI, it will be necessary to combine a plethora of reasoning and learning paradigms, including deduction, induction, abduction, analogical reasoning, non-monotonic reasoning, vague and uncertain reasoning, and so on. This combination of systems and reasoning techniques into something which is "bigger than the sum of its parts" has been identified as a key area of AI research by Bundy (2007) at his Research Excellence Award acceptance speech at IJCAI-07. The philosopher Imre Lakatos produced one such theory of how people with different reasoning styles collaborate to develop mathematical ideas. This theory and suggestions of ways in which people deal with noisy data, revise their beliefs, adapt to falsifications, and exploit vague concept definitions, has much to recommend it to AI researchers. In this chapter we have shown how we might begin to produce a philosophically-inspired AI theory of reasoning.

ACKNOWLEDGMENT

We are grateful to the DReaM group in Edinburgh for discussion of some of these ideas. This work was supported by EPSRC grants EP/F035594/1, EP/F036647 and EP/F037058.

REFERENCES

Aberdein, A. (2005). The uses of argument in mathematics. *Argumentation*, *19*, 287–301. doi:10.1007/s10503-005-4417-8

Abramsky, S. (1994). Proofs as processes. *Theoretical Computer Science*, *135*, 5–9. doi:10.1016/0304-3975(94)00103-0

Abrial, J.-R. (2009). Modelling in Event-B: System and Software Engineering. Cambridge, UK: Cam bridge University Press.

Abrial, J.-R., Butler, M., Hallerstede, S., Hoang, T. S., Metha, F., and Voisin, L. (2009). Rodin: An Open Toolset for Modelling and Reasoning in Event-B. *Journal of Software Tools for Technology Transfer*.

Barton, B. (2009). *The Language of Mathematics: Telling Mathematical Tales. Math ematics Education Library*, *46*. Berlin: Springer.

Bessiere, C., Coletta, R., Koriche, F., & O'Sullivan, B. (2005). A sat-based version space algorithm for acquiring constraint satisfaction problems. *Proceedings of ECML'05*, 23—34.

Bundy, A. (2007). *Cooperating reasoning processes: More than just the sum of their parts*. Research Excellence Award Acceptance Speech at IJCAI-07.

Cauchy, A. L. (1813). Recherches sur les poly`edres. *Journal de l''Ecole Polytechnique*, *9*, 68–86.

Cauchy, A. L. (1821). Cours d'Analyse de l'Ecole Polyechnique. Paris: de Bure.

Charnley, J., Colton, S., & Miguel, I. (2006). Automatic generation of implied con straints. In *Proceedings of the 17th European Conference on AI*.

Colton, S. (2002). *Automated Theory Formation in Pure Mathematics*. Berlin: Springer-Verlag.

Colton, S., & Miguel, I. (2001). Constraint generation via automated theory formation. In *Proceedings of the Seventh International Conference on the Principles and Practice of Constraint Programming*, Cyprus.

Colton, S., & Pease, A. (2005). The TM system for repairing non-theorems. In *Selected papers from the IJCAR'04 disproving workshop* . *Electronic Notes in Theoretical Computer Science*, *125*(3).

Constable, R. & Moczydlowski, W. (2006). Extracting programs from constructive HOL proofs via IZF set-theoretic semantics, (LNCS 4130, pp. 162–176).

Corfield, D. (1997). Assaying Lakatos's philosophy of mathematics. *Studies in History and Philosophy of Science, 28*(1), 99–121. doi:10.1016/S0039-3681(96)00002-7

Davis, P., & Hersh, R. (1980). *The Mathematical Experience*. Harmondsworth, UK: Penguin.

Donaldson, T., & Cohen, R. (1998). Selecting the next action with constraints. In (LNCS 1418, pp. 220–227). Berlin: Springer.

East Lansing, MI: Philosophy of Science Association.

Feferman, S. (1978). The logic of mathematical discovery vs. the logical structure of mathematics. In P. D. Asquith & I. Hacking, (Ed.), *Proceedings of the 1978 Biennial Meeting of the Philosophy of Science Association*, (vol. 2, pp. 309–327).

Freuder, E., & Wallace, R. (1992). Partial constraint satisfaction. *Artificial Intelligence*, (58): 21–70. doi:10.1016/0004-3702(92)90004-H

Frisch, A., Miguel, I., & Walsh, T. (2002). CGRASS: A system for transforming constraint satisfaction problems. In *Proceedings of the Joint Workshop of the ERCIM Working Group on Constraints and the CologNet area on Constraint and Logic Programming on Constraint Solving and Constraint Logic Programming* (LNAI 2627, pp. 15–30).

Gent, I., Rendl, A., Miguel, I., & Jefferson, C. (2009). Enhancing constraint model instances during tailoring. In *Proceedings of SARA*.

Haggith, M. (1996). *A meta-level argumentation framework for representing and reasoning about disagreement*. PhD thesis, Dept. of Artificial Intelligence, University of Edinburgh.

Hayes-Roth, F. (1983). Using proofs and refutations to learn from experience. In R. S. Michalski J. G. Carbonell, & T. M. Mitchell, (Ed.), Machine Learning: An Artificial Intelligence Approach, (pp. 221–240). Palo Alto, CA: Tioga Publishing Company.

Kitcher, P. (1983). *The Nature of Mathematical Knowledge*. Oxford, UK: Oxford University Press.

Laburthe, F. & the OCRE project team (2000). Choco: implementing a CP kernel. In *Proceedings of the CP'00 Post Conference Workshop on Techniques for Implementing Constraint Programming Systems (TRICS)*, Singapore.

Lakatos, I. (1976). *Proofs and Refutations*. Cambridge, UK: Cambridge University Press.

Lakatos, I. (1978). Cauchy and the continuum: the significance of non-standard analysis for the history and philosophy of mathematics. In Worral, J., & Currie, C. (Eds.), *Mathematics, science and epistemology* (pp. 43–60). Cambridge, UK: Cambridge University Press. doi:10.1017/CBO9780511624926

Lakoff, G. & Nuñez, R. (2001). *Where Mathematics Comes From: How the Embodied Mind Brings Mathematics into Being*. New York: Basic Books Inc.

Leuschel, M., & Butler, M. (2008). ProB: an Automated Analysis Toolset for the B Method. *Journal Software Tools for Technology Transfer, 10*(2), 185–203. doi:10.1007/s10009-007-0063-9

McCasland, R., & Bundy, A. (2006). MATHsAiD: a mathematical theorem discovery tool. In SYNASC'06, (pp. 17–22). Washington, DC: IEEE Computer Society Press.

McCasland, R., Bundy, A., & Smith, P. (2006). Ascertaining mathematical theorems. In Electronic Notes in Theoretical Computer Science (ENTCS), 151(1), 21–38.

McCune, W. (1994). *Otter 3.0 Reference Manual and Guide*. Technical Report ANL-94/6, Argonne National Laboratory, Argonne, USA.

McCune, W. (2001). *MACE 2.0 Reference Manual and Guide*. Technical Report ANL/MCS-TM-249, Argonne National Laboratory, Argonne, USA.

McNeill, F. & Bundy, A. R. (2007). Dynamic, automatic, first-order ontology repair by diagnosis of failed plan execution. *IJSWIS (International Journal on Semantic Web and Information Systems) special issue on Ontology Matching, 3*(3), 1–35.

Muggleton, S. (1995). Inverse entailment and Progol. *New Generation Computing, 13*, 245–286. doi:10.1007/BF03037227

Pease, A. (2007). *A Computational Model of Lakatos-style Reasoning*.

Pease, A., Colton, S., Smaill, A., & Lee, J. (2004). A model of Lakatos's philosophy of mathematics. In *Proceedings of Computing and Philosophy*. ECAP.

Pease, A., Smaill, A., Colton, S., & Lee, J. (2009). Bridging the gap between ar gumentation theory and the philosophy of mathematics. *Special Issue: Mathematics and Argumentation. Foundations of Science, 14*(1-2), 111–135. doi:10.1007/s10699-008-9150-y

PhD thesis, School of Informatics, University of Edinburgh. Retrieved from http://hdl.handle.net/1842/2113

Polya, G. (1945). *How to solve it*. Princeton, NJ: Princeton University Press.

Polya, G. (1954). Mathematics and plausible reasoning: *Vol. 1. Induction and analogy in mathematics*. Princeton, NJ: Princeton University Press.

Polya, G. (1962). *Mathematical Discovery*. New York: John Wiley and Sons.

Rissland, E. L., & Skalak, D. B. (1991). Cabaret: Statutory interpretation in a hybrid architecture. *International Journal of Man-Machine Studies, 34*, 839–887. doi:10.1016/0020-7373(91)90013-W

Ruttkay, Z. (1994). Fuzzy constraint satisfaction. In *3rd IEEE Int. Conf. on Fuzzy Systems,* (pp. 1263–1268).

Skalak, D. B., & Rissland, E. L. (1991). Argument moves in a rule-guided domain. In *Proceedings of the 3rd International Conference on Artificial Intelligence and Law*, (pp. 1–11). New York: ACM Press.

Snook, C. F., & Butler, M. (2008). UML-B: A plug-in for the Event-B Tool Set. In E. B¨orger, M. Butler, J. P. Bowen, & P. Boca, (Eds.), ABZ 2008, (LNCS 5238, pp. 344). Berlin: Springer.

Tsang, E. (1993). *Foundations of Constraint Satisfaction*. London: Academic Press.

Tymoczko, T. (Ed.). (1998). New directions in the philosophy of mathematics. Princeton, NJ: Prince ton University Press.

Weld, D. (1994). An introduction to least commitment planning. *AI Magazine, 15*(4), 27–61.

Winterstein, D. (2004). *Using Diagrammatic Reasoning for Theorem Proving in a Continuous Domain*. PhD thesis, University of Edinburgh, Edinburgh, UK.

ENDNOTES

[1] The HRL system incorporates HR (Colton, 2002), which is named after mathematicians Godfrey Harold Hardy (1877 - 1947) and Srinivasa Aiyangar Ramanujan (1887 - 1920), and extends it by modelling the ideas of the philosopher Imre Lakatos (1922-1974).

2 The cards to which we refer in this section are Anglo-American playing cards, consisting of thirteen ranks (Ace, 2-10, Jack, Queen and King) of each of the four French suits (diamonds, spades, hearts and clubs).

3 We do not consider here whether a situation s which does not satisfy the preconditions, $-P_T(s)$, would form a supporting example of the conjecture, as dictated by material implication, or merely be considered irrelevant.

4 Note that this process may appear to be the opposite of the traditional way in which mathematics is thought to be done, since games start in the start state, whereby a conjecture is (presumably) first suggested and then a mathematician tries to show that there is a path from the conjecture to the axioms. In this case, our games analogy seems closer to work by (McCasland and Bundy, 2006; McCasland *et al.*, 2006), where every new statement follows on from the axioms or theorems and is necessarily either a lemma or theorem itself (depending on how interesting it's judged to be). However, games are not normally planned one move at a time, and the typical situation is where a player has a goal/subgoal state in mind, can see how some pieces would get there and forms the hypothesis that it is possible to get all pieces to their required position. The player then works top down and bottom up to form a planned path from current to desired board state, a similar way to that in which mathematicians are thought to work.

5 The British decimal fifty pence coin was replaced by a smaller version in 1997.

Section 3
Computer and Information Ethics

Chapter 11
Deconstructive Design as an Approach for Opening Trading Zones

Doris Allhutter
Austrian Academy of Sciences, Austria

Roswitha Hofmann
WU Vienna, Austria

ABSTRACT

This chapter presents a critical approach to software development that implements reflective compe-
tences in software engineering teams. It is grounded within qualitative research on software engineer-
ing and critical design practice and presents conceptual work in progress. Software development is a
socio-technological process of negotiation that requires mediation of different approaches. Research
on the co-construction of society and technology and on the social shaping of technological artefacts
and processes has highlighted social dimensions such as gender and diversity discourses that implicitly
inform development practices. To help design teams implement reflective competences in this area, the
authors introduce 'deconstructive design'—a critical-design approach that uses deconstruction as a tool
to disclose collective processes of meaning construction. For this purpose, the idea of value-sensitive
design is linked to approaches of practice-based, situated and context-sensitive learning and to the
concepts of 'trading zones' and 'boundary objects'.

INTRODUCTION

The rich research tradition on the social shaping of technology (e.g. Bijker & Pinch, 1984; McKenzie & Wajcman, 1999; Nørbjerg & Kraft, 2002) and on the co-construction of society and technology (e.g. Bowker & Star, 1999; Rip, Misa, & Schot, 1995; Suchman, 2007) illustrates software

development as a socio-technological process in various ways. Firstly, it takes place within organisations and therefore system specifications and their implementation are co-determined by the organisational setting in which they are developed (such as organisational structures, engineering cultures of the respective sector, or work practices) (see Dittrich, Rönkkö, Eriksson, Hansson, & Lindeberg, 2008). Secondly, design decisions—although mediated by methods and

DOI: 10.4018/978-1-61692-014-2.ch011

tools of software engineering—represent the outcome of processes of negotiation and meaning construction (e.g. Akrich, 1995; Floyd, Züllighoven, Budde, & Keil-Slawik, 1992); in this sense everyday knowledge and social discourses become operative in the development process as hidden assumptions and belief-systems. The described 'situatedness' of software engineering in organisational and social contexts raises the question of how structures such as in/formal hierarchies and discursive hegemonies reproduced in everyday practices affect development processes and design decisions (see also Suchman, Blomberg, Orr, & Trigg, 1999).

Grounded in qualitative software engineering research and critical design practice this paper presents conceptual work in progress. It suggests a critical approach to software design that sustainably implements reflective competences in software development teams. We build on previous research that resulted in specifying a collective discourse-analytical method for this purpose (Allhutter, Hanappi-Egger, & John, 2007). This method is called mind scripting and allows one to make visible societal discourses and hidden sense-making that unconsciously shapes system design. On the basis of the above mentioned research tradition, we consider software development as a situated, social process of negotiation requiring the mediation of different viewpoints and approaches (such as views of managers, system designers, graphical and sound designers, programmers). Moreover, design decisions are always based on commonly held beliefs on social contexts. Gender discourse serves as a useful example to illustrate how socio-technological practices emerge from cultural processes of negotiation and meaning construction. The preceding research has shown how implicit discourses on gender and other diversity factors such as age, ethnicity or sexuality provide social meaning to seemingly technology-centred design decisions. In this contribution, we elaborate a 'deconstructive design' approach and highlight how mind script-

ing can gain from approaches to practice-based, situated and context-sensitive learning (Lave & Wenger, 1991) and from the concepts of 'trading zones' (Kellogg, Orlikowski, & Yates, 2006) and 'boundary objects' (Star & Griesemer, 1989). 'Deconstructive design' aims at reflecting collective work practices which unconsciously reproduce hegemonic discourses and by doing this narrow the spaces of innovation. The approach encourages the sustainable implementation of reflective practices. Essentially, 'deconstructive design' not only aims at developing value-sensitive software or artefacts that embody cultural critique (Dunne & Raby, 2001) but it goes beyond this objective. It is meant to enable sustainable practice-based learning in two respects: Firstly, by building competences in the reflective process, it paves a way for implementing constant process improvement. Secondly, by building reflective gender and diversity competences, it inspires value-sensitive innovation.

The guiding questions for our theoretical endeavour are: How can qualitative software-engineering research benefit from approaches to situated and context-sensitive learning? How can software design teams and their organizations broaden their scope of professional action by identifying 'boundary objects' and 'trading zones' in their everyday work routines? How can 'deconstructive design' sustainably foster reflective competences of design teams by making negotiable value-related decisions and development practices? To deal with these issues the paper is organised as follows: The following section locates our research within qualitative software-engineering research and briefly outlines the theoretical underpinning of our deconstructivist methodology. On this basis, we explain the need to integrate value-related design with sustainable learning. Proceeding from the introduction of an elaborate approach to practice-based learning, the third section introduces 'deconstructive design' through a step-by-step description. The approach is illustrated with two case studies that demonstrate its objectives and procedures. Finally, the last section discusses the different levels of learning towards which our approach is directed and provides concluding remarks and suggestions for future research.

SOFTWARE ENGINEERING, (UN)LEARNING AND (DE) CONSTRUCTION

In order to account for a conception of software development as socio-technological activity, several scholars have strongly advocated the need for qualitative approaches to software-engineering research (e.g. Dittrich, 2002; Trauth, 2001). When noting the growing body of literature published within diverse research communities, Dittrich, John, Singer, and Tessem (2007, pp. 533-535) mention the following fields that apply qualitative approaches: (1) Publications in *software engineering* mainly investigate the influence of deploying specific development methods on the outcome of the process. While most researchers use qualitative methods merely for generating hypotheses, which then serve to identify quantifiable relationships between methods and outcome, the sub-field of requirements engineering is found to be more responsive to qualitative methods. (2) In contrast, empirical research in *computer supported cooperative work* has a tradition of using qualitative methods, mostly relying on ethnography and ethnomethodologically informed methods. (3) The intervention-oriented *information systems* discourse seeks to initiate process improvement and quantitatively and qualitatively to evaluate the implemented measures. (4) Eventually, as an exception to the mainly traditionally oriented research in *agile development*, the field has some qualitative studies on work practices and team cultures. To this list, we want to add the respectable number of empirical studies on gender inscriptions to technological artefacts (e.g. Oudshoorn, Rommes, & Stienstra, 2004; Sher-

ron, 2000; Zorn, Maaß, Rommes, Schirmer, & Schelhowe, 2007). Theoretically underpinned by feminist research in *science and technology studies*, this body of literature has highly contributed to strengthen the understanding of how social discourses and gendered everyday practice guide design projects and pre-structure use contexts (e.g. Cockburn & Omrod, 1993; Faulkner, 2001; Haraway, 1991/2001; Elovaara & Mörtberg, 2007; Wajcman, 1994; Weber, 2006). Feminist scholars have argued with the genderedness of software artefacts, of key concepts of computing as well as of processes and methods in software design (e.g. Adam, 1998; Crutzen & Gerrissen, 2000).

Even though empirical design research is a growing field, only few approaches combine qualitative research with the improvement of development methods and processes (see, for example, Dittrich et al., 2008). Embarking on this strategy, *critical design* approaches suggest integrating a reflection of work practices as an essential part of systems development. Reflective and value-sensitive approaches such as 'reflective systems development' (Mathiassen, 1998; 2002), 'critical technical practice' (Agre, 1997), 'value-sensitive design' (Friedman, Kahn, & Borning, 2006), and 'reflective design' (Sengers, Boehner, David & Kaye, 2005) intend to encourage innovation or to raise the accountability of designers. In both respects, 'deconstructive design' adheres to this research tradition; methodologically, however, it uses a deconstructivist approach rather than an interpretive one.[1] Based in discourse theory, deconstructivist methodologies focus on the reproduction of power by tracing the performativity of discourses. As Michel Foucault (1971) and Judith Butler (1990) have illustrated, powerful societal discourses, non-discursive practices and the objectification of these discourses and practices knit together and thereby produce and reproduce societal hegemonies and power relations. Deconstruction questions the normativity of discourses and practices by revealing the constructedness of seemingly 'natural' sense-making. It aims at denaturalizing self-evident causalities which implicitly inform meaning constructions; it seeks absences and silenced contradictions that obscure the mechanisms sustaining this implicit knowledge.[2] Regarding socio-technological processes, 'deconstructive design' therefore suggests analysing and reflecting on cooperative work practices that (re-)constitute social meaning, structures and hegemonies. The notion of 'practices' describes established 'ways of doing'.

As Dittrich et al. (2008, p. 236) explain, these are produced and re-produced through the action of those who take part in the practice. In this way, the individual action is visible and understandable for his or her peers as meaningful behaviour with respect to the common frame of reference a common practice provides [...], it provides a base for ad hoc reactions to situational contingencies.

What we are learning from experiences and latently guiding discourses is deeply inscribed in embodied everyday practices and our cultural beliefs and value-systems (Haug, 1999). At the same time, this means that learning as a social practice strongly relies on processes of unlearning of implicit sense-making and of consciously re-negotiating meaning (see Hedberg, 1981). With regard to gender and diversity, such implicit knowledge may, for example, unconsciously rely on societal hegemonies and power relations to incite stereotypical assumptions on gender-specific or culture-specific, user requirements.

Argyris (1993; 2002) has described different levels of learning as learning loops: Single-loop learning refers to 'if-then'-relations and asks whether we are doing things right; while double-loop learning includes questioning the underlying assumed causality and addresses the question of whether we are doing the right things. Triple-loop learning, a concept introduced by Flood and Romm (1996) adds a third loop: to question value-systems and ask 'Is rightness buttressed by mightiness and vice versa?' Flood and Romm's concept does not reduce organisational learning to structural and procedural changes and to in-

cremental changes, for example, in terms of error reduction. It describes the conscious and repeated questioning of learning routines as an important prerequisite for *sustainable* learning. The authors suggest discussing learning structures and strategies for learning (see also Georges, Romme, & van Witteloostuijn, 1999, p. 440). In this spirit, their approach examines learning practices and the conditions under which learning is possible while also considering the underlying structural hierarchies. Therefore, integrating all three levels of learning should initiate power-critical and change-oriented reflection processes in organisations. The notion of 'mightiness' may refer to formal and informal organisational hierarchies and, as we want to add, to hegemonic discourses or practices. Hanappi-Egger (2006) argues that single-loop learning (i.e. providing functionality) and double-loop learning (i.e. providing the adequateness of the specification) are well-established activities in systems development. The third loop (i.e. questioning implicit assumptions and value-systems) is not yet included but is important to prevent the implementation of very specific perspectives. Besides developing the system, sustaining reflection by establishing a meta-level should thus be an integral part of the software-engineering process.[3]

'DECONSTRUCTIVE DESIGN' TRIPLE-LOOP LEARNING AND BEYOND

Making use of the concept of triple-loop learning in the context of 'deconstructive design' puts forward the need to reflect learning processes in terms of structures and discursive patterns of development teams. As mentioned in the previous section, deconstruction also implies the need to initiate unlearning processes in order to allow for a sustainable value-sensitive development (of the team and its designed artefacts) based on adequate agency of the team members. In the context of 'deconstructive design', the triple-loop learning perspective leads to the following questions: Which social assumptions from specific societal discourses do developers access in the design process? Are these assumptions perceived as right because they are legitimated by in/formal hierarchies and by hegemonic value-systems? Which spaces or 'trading zones' are established to negotiate meanings? Which 'boundary objects' do developers share in their work?

An extremely valuable approach in this respect has been provided by Lave and Wenger (1991) whose concept of 'situated learning' uses triple-loop learning to try and guide cooperation across professional boundaries. The authors conceptualise learning as a social process of participation in communities of practice. Communities of practice are groups of people who share a domain of interest. The members of such communities create relationships in order to share information, resources and experiences. Communities of practice are learning networks or thematic groups that are not limited by formal structures or organizational boundaries. They are important for knowledge creation in and between organizations and for the emergence of learning opportunities that are linked to performance. By focussing on such communities, Lave and Wenger conceptualise learning as a social process informed by societal structures and identity constructions that help to identify power structures as an essential factor for learning. From this perspective, gender and diversity relations—within the organization itself and in its discourses—can be highlighted as crucial elements for learning processes and structures, which can—once identified—be negotiated. Lave and Wenger do not only focus on the structures and processes of learning in organizations (see Flood & Romm, 1996) but on its 'situatedness' and therefore on power structures which inform learning on the personal as well as the discursive level. Referring to their work, Bresnen, Goussevskaia, & Swan (2005, p. 39) found that networks of practice (Brown & Duguid, 2001) create their own logic of action. They can support or resist changes of routines, norms and values,

and therefore, power structures. Consequently, the condition of communities of practice and their repertoire of actions must be considered, when it comes to the negotiation of power structures related to—for example, gender and diversity relations.

In order to highlight the connection between situated learning and power structures, we link the concept of communities of practice to the concept of 'trading zones' developed by Kellogg et al. (2006). 'Trading zones' can be seen as real or virtual spaces of negotiation and learning or agreed procedures of exchange, which are more or less intentionally created by organizations and communities of practices. Such 'trading zones' are determined by power structures and must be identified when learning should be fostered in the cross-disciplinary teams commonly used in software design. The authors refer to the concept of 'trading zones' to highlight how teams and communities of practice use certain spaces to coordinate actions and, also, to exchange and to negotiate ideas, terms, norms, meanings, values and performance criteria (Kellogg et al., 2006, p. 39). Focussing on 'trading zones' of development teams is fruitful for our work for two reasons: Firstly, software design requires the cooperation of different professions. Secondly, the concept provides a conceptual framework to understand the structures for cooperation created and used by communities of practice.

Furthermore, the concept of 'boundary objects' introduced by Star and Griesemer (1989) explains how e.g. communities of practice use objects, symbols or language for their cooperative activities. According to Star and Griesemer (1989, p. 46), 'boundary objects' are objects that are both plastic enough to adapt to local needs and constraints of the several parties employing them, yet robust enough to maintain a common identity across sites. They are weakly structured in common use, and become strongly structured in individual-site use.

Such objects may be quality standards, maps, classification systems, databases, shared vocabulary, etc. Communities of practice or teams share

Figure 1. Model of 'deconstructive design'

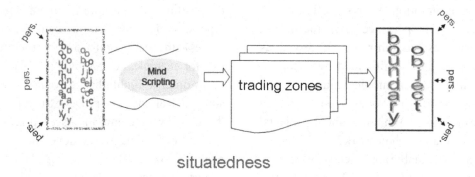

various 'boundary objects' but their members may have different definitions of these objects.

In conducting collective work, people coming from different social worlds frequently have the experience of addressing an object that has a different meaning for each of them. Each social world has partial jurisdiction over the resources represented by that object, and mismatches caused by the overlap become problems of negotiation. (Star & Griesemer, 1989, p. 412)

Both—'trading zones' and 'boundary objects'—are embedded in and informed by societal power structures and hegemonies.

The 'Deconstructive Design' Approach

In order to explain the way in which we use the mentioned concepts, we draw on research results of two case studies conducted with commercial software development teams.[4] The case studies, one of which was based in game development and the second in the field of search-engine technologies, applied the deconstructive method of mind scripting. While accompanying the process of developing a product in each company, the study aimed at investigating how the process and design decisions were influenced by organisational structures as well as social and socio-technical discourses activated by the involved team members. In the company making computer games, special

focus was placed on the interrelation between conceptions of software quality and gender-biases in design decisions; while in the search-engine team, implicit theories and values regarding division of labour were in the spotlight.[5]

To embed mind scripting in a practicable organisational engineering process, we draw on the aforementioned concepts. This move integrates project-related reflection by 'deconstructive design' with the aim of practice-based sustainable learning. The method, as well as the way we use the different learning concepts, will be exhibited in the course of describing the triple-loop learning process. (Figure 1) shows a conceptual sketch making it easier to follow the process and its procedures that will be put forward step by step. The model depicts the methodological concepts guiding the third loop of a learning process, i.e. the sketched detail is part of a cyclical triple-loop learning process.

In brief, a design process is *situated* within specific social and organisational contexts and (temporarily) affiliated team members bring different viewpoints to their common goal. Their partly shared and partly diverging *perspectives* frame their *'boundary objects'*, which may, for instance, be project objectives or concepts and representations guiding the development of an artefact. These perspectives reflect structural positions of team members and socio-technologically constructed meanings, which implicitly inform work practices. In order to disclose established practices and implicit knowledge, *mind scripting* is used to deconstruct collective processes of constructing meaning around these 'boundary objects'. Thereby, Mind Scripting opens *'trading zones'*: Offering a reflective *procedure*, it creates *space* for negotiation and renders negotiable the silenced *issues*. Initially blurred 'boundary objects' to which team members have imputed their views are made explicit; their meaning is re-negotiated and more clearly specified with regard to their value implications. While team members or subgroups of the team still approach the 'boundary object' from their specific perspective, their understanding of their own conceptions and of those of other members are both broadened and specified. Eventually, for all team members, the *negotiated 'boundary object'* still carries diverse but transparent meanings (creating a sort of resonance between the 'boundary object' and team members).

Situatedness and Context-Specificity

As previously mentioned, communities of practice develop agency within a particular societal, economic and organisational framework. Furthermore, their socio-technological work practices are context-specific in that teams apply their established 'ways of doing' in particular projects. Crucial aspects describing the situatedness of the two development teams in question were (1) their professional self-conceptions, including collective cultures linked to their respective sectors as well as individual or subgroup-specific viewpoints of the team members, and, related to this, (2) formal and informal organisation structures.

The first case study was conducted in a small-sized Austrian company developing computer games. The participating team consisted of managers, game designers, graphic designers, sound designers and programmers. As part of the creative industries, the team described its field as being related to fun and self-fulfilment. At the same time, fierce international competition from large companies set the financial and time limits for their creativity. Team members expressed ambivalent views on the importance of 'chaos' and flexible fields of activity in developing their creative potential; simultaneously, they felt a need for more structured working conditions and processes that, however, should not restrict their autonomy. Expressing their image of game development as a creative and non-hierarchical team process, most team members believed that they were granted high autonomy and fair agency within the limits of their functions. However, when it comes to decisionmaking, employees felt that their agency was restricted in terms of deciding on their own authority and that they were over-ruled more often than they could bring in their ideas. Interestingly, the team's wish for a better specification of roles and spheres of competence remained ambivalent: In a sense, it contradicted their belief in autonomy as a prerequisite for creativity and that more clearly defined roles would narrow their scopes of action rather than give them space for self-determination. Within the studied development process, the design of an adventure game, the team sought to significantly improve quality as compared to former productions. This objective, which obviously included a notion of practice-based learning, suggested reflecting on the team's concepts of quality.

Also situated in a small-sized Austrian enterprise, the second case study researched the integration of two subcomponents of the company's refined search-engine technology. The overall project of launching a new version of the company's core product was subdivided into different projects. To integrate a front-end and a back-end component[6], management initiated an internal project. The team, consisting of the CEO, a chief scientist, managers, interface designers and programmers, had a scientific orientation, and strived for innovation and leadership in their field. Based on this positioning, management and employees presented themselves as eager to experiment and to take on new technological challenges. The company's proximity to research and the complexity of the field were underlined by creating the position of a chief scientist who should bring in a holistic view. The team members expressed their professionalism through a high level of abstraction while being interviewed. This collective professional self-conception determined the team's internal perception and assessment of different tasks, which also became structurally manifest in terms of division of labour. According to several team members, the task areas were divided into conceptual tasks, implementation tasks and management. Conceptual tasks were attributed rather high relevance, as they were understood as directly linked to research and innovation. On the contrary, implementation was seen as merely working on tasks that excluded conceptual thinking and active participation in the innovation process. While executive management emphasised that conception and implementation are not distinct areas, several employees voiced their dissatisfaction with what they described as the rather strong division of labour that constricted their area. Even if different opinions have been expressed on this topic, it showed that team members had quite differing information status on their own subproject and, in particular, on the overall project. Coordination difficulties resulting from this situation were part of the problem that eventually led to the failure of the integration project within the planned time frame.

DIFFERING PERSPECTIVES AND 'BOUNDARY OBJECTS'

The example of the search engine development team, showed that the team had implicitly created a 'boundary object'—the prototypical development of a travel information system—in order to accomplish the integration of the front-end and the back-end components of the search engine. The internal project was set up as exemplary ap-

plication to advance the launch of the new version of their core product. In this sense, even though it is a temporary project it is considered a 'boundary object' constituting a common understanding of the core of the team's work content (see also Light & Anderson, 2009). In terms of Star and Griesemer's concept, the project served as an implicit reference point to which team members could connect from different perspectives. However, the implicitness of this procedure did not allow for an explicit specification of project objectives exceeding the idea of its main aim being the integration of two subprojects. In fact, the high level of complexity of the project even made it difficult to establish a common language, which resulted in insufficient communication and uncertain decisions. 'Boundary objects' implicitly serve as communication mechanisms that mostly are unreflected vehicles for commonly held beliefs. In heterogeneous communities of practice, they are essential for mutual knowledge creation and knowledge transfer, thus it is useful to investigate the different representations of the 'boundary object' that team members have constructed for themselves. While diverging viewpoints may hinder common understanding and reaching goals, collectively shared constructions may also silence alternative ways of knowing. Thus, reflecting on individually and collectively shaped constructions of meaning will open negotiations and widen scopes of action.

An example for a collectively shared representation was found in the game-developing team's framing of its 'boundary object' of 'quality'. The team's objective of a major quality leap inspired us to have a closer look at its shared conceptions of 'quality'. Team members explicitly referred to standard concepts of software quality such as error rates, functionality, usability or aesthetics. While the focus of different members clearly was framed by their function within the project, they agreed that they primarily needed to improve the graphical realism of game characters and sets. Implicitly, the team had in mind further aspects that *actually* determine the quality of a game, namely a captivating atmosphere and emotional user-experiences. However, the focus on graphical realism induced them to ignore these user-centred and socio-culturally constructed dimensions in favour of technologically feasible and seemingly objective quality criteria.

In both cases, the 'boundary objects' that represented the teams' key objectives have not been discussed explicitly. Oblivious of the implicit and absent aspects of the 'boundary objects' that informed the projects' work practices, the team obscured their multi-faceted and contradictory character. Referring to Lave and Wenger's power-critical approach, we therefore suggest taking a closer look at the structures and the discursively constructed value-systems that sustain unreflected and established 'ways of doing'. In this spirit, game developers needed to question the discourses that inform their work practices with regard to improving game quality. Whereas the team applied know-how on methods and processes to reach technology-centred quality standards, it was unclear how they decided on design related to the more blurred, atmospheric criteria that they described as subject to artistic talent. Similarly, given the problems arising within the search-engine project, the team was to reflect on the way they made decisions. This enabled the team members to disclose how meaning was given to team culture and structures that have shaped the team's problem-solving strategies.

Opening 'Trading Zones' With Mind Scripting

As previously indicated, reflecting on work practices and their base of implicit knowledge implies disclosing the pre-structuring mechanism of in/formal organisational hierarchies and hegemonic discourses. Clearly, this proposition poses a methodical challenge because such kind of investigative reflexivity demands maintaining a critical distance to one's own practices of constructing meaning. For this purpose, Allhutter and Hanappi-Egger (2006) and Allhutter (forthcoming) suggest the method of mind scripting as a deconstructive tool for software development teams to reflect on their work practices with regard to the reproduction of discursive hegemonies and consequently of societal power structures. This approach focuses on how developers appropriate social structures, everyday experiences and educational and professional backgrounds and on how these collective subjectivation processes translate into inherent professional self-conceptions and work practices that eventually materialise in software artefacts.[7] Since common practices need to be revealed in a process of negotiating meaning within the group of designers, mind scripting is organised as a collective procedure. It enables a team to research its cooperative work practices which are informed by their unconscious constructions of 'boundary objects'. Deconstruction aims at temporarily disclosing an outsider's perspective to the team members and at enquiring the sense-making that permanently re-establishes what has implicitly been taken for granted. Deconstructing 'boundary objects' crucial to situated specification and implementation practices, and investigating how societal discourses implicitly inform seemingly technology-centred concepts and decisions, enables the explicit negotiation of facets that are otherwise silenced. Furthermore, this process helps reveal and question structures, beliefs and value-systems that reproduce dominant viewpoints. Basically, mind scripting works with written texts representing memories that become operative in the actual design process. These so-called mind scripts are understood as narratives that developers use to give meaning to their experiences and practices. The collective deconstruction of the texts and the comparison of their sense-making processes disclose collectively shared meaning constructions.[8]

The Ordinary Mortal User as Surrogate Informant

Given the problems that occurred in the case of the search-engine development, a subject was chosen for mind scripting that should reflect the team's work practices with regard to its communication strategies and problem-solving capacities. The topic of 'When they took a design-decision that was important to her/him' induced writers to narrate how an important or difficult decision has been taken regarding the travel information system to be developed. As mentioned earlier, the team's 'boundary object' was primarily defined by its function as prototypical application; therefore, it was expedient to reflect on who decided on the basis of which information or authority or on the basis of which implicit assumptions. When deconstructing the mind scripts, the team found different representations of project objectives. While management emphasised the system's purpose of serving as demonstration object for marketing, texts of the subgroups developing the front-end or the back-end did not even refer to it as a separate project. The two subgroups had developed very specific perspectives on the common goal of integrating the two components and even if these approaches were not mutually exclusive the different views prevented them from developing a shared understanding and a common language. In the mind scripts, they even used different group-internal names for the travel information system and it showed that nobody seemed to have been explicitly in charge of the interoperable interface of the overall system architecture. In the deconstruction process, this led participants to frame the text analysis in terms of who described himself/herself as in charge of specific tasks and taking responsibility. Different views on their implicit agreements concerning division of labour revealed opposing expectations and resulted in accusations. This particular example sheds light on the influence of contradicting interests, hierarchies and personal antagonism. The text-based

method of mind scripting abstracts from persons and supported a factual treatment of problems as structurally induced difficulties resulting from an unproductive separation of conceptual design and implementation tasks. As affirmed by the deconstruction process, these areas were valued differently within the team; thus, the separation established an informal hierarchy that led to unspoken task sharing and not deliberately negotiated distribution of competencies and responsibilities. These implicit dynamics caused the team members' professional self-conceptions to strongly centre on issues of autonomy and heteronomy. Whereas team members generally thought the company was quite clearly structured, the question of 'who took responsibility' kept coming up during the deconstruction. The process strikingly revealed that the resulting dissatisfaction and ambiguity led to insufficient communication and information deficits. In this respect, mind scripting has hinted at one of the sources of their failure. A further quite peculiar aspect in the mind scripts was the total absence of use contexts for the travel information system. A specification of the target groups seemed dispensable because actual use of the search engine was never part of any of the team members' objectives. In this context, one of the mind scripts brought up an interesting strategy to deal with this situation. As the team worked hard to communicate about and to specify its abstract conceptions, it introduced the role of an 'ordinary mortal user' taken over by a team member in operative management. In contrast to the developers' textual self-presentations as situated experts, the 'ordinary mortal user' was to be technology-illiterate and neutral.[9] The underlying assumption was that if they can make clear their complex assignment to this user, they themselves could accomplish the tasks and develop a mutually understandable language. Moreover, an outsider's perspective would bring in a neutral viewpoint from which it is possible to integrate the different perspectives. Deconstructing the practice of introducing the 'user as informant', the team became aware that its ignorance of use contexts and its failure to come up with a user-centred specification entailed difficulties in translating abstract concepts to tangible design decisions. Indeed, on an intuitive basis, the team had figured out that user-representations serve as important information. Ignoring use contexts obviously caused them problems and also obscured hidden assumptions about future users, which implicitly become operative when breaking down the high level of abstraction to a practical level.[10]

Of Demanding Experts and Average Users

Proceeding from the multi-layered 'boundary object' of 'game quality' and its unspecified component of atmospheric and emotional dimensions, the game development team agreed to write texts entitled, 'When s/he tried out a computer game last time'. While this subject did not impose the problem of 'quality' on the team members, it was chosen to incite a more intuitive and phenomenological approach to their experiences of trying out a computer game. Generally organised around the themes of anticipation and disappointment, the mind scripts thus contained a variety of quality claims to games. As the deconstruction showed, two linguistically and discursively different constructed notions of game quality occurred in the texts: On the one hand, writers demonstrated their professional assessment by referring to criteria such as graphical realism or interaction characteristics of the respective game. These aspects were constructed as checklists that specify standard technology-centred criteria of software quality that can be operationalised and assessed objectively. At the same time, referring to these criteria constructed the expert status of the different team members because each member focused on criteria central to her/his particular area. On the other hand, the writers implicitly evoked conceptions of quality that allude to their preferences on the game's atmospheric and emotional sensations.

While the mind scripts served as a basis for approaching unfiltered and hidden aspects of quality conceptions, most importantly, it is the process of negotiating different perspectives that sheds light on aspects that remain obscured in their explicit understanding. Whereas the participants discussed the first category of quality criteria as resulting from technical-creative solutions and technological competencies, the second category rather was seen as a result of the designers' subjective preferences than of operationalisable standards. While the team had no approaches available on how these implicitly subjectified dimensions could be implemented, team members eventually agreed that these were actually criteria that objectively contributed to the quality of a game. The central construction mechanisms of the team's implicit conception of quality added various hidden assumptions to a collective process of meaning construction, which clearly became operative in their development practices: Excluding subjectified but essential aspects of quality from the team's explicit, technology-centred conception of quality obscured how socio-culturally constructed design decisions indeed played an important role. Even objectified criteria succumb to socio-technological processes of negotiation. Reproducing the hierarchical dichotomy between the technological and the social hindered a productive negotiation on how to break down abstract concepts into specific design decisions. Because the team's central practice for raising game quality was to improve graphical realism, it makes sense, for example, to ask how graphical realism can be implemented in order to contribute to the game's atmosphere or to user experiences. 'Atmosphere' and 'user experiences' also are concepts specified by, for example, game genres and the developers' assumptions on future users. Thus, a further deconstruction of how these conceptions are constructed and become operative in project-specific design decisions can provide a means to operationalise or at least to structure negotiations on the contents of 'atmosphere' and 'user experience'. We can ask which gendered assumptions on future users are inscribed to these concepts and in which way does unconscious stereotyping restrict creativity with regard to their implementation? In this respect, the mind scripting showed that members of the gaming team manifested their expert status by constructing an oppositional image of the 'average' user. The 'average' user implicitly was constructed as being male and having rather mainstream entertainment preferences, which eventually prevented the team from using its full creative potential. This construction was nourished by a combination of conventional beliefs and discourses devaluing the 'average' user as well as special user groups. (For example, they assumed that women do not play computer games, and if they do, then the game must be easy and have a horse.)

The examples of this case study show that the method of mind scripting provided a means for the team to reveal implicit quality conceptions and to discuss how design decisions are made on these subjectified criteria. The deconstructive approach supported understanding how established hierarchical dichotomies such as 'objective/technological' versus 'subjective/social' and 'designers' versus 'users' have framed their perspectives in the context of their ongoing project. Furthermore, the team made visible the mechanism of how hegemonic discourses and value-systems have silently induced them to construct a representation of the 'average' user, and that this representation informs their work practices with regard to the intended advance in quality.

Redefining 'Boundary Objects'

By using mind scripting for disclosing hidden causalities and contradictions in processes of meaning construction, designers can reveal the consequences of unconsciously narrowing down the 'boundary objects' fundamental to their work practices. Implicit power structures and discursive hegemonies are conducive to silently constructing 'boundary objects' as uncontradictory and uncontradicted.

In the case of the search-engine development, the concept of boundary objects provides an adequate framing to show the different perspectives from which team members have approached their common goal. While the multi-layeredness of these perspectives can persist, mind scripting showed what hindered the development of a shared core. Firstly, the informal hierarchy triggered by different positions within the structural separation of conceptual design and implementation led to problems and ambiguities in making decisions. In the mind scripts, these ambiguities left their traces in terms of previously mentioned problem-solving strategies; in the deconstruction process, a 'trading zone' was opened to negotiate the implications of informal hierarchies. A second barrier to defining a shared core of the 'boundary object' was the absence of project objectives with regard to future use contexts. The team had unconsciously accepted the hegemonic discourse that separates the spheres of design and use (Crutzen & Kotkamp, 2006; see also Oudshoorsn & Pinch, 2003). It became visible in their oppositional construction of expert designers versus technology-illiterate users, which eventually induced the team to discuss the consequences of ignoring user-centred objectives and design approaches.

In contrast to the game-developing team's point of departure, the explicitly negotiated and redefined 'boundary object' of 'quality' eventually included a user-centred perspective and took account of the previously silenced social dimensions. It made transparent that 'game quality' is not merely a task to be accomplished by graphical designers and animators. Adding 'atmosphere' and 'user-experience', offered access to the 'boundary object' from the project's various professional perspectives. Mind scripting not only has disclosed the designers' constructions of quality and of different quality criteria but also raised the question of for whose subjective quality requirements the team is developing. Thus, it hinted at the interrelation between quality conceptions and unconscious assumptions about future users and their preferences. Taking this example further, during the translation from abstract to concrete, the questioning of the beliefs and values underlying 'atmosphere' and 'user-experience' allows access to their deeper meaning.

The opening of 'trading zones'—that means the establishment and explicit negotiation of 'boundary objects'—offers a way to integrate heterogeneous viewpoints and implicitly shared perspectives. The case studies provide examples of how obscured components of the 'boundary objects' have become part of the teams' explicit understanding of important reference points for their cooperative work practices. Introducing a procedure for a negotiation of 'boundary objects' makes them a useful resource that enables better communication and diversity within teams. Critical reflection on one's own work practices enlarges capacities for action that have been restricted by the silent reproduction of dominant structures and discourses. Space for value-based innovation can be opened by questioning both established work practices and, also, the beliefs and value-systems on which they are based.

CONCLUSION AND FUTURE RESEARCH

Analysing the function that societal discourses and power structures have in guiding development processes has an impact in a threefold way: Firstly, in the short run, it is a tool to disclose 'boundary objects' and consciously decide on value-related assumptions that otherwise unknowingly become operative in development practices. Secondly, in the medium term, gaining knowledge about the discursive constructedness of existing hegemonies and experiencing how this knowledge changes collective work practices widens capacities for action. And thirdly, in the long run, value-systems as the basis of commonly held beliefs may be challenged and reoccupied. 'Deconstructive design' initiates a process of negotiating who (in/formal hierarchies) and what (discursive hegemonies)

is given normative power on the basis of which values.

The aim of this paper was to introduce a conceptual framework integrating a critical design approach enabling project-related reflection with the objective of introducing a sustainable practice-based learning process in development teams. As has been demonstrated, the concepts of 'boundary objects' and 'trading zones' are useful resources for establishing a method-supported process that integrates deconstruction as a reflective practice of negotiation. Mind scripting provides an analytic and interventionist approach to question work practices and design decisions by disclosing the social dimensions inherent to them. It offers a procedure for development teams to open 'trading zones', i.e. to establish a space for negotiation and to identify layers of 'boundary objects' that have been silenced and are worth negotiating consciously.

The method of mind scripting has been used in cooperation with two commercial development teams and has generated valuable results in analytical terms. While the collectively elaborated results were fed back to the teams, it was not within the scope of the case studies to investigate the impacts of this intervention. As mentioned in the introduction, this contribution presents a conceptual work in progress. In order to advance the described method-supported process and to provide for the intended sustainability of the learning process, we will further elaborate 'deconstructive design' in cooperation with development teams. On the one hand, the practice-based cooperation ensures the learnability and practicability of the procedure; on the other hand, researchers and developers can mutually learn from each other's expertise and viewpoints.

REFERENCES

Adam, A. (1998). *Artificial Knowing: Gender and the Thinking Machine*. New York: Routlegde.

Agre, P. E. (1997). *Computation and Human Experience*. Cambridge, UK: Cambridge University Press. doi:10.1017/CBO9780511571169

Akrich, M. (1995). User Representations: Practices, Methods and Sociology . In Rip, A., Misa, T. J., & Schot, J. (Eds.), *Managing Technology in Society. The Approach of Constructive Technology Assessment* (pp. 167–184). London: Pinter Publishers.

Allhutter, D. (Forthcoming). Mind Scripting. A Deconstructive Method In Software Development. *Science, Technology & Human Values*.

Allhutter, D., & Hanappi-Egger, E. (2006). The Hidden Social Dimensions of Technologically Centred Quality Standards: Triple-Loop Learning as Process Centred Quality Approach . In Dawson, R., Georgiadou, E., Linecar, P., Ross, M., & Staples, G. (Eds.), *Perspectives in Software Quality* (pp. 179–195). London: British Computer Society.

Allhutter, D., Hanappi-Egger, E., & John, S. (2007). *Gendered Software Design. Zur Sichtbarmachung der Gender Scripts in technologischen Artefakten*. Vienna, Austria: WU Vienna, Gender and Diversity in Organizations.

Argyris, C. (1993). *Knowledge for Action. A Guide to Overcoming Barriers to Organizational Change*. San Francisco: Jossey-Bass Wiley.

Argyris, C. (2002). Double loop learning, teaching, and research. *Academy of Management Learning & Education, 2*(2), 206–218.

Bijker, W. E., & Pinch, T. J. (1984). The Social Construction of Facts and Artifacts: Or How the Sociology of Science and the Sociology of Technology Might Benefit of Each Other . In Bijker, W. E., Hughes, T. P., & Pinch, T. J. (Eds.), *The Social Construction of Technological Systems* (pp. 17–50). Cambridge, MA: MIT Press.

Bowker, G. C., & Star, S. L. (1999). *Sorting Things Out. Classification and its Consequences*. Cambridge, MA: MIT Press.

Bresnen, M., Goussevskaia, A., & Swan, J. (2005). Organizational Routines, Situated Learning and Processes of Change in Project-based Organizations. *Project Management Journal, 3*(3), 27–41.

Brown, J. S., & Duguid, P. (2001). Knowledge and Organization: A social-practice perspective. *Organization Science, 12*(2), 198–213. doi:10.1287/orsc.12.2.198.10116

Butler, J. (1990). *Gender trouble. Feminism and Subversion of Identity*. New York: Routledge.

Cockburn, C., & Omrod, S. (1993). *Gender & Technology in the Making*. London: Sage.

Crutzen, C., & Gerrissen, J. F. (2000). Doubting the Object World . In Balka, E., & Smith, R. (Eds.), *Women, Work and Computerization: Charting a Course to the Future* (pp. 127–136). Boston: Kluwer Academic Press.

Crutzen, C. K. M., & Kotkamp, E. (2006). Questioning Gender through Deconstruction and Doubt . In Trauth, E. M. (Ed.), *Encyclopaedia of Gender and Information Technology* (pp. 1041–1047). Hershey, PA: Idea Group Publishing.

Dittrich, Y. (2002). Doing Empirical Research in Software Engineering: Finding a Path between Understanding, Intervention, and Software Development . In Dittrich, Y., Floyd, C., & Klischewski, R. (Eds.), *Social thinking—Software practice* (pp. 243–261). Cambridge, MA: MIT Press.

Dittrich, Y., John, M., Singer, J., & Tessem, B. (2007). Editorial for the special issue on Qualitative Software Engineering Research. *Information and Software Technology, 49*(6), 531–539. doi:10.1016/j.infsof.2007.02.009

Dittrich, Y., Rönkkö, K., Eriksson, J., Hansson, C., & Lindeberg, O. (2008). Cooperative method development. Combining qualitative empirical research with method, technique and process improvement. *Empirical Software Engineering, 13*(3), 231–260. doi:10.1007/s10664-007-9057-1

Dunne, A., & Raby, F. (2001). *Design Noir: The Secret Life of Electronic Objects*. Basel, Switzerland: Birkhauser.

Elovaara, P., & Mörtberg, C. (2007). Design of Digital Democracies—performance of citizenship, gender and IT. *Information Communication and Society, 10*, 404–423. doi:10.1080/13691180701410091

Faulkner, W. (2001). The Technology Question in Feminism. A view from feminist technology studies. *Women's Studies International Forum, 24*, 79–95. doi:10.1016/S0277-5395(00)00166-7

Flood, R., & Romm, N. (1996). *Diversity Management. Triple Loop Learning*. Chichester, UK: John Wiley and Sons.

Floyd, C., Züllighoven, H., Budde, R., & Keil-Slawik, R. (Eds.). (1992). *Software Development and Reality Construction*. Heidelberg, Germany: Springer.

Foucault, M. (1971). *L'archéologie du savoir*. Paris: Gallimard.

Friedman, B., Kahn, P. H., & Borning, A. (2006). Value Sensitive Design and information systems . In Zhang, P., & Galletta, D. (Eds.), *Human-computer interaction in management information systems: Foundation* (pp. 348–372). New York: AMIS.

Georges, A., Romme, R., & van Witteloostuijn, A. (1999). Circular organizing and triple loop learning. *Journal of Organizational Change Management, 12*(5), 439–453. doi:10.1108/09534819910289110

Hanappi-Egger, E. (2006). Gender and Software Engineering . In Trauth, E. M. (Ed.), *Encyclopaedia of Gender and Information Technology* (pp. 453–459). Hershey, PA: Idea Group Publishing.

Haraway, D. (2001). A Cyborg Manifesto. Science, technology and socialist-feminism in the late twentieth century . In Bell, D., & Kennedy, B. M. (Eds.), *The Cybercultures Reader* (pp. 291–324). London: Routledge. (Original work published 1991)

Haug, F. (1999). Erinnerungsarbeit—ein Leitfaden zur Methode . In Haug, F. (Ed.), *Vorlesungen zur Einführung in die Erinnerungsarbeit* (pp. 199–227). Berlin: Argument.

Hedberg, B. (1981). How organizations learn and unlearn. In P.C. Nystrom & W. H. Starbuck (Eds.), Handbook of Organizational Design, (Vol. 1, pp. 3-27). New York: Oxford University Press.

Kellogg, K. C., Orlikowski, W. J., & Yates, J. (2006). Life in the Trading Zone: Structuring Coordination Across Boundaries in Postbureaucratic Organizations. *Organization Science, 17*(1), 22–44. doi:10.1287/orsc.1050.0157

Lave, J., & Wenger, E. (1991). *Situated Learning. Legitimate Peripheral Participation*. Cambridge, UK: Cambridge University Press.

Light, A., & Anderson, T. D. (2009). Research Project as Boundary Object: negotiating the conceptual design of a tool for International Development. In I. Wagner, H. Tellioglu, E. Balka, C. Simone, & L. Ciolfi (Eds.), *Proceedings of the 11th European Conference on Computer Supported Cooperative Work* (pp. 21-41). Berlin: Springer.

Mathiassen, L. (1998). *Reflective Systems Development*. Aalborg, Denmark: Institute for Electronic Systems, Department of Computer Science. Retrieved August 5, 2009, from http://www.mathiassen.eci.gsu.edu/rsd.html

Mathiassen, L. (2002). Collaborative practice research. *Information Technology & People*, *15*(4), 321–345. doi:10.1108/09593840210453115

McKenzie, D., & Wajcman, J. (1999). *The Social Shaping of Technology* (2nd ed.). Buckingham, UK: Open University press.

Nørbjerg, J., & Kraft, P. (2002). Software Practice Is Social Practice . In Dittrich, Y., Floyd, C., & Klischewski, R. (Eds.), *Social Thinking—Software Practice* (pp. 205–222). Cambridge, MA: MIT Press.

Oudshoorn, N., & Pinch, T. (Eds.). (2003). *How Users Matter: The Co-Construction of Users and Technology*. Cambridge, MA: MIT Press.

Oudshoorn, N., Rommes, E., & Stienstra, M. (2004). Configuring the User as Everybody: Gender and Design Cultures in Information and Communication Technologies. *Science, Technology & Human Values*, *29*(1), 30–63. doi:10.1177/0162243903259190

Rip, A., Misa, T., & Schot, J. (Eds.). (1995). *Managing Technology in Society. The Approach of Constructive Technology Assessment*. New York: Pinter.

Sengers, P., Boehner, K., David, S., & Kaye, J. (2005). Reflective Design. *Proceedings of the 4th Decennial Conference on Critical Computing: Between Sense and Sensibility* (pp. 49-58). New York: ACM Press.

Sherron, C. (2000). Constructing Common Sense . In Balka, E., & Smith, R. (Eds.), *Women, Work and Computerization. Charting a Course to the Future* (pp. 111–118). Boston: Kluwer.

Star, S. L., & Griesemer, J. R. (1989). Institutional Ecology, 'Translations' and Boundary Objects: Amateurs and Professionals in Berkeley's Museum of Vertebrate Zoology, 1907-39. *Social Studies of Science*, *19*(4), 387–420. doi:10.1177/030631289019003001

Suchman, L. (2007). *Human-Machine Reconfigurations. Plans and Situated Action* (2nd ed.). Cambridge, UK: Cambridge University Press.

Suchman, L., Blomberg, J., Orr, J. E., & Trigg, R. (1999). Reconstructing Technologies as Social Practice. *The American Behavioral Scientist*, *43*(3), 392–408. doi:10.1177/00027649921955335

Trauth, E. M. (2001). *Qualitative Research in IS: Issues and Trends*. Hershey, PA: IGI Global.

Wajcman, J. (2004). *TechnoFeminism*. Cambridge, UK: Polity Press.

Weber, J. (2006). From Science and Technology to Feminist Technoscience . In Davis, K., Evans, M., & Lorber, J. (Eds.), *Handbook of Gender and Women's Studies* (pp. 397–414). London: Sage.

Zorn, I., Maaß, S., Rommes, E., Schirmer, C., & Schelhowe, H. (Eds.). (2007). Gender Designs IT: Construction and Deconstruction of Information Society Technology. Wiesbaden, Germany: VS.

KEY TERMS AND DEFINITIONS

Boundary Objects: is a concept introduced by Star and Griesemer (1989) referring to objects that serve as interface between people. 'Boundary objects' are any entity shared by people (for example, communities of practice) but defined or used differently by each of them. 'Boundary objects' are means for communication between different professions or social worlds.

Communities of Practice: A group of people who share a concern or a passion for a certain domain and who engage in a more or less regularly interactive process of collective learning, is called a community of practice (Lave & Wenger, 1991). Three elements are crucial for a community of practice: a shared domain, joint activities and, shared resources.

Deconstruction: Based in discourse theory, deconstructivist methodologies focus on the reproduction of power by tracing the performativity of discourses (Foucault 1971; Butler 1990). Deconstruction questions the normativity of discourses and practices by revealing the constructedness of seemingly 'natural' sense-making. It aims at denaturalising self-evident causalities that implicitly inform meaning constructions; it seeks absences and silenced contradictions that obscure the mechanisms sustaining societal hegemonies and power relations.

Deconstructive Design: is an interventionist design approach that integrates project-related reflection with the aim of practice-based sustainable learning. Tying in with the tradition of reflective and value-sensitive critical design approaches, it suggests deconstruction (see mind scripting) as a means to open 'trading zones' for explicitly (re-) negotiating the 'boundary objects' crucial to the cooperative work practices of a development team. 'Deconstructive design' aims at developing value-sensitive software by building reflective process competences. Questioning discursive hegemonies and societal power relations is to inspire innovation by disclosing narrowed capacities for action.

Mind Scripting: is a discourse-analytical and linguistic method for collectively deconstructing and negotiating unconscious meaning constructions that inform processes and design decisions of software development teams (see Allhutter, forthcoming). Applied as critical design practice, it is both a research method and a tool for practitioners to reflect on their work practices with regard to the reproduction of discursive hegemonies and societal power structures. The focus is on how developers appropriate social structures and everyday experiences, educational and professional backgrounds and on how these collective subjectivation processes translate into inherent professional self-conceptions and work practices, which eventually materialise in software artefacts.

Situated Learning: is a concept introduced by Lave and Wenger (1991) that does not only focus on the acquisition of knowledge and, therefore,

it goes beyond cognitive approaches to learning. With their concept, Lave and Wenger place learning in a social context and connect it to processes of co-participation in 'communities of practice'. In this context, learning is a process of social participation and identity building.

Trading Zones: According to Kellogg, Orlikowski and Yates (2006) 'trading zones' are coordination structures, procedures, negotiable issues and, resources (such as time) for cross-boundary work between different practitioners. Such coordination structures are ongoing accomplishments of the actors involved and not a static characteristic of an organization. Therefore, 'trading zones' are always in the making (see Kellogg et al., 2006, p. 39).

ENDNOTES

[1] For a more detailed account of methodological differences, see Allhutter (forthcoming).

[2] While cognitive approaches to knowledge and learning have used the notions of 'implicit knowledge' or 'tacit knowledge' to denote a (hidden) inventory of knowledge or expertise, a discourse-theoretical approach implies the performativity of discourses. In this spirit, our use of the term 'implicit knowledge' refers to the permanent reappropriation of discourses in processes of subjectivation.

[3] For a graphical model and a more detailed description of triple-loop learning as evolutionary development approach, see Allhutter and Hanappi-Egger (2006).

[4] The case studies are part of the research project 'Gendered Software Design' (2005–2007) which has been conducted by Allhutter, Hanappi-Egger and John and financed by the Austrian Ministry of Education, Science and Culture. The presented results were generated with semi-structured interviews and mind scripting.

5   The extra benefits of this focus, so to speak, was that the results gained in the cooperation with the teams were not only meant to reflect work practices and inform practice-based development but served to rethink methods, underlying concepts and theories of applied informatics (e.g. 'quality standards').

6   The front-end is the part of a system that interacts directly with the user, and the back-end comprises the components that process the output from the front-end. This separation of software systems is an abstraction that serves to keep separated the different parts of the system.

7   Mind scripting is based on 'memory work' (see Haug, 1999), a socio-scientific method for investigating how individuals and collectives construct themselves into existing social relations and how they reproduce these through their everyday theories and sense-making. For a detailed description of mind scripting as well as of its theoretical and methodological background, see Allhutter (forthcoming).

8   In brief, mind scripting consists of the following steps: Participants identify a boundary object crucial to the actual design process or latently present in organisational culture or work practices of the team. They agree on a subject that, for example, relates the boundary object to a particular design phase, project aims, important or unclear design decisions, or any context-specific and actual issue. All participants write a short text that records actual memories of a situation referring to the agreed upon topic, for example, memories of making a design decision. Then begins the actual mind scripting process—the deconstruction and comparison of texts. Through collective deconstructing all mind scripts, participants search for representations of subjects, activities, emotions, motivations, relations and communication occurring in the texts. Deconstructing a text means taking it apart, separating content and formal aspects under the focus of how the author constructs himself/herself in the described situation, how work practices are given meaning and how concepts relating to the respective development context (e.g., quality issues) are constructed. The deconstruction sessions are recorded in writing (or on tape) and eventually analysed comparatively according to the reading negotiated between participants.

9   This kind of collective identity building clearly has implications for the negotiation of 'boundary objects'.

10 For an analysis of the gendered dimensions of user-representations, see Allhutter (forthcoming).

Chapter 12
Scientific Authorship and E-Commons

Luc Schneider
Institut Jean Nicod (CNRS, EHESS, ENS), Paris, France & Institute for Formal Ontology and Medical Information Science, Saarbrücken, Germany

ABSTRACT

This contribution tries to assess how the Web is changing the ways in which scientific knowledge is produced, distributed and evaluated, in particular how it is transforming the conventional conception of scientific authorship. After having properly introduced the notions of copyright, public domain and (e-)commons, the author will critically assess James Boyle's (2003, 2008) thesis that copyright and scientific (e-) commons are antagonistic, but the author will mostly agree with the related claim by Stevan Harnad (2001a,b, 2008) that copyright has become an obstacle to the accessibility of scientific works. He will even go further and argue that Open Access schemes not only solve the problem of the availability of scientific literature, but may also help to tackle the uncontrolled multiplication of scientific publications, since these publishing schemes are based on free public licenses allowing for (acknowledged) re-use of texts. However, the scientific community does not seem to be prepared yet to move towards an Open Source model of authorship, probably due to concerns related to attributing credit and responsability for the expressed hypotheses and results. Some strategies and tools that may encourage a change of academic mentality in favour of a conception of scientific authorship modelled on the Open Source paradigm are discussed.

INTRODUCTION

In this contribution, I try to gauge the impact of the Web on the production and distribution of scientific knowledge, especially on the notion of scientific authorship. In particular I will venture some extrapolations as to a more open, i.e. collaborative, form of scientific authorship modelled on the Open Source paradigm in software engineering.

The background section sets the stage by providing a conceptual analysis of the intertwined notions of copyright, public domain and what

DOI: 10.4018/978-1-61692-014-2.ch012

one may call, after Lessig (2001, 2002) and Boyle (2003, 2008), the "electronic commons" or "e-commons", which covers both the public domain and resources that are distributed under free public licenses.

The main section of this chapter assays two recent reflections as to the need for redefining the scope of intellectual property in the digital era for the sake of protecting the freedom of scientific research. The one pertains to scientific endeavour as a whole, while the other focuses on scientific authorship. First, I will assess James Boyle's (2003, 2008) criticism of what he calls the "second enclosure movement", a general tendency in current national and international legislations to carve up the public domain, and I will qualify his worry that this evolution may stifle intellectual and scientific creativity by reducing the "commons" of freely available research results and data.

Second, I will discuss Stevan Harnad's (2001a,b, 2009) defense of Open Access scientific literature. Harnad pleads for keeping apart protection from theft of ideas (plagiarism) and protection from theft of text (piracy). He argues that only the former is relevant for scientific authorship that aims for impact and not for income. I will take up this line of thought and ask whether one can go further and apply the Open Source model to scientific writing. However, it seems that there are considerable obstacles to this move, not so much on the side of copyright, since sufficiently liberal free public licenses are available, than on the side of scientists themselves. In the absence of empirical studies, one can only venture some plausible hypotheses as to reasons for the general resistance of academic mentality to an open form of authorship.

The section on Future Issues proposes some strategies and tools that may overcome academic reticence regarding an open and collaborative form of authorship. In particular I will emphasize the need to refine the notion of contributing to a scientific publication and to adopt a modular conception of scientific works. As an example of a current initiative to integrate these strategies and tools I introduce the European project „Liquid Publications".

BACKGROUND: COPYRIGHT, PUBLIC DOMAIN AND (E-)COMMONS

Copyright

Copyright is a kind of intellectual property, the other two categories being patents and trademarks (Koepsell, 2000). The rationale of patent law is to protect the exclusive rights as to the exploitation or distribution of inventions, i.e. new products, devices and processes, or improvements thereof, with the explicit exclusion of ideas and methods of operation, e.g. the buttons on a radio (ibid.). Trademark protection aims at the exclusive right to use a certain product name (ibid). The scope of copyright is original expressions (ibid.).

More precisely, the purpose of copyright is to grant the author of an original work exclusive rights for a limited time period with respect to the publication, distribution and adaptation of that work. After that period time the work enters the public domain (Berry & McCallion, 2001). However, most legislations allow for "fair" exceptions to the author's exclusive rights, and concede certain rights to the public, such as to make copies for private use or to quote from published works, under the condition to give credit to their authors.

Copyright applies to the expression of any idea or piece of information that is sufficiently original. In other words, copyright does not concern ideas or bits of information, but primarily the manner in which they are expressed (Koepsell, 2000). As such, a wide range of creative, intellectual, or artistic forms are covered, including news paper articles, poems, scientific papers, academic theses, plays, novels, personal letters, but also movies, dances, musical compositions, recordings, paintings, drawings, sculptures, photographs, software, radio and television broadcasts.

A detailed account of the evolution of copyright is beyond the scope of this chapter, so some indications have to suffice. Copyright law has its origin in the monopolies that appeared with the development of presses: publishers and bookbinders were organized in guilds and protected their primacy in information dissemination by keeping their manufacture methods secret (Koepsell, 2000; Chartier, 1987). The Statute of Anne (1710) in Britain can be regarded as the first copyright act; it established both the author of a work and its publisher as owners of the right to copy that work for a period of time of 21 years (Koepsell, 2000; Geller, 2003). In 1886, on the initiative of Association Litteraire et Artistique Internationale (AIAI) and its president, the French poet and novelist Victor Hugo, the Berne Convention first established a form of international recognition of copyrights. It has been influenced by the French legal concept of "droit d'auteur" that attributes the exclusive ownership of a work to its author. In the more than 160 countries currently adhering to the Berne Convention, creative works are copyrighted as soon as they have physically taken form, unless the author explicitly abandons any claim on them, or until the copyright expires and the work falls into the public domain (Geller, 2003). Since the regulations of the Berne Convention have been part of the WTO's 1995 TRIPS agreement, their validity has been practically world-wide (ibid.).

Public Domain

The notion of public domain stems from the French "domaine public" which made its way into international and national law through the Berne Convention (Litman, 1990; Boyle, 2003). David Lange (1981) was the first to raise the issue of the necessity to delimit and defend the public domain. Lange (1981) argues that the very imprecision of the notion of intellectual property is one of the major reasons for its unshackled expansion; the remedy is to acknowledge a no-man's land at the confines of intellectual property (Lange,1981).

However, Lange does not provide a further clarification of the concept of public domain, nor what individual rights exist within it (Boyle, 2003).

Lange's article triggered a whole literature on the topic of public domain. Lindberg and Patterson (1991), for instance, proposed to view copyright as a set of temporary and constrained privileges that feeds the public domain with works as their copyrights expire. Jessica Litman (1990) contends that the main role of the public domain is to allow for copyright law to function despite the unrealistic conception of individual creativity it presupposes. She defines the public domain as a commons including uncopyrighted aspects of copyrighted works (Litman, 1990). That is, according to Litman's definition, the public domain comprises the re-usable unprotected elements in copyrighted works as well as works that are completely unprotected (Boyle, 2003).

Yochai Benkler's (1999) approach to the evasive notion of public domain is comparatively pragmatical: the public domain is the totality of all uses, works and aspects of works that can be identified as free by lay people without carrying out a sophisticated legal inquiry into individual facts (ibid.). According to Boyle (2003), Benkler's definition is intended to raise the issue whether lay people really have reliable intuitions as to whether a certain resource is free, i.e. both uncontrolled by someone else and free of charge. Boyle (ibid.) takes a contextualist, if not sceptical stance, on this issue: the delimitation of the public domain depends largely on our views and desires regarding the public domain, the freedom or creativity it stands for and which dangers it holds at bay; hence a certain pluralism about the notion of public domain must be allowed for.

E-Commons

The term "commons" has come to denote areas of creativity that lie outside of the boundaries of intellectual property, as for instance the Internet (Boyle, 2003). As such "commons" or "e-commons" and "public domain" would appear to be synonymous. But Larry Lessig (2001, 2002) proposes a more restrictive definition: "e-commons" is the totality of works or information the uses of which are perhaps not for free, but are such as to be unconstrained by the permission or authorisation of somebody else, certain liability rules excepted.

A similar delineation of the concept of commons is proposed by Benkler and Nissenbaum (2006). The focus is on control and the freedom from the will of another, rather than on absence of costs: intellectual property should not restrain innovation in the form of a monopoly (Boyle, 2003). Hence being in the e-commons is compatible of being owned individually or collectively. A good example is open-source software that is available under so-called free public licenses, like the GNU licenses (http://www.gnu.org) or those offered by Creative Commons (http://creativecommons.org). Free public licenses actually are copyright licenses granting end-users the right to modify or copy the software or any other expression of content as long as these uses comply with the initial license.

The distinction between public domain and e-commons is that the first is based on the dichotomy between the domain of property and the domain of the free, while the second draws the dividing line between the domain of individual control and the domain of distributed production and management (Boyle, 2003). Not only is the e-commons compatible with constraints, but the successful examples of e-commons, like open source software, actually presuppose constraints, be they legal - in the form of liability rules - or based on shared values and norms as well as on prestige networks (ibid.).

It is important to note that the e-commons is "outside" of the domain of intellectual property not in the sense that it excludes property rights, but only in the sense that it precludes that they may become an obstacle to innovation and intellectual creativity. Free public licenses, the backbone of the e-commons, actually exploit intellectually

property rights in order to prevent the abuse of the very same rights. Thus, the e-commons stands squarely on the ground of intellectual property. However, in a more liberal reading, which is adopted by Boyle (ibid.), the notion of e-commons covers both resources subject to intellectual property but are distributed under a free public license and resources that are free in the sense of being part of the public domain. That is, the e-commons in the wider sense includes the public domain, while stretching over into the area of intellectual property.

E-COMMONS AND SCIENTIFIC RESEARCH

The Enclosure of the E-Commons

The Tragedy of the Commons

The patenting of the human genome (Boyle, 2003) and the European Database Protection Directive which extends intellectual property rights over mere compilation of facts (Boyle, 2003; Boyle, 2005), are in the eyes of James Boyle only two examples for what he calls the "enclosure of the intangible commons of the mind". This phrase, which is similar to one used by Yochai Benkler (2006), refers to the expansion of intellectual property into the area of uses, works or aspects of works that used to be regarded as uncopyrightable. The traditional frontiers of intellectual property rights are under attack (Boyle, 2003; Boyel 2008), questioning the old assumption that the raw materials of scientific research, i.e. ideas, data and facts, should remain in the public domain and not become proprietary (ibid.).

Now even if the enclosure of the e-commons in some ways parallels the state-promoted transformation of common land into private property in the late 18th and the early 19th century (Thompson, 1991; Boyle, 2003), there are also dissimilarities between the commons of the mind and its earthy counterpart. Indeed common land is a rival resource inasmuch as many individual uses of the latter mutually exclude each other. Herdsmen who roam the same common pasture compete with each other as to its use and may eventually ruin it: since it is to the immediate benefit of an individual herdsman to add one more cow to his herd, there is no incentive for each one of them to prevent over-grazing of the commons. A "tragedy of the commons" seems to be the outcome: rival resources that are not individually owned inevitably are overexploited (Boyle, 2003; Lessig, 2001). However, such a tragedy does not occur with respect to a commons that is non-rival - such as in fact the e-commons: there is no limit as to how many times an MP3 can be downloaded or a poem read on the Web (Boyle, 2003).

Arguments for and Against the Sustainability of the E-Commons

Defenders of the enclosure of the e-commons therefore prefer to argue that the problem with the informational commons is that there is no incentive to create this resource in the first place. Indeed, information resources are not only non-rival, but also non-excludable: one unit of such a good may satisfy an unlimited number of users at no marginal cost at all (Boyle, 2003). Boyle quite plausibly objects that the Internet compensates this apparent deficiency by also reducing production and distribution costs, while enormously enlarging the market (ibid.). Moreover, the technologies of the Internet also facilitate quick detection of illegal copying, such that it is not obvious that copyright holders see their privileges diminished through the advent of the Web (ibid.).

Another argument in favour of the enclosure of the e-commons is the growing impact of information-based products in the world economy. However, one may reply that since information products are built out of parts of other information products, and thus every information item consti-

tutes the raw material for further innovation, each additional extension of individual property into the e-common reduces access to and increases the cost of each new product and innovation. Hence, the enclosure of the e-commons may do more harm to innovation than good (Boyle, 2003).

As to the question what incentives or motivations there are for building the resources that make up the e-commons - whether it is for prestige, improving one's resume, the satisfaction of exerting one's skills and creativity, or at least partly because of sheer altruistic virtues and values, as claim Benkler and Nissenbaum (2006) - it appears be spurious. Indeed, in a global network with a large number of members, there will be always enough talented people that will be willing to contribute to the creation and evaluation of information products, if production and distribution costs are near to zero (Boyle, 2003). Under one condition, however: without centralised supervision, large-scale projects have to be modular in order to allow for an efficient division of labour (ibid.). Open source development is the paradigm of a distributed, non-proprietary creation, a commons-based peer production (Benkler & Nissenbaum, 2006), but so has been scientific research and the development of artistic movements long before the existence of the Internet (Boyle, 2003).

Distributed creation is also appropriate for capital-intensive projects, at least in the case of science, which more and more relies on data- and processing-intensive models. Lay volunteers have been successfully recruited to the task of distributed data scrutiny, as for example in NASA's "Clickworkers" experiment which recurred to volunteers for the analysis of data sent by Mars probes (http://clickworkers.arc.nasa.gov). Another example for large-scale distributed information production in the field of bioinformatics is the open-source genomics project (http://www.ensembl.org) (Boyle, 2003; Bricklin, 2006; Benkler & Nissenbaum, 2006). Thus, against economical prejudice in favour of free market competition based on individual property, distributed creativity in an information commons is certainly viable (Boyle, 2003).

A False Manichaeism?

According to Boyle (2003, 2008), the enclosure of the commons of the mind is dangerous because propertisation is a vicious circle. He argues that in order to achieve optimum price discrimination with proprietary information goods that have no substantial marginal costs, the holders of intellectual property rights will demand ever greater extension of the realm of individual property into the information commons (Boyle, 2003; Boyle, 2000). However, the real motivation behind the tendency to transform the e-commons into a private property may be a cognitive bias against openness of systems and networks as well as against non-proprietary creation - an aversion which may be due to the fact that our everyday experience of property is that over tangible resources for which the "tragedy of the commons" indeed holds (Boyle, 2006). Our conceptions of property have still to be adapted to the non-tangible commons of the mind (ibid.).

While one may agree with Boyle's general concern about the enclosure of the e-commons and deplore the propertisation of the raw material of scientific research, it is appropriate to qualify an excessively Manicheistic view of the relation between intellectual property and e-commons. In fact, the notions of public good and private ownership are by no means mutually exclusive. A classical example of non-excludable private goods are privately owned lighthouses in 19th century Great-Britain: the service provided by a lighthouse, namely the aid for navigation through the emitted light- or sound signal, cannot be reserved to a few ships (Foldvary, 2003; Coase, 1974). In a sense, e-commons resources are digital-era examples of (possibly) private goods that are non-excludable.

It is certainly true that in a first stage reducing the extent of the public domain also means pushing

back the frontiers of the e-commons. However, as Boyle himself concedes, the e-commons not only stretches into the area of intellectual property, but actually presupposes intellectual property rights in a crucial respect. As we have seen, free public licenses, that underly most of the e-commons, actually are copyright licenses that are designed to neutralise the monopolistic tendencies inherent in intellectual property. While it is true that intellectual property and public domain correspond to each other like figure and background, and hence each widening of the scope of the former diminishes the extent of the latter, this is not so for the relation between intellectual property and the e-commons. Paradoxically, the extension of copyright means a potential increase of the commons of the mind, provided free public licensing keeps up with propertisation.

Furthermore, e-commons and intellectual property do not exclude each other in terms of their associated business models: indeed, there is (maybe anecdotal) evidence that some information goods may well be simultaneously available both in the e-commons and on the proprietary market, without any prejudices to sales in the latter (Boyle, 2007). Not only academic works like Yochai Benkler's (2006) "The Wealth of Networks" and James Boyle's (2008) "The Public Domain", but also science fiction novels like "Down and Out in the Magic Kingdom" by Cory Doctorow have sold considerably well despite being available either in the public domain or under a Creative Commons license (Boyle, 2007).

The explanation of this peaceful co-existence may of course reside in the fact that at present, paper copies and electronic copies of a text have complementary uses: pdf-copies are easier to search and quote, while books are more comfortable to carry around or to keep on the bedside table (even more so than print-outs). Of course, the future dissemination of e-book readers may alter this equilibrium. In the case of other media, like music, the comparative advantages of having a hard copy besides the electronic copy may be too marginal to allow for such a harmonious co-existence. For example, the quality of the music as registered on a CD may still be higher than that of an MP3, but for anyone save aficionados of classical music, i.e. for the large majority of consumers that enjoy music as a mere entertainment, it makes no difference to listen to a CD player instead of enjoying the same piece or song on a MP3 player, which has the additional advantage of huge storage capacities.

SELF-ARCHIVING AND OPEN ACCESS

Authorship vs. Copyright

A distinction which goes often unnoticed is the one between authorship and copyright (Harnad, 2001a). Authorship is intellectual priority or "parentship" with respect to an idea or set of ideas, while copyright is the ownership with regard to its expression. Infringement of copyright is theft of text or piracy, while infringement of authorship is theft of ideas or plagiarism. If someone publishes, e.g. reprints, a text without asking the permission of the copyright owner, she may not necessarily also be guilty of plagiarism, which would be the case if she would republish the text under her name. Also, in contrast to copyright, which may be transferred, authorship is unalienable: you can never loose the authorship of your own discoveries and ideas, whereas, in the case of copyright, you can decide to sell or give away the rights on your writings.

The modern conception of scientific authorship was shaped around the birth of the Royal Society and its publication series, The Philosophical Transactions, started in 1665. The community of natural philosophers that founded the Royal Society established some standards and practices related to scientific authorship that are still in force today. For example, they decided that a scientific author cannot "own" his or her discovery: Scientific writing is a way of reporting facts of nature, and nature – so the common lore – cannot be subject to copyright. The members of the Royal Society also introduced an early form of peer-review: new ideas or discoveries were "informally" discussed in the meetings of the Royal Society, and, upon approval by the community of peers, published in the Philosophical Transactions (Biagioli, 2003).

The distinction between authorship and copyright is crucial for scientific literature, which is, in contrast to the majority of the published works, a give-away literature: authors of research papers and books do not seek (and generally do not receive) any royalties, but impact, that is the distribution, recognition and exploitation of their work by their peers. It is on the basis of impact that academics built their career and hence their income (Harnad, 2001a,b; Harnad, 2009).

This means that unlike authors of non-give-away works who earn their keep in form of royalties, researchers are less worried about piracy than about plagiarism, i.e. the denial of authorship, since their main concern is that their ideas circulate and gain recognition among their peers. Of course, this does not entail that authors of scientific works would be delighted if their papers and books were pirated; in most cases, they still want to retain control over where their work appears, whether credited or not. However, any obstacle to accessing their works and hence to the impact of their ideas jeopardises their main source of income (Harnad, 2001a,b).

Self-Archiving and Open Access

Based on this insight, Stevan Harnad has been one of the most vocal critics of the traditional subscription-based business model for peer-reviewed scientific journals. Subscription fees have reached a level of about 2000 Euros, which means that research institutions not only in the developing countries are experiencing serious difficulties in paying access to refereed journals for their members (Harnad, 2001a,b). In other words, subscription tolls have become access barriers and thus also impact barriers.

Now, peer review is essential for the assessment and certification of the scientific quality of research papers or books and thus for the academic reputation of their authors. As such, peer review is the only service provided by scientific journals which researchers are really interested in (ibid.). But it has been estimated that the review costs only constitute about 10 percent of the total subscription tolls (ibid.). The long-term solution advocated by Harnad is the spreading of electronic open-access journals, where publication costs are minimized and are paid by the institutions that host the authors, such that readers can access papers for free (Harnad, 2009).

But there is a cheaper alternative: self-archiving of pre- and post-prints in institutional eprint archives, like EPrints (http://www.eprints.org) or HAL (http://hal.archives-ouvertes.fr/), which has been practised by physicists since 1991. Some scientific publishing companies, like Springer or Elsevier, provide copyright transfer agreements that explicitly authorize authors to self-archive a personal copy of the refereed and published version, i.e. the so-called post-print, of their paper (Harnad, 2001a; personal communications by Ralf Gerstner from Springer and Barbara Kulemenos from STM Association). In case no such clause can be negotiated, or an embargo is imposed on post-prints, there is a simple and completely legal strategy to circumvent restrictive copyright, namely the so-called "Harnad-Oppenheim strategy" (Harnard, 2001a; Oppenheim, 2001): simply self-archive the preprint and the corrigenda of the post-print separately. Of course, this strategy applies only if the copyright transfer agreement does not stipulate an embargo on preprints too.

Importing the Open Source Philosophy Into The World Of Scientific Publishing

Though in the last decade the scientific community has increasingly realised that Open Access greatly facilitates the circulation of ideas and scientific results, the academic world does not seem to have yet fully grasped the potential of the e-commons for reducing the reckless multiplication of the scientific literature. This problem could at least partially be addressed by introducing the practice of re-use in the production of scientific texts. Now, the free public licenses underpinning some Open Access schemes do actually permit such a practice. The peer-reviewed Open Access journal PLoS One (http://www.plosone.org) and Springer's Open Choice scheme, for instance, recur to Creative Commons Attribution (http://creativecommons.org/licenses/by/3.0/) and Creative Commons Attribution Non-commercial (http://creativecommons.org/licenses/by-nc/3.0/) respectively, which both explicitly allow for re-use of text. Nonetheless, the scientific community is still far away from applying the Open Source philosophy to its publications, with the exception of teaching and reference material.

As has been pointed out above, free licensing is the *conditio sine qua non* for commons-based peer production, i.e. for the distributed creativity that has been the reason why open source software development has been so successful. The license to re-use and modify, together with a peer review in vast global communities, allows for a large-scale incremental optimization of any resource in the e-commons. But while science has applied this model of optimization for the development of ideas and theories, scientific writing is still largely based on the cooperation of small numbers, if not on the romantic cliché of solitary creation.

Online collaborative encyclopaedias such as Wikipedia (http://en.wikipedia.org) are examples that large-scale commons-based distributed production can also be harnessed to the creation and improvement of texts. But while this strategy has been applied to manuals and tutorials under the GNU Free Documentation License (http://www.gnu.org/copyleft/fdl.html), especially in Computer Science, even before the Wikibooks initiative (http://en.wikibooks.org), this is patently not the case for original research literature.

It seems that it is the prevailing mentality in academia which does not allow for re-use of text: it is still unthinkable for most academics that one could rewrite a scientific article, correcting some of its flaws (say, a gap in a proof), and publish the new derived version under one's own name, even if one acknowledged the author of the original paper. Instead one has to write a completely new article that must not substantially overlap with the old one. Of course, one may contact the author as the holder of the copyright and negotiate to write a common, improved article. But in even this case, there is an unnecessary waste of time and resources. Conversely, it is still not part of the academic mindset to publish a note for others to re-use and develop, though under a free public license, priority of authorship would be safeguarded and derived versions would be iteratively traceable, such that one could in principle gather credits for having sown the seeds of a series of (hopefully) high-quality papers based on one's original note.

In the absence of empirical findings on this topic, one may only speculate with more or less plausibility on the reasons why commons-based peer production is not applied to original research literature. First, many academics, especially but not exclusively in the humanities, regard the actual writing of the text not just as a passive registration of ideas, but as contributing to the development of these ideas. That is, in the eyes of many scientists, there may not be a clear-cut separation between the creation of scientific ideas and the production of the texts in which the former are embedded. Since authorship of ideas is not negotiable for researchers since it is career-building, the ideology of the inseparability of ideas and texts, form and content, would partly explain why scientific authors, unlike software designers, do not open up their works for others to modify freely.

Another obstacle to importing the open software philosophy to the production of scientific writings is the fact that the author of the original work may not agree with the ideas expressed in derivative works. Indeed, the author of the original work would need to be included in the list of the author(s) of the derived work, and hence would be attributed responsibility for the ideas expressed in the latter, at least under the current conception of authorship.

Finally, such an innovative way of producing scientific articles would presuppose changes in the review and crediting process. E.g., drafts intended as seeds of more developed research papers would have to be evaluated differently as fully written-out articles.

All three points raised as possible obstacles to applying commons-based peer-production to original research literature, namely the (apparent) inseparability of the creation of ideas and the creation of texts, the problems of attributing responsibility for the derived works in the current authorship model and the necessary transformation of the crediting process point to the necessity of changing academic mentality towards a more collaborative conception of scientific writing and an open model of authorship akin to the philosophy of Open Source.

FUTURE ISSUES

However, in order to initiate a change from the traditional closed model of scientific authorship to an open model that is more appropriate for e-commons-based peer-production, not only a change in mentality is required, but also strategies and tools that facilitate the open source creation and peer-review of scientific works.

First, the classical notion of scientific authorship has to be refined and replaced by a manifold of different roles, each reflecting a distinct aspect of contributing to a scientific publication: maintainers (editors), contributors, commentators, reviewers, etc.. Identifying these roles and the different aspects of the creation, dissemination and evaluation of scientific knowledge they are involved in would be the first step towards the development of process models for distributive authoring and reviewing of academic texts.

Second, such distributive role and process models for scientific publications in turn presuppose that the idea of a monolythic paper or monograph is substituted by the paradigm of a modularized scientific knowledge distribution object, along the lines suggested by Anita de Waard (2006, 2007, 2008). Indeed, scientific texts are actually highly complex artifacts that – thanks to online publishing - are increasingly integrating multimedia elements of different sources. That is, scientific works are becoming multi-source composite objects the components of which are distributed over the Internet, and hence will be essentially multi-authored. Furthermore, a versioning system akin to the ones used in software development would be help to track changes and assess the weight and thus credit of each contribution.

Third, a collaborative and distributive production of scientific texts requires a change in the current practices of evaluation and credit attribution. Given a refined notion of (co-) authorship in a highly distributed setting, we need to find ways to properly assess and reward any aspect and degree of participation in the evolution of a scientific text. Moreover, in order to mobilize a large number of reviewers in the community, Social Web tools or derivatives thereof would have to be recruited.

Last, but not least, the import of the open source model into the world of scientific publications would be made easier by easy to use collaborative web-based platforms not only for the evolution, but also for the peer evaluation and distribution of research literature. Here again lessons have to be learned from the Social Web: in order for such platforms to be effective and widely accepted, they should be designed for intuitive use by non-technicians.

A current attempt to address the issues raised above and to integrate the strategies and tools that allow for a commons-based collaborative future of scientific publishing is the project „Liquid Publications" (http://project.liquidpub.org) funded under the Future and Emerging Technologies (FET) programme within the Seventh Framework Programme for Research of the European Commission. This project envisages the innovative notion of so-called liquid publications, that are evolutionary, collaborative, and composable units of scientific knowledge production and communication. Recruiting the similarities between scientific knowledge artifacts and software artifacts, the project aims at pulling together the experiences gathered in open source software development as well as regarding the Web 2.0. Acknowledging the role of the scientific publishing industry, it interestingly also sets out to develop innovative services and business models.

How far this and similar initiatives, such as the grassroots project LogiLogi (http://en.logilogi. org/), will actually change the way scientific literature is authored, distributed and evaluated is of course impossible to predict. That the landscape of scientific publishing is changing in an Open Access world, however, cannot be questioned.

CONCLUSION

That the Web is changing the ways in which scientific knowledge is produced and distributed and is transforming the conventional conception of scientific authorship certainly constitutes a blatant truism. To assess its impact however, is a more difficult task. One the one hand, the usual opposition between copyright and scientific (e-) commons is certainly too manicheistic: the commons of the mind is largely grounded on free public licenses that are themselves firmly rooted in copyright law. However, it may be argued that academic authors may be more concerned with questions of priority than questions of copyright and that coypright becomes a liability if it directly or indirectly becomes an obstacle to the accessibility of scientific works and thus their impact on which the reputation of their authors is built. Open Access models certainly solve the problem of the availability of scientific literature, but also contain elements that may help to tackle the quasi opposite concern, namely the uncontrolled and often spurious multiplication of scientific texts. Indeed, most Open Access schemes are based on licenses that allow for the re-use of text. It seems, however, that the scientific community is yet not prepared to move towards an Open Source model of authorship. Given the existence of appropriate licensing schemes, plausible reasons for academics to resist this move are problems related to attributing credit and responsability for the expressed hypotheses and results. Some strategies fostering a change of academic mentality in favour of recasting scientific authorship according to the Open Source paradigm have been discussed, especially a refinement of the notion of co-authorship alongside a modular conception of scientific publications, both allowing for a more targeted credit attribution scheme. Finally, the need for intuitive web-based platforms for the collaborative production and evaluation of scientific literature, like the one aimed at in the European project „Liquid Publications", has been emphasised.

ACKNOWLEDGMENT

The author would like to thank Aliaksandr Birukou (Trento), Fabio Casati (Trento), Roberto Casati (Paris), Anita de Waard (Utrecht), Ralf Gerstner (Heidelberg), Fausto Giunchiglia (Trento), Barbara Kulemenos (Munich), Gloria Origgi (Paris), Carles Sierra (Barcelona), Joe Wakeling (Fribourg) and Wybo Wiersma (Groningen) for discussion and many helpful suggestions. Research leading up to the present article has been supported by the FET-Open grant nr. 213360 within the Seventh Framework Programme for Research of the European Commission.

REFERENCES

Benkler, Y. (1999). Free as Air to Common Use: First Amendment Constraints on Enclosure of the Public Domain. *New York University Law Review, 74*, 354–446.

Benkler, Y. (2006). *The Wealth of Networks*. New Haven, CT: Yale University Press.

Benkler, Y., & Nissenbaum, H. (2006). Commons-based Peer Production and Virtue. *Journal of Political Philosophy, 14*(4), 394–419. doi:10.1111/j.1467-9760.2006.00235.x

Biagioli, M., & Galison, P. (2003). *Scientific Authorship: Credit and Intellectual Property in Science*. New York: Routledge.

Boyle, J. (2000). Cruel, Mean, or Lavish?: Economic Analysis, Price Discrimination and Digital Intellectual Property. *Vanderbilt Law Review, 53*, 2007–2039.

Boyle, J. (2003). The Second Eclosure Movement and the Construction of the Public Domain. *Law and Contemporary Problems, 66*, 33–74.

Boyle, J. (2005). Public information wants to be free. *Financial Times*, February 24, 2005. Retrieved September 30, 2009, from http://www.ft.com/cms/s/2/cd58c216-8663-11d9-8075-00000e2511c8.html

Boyle, J. (2006). A closed mind about an open world. *Financial Times*, August 7, 2006. Retrieved September 30, 2009, from http://www.ft.com/cms/s/2/64167124-263d-11db-afa1-0000779e2340.html

Boyle, J. (2007). Text is free, we make our money on volume(s). *Financial Times*, January 22 2007. Retrieved September 30, 2009, from http://www.ft.com/cms/s/b46f5a58-aa2e-11db-83b0-0000779e2340.html

Boyle, J. (2008). *The Public Domain. Enclosing the Commons of the Mind*. New Haven, CT: Yale University Press.

Bricklin, D. (2006). *The Cornucopia of the Commons: How to get volunteer labor*. Retrieved September 30, 2009 from http://www.bricklin.com/cornucopia.htm

Chartier, R. (1987). *Lectures et lecteurs dans la France de l'Ancien Regime*. Paris: Seuil.

Coase, R. (1974). The Lighthouse in Economics. *The Journal of Law & Economics, 17*, 357–376. doi:10.1086/466796

De Waard, A. (2007). A pragmatic structure for research articles. In S. B. Shum, M. Lind & H. Weigand, (Eds.), *Proceedings of the 2nd International Conference on Pragmatic Web (ICPW 2007). ACM International Conference Proceeding Series 280*, (pp. 83-89). New York: ACM.

De Waard, A., & Kircz, J. (2008). Modeling Scientific Discourse - Shifting Perspectives and Persistent Issues. In L. Chan & S. Mornatti (Eds.). *Open Scholarship: Authority, Community, and Sustainability in the Age of Web 2.0. Proceedings of the 12th International Conference on Electronic Publishing* (223-233). Berkeley, CA: bepress.

De Waard, A., & Tel, G. (2006). The ABCDE Format. In M. Völkel & S. Schaffert (Eds.), *SemWiki2006. First Workshop on Semantic Wikis - From Wiki to Semantics. CEUR Workshop Proceedings*. Retrieved September 30, 2009, from http://www.ceur-ws.org/Vol-206/paper8.pdf

Foldvary, F. (2003). The Lighthouse as a Private-Sector Collective Good. *The Independent Institute Working Paper* 46. Retrieved September 30, 2009, from http://www.independent.org/publications/working_papers/article.asp?id=757

Geller, P. E. (2003). *International Copyright Law and Practice*. Albany, NY: Matthew Bender.

Harnad, S. (2001a). *Skyreading and Skywriting for Researchers: A Post-Gutenberg Anomaly and How to Resolve it*. Retrieved September 30, 2009, from http://www.text-e.org/conf/index.cfm?fa=texte&ConfText_ID=7

Harnad, S. (2001b). The self-archiving initiative. *Nature, 410*, 1024–1025. doi:10.1038/35074210

Harnad, S. (2009). The Postgutenberg Open Access Journal . In Cope, B., & Phillips, A. (Eds.), *The Future of the Academic Journal*. Oxford, UK: Chandos.

Koepsell, D. R. (2000). *The Ontology of Cyberspace*. Chicago: Open Court.

Lange, D. (1981). Recognizing the Public Domain. *Law and Contemporary Problems, 44*, 147–178. doi:10.2307/1191227

Lessig, L. (2001). *The Future of Ideas*. New York: Random House.

Lessig, L. (2002). The Architecture of Innovation. *Duke L. J., 51*.

Lindberg, S. W., & Patterson, L. R. (1991). *The Nature of Copyright: A Law of Users' Rights*. Athens, GA: University of Georgia Press.

Litman, J. (1990). The Public Domain. *Emory Law Journal, 39*, 965.

Oppenheim, C. (2001) The legal and regulatory environment for electronic information. *Infonortics*. Retrieved September 30, 2009, from http://www.infonortics.com/publications/legal4.html

Thompson, E. P. (1991). *The Making of the English Working Class*. London: Penguin.

KEY TERMS AND DEFINITIONS

Authorship: the property of being the originator of an idea or procedure

Copyright: a form of intellectual property; the

ownership as to an original work whether literary, scientific or artistic

Public domain: the set of resources or aspects of resources that are not or not anymore protected by copyright

Commons: the set of resources that are in the public domain or are distributed under a free public license

Free public license: a license under which the copyright holder of a given resource grants the public the right either to copy, distribute, re-use or modify the latter freely often under certain conditions, such as to acknowledge authorship or to share derivatives under the same or compatible license.

Commons-based peer production: the collaborative creation of a resource belonging to the commons under a free public license

Open Access: a publishing scheme under which a work is made freely accessible to the public, the copyright remaining in the hands of the author(s) or the publisher (in case copyright has been transferred)

Chapter 13
Armchair Warfare 'on Terrorism':
On Robots, Targeted Assassinations and Strategic Violations of International Humanitarian Law

Jutta Weber
University Uppsala, Sweden

ABSTRACT

In the 21ˢᵗ century, militaries are not competing for military dominance through specific superior weapon systems alone but also through networking these systems via information and communication technologies. The 'Revolution in Military Affairs' (RMA) relies on network centric warfare, 'precision' weaponry and 'intelligent' systems such as uninhabited, modular, globally connected robot systems. While some Western forces (and the U.S. Central Intelligence Service C.I.A.) claim that robots help to avoid the death of one's soldiers (respectively agents), NGOs point out the increase of killed civilians. In my paper, I discuss the deployment of uninhabited combat aerial vehicles (UCAV) in Western 'wars on terror' and their political and techno-ethical consequences. The question arises whether the new military philosophy, network centric (armchair) warfare, targeted assassinations and robot technology work towards the weakening of international humanitarian law.

INTRODUCTION

In the 21ˢᵗ century, militaries are not competing for military dominance through specific superior weapon systems alone but also through networking these systems with the help of information and communication technologies (Kaufmann, 2006). In the course of the 'Revolution in Military Affairs', concepts of network centric warfare,

transparent battle space, a logic of precision strikes with autonomous resp. 'intelligent' systems and munitions are becoming dominant in western warfare. In the configuration of high-tech militaries, robotic systems play a decisive role. Uninhabited, modular, globally connected, and tele-operated as well as increasingly autonomous, multi-mission systems are regarded as crucial means of warfare. They are faster, cheaper and supposedly more adaptable systems which are claimed to help avoid the death of one's soldiers

DOI: 10.4018/978-1-61692-014-2.ch013

and cope with non-conventional/asymmetric wars. Rarely anybody considers that armchair warfare with tele-operated robots firing missiles from thousands kilometres away from the battlefield has severe consequences with regard to human rights and mirrors problematic changes in recent military philosophy. However, robotic precision weaponry such as uninhabited combat aerial vehicles (UCAVs) not only poses a permanent threat for local populations in everyday life, but leads to an increase of the number of killed civilians (Münkler 2002). The 'revolution in military affairs' (RMA) as well as the invention of network centric warfare seem to come with a new military philosophy that works towards the weakening of human rights standards in laws of war and rules of engagement which could in the long run endanger international humanitarian law.

In my paper, I will discuss the deployment of uninhabited combat aerial vehicles (UCAV) and their political, sociocultural and technoethical consequences.

KILLER ROBOTS
TARGETING CIVILIANS?

Today, UCAVs are deployed by the US and the NATO militaries in the war in Afghanistan, Iraq and Pakistan, and by the Israel military for targeted killings in Palestinian occupied territories.

The deployment of new robotic technologies for aerial attacks intensified massively in the last years (Cordesman, 2008; Fischer, 2008; Singer, 2009; Weber, 2009)[1] and the number of killed civilians is rising (UN News Center 2009). Especially interesting is also the deployment of US drones in Pakistan, where not only the military but also the C.I.A. operates uninhabited combat aerial vehicles: "it represents a radically new and geographically unbounded use of state-sanctioned lethal force. And, because of the C.I.A. program's secrecy, there is no visible system of accountability in place, despite the fact that the agency has

killed many civilians inside a politically fragile, nuclear-armed country with which the U.S. is not at war." (Mayer 2009, 39)

Estimates of killed civilians differ widely. According to the survey of Peter Bergen and Katherine Thiedemann from the think tank 'The New America Foundation' 82 drone attacks were undertaken in Pakistan between January 2006 and mid October 2009 in which between 750 – 1000 people were killed. Bergen and Thiedemann (2009) estimate that 250 – 320 of these had been civilians (31-33%). 'The News' – a Pakistani newspaper – reported in April 2009: "Of the 60 cross-border predator strikes carried out by the Afghanistan-based American drones in Pakistan between January 14, 2006 and April 8, 2009, only 10 were able to hit their actual targets, killing 14 wanted al-Qaeda leaders, besides perishing 687 innocent Pakistani civilians." (Mir 2009, np). There are diverse counts of killed civilians in Pakistan as official numbers are not available and Pakistan's tribal areas have become largely forbidden terrain for media organizations.

The number of US air strikes in Iraq rose from 285 to 1119 (per year) between 2004 und 2007 and from 6495 to 12,775 in Afghanistan. As the number of flying hours of uninhabited combat aerial vehicles (UCAVs) tripled between 2003 und 2007, while the number of surveillance flights in Iraq and Afghanistan rose only very slightly, it is very likely that air attacks by UCAVs in Afghanistan and Iraq also massively increased lately (see also Cordesman 2008, Rötzer 2008).

A study on the weapons that killed civilians in the Iraq war from 2003-2008 (using the detailed and extensive data base of Iraq Body Count) published in the internationally renowned *New England Journal of Medicine* states: "*Female Iraqis and Iraqi children constituted the highest proportions of civilian victims when the methods of violence involved indiscriminate weapons fired from a distance: air attacks* and mortars. That air attacks, whether involving bombs or missiles, killed relatively high proportions of female civilians and children is additional evidence in support of the argument that these weapons, ..., should not be directed at civilian areas because of their indiscriminate nature." (Hsiao-Rei Hicks et al. 2009, 1587; my emphasis)

With regard to the deployment of UCAVs in the Palestinian occupied territories, Guardian reporter Clancy Chassay states: "During the [Israeli] 23-day offensive, 1,380 Palestinians perished, 431 of them children, according to figures published by the World Health Organisation. A Guardian investigation into the high number of civilian deaths has found Israel using a variety of weapons in illegal ways. Indiscriminate munitions, including shells packed with white phosphorus, were fired into densely populated areas, while precision missiles and tanks shells were fired into civilian homes. *But it is the use of drones in the killing of at least 48 civilians that appears most reprehensible. The drones are operated from a remote position, usually outside the combat zone. They use optics that are able to see the details of a man's clothing and are fitted with pinpoint accurate missiles. Yet they killed Mounir's family sitting in their courtyard, a group of girls and women in an empty street, two small children in a field, and many others.* ... The attack on this home in Gaza City is just one of more than a dozen incidents recorded by Amnesty International where Israel's unmanned aerial vehicles (UAVs) – or drones – killed one or more civilians. " (Chassay 2009; my emphasis; see also Human Rights Watch 2009)

Trying to explain the increasing killing of civilians in western war 'on terror', some theorists point to the aggressive Israeli[2] or US conduct of war as responsible[3], while others claim a broader and problematic shift in military philosophy. For example, the former head of the International Law Division (ILD) of the Israeli Army, Colonel Daniel Reisner, conceded – according to the already mentioned report in *The Guardian* – that ILD is "pushing the boundaries of what is acceptable in war. *'What we are seeing now is a revision of international law,*" Reisner said. "*If*

you do something for long enough, the world will accept it. The whole of international law is now based on the notion that an act that is forbidden today becomes permissible if executed by enough countries. *International law progresses through violations. We invented the targeted assassination thesis and we had to push it*." (Chassay 2009; my emphasis)

Targeted assassinations of terrorist suspects without juridical investigations are especially easy to conduct with the help of UCAV technology. These assassinations are frequently conducted in the Western war 'on terror' – not only in Palestine Occupied territories but in Afghanistan, Pakistan and Iraq. They undermine international law and human rights issues and come with a reconfiguration of military philosophy in the course of the Revolution in Military Affairs. While some philosophers, peace researchers, military personnel and roboticists discuss the ethical consequences of combat robots and problems of arms control (Altmann 2009, Arkin 2007, 2008, Asaro 2008, Blackmore 2005, Capurro / Nagenborg 2009, Cerqui / Weber / Weber 2006 ; Lin et al. 2009, Singer 2009, Sharkey 2007, Sparrow 2007, Tamburrini 2009, Weber 2009), the complex of RMA, high-tech weaponry and the weakening or 'revision' of international humanitarian law is still rarely discussed.[Finn 2008,, Zwanenburg et al. 2005). Only recently Philip Alston, the UN Special Rapporteur on extrajudicial, summary or arbitrary executions criticized in a report to the US government the increasing usage of CIA drones for attacks in Pakistan and asked whether they are compatible with international humanitarian law (Alston 2009)

Given the biased character of western media coverage of U.S. / NATO and Israeli wars 'on terror', adequate public attention and discussion of the juridical, ethical and sociocultural problems of these wars are missing.

A SHORT HISTORY OF WESTERN UCAV TECHNOLOGY

In 2001 when military technology boomed massively, the US Congress decided that the armed forces should develop remote control techniques so that in 2010 one third of the attack aircraft and in 2015 one third of the ground combat vehicles can be operated uninhabited. Today, 50 countries all over the world are working on the development of uninhabited systems (Altmann 2009). At the same time, uninhabited systems, which were used before for surveillance only, got armed with air-to-ground and air-to-air missiles (Weber 2009).

In 2007 the first unmanned combat aircraft wing, the 432nd Wing of the U.S. Air Force, had its first inauguration, operating the MQ-1 Predator and MQ-9 Reaper drones from their basis in the United States (Hanley 2007).

The second biggest developer of UCAVs is Israel. Israel deployed UCAVs from the Hermes series (Elbit Systems Ltd.) in 2006 in the war against Lebanon, but also for surveillance, targeted killings and war operations in the West Bank and the Gaza strip. The Israeli Air Force also has its own UAV squadron, equipped with Hermes 450s.

Today, uninhabited aerial vehicles for surveillance as well as combat are extensively used in NATO and military operations and are regularly deployed and used by the U.S. Forces in the Afghanistan and Iraq wars (Barry/Zimet 2001; Sparrow 2007, Weber 2009)

Recently, the Department of Defense (2009) released its twenty five year research plan for military robots, the 'Unmanned Systems Integrated Roadmap 2009-2034', for which expenditures of $21 billion are foreseen for the first five years of research.

The development in military robotics in Europe is immensely influenced by the US Forces. Now, the air forces of the U.K., Italy, Germany and some other European countries deploy uninhabited aerial vehicles but also develop first prototypes of uninhabited combat aerial vehicles[4]. Uninhabited aerial vehicles are the majority of already existing military robots (Sparrow 2007). More than 250 types are already in service or market-ready. (van Blyenburgh 2008). "At present, more than 50 countries develop or produce UAVs. Armed UAVs are possessed by the USA (Predator, Sky Warrior, Hunter, Reaper), Israel (Harpy, CUTLASS), Iran (Ababil-T). Unmanned combat air vehicles (UCAVs) proper are in development in the USA (UCAS-D); Great Britain (Corax), France (nEuron, with partner countries [Greece, Italy, Sweden, Spain and Switzerland]), Germany (Barracuda), and Russia (Skat) (Jane's 2007). One need not be a prophet to predict that other producers of military aircraft and UAVs, e.g. China, India, Pakistan, Brazil will put weapons on UAVs or develop full-blown UCAVs, also for export." (Altmann 2009, 72) UCAVs are predicted to be the future of military aircraft (Sparrow 2007).

A Vaccuum? STS and Technoethics of Military R&D

A discussion of uninhabited military systems (UMS) in general and especially of Uninhabited Combat Aerial Vehicles (UCAVs) is urgently needed from a technoethics and science and technology studies (STS) perspective: Not the least because "in-depth technology assessment of military uses of cognitive science and IT, and studies of preventive arms control are missing. Due to its time urgency, in particular the area of autonomous combat systems should be investigated." (Altmann 2006?).

The social pervasiveness and technoethical problem that come with the robots are immense: With regard to arms control, peace studies expert Juergen Altmann points out that "[t]he history of technological arms races, in particular the Cold War, shows many examples where after one side had introduced a military innovation, potential opponents followed suit after only a few years. In many such cases, *the mutual threat had increased, warning and reaction times had decreased, and stability was reduced.* In those few cases where such developments could be reversed, it took many years for negotiations to begin and many more to come to a treaty." (Altmann 2009, 71; my emphasis) In the introduction I pointed out that UCAVs increased the number of killed civilians in the so-called war on terrorism (Boes 2006, Rötzer 2007a, 2007b, Sparrow 2007, Weber 2009). It is also the question whether the increased usage of UCAVs – which makes targeted assassinations a relatively safe 'business' – lead to the undermining of international humanitarian law.

The Technology of Uninhabited Air Vehicles (UAVs)

Uninhabited Combat Air Vehicles are aircraft which can be operated by remote control or autonomously.. UCAVs consist of three components: an airplane with sensors and weapon systems, a ground control station from which it is tele-operated and a communication infrastructure such as radio communication or satellite link. As Altmann points out, 'flight control is done by on-board processing, but general directions and in particular attack decisions are given by remote control, often via satellite link from hundreds to many thousands of kilometres away." (Altmann 2009, 69). As an integral part of network centric warfare, UCAV video images are transferred to ground troops, helicopters or ground vehicles. For example, the MQ-9 Reaper of the U.S. forces is an up-graded and enlarged version of the UCAV MQ-1 Predator, with 11 meters length and 20 meters wingspan. Possible payload mass is 1702 kg. The MQ-9 Reaper is capable of 14 hours non-stop flying – the traditional jet fighter-bomber F-16 is capable of 2-3 hours flying but at much faster speed. MQ-9's maximum speed is 400 km/h, service ceiling is 15,000 meters. Most of these UCAVs are guided from bases in the United States – thousands of kilometres away. Only the take-offs and landings are operated from Afghan or Iraq bases. One Reaper system (a ground sta-

tion and 4 planes) costs about 69 million dollars. The tactical aim of UCAVs is described by the military to threaten the local population as well as to hold a huge amount of ammunition on call for short-notice strikes. They are used for targeted killing missions and 'precision attacks' and thereby combine surveillance and combat tasks.

The 'Unmanned Systems Roadmap' of the U.S. Department of Defense states that the latest US wars have been a most welcome test bed for the weapon technologies for engineers and military strategists and that they support further development and fund raising "For defense-related unmanned systems, the series of regional conflicts in which the United States has been engaged since the end of the Cold War has served to introduce and expand the capabilities of unmanned systems technology to war fighters. *This conflict-driven demand has ensured the technology's evolution and continued funding, with each new conflict reinforcing the interest in such systems.* Global Hawk owes its appearance over Afghanistan to the performance of Predator over Bosnia and Kosovo, which in turn owes its start to the record establishes by Pioneer in the Persian Gulf War." (Department of Defense 2007, 47; my emphasis).

Tele-Operated Combat Drones and International Humanitarian Law

Uninhabited aerial combat systems are advocated by the military because of their efficiency, speed and low costs. Another advantage is seen in the possibility to spare or save the lives of one's own soldiers and to more efficiently kill insurgents (Barry/Zimit 2001, Arkin 2007, Asaro 2008, Lin et al. 2009).

While *tele-operated systems* today can supposedly distinguish reliably between soldiers, surrendering soldiers and civilians (Altmann 2003, Boes 2005, Sparrow 2007, Weber 2009), some also argue that *future autonomous systems* may even be able to discriminate reliably between civilian and military targets, therefore using them might be morally superior to ordinary weapons – as well as human beings (Meilinger 2001, Arkin 2007).

But when you look closer at recent developments, the picture given by the military is turned upside down: With the excellent cameras of today's tele-operated systems it is possible to monitor the battlefield very closely. The already mentioned Guardian investigation quotes the report of the Israeli Major Gil, deputy commander of the first Israeli UAV squadron, in the online version of an Israeli Army magazine, where he describes drone attacks during the 23-days Gaza offensive against .... "'We were able to monitor each of the soldiers at any minute and identify any threats to them," he said. He also *describes being able to clearly distinguish fighters from women and children and other civilians*: 'When there were innocent people around, we would wait for the terrorist to leave the child and then hit him,' he said. Lieutenant Tal, an operator and intelligence officer in the UAV squadron, describes the details the drone cameras can see. 'We identified a terrorist that looked like an Israeli soldier. Our camera enabled us to see him very clearly. He was wearing a green parka jacket and was walking around with a huge radio that looked exactly like an army radio. It was very clear he wasn't a soldier.' (Chassay 2009)

On the one hand, there is the obvious problem of a 'correct' interpretation of the data and images – how does wearing an army radio indicate that someone who looks like a soldier is a terrorist? On the other hand – if there is no doubt that the (tele-)operator of a today's UCAV can easily differentiate between soldiers, surrendering soldiers and civilians, one has to wonder why the number of killed civilians permanently increased in the last years of Western wars 'on terrorism' – especially with regard to air attacks. While Hsiao-Rei Hicks et al. 2009 argue that the indiscriminate nature of air attacks either with bombs or missiles causes civilians deaths, one could get the impression that UCAV and guided missiles– despite their discriminate nature - were used in the Gaza offensive *for killing them on purpose*. This might be

an indicator of the weakening of the international humanitarian law in western wars 'on terror'.

At the same time, the highly sophisticated possibilities of UCAV technology might pose a seduction to today's armed forces to use it for eliminating 'disobedient' or unwanted persons – let it be terrorists, surrendering enemies or civilians – *exactly because it is a perfect means for remote-controlled killing which doesn't endanger one's own life*. Controlling UCAVs from beyond the battlefield via computer game-like interfaces seems to lower the threshold of killing or even encourage a practice of of push-button killing.

Therefore, given these developments in western wars on terror in Palestine as well as in Afghanistan, Pakistan and Iraq, it is highly questionable that UCAV technology helps to reduce the killing of civilians. On the contrary, it seems *that the usage of UCAVs and other means of digital warfare come at the same time with a neglect of international humanitarian law. In some cases one gets the impression that these armchair warfare weapons are used on purpose and quite effectively to terrorize and kill not only enemy soldiers but also the civilian population.*

The targeted killings of Palestine terrorist suspects is not a new phenomenon. Between 2000 and 2006 three hundred people characterized as terrorists were killed together with 129 civilians (Case 2008). In face of this development, Israeli Human Rights Groups filed a lawsuit against the government. They argued that *'targeted killing' is an illegal use of force* – according to Israeli as well as international law. To kill suspects without trial is not acceptable. "In December 2006, the Israeli Supreme Court issued a landmark decision in the case. While the court stopped short of an outright ban on Israel's assassinations program, it ruled that *international law constrains the targeting of terror suspects*. Currently, in order to justify a strike, Israel must have reliable information that the suspect is actively engaged in hostilities (such as planning a terrorist attack) and must rule out an arrest as being too risky. The court also requires that there be an independent investigation after each strike." (Case 2008; my emphasis)

Amnesty International protested to George W. Bush against targeted killings by the U.S. forces and the CIA in Iraq, Pakistan and Afghanistan – very often deployed via UCAVs. Amnesty International claims that extrajudicial executions are prohibited under international human rights laws (Alston 2009). Beyond the question of the juridical status of targeted assassinations, it is important to remember that air surveillance mostly takes place several times before the targeted killings. Therefore it is highly likely that those who ordered the attacks were very well aware of the presence of women, children and other innocent people close to the envisioned target. In many cases the proportionality of the military aim of the attack and the collateral damage is questionable when you think of the bombing of a double marriage, of a school and other incidents in Pakistan (Weber 2009).

This situation has not changed under the new U.S. presidency of Barack Obama – regardless of the Nobel Peace Prize award – because he did not stop the practice of targeted killings in the U.S. war on terror. On the contrary, since he took office the number of UCAV deployments and targeted killings has risen (Mayer 2009) and Obama explicitly supports the development of robots and their increasing deployment in Afghanistan and Iraq.

Autonomous Killer Drones?

Tele-operated UCAVs are frequently used to spare the lives of friendly soldiers, but at the same time it seems that the deployment of UCAVs does not only lead to the increasing accidental killing of civilians but that it can also result in the wantonly negligent or even intentional killing of civilians. In face of the rising numbers of killed civilians in the Israeli-Palestine conflict as well as in the western 'wars on terror' in Afghanistan, Iraq and Pakistan, *the question arises whether RMA, network centric warfare and high-tech weapon technology such* *as tele-operated UCAVs come with a weakening of international humanitarian law.*

Tele-operated UCAVs are equipped with excellent cameras so that pilots can very well differentiate between adults and children, between combatants and civilians. The new high-tech weaponry is often used either to assassinate suspect terrorists seemingly without regard for civilians nearby or even to kill not only soldiers but civilians on enemy territory without any differentiating. In other cases, UCAVs are used as easy pushbutton weapon to blow up houses with little regard for the possible civilians inside and for operating them in regions which are not even declared enemy's territory – such as Pakistan where the government at least officially withdraw its acceptance of US-UCAV attacks in the beginning of 2009.

The next question is how this scenario would look like with the use not of tele-operated but autonomous UCAVs? The question already discussed by ethicists, peace activists and military is, whether they can be deployed according to international humanitarian law at all. Autonomous UCAVs work on the basis of object recognition systems which can only differentiate between the members of one's own army and everybody else – with the help of identification friend-foe systems. Insofar as autonomous systems can't differentiate between soldiers, surrendering soldiers and civilians, they contradict the laws of war. As many pro and con arguments for autonomous weapons are related to the autonomy of the weapon systems, we need to have a closer look at what 'autonomy' means here and how it influences the ethical discussion on UCAVs.

As the state of military development is kept at least partially secret, it is difficult to judge the degree of autonomy already realized and deployed in recent UCAVs. General Atomics – producer of MQ-9 Reaper – states that the system has "robust sensors to *automatically find, fix, track and target critical emerging time sensitive targets*." (General Atomics 2007; my emphasis)

At the moment there seems to be no fully operational autonomous systems with software enabling them to make autonomous decisions on their targets on the basis of pre-given information and variables. But there are discussions on humans 'on' the loop instead of 'in' the loop which might become a reality in a few years. Up to now, UCAVs are 'only' able to act independently in the sense of calculating their own trajectory towards the target as already known from long-range systems[5]. Up to now, the U.S. Department of Defense claims that until the resolution of certain legal and safety concerns, killing will not be fully automated: "Because the DoD complies with the Law of Armed Conflict, there are many issues requiring resolution associated with the employment of weapons by an unmanned systems. For a significant period into the future, the decision to pull a trigger or to launch a missile from an unmanned system will not be fully automated, but it will remain under the full control of a human operator." (DoD 2009, 24)

This statement suggests that the state of art in UCAV technology already would allow the deployment of autonomous ones at least in principle. Only for legal and safety issues the (U.S.) military (says it) can't. Given the interest in autonomous UCAVs, the tendency towards the weakening of international humanitarian law and the well-known effects of arms race, the danger that autonomous killer drones might become a reality (soon) is quite high. The introduction of the 'Unmanned Systems Roadmap' of the U.S. Department of Defense of 2009 consequently states: "In response to the Warfighter demand, the Department has continued to investigate aggressively in developing autonomous systems and technologies. That investment has seen unmanned systems turned from being primarily tele-operated, single-mission platforms to platforms into increasingly autonomous, multi-mission platforms. The fielding of increasingly sophisticated reconnaissance, targeting, and weapons delivery technology has not only allowed unmanned systems to participate in shortening 'the sensor to shooter kill chain', but it has also allowed them to complete the chain by delivering precision weapons on target." DoD 2009, xiii)

If UCAVs will be entrusted with decisions about target identification and destruction, severe problems with regard to the question of responsibility – and therefore international humanitarian law – will arise: Who should be held responsible for the death of civilians or soldiers that had surrendered in case of faults and atrocities? Many ethicists and peace researchers arguing from diverse theoretical backgrounds have pointed out that responsibility for killing is a main condition for jus in bello[6]: "If the nature of a weapon, or other means of war fighting, is such that it is *typically* impossible to identify or hold individuals responsible for the casualities that it causes then it is contrary to this important requirement of *jus in bello*. (Sparrow 2007; emphasis given). If responsibility is no longer considered a critical issue, this might have severe consequences for the way wars with autonomous weapon systems (AWSs) will be fought

As I already stated, to avoid the accusation of undermining international humanitarian law via autonomous robots, the U.S. forces claim that UCAVs will only be deployed under the supervision of human (military) operators[7]. There is an internal tension to this claim. On the one hand, why should one want to build fully autonomous systems and only use them as more or less remote-controlled systems? One of the main reasons for building autonomous systems is to heighten the speed on the battlefield. So why would you stay with human operators who slow down fully autonomous network-centric warfare? Consequently, the United States Air Force write in their latest Unmanned Aircraft Systems Flight Plan 2009-2047: "The vision is the USAF [United States Air Force; JW] postured to harness *increasingly automated*, modular, globally connected, and sustainable multi-mission unmanned systems resulting in a leaner, more adaptable, and efficient air force ..." (United States Air Force 2009, 14, emphasis J.W.)

On the other hand, it is also very likely, that from the moment an enemy will deploy totally autonomous systems, its enemy will also use them. In this case, the battle could get out of control very easily.

Last but not least there is a strong technical reason to use fully autonomous UCAVs because remote control requires a communication infrastructure which might be threatened by the enemy. It is highly probable that hostile forces will engage in disabling the robot systems by jamming or hacking its communication infrastructure – one of the vulnerable spots in autonomous systems (see Altmann 2003, Sparrow 2007; Weber 2009). Hacked autonomous systems would be highly dangerous not only to the soldiers of one's own forces but also to civilians. As the military is also aware of this great danger, it is also likely that uninhabited combat vehicles will be used in full autonomy in the near future so that they are not dependent on communication systems.

This development is not only highly problematic with regard to the question of responsibility, but also with regard to the heightened speed of warfare where wrong decisions can no longer be cancelled or changed.

But there are several other propositions by the military how to ensure responsibility with regard to autonomous systems – either to address responsibility towards the programmer, the machine or the commanding officer. As autonomous systems will show unpredictable behaviour, some argue that the responsibility lies with the programmer and / or manufacturer. Yet if the manufacturer were to give appropriate information about the risks of autonomous weapons, the manufacturer cannot likely be held responsible for a machine's failure. Think for example of the destruction of the wrong target as an outcome of the autonomous behaviour of the system. If a system is supposed to act increasingly autonomouslyy and the system does so, the programmer cannot be held respon-

sible for the negative outcome of the unpredictable behaviour of an autonomous system. The programmer could only be held responsible – at least in a legal sense – in the case that autonomous weapon systems will be banned internationally (for example by an appendix to the Geneva Convention) (Nagenborg et al. 2008, Weber 2009). To hold an autonomous machine responsible in the literal sense doesn't make sense as the system is always pre-programmed by human beings – even if it is programmed to execute unpredictable behaviour.

The preferred approach of the military is to attribute the responsibility to the commanding officer – as it is the case with long-range weapons. This seems to be a non-satisfying and possibly incorrect solution of the problem because autonomous systems choose their targets on the basis of their programmed parameters, categories and variables. Thus it would seem that officers should not be held responsible for weapons which they do not control. (Sparrow 2007, 71)

In the face of the immense ethical and juridical problems of military robots and their possible prohibition under international humanitarian law, research on ethics for military robots as well as so-called 'ethical' software is sponsored by the U.S. Army Research Office and the U.S. Office of Naval Research (Arkin 2007, Arkin 2008, Canning 2006; Moshkina/Arkin 2008, Lin et al.2009). For example, Ronald Arkin, a roboticist at the Georgia Institute of Technology, in a project funded by the military, proposes that *future* robots will be more ethical than humans because they don't have emotions or a drive for self-preservation (Arkin 2008). He is facilitating the idea that *future* robots might have a better technical equipment – such as better sensors, processor, rules, memory etc. – to decide whether a target is legitimate. Astonishingly, he makes the point that robots do not suffer under the pressure of 'scenario fulfilment' – they don't interpret their input according to a given schema, fixed expectations and a pre-given frame of thought. But that is exactly how software programs work – on pregiven schemes, values and perspectives which in action can't be put into question. Even behaviour-based robotics which (partly) builds on emergence, unpredictability and system-environment coupling nevertheless builds on pre-programmed software. And robots are not able to question their own framework and decisions while humans in principle have the potential to do so.

Arkin doesn't argue that robots might become perfect – but that they will perform better than humans. He makes the point that robots compute more information in shorter time. Therefore they would have more time for reasoning about lethal decisions (Arkin 2007, 6f).

In the face of the massive violations of the laws of war during western war 'Operation Iraqi Freedom' (Surgeon General's Office 2006[8]), Arkin argues for a technological fix: In the face of advanced weapon technology he calls for an 'automated ethics' instead of reflecting the failure of the U.S. forces to train their soldiers in a way to respect and apply the international and national humanitarian law. To think of ways to change this behaviour in principle to make warfare more secure for civilians, surrendered insurgents, etc. seems to be out of sight.

What is usually left out of this approach is the underlying epistemological and ontological foundations. For example, Arkin takes for granted that robot systems have at least as much information as soldiers. He does not discuss the meaning of 'information' and whether information is identical with meaning, knowledge or even understanding. Second, he proposes systems that can resist unethical acts and even explain why. If the resistance is overridden by the commanding officer, the latter is responsible for the system's actions. This approach either suggests *highly intelligent* systems that will not become reality in the next decades (Sharkey 2007, Tamburrini 2009) or this mechanism of resistance works on a very reductionist level. The third assumption of Arkin's approach is the capability of autonomous weapon systems to distinguish between soldiers,

surrendering soldiers and civilians – an assumption that is highly unlikely at least in the near future.

Implicitly he also takes for granted *that every possible complex situation can be formalized correctly and computed in real time – a very old fairytale of Artificial Intelligence*. He does not discuss problems of navigation, object recognition as well as the scaling-up problem (parallel computing of many behaviours in one system) in real and complex worlds; these problems of robotics will not be solved in a satisfying manner soon. But nevertheless, being aware of some difficulties, Arkin proposes that a system should never be allowed to make lethal decisions in situations which are not covered by ethical prescriptions. *But how do you make sure that a system is applying its rules adequately to a given situation?*

Arkin also avoids the *problem of formal verification – that is the problem of software mistakes or bugs*. How can you make sure that there are no bugs in the software of autonomous lethal systems? Formal verification of software for systems as complex as combat robots is not possible in a reasonable amount of time – if at all. So how can one think of 'ethical' warbots?

The uncritical discussion of ethical software for killer robots produces the impression that it is mostly about raising the acceptance in western countries for these new weapon systems rather than to solve the humanitarian problems of high-tech automated warfare which does not only endanger the lives of many civilians but also destabilizes the military situation between opponents and contributes to further arms races, proliferation of weapons, and undermines international law of warfare.

In contrast, Noel Sharkey, British roboticist, calls for more responsibility of computer scientists and engineers to make the unsolved and profound technical problems of military robotic systems visible for the public. Engineers and computer scientists should resist generous funding for military robots and criticize the old salvation stories of AI. As Sharkey writes: "Computer professionals and engineers have a duty to ensure that the funding bodies, policy makers and – if possible – end users know the current limitations of AI technology, including potential mishaps in the complexity of unpredictable real-world events. *Do not be tempted to express your opinions or future predictions of AI as if the technology were already in place or just around the corner.* The consequences of playing the funding game are too serious. Ultimately, we must ask if we are ready to leave life-or-death-decisions to robots too dim to be called stupid." (Sharkey 2007, 123; my emphasis).

Economy, Technology Development and Codes of Ethics

But traditionally, international professional associations such as the IEEE or ACM (Association for Computing Machinery) have avoided the topic of the intertwinement of engineering and the military. For example, in their 'Codes of Ethics", engineers declare themselves as responsible for their systems, products and artefacts so they will not threaten the safety, health and welfare of the public. The Code of the ACM even states: „When designing or implementing systems, computing professionals must attempt to ensure that the products of their efforts will be used in socially responsible ways, will meet social needs, and will avoid harmful effects to health and welfare." (ACM Code of Ethics and Professional Conduct 1992, 1)

It seems too easy to put the burden of the ethical solution of this highly complex problem primarily on the shoulders of engineers (von Schomberg 2007). Nevertheless, it is necessary to discuss these conflicts also in reference to the Code of Ethics of professional associations.

Up to now the field of autonomous combat systems is virtually ignored by ethics in general and therefore roboticists should have a strong motivation to develop professional techno-ethical regulation in this new and emerging field. We know that technology assessment and ethics are effec-

tive means to construct our technological future. Techno-ethical analyses and regulations are partly instruments to govern policies, to shape research strategies as well as to prepare legal certainty for research, development and commercialization of new products and systems (Schaper-Rinkel 2006). These aspects need to be kept in mind with regard to the discussion of techno-ethical issues.

In robotics – as in many other technosciences – we have no clear-cut borders between the technoscientific, military, economic and the industrial complex. For example, there are rarely any US robotic labs which are not funded directly or indirectly by the military in the US. This is also a problem in Europe – but the impact of the military is (still) lower.

Financing and Motivating (Future) High-Tech Armchair Warfare

The political and ethical problems of UCAVs are related to issues of arms control. One might expect arms control to become a minor issue after the end of the Cold War in 1989, but after a short decline of military expenses in R&D, the latter grew rapidly since the mid90s – especially in the US. The US military budget comprises nearly half of the world's total expenditures on the military. By the fiscal year 2008, the U.S. military budget had "doubled since Bush took office in 2000 and is now higher in real terms than any other year in the last half-century." (Kumar Behera 2008). Robert Higgs, U.S.-American economist and political scientist at The Independent Institute in California considers the real defense budget of the USA for 2006 – to include not only the budget of the Department of Defense ($499.4 billion), but also defense-related parts of the Department of Energy budget ($16.6 billion), the budget of the Department of Homeland Security ($69.1 billion), the budget of the Department of State and international assistance programs for activities arguably related to defense purposes ($25.3 billion), the Department of Veterans Affairs ($69.8 billion), the Department of the Treasury (Military Retirement Fund of $38.5 billion) as well as the National Aeronautics and Space Administration's outlays which are at least as indirectly defense-related. "When all of these other parts of the budget are added to the budget for the Pentagon itself, they increase the fiscal 2006 total by nearly half again, to *$728.2 billion*." (Higgs 2007; my emphasis) During the presidency of Barack Obama, a decline of the US military budget is expected in general (Mayer 2009), but at the same time Obama is known for favouring military robots. For Fiscal Year 2009 the US Congress originally approved 3.6 billion dollars for the Future Combat System (FCS) alone (Washington Post, 13/10/2008). Now the FCS was determined but the research on sensors, unmanned aerial and ground vehicles, the Non-Line-of-Sight Launch System, and a modified FCS network was shifted to the New Army Brigade Combat Team Modernization strategy (https://www.fcs.army.mil/).

On the economic level UCAVs are regarded as a key technology for the future global market. The USA already sold and still sells their MQ UCAVs to France, Italy and other countries. The USA spent several billions every year on drones. For example, one of the mentioned MQ-9 Reaper systems (with four aircraft) costs about 70 million dollars. Experts estimate that UCAVs will be sold from 2015 on for about five billion dollars every year (Nikolei 2005). *Given the huge techno-ethical problems, Europe should engage in preventive arms control to regulate the development of this market and to hinder an arms race in the near future and to work against a further increase of the numbers of killed civilians.*

One important question underlying others is: Do robot systems fall under the categories of existing arms control. Arms control expert Jürgen Altmann describes the problems of UCAVs for example with regard to the Conventional Forces in Europe Treaty in the following way: "The Treaty on Conventional Armed Forces of 1990 limits the holdings in five major weapons classes for the NATO member states and Russia; its definitions of battle tanks, armoured combat vehicles, artillery, combat aircraft and attack helicopters intentionally do not mention personnel on board, so that crewless versions would fall under the same rubrics, would count in the national holdings, would have to be notified to the Treaty partners, would be subject to inspection etc. However, *one can foresee a debate which types of armed UAVs would constitute a combat aircraft*. Whereas the definition is quite general, arguments might be made that converted surveillance drones or very small crewless aircraft do not fall under this heading. The situation with respect to "combat helicopters" is similar. […] Thus, a grey area of uncounted and unlimited combat systems might develop. A fundamental problem is that similar limitations of conventional armaments are not in force in other continents." (Altmann 2009, 74-75, emphasis J.W.)

One of the more pressing socio-political concerns about autonomous combat systems is that they might make going to war much easier. Up to now in Western democracies, politicians had to convince their people to participate in a war. How will this change if it is only or mostly about pushing buttons from a remote place? Also deciding whether to disobey inhumane orders will no more happen in robot wars and this is (or was?) a crucial part of at least a bit more human way of warfare. We know of soldiers who pointed their guns into the air because they didn't want to kill. Robots will always execute what they are programmed for aside from systems failure. Many philosophers such as Paul Virilio or Friedrich Kittler also ask how our self-understanding, and more generally the relation between human and machine might change, if weapon systems decide on their targets and when to destroy them (including human beings). The autonomy of a weapon system comes with the depersonalization and anonymization of power and control. Following the argument of Virilio and Kittler, some are concerned that autonomous weapon systems might gain the status of subjects as they are the ones in power (Kittler 1988, 355; Virilio 2000). This would mean a clear shift of power in the relation between humans and machines where the latter are the autonomous ones. I think that we need a closer analysis of these processes.

STS and ethics today must address the consequences of unintended side-effects as well as societal and political decisions in our highly complex societies. These techno-scientific issues cannot only be addressed by single engineers and philosophers, but must be integrated in a broad sociotechnical discussion including a broad public debate on socio-political and techno-ethical issues, deliberative technology assessment procedures like consensus conferences (von Schomberg 2007) as well as international political actions and policies for the integration of issues of military robotics into preventive arms control. In the field of autonomous weapon systems more interdisciplinary research is needed "on the risks of misuse of new technologies and consequences for international security, explicitly including military applications and civil-military interaction/exchanges, considering also the capabilities of small groups and second-level arms-producing countries." (Altmann 2006, 44)

But of great importance is also to analyse further the relation between contemporary warfare and the killing of civilians in the context of the 'Revolution in Military Affairs' and high-tech weapons (such as combat robots). High-tech weaponry seems to make possible and probably increasingly intense extra-judicial killings (organized, targeted assassinations) in the Israeli-Palestine conflict as well as in western wars on terror. In case this is leading to a silent 'revision' of international humanitarian law, urgent action is needed. To ban UCAVs could be a first step to secure international humanitarian law.

ACKNOWLEDGMENT

I wish to thank Cheris Kramarae, Juergen Altmann and Lucy Suchman very much for helpful comments and discussions on earlier drafts of this paper.

REFERENCES

Alston, P. (2009). *Information to the Third Committee (Social, Humanitarian and Cultural) of the UN General Assembly*, 27 Oct. 2009; Retrieved 20th of November, 2009 from http://reliefweb.int/rw/rwb.nsf/db900sid/MYAI-7X94DK?OpenDocument

Altmann, J. (2003). Roboter für den Krieg? *Wissenschaft und Frieden*, *21*(3), 18–22.

Altmann, J. (2006). Trends in Cognitive Science and Information Technology. In S. Pullinger (ed.), *Annex to Study: EU research and innovation policy and the future of the Common Foreign Security Policy. A Report Commissioned by the Science and Technology Foresight Unit of DG Research, European Commission* (October 2006). Retrieved October 14, 2009, from http://www.isis-europe.org/pdf/reports_11.pdf

Altmann, J. (2009). Preventive Arms Control for Uninhabited Military Vehicles. In Capurro, R., & Nagenborg, M. (Eds.), *Ethics and Robotics* (pp. 69–82). Amsterdam: IOS Press.

Arkin, R. (2007). *Governing Lethal Behaviour: Embedding Ethics in a Hybrid/Deliberative/Reactive Robot Architecture*. Mobile Robot Laboratory, College of Computing, Georgia Institute of Technology. Retrieved October 14, 2009, from http://www.cc.gatech.edu/ai/robot-lab/online-publications/formalizationv35.pdf

Arkin, R. (2008). *On the Ethical Quandaries of a Practicing Roboticist: A first-hand Look*. Retrieved October 14, 2009, from www.cc.gatech.edu/ai/robot-lab/online-publications/ArkinEthicalv2.pdf

Asaro, P. (2008). How Just Could a Robot War Be? In Brey, P., Briggle, A., & Waelbers, K. (Eds.), *Current Issues in Computing And Philosophy*. Amsterdam: IOS Publishers.

Association for Computing Machinery. (1992). *ACM Code of Ethics and Personal Conduct*. New York: Author. Retrieved October 14, 2009, from http://www.acm.org/constitution/code.html

Atomics, G. (2007). *MQ-9 Reaper. Predator-B Hunter-Killer UAV*. Retrieved October 14, 2009, from www.defense-update.com/products/p/predatorB.htm

Barry, C. L., & Zimet, E. (2001). UCAVs – Technological, Policy, and Operational Challenges. *Defense Horizons, 3*, 1–8.

Bergen, P., & Tiedemann, K. (2009. October 19). Revenge of the Drones. An Analysis of Drone Strikes in Pakistan. *New America Foundation*. Retrieved October 22, 2009 from http://www.newamerica.net/publications/policy/revenge_drones

Berglund, E. (2008). *The Potential of UAS for European Border Surveillance*. Retrieved October 22 from http://www.uvs-info.com/Yearbook2008/042_Contributing-Stakeholder_FRONTEX.pdf

Blackmore, T. (2005). *War X*. Toronto, Canada: University of Toronto Press.

Boes, H. (2005). *An der Schwelle zum automatischen Krieg*. Retrieved October 14, 2009, from http://www.heise.de/tp/r4/artikel/21/21121/1.html

Canning, J. S. (2006). Concept of Operations for Armed Autonomous Systems. *The Difference between 'Winning the War' and 'Winning the Peace'*. Retrieved October 14, 2007, from www.dtic.mil/ndia/2006disruptive_tech/canning.pdf

Capurro, R., & Nagenborg, M. (Eds.). (2009). *Ethics and Robotics*. Amsterdam: AKA/IOS Press.

Case, D. (2008). *The U.S. Military's Assassination Problem*. Retrieved January 1, 2009, from http://www.motherjones.com/commentary/columns/2008/03/the-us-militarys-assassination-problem.html

Cerqui, D., Weber, J., & Weber, K. (Eds.). (2006). Ethics in Robotics. *International Review of Information Ethics 2/2006*. Retrieved October 14, 2009, from http://www.i-r-i-e.net/inhalt/006/006_full.pdf

Chassay, C. (2009, March 23). Cut to pieces: the Palestinian family drinking tea in their courtyard. Israeli unmanned aerial vehicles – the dreaded drones – caused at least 48 deaths in Gaza during the 23-day offensive. *The Guardian*. Retrieved October 14, 2009 from http://www.guardian.co.uk/world/2009/mar/23/gaza-war-crimes-drones/print

Cordesman, A. C. (2008, March). *Air Combat Trends in the Afghan and Iraq Wars. Center for Strategic & International Studies (CSIS)*. Retrieved December 14, 2008 from http://www.csis.org/media/csis/pubs/080318_afgh-iraqairbrief.pdf

Department of Defense. (2007). *Uninhabited Systems Roadmap 2007-2032*. Washington, DC: Author. Retrieved October 14, 2009, from http://www.acq.osd.mil/usd/Uninhabited%20Systems%20Roadmap.2007-2032.pdf

Department of Defense. (2009). *Unmanned Systems Integrated Roadmap, 2009-2034*. Retrieved October 14, 2009 from http://www.acq.osd.mil/uas/docs/UMSIntegratedRoadmap2009.pdf

Finn, A. (2008). Legal considerations for the weaponisation of Unmanned Ground Vehicles. *Int. J. Intelligent Defence Support Systems, 1*(1), 43–74. doi:10.1504/IJIDSS.2008.020273

Fischer, H. (2008). Iraqui Civilian Death Estimates. *CRS report for Congress,* August 2008. Retrieved October 14, 2009 from http://www.fas.org/sgp/crs/mideast/RS22537.pdf

Hanley, Ch. J. (2007). Robot Air Attack Squadron Bound for Iraq. *Associated Press,* July 16, 2007. Retrieved October 14, 2009 from http://www.commondreams.org/archive/2007/07/16/2570

Higgs, R. (2007, March 15). *The Trillion-Dollar Defense Budget Is Already Here.* Retrieved October 14, 2009 from http://www.independent.org/newsroom/article.asp?id=1941, Oct 11th 2009.

Horowitz, A., & Weiss, P. (2009). American Jews Rethink Israel. *The Nation,* Oct. 14th 2009. Retrieved at Oct. 2009 at http://www.thenation.com/doc/20091102/horowitz_weiss/single

Hsiao-Rei Hicks, M., Dardagan, H., Guerrero Serdán, G., Bagall, P. M., Sloboda, J. A., & Spagat, M. (2009, April 19). The Weapons that Kill Civilians – Death of Childrens and Non-Combatants, 2003-2008. *The New England Journal of Medicine, 360*(16), 1585–1588. doi:10.1056/NEJMp0807240

Huang, H.-M., Pavek, K., Novak, B., Albus, J., & Messina, E. (2005). A Framework for Autonomy Levels for Uninhabited Systems (ALFUS). In *Proceedings of the AUVSI's Uninhabited Systems North America 2005, June 2005,* Baltimore. Retrieved September 21, 2007 from www.isd.mel.nist.gov/documents/huang/ALFUS-auvsi-8.pdf

Human Rights Watch. (2009). *Precisely Wrong. Gaza Civilians Killed by Israeli Drone-Launched Missiles.* Retrieved October 14, 2009 from http://www.hrw.org/en/reports/2009/06/30/precisely-wrong?print

Kaufmann, S. (2006, Nov.). Land Warrior. The Reconfiguration of the Soldier in the 'Information Age'. *Science . Technology and Innovation Studies, 2,* 81–102.

Kittler, F. (1988). Signal-Rausch-Abstand. In H. U. Gumbrecht, & K. L. Pfeiffer (eds.) Materialität der Kommunikation, (pp. 342 - 359). Frankfurt a.M., Germany: Suhrkamp.

Kumar Behera, L. (2008). *The US Defence Budget for 2008. IDSA strategic comments.* Retrieved October 14, 2009 from http://www.idsa.in/publications/stratcomments/LaxmanBehera210207.htm

Lin, P., Bekey, G., & Abney, K. (2009). Robots in War. Issues of Risk and Ethics . In Capurro, R., & Nagenborg, M. (Eds.), *Ethics and Robotics* (pp. 49–68). Amsterdam: AKA / IOS Press.

Marsiske, H.-A. (2007), An der langen Leine. Roboter im Sicherheitsdienst. *c't – magazin für computertechnik, 9.*

Marte, A., & Szabo, E. (2007). *Center for Defence Information: Fact Sheet on the Army's Future Combat Systems, August 7, 2007.* Retrieved October 14, 2009 from http://www.cdi.org/program/issue/document.cfm?DocumentID=4058&IssueID=221&StartRow=1&ListRows=10&appendURL=&Orderby=DateLastUpdated&ProgramID=37&issueID=221 Oct. 15th 2009

Mayer, J. (2009, October 26). The Predator War. What Are the Risks of the C.I.A.'s Covert Drone program? *New Yorker (New York, N.Y.),* 36–45.

Meilinger, Ph. S. (2001). Precision Aerospace Power, Discrimination, and the Future of War. *Aerospace Power Journal, 15*(3), 12–20.

Mir, A. (2009, April 19th). 60 drone hits kill 14 al-Qaeda men, 687 civilians. *The News.* Retrieved October 14, 2009 from http://www.thenews.com.pk/top_story_detail.asp?Id=21440

Münkler, H. (2002). *Die neuen Kriege.* Reinbek, Germany: Rowohlt.

Nagenborg, M., Capurro, R., Weber, J., & Pingel, C. (2007). Ethical Regulations on Robotics in Europe. *AI & Society*, ▪▪▪, 349–366.

Nikolei, H.-H. (2005). *Milliardenmarkt Drohnen*. Retrieved January 1, 2006 from www.n-tv.de/544984.html

Post, W. *Balancing Defense and the Budget. After Eight Boom Years for Spending on Military Equipment, Contractors Expect a Slowdown. (Materials from a September 2008 report by the Institute for Policy Studies; report by the Center for Arms Control and Non-Proliferation; and government documents.)* (2008). Retrieved October 14, 2009 from http://www.washingtonpost.com/wp-dyn/content/graphic/2008/10/13/GR2008101300651.html?sid=ST2008101300698

Rötzer, F. (2007a). *Einsatzregeln für Kampfroboter*. Retrieved October 14, 2009 from www.heise.de/tp/r4/artikel/25/25117/1.html

Rötzer, F. (2007b). *Schwärme von Kampfdrohnen sollen Aufständische bekämpfen*. Retrieved October 14, 2009 from http://www.heise.de/tp/r4/artikel/25/25722/1.html

Rötzer, F. (2008). *Der Luftkrieg im Irak und in Afghanistan*. Retrieved October 14, 2009 from http://www.heise.de/tp/r4/artikel/27/27180/1.html

Schaper-Rinkel, P. (2006). Governance von Zukunftsversprechen: Zur politischen Ökonomie der Nanotechnologie. *PROKLA 145 " Ökonomie der Technik", 36*(4), 473-96

Sharkey, N. (2007). Automated Killers and the Computing Profession. *Computer, 40* (11), 124, 122-123.

Singer, P. (2009). *Robots at War: The New Battlefield*. Retrieved October 14, 2009 from http://www.wilsoncenter.org/index.cfm?fuseaction=wq.essay&essay_id=496613

Sparrow, R. (2007). Killer Robots. *Journal of Applied Philosophy, 24*(1), 62–77. doi:10.1111/j.1468-5930.2007.00346.x

Surgeon General's Office. (2006). *Mental Health Advisory Team (MHAT) IV Operation Iraqi Freedom 05-07*, Final Report, Nov. 17, 2006. Retrieved October 14, 2009 from http://www.house.gov/delahunt/ptsd.pdf

Tamburrini, G. (2009). Robot Ethics: A View from the Philosophy of Science . In Capurro, R., & Nagenborg, M. (Eds.), *Ethics and Robotics* (pp. 11–22). Amsterdam: IOS Press.

UN News Center. (2009). Civilian casualties in Afghanistan keep rising. Retrieved October 14, 2009 from http://www.un.org/apps/news/story.asp?NewsID=31636&Cr=afghan&Cr1=civilian#

United States Air Force. (2009). *Unmanned Aircraft Systems Flight Plan 2009-2047*. Unclassified. Updated version. Washington, DC: Author. Retrieved December 10th, 2009 from http://www.govexec.com/pdfs/072309kp1.pdf
van Blyenburgh, P. (ed.), (pp. 2008). *UAS – Unmanned Aircraft Systems – The Global Perspective 2008/2009*. Paris: Blyenburgh & Co.

Virilio, P. (2000). *Strategy of Deception* (Turner, C., Trans.). New York: Verso.

von Schomberg, R. (2007). *From the Ethics of Technology towards an Ethics of Knowledge Policy & Knowledge Assessment*. European Commission, Community Research, Working Document, EU 22429. Retrieved December 1st, 2009 from ec.europa.eu/research/science.../ethicsofknowledgepolicy_en.pdf

Weber, J. (2009). Robotic Warfare, Human Rights & the Rhetorics of Ethical Machines. In R. Capurro & M. Nagenborg (Eds.), Ethics and Robotics, (pp. 83-103). Heidelberg, Germany: AKA, Amsterdam: IOS Press.

Zwanenburg, M., Boddens Hosang, H., & Wijngaards, N. (2005). Humans, Agents and International Humanitarian Law: Dilemmas in Target Discrimination. In *Proc. 4ᵗʰ Workshop on the Law and Electronic Agents – LEA*. Retrieved December 5ᵗʰ 2009 from http://www.estig.ipbeja.pt/~ac_direito/ZwanenburgBoddensWijngaards_LEA05_CR.pdf

ENDNOTES

[1] At the same time uninhabited vehicles are increasingly used by US Homeland Security to monitor the Mexican / US American or US-American-Canadian borders. Recently the European agency for border security Frontex also plans to monitor European borders by drones; see Berglund 2008.

[2] For the growing Jewish criticism of Israel's policy in face of its brutal invasion in December 2008/January 2009 see Horowitz / Weiss 2009

[3] Arkin 2007

[4] It is probable the case today that aerial vehicles can easily be switched from the remote control mode to one of full autonomy. Full autonomy means either that route and target details are pre-programmed and the assassination is conducted without the help of human operators or that UCAVs are pro-vided with software that enables the system to search a given space for valuable targets and 'decides' on possible lethal attacks on the basis of its program (see chapter on 'Autonomous Killer Drones?').

[5] Key representative practitioners from the U.S. Departments of Commerce, Defense, Energy and Transportation are working on a "Framework for Autonomy Levels for Uninhabited Systems (ALFUS)" see Huang et al. 2005

[6] Jus in bello is about the ,proper' conduct of war, while jus ad bellum is about acceptable justifications to enter war. Both are part of the laws of war.

[7] See also Marsiske 2007, Sparrow 2007

[8] The report interviewed Army soldiers and marines with regard to their battlefield ethics. No more than 47% of Army soldiers and 38% of marines agreed that non-combatants should be treated with respect, less than half of the respondents would report a team member for an unethical behaviour and over a third of them thought that torture should be allowed if the life of a fellow soldier could be saved or important information about insurgents obtained.

Chapter 14
Information Technology:
The Good and Modernity

Pak-Hang Wong
University of Twente, The Netherlands

ABSTRACT

In Information and Computer Ethics (ICE), and, in fact, in normative and evaluative research of Information Technology (IT) in general, researchers have paid few attentions to the prudential values of IT. Hence, analyses of the prudential values of IT are mostly found in popular discourse. Yet, the analyses of the prudential values of IT are important for answering normative questions about people's well-being. In this chapter, the author urges researchers in ICE to take the analyses of the prudential values of IT seriously. A serious study of the analyses, he argues, will enrich the research of ICE. But, what are the analyses? The author will distinguish the analyses of the prudential values of IT, i.e. the prudential analysis, from other types of normative and evaluative analysis of IT. Then, the author will explain why prudential analyses are not taken seriously by the researchers in ICE, and argue why they deserve more attentions. After that, he will outline a framework to analyse and evaluate prudential analyses, and he will apply the framework to an actual prudential analysis. Finally, he will briefly conclude this chapter by highlighting the limits of the proposed framework and identifying the directions for future research.

INTRODUCTION

In "Is Google Making Us Stupid?", an article published in *The Atlantic*, Nicholas Carr (2008) described the possible impact of Information Tech-

nology (IT) on people's cognition. He argued that the Internet has altered the way in which people read and think that makes a specific way of reading and thinking, i.e. *deep reading* and *deep thinking*, difficult. The aim of Carr's article, in other words, is to explicate what he believed to be one of the detrimental effects of the Internet on a person's

DOI: 10.4018/978-1-61692-014-2.ch014

quality of life. It should be clear that the aim of Carr's article is *normative*, as he explicitly argued against a particular form of online practice. If one understands *morality* in the broad sense, which encompasses the questions about *how one should live*, then Carr's argument should also be included in the domain of morality. While Carr's article has generated heated debates on the Internet, researchers in Information and Computer Ethics (ICE) have not responded as enthusiastically. In fact, Carr's article is only one of the more visible examples among various appraisals of IT.[1] As the amount of similar appraisals of IT continues to grow, I think, more attentions should be given to them. The insufficient attentions to the appraisals of IT seem to reiterate Charles Taylor's characterisation of contemporary moral philosophy, which he claimed "tended to focus on what is right to do rather than on what is good to be, on defining the content of obligation rather than the nature of the good life" (Taylor 1989, 3), and, as a result, the domain of morality in contemporary moral philosophy becomes "cramped and truncated" (*ibid.*). By turning the focus to the appraisals, which discuss the possible impacts of IT on people's quality of life, it will broaden the scope of ICE and alleviate the worry expressed by Taylor.

Hence, the aim of this paper is to urge researchers in ICE to take seriously the appraisals similar to Carr's. A serious study of the appraisals will enrich the research in ICE. Yet, what exactly are the appraisals? Using Brey's categorisation (Brey 2007), I distinguish Carr's and similar appraisals from other types of normative analysis of IT. And then, I will explain why the appraisals are not taken seriously by the researchers in ICE, and argue why they deserve more attentions. After that, I will outline a framework to analyse and evaluate the appraisals, and apply the framework to Carr's appraisal. Finally, I will conclude this chapter by highlighting the limits of the proposed framework proposed and identifying the directions for future research.

PRUDENTIAL ANALYSIS OF INFORMATION TECHNOLOGY

I have pointed out that the aim of Carr's appraisal of the Internet and other appraisals similar to his are normative. Yet, an important question remains, that is – *what distinguish the appraisals from other normative analyses of IT?* According to Brey (2007), the current normative and evaluative research of IT can generally be divided into four types, namely ethical analysis, normative political analysis, aesthetic analysis and epistemological analysis. Brey's division is based on the observation that these analyses are guided by different *ideals*. For example, ethical analyses of IT are generally grounded in ethical theories such as deontology, utilitarianism and virtue-based theories, and IT-related ethical issues, e.g. issues on privacy and anonymity, intellectual property, etc. are scrutinised using these ethical theories.[2] Accordingly, the guiding ideal for ethical analyses of IT is *the Right*. Similarly, for their specific domains of inquiry, the guiding ideals for normative political analyses, aesthetic analyses and epistemological analyses are *the Just*, *the Beauty* and *the True* respectively. (Brey 2007)

However, as Brey rightly pointed out, the division as such does not exhaust all forms of normative and evaluative research that are currently being undertaken. Particularly, he has identified what he labelled 'cultural critique' as a specific form of normative and evaluative analyses of IT that is distinct from the aforementioned types. According to Brey, cultural critiques are directed at the culture itself. And, in the current context, cultural critiques of IT take cultural issues generated by the development and use of IT as their object of inquiry. Yet, what precisely distinguishes cultural critiques from other types of normative and evaluative analysis of IT is not merely its object of inquiry, but, rather, it is the different guiding ideal. Cultural critiques are different from other types of normative and evaluative analysis, precisely because they are "governed by our most general ideal, which is the Good." (Brey 2007, 4)

While Brey's notion of cultural critiques provides an important alternative to classify a family of normative and evaluative analysis of IT that does not readily fit into the four aforementioned types, the guiding ideal of cultural critiques, i.e. the Good, nonetheless appears to be too general and too abstract to capture what is unique to the appraisals such as Carr's. Those appraisals, undoubtedly, are about IT-related cultural issues, but it is not immediately clear that they are about what is the Good of IT *per se*. The central concern in the appraisals, as it appears, is mostly limited to what the current, as well as possible, effects of IT can have on people. Particularly, they are about whether, and to what extent, IT is *good for* (or *bad for)* people. In other words, the appraisals are about the prudential values or disvalues of IT. Here, following Griffin (1996), the term 'prudential values' refers to "everything that makes a life good simply for the person living it." (Griffin 1996, 19) For example, in his article, Carr attempted to argue that the Internet has diminished people's ability to concentrate. He argued that the Web, which contains numerous hyperlinks within a single page, has changed people's reading and thinking habit. He lamented people's disability to focus on reading longer texts, e.g. literary classics, and argued that such a change is a loss for people. As such, the conclusion he drew from his observation is that the Internet is *bad for* people. In short, Carr's and similar appraisals aim to analyse the prudential values and/or disvalues of IT, and it should be clear by now that the guiding ideal of the appraisal is *the Well-being* of the people. In other words, the appraisals are governed by a specific ideal, i.e. *the Well-being*, and they proceed by analysing the prudential values and/or disvalues of IT. Given their unique guiding ideal, the appraisals should be placed into a separate category. Since they focus on the prudential values and/or disvalues of IT, I shall call them *prudential analyses of IT* (or, prudential analysis for short).

So far, I have placed the appraisals of IT similar to Carr's into a separate category, i.e. prudential analysis, and pointed out that the prudential analyses are primarily about IT's impacts on people's well-being. Theoretically, the prudential analyses have to be backed by a specific view of well-being. Hence, before moving further, it is necessary first to provide a brief summary of the major views of well-being that are currently available. For the purpose of the current chapter, I shall restrict my scope to the philosophical theories of well-being.[3] It should be noted that philosophical theories of well-being can be merely descriptive. The task for a descriptive theory of well-being is to provide an analysis of the concept of well-being. But, a theory of well-being as such is not by itself normative. A theory of well-being is normative, when it also tackles the question: *how should I live?* Since prudential analyses belong to the domain of normative inquiry, they require, at the foundation, a normative theory of well-being. So, in the remaining of this section, I will concentrate mainly on the normative theories of well-being.

In philosophy, theories of well-being generally fall into one of the following types, i.e. *hedonism, desire theories* and *objective list theories*.[4] Hedonism, in its simplest formulation, maintains that the greater the pleasure and the fewer the pain a person has, the better will be the person's life. A person's well-being, according to hedonism, lies in his maximisation of pleasure and minimisation of pain. While hedonism equates a person's well-being with his acquisition of pleasure and avoidance of pain, a naïve desire theory argues that a person's well-being consists of the fulfilment of his desires. In other words, a person's life is at its best if he can satisfy all of his desires. Finally, objective list theories maintain that a person's well-being is determined by a list of goods that may be independent to anyone's acquisition of pleasure or fulfilment of desires. An objective list theory is objective, precisely because of the list of goods specified by the theory is supposed to be required by every person's well-being regardless of who he is. Typically, goods such as knowledge, friendship and other virtuous characters are proposed to be included in the list. Accordingly, a person's life is good when he obtains the goods that are included in the list.

The brief summary provided above is admittedly brief. Numerous objections against hedonism, desire theories and objective list theories are proposed, and it remains a heated debate as to which theory best characterises people's well-being. Sophisticated versions of hedonism, desire theories and objective list theories are developed and defended by philosophers to answer the objections against their preferred theory. Although the philosophical debate on the theories of well-being is an interesting and important topic, it is not the place to discuss the complications in this section. The point of outlining the philosophical theories of well-being is simply to illustrate the relation between prudential analyses and the theories of well-being. As I have noted, prudential analyses, being normative, require a normative theory of well-being as their basis. Therefore, the conclusion one draws from his prudential analysis is essentially effected by which theory of well-being he subscribes. For example, if a person maintains a naïve desire theory to be the true theory of well-being, barring various complications, he will conclude that IT, or a specific IT-related practice, is good for the people as long as it helps them to satisfy their desires. The conclusion will obviously be different, if he holds a different theory of well-being, e.g. objective list theory, which requires something other than the fulfilment of desires to be conducive to people's well-being.

WHY PRUDENTIAL ANALYSIS IS BEING NEGLECTED AND WHY IT SHOULD NOT BE

Having distinguished prudential analyses from other types of normative and evaluative analysis of IT and explained their relation to philosophical theories of well-being; in this section, I will offer two reasons of why prudential analyses are being neglected by researchers in ICE. The first reason is based on a relatively casual observation of the style of writing of prudential analyses. It is linked to the way in which the appraisals such as Carr's are *actually* presented. And, the second reason is derived from the nature of the theories of well-being itself. I will show neither of the reasons warrants the negligence of prudential analyses. I will argue that prudential analyses are a necessary complement to the theories of well-being if one is to provide answers to the normative question: *how should one live?* Particularly, if one wants to provide answers to this question with respect to the impacts of IT, one has to go beyond the philosophical theories of well-being and to consider the concrete insights provided by prudential analyses.

A casual observation of the venues where the prudential analyses, which take the form of an appraisal such as Carr's, are published may provide a hint of why they are not taken seriously by researchers of ICE. The appraisals are generally found in popular journals or are published by popular press (and, the subsequent discussions of the appraisals usually take place on non-academic venues, e.g. Blogs). The intended readership of the appraisals, therefore, is understandably different from those of academic journals or books. As the appraisals are written for the general public, they demand a different style of writing; unlike academic scholarships, which emphasise the structure and explicitness of arguments, the appraisals express arguments and/or claims by extensive use of concrete examples, stories or anecdotes. Also, they seldom examine the theoretical and/or empirical supports for the arguments and/or claims. Theories and/or empirical evidence, if the appraisals contain any of them at all, are often mentioned only in passing. While the structure and explicitness of arguments and the theoretical and/or empirical supports for one's conclusion are essential to academic research, they may be considered as excessive information for an article intended for the general public.

The style of writing as such, I believe, leads to the impression that the appraisals do not constitute serious scholarships that are worthy of scrutiny. And, the impression of semi-seriousness of the appraisals is boosted by the metaphorical and oft-hyperbolic expressions in the appraisals. The title of Carr's article, i.e. "Is Google Making Us Stupid", is one of the clear examples. Others, such as the title (and subtitle) of the books by Andrew Keen (2007) and Mark Bauerlein (2008), namely *The Cult of the Amateur: How blogs, MySpace, YouTube, and the rest of today's user-generated media are destroying our economy, our culture, and our values* and *The Dumbest Generation: How the Digital Age Stupefies Young Americans and Jeopardizes Our Future (Or, Don't Trust Anyone Under 30)*, provide other vivid examples of the metaphorical and hyperbolic language being used in the appraisals. As a result, I think, the appraisals inevitably invite suspicion to their seriousness and worthiness.

The impression of unimportant and unworthy for serious scholarships generated by the style of writing of the appraisals, however, is unfortunate. For, although the appraisals may lack in their arguments the structure, explicitness and/or adequate supports, they nevertheless provide important insights for answering the question: *how one should live (with respect to the development and use of IT)?* Particularly, the appraisals provide *actual* cases for researchers to reflect on the impacts of IT on a person's quality of life. A serious investigation of the appraisals, therefore, will enable researchers to better understand how people believe IT, in reality, may affect a person's quality of life.

While the reason offered above is based on a stipulation of the researchers' attitude and reaction towards the appraisals, I want to provide a more substantial reason that is derived from the nature of philosophical theories of well-being itself. There is, I believe, a natural tendency for the philosophical theories of well-being to ignore prudential analyses. Let us recall the distinction between descriptive and normative theories of well-being. As I have noted, a descriptive theory of well-being aims to provide a conceptual analysis of the concept of well-being, and a normative theory of well-being, which seeks to answer the question "how should one live?", has to know what constitutes a person's well-being before it can provide any answer to the question. In this sense, the descriptive project is prior to the normative project. But, a reflection on the nature of the descriptive project will reveal that it is not immediately compatible with prudential analyses.

The task of descriptive project, as Tiberius (2004) pointed out, is "to give an analysis of the nature of well-being [by] articulat[ing] the criterion (or criteria) that anything must meet in order to count as a source or cause of wellbeing." (Tiberius 2004, 295-296) In other words, the project strives to define a universalistic concept of well-being. For example, *hedonism* defines 'well-being' as the acquisition of pleasure and avoidance of pain. Such a definition, however, is presumed by its defenders to be applicable to everyone across various cultural, social, historical and personal circumstances. The same is true for desire theories, which hold that the fulfilment of desires is conducive to a person's well-being to be an invariable fact. Finally, objective list theories, while being more substantive in their analyses of 'well-being', they still aim to specify the list of goods that are necessary (and sufficient) for *any* person's well-being. The tendency to conceive 'well-being' as a universalistic concept, I think, has led researchers to formulate well-being in minimalistic terms and to construct the theories in the most context-free manner. Disconnecting the cultural, social, historical and personal circumstances, the resulting analysis from the philosophical theories of well-being is bounded to be abstract and theoretical. If a normative theory of well-being is built on its descriptive counterpart, then it is going to share the universalistic tendency inherited in the descriptive project.

On one hand, the philosophical theories of well-being strive to provide an analysis that is clear of particulars, i.e. they strive to provide a concept of well-being that is applicable to any circumstance. On the other hand, prudential analyses mostly restrict themselves to actual cases of IT-related issues and are limited to specific values (or the activities that are believed to be valuable). For example, the impacts of the Internet on a person's reading and thinking habits (Carr 2008), the proliferation of 'amateur content' on blogs, YouTube, etc. (Keen 2007), and the effects of IT to a generation entirely dependent on them (Bauerlein 2008). Given the different nature of philosophical theories of well-being and prudential analyses, the apparent tension between the universality of the former and the particularity of the latter is obvious. As the philosophical theories of well-being deploy a universalistic concept of well-being, it seems that they are warranted to ignore prudential analyses, which emphasise particularity and, thereby, appear to be irrelevant to either the descriptive project or the normative project.

However, it should be reminded that normative theories of well-being also attempt to answer the question "how should one live?" In the current context, the principal question for a normative theory of well-being, therefore, concerns with a person's quality of life provided that she has and uses, or does not have and/or use, a specific IT. Here, normative theories of well-being, as I have characterised above, do not seem adequate to provide answers to this question because they are devoid of circumstantial factors that are important for offering practical advice. The problem of normative theories of well-being as such is best captured by Williams's (2005) objection to contemporary moral theory, as he pointed out "it is too abstract and theoretical to provide any substance to ethical life…, and it is precisely the use of "thick" ethical concepts, among other

things, that contributes to a more substantive type of personal ethical experience than theory is likely to produce." (2005, 48) The stronger claim from Williams is that moral theories, which analyse ethical concepts by using the most general terms, are bounded to fail. But I think it is not necessary to follow Williams and declare the whole enterprise of descriptive and normative theories of well-being as a failure. A moderate lesson can be drawn from Williams's objection. If a theory of well-being seeks to answer the question "how should one live?", it has to go beyond the minimalistic concept of well-being and to include other factors such as cultural, social, historical and personal circumstances in its consideration. In this way, prudential analyses, which situated themselves in a particular circumstance, provide an important complement to the theories of well-being in answering IT-related normative questions.

Now, I shall illustrate, in more detail, the role prudential analyses can play in complementing the philosophical theories of well-being. Instead of showing what role they play in hedonism, desire theories and objective list theories separately, I will classify those theories into two types, i.e. objective theories and subjective theories, and explain the role prudential analyses can play in them. The distinction between objective and subjective theories is summarised by Sumner (1995) as the following: objective theories of well-being state that there is a list of goods for people's well-being regardless of whether a person approves it or not; and, subjective theories state that a person's well-being ought to be determined by the person himself. Accordingly, objective list theories are clear instances of objective theories, and hedonism and desire theories are mostly subjective theories.

It is, I think, relatively easy to discern the role prudential analyses can play in objective theories of well-being. As the characterisation of objective theories suggests, there is a specific list of the goods regardless of any individual's pro-attitudes towards them. In other words, a true objective theory implies the existence of objective goods that are independent of the people. Still, without taking people's circumstances into account, the list of goods specified by an objective theory of well-being is likely to remain abstract and theoretical. Here, prudential analyses can supply the objective theory with IT-related values that are specific to certain social, cultural, historical and/or personal circumstances. In turn, they can consolidate the objective theory by offering the supports that are essentially connected to *actual* cases. There is, therefore, a mutual relation between objective theories and prudential analyses. A true objective theory will provide the normative foundation for prudential analyses, and prudential analyses will specify the values that are connected to a particular situation and help providing practical advice based on the more substantial values. The task of an objective theory, in this case, is to elaborate the conceptual relations between the abstract, theoretical values and the more substantial ones. Here, a true objective theory of well-being will also enable us to verify the truth or falsity of prudential analyses. Where the substantial values presupposed by a prudential analysis cannot be derived from the list of goods specified in the objective theory, it is reasonable to conclude that such an analysis is based on a false foundation.

For subjective theories of well-being, however, it may not be immediately clear why prudential analyses do matter at all. For instance, prudential analyses aim to illustrate what good IT is for a person; the *good for* here, however, according to a subjective theory of well-being, is a subjective matter. So construed, one person's prudential analysis may be completely irrelevant to another, because what is *good for* the first person may not be the same as the second one, that is – something is good for a person if and only if he determines that it is so, and, in any case, he can decide that something is *not* good for him. In this sense, a prudential analysis may be reduced to an idiosyncratic opinion of what good IT is for the person who performs the analysis. Of course, it is possible to criticise the above characterisation

of prudential analyses by evoking views such as a false picture of people. Those who argue with the notion of false picture of people will point out that a person's decision cannot be entirely separated from the community, thus, he will inevitably be influenced by the community's evaluative standard. As a result, what good IT is for a person as specified in a prudential analysis cannot just be an idiosyncratic opinion in the radical sense. I think this objection to such a characterisation of prudential analyses is a plausible one, but I will not explore this option further. Instead, I will argue that, even if prudential analyses are akin to subjective opinions, a careful investigation of them can still enrich subjective theories of well-being.

Before proceeding to my claim, however, it is necessary to point out that the simplistic formulations of both hedonism and desire theories provided above are untenable. For example, one of the most prominent arguments against naïve hedonism is *the argument from false pleasure*. There are various formulations of the argument, but what they have in common is the basic assumption that a person can be deceived into thinking his life to be a pleasurable life; but, since false pleasure is not conducive to a person's well-being, without the ability to distinguish false pleasure from real, authentic pleasure, simplistic hedonism is an untenable account of well-being.[5] Similarly, naïve desire theories have been accused of not being able to separate false desires, i.e. desires induced by external factors that are against or unrelated to a person's own will, from real, authentic ones.

In response to the objections, more plausible formulations of both hedonism and desire theory are developed and defended by philosophers. For example, Feldman (2004) has proposed a version of hedonism, which only takes a specific form of pleasure, i.e. *truth-adjusted (attitudinal) pleasure*, to be conducive to a person's well being. In Feldman's theory, attitudinal pleasure is one that corresponds to the states of affairs, and only the pleasure derived from *true* states of affairs will be conducive to a person's well being. Similarly,

Griffin (1986) has argued for what he called *informed desire theory*, in which only the fulfilment of one's rational and informed desires will contribute to his well-being. What distinguishes the simplistic hedonism and naïve desire theories from the more sophisticated formulations of Feldman's and Griffin's, as we can see, is the additional requirement on the type of pleasure and desires a person has in order for them to be conducive to his well-being. Despite the differences between Feldman's and Griffin's theory, the additional requirement seems to be the same, that is – both re-formulations have stressed the importance of the person's rational scrutiny (of the pleasure or of the desires). I shall call this additional requirement 'rational requirement'.

The rational requirement in subjective theories of well-being requires a person to determine her own criterion (or criteria) of well-being rationally. However, even if a subjective theory is true, it does not by itself provide the resources to facilitate the person's rational thinking. The additional requirement in Feldman's and Griffin's sophisticated formulations is only a formal condition on the type of pleasure or desires a person should acquire or satisfy, but they provide no way, either in theory or in practice, to identify the appropriate type of pleasure or desires. Missing the resource, a subjective theory of well-being cannot provide any practical advice to people. Here, prudential analyses can complement a true subjective theory of well-being with the information needed to discern the appropriateness of pleasure or desires, even if they merely appear as a form of subjective opinion. In other words, prudential analyses are a necessary complement to subjective theories of well-being if the latter are to provide practical advice to people. Prudential analyses supply information from *actual* cases to people for them to better defend their own view of well-being. In short, prudential analyses provide the required information (or justifications) to *rationally* determine their own view.

THREE DIMENSIONS OF PRUDENTIAL ANALYSIS

I have argued, in the previous section, that for both objective and subjective theories of well-being, if they are to answer the normative question about the people's well-being, they need to pay more attention to prudential analyses. However, as I have also noted, with the style of writing that is intended for the general public, the insights of the appraisals such as Carr's are not readily transferrable to the academic research. Hence, to be able to utilise the appraisals, a better framework has to be developed for the analysis and evaluation of them.

Brey (2006) has developed a useful framework for analysing and evaluating the beliefs about the Internet's benefits and harms. Since his framework can readily be extended to analyse and evaluate of prudential analyses, I shall provide a brief overview of it. Brey has distinguished two types of analysis and evaluation in his framework, i.e. descriptive analysis and critical analysis. In the descriptive analysis, the goal is to better understand an appraisal by clarifying the meanings of concepts in the appraisals, identifying the presupposed values and implied empirical claims and examining the evidence for the implied empirical claims. And, in the critical analysis, one begins to critically scrutinise the appropriateness of the meanings of concepts as well as the legitimacy of the presupposed values in the appraisals. (2006, 7-8) Accordingly, it is possible to differentiate three dimensions in a prudential analysis; they are *the empirical dimension*, *the conceptual dimension* and *the evaluative dimension* respectively.

The empirical dimension of an analysis refers to those statements that are about the (possible) consequences of the development and use of IT, e.g. Carr's claim that the Internet has altered people's reading and thinking habit. To analyse and evaluate the empirical dimension, one has to examine the purported facts suggested by the analysis and verify their truth or falsity. Thus, the empirical dimension can only be investigated by looking at the actual cases themselves. The conceptual dimension, on the other hand, is about the concepts deployed in an analysis, and especially relevant to prudential analyses is the *nature* of IT in question. The IT in question can be seen as value-laden or value-free, and/or it can be seen as deterministic, etc. Hence, the conceptual dimension of an analysis has to be investigated against the background of philosophical theories of technology.

Finally and, perhaps, the most important for the current chapter, is the evaluative dimension of an analysis. The evaluative dimension specifies what good (or bad) IT is for people's well-being and why. As I have shown, the judgments on what good (or bad) something is for a person's well-being depends on the theory of well-being a person maintains. Moreover, I have also pointed out that the values go well beyond the abstract and theoretical values in prudential analyses, because prudential analyses are essentially about actual cases. Hence, to analyse and evaluate the evaluative dimension, it is necessary to identify the substantial values specific to those cases. But, what are those values? As Brey (2006) rightly pointed out, the values presupposed by people's evaluative claims are often shared by a large group of people. Following Rawls, he called systems of values shared by the people *comprehensive doctrines*, i.e. "systems of value, be they religious, moral or ideological, that contain values concerning what is good and bad, and are often accompanied by norms for conduct and a system of (metaphysical) beliefs." (2006, 8) As such, to truly understand the evaluative dimension of a prudential analysis, it is necessary to study the substantial values embedded in it, where those values are socially, culturally and historically dependent.

MODERNITY AND THE EVALUATIVE DIMENSION OF PRUDENTIAL ANALYSIS

The substantial values appear in the evaluative dimension of a prudential analysis come from a rich cultural, social and historical context. And, to see how those substantial values become constitutive of people's view of well-being, a study of the origin of these values has to be done. In this section, I will show how such a study can be done by looking at the study of the modern sources of *the good* embarked by Charles Taylor (1989) in *Sources of the Self: The Making of Modern Identity*.

In *Sources of the Self*, Taylor provided an interesting account of modern identity. The notion of 'identity' refers to the way in which people understand and interpret *the self*. In turns, this notion of identity underpins the substantial values for the people, because it provides an image of the proper (and ideal) way to be *a person*, that is – it states the defining characteristics of being a self. Taylor's discussion is rich in details, and I will confine myself to the two strands of modern self identified by him. The first strand may be called the 'disengaged self', which was first expressed in its most complete form by Descartes. And, the second strand is called the 'expressive self', which had Rousseau and the Romantics as its origin. In what follows, I will explain the defining characteristics of these two strands of the self, and state what are the substantial values derived from them.

According to Taylor, the disengaged self is characterised by its disengagement stance, i.e. the separation of subject and object (of inquiry), its primacy of instrumental reason, and an accompanied procedural conception of reason. This strand of the modern self portrays its ideal as an autonomous, rational and moral agent, who is self-determining and self-responsible, and whose acts ought to be determined by reason and reason alone. The formulation of agency as such places human dignity at the centre of the disengaged self. And, in many ways, the expressive self can be seen as a reaction to the disengaged self. While the ideal of the disengaged self is driven by rationality alone, the expressive self rejects the disengaged self's lone emphasis on reason and embraces a broader notion of nature as inner voice, which takes seriously one's feeling as a guide to their ideals. The defining characteristics of the expressive self, as Taylor noted, is sufficiently captured by the Romanticism's doctrines, i.e. the right of the individual, the power to creative imagination and the importance of feelings for a meaningful life. (Taylor 1989, 368)

There are two different pictures of (ideal) human nature behind the two strands of modern self. Human nature in the disengaged self can be defined exhaustively by the subject's rational nature alone, and hence "individual differences are only unimportant variations within the same basic human nature". The picture is different in the expressive self, individuals are essentially different, and the differences "entail that each of us has an original path which we ought to tread; they lay the obligation on each of us to live up to our originality". (Taylor 1989, 375) The defining characteristics of the two strands of modern self and the human nature behind, in turns, become the basis of the substantial values. Here, the ideal of the disengaged self draws support from the practices of rational enquiry, and the ideal of the expressive self draws its power from various forms of artistic imagination. Albeit the differences, the two strands of modern self place the person, i.e. the subject, at the most important position. And, emerging from the two strands of modern self is two different sets of values.

To start with, knowledge, especially practical knowledge and technical knowledge, is promoted by the disengaged self to be valuable to all humankind. It is believed that only through the acquisition of knowledge people can exert control over their surroundings. This concept of knowledge presumes a specific standard that is modelled on rational inquiries. Anything that fails to contribute to the development of practical or technical

knowledge or to satisfy the criteria adopted in rational inquiries, e.g. clarity and distinctness, is considered to be inferior. This is so, because human progress is to be assessed by the degree of control over their surroundings. Autonomy is another value that has assumed fundamental position in the disengaged self. Here, an autonomous being is defined as a subject, whose assent of his own actions, as well as the rules for such actions, must be a result of his own rational reflection. In other words, to be an autonomous being, one has to be a rational being. Since it is the subject's rational nature that constitutes his autonomy, the subject is deemed to have determined his own course of actions, and, thus, is responsible for his choices and actions. From the outlook of the disengaged self, every subject must be a rational being. And, because of this, every subject are in essence the same, therefore, they ought to be treated equally and impartially. Moreover, rational decisions and actions from different subjects should be seen as analogously acceptable because they can be justified by the same standard. This gives rise to a sense of tolerance, because a person's rational decisions and actions are legitimate whether they are liked by the others or not. In summary, knowledge, autonomy, equality, impartiality and tolerance are the key values promoted by the disengaged self.

The importance of autonomy and equality is also shared by the expressive self. Underlying the ideal of the expressive self is the notion of authenticity, i.e. to be true to one self. To be authentic, the subject must be free from externalities and to be able to act on their own will. While the disengaged self defines the subject by universalised reason, the expressive self points to individuals' differences. In such outlook, individuality is not to be disregarded, but rather to be valued. In other words, every individual should be considered equal precisely because of their uniqueness. Authenticity, together with the respect for differences, lead to the valuing of diversity: the subjects ought to be respected by and recognised as who they really are. So, diversity ought to be preserved. For the expressive self, its ideal can only be attained through self-expression or self-articulation of the individual's unique inner nature; such disclosure is not be to guided by reason, but rather it is a creative endeavour. Creativity, therefore, is another key value of the expressive self. Although the creative endeavour is not to be guided by (instrumental) reason, it does not entail that such an endeavour is without any standard. As Taylor has pointed out, for the purpose of self-discovery, the creative endeavour has to be epiphanic, where "the locus of a manifestation which brings us into the presence of something which is otherwise inaccessible". (Taylor 1989, 419) In other words, to satisfy the standard of the expressive self, the creative effort should not only be representational, it ought to be revealing as well. The key values of the expressive self, therefore, are authenticity, autonomy, individuality, equality, diversity and creativity.

"IS GOOGLING MAKING US STUPID" AS A PRUDENTIAL ANALYSIS

Once we realise the substantial values in prudential analyses are grounded in a culturally, socially and historically rich notion of identity, it is possible to recast the analyses in terms of the key values embedded in them. By doing so, it does not only clarify the normative basis of the evaluative claims in the prudential analyses, it also enables us to better understand those claims, thereby, allows us to accept or dismiss them more fairly. In this section, I will provide an example of recasting a prudential analysis with the two strands of modern self discussed. I will focus on Nicholas Carr's appraisal of the Internet's impacts to the people's reading and thinking habit.

The main claim made by Carr in his appraisal of the Internet can be summarised as the following: the Internet, in particular, the Web, with its information-thick and hyperlinks-rich environ-

ment, has transformed people's reading habit. He argued that reading online, which jumps from one point to another, is a completely different activity from reading in the traditional sense. The result, he noted, is that a person can no longer concentrate on longer texts, which makes deep reading difficult. He believed that this is bad for people, because people's reading habit directly influences their thinking habit. Hence, when deep reading is no longer possible, so is deep thinking. Accompanied with this major claim, Carr also criticised the design of the Internet itself. He believed that its very vision of design predetermines the exclusion of deep reading and deep thinking, as he summed up Google's vision, i.e. "the more pieces of information we can "access" and the faster we can extract their gist, the more productive we become as thinkers." (Carr 2008)

How are we going to evaluate the evaluative dimension of Carr's appraisal? Particularly, how are we going to evaluate his claim that the Internet, because of its design, is *bad for* people; and, also the claim that deep reading and deep thinking are essential to people? Here, Carr's appraisal can be recast in terms of the key values embedded in the two strands of modern self outlined in previous section. The vision of the Internet's design summed up by Carr is, in effect, the disengaged self's notion of knowledge. Knowledge, so conceived, is merely technical or practical, and its purpose is to enable human being to gain control. In other words, Carr's negative appraisal of the Internet's design is precisely an argument rooted in the discontent of such a notion of knowledge. If the disengaged self's notion of knowledge is indeed insufficient, then Carr's point should be rightly taken.

Similarly, the importance of deep reading and deep thinking can be grounded in the key values embedded in the expressive self. Recall the expressive self's valuing of authenticity, individuality and creativity, these values are clearly noticeable in Carr's praise of deep reading and deep thinking, as he wrote,

"The kind of deep reading... is valuable not just for the knowledge we acquire from the author's words but for the intellectual vibrations those words set off within our own minds... for that matter, we make our own associations, draw our own inferences and analogies, foster our own ideas." (Carr 2008)

What is so important about deep reading, accordingly, is that it allows a person to exercise his *creativity* to formulate his *unique thoughts* that belong only to him. Deep reading is, in this sense, necessarily *epiphanic*. In short, Carr's appraisal of the Internet is one that being issued from the perspective of the expressive self. By revealing the normative basis of Carr's claim, e.g. the key values underlying 'deep reading' and 'deep thinking', we are in a better position to judge its plausibility. By revealing the key values implicit in the prudential analyses and making explicit the relation between the key values embedded in different notions of the self and the values the prudential analyses refer to, we have provided a firmer ground for the evaluative claims in prudential analyses. As such, recasting prudential analyses with the two strands of modern self allows us to reformulate the arguments in prudential analyses with better details and to utilise their insights in other contexts.

CONCLUSION: THE FUTURE RESEARCH ON PRUDENTIAL ANALYSIS

In this chapter, I have argued that appraisals of IT similar to Carr's constitute a separate type of normative and evaluative analysis of IT. They are, as I called them, the prudential analyses of IT. I have also pointed out, and then rejected, the reasons why they are being neglected by researchers in ICE. Particularly, I have argued that if a theory of well-being is to provide practical guidance to people with respect to the development and/or use of IT, it ought to incorporate the insights of prudential analyses, because the analyses provide

contextually-rich information that is complementary to the abstract and theoretical nature of the philosophical theories of well-being. I then apply a framework I drew from Brey (2006) to analyse and evaluate Carr's appraisal of the Internet as an example of how such an investigation can be done. I hope, in this chapter, I have provided sufficient motivations for researchers in ICE to paying more attentions to the prudential analyses.

However, by choosing to analyse and evaluate Carr's "Is Google Making Us Stupid", I have restricted myself only to the values related to a person's well-being. Ideally, it is possible to employ the same framework to analyse and evaluate appraisals of IT that are about its impacts on a *society* as well. Since the key values, which form the normative basis of prudential analyses, are culturally, socially and historically dependent, to analyse and evaluate appraisals related to societal well-being (or, the *goodness-for or badness-for* a society), it requires an in-depth investigation the origin of the key values for a good society as well as a study of various theories of good society.

Moreover, I have also confined myself to an analysis assuming a (Western) modern perspective. However, it should be nothing but obvious that appraisals of IT as such can be delivered by people from different perspectives, i.e. Confucian perspective, Buddhist perspective, Islamic perspective, etc. Hence, to fully utilise the framework developed in this chapter, it is necessary to go beyond the (Western) modern perspective and to study the comprehensive doctrines in various cultures. In this way, a study of various prudential analyses will enable us to see how IT affects the quality of life of people in different cultures. More importantly, by drawing insights from different cultural perspectives, it will undoubtedly enrich both the theoretical and practical resource to answer the question: *how should one live in an Information Society.*[6]

REFERENCES

Bauerlein, M. (2008). *The dumbest generation: how the digital age stupefies young Americans and jeopardizes our future (or, don't trust anyone under 30)*. New York: Jeremy P. Tarcher/Penguin.

Brey, P. (2006). Evaluating the social and cultural implications of the internet. *SIG-CAS Computers and Society, 36*(3), 41–48. doi:10.1145/1195716.1195721

Brey, P. (2007). Theorizing the Cultural Quality of New Media. *Techné: Research in Philosophy and Technology, 11*(1), 1–18.

Bynum, T. (2008) Computer and Information Ethics. *Stanford Encyclopaedia of Philosophy*. Last retrieved 6 September, 2009, from http://plato.stanford.edu/entries/ethics-computer/

Carr, N. (2008). Is Google Making Us Stupid. *The Atlantic*. Last retrieved 6 September, 2009, from http://www.theatlantic.com/doc/200807/google

Crisp, R. (2008) Well-Being. *Stanford Encyclopaedia of Philosophy*. Last retrieved 6 September, 2009, from Last retrieved http://plato.stanford.edu/entries/well-being/

Feldman, F. (2004). *Pleasure and the good life: concerning the nature, varieties, and plausibility of hedonism*. Oxford, UK: Clarendon Press.

Gasper, D. (2004) 'Human Well-being: Concepts and Conceptualizations', *ISS Working Papers, No. 388*.

Griffin, J. (1986). *Well-being: its meaning, measurement and moral importance*. Oxford, UK: Clarendon Press.

Griffin, J. (1996). *Value Judgement: improving our ethical beliefs*. Oxford: Clarendon Press.

Himma, K. E., & Tavani, H. (Eds.). (2008). *The Handbook of Information and Computer Ethics*. Hoboken, NJ: Wiley. doi:10.1002/9780470281819

Keen, A. (2007). *The cult of the amateur: how today's internet is killing our culture*. New York: Doubleday/Currency.

Schroeder, M. (2008). Value Theory. *Stanford Encyclopedia of Philosophy*. Last retrieved 6 September, 2009, from http://plato.stanford.edu/archives/fall2008/entries/value-theory/

Sumner, L. W. (1995). The Subjectivity of Welfare. *Ethics, 105*(4), 764–790. doi:10.1086/293752

Taylor, C. (1989). *Sources of the self: the making of modern identity*. Cambridge, UK: Cambridge University Press.

Tiberius, V. (2004). Cultural differences and philosophical accounts of well-being. *Journal of Happiness Studies, 5*, 293–314. doi:10.1007/s10902-004-8791-y

Tiberius, V. (2006). Well-Being: Psychological Research for Philosophers. *Philosophy Compass, 1/5*, 493–505. doi:10.1111/j.1747-9991.2006.00038.x

van den Hoven, J., & Weckert, J. (Eds.). (2008). *Information Technology and Moral Philosophy*. New York: Cambridge University Press. doi:10.1017/CBO9780511498725

Williams, B. (2005). *In the beginning was the deed: realism and moralism in political argument*. Princeton, NJ: Princeton University Press.

KEY TERMS AND DEFINTIONS

Prudential analysis of Information Technology: is an analysis of the prudential values and/or disvalues of Information Technology. The guiding ideal of prudential analyses of IT is *the Well-being* of the people.

Prudential value: according philosopher James Griffins, refers to everything that makes a life good simply for the person living it.

Hedonism: is a family of theories of well-being that maintains that the greater the pleasure and the fewer the pain a person has, the better will be the person's life.

Desire theories: is a family of theories of well-being which states that a person's well-being consists of the fulfilment of the person's desires.

Objective list theory: is a family of theories of well-being that maintains a person's well-being is determined by a list of goods, which can be independent to any person's acquisition of pleasure or fulfilment of desires.

Objective theories of well-being: state that there is a list of goods for a person's well-being regardless of whether *that* person approves it or not.

Subjective theories of well-being: state that a person's well-being *ought* to be determined *only* by the person himself.

Comprehensive doctrines: are shared sets of values (or, systems of values), which characterise, either explicitly or implicitly, what is good and bad. They often accompanied by a set of norms and/or code of conducts and a systems (metaphysical) beliefs. Comprehensive doctrines are also known as *ideologies*.

ENDNOTES

[1]	The other notable examples include Andrew Keen (2007) and Mark Bauerlein (2008).

[2]	For an overview of the current topics in Information and Computer Ethics, see Bynum (2008), Himma & Tavani (2008) and van den Hoven & Weckert (2008).

[3]	See, Tiberius (2006) for an overview of the psychological research on well-being. Her discussion is particularly helpful here because she mapped out the similarities and differences between philosophical and psychological research. See also, Gasper (2004) for a general overview of the concept of well-being.

[4]	It is beyond my scope in this chapter to offer a comprehensive study of various theories of well-being. For a comprehensive review of theories of well-being, see Crisp (2008) and Schroeder (2008).

[5]	For an extensive discussion of various objections and replies to hedonism, see Feldman (2004, Chapter 3).

[6]	Early versions of this chapter were presented at ECAP 09 (Universitat Autonoma de Barcelona, 2009) and SPT 2009: Converging Technologies, Changing Society (Universiteit Twente, 2009). I would like to thank my audiences for helpful remarks and suggestions. I would also like to thank Philiip Brey, Adam Briggle, Edward Spence and Johnny Soraker for their valuable comments.

Section 4
Simulating Reality?

Chapter 15
Computing, Philosophy and Reality:
A Novel Logical Approach

Joseph Brenner
CIRET, France

ABSTRACT

The conjunction of the disciplines of computing and philosophy implies that discussion of computational models and approaches should include explicit statements of their underlying worldview, given the fact that reality includes both computational and non-computational domains. As outlined at ECAP08, both domains of reality can be characterized by the different logics applicable to them. A new "Logic in Reality" (LIR) was proposed as best describing the dynamics of real, non-computable processes. The LIR process view of the real macroscopic world is compared here with recent computational and information-theoretic models. Proposals that the universe can be described as a mathematical structure equivalent to a computer or by simple cellular automata are deflated. A new interpretation of quantum superposition as supporting a concept of paraconsistent parallelism in quantum computing and an appropriate ontological commitment for computational modeling are discussed.

INTRODUCTION: PHILOSOPHY OF SCIENCE

This Chapter is the outcome of my collaboration and joint presentation at ECAP09 with Michael Nicolaidis, in which I contrasted his computational model of the universe and view of quantum superposition with a number of other current models based on the logical approach I call "Logic in Reality" (LIR). I also made a critique of his positions on some issues in quantum physics. This is repeated here and the interested reader can compare it with his statement on the relation of his theory to LIR in his Chapter. It was and is our feeling that the "strongest possible theory of reality" (the working title of our contribution) is one which would incorporate both computational and non-computational perspectives.

DOI: 10.4018/978-1-61692-014-2.ch015

In my view, an adequate philosophy of science should include, as a minimum, the following:

- A view of reality, that is, the ontology of the physical universe, independently of whether and how it can be effectively or adequately modeled;
- A view of models of the physical universe, that is, whether it can be modeled independently of what it is or may be in itself.

The situation regarding computer science is particularly interesting, since many recent conceptions of both reality and models of reality are computational. The juxtaposition of the terms computing and philosophy in this venue thus strongly implies that computational models and approaches should include explicit statements of the worldview underlying them, given the fact that reality has both computational and non-computational aspects. The primary objective of this Chapter is to address the first of above points, although implications for the second will also emerge.

I begin in Section 2 by outlining several current cosmological theories of various types. Section 3 revisits the issue of computability and non-computability. Section 4 summarizes the key concepts of Logic in Reality (LIR) and its implications for outstanding issues in philosophy and science. Section 5 discusses each of the cosmological theories and their corresponding ontological commitments from the perspective of LIR, and Section 6 makes some brief comments on models.

CURRENT THEORIES OF THE UNIVERSE

Since the advent of quantum mechanics and the computer, the classical dichotomy between a universe based on energy or position, deterministic or indeterministic, continuous or discontinuous, has been recast into three or four major kinds of theories, with widely varying degrees of ontological commitment, as shown in the following Table. Many of these issues are also surfacing in another form, namely in connection with natural computation or computing, in which an understanding of their ontology can be critical to the use of natural phenomena as components of a computing process.

The first three types of theories have one thing in common – they fail to take into account or acknowledge that there might be something fundamentally true about the opposing theory, and, even if this is recognized, have no mechanism to handle the relationship. In addition, the motivation of many of these theories is to "deliver" the epistemic agent, that is, *also* to provide a basis for qualia, intentionality and free will. In my view, however, no ontological commitment is made that enables this. The generally low level of ontological commitment in the first three types, for various reasons, including the belief that one cannot know at least some of the attributes of reality, creates more problems than it solves for a scientific realist.

Table 1.

Theories of Reality		
Model Exponents Ontological Commitment		
Mathematical/Digital		
Tegmark Platonic		
Zuse ditto		
Wheeler "It from Bit"		
Wolfram Agnostic (Cellular Automata)		
Nicolaidis Agnostic (Meta-objects)		
Mathematical/Analogue		
Longo Continuum Hypothesis		
Thom/Petitot Continuity		
Epistemological/Informational		
Floridi Agnostic (ISR)		
Ladyman *et al.* Informational Patterns		
Logical-Dynamic		
Brenner New Energy Ontology		

COMPUTATIONAL APPROACHES AND LIR

At ECAP08, I suggested that reality, the extant domain or everything that exists, includes both computable and non-computable sub-domains that can be differentiated according to the logics applicable to them. A new "Logic in Reality" (LIR) was proposed as best describing the dynamics of real, non-computable processes.

In making this division I have taken as primitive the limitations placed on computability by computer scientists themselves. It is possible to disagree on whether any specific phenomenon is now, is not now or could never be reproduced *via* an appropriate algorithm. I do not consider this a problem, since complete agreement or absolute certainty is not required in my logic. In fact, I predict that on-going disagreement between people is inevitable, on computability and other issues.

The impulse for this Chapter was a statement in the presentation by Michael Nicolaidis at ECAP08 regarding the principle of superposition of states in quantum mechanics. He argued that this principle was not tenable since it conflicted with the axiom of non-contradiction in standard logic. A second thesis, for which he has just presented additional arguments in the preceding two papers, is that since standard quantum mechanics requires this principle, one of its corollaries, namely, that a quantum computer could be built with infinite computing power must be rejected as a *reductio ad absurdum*.

I argue here that LIR is the missing ingredient in the debate over whether the reality or the universe is digital, analogue or informational or involving a metaphysical and metalogical but still physical principle of dynamic opposition (PDO). Comparative analysis of the domains from the computational standpoint is made that includes a state-transition description of the abstract domain of computer operations (that is, the manipulation of abstract entities) that follows neo-classical binary logic, and a logical-dynamical description of the process entities of the real domain. In discussions with Nicolaidis, we came to the realization that our approaches were, in a significant sense, complementary. Neither alone gives a picture of reality that includes both computational and non-computational domains. Rather, we believe that a "strongest possible theory of reality" (the working title of our presentation) should combine the two viewpoints.

LOGIC IN REALITY

Logic in Reality (LIR) is a new kind of logic (Brenner, 2008) grounded in a particle/field view of the universe, whose axioms and rules provide a framework for analyzing and explaining real world entities, extending the domain of logic to real processes and complex interactions at biological, cognitive and social levels of reality or complexity. LIR is an up-dating and extension of the theory of the Franco-Romanian philosopher Stéphane Lupasco (Bucharest, 1900–Paris, 1988).

The term "Logic in Reality" (LIR) is intended to imply both 1) that the principle of change according to which reality operates is a *logic* embedded in it, *the* logic in reality; and 2) that what logic really *is* or should be involves this same real physical-metaphysical but also logical principle. The major components of this logic are the following:

- The foundation in the physical and metaphysical dualities of nature
- Its axioms and calculus intended to reflect real change
- The categorial structure of its related ontology
- A two-level framework of relational analysis

Stated very rapidly, the most important concepts (Lupasco, 1987) of LIR are that 1) every real complex process is accompanied, logically and functionally, by its opposite or contradiction, but only in the sense that when one element is (predominantly) present or actualized, the other is (predominantly) absent or potentialized, alternately and reciprocally, without either ever going to zero (principle of dynamic opposition, PDO); and 2) the emergence of a new entity at a higher level of reality or complexity can take place at the point of equilibrium or maximum interaction between the two.

Details of the axioms, non-standard semantics and ontology of LIR are provided in my book and in other recent publications (Brenner, 2009) and will not be reproduced here. Basically, LIR should be seen as a process logic, a process-ontological view of reality (Seibt, 2009), applying to trends and tendencies, rather than to "objects" or the steps in a state-transition picture of change (Brenner, 2008). Stable macrophysical objects and simple situations, which can be discussed within binary logic, are the result of processes of processes going in the direction of a "non-contradictory" identity. Standard logic underlies, rather, the construction of simplified models which fail to capture the essential dynamics of biological and cognitive processes, such as reasoning (Magnani, 2002). LIR does not replace standard bivalent or multivalent logics but reduces to them for simple systems. These include chaotic systems which are not mathematically incomprehensible but also computational or algorithmic, as their elements are *not* in an appropriate interactive relationship. Such interactive relationships, to which LIR applies, are characteristic of entities with some form of internal representation, biological or cognitive.

Categorial Non-Separability in The Ontology Of Lir

The third major component of LIR is the categorial ontology that fits its axioms.

Material Category
Energy/Quantum Field

Formal Categories
Process
- ○ Emergence, Closure and Downward Causation
Dynamic Opposition
- ○ Separability and Non-Separabilty
Subject, Object and Subject-Object
T-state (emergent included middle)

In this ontology, the sole material category is Energy, and the most important formal category is Dynamic Opposition. From the LIR metaphysical standpoint, for real systems or phenomena or processes in which real dualities are instantiated, their terms are *not* separated or separable! Real complex phenomena display a contradictional relation to or interaction between themselves and their opposites or contradictions. On the other hand, there are many phenomena in which such interactions are not present, and they, and the simple changes in which they are involved can be described by classical, binary logic or its modern versions. The most useful categorial division that can be made is exactly this: phenomena that show non-separability of the terms of the dualities as an essential aspect of their existence, at their level of reality and those that instantiate separability.

LIR thus approaches in a new way the inevitable problems resulting from the classical philosophical dichotomies, appearance and reality, as well as the concepts of space, time and causality as categories with *separable categorial features*, including, for example, final and effective cause. Non-Separability underlies the other metaphysical and phenomenal dualities of reality, such as determinism and indeterminism, subject and object, continuity and discontinuity, and so on. This is a 'vital' concept: to consider process elements that are contradictorily linked as separable is a form of category error. I thus claim that non-separability at the macroscopic level, like that being explored at the quantum level, provides a principle of organization or structure in macroscopic phenomena that has been neglected in science and philosophy.

Stable macrophysical objects and simple situations, which can be discussed within binary logic, are the result of processes of processes going in the direction of non-contradiction. Thus, LIR should be seen as a logic applying to processes, to trends and tendencies, rather than to "objects" or the steps in a state-transition picture of change.

LIR is thus a valid logical system with a formal part –axioms, semantics and calculus; an interpreted part – a metaphysics, categorial ontology and a contradictorial, two-level framework for analysis with applications in philosophy and science. I distinguish LIR from logics that employ standard linguistic concepts of truth, falsity and logical operations. Despite its application to the extant domain, LIR is neither a physics nor a cosmology. It is a logic in the sense of enabling stable patterns of inference to be made about processes, without reference to propositional variables. LIR resembles inductive and abductive logics in that truth preservation is not guaranteed. The elements of LIR are not propositions in the usual sense, but probability-like metavariables as in quantum logics. Identity and diversity, cause and effect, determinism and indeterminism and time and space receive non-standard interpretations in this theory.

The principle of dynamic opposition (PDO) in LIR extends the meaning of contradiction in paraconsistent logics (PCL), *defined* such that contradiction does not entail triviality. LIR captures the logical structure of the dynamics involved in the non-separable and inconsistent aspects of real phenomena, e.g. of thought, referred to by Graham Priest (2002).

LIR thus applies to all real dualities, between either classes of entities or two individual elements. Examples are theories and the data of theories, or facts and meaning, syntax and semantics. Others are interactive relations between elements, relations between sets or classes of elements, events, etc. and the descriptions or explanations of those elements or events.

LIR does not replace classical binary or multi-valued logics, including non-monotonic versions, but reduces to them for simple systems. These include chaotic systems which are not mathematically incomprehensible but also computational or algorithmic, as their elements are *not* in an adequately contradictorial interactive relationship.

LIR permits a differentiation between 1) dynamic systems and relations *qua* the system, which have no form of internal representation (e.g. hurricanes), to which binary logic can apply; and 2) those which do, such as living systems, for which a ternary logic is required. I suggest that the latter is the privileged logic of complexity, of consciousness and art, of the real mental, social and political world.

Ortho-Dialectic Chains of Implication

The fundamental postulate of LIR and its formalism can also be applied to logical operations, answering a potential objection that the operations themselves would imply or lead to rigorous non-contradiction. The LIR concept of real processes is that they are constituted by series of series of series, etc., of alternating actualizations and potentializations. However, these series are not finite, for by the LIR Axiom of Asymptoticity they never stop totally. However, in reality, processes *do* stop, and they are thus not infinite. Following Lupasco, I will use the term transfinite for these series or chains, which are called ortho- or para-dialectics.

The terms develop into a transfinite series of disjunctions of implications. However, every implication implies a contradictory negative implication such that the actualization of one entails the potentialization of the other and that the non-actualization non-potentialization of the one entails the non-potentialization non-actualization of the other. This development in chains of chains of implications must be finite but unending, that is, transfinite, since it is easy to show that if the actualization of implication were infinite, one arrives at classical identity (tautology). Any phenomenon, insofar as it is empirical or diversity or negation, that is, not attached, no matter how little, to an identifying implication of some kind suppresses itself. It is a theorem of LIR that both identity and diversity must be present in existence, to the extent that they are opposing dynamic aspects of phenomena and consequently subject to its Axioms.

Implications for Philosophy Determinism And Non-Separability

Many theoretical arguments depend on some form of absolute separability of dichotomous terms *via* the importation, explicit or implicit, of abstract principles of propositional binary logic into exemplified, in the standard notions of time, space and causality. LIR discusses philosophical problems in physical, dynamical terms that do not require abstract categorial structures that separate aspects of reality. The critical categorial feature of the LIR process ontology is the *non-separability* of opposing phenomena, *e.g.*, two theories or elements of phenomena, *e.g.*, syntax and semantics, types and tokens.

The philosophy of LIR can be very rapidly characterized as a non-naïve dualistic realism that assumes a real, interactive relation between all the classic dualities when they are instantiated in reality. It is part of a new ontological turn in philosophy. The LIR view on determinism, critical for any discussion of free will, is that the world is both deterministic and indeterministic, in the contradictorial relation suggested above. All processes are deterministic, in the sense that the trajectory of all particles could in principle be followed since their creation; indeterminacy is epistemological, not ontological. The possible exception is that of the timing of radioactive decay[1], but this does not affect the further argument. The key idea is that starting at the quantum level it is the potentialities that are the carriers of the causal properties necessary for the emergence of new entities at higher levels. Other randomness is epistemological and the cognitive result is a deterministic reality – classically, necessity - dialectically linked to the appearance of chance.

The obvious and often stated concept that no theory, including LIR, is 100% true has ontological value as part of its core thesis. *No* complex real process is totally instantiated or instantiated in all cases *vs.* some alternative – entity or construct as the case may be. The only exceptions to this rule are either trivial or outside the domain of human existence, that is, of thermodynamic change. There are no exceptions to the law of gravity or the inverse square law of electromagnetic radiation.

My philosophical approach is an ontological one, and examples of specific real processes one can take the creation of a computer program; a presidential election; or a conflict over global warming. I then look, as accurately as I can, at the dynamics of the changes involved, a difficulty in resolving a knotty problem or choosing between length and elegance, a shift of government from right to left, a refusal to establish new pollution norms, and so on and assign a structure to them, on the basis that the changes all follow the same pattern of alternating actualization and potentialization of the elements in opposition or conflict, internal or external.

For the time being, there is an informal calculus, originally proposed by Lupasco, to describe processes of change, as indicated, but unfortunately, no good mathematics. This makes the computation of some aspects of my logical description even more inaccessible than they might otherwise have been, but I am hopeful that a mathematization of LIR can be achieved.

LIR and Non-Computability

As a final point of this summary of aspects of LIR, I will summarize from the ECAP08 paper (unpublished) the implications of LIR for computability, namely, as a way to differentiate the domains of reality that are in principle computable and those that are not.

Based on the same postulates of LIR, I proposed a rationale for the equivalence of different formalizations of computability, and an approach to exploring the interface between mathematics and reality. The physical interactions of the elements of non-Markovian processes, in particular those of living systems, will in general not be computable. Their essential aspects cannot be captured by propositional or predicate logics or their modular or paraconsistent extensions but they can by my contradictorial logic of reality.

The reasons that the LIR variables are non-computable are thus the following:

- they are not context-free: context and content interact contradictorially.
- one is not dealing with binary strings.
- recursion is excluded
- no value depends only on the preceding one (non-Markovian processes).
- some sub-processes move in the direction opposite to the main tendency.

In the LIR interpretation, all the critical, interactive process aspects of living systems growth, reproduction, morphogenesis, and cognition – are emergent and conform to the LIR Axiom of the Included Middle. If this thesis is correct, such life processes are non-Markovian and accordingly non-computable. In other words, if the LIR principle of dynamic opposition holds throughout all levels of reality, not as a "theory of everything" but a "theory for everything real", then no emergent process is computable.

I should not like the reader to think this view overly pessimistic. For some processes in which the degree of actualization and potentialization of opposing entities is relatively easily determined, some computer modeling of the chains of implication referred to above may be possible. There will always be *some* non-computable processes, but the PDO I have suggested for their logics may itself suggest new approaches for hypercomputational

algorithms, applicable to or capable of modeling portions of such processes or others.

CRITIQUE OF CURRENT THEORIES

I will now go back over my original grouping of theories and give an LIR interpretation of some of the key issues in each based on the LIR ontology of energy (New Energy Ontology – NEO). What I claim in each case, to repeat, is that the application of the principle of dynamic opposition is necessary but also sufficient to guarantee that the domain in question belongs to the real and not the digital world. From the LIR point of view, the elements of digital and computational pictures are abstractions that model *part* of a reality that, to return to the distinction I made at the beginning is not in and of itself digital, computational or informational in the limited sense indicated.

To "prove" this, it is necessary to show only that either 1) no ontology is expressed or implied or 2) it is classical without the interactive, dialectic characteristics for which LIR gives the logical and physical foundation. For each theory I will indicate one or two major ontological claims and my refutation of them. I hope that this approach, which will give the reader the opportunity to agree with or refute my refutation, will focus discussion of the potential applicability of my approach to the key issues in this Chapter.

The existence of a mind-independent reality is substantially accepted, but pictures of that reality obtained by human beings processing the information available from the ultimate structures of the universe is considered to constitute a separate mind-dependent reality. This is the position even of people who argue for elimination of the disjunction between the observer and the observed, since this is understood only in an epistemological sense.

In my view, this artificial separation, that fails to take into account that "our" structures might be the same as "its" (the world's) structures, is a new form of anthropocentrism. It is supported by the "computational turn" in ontology due to the lack of good candidates for the underlying ontological structures and their relation to the way in which they are expressed epistemologically.

Digital Ontology

For some reason I don't understand too well, many people seem to like the idea that the universe moves in a regular manner from one state to the next. We are not able to predict such an evolution, due to the vast number of variables involved, but we can make a computational model of it and describe it mathematically. Digital ontology is the position that the ultimate nature of reality is digital, and the universe is a computational system equivalent either to a Turing machine, or something more powerful because based on natural processes (natural computation), but still computational. Now, I personally think that this approach to reality is incomplete, given the existence of complex dynamic processes – biological, cognitive and social – the value of whose variables do not, in a simple Markovian way, depend solely at time t at their state at t-1.

Digital ontology, and its prestige, can be traced back to John Wheeler's 'It from bit' thesis.

- 'It from bit' symbolizes the idea that every item of the physical world has at bottom an immaterial source and explanation;
- Every 'it' – every particle, every field of force, even the space-time continuum itself – derives its function, its meaning, its very existence entirely – even if in some contexts indirectly – from apparatus-elicited answers to yes-or-no questions, binary choices, bits.
- That which we call reality arises in the last analysis from the posing of yes-no questions and the registering of equipment-evoked responses; in short, that all things physical are information-theoretic in origin.

The LIR position is that this thesis fails to provide basis for continuity (analogue ontology) as well as discontinuity. There is no logical *need* to eliminate 'its' as fundamental since they are not individuals in the classic sense.

There are parts of the universe, however, to which this picture clearly applies, and those are digital computers, both those operating on standard electronic platforms and others executing the same functions on other substrates. Any theory of reality, accordingly, should be able to deal with the two domains, unless it can be shown that what I describe as irregular or even inconsistent in the universe is actually ontologically reducible to a computational process model.

It is also possible to describe the elements involved in biological and cognitive processes as executing a form of 'computation' in which complex, non-Shannon information is transferred, as for example in an antigen-antibody interaction. Such descriptions constitute in part the emerging paradigm of natural computation. None of these developments, however, talk to the properties of the fundamental physical substrate of our world. However, such a functional dualism and process logic as I propose is consistent with them and what its consequences might be at the macroscopic level.

Analogue Ontology

As noted previously, analogue ontologies assume that the universe is fundamentally a continuum. The continuum hypothesis refers to a conception of the universe founded on geometry, the Cantor-Dedekind view, as discussed by Giuseppe Longo (1999), which sees not only in mathematics, but everywhere, continuity as ontologically preceding the discrete: "The latter is merely an accident coming out of the continuum background."

This approach fails, from the LIR standpoint, using the same reasoning as in the digital case: there is no basis for the emergence of *discontinuity*. This model is closely related to the geometric view that states which states that physical reality is a mathematical structure that determines a geometry into which matter/energy "fits" in some manner; and 2) Alain Connes' (1994) concept of a non-commutative geometry as being capable of defining the essential properties of the fine structure of space-time described in the standard model of general relativity. It is a geometrical way of thinking about matter itself. Both of these approaches beg the question, however, of whether energy, including quantum gravity, has properties of its own that are *not geometrical* and hence not captured by the model.

The Mathematical Computational Universe

The Tegmark Approach

The Mathematical Universe Hypothesis of Max Tegmark (2007) is relevant since it leads to a Computational Universe Hypothesis that states that "the mathematical structure that *is* our universe is computable and hence well-defined in the strong sense that all its relations can be computed. There are thus no physical aspects of our universe that are uncomputable/undecidable, eliminating the … concern that Gödel's work makes it somehow incomplete or inconsistent." Extending this picture further, one can make the claim that the universe "is" itself a computer that requires only a very simple set of algorithms to "function", because the structure of quantum field theory is mathematically equivalent to that of a spatially distributed quantum computer.

It is easy to see, however, that such a computational model of the universe is an ideal, abstract or if one prefers a neo-Platonist one. Tegmark assumes that either the mathematical structures he sees could be computable "if infinitely many computational steps were allowed", or The mathematical structure that is our external physical reality is defined or described by computable functions or computations by evaluating its relations, but do not evolve the universe as such. Here computable structures are those whose relations are defined

by halting computations. If the Computational Universe Hypothesis is false, Tegmark retreats to a picture of a Computable Finite Universe whose structures are trivially computable.

The justification of such a complicated picture is weak, since it is introduced only *in order to avoid the known paradoxes of existing theories* that are applicable to the highest level (IV) or most complex multiverse that can be imagined consisting of the countably infinitely many computable mathematical structures.

The Nicolaidis Approach

The Chapter by Michael Nicolaidis describes computational models in this category. By clearly establishing that the nature of the meta-objects executing the computation are outside the thermodynamic, phenomenal world, Nicolaidis provides the basis for the "world of the computer", with conclusions about both the capabilities and limitations on key issues such as quantum computation and computation to which I return below.

Nicolaidis shows that the computational characteristics of the quantum domain are *constitutive* for machine, or rather digital computing and relates them to special relativity. His consequent concept of quantum computation avoids the paradoxes in standard logic consequent on the requirement that quantum systems be in a superposition of actual states. Nicolaidis proposes that a statistical view of quantum mechanics, related to special relativity is a basis for quantum mechanics that provides a satisfactory basis for quantum computing.

The model of Nicolaidis has one significant advantage over the other computational models: it states 1) that its validity depends on the existence of unknown objects capable of executing the computation but 2) frankly admits that we can have no knowledge of such objects

The work of Nicolaidis (in press) raises two different kinds of objections to the standard theory of quantum computing: 1) it requires superposition of states in conflict with the principle of non-contradiction in classical logic; and 2) it implies that quantum systems would have infinite computing power. The concept of superposition can be replaced by computations over stochastic processes, avoiding both the counter-intuitive aspects of the "many-worlds" hypothesis used to correct the anti-realism implied by quantum superposition as in the Copenhagen model.

The LIR view of conditional contradiction and an included middle offers an alternative interpretation of quantum superposition and supports a concept of paraconsistent parallelism in quantum computing.

Paraconsistent logics (PCL) are *defined* such that contradiction does not entail triviality (Carnielli 2005) and provide an alternate basis for quantum computation using quantum circuits. Superposition is allowed, and quantum parallelism can be achieved by calculation on all the elements of a superposition state. LIR bears some resemblance to paraconsistent logics (PCL), in which the law of non-contradiction fails. According to the LIR axiom of Conditional Contradiction, however, if A and non-A are present at the same time, it is only in the sense that when A is (predominantly) actual, non-A is (predominantly) potential. Following the LIR axiom of the Included Middle, LIR replaces the superposition of actual states in PCL with states that are semi-actual and semi-potential.

Newton Da Costa and Décio Krause have applied PCL to complementarity and the characteristics of quantum particles. They show that such particles both *are* and *are not* individuals, or both parts *and* wholes. LIR both supports the dualities described by paraconsistent quantum logics and permits this extension.

The PDO principle of LIR thus removes the first of Nicolaidis' objections to superposition in a way that is preferable to PCL. In LIR, in addition, since PCL makes no ontological commitment, one can talk of real physical systems instantiating quantum computation which thus could never be "perfect", removing the second

objection. Current difficulties in the preparation of efficient computing systems are not necessarily a reflection of the state of technology, but of the real properties of the physical world. Advances beyond the limitations of Turing machines are possible in principle, as indicated by concepts of using physical systems for hypercomputation, but this remains at the level of speculation.

Informational Structural Realism

Other recent relevant approaches are those of Informational and Information-Theoretic Structural Realism, as emerging from the work in particular of Luciano Floridi and James Ladyman and their respective associates. Although these approaches, which are in Gianfranco Minati's term "beyond computationalism", differ in the emphasis on epistemic aspects, they retain much of the language and structure of digital ontology.

Luciano Floridi (2009), makes a critique of a digital ontology, a position defined as saying that the ultimate nature of reality is digital, and the universe is a computational system equivalent either to a Turing machine, or something more powerful because based on natural processes (natural computation), but still computational. The work of Luciano Floridi is an example of the informational turn in the philosophy of computer science, and it supports a kind of structural realism that is unavoidable for the logico-philosophical theory reality of the kind I am proposing.

In Floridi's informational ontology or Informational Structural Realism (ISR), he proposes partially or completely unobservable informational objects at the origin of our theories and constructs. Structural objects work epistemologically like constraining affordances: they allow or invite constructs for the information systems like us who elaborate them.

In ISR, the simplest structural objects are *informational objects*, that is, cohering clusters of *data*, not in the alphanumeric sense of the word, but in an equally common sense of *differences de re*, i.e. mind-independent, concrete points of lack of uniformity. In this approach, a datum can be reduced to just a lack of uniformity, that is, a binary difference, like the presence and the absence of a black dot, or a change of state, from there being no black dot at all to there being one. The relation of difference is binary and symmetric, here static. The white sheet of paper is not just the necessary background condition for the occurrence of a black dot as a datum; it is a constitutive part of the datum itself, together with the fundamental relation of inequality that couples it with the dot. In this specific sense, nothing is a datum *per se*, without its counterpart, just as nobody can be a wife without there being a husband. It takes two to make a datum. So, ontologically, data (as still unqualified, concrete points of lack of uniformity) are purely relational entities.

Floridi's ISR is thus primarily epistemological, leaving the relation to the energetic structure of the universe largely unspecified, even if, correctly, the emphasis is shifted from substance to relations, patterns and processes. However, it points at this level toward the dynamic ontology of LIR in which the data are the processes and their opposites or contradictions.

Information Theoretic Structural Realism

In the Information-Theoretic Structural Realism of James Ladyman, Don Ross and their colleagues (Ladyman & Ross, 2007), the notion of individuals as the primitive constitutents of an ontology is replaced by that of real patterns. A real pattern is defined as a relational structure between data that is informationally projectable, measured by its logical depth, which is a normalized quantitative index of the time required to generate a model of the pattern by a near-incompressible universal computer program, that is, one not itself computable as the output of a significantly more concise program.

In replacing individual objects with patterns, the claim that relata are constructed from relations does not mean that there are no relata, but that relations are logically prior in that the relata of a relation always turn out to be relational structures themselves.

An area of overlap between ITSR and LIR is Ladyman's definition of a "pattern" as a carrier of information about the real world. A pattern is real iff it is projectable (has an information-carrying possibility that can be, in principle, computed) and encodes information about a structure of events or entities *S* which is more efficient than the bitmap encoding of *S*. More simply: "A pattern is a relation between data." Ladyman's position is that what exist are just real patterns. There are no 'things' or hard relata, individual objects as currently understood. It is the real patterns that behave like objects, events or processes and the structures of the relations between them are to be understood as mathematical models.

But then Lupasco's question "What is a structure?" still appears, as if the only answer to it were a set of equations! His answer (Brenner 2008) was that structures are also dynamic processes, subject to the same logical rules of evolution as other complex processes, moving toward non-contradiction or contradiction.

The indirect answer of Ladyman and Ross is in terms of science as describing modal structures including unobservable instances of properties. What is not of serious ontological account are unobservable *types* of properties. Thus seeing phenomena not as the 'result' of the existence of things, but their (temporary) stability as part of the world's modal structure, necessity *and* contingency, is something that is acceptable in the LIR framework, provided that the dynamic relation of necessity and contingency is also accepted. There is information carried by LIR processes from one state (of actualization and potentialization) to another, describable by some sort of probability-like non-Kolmogorovian inequalities, although it may not be easily 'computable'.

The theories of mathematical structural realists like Daniel McArthur, and ontic realists like Ladyman and his colleagues might thus benefit from something like my view of structures as dynamic entities. As in the LIR process logic, these are the sets of processual relations themselves rather than sets of equations semantically equal to a theory. As Ladyman points out, the structuralist faces a challenge in articulating his views to contemporary philosophers schooled in modern logic and set theory, which retains the classical framework of individual objects represented by variables subject to predication or membership respectively. "*In lieu of a more appropriate framework for structuralist metaphysics, one has to resort to treating the logical variables and constants as mere placeholders which are used for the definition and description of the relevant relations even though it is the latter that bear all the ontological weight* (emphasis mine)." This is where I see a major contribution of the LIR approach as a Scientific Structural Realism (Brenner, 2008)". The mutual exclusivity of the logical variables and the description of the relevant relations is lifted: the relations are the logical variables in different states of actualization and potentialization, without the need for any kind of intermediate entity.

Two Further Quantum Cosmologies

Although they do not refer to logic as such, I find a close parallel LIR in the cosmology of Mauro Dorato and Massimo Pauri (in press) and the elimination of time by Carlo Rovelli (2008). The first authors propose a new kind of *holistic and structuralist* conception of spacetime, including elements common to the tradition of both *substantivalism* (spacetime has an autonomous existence independently of other bodies or matter fields) *and relationism* (the physical meaning of spacetime depends upon the relations between bodies or, in modern language, the specific reality of spacetime depends also upon the matter/fields it contains). Substantivalism and relationism, as they were

understood before the advent of relativity or even before the electromagnetic view of nature, simply do not fit in well within the main features of the general theory of relativity, reinforcing the need of advancing a *tertium quid* between these two positions, which tries in some sense to overcome the debate by incorporating some claims of both sides.

Rovelli develops a formalism for quantum gravity and cosmology in which the notion of time plays no primitive role. He interprets mechanics, both classical and quantum as a relation between variables, instead of an evolution of the variables in standard time. The properties or macroscopic parameters of phenomena normally classified under "time" are of thermodynamic origin, exactly as proposed in LIR. In the detailed LIR theory of time and space (Brenner 2008), both emerge from the underlying matter/energy field, but LIR adds, in addition, the basis for the emergence of new entities based on the Pauli Exclusion Principle for fermions, as well as the movement between actuality and potentiality which is necessary for a description of change at the macroscopic level.

MODELS: COMPUTATIONAL AND NOT

Models have many roles to play in science (Frigg & Hartmann, 2006), and LIR can be used to analyze the relation between objects and their models in general and computational models in particular. Nicolaidis' development of a computational model for the properties of quantum entities that could enable quantum computing is a pertinent example of a clear fit between a model and the modeled phenomenon. Here, the model refers only to its instantiation in the binary "world" of the computer.

John Symons (2008) has shown how computational models are even more "screened off" from the phenomena they attempt to describe than other types of models. Computational models that address the most general possible issues of the structure of the universe, that is, those that concerned us above have severe limitations. LIR provides for *non-computational* models that have a high degree of generality for explanation without the weaknesses of cataloging or "theory of everything" projects.

Maximal theories are made *vs.* abductive inference to the best (scientifically) generally valid explanation. Computational models thus occupy a modest niche for selected medium-scale phenomena, but LIR avoids burdening them with explanatory possibilities they are not designed to carry. LIR establishes the relation between synchronic downward causation, validating the Symons project, in the following manner: it is the principle of dynamic opposition operating between parts and wholes, carried by the structure of the whole, which is the basis for the effect of the structure on its constituents that is distinct from the powers of those same constituents. In the probabilistic, antagonistic system of cause (or cause/effect), one can propose an account of this effect 'taking place' that is both synchronic and diachronic.

SUMMARY AND CONCLUSION

I have proposed a dynamic logic of and in reality as filling the explanatory gap between computational and informational theories and models of reality and that reality. It is a basis for removing an otherwise obligatory dichotomy or absolute separation between models and the reality they model, at least in the complex biological, cognitive and social processes of primary interest.

The aspect of fundamental postulate of Logic in Reality that physical states are not fully actual, but always instantiate both actuality and potentiality permits a new reading of quantum superposition. The opposing superposed states are in fact semi-actual and semi-potential to the same degree, explicating the paraconsistent logical interpretations that both *can* be present at the same time.

For the real process phenomena described by LIR, the most important categorial feature is the non-separability of the opposing or contradictorially related process elements. The difference with classical category theory, which requires that categories be exhaustive and exclusive, should be clear.

The fact that I have had to include explicitly, in this Chapter, insights and points of view from a wide variety of disciplines – physics, logic, philosophy, computer science, epistemology and perhaps implicitly several others – in order to adequately address critical unresolved issues is not intended as a complication. The transdisciplinarity and transspeciality of *all* thought seems more and more necessary, and I could adduce several additional fields, both abstract, such as symmetry, and pragmatic, such as ethics and evolutionary social theory, in which this factor can be clearly seen.

LIR is thus a substantially new approach, looking at the dynamics of processes and changes from a logical as well as physical perspective. It provides a way of differentiating between the philosophical foundations of digital computer science and those necessary for the part of the world which cannot be captured by binary logical principles. Together with carefully circumscribed computational and informational views, such as those of Nicolaidis and Floridi respectively, it could be part of a potential "strongest possible theory of reality".

REFERENCES

Agudelo, J. C., & Carnielli, W. (2006). *Quantum Computation via Paraconsistent Computation*. arXiv:quant-ph/0607100v1 14 Jul 2006.

Brenner, J. E. (2008). Dordrecht: Springer.

Brenner, J.E. (2009). Prolegomenon to a Logic for the Information Society. *triple-c* 7(1): 38-73. www.triple-c.at.

Carnielli, W. (2005). Logics of Formal Inconsistency. In CLE e-Prints, 5, 1.

Connes, A. (1994). *Non-Commutative Geometry*. San Diego, CA: Academic Press.

Contemporary Phenomenology and Cognitive Science. Stanford, CA: Stanford University Press.

Da Costa, N. C. A., & Krause, D. (2006). The Logic of Complementarity . In *The Age of Alternative Logics: Assessing the Philosophy of Logic and Mathematics Today*. Dordrecht: Springer.

Dorato, M., & Pauri, M. (in press). Holism and Structuralism in Quantum GR . In French, S. (Eds.), *Structuralism and Quantum Gravity*.

Floridi, L. (2009). Against digital ontology. *Synthese*, *168*, 151–178. doi:10.1007/s11229-008-9334-6

Frigg, R., & Hartmann, S. (2009). Models in Science. In Edward N. Zalta (Ed.), *Stanford Encyclopedia of Philosophy*. Retrieved from http://plato.stanford.edu/archives/sum2009/entries/models-science/

Krause, D., & French, S. (2007). Quantum Sortal Predicates. *Synthese*, *154*, 417–430. doi:10.1007/s11229-006-9127-8

Ladyman, J., & Ross, D. (2007). *Every Thing Must Go. Metaphysics Naturalized*. Oxford, UK: Oxford University Press. doi:10.1093/acprof:oso/9780199276196.001.0001

Longo, G. (1999). The Mathematical Continuum . In Petitot, J. (Eds.), *Naturalizing Phenomenology. Issues in*.

Lupasco, S. (1987). *Le principe d'antagonisme et la logique de l'énergie*. Paris: Editions du Rocher.

Magnani, L. (2002). Preface . In Magnani, L., & Nersessian, N. J. (Eds.), *Model Based Reasoning: Science, Technology, Values*. Dordrecht, The Netherlands: Kluwer.

Nicolaidis, M. (in press). A Computational Vision of the Universe . In Valverdu, J. (Ed.), *Thinking Machines and the Philosophy of Computer Science: Concepts and Principles*. Hershey, PA: IGI Global.

Priest, G. (2002). *Beyond the Limits of Thought*. Oxford, UK: Clarendon Press.

Rovelli, C. (2009). *Forget Time*. Retrieved from arXiv:0903.3832v3 27 Mar 2009.

Seibt, J. (2009). Forms of emergent interaction in General Process Theory. *Synthese*, *166*, 479–512. doi:10.1007/s11229-008-9373-z

Symons, J. (2008). Computational Models of Emergent Properties. *Minds and Machines*, *4*, 475–491. doi:10.1007/s11023-008-9120-8

Tegmark, M. (2007). *The Mathematical Universe*. Retrieved from arXiv:0704.064v2 8 Oct 2007

KEY TERMS AND DEFINITIONS

Computational models: models of complex entities, *e.g.*, consciousness or the universe, which attempt to capture their structure in terms of algorithms.

Informational ontology: a new ontology that proposes informational objects as the ground of theories and constructs.

Logic in Reality (LIR): an extension of the concept of a logic to real-world processes and systems, describing their evolution, in terms of interactive actual and potential states and an emergent intermediate state.

Non-Computability: a property of real systems for which no simple algorithm is possible in principle or, if possible, would require unrealizable computational resources.

Non-Separability: a category in the ontology of LIR (*q.v.*) that refers to the property of complex real phenomena always being associated with their opposites or contradictions.

Ontology of LIR: a new ontology in which energy is the sole material category.

Principle of Dynamic Opposition (PDO): the key principle of LIR, stating that elements of real processes are always accompanied by their opposites or contradictions (counteractions).

Process logic: logic in reality in the sense that all its elements are real processes, processes of processes, etc.

Quantum superposition: superposition of quantum states in quantum phenomena before measurement of a specific property.

Standard logic: classical bivalent propositional or predicate logics and their modern multivalent modal, fuzzy, deontic, paraconsistent or paracomplete versions.

Chapter 16
Computational Space, Time and Quantum Mechanics

Michael Nicolaidis
TIMA Laboratory (CNRS, Grenoble INP, UJF), France

ABSTRACT

The author starts this article by introducing an ultimate limit of knowledge: as observers that are part of the universe we have no access on information concerning the fundamental nature of the elementary entities (particles) composing the universe but only on information concerning their behaviour. Then, th authors use this limit to develop a vision of the universe in which the behaviour of particles is the result of a computation-like process (not in the restricted sense of Turing machine) performed by meta-objects and in which space and time are also engendered by this computation. In this vision, the structure of space-time (e.g. Galilean, Lorentzian, ...) is determined by the form of the laws of interactions, important philosophical questions related with the space-time structure of special relativity are resolved, the contradiction between the non-locality of quantum systems and the reversal of the temporal order of events (encountered in special relativity when we change inertial frames) is conciliated, and the "paradoxes" related with the "strange" behaviour of quantum systems (non-determinism, quantum superposition, non-locality) are resolved.

INTRODUCTION

In this article we present a computational vision of the universe aimed at resolving the paradoxes of modern physics. The computational universe idea introduced by Konrad Zuse (Zuse, 1969, Zuse, 1970) and further developed by Jurgen Schmidhuber (Schmidhuber, 1997), considers that the universe can be engendered by a computation. However, to be convincing, such an approach should explain:

1. Why we perceive a real space and time in our every-days life if the world is the result of a computation?

DOI: 10.4018/978-1-61692-014-2.ch016

2. How space and time could emerge from a computation and why we could not distinguish them from a space and a time that would be primary ingredients of the universe?
3. How a relativistic 4D space-time could emerge in a computational universe?
4. What could be a computational model of quantum systems?

Since several millennia we consider that our universe is composed of objects immersed in a veritable space and evolving with the flow of a veritable time (merged in space-time according to relativity). Thus, in this vision, objects, space and time are primary ingredients of the universe. But, is this vision compatible with the behaviour of our world as it is described by modern physics? Several questions concerning the non-determinism, the state superposition and the non-locality of quantum systems, and the structure of space-time described by special relativity, seem to indicate the opposite.

Non-locality of quantum systems raises an important philosophical question concerning the nature of space. In entangled particles, a measurement performed on the one impacts instantaneously the state of the other, whatever is their distance. But, the essence of space is to separate objects. The extent of this separation is referred as distance. The essence of this separation is to take time for two distant objects to interact. The more distant are two objects the more time they need to interact. So, the instantaneous "communication" between distant entangled particles annihilates the very essence of a veritable space, that is, the existence of a veritable separation between distant objects.

Quantum superposition also raises important philosophical questions. What exactly this superposition means? For instance what is this state where an object can be simultaneously on infinite number of space positions?

The nature of space-time described by special relativity raises also several philosophical ques-tions. We imagine time to flow from past to future through the present. But in relativity there is not clear distinction between past, present, and future. This question raises a fundamental dilemma, as expressed with clarity in the foundation text of the International Conference on the Nature and Ontology of Spacetime (Space-Time conference web site, 2004):

"A 3D world requires not only a relativization of existence, but also a pre-relativistic division of events into past, present, and future. Therefore, it appears that such a world view may not be consistent with relativity. However, the alternative view – reality is a 4D world with time entirely given as the fourth dimension – implies that there is (1) no objective time flow (since all events of spacetime are equally existent), (2) absolute determinism (at the macro scale), and (3) no free will. It is precisely these consequences of the 4D world view that make most physicists and philosophers agree that a world view leading to such implications must be undoubtedly wrong. But so far, after so many years of debate, no one has succeeded in formulating a view that avoids the above dilemma and is compatible with relativity."

Yet another quote (Lusanna, Pauri, 2006) reveals the importance of this question for the philosophy of science: "the conventional nature of the definition of distant simultaneity that follows from the analysis of the basic structure of causal influences in SR seems to conflict with every possible notion of /3-dimensional reality / of objects and processes which stands at the basis of our phenomenological experience since it entails that no observer- and frame-independent notions of simultaneity and instantaneous 3-space be possible. There is, therefore, a deep contrast between the formal inter-subjective unification of space and time in the scientific relativistic image, on the one hand, and the ontological diversity of time and space within the subjectivity of experi-ence, on the other. This appears to be the most important and difficult question that physics raises to contemporary philosophy, since it reveals the core of the relation between/ reality /of /experience /and /reality-objectivity /of /*knowledge/*. "

The 4D world vision leads other authors (Tegmark, M. 2007). to consider that the whole 4D structure of the universe (i.e. its whole history) exists altogether, like a film stored in a DVD. Our everyday's perception of the world corresponds in this case to the visualization in a screen of the film stored in the DVD.

To reveal another paradox, let us combine the non-locality of quantum systems with the absence of objective time flow in special relativity. Consider two observers performing measurements over two distant entangled particles. The measure performed first will determine the state of the measured particle but also of its entangled counterpart. But due to the absence of objective time flow in special relativity, it is possible that the two observers experience a different temporal order for the measurement events. According to the first observer, it is her/his measurement that occurs first. So, for her/him, her/his measurement determines the states of the particles. But for the second observer it is the opposite. Furthermore, according to the special relativity, each one of these points of view is as well valid as the other. Thus, two incompatible situations « the action of the first observer determines the states of the particles » and « the action of the second observer determines the states of the particles » will both be valid!

These questions challenge the pertinence of the above-mentioned thousands-years-old vision. That is,, it becomes natural to raise the question about the pertinence of this vision and the related nature of space and time, which, by the way, are involved in all these questions.

From a very generic perspective, not restricted to the Turing paradigm, a computation can be viewed as a process where the states of a system (referred as computer) evolve according to certain rules (which in the case of digital computers are coded by the software). In this respect, a natural process can be viewed as a kind computation, where the states of a natural system evolve according to certain rules (the laws of physics). This could be extended to the process of evolution of the whole universe, and we could consider its evolution as a computation where the state of the universe evolves according to the laws of physics. However, the simple fact to call the process of evolution of the universe "a computation" does give a clue for understanding our world. In particular, calling computation the evolution in a veritable space of a set of objects composing a natural system does not help understanding paradoxes like non-locality, position superposition, etc. A more radical move from the current vision of the universe and in particularly of the nature of space and time will be required, in which the concept of computing systems could play an essential role. In particular, considering the positions of particles not as veritable positions in a veritable space, but as state "variables" evolving according to certain laws, could allow treating behaviours such as non-locality, position superposition, length contraction, time dilatation, etc. as computational problems. However, in this case, space becomes virtual, while our experience convinces us about its reality. So, any convincing attempt to introduce such a computational vision should first treat this problem.

We treat this problem by giving a very central role to the observers that are part of a universe. That is, observers composed of the same elementary entities (particles) that compose any structure of the universe. For such observers we derive a fundamental limit of knowledge according to which they can access information concerning the behaviour of these entities but by no means information concerning their veritable nature. Due to this limit, such observers could not distinguish a universe in which particles evolve in a veritable space from a computational universe where the positions of particles are state variables evolving according to certain laws. Then, we can create a vision in which:

- The instantaneous "communication" between distant entangled particles can be treated as a computational problem and lose its paradoxical status.
- The interpretation of quantum mechanics based on the quantum superposition concept is replaced by a computational model consisting on computing certain deterministic functions acting on stochastic signals.
- Lorentz transformations do not reflect the veritable structure of a veritable space-time but become a consequence of the interaction laws used to compute the evolution of the states of particles and the measurement means that we dispose as observers that are part of the universe. This re-establishes an objective time flow resolving the related paradoxes.

The general principles of the proposed computational model including the emergence of space and time were first described in a lab report (Nicolaidis, 2003), while both these principles and the models for special relativity and quantum mechanics were presented in a book (Nicolaidis, 2005).

INTERNAL OBSERVERS, OBJECTS AND BEHAVIOURS

In this section we establish an ultimate limit of knowledge stating that we can access information concerning the behaviour of elementary particles but not information concerning the nature of the "objects" which produce this behaviour. This limit is implied by the fact that the nature of information that we can access is conditioned by our position as *internal observers of the universe (in the sense that we are constituted by the same elementary entities (particles) that compose any structure of the universe)*. As a consequence, the information collected by our sensorial systems, as well as by the systems we built to observe nature, comes from the interactions of the particles composing these systems with other particles (like photons, electrons,....). The later having interacted previously with the objects that we want to observe, their states are modulated by these interactions and bring to us information which is the outcome of these interactions. But the interactions represent the behaviour of the particles.

To better understand the foundations of this limit let us consider a system made of several entities represented by light blue circles in figure 1. Each of these entities is an object which comprises a state and exhibits a certain behaviour produced in the following manner. Each entity interacts with other entities (interactions illustrated schematically by plain gray lines) and receives information concerning their state. It determines its next state as a function of its present state and of the present and/or past states of the entities with which it interacts. Entities described in such generic terms could correspond to various interacting objects, including the cells of a cellular automata, the nodes of a parallel processor, software agents, the elementary particles of our universe ... We can call the rules that the entities use to determine their next state, while interacting with other entities, laws of interactions. Let us consider in this system a set A of entities (for example those surrounded by a circle in gray dashed line in (Figure 1) and the set B of entities external to A. We observe that the information the entities of set A receive from the entities of set B concerns the states of the later and the way in which these states evolve. Thus, for determining their next state, the only information that the entities of set A could receive concerning the entities of set B are related to the states of the later and the way these states evolve. But the state of an entity and the way this state evolves represent its behaviour. Consequently, the states of the entities of set A can contain information concerning the behaviour of the entities of set B but they can not contain information concerning the intimate nature (or structure) of the objects which produce this behaviour.

Let us now consider that the entities of set A are the elementary particles which compose a sensory organ (for example the eye) of an observer, as illustrated in (Figure 2).

The particles of this sensory system interact with other particles and via these interactions they collect and transfer information to the particles that compose the mental structures of this observer. Thanks to this kind of information these structures form images (perceptions) of all kinds of objects of the world in which belongs the observer. For reasons which we have just explained, the states of the particles of these sensory and mental structures can contain only information concerning the behaviour of elementary particles. Thus, this discussion highlights *an ultimate limit of our knowledge*: as observers composed of the same kind of elementary particles as those composing any object of our universe (observers that are part of the universe or internal observers), we can have access to information concerning the behaviour of the elementary particles but by no means to information concerning the nature of the objects which produce this behaviour[1]. Therefore, these objects are *meta-objects* for the internal observers. We will refer to this limit as the ultimate limit of knowledge for internal observers (ULKIO).

System Closure vs. Internal Observers

In this section we consider a system structure more suitable for proposing a computational model of quantum systems (as the one described later in section 6). Let us consider that the system in (Figure 1) and (Figure 2) is closed and that the state of each entity of this system is determined from its own state and the states of the entities with which it interacts, following certain rules (interaction laws). The internal observer could observe a large number of times the state of any entity and of the entities with which it interacts. Through interactions, he/she may also force the states of these entities at particular configurations and observe the outcome. Then, after a sufficient number of observations and with a certain amount of intelligence she/he could extrapolate the interaction laws. Afterwards, once he has observed the state of a closed set of entities (i.e. not interacting with any other entities), he can use these laws to predict their future states.

Let us now consider the system of (Figure 3). In this system each entity is composed of two parts, the first represented by a light blue circle and the second by a gray circle. In this system certain (interaction) laws determine the state of the first (blue) part of each entity from the state of this part; the state of the second (gray) part of the entity; and the states of the first (blue) parts of

Figure 1. A system composed of a set of interacting entities

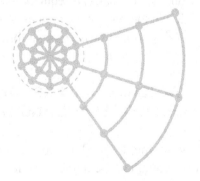

Figure 2. Objects and observer being part of a system

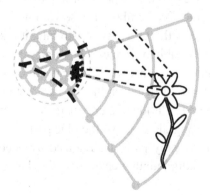

Figure 3. System closure versus internal observers

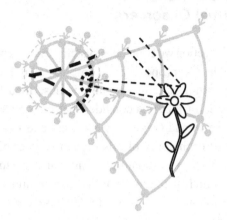

the entities with which it interacts. Consider also that the second (gray) part is autonomous. That is, the future state of a gray part does not depend on the state of any other part of any entity. For instance, the gray part could be an autonomous pseudorandom generator or a random generator. We observe that for an internal observer of this system:

- Similarly to the states of the entities of (Figure 1) and (Figure 2), in (Figure 3) the states of the blue parts of the entities are observable and may also be forced at particular configurations.
- An internal observer has no means for performing experiments in which he/she forces the states of the gray parts at selected values, neither observe these states.
- It may be impossible to extrapolate the state of the gray parts by observing the states of the blue parts, or it may require an intractable number of observations.
- Due to the previous constraints, it may be impossible or it may require an intractable number of observations for the internal observer to discover the law governing the state evolution of a gray part by simply observing the states of the blue parts,
- If the gray parts are realized by adequate pseudorandom generators, the behaviour

of the blue parts as well as the behaviour of the whole system and the properties emerging in it may be indistinguishable with respect to the case where the gray parts are realized by truly random generators.

- The knowledge of the state of the blue part of an entity and of the states of the blue parts of the entities with which it interacts may not be sufficient for determining the next state of this blue part (since it also depends on the unobservable and unpredictable state of the gray part). However, it may be possible to restrict the set of possible values of this state (potential values). The unknown and unpredictable value of the state of the corresponding gray part will determine which particular value among these potential values will become the actual state of the blue part (actualization). Thus, an internal observer disposing a sufficient number of observations will not be able to extrapolate laws allowing her/him to predict the exact value provided by the blue part of an entity (or of a set of entities), but only laws allowing him to predict the set of possible (potential) values.

We observe that, though the system of (Figure 3) can be closed and possibly deterministic (e.g. when the gray parts are deterministic autonomous generators such as pseudorandom generators), for its internal observers the system will be seen as non closed and non deterministic, since some information not accessible to them (the values coming from the gray parts) is required to predict the evolution of the state of the system. For these observers, this information is a meta-information.

COMPUTATIONAL UNIVERSE AND EMERGENCE OF SPACE AND TIME

According to the ULKIO (ultimate limit of knowledge) limitation, we can access information concerning the behaviour of elementary particles but not information concerning their profound nature. As a consequence, we are not able to know if they are veritable particles immersed in a veritable space or if their behaviour is the result of a computation-like process such that:

- The evolution of the state of the particles is determined by "computation" rules identical to what physics calls interaction laws.
- The position of each particle is determined by the values that this process attributes to a position variable, rather than being a veritable position in a veritable space.

To illustrate this vision, let us consider that the meta-system making the above computations is a cellular network, as shown in (Figure 4), composed of a set of cells (the meta-objects of the previous section) that compute the evolution of the states of elementary particles. Each cell uses its computational means to determine the next values of the state variables of a "particle" (including its position variable), as a function of the current values of these variables and of the current and/or past values of the state variables of the "particles" with which it interacts. The computation is performed following certain rules that we can call interaction laws.

It is worth to point out that the distance between "particles" does not correspond to the distance of the corresponding cells in the cellular network,

but to the numerical distance, determined by the values of the position variables of the "particles". Thus, in (Figure 4), two cells a and b are close in the network, but their position variables have very different values. In this case, in the universe engendered by the cellular network, the corresponding "particles" a' and b' will have very distant positions. On the other hand, the cells b and c are very distant in the network but their position variables have very close values. As particles corresponding to distant cells in the network may interact, the network will dispose communication means to exchange information between distant cells as required by the interactions.

Emergence of Space

In the illustration example given previously, the cells of the cellular network determine at each computation step the values of the position variables of the particles. If we consider that the values of the position variables represent positions in a multi-dimensional system of Cartesian co-ordinates (e.g. in a four-dimensional system) corresponding to a virtual multi-dimensional space with Euclidian structure, then, the values of the position variables determined by all the cells will lie in a subspace of this virtual space. This subspace will have a certain form (e.g. the form of a curve of three dimensions in a four-dimensional space, illustrated in (Figure 5) by the surface of a sphere of two dimensions). In this sense, the values of

Figure 4. Cellular network and computational universe

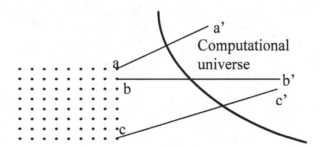

the position variables computed by the cells of the cellular network determine the form of the space engendered by this computation.

However, this space is virtual for any observer external to this universe, because she/he will be able to perceive its computational nature. Thus, space could be perceived as real only by the internal observers of the computational universe. On the other hand, in the computational universe, all structures (including the sensory and mental structures of its internal observers) are shaped by the states of the particles composing them and by their evolution. These states also determine the representations of the world emerging in these mental structures. If the computation rules used in a computational universe are identical to the laws of interactions of a non-computational universe (in the sense that particles are immersed in a veritable space), then, the states of similar sets of particles will evolve similarly, creating similar structures and similar state configurations in both universes. Thus, in the mental structures of internal observers of the computational universe, the states representing the form of an object, the relative positions of a configuration of objects, etc., will be similar to the states representing the form of a similar object, the relative positions of a similar configuration of objects, etc … in the mental structures of internal observers of the non-computational universe. Therefore, the representations of the "computational" objects and of the "computational" space emerging in the mental structures of the observers of the "computational" universe will be similar to the representation of the "veritable" objects and of the "veritable" space in the mental structures of the observers of the non-computational universe. Thus, the perception of space and of objects emerging in the mental structures of the observers of the "computational" universe will be identical to the perception of space and of objects emerging in the mental structures of the observers of the non-computational universe. Therefore, nothing could differentiate these perceptions. Thus, the observers of the "computational" universe could believe that they live in a world composed of veritable objects immersed in a veritable space and nothing could prove to them that this is not true. For the similar reason, we could not prove that we do not live in a world composed of "computational" objects immersed in a "computational" space rather than in a world composed of veritable objects immersed in a veritable space. This resolves the questions i. and ii. stated in the beginning of the introduction.

Emergence of Time

In this section we address a fundamental question concerning the nature of time: is time an autonomous entity which has an existence per se

Figure 5. Emergence of space in a computational universe

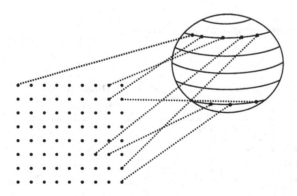

and which paces the changes in the Universe? or time does not exist a priori but it is a by-product of the evolution of the structures and processes of the universe, in the sense that this evolution creates the notion of time in our minds? We are interested about the internal time of a universe and more generally of a system, that is, the time experienced by its internal observers. Such observers are agents that anticipate the evolution of a process taking place in the system by comparing it with other processes taking place in the system and selected as time references.

A Necessary and Sufficient Condition

Let us first discuss the sufficient condition that enables the emergence of internal time in any system (including a universe). We can find that the notion of the internal time (hereafter simply referred as time) is closely related to a well known invariance, which seems to govern the evolution of our universe. To describe this invariance let us consider a process H (for example the evolution of a clock) and k consecutive states h_1, h_2, h_3, ..., h_k of this process. Let us consider a second process G (for example the fall of a water drop) and k successive states g_1, g_2, g_3 ... g_k of G, which are respectively synchronous to the states h_1, h_2, h_3 ... h_k of H. Suppose that the processes H and G take again place under exactly the same conditions as before and that the state g_1 of G is synchronous to the state h_1 of H. Then, according to this invariance, the states g_2, g_3 ... g_k of G will be synchronous to the states h_2, h_3 ... h_k of H. In fact, this synchronism will not be perfect due to the quantum indeterminism, but will be verified with a high degree of accuracy if H and G describe the evolution of macroscopic systems. Thus, this invariance states that each time any two processes H and G take place and their initial states h_1 and g_1 are synchronous, their states h_2, h_3 ... h_k and g_2, g_3 ... g_k will also be synchronous. Therefore, if we observe once the two processes, we will be able whenever the two processes occur to antici-

pate the evolution of process G by observing the evolution of clock H.

The above discussion is not limited to our universe but determines a *sufficient condition* for the emergence of time for observers that are part of any system or "universe", including a computational universe. Indeed, let us imagine a world in which there is always the same relationship between the paces of evolution of two processes, whenever and wherever these processes take place. In such a world we can speak about time, because:

1. we can choose a process as time reference, and

2. after having observed once the correspondences between the different events of this process and the events of another process we can:

   ° use the reference process to predict the instant (event of the reference process) in which each event of the second process occurs.

   ° measure the duration of a process, by observing the events of the reference process in which the process under measurement starts and finishes.

As concerning the *necessary condition* for the emergence of (internal) time, let us imagine a world in which:

• certain times the zebras are incomparably faster than the lion and certain times the opposite,

• a car being at several kilometres of distance covers suddenly this distance in a fraction of a second and crushes us,

• the earth carries out hundreds of evolutions around the sun without your biological age being advanced, while several generations of people already passed, and suddenly you age of a hundred years in a fraction of a second,

• ......,

Let us imagine a world (or system) in which processes evolve arbitrarily the one with respect to the other, and thus, there is no invariant correlation between the paces of evolution of the different processes. In such a world, the observation of the changes would not lead an intelligent observer to form the notion of time. Moreover, it would be improbable that such a universe will engender the intelligence. In fact, an intelligent being could not act by anticipation to protect itself from a natural phenomenon, because the speed of evolution of the phenomenon would be completely unpredictable; a herbivore could not escape a carnivore thanks to its speed, nor the carnivore catch the herbivore thanks to its speed, its strategy and its power, because the relative speed of these animals would change in a unpredictable way. For the same reason, the intelligence could emerge, and in any case its existence would not have any sense: what would be the utility of intelligence if it could not anticipate any event?

In a system whose state evolves according to certain rules (laws), it is easy to check that the invariance of these laws is the necessary and sufficient condition that implies the invariance of the ratios of the paces of evolution of the processes that take place in this system. Thus, *the invariance of the laws governing the evolution of the system is the necessary and sufficient condition for the emergence of (internal) time*. In the case of a universe constituted of particles taking positions in a space (veritable or computational), this condition can be stated as: the laws that govern the evolution of the states of the particles are invariant (i.e. they are independent of the values of the position variables of the particles, and remain unchanged throughout the evolution of this universe). Indeed, in this case, the correspondence between the events of two processes will remain the same whenever and wherever these processes take place.

However, it is worth to note that this condition could be somehow relaxed without preventing the emergence of time in the mental structures of an internal observer. Indeed, the variation of the

laws which govern the evolution of a universe will not prevent this emergence as long as this variation remains sufficiently weak or sufficiently slow to allow the prediction of the events with a sufficiently small margin of error.

We can conclude from the above discussion that the internal time of a system (or a universe) is not an autonomous category but can exist if and only if the laws governing its evolution are invariant.

Quantitative Principle Governing the Internal Time

We will notice that the above invariance is not dependent on the very particular form of the laws which govern the evolution of a system/universe, but on a generic principle of invariance of these laws. This invariance is the qualitative principle that underlies the emergence of time (the necessary and sufficient condition for its emergence). On the other hand, the particular correspondence between the states of two processes H and G is determined by the particular laws which govern the system/universe. For instance if process H is governed by an electromagnetic interaction having a given expression and process G is governed by a gravitational interaction having another expression, the particular expressions of these laws will determine the relation of the pace of evolution of process G with respect to the pace of evolution of process H. Therefore, the particular form of the laws governing a universe determines the quantitative manifestation of time (quantitative principle). It is also this form that determines the structure of time and consequently of space-time (e.g. Galileo or Lorentz transformations), as we show elsewhere (Nicolaidis, 2007, Nicolaidis, 2009-1).

Time vs. Meta-Time

In the previous sections we have seen that the invariability of the laws implies the emergence of internal time in a system/universe. *Nevertheless, the emergence of time presupposes that the state of this system evolves.* This assumption means that there is a cause that makes the system changing its states. We can call it engine of change or external time or meta-time. Whatever is the word we use the fact is that we tried to understand the nature of internal time by implicitly introducing a "meta-time". Since this "meta-time" is a metaphysical category (thus of inscrutable nature), we could conclude that this attempt has no sense since it replaces the question of the nature of time by the question of the inscrutable nature of a meta-time. This conclusion will be correct if time is a simple translation of meta-time. But this can not be the case, since we have seen that both qualitatively and quantitatively time is determined by the laws governing the evolution of the states of the system. We can use the computational universe vision to make this fact more clear. This vision is very useful for illustrating the related ideas, as it allows us to give a simple and clear example of an external time of a system/universe and the independence of the internal time from the external time. Let us consider that the universe is engendered by a (meta)computing system which is paced by a temporal dimension that we call meta-time. Let us suppose that this system is synchronous and its computations are paced by a meta-clock whose period corresponds to a duration T of meta-time. That is, T corresponds to the meta-time duration that the meta-system disposes for carrying out one step of computation (e.g. for exchanging information between meta-cells and computing the new states of the meta-cells). This step of computation will carry the minimal changes that can occur in the engendered universe. Therefore it will correspond to a minimal duration of time t_h in this universe. Let us now consider that the clock period T is variable.

This is illustrated in (Figure 6), where the period T of the meta-clock takes two different values T_1 and T_2 in two different cycles of computation. In this figure, the old and new states of each cycle are represented by the high and the low position

of a water drop. Because at each clock cycle the meta-system carries out one cycle of computation, corresponding to the minimal time duration t_h of the universe, then, the same time duration of the universe (t_h) will correspond to two different durations T_1 and T_2 of meta-time. Thus, stopping, decelerating, or accelerating the meta-clock will not have any influence on the time experienced by the observers that are part of the universe. We can arrive in the similar conclusion if we consider continuous time. But we will not develop further this case for space reasons.

Time, Meta-Time, Synchronism and Meta-Synchronism

We were obliged to introduce the category referred as engine of change or meta-time or external time, because we consider dynamic systems, like the universe, having evolving states. The second fundamental reason for introducing such a category (not mentioned explicitly so far), is the fact that the emergence of internal time requires correlating the paces of evolution of two processes, that is correlating the events of these processes. Indeed, to introduce the condition enabling the emergence of internal time, we used the following proposition: "let us consider a process H (for example the evolution of a clock) and k consecutive states $h_1, h_2, h_3, ..., h_k$ of this process. Let us consider a second process G (for example the fall of a water drop) and k successive states $g_1, g_2, g_3 ... g_k$ of G, which are respectively synchronous to the states $h_1, h_2, h_3 ... h_k$ of H.". The existence of certain correlations (synchronism) in the evolution of the states of the different parts of the system is necessary, because if such a correlation does not exist, the paces of evolution of different processes could not be put in relation and internal time could not emerge. The source of this correlation should be associated with the source of change, that is with the meta-time, and this correlation will be referred as meta-synchronism or fundamental synchronism. As an illustration, in the example

Figure 6. Independence between time and meta-time

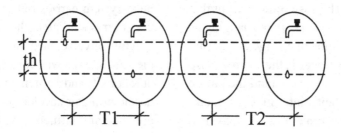

of the cellular network considered previously, the cells of the network can compute new states of the particles at each cycle of a meta-clock, resulting on the correlation (meta-synchronism) of the states computed at the same cycle. This determines a fundamental synchronism. However, this synchronism does not determine the internal time, which is determined by the rations of the "amount of change of the states" of different processes encountered at each computation step, and these ratios are determined by the form of the laws of interactions. The same is valid if the states of the system evolve following continues meta-time. In this case the internal time will be determined by the rations of the "amount of change of the states" of different processes encountered during infinitesimal meta-time durations dT. These ratios again are determined by the form of the laws of interactions. Furthermore, the fundamental synchronisatiion does not determine the synchronisation experienced by the internal observers. By using reference processes as clocks and by synchronizing distant clocks, these observers will alter the fundamental synchronism in a way determined by the form of the laws governing these processes (i.e. the laws of interactions). This may lead to a synchronism that is different from one observer to another and from the fundamental synchronism. The way this can happen in practice becomes more clear when we treat special relativity (Nicolaidis, 2007, Nicolaidis, 2009-1).

To summarize, the above discussions show that *the time experienced by an observer that is part of a system/universe (i.e. the internal time of a system/universe), is governed by three principles:*

- *The principle of the qualitative emergence of internal time (determined by the invariance of the laws that govern the change of the states of the system/universe);*
- *The principle of the quantitative expression of the internal time (determined by the particular form of the laws which govern the change of the states of the system/universe);*
- *The principle of independence of the internal time from the "external time" (or the "engine of change").*

The morality is that the existence of the time we experience as observers internal to the universe can not be identified with change. Also, this time has not an existence per se, since its qualitative emergence becomes possible only if the laws governing a system/universe are invariant, and qualitatively it is determined by the form of these laws. But these laws are not enough for the emergence of what we experience as time. A category (that we call external time or meta-time), having the attributes of an engine of change and of correlating the events of different processes, is also needed. Note that known approaches considering that time is a by product of relations miss the consideration of a source of change and the necessity of a fundamental correlation between the states of different processes. By doing so, they disregard the fact that without considering any pre-existing correlations it is impossible to introduce any relations between different processes. Thus, in many papers the need for a fundamental correlation is hidden in the text. For instance, some otherwise very interesting developments on the relations-based modelling of physics (Rovelli, 2009) start with the proposition: "*let α be the reading of the device measuring the elongation of the pendulum and β be the reading of the clock ... Call the variables α and β the partial observables of the pendulum. A physically relevant observation is a reading of α and β, together*". Here, "reading α and β, together" is necessary for establishing relations between different processes. However, the hypothesis of pre-existing correlations (synchronism) between the events of the considered processes is hidden in the phrase "reading α and β, together". Also, by trying to ignore the fundamental synchronization, relations-based approaches develop models of physics, and particularly of quantum mechanics, accounting for the multitude of observer-depending time flows, which may result on unnecessary complexities. Thus, they miss the fundamental interest of a relations-based approach, which could simplify physics by attributing the multitude of time flows to relations and use a single (fundamental) time-flow for developing models of physics, including quantum models. More generally, known approaches considering the universe as by-product of relations miss a background supporting the emergence of processes and the associated relations. Without such a background this emergence looks like a Deus ex machina. Establishing the foundations of such a background was the goal of sections 2 and 3.

COMPUTATIONAL UNIVERSE AND INTERPRETATION OF MODERN PHYSICS

In order to illustrate the vision of a computational universe in a simple way, in the previous sections we used some examples of computing system. These examples should be viewed only as illustrations of the ideas that support the suggested vision and not as proposals for computational models of the universe. The ultimate goal of this vision would be to propose a new framework for interpreting modern theories of physics and circumvent the hard philosophical questions that they are raising. Certain answers concerning these questions are addressed in the next sections and in referenced articles. For example, we show that:

- The structure of space-time described by Lorentz transformations can emerge in a system in which each particle determines its state while interacting with other particles, provided that the laws of interactions obey a certain condition.
- The interpretation of quantum mechanics based on the superposition concept is replaced by a computational model.
- The non-local behaviour exhibited by entangled particles can be reproduced by simple communication mechanisms acting between the cells of a cellular system.

These results eliminate the paradoxes of modern physics discussed in the introduction. However, these are just initial steps, as we have still to go a long way before establishing a complete computational vision integrating and unifying all aspects of physics.

EMERGENCE OF RELATIVISTIC SPACE-TIME IN A COMPUTATIONAL UNIVERSE

As discussed earlier, the structure of space and time perceived by an internal observer of a computational universe is determined by the form of the laws of interactions. Then, Lorentz transformations should be attributed to this form, rather than to an a priori structure of space-time as considered by the current vision of special relativity. This problem is treated in some other articles (Nicolaidis, 2007, Nicolaidis, 2009-1). In these articles we show that according to the form of the laws of interactions, time and space measurements of internal observers will obey different transformations: the Galileo transformations, if the intensity of interactions does not depend on the velocity of the interacting objects; the Lorentz transformations if these intensities depend on the velocities of the object following a particular condition referred as *Relativistic Constraint of Accelerations*. In particular, the measurement means (length units, time units, and clock synchronization principles) that dispose the observers internal to a system/universe play an essential role in the emergence of Lorentz transformations. It results a formulation of special relativity in which:

- There is a fundamental inertial frame and a fundamental time, establishing an objective time-flow.
- All measurements performed by observers internal to the universe obey Lorentz transformations.
- The fundamental principle of special relativity (the laws of physics are invariant with respect to Lorentz transformations for the transition from one inertial system to any other arbitrarily chosen inertial system) is replaced by: the laws of our universe are such that they appear (create the illusion) to its internal observers to be invariant with respect to Lorentz transformations for the transition from one inertial system to any other arbitrarily chosen inertial system.

Note that there are some similarities of the above interpretation with the Neolorentzian interpretation of special relativity. However, the later is subject to certain strong objections stating that this interpretation is based on principles borrowed from the space-time interpretation that is supposed to refute (Balashov, (Janssen, 2002), such as:

- The speed of light is same in all inertial frames.
- The laws of physics are invariant with respect to Lorentz transformations for the transition from one inertial frame to any other inertial frame.

These objections do not apply on our computational interpretation of special relativity as we do not assume any invariance of the laws of physics with respect to Lorentz transformations (we only consider a system composed of entities which compute their states variables according to certain computation rules), neither any invariance of the speed of light (we synchronize distant clocks by using synchronization objects composed of entities computing their states as above, instead of light beans).

A critic of the proposed formulation of special relativity could be that it does not provide added value, as its predictions are identical to those of its current formulation. However, its added value has to be seen not in the context of special relativity alone but in its combination with quantum mechanics. In particular, by re-establishing the existence of objective time-flow, this formulation resolves the philosophical dilemma concerning the 3D/4D world visions, as well as the question raised when we combine the lack of fundamental time-flow with the quantum non locality. Resolving this question has very important implications on modern physics. Indeed, attempts to reformulate quantum mechanics to make them coherent with the current interpretation of special relativity, lead to very complex models that ultimately fail to provide coherent physical theories. As an example, an important progress on creating such coherent models is the relativistic version of the Ghirardi–Rimini–Weber model of spontaneous wavefunction collapse, proposed recently by Roderich Tumulka (Tumulka, 2006). However, as noticed by David Albert (Albert, 2009) "No one has yet been able to write down a satisfactory version of Tumulka's theory that can be applied to particles that attract or repel one another. Moreover, his theory introduces a new variety of nonlocality into the laws of nature—a nonlocality not merely in space but in time! To use his theory to determine the probabilities of what happens next, one must plug in not only the world's current complete physical state (as is customary in a physical theory) but also certain facts about the past."

By showing the illusory status of the 4D world view and re-establishing the existence of an objective time-flow, we greatly simplify the problem. In fact, as the issue of the compatibility of quantum non-locality with special relativity is resolved, quantum models developed in the context of a world view based on the consideration of a fundamental time can become fully compatible with special relativity (Nicolaidis, 2007, Nicolaidis, 2009-1). In particular, any quantum mechanics theory, which is compatible at the macroscopic level with the *Relativistic Constraint of Accelerations* (i.e. this condition is verified at the level of the mean values of the physical observables), becomes fully compatible with special relativity. Indeed, as this condition engenders Lorentz transformations, such a theory absorbs special relativity in the sense that it contains it and provides a single theory for quantum mechanics and special relativity. In this sense, existing quantum theories, like for instance quantum electrodynamics, which give mean values of observables compatible with Lorentz transformations, absorb special relativity.

Concerning general relativity, conceptually, applying the same approach will consist on saying that the relationships attributed by general relativity to a veritable curvature of space-time, are in fact due to the impact of the gravitational interaction on the shapes of objects, on the shapes of object trajectories, on the paces of evolution of processes and on clock synchronization. By modifying these relationships, gravitation changes the results of spatial and temporal measurements performed by the internal observers of the universe. These changes give rise to measurement

relationships, which were formalized by general relativity into a geometric form and attributed to a veritable structure of space-time. Thus, conceptually, the approach adopted for special relativity could also be used to incorporate general relativity in the vision of the computational universe. It will consist on providing a formulation of a macroscopic 3D-world gravitation interaction law that engenders the above relations. This is an extremely complex task and substantial work has to be done for transforming this conceptual vision into a formal theory. However, achieving this goal may be the good strategy for simplifying the development of a quantum theory of gravitation, as it will require developing a 3D-world quantum theory, producing at the macroscopic level (i.e. on the mean values of the observables) the effects of the 3D gravitation law obtained in the previous step. The existence of a non-geometric interpretation of general relativity may seem dubious. However, if the Graal of physics is the unification of all interactions, meaning that all interactions are fundamentally of the same nature, how can we consider at the same time that gravity is of very different nature, as it has the singularity to modify the veritable structure of space-time? Isn't it more rational to consider that, as it is the only interaction that affects similarly all particles (due to the equivalence of inertial and gravitational mass/energy), it is the only one that could allow a geometrical formulation of its effects (as such a formulation has similar effects on all particles)?

QUANTUM MECHANICS AND STOCHASTIC COMPUTATIONS

This section treats the question of a computational model able to reproduce the non deterministic behaviour of quantum systems. Let us start with a short remind of the basic concepts of quantum mechanics. For a particle being in a given environment (e.g. determined by a function of potential), its wave function ψ is determined as the solution of an equation like Schrödinger's, or one of its relativistic analogues (such as Klein-Gordon, Dirac ...). This function determines the statistical distributions of the observables of the particle, such as its position, its momentum, its energy, etc. More precisely these distributions are determined by using the algebra of operators according to the following rules:

- At each observable A is associated a Hermitian operator $\hat{A}$ (whose form has a certain relation with the expression of the observable in non-quantum physics, i.e. Newtonian or relativistic).
- The possible values α_1, α_2, ..., of an observable A are the eigenvalues of the operator $\hat{A}$ of this observable.
- The probabilities associated to these values are $P_1 = |c_1|^2$, $P_2 = |c_2|^2$, ..., with $c_i = \langle \psi_i | \psi \rangle$ $\forall$ $i \in \{1, 2, ...\}$, (the inner product of eigenvector ψ_i and the wave function ψ).

The above rules concern observables, like energy, having discrete spectrum. Similar rules are valid for the case of observables having continuous spectrum, such as the position or momentum. In this case the statistical distribution is described by a probability density P(a). For instance, the probability density of position is equal to $|\psi|^2$. In the following, in order to simplify the discussion, we will use the conventions related to observables having discrete spectrum, but the arguments used are also applicable to the case of observables having continuous spectrum.

When we measure an observable A, the obtained value is not the result of a deterministic process but can take any value among the eigenvalues α_1, α_2, ... of operator $\hat{A}$. The probability to obtain a value α_i among these eigenvalues is equal to P_i. This measurement acts on the state of the particle by modifying its wave function ψ. Thus, after the measurement, the wave function becomes equal to ψ_j, where ψ_j is the eigenvector of

$\hat{A}$ corresponding to the eigenvalue α_j obtained as result of the measurement. Thus, a new measurement of observable A will give again α_j as result. Before the measurement the system is said to be in coherence. We observe that, after measurement of A, the wave function ψ collapses into one of the eigen-vectors of $\hat{A}$. Thus, the measurement destroys the state of coherence. It is important to mention here that *the concepts and mathematical formalism described above are the strictly necessary ones required for describing the observable behaviour of a quantum system*. But the state of coherence is strange, since we cannot allocate to the observable a unique value as in the macroscopic world. To give it a sense, *this state was interpreted by saying that the observable is in a superposition of a plurality of values*. (Figure 7) illustrates the quantum superposition idea by showing the observable A to be simultaneously on several values α_1, α_2, ..., α_n, ... to which correspond certain probabilities p_1, p_2, ..., p_n, ...

But the state of superposition raises various philosophical questions which could be resolved if we eliminate it. However, it is not possible to eliminate this concept within the vision considering that the universe is composed of objects immersed in a veritable space. Indeed, when a statistical distribution is associated to the position of a particle instead of a particular value, we can either consider that the particle is nowhere in space or that the particle is in superposition on all possible positions determined by this statistical distribution. But in a space-centric vision an object can exist only within space. Thus, we can either admit the superposition hypothesis or abandon the space-centric vision. The computational vision proposed in this paper offer such an alternative. Nevertheless, there is a strong technological argument which seems to give factual support to the superposition state: the power of quantum computing is due to the fact that quantum algorithms perform a parallel computation over a plurality of values (the superposition values). So, we also

Figure 7. State superposition and action of measurement

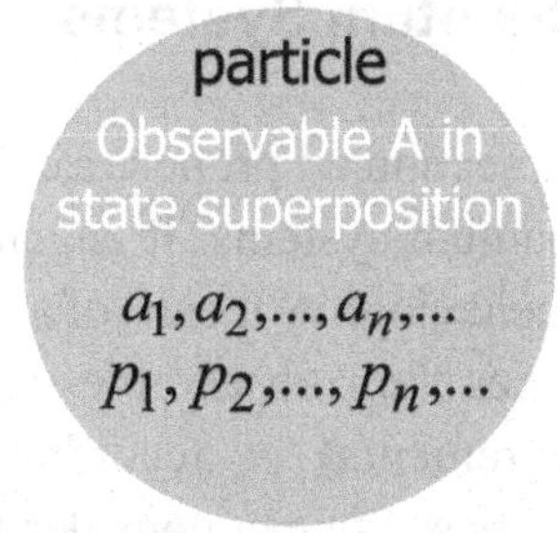

Measurement of observable A $\rightarrow$ result = $\alpha_i \in \{\alpha_1, \alpha_2, ...\}$, $\psi = \psi_i$

have to ask the question: is quantum computing a truly parallel computing? As these questions are related we will treat them conjointly.

State of Superposition and Quantum Computers

Let us first remind in few words how quantum computing is supposed to process information by exploiting quantum superposition. A q-bit corresponds to an observable A of a quantum system, which can be in two possible states represented by 0 and 1. According to the superposition concept, a q-bit can be at the same time on state 0 and on state 1. Thus, n q-bits can be simultaneously on 2^n states. A quantum algorithm comprises a certain number of steps which transform the state of n q-bits. Then, according to the superposition concept, the power of quantum computing is due to the fact that a quantum algorithm could manipulate at the same time the 2^n superposition values of n q-bits, while a traditional algorithm manipulates only one of these values. Thus, it seems that we are obliged to accept the superposition as a factual state and the idea that quantum computers perform a truly parallel computation as valid. In the following we argue that this is not the case.

Firstly a truly parallel computer (i.e. a computer able to perform parallel computations over N values), can treat a problem by means of a black-box approach. That is, without considering the particular structure of the data of the problem.

For instance, to find a particular value within a list of N values, it can compare in parallel the particular value with all the values in the list, and find the solution within one parallel computation step. On the other hand, if we do not exploit the structure of the data in the list (e.g. the fact that the list could be ordered), traditional non-parallel computing needs on the average N/2 computation steps for the same search. Thus; a truly parallel computer achieves exponential acceleration. Thanks to these capabilities a truly parallel computer solves NP-complete problems in polynomial time. As concerning quantum computing, there is no quantum algorithm achieving exponential acceleration for black-box problems (there is not even known algorithm solving NP-complete problems in polynomial time (Aaronson, 2008)). Shor's factoring algorithm (Shor, 1994) and Grover's search algorithm (Grover, 1996) are good illustrations of the fact that known quantum algorithms do not deliver the computing power of truly parallel computers. Shor's algorithm speeds exponentially the resolution of the factoring problem. But there is no evidence that factoring is a NP-complet problem. In fact, factoring has special properties that don't seem to be shared by NP-complete problems[8]. In particular the quantum part of Shor's algorithm uses the Quantum Fourier Transform, to transform a quantum state encoding a periodic sequence to a quantum state encoding the period of that sequence. It works because it exploits specific properties of periodic sequences. Thus, it is not a black-box approach, since it relies on such special properties. Grover's algorithm treats a black-box problem. It provides a significant acceleration ($\sqrt{N}$ instead of $N/2$), but this is still far from the exponential acceleration achieved by a truly parallel algorithm. In fact, the $\sqrt{N}$ complexity of Grover's algorithm matches the best performance that can achieve quantum computers for solving black-box problems (Bennett, 1997). So, quantum computing is far from reaching the computing power of truly parallel computers. Thus, it can not caution the existence of a veritable superposition. Further reasons for contesting the existence of a veritable state of superposition are:

- The superposition is a meta-physical state since there are no means for observing directly this state: any attempt to do so leads to decoherence and provides as result a single value.
- As already noticed, the concepts and mathematical formalism described in the beginning of this section are the strictly necessary ones required for describing the observable behaviour of a quantum system. Thus the state of superposition is not among the strictly necessary concepts for describing this behavior
- Since the state of superposition is meta-physical and does not belong to the strictly necessary concepts that describe the behavior of quantum systems, it is a non-mandatory interpretation of the state of coherence.
- Observables of continuum spectrum, like position and momentum (but also some observables of discrete spectrum like energy), have infinite number of eigenvalues. They imply the superposition of infinite number of values and, correspondingly, infinity memory capacity and computing power!

A Computational Model of Quantum Systems

In this section we propose a computational model of quantum systems. It engenders their observable behaviour by means of a computation which produces their observable states (the results of measurements) in accordance with quantum mechanics. We can consider that this computation is taking place in a meta-object, as nothing concerning this object is observable except the states it returns when a measurement is performed. Thus, this computing meta-object (CMO) is not part of our observable universe and corresponds to the meta-objects of the ULKIO (ultimate limit of knowledge) principle. But, what kind of computation this object should perform? Let us first notice that probabilistic computations (Kaye, 2007), where the transition from state i to state j is performed with a given probability, engender a stochastic process like quantum systems. However, they miss the way a quantum system determines during coherence the statistical distributions of its observables. So we need a different computational model.

The proposed model is illustrated in (Figure 8a). In this model the CMOs produce the observable behaviour of quantum systems by means of computations which use deterministic functions to transforms stochastic meta-signals into signals that provide the values of the observables during their measurements. Note that these meta-signals can not be considered as hidden variables because they are stochastic. Also, the values they bring can not be determined by observing them neither be predicted (any cause-effect relation between the values they could take in the future and the present or past states of the quantum object and its environment is excluded since they are stochastic, but also because their states and their production laws are unknown). As shown in (Figure 8a), a CMO comprises two computing blocks:

Figure 8. Proposed computational model (a) versus superposition model (b)

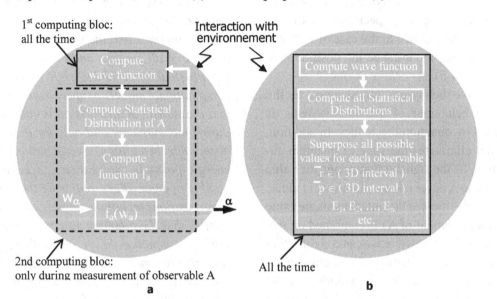

- The first computing bloc computes the wave function by resolving a differential equation (e.g. Schrödinger's equation) for a function of potential corresponding to the CMO's environment (ultimately determined by the states of the other CMOs with which it interacts). *The wave function represents at any time the state of the CMO.*

- The second bloc performs computation only during "measurements": each time an observable A is measured this block computes a deterministic function f_a and uses this function to transform a stochastic meta-signal w_a into a stochastic signal $\alpha = f_a(w_a)$. The later provides the result of the measurement of observable A. As the function f_a transforms a unique value (the current value of w_a) to produce the current value of α, signal α will return a unique value during measurement.

In addition, during the measurement of A, the first computing bloc computes a new wave function which is equal to the eigen-function associated to the eigen-value $\alpha = f_a(w_a)$ obtained on signal α during the measurement. This influence of the value of signal α on the computation of the wave function is represented in (Figure 8a) by an arrow which brings the value of signal α to the input of the first computing bloc.

The function f_a is computed in a manner that the statistical distribution (values α_1, α_2, ... and the corresponding probabilities p_1, p_2, ...) of signal α produced by the transformation $\alpha = f_a(w_a)$ is identical to the statistical distribution of the corresponding observable A determined by the rules of quantum mechanics. This computation will be possible if, for any statistical distribution $p(\alpha)$ of an observable A, it exists a deterministic function f_a which transforms the stochastic signal w_a to a stochastic signal α that has the statistical distribution $p(\alpha)$. We have shown (Nicolaidis, 2008, Nicolaidis, M. 2009-2) that for a signal w_a having an arbitrary but given statistical distribution of continuous spectrum $s(w_a)$ and for any statistical distribution $p(\alpha)$, it always exists a function f_a which produces a signal $\alpha = f_a(w_a)$ whose statistical distribution is equal to $p(\alpha)$. The same articles provide the computation steps required for determining function f_a. These results are valid for statistical distributions p(α) of discrete spectrum as well as of continuous spectrum. This result can be easily generalised to the case of vectorial observables (like for instance the position $\bar{r}$ or the momentum $\bar{p}$).

The above behaviour corresponds to the observable behaviour of quantum systems as determined by quantum mechanics. In addition, this model eliminates the state of quantum superposition, as the signal α that brings the value of observable A never takes a plurality of values: either no value (most of the time) or a single value (during measurement of A) is computed on this signal. From this discussion we can conclude that the concept of superposition can be eliminated, since it exists a stochastic computational model that provides the same observable behaviour of quantum systems as the one described by quantum mechanics.

(Figure 8b) shows the computations that would correspond to a model based on the superposition concept. In this model *the wave function has to be computed all the time,* as in the model of (Figure 8a). However, *this model should also compute all the time the statistical distribution and create a superposition state for each observable A.* This superposition comprises all the values that have no nil probability (or no nil probability density) in the statistical distribution of the observable A, together with the associated probabilities (or probability densities). This superposition has to be done for each physical observable (such as position, translational momentum, orbital angular momentum, spin, total angular momentum, energy) but also for any "observable" corresponding to an orthonormal basis. This is because in theory any of these observables could be measured and because in the superposition concept the result of any measurement is a value among the superposition values pre-existing to the measurement. Note that, the feasibility of the measurement of the observable corresponding to any discrete unitary operator was shown as early as 1994 (Reck, 1994)).

We observe that *the superposition model requires much heavier computations as the statistical distributions and the superpositions have to be realised all the time and for all physical and non physical observables, while in the proposed computational model no superposition is realised and the statistical distribution is computed only during measurement and only for the measured observable. In addition, several observables (like energy, position, momentum ...) have infinite number of eigenvalues, requiring the creation of superpositions on infinite number of values. This implies that the quantum system should employ infinite computing power and infinite memory resources for each of these observables!* Attributing infinite computing power to the process that engenders the behaviour of a physical system does not seem reasonable. Also, as this behaviour can be engendered by a much simpler process (e.g. the one described by the proposed computational model), considering the superposition concept will mean that nature employs a very inefficient process wasting infinite amount of resources. This seems also unreasonable. Furthermore, the existence of a veritable superposition is necessary for a quantum computer to be able to perform truly parallel computations. Hence, this is another reason for contesting the parallel computing interpretation of quantum computers.

From the mathematical point of view the interpretation of quantum mechanics based on the superposition concept is complete as it provides all the rules needed to determine the statistical distributions of observables. However, in nature, each measurement of an observable provides a particular value among the ones allowed by its statistical distribution. That is, during each particular measurement there is something that selects a particular value among the possible ones. The interpretation based on the superposition concept does not provide such a selecting mechanism. Thus, from the physical point of view the superposition interpretation is incomplete, while the proposed computational model is complete as it provides such a mechanism: the result of the measurement is the value $\alpha = f_a(w_a)$ corresponding to the current value of the stochastic meta-signal w_a.

To be fair, it is worth noting that such a mechanism is not required in the Everett-Deutsch many-worlds interpretation (Everett, 1957, DeWitt & Graham, 1973). Indeed, in this interpretation there is no need to select one of the superposition states during each measurement, since after the measurement the universe is split in as many universes as the number of states in superposition and each of these states is realized in one of these universes. However, this interpretation introduces a number of parallel universes that increases exponentially over time, and which additionally are not observable.

One objection to the proposed computational model could be the fact that it introduces meta-objects and meta-signals (w_a) that are not part of the universe. This is in contradiction with a view of the universe as a closed system, which should include everything that can affect the evolution of its state. But this contradiction is only apparent. Firstly, due to the ULKIO principle, any observer that is part of the system that he/she observes can only access information related to the behaviour of the entities composing this system but not related to the nature of the objects producing this behaviour. *Thus, the point of view of the internal observer of the universe (and of any other system) necessarily introduces the existence of meta-objects. Nevertheless, though for the internal observers these meta-objects do not belong to their "observable universe", they still belong to the universe in its broader sense (i.e. the system that includes not only the information that is accessible to its internal observers but also what produces this information).* Secondly, according to the system structure shown in (Figure 3), section 2, and the related discussion, the computing meta-objects can be divided into two parts (represented in (Figure 3) by gray and blue circles). In this representation, the signals w_a of

the computational model of (Figure 8a) bring to the blue parts of the computing objects the values of the states of the gray parts. *Thus, the gray parts and the signals w_a that they produce are parts of the computing objects and thus of the universe in its broader sense. This universe not only is closed but can even be deterministic[2].* Indeed, if the gray parts of the computing objects are pseudorandom generators of sufficient complexity and randomness, the computational model will produce a behaviour that is observably indistinguishable from the behaviour produced when the gray parts generate truly stochastic values. Thus, considering the limited observability of the observers that are part of the observed system is essential for proposing a consistent "computational" interpretation of quantum mechanics associated with a closed model of the universe. Also, it is generally considered that the non-local behaviour of entangled particles becomes necessary due to the non-determinism of quantum systems. Thus, *it is important to stress that in the system shown in (Figure 3), entanglement will imply non-locality even if the gray parts of the particles correspond to pseudorandom generators.* Indeed, in this case we can have two possible scenarios:

- The operation of the system shown in (Figure 3) is such that at the instant of entanglement the states of the pseudorandom generators of the entangled particles are not forced at correlated states. In this case, their values can not be used to correlate the states of the particles when a measurement is performed on one of them. Thus, entanglement will still requite spooky action.

- The system shown in (Figure 3) is such that at the instant of entanglement the states of the pseudorandom generators of the entangled particles are forced at correlated states. Thus, their states will remain correlated at any instant after the entanglement (e.g. they produce identical states). One could think that this can be used to avoid spooky action. But for this correlation to be exploited, particles should use the states of the two pseudorandom generators at exactly the same instant. Thus, when a measurement is performed on one particle, and this particle uses the state of its pseudorandom generator to determine the result of the measurement, the other particle should be informed instantaneously in order to use the content of its pseudorandom generator at exactly the same instant.

To summarize, the previous discussion pleads for abandoning the idea that during the state of quantum coherence exists a veritable superposition over a plurality of states. It suggests instead a computational interpretation of quantum mechanics, where the behaviour of quantum systems is engendered by deterministic computations performed over stochastic (or pseudo-stochastic) signals. It also pleads that the concept of quantum superposition is not pertinent for explaining the power of quantum algorithms, as analysing carefully quantum computing does not reveal a truly parallel computation performed over a plurality of values. Accordingly, the power of quantum computing is not due to a hypothetical parallel process, which manipulates simultaneously a plurality of values, but to the ability of quantum systems to evolve their wave function in a very complex manner. Thus, a quantum algorithm would consist in a judicious technique allowing to constraint quantum processes to produce pertinent results by manipulating what is deterministic in these processes, that is, their wave function and the related statistical distributions.

Preparing a presentation on this topic, first for ECAP09 and the for this book, was motivated by several discussions I had with Joseph Brenner on the relations between my computational approach (in particularly the quantum mechanics computational model) and LIR, which led to a shared session at ECAP09. My conclusions on the relationships between my computational model and LIR are:

While the computational processes underlying this model are in conformity with the non contradiction principle, and thus the reasoning leading to and supporting this model is based on classical logic, the behaviour of real quantum systems that emerges from this model seems to be in conformity with LIR.

The similar seems valid for the superposition model. Indeed, as the superposition values are part of the internal state of the particle (since they are not observable), they can be viewed as values allocated to a plurality of state variables (like the registers of a computer) from which one value is selected during measurement. So, each of these variables has a unique value and at this level of description we can use classical logic. But when we look on the behaviour of the quantum system that emerges from this description, LIR seems more adapted. However, there is a problem related with the "asymptoticity" axiom of LIR. During coherence, the superposition values of each observable truly exist. Their existence is clearly testified by the interpretation of quantum computing based on the superposition concept. According to this interpretation, a quantum algorithm performs a computation over each of the superposition values. Thus, the superposition values are 100% realized in the internal state of the quantum system; though they are hidden (i.e. they can not be observed). We have a 100% actualization, which is not compatible with one of LIR's axioms (LIR6: Asymptoticity: No process of actualization or potentialization of any element goes to 100% completeness) (Brenner, 2008).

On the other hand, in the computational model, during coherence the state of the system is described by the wave function alone. Therefore, the potential values of each observable are not realized, as in the superposition model. Thus, these values are predominantly potentialized. At the same time, they are in a certain degree of actualization, as all these values are captured by the wave function (in the sense that they are completely determined by it). Thus, potentialization dominates this state, but it is not a pure potentialization, making the computational model compliant with LIR.

Quantum Entanglement

The model of (Figure 8a) can be extended to include a computation mechanism that incorporates quantum non-locality. As this computation takes place in a substrate external to our observable universe, the related computation mechanism is not based on means available in our observable universe (meta-means). Nevertheless, for the shake of illustration, let us consider the example of a mechanism using means available in our observable universe. It comprises: an identification value ID unique to each meta-object; an entanglement variable EV; and a mechanism of Hertzian emission/reception using in emission a modulation frequency equal to the value of the identification value of the meta-object and in reception a demodulation frequency equal to the value of the entanglement variable of the meta-object. This is illustrated in (Figure 9). In this figure, particles i and j are entangled. At the instant of entanglement, particle i assigns the identification value ID_j of particle j to its entanglement variable EV_i ($EV_i = ID_j$). Similarly, particle j assigns the identification value ID_i of particle i to its entanglement variable EV_j ($EV_j = ID_i$). Then, if observable A of particle i is measured, i emits information that a measurement happened and the result of the measurement. Particle j uses as demodulation frequency the value of its entanglement variable ($EV_j = ID_i$). Thus, it immediately receives this information and adapts its state. In a similar manner, particle i can immediately adapt its state to a measurement performed on particle j. Therefore, this computation reproduces the behaviour of entangled particles and combined with the computation illustrated in (Figure 8a),

it provides a model (illustrated in Figure 9) that produces a behaviour identical to the one described by quantum mechanics. In particular, this behaviour is non-deterministic (statistical distributions and measurement results identical to the ones described by quantum mechanics), non-local and without hidden variables.

One could however object that the proposed entanglement mechanism requires a certain time for transmitting "information" from the particle that undergoes a measurement to its entangled counterpart, while in quantum mechanics the states of the entangled particles change simultaneously. To circumvent this objection let us remind that in the proposed model the states of particles are determined by a computing meta-system. Each computation step of this system can include: the meta-time for computing the new state of the particle that undergoes the measurement; the meta-time required for transmitting "information" from this particle to its entangled counterpart; and the meta-time for computing the new state of the later. As the news states of the entangled particles are computed within the same computation step, then, for the observers that are part of the universe, their states change simultaneously. Remind also from section 3.2 that the meta-time duration of each computation step of the computing meta-system engendering the universe has no effect on the time observed in the universe (even if this duration varies from one computation step to another).

CONCLUSION

In this article we proposed a computational vision of the Universe. Our starting idea is that as observers that are part of the Universe we can not distinguish between a universe having existence per from a universe engendered by a computation. To support this idea we have shown that for any observer that is part of the observed system (or universe), there is an ultimate limit of knowledge

Figure 9. Computational model for entangled particles

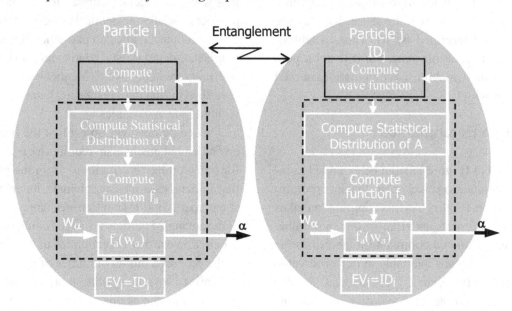

(referred as ULKIO). This limit allows observers that are part of the observed system to receive information concerning its behaviour but by no means information concerning its veritable structure (or nature). The consequence is that, as observers that are part of the Universe we have no means allowing us to distinguish whether our perceptions correspond to a universe composed of veritable particles immersed in a veritable space or of a universe engendered by a computation-like process that takes places in a meta-substrate (a substrate that is not part of our observable universe). The interest of the computational vision is that it allows us resolving several philosophical questions raised by modern theories of physics.

In the case of quantum mechanics this vision allows proposing a computational model for quantum systems that eliminates the paradoxes related with the non-deterministic and non-local behaviour of quantum systems and with the "strange" concept of superposition. This model represents the universe as a closed system, though for us it may not be closed due to the ULKIO principle. The price we paid for eliminating these paradoxes is to renounce the existence of a veri-

table space. Indeed, modelling quantum systems by a computation-like process, as illustrated in figures 8a and 9, is not possible in the context of a veritable space, since a computation could not produce as result a position in a veritable space. Renouncing the existence of a veritable space may appear absurd. But what could be the sense of a veritable space in which an object could be simultaneously on an infinity of positions, or in which very distant objects could influence each other instantaneously? Is there any reason for maintaining the idea of a veritable space, once the state of quantum superposition and the behaviour of entangled particles emptied it of any sense that we could attribute to a veritable space?

Furthermore, this vision allows proposing a computational model for special relativity re-establishing an objective time flow, while maintaining the validity of Lorentz transformations for the internal observers of the universe. Thus, this model resolves the philosophical question related with the non-existence of objective time flow in special relativity as well as the contradiction between the non-locality of quantum systems and the reversal of the temporal order of events in special relativity. It also simplifies the unification of modern physics.

The proposed vision could be categorized as a relations-based vision. Other approaches considering time and more generally the universe as by-product of relations (e.g. Tegmark, 2007, Rovelli, 2009) miss a substrate enabling the emergence of processes and the associated relations. The foundations of such a Substarte/background were established in sections 2 and 3. The resulting vision allows viewing our time (more precisely the internal time of the universe that is subject to our experience) not as a metaphysical category but as a category that emerges from physical processes. By distinguish this time from the cause of changes (external time or metatime), we were able to determine the qualitative principle that underlies the emergence of our time (the invariance of the laws of physics) as well as the quantitative principle that determines its structure (the form of these laws).

Thought the proposed vision and its use to treat quantum mechanics and special relativity allowed us resolving several philosophical questions raised by modern physics, this vision is still incomplete as its ultimate goal should be to propose a computational vision integrating and unifying all aspects of physics. The results obtained simplify the efforts for this unification, but there is a long way to go before reaching such an ambitious goal.

REFERENCES

Aaronson, S. (2008, March). The Limits of Quantum Computers. *Scientific American.*

Albert, D. Z. & Galchen, R. (2009, March). Was Einstein Wrong?: A Quantum Threat to Special Relativity. *Scientific American Magazine.*

Balashov, Y., & Janssen, M. (2002). *Presentism and Relativity.* Philosophy of Science Archives.

Bennett, C. H., Bernstein, E., Brassard, G., & Vazirani, U. (1997). Strengths and Weaknesses of Quantum Computing. *SIAM Journal on Computing, 26,* 1510–1523. doi:10.1137/S0097539796300933

Brenner, J. E. (2008). *Logic in Reality.* Dordrecht: Springer. doi:10.1007/978-1-4020-8375-4

DeWitt, B. S., & Graham, R. N. (Eds.). (1973). *The Many-Worlds Interpretation of Quantum Mechanics.* Princeton, NJ: Princeton University Press.

Everett, H. (1957). Relative State Formulation of Quantum Mechanics. *Reviews of Modern Physics, 29,* 454–462. doi:10.1103/RevModPhys.29.454

Grover, L. (1996). A Fast Quantum Mechanical Algorithm for Database Search. In *Proceedings of the 28th ACM Symposium on the Theory of Computing (STOC),* (pp. 212-219).

Kaye, P., Laflamme, R., & Mosca, M. (2007). *An Introduction to Quantum Computing.* New York: Oxford University Press.

Lusanna, L., & Pauri, M. (In press). Dynamical Emergence of Instantaneous 3-Spaces in a Class of Models of General Relativity . In van der Merwe, A. (Ed.), *Relativity and the Dimensionality of the World.* Dordrecht: Springer.

Nicolaidis, M. (2003). *Une Philosophique Numérique de l'Univers.* Technical Report, TIMA Lab, ISRN TIMA-RR-03/04-02-FR, Avril 2003.

Nicolaidis, M. (2007). *Emergence of Relativistic Space-Time in a Computational Universe.* Grenoble, France: TIMA Laboratory.

Nicolaidis, M. (2008, June 16-18). *On the State of Superposition and the Parallel or not Parallel nature of Quantum Computing: a controversy raising view point.* Paper presented at the 2008 European Computing and Philosophy Conference, (ECAP'08), Montpellier, France.

Nicolaidis, M. (2009-1). Simulating Time. In *Proceedings 2nd Computing and Philosophy Symposium, 2009 AISB Convention,* Edinburgh, UK. Hove, UK: SSAISB: The Society for the Study of Artificial Intelligence and the Simulation of Behaviour.

Nicolaidis, M. (2009-2). *On the State of Superposition and the Parallel or not Parallel nature of Quantum Computing.* Tech. Report TIMA Lab., ISRN TIMA-RR--09/09--01-FR.

Nikolaidis, M. (2005). *Une Philosophie Numérique des Univers.* Grenoble, France: TIMA Editions.

Reck, M., Zeilinger, A., Bernstein, H. J., & Bertani, P. (1994). Experimental Realization of Any Discrete Unitary Operator. *Physical Review Letters, 73*(1). doi:10.1103/PhysRevLett.73.58

Rovelli, C. (2009, March). *Forget time.* arXiv:0903.3832v3 [gr-qc] 27

Schmidhuber, J. (1997). *A Computer Scientist's View of Life, the Universe, and Everything, (LNCS 201-288).* Berlin: Springer.

Shor, P. (1994). Algorithms for Quantum Computation: Discrete Logarithms and Factoring. In *Proceedings of the 35th Annual Symposium on Foundations of Computer Science,* (pp. 124-134). *Space-Time Conference web site.* (2004). Retrieved from http://alcor.concordia.ca/~scol/seminars/conference/minkowski.html

Tegmark, M. (2007). *Shut up and calculate.* arXiv:0709.4024v1 [physics.pop-ph]

Tumulka, R. A. (2006 November). Relativistic Version of the Ghirardi–Rimini–Weber Model. *Journal of Statistical Physics, 125*(4), 821-840(20).

Zuse, K. (1969). *Rechnender Raum.* Braunschweig, Germany: Friedrich Vieweg & Sohn.

Zuse, K. (1970). *Calculating Space, MIT Technical Translation AZT-70-164-GEMIT.* Cambridge, MA: Massachusetts Institute of Technology.

KEY TERMS AND DEFINITIONS

Computational Universe: A vision in which all objects, structures and processes of the universe, as well as the space-time in which they are immersed/evolve, emerge from a computation-like process.

Internal Observers (also referred as observers that are part of a system/universe): These are observers that are part of the system/universe and are therefore composed of the same elementary entities (particles) that compose any structure of the system/universe.

ULKIO (ultimate limit of knowledge for internal observers): Internal observers receive information coming through the interactions of the particles composing their sensorial systems with the particles composing the objects they observe. As the information coming through interactions is related with the behaviour of the elementary entities/particles, these observers have access to information concerning this behaviour but by no means to information concerning the intimate nature of the objects producing this behaviour.

Meta-Objects: As the internal observers of a system/universe have no access to information concerning the intimate nature of the objects producing the behaviour of the elementary entities/particles (see ULKIO key term), these objects are meta-objects for these observers.

Internal Time: The time perceived by the internal observers of a system/universe and measured by comparing processes with a reference process. This time is qualitatively and quantitatively determined by the laws governing the evolution of the elementary entities/particles (interaction laws).

Meta-Time (also referred as external time and engine of change): Because we consider dynamic systems/universes having evolving states we are obliged to introduce a category that causes this change.

Computational Model of Quantum Systems: A model reproducing the behaviour of quantum systems by means of deterministic computations performed over stochastic signals.

Computing Meta-Object (CMO): The meta-object related to the ULKIO limitation (see keyterm meta-object), which performs the computations producing the behaviour of a quantum system.

Stochastic Meta-Signals: Stochastic signals transformed by the computing meta-objects (see their definition in the keyterms) in order to produce the measured values of the physical observables.

Non-Locality: The property of particles to correlate instantaneously their state with the result of a measurement performed over their entangled counterparts, whatever is the distance separating them.

Quantum Superposition: A state in which an observable of a quantum system is supposed to be at a plurality of values.

Inconsistency between Quantum Non-Locality and Special Relativity: When two observers measure two entangled particles, the first measurement determines the state of both particles. But in special relativity it is possible that for each observer it is his/her measurement that occurred first. So, for each observer it is his/her measurement that determined the state of the two particles, resulting in two contradictory perceptions coming from situations that are both valid in special relativity.

Fundamental Principle of Special Relativity: The laws of physics are invariant with respect to Lorentz transformations (for the transition from one inertial system to any other arbitrarily chosen inertial system).

Modified Fundamental Principle of Special Relativity: The laws of our universe are such that they appear (create the illusion) to its internal observers to be invariant with respect to Lorentz transformations (for the transition from one inertial system to any other arbitrarily chosen inertial system).

ENDNOTES

[1] This principle does not apply on objects composed of several elementary particles. The structure of such an object (i.e. the elementary particles composing an object and the way these particles are structured to form it) can be determined thanks to information collected by our sensorial systems and by systems we built to observe nature.

[2] Ideally, from the information point of view, we should consider as closed a system in which its future state is determined only from information residing in it (its present and past states). If a system is governed by truly stochastic laws, we can only determine from its past and present states the statistical distribution of its future state. However, when a particular value among the values allowed by this distribution is actualized, at this instant, there is something that selects this particular value among the allowed ones. This something is not information that resides in the system itself (it is external to the system otherwise the actualized values could be predicted deterministically). As a matter of fact, ideally, a closed system should be deterministic and a stochastic system should not be considered as closed. Nevertheless, a pseudo-stochastic system, whose behaviour could not be practically distinguished from the stochastic one, can be an ideally closed system.

Chapter 17
Seeing for Knowing:
The Thomas Effect and Computational Science

Jordi Vallverdú
Universitat Autònoma de Barcelona, Spain

ABSTRACT

From recent debates about the paper of scientific instruments and human vision, we can conclude that we don't see through our instruments, but we see with them. All our observations, perceptions and scientific data are biologically, socially, and cognitively mediated. So, there is not 'pure vision', nor 'pure objective data'. At a certain level, we can say that we have an extended epistemology, which embraces human and instrumental entities. We can make better science because we can deal better with scientific data. But at the same time, the point is not that be 'see' better, but that we only can see because we design those cognitive interfaces. Computational simulations are the middleware of our mindware, acting ad mediators between our instruments, brains, the worlds and our minds. We are contemporary Thomas, who believe what we can see.

INTRODUCTION

"Except I shall see in his hands the print of the nails, and put my finger into the print of the nails, and my hand into his side, I will not believe", The New Testament, St John, 20: 24.

DOI: 10.4018/978-1-61692-014-2.ch017

I propose you a simple activity: try to think whatever you want and imagine that situation, calculation or feeling for several seconds, I'll wait. Surely, you've used several images to think and imagine it, and I remember you that a letter is an image. And I propose you a second mental exercise: are you able to think any *concept* without images? Even the word's letters you use are strongly associated to visual aspects (typography, size, design…). We think with images, and all our language is full of visual words to mean 'known': 'clear demonstration', 'illuminating proof', 'I see' (meaning "I understand you'), etc.

Only blind born people develop their relationship with the world from touch sense. In March 2ⁿᵈ 1692, the Irish William Molyneux wrote a letter to John Locke in which he finished his comments with this text:

"I will conclude my tedious lines with a jocose problem, that, upon discourse with several, concerning your book and notions, I have proposed to divers very ingenious men, and could hardly ever meet with one, that, at first dash, would give me the answer to it which I think true, till by hearing my reasons they were convinced. It is this: "Suppose a man born blind, and now adult, and taught by his touch to distinguish between a cube and a sphere (suppose) of ivory, nighly of the same bigness, so as to tell when he felt one and t'other, which is the cube, which the sphere. Suppose then the cube and sphere placed on a table, and the blind man to be made to see; query, 'Whether by his sight, before he touched them, he could now distinguish and tell, which is the globe, which the cube?' I answer, not: for though he has obtained the experience of how a globe, and how a cube affects his touch; yet he has not yet attained the experience, that what affects his touch so or so, must affect his sight so or so; or that a protuberant angle in the cube, that pressed his hand unequally, shall appear to his eye as it does in the cube."[1]

Their following letters were centered on this topic, later denominated *Molyneux's problem*. Although they were discussing the limits and nature of empiricist's philosophy, the problem of relationships between vision-knowledge

reached an own status. Later, Étienne Bonnot, Abbé de Condillac, with his *Treatise on Sensations* of 1754, tried to answer to the Molyneux's question, by asking his readers to consider an originally inanimate and insentient human being (a "statue" of a human being) and to consider what this being could come to know were it to acquire each of the senses in isolation from the others, or each in combination with just one or two others. In proposing this question Condillac was asking a more radical version of the question Molyneux had posed to Locke: would a person born blind to perceive spatial features well enough upon first sight to be able to identify cubes and spheres without touching them? But this is not a paper on the history of empiricist philosophers and their arguments and counterarguments about epistemology's senses. But, yes, we discuss about epistemology and about how our senses, basically the sight, define the instruments we use to reach knowledge.

What do we know about vision? Approximately 60% of the human brain's sensory input comes from vision (Humphreys, 2004). Therefore, there is a strong relationship between vision and cognition (Latour, 1986). Images and animations are valuable tools in both producing and learning scientific topics, because they help users with important conceptual relationships (Brodie, 1992). To think is to establish visual relationships in our minds. Even for non classical reasoning ways, like those of mathematician S. Ramanujan, A. Kekulé (and his dream about benzene atomics structure) or J. von Neumann, they told us that they 'see' the result. But at the same ime, we see things that we don't percept directly, like invisible motion (Moutoussis & Zeki, 2006). Vision is a very, very complex process. Just an example: wehen Stanford scientists tried to create a robot with artificial vision, Shakey, it revealed the difficulty of the whole project. In fact, shakey was something else: it was the first robot to combine problem solving, movement and perception.

WHEN WE CANNOT LOOK, NOR SEE

From recent debates about the paper of scientific instruments and human vision (Hacking, 1981), we can conclude that we don't see *through* our instruments, but we see *with* them. From classic conception of vision (Marr, 1982; Mar & Hildreth, 1980), it is a representational activity constrained by natural structures (neurological basis), hierarchically organized, where it is produced a modularity of visual processing in the brain. As Polger (2004): 1000 tells about Marr's Computational theory of vision, "visual perception begins by taking as input the stimulation of retinal photoreceptors and deriving a representation of the three-dimensional scene before the perceiver. This process has three stages. First, the retinal response is processed to produce a primal sketch that makes explicit the two-dimensional information in the scene. Derivation of the primal sketch begins by locating the luminance boundaries ("edges") in the image projected onto the retina, forming the raw primal sketch. Then the luminance boundaries are grouped into objects and shapes, yielding the full primal sketch. Next, the full primal sketch is enriched to include information about the depth and orientation of contours in a viewer-centered framework. And, finally, a three-dimensional model is constructed to represent the objects and their spatial organization in an object-centered framework". Therefore, psychological states supervene on neural states (Morton, 1993). But current theorizing within visual neuroscience vindicates psychological descriptions of the visual system (van Eck *et al*, 2006: 175). There is no place for confrontation between 'mind' and 'brain' when we study vision processes. At the same time, a new conception of vision is emerging, which affirms that besides perceptual functions, the visual system has deep roots into to the visual guidance of motor behavior. Vision evolved to enable organisms to move about and navigate their surroundings. It therefore seems a plausible assumption that vision initially served action purposes and preceded representational vision (Haffenden and Goodale, 1998; Goodale & Humprey 1998). Therefore, the common actual idea is that vision subserves both perceptual and visuomotor goals (van Eck *et al*, 2006:179).

All our observations, perceptions and scientific data are biologically, socially, and cognitively mediated (Pinker, 1997, specially chapter 4, "The Mind's Eye"). So, there is not 'pure vision', nor 'pure objective data'. Paul Feyerabend, in his book *Against Method,* explain the typical case of the person who makes her/his 'first look' through a microscope. Usually, all is blurry, without clear sense, which appears after consulting detailed textbook drawings. With the mental map of what we should see, we can then look things with the microscope. We learn to perceive, as said the Medicine Nobel Prize, Sir Peter B. Medawar[2], from his practical experiences.

In the middle of XXth Century a new scientific phenomenon appeared, that is, *Big Science.* The Manhattan project for the creation of an atomic bomb, the Apollo mission to the Moon, NASA's Voyager project for planetary exploration on a grand scale, particle accelerators or the Human Genome Project are different and consecutive historical examples of that process (Capshew & Rader, 1992). Their scientific, budgetary, and technological immensity make these research projects as archetypical big science.

The same century experienced another important occurrence: the development of electronic computer machines. Following on from the seminal ideas of Alan Turing and John von Neumann, several huge computer machines were created and employed initially for military uses, but the transistor and microprocessor revolution enabled the creation of microcomputers, facilitating the implementation of computers in all kind of situations. Finally, the communication revolution of satellite technologies and the development of the Internet connected all these machines together and enabled a new way of life and thinking.

Thus, science has turned into e-Science (Hey & Trefethen, 2005), that is, computationally intensive science. This new kind of science is also the type of science that is carried out in highly distributed network environments, or science that uses immense data sets that require grid computing.

Then if we consider the high intensive use of computers in contemporary science and e-science, and their design as visual workstations, we must consider the great paper of vision (real or simulated) in our processes of knowledge acquisition (Giere, 2003). Most computational interfaces are visually-oriented.

But the nature that we study with our computational devices is different from the nature described by Hacking or Medawar, and microscopes or telescopes have another cognitive relationship with us: (a) first of all, because with them we could look to the world, (b) second, because they were extended and passive tools of our cognition, (c) third, we could *understand* and *calibrate* their functioning. Our actual paradigm of scientific research finds another situation: (a) the vast amount of data (the quantitative world) cannot be looked by scientists, (b) although they are an extended part of our minds, they develop also active roles in the knowledge acquisition, as we can see in expert systems and AI, (c) finally, the difficulty of calculus and complexity if data impedes us not only to understand the computing process (creating 'black boxes'), nor discover the errors happened through the process. Humphreys (2004):147, define it as "epistemic opacity". That opacity has two sources: first, when a computational process is too fast to follow for humans; second, when occurs a computationally irreducible process (Wolfram 2002, 737-750).

But we were talking about vision, not about computer epistemology, although both topics are strongly related themselves.

VISUAL THINKING AND VISUAL COGNITION

There is a chapter of the superb BBC comedy *Blackadder,* "Potato" Chapter – Blackadder II, that begins with this dialogue between the noble Blackadder (BA) and his servant Baldrick (B)[3]:

BA: Right Baldrick, let's try again shall we? This is called adding. If I have two
beans, and then I add two more beans, what do I have?
B: Some beans.
BA: Yes...and no. Let's try again shall we? I have two beans, then I add two more
beans. What does that make?
B: A very small casserole.
BA: Baldrick, the ape creatures of the Indus have mastered this. Now try again.
One, two, three, four. So how many are there?
B: Three
BA: What?
B: And that one.
BA: Three and that one. So if I add that one to the three what will I have?
B: Oh! Some beans.
BA: Yes. To you Baldrick, the renaissance was just something that happened to
other people wasn't it?

The certain thing is that the human being has not an immediate perception of numbers superior to 4 (Ifrah 1999, Chapter 1). That is to say, that he has a direct clear knowledge from the 1 to the 4. We even can remember that diverse native groups, not civilized westernly, of the Australian Continent, Asia, America and Africa only have in their respective languages terms like "one", "two" and "many" ('some' for Baldrick). Therefore, if we were mesopotamic shepherds with a flock gazing at our sheeps at the shore of the Euphrates, four thousand years ago, we would know to say how many sheep exactly are there in each side of the grass?

Figure 1. To glancing at the image: how many sheep do can you see?

It is clear that the shepherd could see quickly that in the left there were two sheep, but in the right … is more complicated. We must count, to develop some strategy to process the information that we just 'see', since the mere glance does not offer to us more than information than… "many" or "some". To see implies a complex process of analysis of the data with which we try to do something, and our cognitive weaknesses are many. Continuing with the numbers, generally people difficulty remember greater numbers than those of nine units (that is, for example, 798428197) (Miller, 1956). Our minds and our senses have physical characteristics that determine our relation with the data of the world. But on the other hand, although everybody knows that in the horizon the parallel bars of a train route never touch themselves, nevertheless, they seem to indicate it to our senses. Becoming aware of that fact, many artists have delighted us with their visual deceits (all simulation of 3 dimensions in a sheet of paper that only has 2 is a deceit of this type), from the false ceilings in the Renaissance (made by great artists like Rafael, Vignola or Mascherino) to the visual paradoxes of M.C. Escher, already in the middle of 20th century (Kemp 1990, 2001). On a paper titled "Theoreticians, Artists and Artisans" (1996), and in his book *Farewell to Reason* ("Progress

in Philosophy, the Sciences, and the Arts"), Paul Feyerabend talks about the relationships between Art and Science, demonstrating the deep *visual* relationships between both worlds. In fact, if you think about the similarities between Science and Art, you can find some like: (a) both value the careful observation and the new ways to collect the data by the senses, to process them into original new results (theories or artworks), (b) both value the creativity, (c) both propose the introduction of the change, the innovation, or the improvement on own disciplines, (d) both use abstract models to understand the world, (e) both aspire to create ideas of universal relevance. From ancient times scientists typically use a variety of representations, including different kinds of figures, to present and defend hypotheses. In order to understand the justification of scientific hypotheses, it is essential to understand how visual representations contribute to scientific arguments. Since the logical understanding of arguments involves the truth or falsity of the representations involved, visual representations must have the capacity to bear truth in order to be genuine components of arguments (Perini, 2005). As a consequence, we can conclude that *seeing*, *thinking* and *knowing* have common roots (Carsetti, 2004), and that the metaphor of *vision* as representing theoretical knowledge is a good one, like made Thomas Kuhn when he assimilated theoretical change to a gestalt reorganization of vision (Scheffler, 1972): "what were ducks in the scientists' world before the revolution are rabbits afterwards. The man who first saw the exterior of the box from above later sees its interior from below" (Kuhn, 1962: 110). At a certain level, we can see what we can understand; therefore, we need to see to be able to know, and knowledge is a special kind of vision.

The world perceived at the visual level is constituted not by objects or static forms, but by processes appearing imbued with meaning (Carsetti, 2004). Perceive something is equal to reconstruct it with our cognitive tools, by those biologically (by natural evolution) embedded in our bodies or by those extended technologically as a result of our capacity to create powerful tools to modify, analyze and look to the world. With these visual means of displaying information, researchers have the capability to comprehend visual patterns and dynamical relationships of great complexity, providing them with profoundly useful tools for understanding scientific data.

Saving the contextual, temporary and cultural distances, nowadays we were in the same situation that the mesopotamic shepherd. We have happened to have few sheeps (the scientific data) to great, enormous and huge flow of data petabytes of difficult handling. To put an example, a simulation of the behavior of the flow of gas near a black hole generates, over 10.000 time steps, a solution of 1.25 billion numerical values (Humphreys 2004, 113). We must return to remember that the work of mapping of the human genome works with 3000 million pairs of bases. It is therefore necessary to develop to interfaces and visual systems that allow to an interaction between human beings and data, considering this aspect like a key element of the epistemological process of knowledge creation. In a nutshell, visualization allows people to comprehend visual representations of data much more easily and rapidly than they can process huge amounts of raw data (text,

numbers). Better visualizations allow a greater depth in the understanding of the nature that we tried to know. It is not strange that has appeared specialized journals like *Computing and Visualization in Science*, dedicated to the detailed study of the relations between the new computational tools and the possibility of seeing in a more 'human' way.

It is almost contradictory: the more computerized is a complex model with many data, the more human is the information that provides, because it adapts to our cognitive abilities, specially the eyesight. Simulations and visualization systems (*SciVis*), are at the core of actual scientific knowledge production, made with a big range of computational tools.

Designing Visualization:
Cognitive Fitness

At the same time that we analyze the strong relationships between seeing and knowing, we must be aware about a key factor: information can be presented under different visual 'dresses'. We receive information on different ways, and each of them, due to their *cognitive fitness*, has an impact on our final epistemological process. Simulation provides us greater levels of understanding or, to be honest, the only way to process a huge amount of information. For example: the new CERN particles accelerator, the LHC, will generate two petabytes of data every second. Not all of this is needed - but 10 petabytes will be retained every year during the 10-year project, which would require the power of 100,000 of today's fastest PCs to process. So, we need visualization and processing computational technologies that enables us to think about reality and produce new knowledge: computer-aided vision and thinking. Both activities (seeing and thinking) are deeply entwined.

When I say "cognitive fitness", I'm not talking about psychological techniques to profiling *cognitive* preferences and flexibilities of thinking styles, reduce anxiety or improvement of elderly mental activities. I refer to the creation of tools which are *well-adapted* to human cognitive skills. For example, MS-Dos interfaces were less adapted to human cognition than are now Windows ones. Information is more easy to use and to manipulate with modern computer interfaces that with old ones. At the same time, the increasing computer power enables us to design 3D or three-dimensional modeling in chemistry, industry, genomics, etc.

Those systems make possible that we reduce the epistemic opacity and, at certain level, to think about reality. That cognitive fitness includes, at the same time, the possibility to deal intuitively with huge amounts of data, and to improve the efficiency of our cognitive processes oriented towards scientific knowledge production.

Projects like HIPerWall[4] or Visual Complexity[5] are an answer to the new necessities of contemporary forms to interact with information. We must remember that nearly all our workstations are embedded on visual interfaces. HIPerWall, as example, provide new vistas in scientific visualization, and build a large, collaborative visualization platform capable of displaying static images, image sequences in the form of movies and animations, and three-dimensional, time-varying data in real time.

'Usability' is just a term do designate good designs but it cannot deal with the basic idea of visualization and cognition. Cognitive fitness has a more deep meaning: it appeals to the whole process of cognitive activity necessary to create new knowledge. But let me first propose a metaphor to delimitate the field.

The Thomas' Effect

Most of you know the history of the Christianity founder's resurrection. Three days after his death, he appeared to his disciples and celebrated with them the new human era[6]. But one of the elf remaining disciples (because the 'twelfth', the traitor, had committed suicide), was not there.

He was Thomas, called Didymus. Thomas could not believe until he saw his master, as happened one day later.

The point is: do we can believe things that we don't see? And the most important, do we can think things that we cannot see? First question has a definitive answer: yes. Quantic physics is the realm of non-observable entities, although we can infer their existence by other means. The second question is not so easy. We come back to the Molyneux debate. Blind by birth, some humans has never seen shapes, forms and colours. From their touching experiences (some of them from Braille reading process), they conceive shapes and spatial relationships.

Do blind people see in their dreams? Do they see in colour? We can answer that congenitally blind dreamers and those who became blind in infancy do not have visual imagery in their dreams, just sounds (Kerr & Domhoff, 2004). It's a world without light, but although they cannot dream visual imagery, dreaming or being awake, it is true that they can think.

Yes, blind people can think without seeing, but do we can too? We can think what we can see. There is no knowledge beyond those visual simulations, models or signs. The more visualized is one fact, the more (easily) can be it known.

And the great amount of data that contemporary scientific projects must process requires the use of high-intensive computing tools. Simulations, virtual reality, augmented reality and visual interfaces are the day-to-day situation in knowledge development.

As in the microscope, we don't see through them, but with them. They are cognitive extensions of us, according to the extended mind model (Clark, 2003). This advocates a special sort of externalism, an active externalism, based on the active role of the environment in driving cognitive processes. Environmental supports develop a crucial role in knowledge production. We are extending ourselves with these new instruments, consequently we should understand how the apparatus operates, and include its results in our own scientific abilities. We know and think with the helpful contribution of machines, so we should include them in our cognitive models. They are not only the instrument through which we achieve results from nature, but they are part of our minds and design the shape of our thoughts. Imaging computational tools are an example of that idea. 3-D visualizations have enabled profound progress in the scientific use of vast amounts of difficult data, and user-friendly interfaces help us to make better representations of the world. The purpose of the Scientific Visualization experts is to provide cutting-edge tools and techniques for analyzing and visualizing complex scientific data. With the powerful graphics workstations and other equipment, researchers are able to view results using high resolution, true color graphics, three dimensional solid modeling, even animation. As Thomas, we don't believe, nor think, without images.

Visual-spatial thinking has been an aspect of science overlooked by educators (Mathewson, 1999), although there are relevant arguments in favour of its importance in the scientific bibliography (Churchland, 1995; Comoldi & McDaniel, 1991; Kosslyn, 1994; Marr, 1982; Pinker, 1997). Images are coherent encodings of experience, and the computational ways by which they are produced in the scientific process, belong to extended human cognition. We know that successful visual resources support important cognitive processes, and recent surveys of computer science educators suggest a widespread belief that visualization technology positively impacts learning (Tversky, B., Morrison, J.B., Betrancourt, M., 2002). If visualizations are now a cornerstone of most scientific endeavours, they must be soundly based on an understanding of cognition, which is provided by cognitive psychologists and philosophers (Gilbert, 2005). The merging of scientific fields with disciplines such as art, psychology, and technology can result in visualizations that are not only effective in communicating concepts, but are also easily interpreted by new students. These interdisciplinary collaborations are important for visualizations of the particulate level of matter to be effective learning tools. We must also consider that the cognitive advantages of visual models and their ability to explicitly show, in a single unified view, the relationships between a large number of diverse elements, makes them an indispensable part of the knowledge integration process. The goal of knowledge integration is to enable an emergent level of intelligence in the face of scientific complexity. *Knowledge integration* is the process of fitting our ideas – our theories of how-the-world-works – together into a coherent structure. That coherent structure, and the *process* of bringing knowledge together, has a number of critically important, yet under-appreciated, uses: (a) as we expand the scope of our thinking we may come across just the idea, or combination of ideas, that enables progress on the seemingly intractable problems we face; (b) as we reconcile conflicting ideas we can force into the open, hidden assumptions and logical inconsistencies (c) as we synthesize diverse perspectives we can clarify our thinking and highlight areas of (in) coherence, (dis)agreement, or (un)certainty; (d) as we connect ideas we can create a whole that is greater than the sum of its parts.

'WHO' DO SEE WHAT?

We've established at this point several things: human beings think with images, and actual scientific visualization processes are embedded on computational tools. But we would not be honest if we accepted uncritically those computing images. There is no a 'pure' vision, but an active mind process to achieve visual meanings. It happens not only at our cognitive level (neurons, brain), but also at an extended level: our instruments develop a certain 'sight' over the information. We can show information in several different ways and cognitive biases in imaging technologies can happen (Giere, 2003; Rapp, 2003).

More critically, visualization can be considered as an unnecessary 'human distortion of data' (Humphreys, 2004). Therefore, must be our simulations real or symbolic? (Sidiropoulos & Vasilakos, 2006). There is also the problem of uncertainty visualization: uncertainty or errors are introduced into information visualization as data are collected, transformed and integrated. In the absence of integrated presentation of information and its associated uncertainty, the analysis of the visualization is incomplete at best, and may lead to inaccurate or incorrect conclusions. Therefore, the use of imaging technologies requires a critical point of view about *electronic common-sense*. We know that what we see with our eyes it's not the true reality, but the kind of information that our senses and cognitive situation can offer us. We are not naïve about our eyes, and we must also be honest with our computational visualization extensions. But the role of synthetic models in our knowledge process is a controversial topic.

It is a common belief to consider that a model and its target have to be isomorphic (van Fraassen 1980; Suppes 2002) or partially isomorphic (Da Costa & French 2003). Computer simulation models are part of a new methodology (Winsberg 1999, 2001, 2003) that can be understood as an upper step into scientific knowledge acquisition (Humphreys 1991, 1995, 2002). Nevertheless, the credibility of digital computer simulations has always been a problem. Today, through the debate on verification and validation, it has become a key issue. Varenne (2001) showed clearly that, due to the role of epistemological beliefs in science, no general agreement can be found on this matter. Simulations can be epistemologically considered as experiments, tools or an intermediate between theory and experiment, but, at the end, their use is increasing every day and their success is based on their visual capacities. Therefore, computer simulations present a good cognitive fitness.

But at the same time, they present several problems that have deep epistemological questions, being perhaps the most important, that related to its true value:

At the same time, we could argue about the ontological status of a simulation, because the credibility of digital computer simulations has always been a problem (Varenne, 2001). Is A life a true simulation? And which are the epistemic values of simulations? From an historical point of view, the question of computer simulation credibility is a very old one and exist different possible standpoints on the status of simulation: they can be considered as a genuine experiment, as an intermediate step between theory and experiment or as a tool.

From a pragmatical philosophical perspective, I propose this lema: "does it works?" (a pragmatic view yet present in the work of Larry Laudan and science as a 'problem solving activity'). Let me present an example: Alife simulations, at least L-systems, reproduce and explain plant development. In our relationship with the world the way to obtain truths is mediated by our models, and we know that our models fit well with the world when they show a similar behavior, an homogeneous nature. Science solves problems and explains the nature of these problems. The prehistory of individual plant simulation can be referred to the Ulam's digital computer simulations on branching patterns with the cellular automata, at the beginning of the 1960's. Then Lindenmayer's work on substitution formal systems - the so-called L-systems -, which were first published in 1968, helped some biologists to accept such a formal computer modeling. In 1979, De Reffye produced and published through his Ph.D. thesis the first universal 3D simulation of botanical plants. He could simulate them, whatever their "architectural model" in the sense of the botanist Hallé. From a conceptual point of view, the new architectural vision, due to Hallé's work in the 1970's, enabled De Reffye to consider plants as discrete events generated discrete trees and not as chemical factories.

Then, the question is "what kind of existence does the scientist ascribe to the mathematical or logical equivalent he is using to model his phenomenon?". My point is: if the model fits well with reality, it shares an important amount of *essence* with the real world. So, it is *the real world*, at least at some levels of its reality. We don't ask all the possible questions to the real world, just the ones we are able to think in a formal way. So, if our approach to the reality of the facts is limited by our questions, and the world is never all the possible world but just the *thinkable* world, then simulations (or good simulations) are true experiments. We must also to admit that the best map of the world is the world itself. Then, to operate properly with the world we should use the whole world, something impossible. Consequently, we reduce parts of the world to simple models, which can be 'real' (one plant as example of all plants) or 'virtual' (a L-system representation of a plant). The problem is not the nature of the model, but its capacity to represent the characteristics of the world that we try to know (and to learn/teach).

As a consequence, we can consider Alife simulations as true real life observations. They are as limited as are our own theoretical models. There is nothing special in virtual simulations which cannot enable us to use them as true models of the world. The only question is to be sure about the limits of our virtual model, in the same way that when we go to the laboratory and analize *1* plant (or limited series of them), that one it's not the whole specie, just a specific model. Although that plant is *real* we use them in the laboratory as a model representation of all the same items in the world. Consequently, we can suppose that the rest of similar plants manifest a similar structure and behavior, if our chosen model is a good one (could be a special mutation, or an ill exemplar,...). The virtual model reaches a different level of abstraction, but it is also a model. The crucial question is about the accuracy of the similitudes (and the successful final research) between the virtual model and the real world, not

about the biological o digital nature of the studied object. The use on imaging computational tools led not only to a direct animation, but also to the visualization of the *hidden* properties under real analysis, properties that would not be accessible to classical experimental observation. In microscopy, for example, researchers can obtain structural information but usually without the energetics. Through simulation, however, they can have both.

There are also more problems to be considered as epistemological problems in these kind of visualizations: the lost of control, the tyranny of scales, the verification and validation process with ongoing updating databases (and the provenance of data), the epistemic opacity of computational proofs, the real-time visualization, data distortion and imaging bias, …

END REMARKS AND THE TRANSCOGNITIVE MODEL

If we consider last fMRI studies about vision and the deep structural changes suffered by contemporary science (computational science, e-science), we can conclude that visualization not only develops a key role in the process of knowledge acquisition, but also that we need to create better imaging frames for a comprehensive knowledge.

At a certain level, we can say that we have an extended epistemology, which embraces human and instrumental entities. We can make better science because we can deal better with scientific data. But at the same time, the point is not that be 'see' better, but that we only can see because we design those cognitive interfaces. Computational simulations are the middleware of our mindware, acting ad mediators between our instruments, brains, the worlds and our minds.

In this moment we need a stable paradigm of visualization (Kitano, 2003), as a precautionary measure to not to be overloaded by different platforms. User intuition is a complex and hard process and we should not spare our time learning different ways of common sense in front of computational visualizations. At the same time, we must note that with these changes, our model of cognition has evolved from a pure human-centered perspective to an extended one: computational tools and environments (AI, expert systems, imaging, simulations,…) have extended cognition to the computational kingdom. We are in the next cognitive step, the transcognitive model: we can think in a certain way because of our visualization (smart) machines. Therefore, cognition is not a human-centered process, but also a machine-centered process. Although they are outside out bodies, contemporary visualization tools constitute part of our thoughts. The representation of data graphically as a means of gaining understanding and insight into the data, allows the researcher to gain insight into the system that is studied in ways previously impossible.

As extended Thomas, we can belief what we can (computationally) see.

ACKNOWLEDGMENT

This work was partly supported by the TECNO-COG research group (at UAB) on Cognition and Technological Environments, [FFI2008-01559/FISO]. Thanks to my computer and engineering students from the course *Philosophy and Computing* for their online comments, and to Peter Skuce for their interesting questions and suggestions.

REFERENCES

Brodie, R. W. (1992). *Scientific Visualization*. Berlin: Springer Verlag.

Capshew, J. H., & Rader, K. A. (1992). Big Science: Price to the Present. *Osiris, 2*(7), 14–22.

Carsetti, A. (Ed.). (2004). *Seeing, Thinking and Knowing: Meaning and Self-Organisation in Visual Cognition and Thought*. Dordrecht, The Netherlands: Kluwer Academic Publishers.

Churchland, P. M. (1995). *The engine of reason, the seat of the soul*. Cambridge, MA: MIT Press.

Clark, A. (2003). *Natural-born cyborgs. Minds, technologies, and the future of human intelligence*. Oxford, UK: Oxford University Press.

Comoldi, C., & McDaniel, M. A. (Eds.). (1991). *Imagery and cognition*. New York: Springer.

Da Costa, N., & French, S. (2000). Models, Theories, and Structures: Thirty Years On. *Philosophy of Science, 67*(Supplement), S116–S127. doi:10.1086/392813

Feyerabend, P. (1996). Theoreticians, Artists, and Artisans. *Leonardo, 29*(1), 23–28. doi:10.2307/1576272

Giere, R. (2003). The role of computation in scientific cognition. *Journal of Experimental & Theoretical Artificial Intelligence, 15*, 195–202. doi:10.1080/0952813021000055216

Gilbert, J. K. (Ed.). (2005). *Visualization in Science Education, Series: Models and Moxdeling in Science Education* (*Vol. 1*). London: Springer Verlag.

Goodale, M. A., & Humphrey, G. K. (1998). The Objects of Action and Perception. *Cognition, 67*, 181–207. doi:10.1016/S0010-0277(98)00017-1

Hacking, I. (1981). Do We See With Microscopes? *Pacific Philosophical Quarterly, 62*, 305–322.

Haffenden, A. M., & Goodale, M. A. (1998). The Effect of Pictorial Illusion on Prehension and Perception. *Journal of Cognitive Neuroscience, 10*, 122–136. doi:10.1162/089892998563824

Hey, T., & Trefethen, A. E. (2005). Cyberinfrastructure for e-Science. *Science, 308*, 817–821. doi:10.1126/science.1110410

Humphreys, P. (1991). Computer Simulations. In Fine, A., Forbes, M., & Wessels, L. (Eds.), *PSA 1990 (Vol. 2*, pp. 497–506). East Lansing, MI: Philosophy of Science Association.

Humphreys, P. (1995). Computational Science and Scientific Method. *Minds and Machines*, *5*, 499–512. doi:10.1007/BF00974980

Humphreys, P. (2002). Computational Models. *Philosophy of Science*, *69*, S1–S11. doi:10.1086/341763

Humphreys, P. (2004). *Extending Ourselves. Computational Science, Empiricism and Scientific Method*. New York: OUP.

Ifrah, G. (1999). *The Universal History of Numbers: From Prehistory to the Invention of the Computer*. Chichester, UK: Wiley.

. .Kemp, M. (1990). *The Science of Art: optical themes in western art from Brunelleschi to Seurat*. New Haven, CT: Yale University Press.

Kemp, M. (2001). *Visualisations: The Nature Book of Art and Science*. Oxford, UK: Oxford University Press.

Kerr, N., & Domhoff, G. W. (2004). Do the blind literally "see" in their dreams? A critique of a recent claim that they do. *Dreaming*, *14*, 230–233. doi:10.1037/1053-0797.14.4.230

Kitano, H. (2003). A Graphical Notation for Biochemical Networks. *BIOSILICO*, *1*(5), 159–176. doi:10.1016/S1478-5382(03)02380-1

Kosslyn, S. M. (1994). *Image and brain. The resolution of the imagery debate*. New York: Free Press.

Kuhn, T. S. (1962). *The Structure of Scientific Revolutions*. Chicago: University of Chicago Press.

Latour, B. (1986). Visualization and Cognition: Thinking with Eyes and Hands. *Knowledge and Society*, *6*, 1–40.

Marr, D. (1982). *Vision: A Computational Investigation into the Human Representation and Processing of Visual Information*. San Francisco: Freeman.

Marr, D., & Hildreth, E. (1980). Theory of Edge Detection. In *Proceedings of the Royal*

Mathewson, J.H. (1999). Visual-Spatial Thinking: An Aspect of Science Overlooked

Miller, G.A. (1956). The Magical Number Seven, Plus or Minus Two: Some Limits on

Morton, P. (1993). Supervenience and Computational Explanation in Visual Theory.

Moutoussis, K., & Zeki, S. (2006). *Seeing invisible motion: a human FMRI study*. Current.

Our Capacity for Processing Information. *The Psychological Review*, *63*,

Perini, L. (2005). The Truth in Pictures. *Philosophy of Science*, *72*, 262–285. doi:10.1086/426852

Philosophy of Science, *60*(1), 86–99. doi:10.1086/289719

Pinker, S. (1997). *How the Mind Works*. New York: W.W. Norton & Company.

Polger, C. W. (2004). Neural Machine and Realization. *Philosophy of Science*, *71*, 997–1006. doi:10.1086/425948

Rapp, D. N. (2003). The impact of digital libraries on cognitive processes: psychological issues of hypermedia. *Computers in Human Behavior*, *19*, 609–628. doi:10.1016/S0747-5632(02)00085-7

Scheffler, I. (1972). Vision and Revolution: A Postscript on Kuhn. *Philosophy of Science*, *39*(3), 366–374. doi:10.1086/288456

Sidiropoulos, G., & Vasilakos, A. (2006). Ultra-real or symbolic visualization? The case of the city through time survey. *Computers & Graphics*, *30*, 299–310. doi:10.1016/j.cag.2006.01.034

Society of London B 207, 187–217.

Suppes, P. (2002). *Representation and Invariance of Scientific Structures*. Stanford, CA: CSLI Publications.

Tversky, B., Morrison, J.B., Betrancourt, M., (2002). Animation: Can it facilitate? *International Journal of Human-Computer Studies, 57*, 247–262. doi:10.1006/ijhc.2002.1017

van Eck, D., De Jong, H. L., & Schouten, M. K. D. (2006). Evaluating New Wave Reductionism: The Case of Vision. *The British Journal for the Philosophy of Science, 57*, 167–196. doi:10.1093/bjps/axi153

van Fraassen, B. (1980). *The Scientific Image*. Oxford, UK: Oxford University Press. doi:10.1093/0198244274.001.0001

Varenne, F. (2001). What does a computer simulation prove? In N. Giambiasi & C. Frydamn, (ed.), *Simulation in Industry, Proc. of The 13th European Simulation Symposium,* Marseille, France, *October 18-20th*, SCS Europe Bvba, Ghent, (pp. 549-554).

Winsberg, E. (1999). Sanctioning Models: The Epistemology of Simulation. *Science in Context, 12*, 275–292. doi:10.1017/S0269889700003422

Winsberg, E. (2001). Complex Physical Systems and their Representations . In *Philosophy of Science 68 (Proceedings)* (pp. 442–454). Simulations, Models and Theories.

Winsberg, E. (2003). Simulated Experiments: Methodology for a Virtual World. *Philosophy of Science, 70*, 105–125. doi:10.1086/367872

Wolfram, S. (2002). A New Kind of Science. Champaign, Il: Wolfram Media.

KEY TERMS AND DEFINITIONS

Cognition: Cognition is the scientific term for "the process of thought". Its usage varies in different ways in accord with different disciplines. It is the result of high-level functions carried out by the human brain, including comprehension and use of speech, visual perceptions and construction, calculation ability, attention (information processing), memory, and executive functions such as planning, problem-solving and self-monitoring.

Visualization: Any technique for creating images, diagrams, or animations to communicate a message. Visualization through visual imagery has been an effective way to communicate both abstract and concrete ideas since the dawn of man. Typical of a visualization application is the field of computer graphics. The invention of computer graphics may be the most important development in visualization since the invention of central perspective in the Renaissance period. The development of animation also helped advance visualization.

Imaging: Computer imaging is a wide field that includes digital photography, scanning, and composition and manipulation of bit-mapped graphics. A field of computer science covering digital images - images that can be stored on a computer, particularly bit-mapped images.

Computational: Of or involving computation or computers. Computation is a general term for any type of information processing. This includes phenomena ranging from human thinking to calculations with a more narrow meaning.

Thomas Effect: As modern Thomas, we can belief what we can (computationally) see. And we don't see *through* our instruments, but we see *with* them. All our observations, perceptions and scientific data are biologically, socially, and cognitively mediated. So, there is not 'pure vision', nor 'pure objective data'. At a certain level, we can say that we have an extended epistemology, which embraces human and instrumental entities. We can make better science because we can deal better with scientific data. But at the same time, the point is not that be 'see' better, but that we only can see because we design those cognitive interfaces.

ENDNOTES

[1] (1824) *The Works of John Locke in Nine Volumes,* London: Rivington, 12th ed., Vol. 8.

[2] (1961) *The Strange Case of the Spotted Mice*, Oxford: OUP, Chapter 2.

[3] The complete original can fe found at http://www.bbc.co.uk/comedy/blackadder/.

[4] http://cg.calit2.uci.edu/mediawiki/index.php/Research_Projects:_HIPerWall

[5] http://www.visualcomplexity.com/vc/.

[6] *The New Testament,* St John, 20: 24.

Chapter 18
Computer Simulations and Traditional Experimentation:
From a Material Point of View

Juan M. Durán
SimTech - Universität Stuttgart, Deutschland

ABSTRACT

In this work I expect to revisit Francesco Guala's paper Models, simulations, and experiments in order to cast some doubts upon the so-called 'ontological account' of computer simulations and experiment described in his work. Accordingly, I will develop my argument in three (plus one) steps: firstly, I show that Guala's conception of 'experiment' is too narrow, suggesting a more accurate version instead. Secondly, I object to his notion of 'simulation' and, following Trenholme, I make a further distinction between 'analogical' and 'digital' simulations. This distinction is also meant to enrich the concept of 'experiment'. In addition, I suggest that Guala's notion of 'computer simulation' is too narrow as well. All these arguments have the advantage of moving the 'ontological account' into a new ontological map, but unfortunately they cannot get rid of it. Hence, as a third step I discuss cellular automata as a potential solution of this new problem. Finally, I object to his conception of 'hybrid simulations' as another way of misrepresenting computational activity.

INTRODUCTION

Computer science has undoubtedly introduced a new, possible radical, way of performing scientific research. Many philosophers, consequently, tend to refer to certain computational practices, such as computer simulations, as the 'third pillar' of scientific practices, along with theory and experi-

mentation. This is a strong claim that has been philosophically questioned on different grounds: epistemological, ontological, methodological, semantic, among others. Each one of this raises new and revives old philosophical issues. In this work I will narrow down the possible set of discussions, focusing myself specifically on the differences and proximities between computer simulations and traditional experimentation. The general idea is to understand if there exists a clear

DOI: 10.4018/978-1-61692-014-2.ch018

division line that divorces computer simulations from experiments, or the distinction is so abstruse that any attempt is condemned to fail.

Probably, one of the most controversial discussions today is about the so-called 'materiality' of computer simulations. Briefly, the claim goes as follows: an experiment differs from a computer simulation in terms of the causal relations present in each; and since the materiality (i.e. the causal relations) of the experiment is expected to be similar to those of the phenomena, then a computer simulation must be epistemically defective. The bare bones of this argument consist in claiming for an ontological difference that authorizes drawing conclusions on epistemic grounds. The advocates for this argument, that from now on I will be referring to as the 'ontological account'[1], usually try to kill two birds with one stone: they pretend to solve the controversy with the 'epistemological account', and to settle the dispute about computer simulation once and forever.

The general idea behind this work consists in raising some questions on certain assumptions that rest in the heart of the ontological argument. In order to achieve this task, I will be discussing Francesco Guala's paper *Models, simulations, and experiments*. This work on computer simulations and experimentation has the benefit of presenting the ontological account in a radical way such that it is possible to deal with a clean, general picture, free of subtleties.

One of Guala's main motivations for writing his paper was his rejection to the 'epistemological account'. Briefly, the epistemological account establishes a degree of epistemic 'fertility' or 'reliability' to the outcome of a computer simulation; therefore what matters is finding epistemic credentials that will increase the perspectives of a computer simulation to become a real experiment. It is interesting to follow the different philosophical positions attached to this epistemological account: the more devotees believe, not without a lot of controversy, that we could fully rely on computer simulations for our understanding of

the world insofar our access to the world is, ultimately, through models. In the end, these same philosophers may also suggest that, sometime soon we could just completely depend on computer simulations and leave experimentation out of the realm of scientific activity once and for all. They recognize, however, that before this could happen, a proper epistemology and metaphysics must be in place. On the other hand, a more conservative follower, but still a confident one, would suggest that computer simulation do not need to compete with experiment in such a radical way; instead it is possible to deal with each activity in its own domain, making no differences in their (comparable) epistemological power. Their favorite example is the understanding of astronomical phenomena, where experimentation can hardly be performed (if it can be performed at all). However, when this philosopher is asked about the many cases where computer simulations and experimentation are somehow competing on the same domain, his choice is usually inclined to favor experimentation over simulations. This reaction is based on the philosophical assumption that there exists a deep, possibly causal, relation that experiments maintain with the world. Finally, there is a third category of philosophers that believe that computer simulations are nothing but some sort of huge *abacus* for helping the scientist make his calculations quicker and more precise. It follows, according to this philosopher, that computer simulations are not epistemically important *per se*, but only as a tool, just in the same way a microscope or a pipe is a tool in the scientist's lab.

Independently of the epistemological position, all these philosophers agree that the question about the differences between computer simulations and experimentation can be solved on epistemological grounds, namely, on the degree (positive or negative) of 'reliability' of the knowledge obtained by running a computer simulation. On the contrary, Guala believes that this difference cannot be answered from pure epistemological grounds, but instead from an ontological one. In Guala's own terms "the interesting question, however, is whether the epistemic difference is fundamental from a semantic viewpoint or whether it is just a byproduct of some more basic difference between experiments and simulations" (Guala, 2002, pp. 63). Here is where the ontological argument comes into play: there is a radical, insuperable, difference rooted in the very nature of experiments and computer simulations. According to Guala, this difference is the key for understanding the whole epistemic dilemma: equal ontology, equal epistemic power. Due to this ontological principle, his whole work will not only focus on the development of this fundamental distinction, but also emphasize the philosophical priority of the ontological argument.

In this paper I will be developing three (plus one) arguments. Firstly, I will show that Guala's conception of experiment is misleading, isolating and demanding from experiments something that it could not be given, v. gr. 'purity'. I will replace his notion with what I believe is a more accurate representation of scientific experiment and scientific experimentation. At this point of analysis all it will be shown is that experimentation is a complex activity that involves, among many other things, formal models[2]. Secondly, it will be necessary to clarify Guala's notion of computer simulation. Moreover, I object to his conceptualization on the ground that it is, ironically, an ontological hodgepodge of different, unrelated, ideas of what a simulation is. Instead, I urge for a further distinction between 'analogical simulations' and 'digital simulation'. In doing so, I will shed some light on the claim that simulations (as a whole) are ontologically different than experiments. Nevertheless, splitting the concept of simulation into two new classes is not enough for undermining the ontological argument. Therefore I will draw a further distinction into the class 'computer simulations' as an attempt to bring back computer simulations into the experimental realm. The 'plus' argument discusses the so-called *hybrid simulations*. My work here will be very

simple and quick: I will show that Guala's idea of this kind of simulation is, again, not accurate, failing to take into consideration many types of hybrid simulations.

EXPERIMENTS, SIMULATIONS AND A LOT OF CONFUSION

In 2002 Francesco Guala published a paper where he defends a profound and insuperable difference between computer simulations and traditional experiments. In this work he criticizes the view according to which this difference is not fundamentally epistemic in character but, instead, ontological. In order to carry out his claim three things must be in place: a conception of experiment, a conception of simulation and an idea of how these two relate to each other. In the following I show that his conception of experiment as well as his conception of simulation is confusing, mainly due to this ontological account. As for the relationship between these two, I claim that it is more complex and it is more interweaved with scientific experimentation than Guala suggests.

Experiments and Simulations: What's All About?

To Guala the particularity of experiments is straightforward: they are developed and carried out by using the *same* materiality present in the phenomenon under study. In other words, it is expected from a regular experiment makes use of materiality *vis-à-vis* the phenomenon studied. However, what does 'materiality' mean in this context? Materiality here refers to the causes that bring the phenomenon about. In this sense, an experiment is some sort of causal copy used for manipulating, in a controlled setup environment, a phenomenon. In Guala's own words, "in a genuine experiment the same 'material' causes as those in the target system are at work" (Guala, 2002, pp. 67). Clearly his conception of experiment is of some specific configuration where the components are, due to its nature, guarantees of true access to the world. If an experimenter is interested in learning about light waves, she must run an experiment using a light beam. This way of dealing with phenomena has the comfortable consequence of guaranteeing the manipulation of the same causes at work in both, the experiment and the real phenomenon. Therefore, materiality and causality are complementary in laboratory experimentation, allowing a truly and unique way of dealing with real phenomena.

However, it seems to be a conceptual error based on the dual use of 'phenomena', both as the system *under* study (the experiment) and the system *to* study (the real phenomena). Although the identification made by Guala is not, strictly speaking, incorrect, at least seems to misinterpret current scientific experimentation. If an experimenter makes use of a beam of light for understanding the properties of light, he is manipulating 'the same thing' in an obvious sense: the object/phenomenon under study is identical and, consequently, so are the causes that bring it about[3]. Consequently prediction, and eventually explanation, seems to be a much easier task to perform. However this identification leaves a bad taste in one's mouth: it seems that a more accurate evaluation of experimentation takes into account the role instruments play in scientific activity, the place 'noise' and 'error' has during the execution as well as in the result of an experiment, the importance of data collection, among other things. These few comments on the surroundings of experimentation should give us the key for two claims: firstly, that our way of understanding an experiment and, consequently, evaluating its epistemic power, is not as straightforward as Guala suggests; and secondly, that the dual use of 'phenomena' is misleading and should be abandoned.

Moreover, this is not the only, let alone the primary way that current scientific activity is performed. Indeed, not every scientific experiment is related to materiality: a thought experiment[4]

is a good example of this last category, or an experiment where it is impossible to manipulate the real phenomenon, like galaxies or atoms. Moreover, not only micro or macro phenomena can be used as examples. There are simple and accessible phenomena that might be studied without direct mediation of the same materiality. This is an interesting point that Guala calls for our attention, although in a more radical way: when the system used for studying a particular phenomenon is made of *different* materials than those of the real phenomenon, then the situation changes drastically. The experimental activity previously defined must be set aside for a more suitable conception, namely, a *simulation*. What a simulation is and, perhaps more importantly, how does it differs from a regular experiment, will be explained using his own example:

A material model of the propagation of light, according to the wave theory, can be build with the aid of water in a ripple tank. At a general level of analysis any kind of wave can be modeled as a perturbation in a medium determined by two forces: the external force producing the perturbation, and the reacting force working to restore the medium at rest. General relationships such as Hooke's law or D'Alembert's equation may hold for all kind of waves. More fundamental relationships, such as Maxwell's equation, describe the properties of the electric and the magnetic field only. The values given by Maxwell's equation can be used in D'Alembert's wave equation in order to obtain, for instance, the velocity of propagation of an electromagnetic wave, because electricity behaves like a wave, although the fundamental principles at work are different from those at work in case of, e.g., water waves. The terms appearing in the equation describing the target and the model-system are to be interpreted differently in the two cases: the forces are different in nature, and so are the two media in which waves travel. The similarity between the theoretical model of light waves and he ripple-tank model holds at a very abstract level only. The two systems are made of different 'stuff': water waves are not light waves. Because of the formal similarity, though, the behavior of light waves can be simulated in a ripple tank. Both light waves and water waves obey the same non-structural law, despite their being made of different 'stuff'. This is due to different reasons in each case: different underlying processes produce similar behavior at an abstract level of analysis. (Guala, 2002, pp. 66)

According to this, a simulation is some sort of theoretical model[5] in mathematical form, relating the various properties exhibited by the phenomena under study. If this is the case, then the relation held with the phenomena is not of direct access but rather mediated by the model. The ontological difference between an experiment and a simulation can be highlighted in the following quote: "the difference lies in the kind of relationship existing between, on the one hand, an *experimental* and its *target* system, and, on the other, a *simulation* and its target system. In the former case, the correspondence holds at a 'deep', 'material' level, whereas in the latter the similarity is admittedly only 'abstract' and 'formal'"[6] (Guala, 2002, pp. 67). It is exactly this conceptual dichotomy that is not working. As we shall see later, those boundaries well delimited by Guala must be relaxed if we expect to get a more accurate picture of experimentation and, probably more important due to its unfamiliarity, of computer simulations.

The example of the ripple-tank is paradigmatic and will give us an idea of Guala's dichotomy: it is not the presence of materiality what dominates the simulation, but quite the opposite, it is the presence of a formal entity in-between the beam of light and the ripple tank that it is prominent. Since there is no material equivalency, there is no equal causal manipulation. Since there is no equal causal manipulation, there is no genuine experiment. Instead, a formal connection, a theoretical model takes place and clears the path to what can only be a defective access to the phenomenon

under study. It is possible to track this idea even in the smallest details, for instance, in claiming that there is no reductionist story compelling enough for making the idea of a ripple-tank become an experiment[7].

The activity so far depicted clearly divorces experimentation from simulation. The question is, of course, whether this is the case. A closer look into scientific activity shows that this divorce cannot be simply carried out. In the following I will briefly discuss the case of instruments in the laboratory, but as I have mentioned before, scientific activity is a rich and complex activity involving several other features.

If it is correct that most experiments (if not all of them) are performed in a laboratory, where different instruments are involved in the development of phenomena[8], then it is legit to ask the following question: can we experiment in a pure, genuine and direct way as Guala suggests?[9] I believe that this question has a negative answer. It is not possible, and maybe not even desirable, to have a pure access to the phenomenon. It seems that the more complex the phenomenon gets, the more instruments, theoretical means and different sorts of materials will be necessary for carrying out an experiment. The number of highly sophisticated machinery involved in the development, observation, manipulation or whatever investigation an experimentalist pretends to carry out on a single phenomenon is enormous. In any regular laboratory it is possible to find tubes, pipes, computers, microscopes, among several offices, tables and laboratories, some of them explicitly needed for the success of the experiment, some of them just playing a secondary role.

Consider for instance a wind tunnel: a highly controlled test chamber where an aircraft flight is simplified in order to reduce secondary factors as crosswinds, updraft and downdraft, pilot maneuvering, and engine variations. All those removed factors are neglected in this simplified environment with the expectation that they will not affect the understanding of the underlying phenomena. Chambers like the one described here make use of a real airplane wind, a real wind flow, a real perturbation in the fuselage, and other paraphernalia for resembling the flight as realistically as possible. This example of wind tunnel is an experiment in Guala's sense: it is made of a real wing[10], real air flow, real resistance, real pressure and a real so on.

Such experimental control yields, due to the neglected factors already mentioned, raw data measurements that are relatively uncontaminated reflections of the principal flight components. As Norton and Suppe point out, "the measurements are systematically inaccurate. Experimental control introduces artifact (systematic errors) into the data (...) Walls [in the wind tunnel] introduce turbulence affecting airflow past models, causing systematic airflow variations (...) Mathematical models are applied to correct data." (Norton & Suppe, 2001, pp. 71). However precise and accurate in their resolution, instruments are prone to systematic errors in data collection that must be corrected. And this is a fact in most of the current experimental activity: the design of an experiment depends on instruments that introduce artifactual effects that must be identified and removed. Incidentally, those effects can be rectified by using theoretical models. In this sense, and despite what it has been suggested by Guala, a large number of so-called experiments are unconditionally related to instruments, its apparatus and, ultimately, to theoretical models. Moreover, in many cases there are no experimental results unless there is some theoretical model involved in the data correction, artifactual rectification, instrument calibration, etc. In the end we must live with the fact that certain phenomena is not fully accessible, let alone manipulable, unless experimenters include as object of their work a simplified, possibly highly constrained by instruments, version of the real phenomenon.

It should be notice, however, that the presence of theoretical modeling in experimentation does not mean *simulation*, not in Guala's terms.

Consider the case of the ripple-tank again. The particularity of this case is that different materiality is involved. So, recalling the ontological argument once more, if different materiality is present, then the relationship must be only formal, *through* a theoretical model. Moreover, as the ontological account continues, it is due to the presence of a theoretical model that the philosopher is allowed to draw fundamental differences between a simulation and an experiment. Therefore, the priority of the ontological argument is to focus on the materiality or on the lack of it, and any disagreement must be based upon this difference.

Nevertheless, the case of the wind tunnel is somehow different. It shows that the same materiality is present (making a case for the ontological argument) while the whole experiment depends upon reliable formal models (making the exact opposite case). This ultimately shows that the claim materiality is vacuous and misguided. The wind tunnel example shows an evident clash between Guala's idea of pure experiment and a conception of instrument-mediated experimentation. This clash ultimately suggests that Guala's conception of experiment is too narrow for dealing with current scientific activity. Alternatively, a more accurate conception would be one that considers experiments entailing theoretical models[11], whether that may be in a primary level, setting the experiment up, or in a secondary level, just modifying the experiment's outcome. Our access to the world is so deeply grounded on models, that an access without them seems impossible. Of course this mediation raises new and crucial questions, although it is not my intention to answer them here. What I would like to point out though, is that sometimes it seems that Guala's intention is to divorce experimentation from the use of instruments, and, in doing so, also from measurement, observation and virtually from the wider body of scientific practice performed by laboratory equipment. If this is so, the problem seems clear: there is little (or none) experimental activity without entailing, in one way or another, theoretical modeling; in this sense, a grey zone where experiments and simulations overlap is unfolded.

Another Categorical Mistake

Deep down, it seems that Guala is treating experiments as a mysterious and truly unique way of accessing any phenomena: the more real it gets, the more obscure it becomes. This can be confirmed not only by his concept of direct experimentation, but also by the claim that there exist strong epistemic levels related to those scientific concepts. To quote in extent:

(...) why do scientists slip from 'experiment' talk, to 'model' and to 'simulation' talk? A plausible answer is that the difference is purely epistemic in character: 'experiment' and 'theory' being the pillars upon which all proper science should stand, scientists signal their epistemic doubts using a special terminology. An incomplete or less than certain theory becomes a 'model'; a dubious experiment becomes a 'simulation', and so on. (Guala, 2002, pp. 60)

Regarding this quote, I would like to point out two things: firstly, that a theory seems to be (partially) divorced from models; secondly, and more important to my claim, that Guala considers simulations as being epistemically *defective* compared with experiments. The first claim is related to his conception of models as *mediators* or as *autonomous agents*, a point of view endorsed by Morgan and Morrison (Morgan & Morrison, 1999) and quite appropriate for this kind of studies. The second claim is a little more controversial, therefore I would like to discuss it in extent.

What exactly does Guala mean by a "dubious experiment becomes a 'simulation'"? *Prima facie,* given the disdain for treating certain kind of experiments (and therefore simulations), it seems to suggest that our knowledge fades away more and more as we get into the abstract world. The

further we get relying on theoretical models, the less epistemic power we can expect. This idea is supported by the use of concepts such as 'previous knowledge' or 'fully specified' (Guala, 2002, pp. 67), two key terms that have a long and interesting history in philosophy of science, mostly related to *theory-laden* or *theory-guided* conceptualizations of experiments. Hence, to Guala the former question has a simple answer: a simulation is a poor way of performing an experiment due to its incapacity of being carried out without any previous minimal knowledge of the phenomenon under study. Although this might be true of simulations (and certain kind of experiments), it seems too strong to claim that the epistemic power decreases just for the fact that it is an abstract entity. Moreover, given this background conceptualization, it is not difficult to find examples from history of science which fail to fit into either of Guala's categories.

The Becquerel Example

Well known cases of fortunate strikes places the experiment (and the experimenter) in an unusual position. Such is the case of experiments in radioactivity and in the photoelectric phenomenon; from Röntgen to the Curies, just to mention the beginning of this important epoch for physics and chemistry, the presence of happy endings (at least for the history of science) tells us a little more about the relationship between theory and experiment.

During the last years in the 19th century, and with the use of Wilhem Röntgen's work on X-Rays, Henri Becquerel discovered one astonishingly phenomenon, absolutely unknown until then: the discovery of spontaneous radioactivity, for which he was awarded with half of the Nobel Prize in Physics in 1903.

Becquerel's earliest work was concerned with the plane polarization of light, with the phenomenon of phosphorescence and with the absorption of light by crystals. During the year 1896, he finally discovered the phenomenon of spontaneous radioactivity, overshadowing his own previous work, and opening the door to an unknown, incomprehensible, new phenomenon. Working with the recently discovered X-rays and a type of phosphorescence in the vacuum tube, Becquerel decided to investigate whether there was any connection between X-rays and naturally occurring phosphorescence. By using his father's uranium salts, and expecting them to phosphor when exposed to light, he came across salts that, when placed near to a photographic plate covered with opaque paper, fogged the plate. The surprise specially came when for two consecutive days he could not expose them to the sunlight because it was not shining, but on the third day, when he develop the plates anyway expecting to see little or no effect, he finds out that the plates were as black as if they had been exposed to full sunlight.

The discovery of a new, powerful and, by that time, supposed infinite source of energy fascinated the entire world. But the question about the origin of that energy was not answered until Einstein came along with his famous equation. The historical remark is that Einstein, working in a completely different area, wrote a three-page article where he presents the equation bonding energy with mass and the speed of light. It is possible to explain he relative radiation of a body in terms of his equation (Cf. Einstein, 1905).

There is little doubt that Becquerel's discovery of radiation was a fortuitous one. However, it is a perfect example of how scientific experimentation works sometimes: by hunches, by intuition, by lucky guesses...

This example allows me introduce the concept of 'non-pure' experiment, which will contrast with the idea of 'pure' or 'direct' experiment discussed earlier. Therefore, a 'non-pure' experiment would be a regular experiment that uses certain materiality for explaining a phenomenon made by another, totally different, materiality. Of course, a 'non-pure' experiment can make use of previous knowledge (or not), just like in the case of a 'pure' experiment.

It might be objected that I am just playing with words; that, deep down, what I have called 'non-pure' experiment is just Guala's concept of 'simulation' and nothing more. Not so. Making use of the triad 'experiment, simulation, previous knowledge' it is possible to show that the photoelectric effect is an example that falls out of Guala's categories. Indeed, it is certainly not a 'pure' experiment because it makes use of a different materiality for bringing the phenomenon about; but it is not a simulation either because, for being so, it is mandatory certain 'previous knowledge', totally absent in Becquerel's experiment. None of these two categories are enough for holding in a 'non-pure' experiment simply because it fulfills both requisites: it is an experiment in the sense that there is no previous knowledge guiding and explaining what it is going on, and it is a simulation in the sense that it does not uses the same materiality as the phenomenon brought about. But in Guala's terms, it is neither.

By now it should be clear that there is only one explanation for this (and any previous) counter-example: Guala's categories are too narrow both for experiments and for simulations. We have seen before that his idea of experiment is too narrow for the actual practice of science: the first argument begs the question for a non-mediated access to the phenomena, raising the suggestion that most experimental practice requires the use of instruments and, therefore, some presence of models. Now this categorical mistake begs the question for the 'purity' of an experiment, pointing out that there are several scientific experiments that are in some kind of limbo imploring for an identity. Both arguments call into question Guala's ontological difference between experiments and simulations. Moreover, every objection suggests that simulations and experiments are much closer to each other than Guala suggests.

But enough about experiments and simulations; the claim that computer simulations and experiments are different seems to be, at least, on the right track. In the following I would like to explore the possibility of drawing a new ontological map based on the analysis of computer simulations.

Computer Simulations

Just like the case of the ripple-tank, a computer simulation is also based on a theoretical level, v. gr. A theoretical model in mathematical (or logical) form, or at least this is the way Guala considers it. In order to show how a computer simulation works, he presents Stratagem (Guala, 2002, pp. 68), a computer-based modeling package used by geologist working on stratigraphy. The presentation of Stratagem is as follows:

This simulation device works on the basis of a number of structural equations taken from the theory of 'sequence stratigraphy'. The equations model the system's outcome (the actual sedimentation) as a function of a number of variables including the hydrodynamics of sediment deposition, the subsidence patterns, the global sea level, the amount of sediment supplied to the basin, etc. The outcome of the simulation is dependent on the approximate validity of the theory of sequence stratigraphy, and also on the correct specification of the initial conditions and of the values assigned to the free parameters in the equations. (Guala, 2002, pp. 69)

Typically, simulations are used in one of two different ways: either (1) to bootstrap from the fact that a given effect (which we have observed in system A) can be produced by means of simulation B, to the fact that the relations governing the behavior of B also govern the behavior of A. Or (2) to argue that a certain effect observed by simulating with B will also be observed in the case of A because the two are governed by similar relations (Guala, 2002, pp. 67)

As we can see, a computer simulation consists of a theoretical model which represents formally a well-known theory such as stratigraphy. The result of the computer simulation, which comes from solving the theoretical model, depends explicitly on the validity of the theory (plus some initial and boundary conditions). We have already seen how the ripple-tank case is defended, and we can also see that the case of computer simulations is not different at all: both share the same kind of theoretical structure (i.e, an abstract representation of the real phenomena), and both are used for the same purposes, namely, to create epistemic bonds with the phenomena. Moreover, computer simulation, as expected, also require previous knowledge of the system simulated: "Geologist try to simulate system A (real-world geological structures) by means of a computer-model B, and all the fundamental relation in B must be known and specified in advanced" (Guala, 2002, pp. 68). In short, computer simulations and the ripple-tank type of simulations are, ontologically (and, accordingly, epistemically) speaking, identical.

This identity clashes with our intuition of a ripple-tank (not) being a computer simulation. I believe this apparent disparity can be overcome by making a further distinction: simulations such as the ripple-tank should be conceived as 'analogical simulations', whereas simulations such as Stratagem should be conceived as 'digital simulation'. As ironically as it might seem, this distinction will not only fulfill our more basic philosophical intuitions about simulations, but also help to understand in more clear terms the ontological claim[12].

Russell Trenholme (Trenholme, 1994) presents an interesting and elaborated dichotomy between analogical simulations and digital simulations (renamed by him as *symbolic simulations*). Trenholme' strategy is to shift the focus from a dichotomy based on the type of numerical representation, which is the classical way of dealing with this kind distinction, to one based on the type of processes involved. Following this switch, it is possible to make clear the intuition (and *a fortiori* the certainty) that *analogical* and *symbolic* processes are two, distinct and philosophically relevant processes. In a few words, the dichotomy is based on the notion of an analog processes characterized by parallel causal-structures isomorphic to the phenomenon simulated[13], whereas digital simulations behaves as symbolic processors, that is, "only if a symbolic theory which is coded into them adequately describes some aspect of the world."[14] (Trenholme, 1994, pp. 118).

Summarizing Trenholme's ideas, a *symbolic simulation* "is characterized by a mapping between a syntactically expressible inference relation of a theory and physically definable transition states between causally discrete components of a digital device" (Trenholme, 1994, pp. 118) In other words, a symbolic simulation is a twofold mapping: on one hand, there is a mapping between a theoretical structure, such as an algorithm, to the hardware structures and, on the other hand, there is a mapping between the same theoretical structure to extra-computational phenomena. The first mapping, called *symbolic processing*, is a "syntactic relation among symbols of the theory onto causal relations among elements of the hardware"[15] (Trenholme, 1994, pp. 119). In this sense, it is completely independent of the soundness or representativeness of the theory of any phenomena. It allows to create a 'world of its own' in the computer realm, just as the mathematician is able to create his own world of mathematical entities without worrying about the true existence or representativeness of those entities in the world. Moreover, at this level of analysis, the correctness or incorrectness of the theoretical model regarding some external phenomenon is absolutely irrelevant to the concept of symbolic processing. Instead, the correctness of the model is exclusively a formal matter and, hence, subjected to the realm of formal semantics. The second type of mapping, however, involves a 'model-world' relationship, where the structure of the theoretical model relates to extra-computational phenomena. This last type of mapping limits the scope of computer simulation to those theoretical models that are, to some intended level, realistic representation of real phenomena.

In contrast, an analog simulation "is defined by a single mapping from causal relations among elements of the simulation to causal relations among elements of the simulated phenomenon" (Trenholme, 1994, pp. 119) Here the relationship is direct, causal and resembles the real phenomenon. According to this conception, analog simulations provide causal information about aspects of the physical process being simulated. In fact, as Trenholme claims, "their internal processes possess a causal structure isomorphic to that of the phenomena simulated, and their role as simulators may be described without bringing in *intentional concepts*" (Trenholme, 1994, pp. 118, my emphasis). This lack of intentionality tries to underline the fundamental aspect of analogical simulations: they do not require an epistemic agent, as in the case of symbolic simulation, for representing the fundamental structures of the real phenomena.

Under these new categories the ripple-tank simulation might depend on a prior and more fundamental relation with light waves: it is at the level of the isomorphic causal-structures they share, and not at their formal representational level, where water waves behaves as if they were light waves. The formal level is just a second-level relationship that we use to describe, using mathematical terminology, the more fundamental causal-structures. Confusion rises when this formal level is interchanged with the causal level as, I believe, it is in the heart of the ontological argument.

This new dichotomy has the advantage of fulfilling our previous intuition, namely, that (analogical) simulations, as well as experiments, do not necessarily require previous-knowledge, just as Becquerel's experiment shows. In addition, it helps to overcome the evident clash between a concept of simulation made of real 'stuff' and a concept of simulation made of pure mathematical (or binary code). Accepting this, it follows not only that analogical simulations are legit experiments in Guala's terms, but also fits into a more accurate picture of scientific activity.

The new ontological map is as follows: the concept of experiment must be extended and must include theoretical models as part of it. Additionally, the conceptualization of *simulations* made by Guala must be absorbed by his own conceptualization of *experiment*. This new map shows that Guala is correct in pointing out the ontological difference between an experiment (and, in our case, an analogical simulation), and a computer simulation, although it makes no direct implications about epistemic claims. Hoping that I have not reached a dead end, I will fight the idea of computer simulations just as sets of equations that must be solved. If I am correct about this, there might still have some room for considering computer simulations as experiments.

Again, What was it All About?

The conception of a computer simulation *as* structural equations is currently the most spread among philosophers. It leads to the conclusion that the set of equations that constitute the simulation must be solved either by numerical calculus or by other means, such as a replacement of the original theoretical model by a computable model. Whatever the means, every philosopher agrees that computer simulations are, at best, a highly accurate and powerful instrument. On the other hand, there is an increasing number of scientist and philosophers that believe that a cellular automaton (CA), a computer simulation par excellence, considerably differs from the previous kind of simulation in many respects. If so, it is worth discussing.

A CA is a D-dimensional lattice with a finite automation residing at each lattice site. Each automaton consist of a finite set of *states*, a finite *input alphabet*, and a *transition function*, which is a mapping from the set of neighborhood state to the set of cell states. (Langton, 1990, pp. 13) The whole idea behind a CA is "to discover and

analyze the mathematical basis for the generation of complexity, one must identify simple mathematical systems that capture the essence of the process" (Wolfram, 1986). In general, a CA imitates the evolution of a system in which space and time are discrete (rather than continuous, as in the case of differential equations used by Stratagem) and logical steps are performed by the transition rules (rather than mathematical as in differential equations). In this sense, there has been performed a deep conceptual change here: from a quantitative representation of phenomena, leaded by computer simulations like Stratagem, to a more qualitative representation; from a mathematical syntax to a logical syntax[16].

How does this affect our discussion on the ontological account? I believe radically. To start with, given the nature of CA, their results are always exact (Cf. Toffoli 1984), unlike the set of errors a mathematical-based simulation must deal with (round-off errors, truncation errors, transformations, etc)[17]. Therefore, since there are no approximations involved in applying the theory, any disagreement between the model and the empirical data can be blamed directly on the theory which the model realizes (Rorhlich, 1990). In other words, what it has been suggested until now is that the main feature of symbolic simulations discussed earlier, v.gr. the twofold mapping, might disappear, unifying ontologically both types of simulations and, afterwards, experimentation as well. Quoting Fox-Keller:

"[CA are] employed to model phenomena that lack a theoretical underpinning in any sense of the term familiar to physics -phenomena for which no equation, either exact or approximate, exist (...) or for which the equation that do exist simply fall short (...) Here, what is to be simulated is neither a well-established set of differential equations (...) nor the fundamental physical constituents (or particles) of the system (...) but rather the phenomenon itself". (Fox-Keller 208)

A few more words are needed about this issue. One can appreciate that the big philosophical puzzle here seems to be that CA models works in a phenomenological level, whereas mathematical-based simulations works on a more or less fundamental level. Evidently it is not the use of models, nor the use of mathematics which characterize certain kind of computer simulations, but the very *nature* of their representation and the metaphysical status of the world, which characterizes this kind of computer simulation. Many scientist and philosophers suggest the possibility that the physical world really is a discrete machine evolving according to simple rules capable of representation by a CA. Although there is no need to get into this train of thought, this conception helps to see in what extent old philosophical ideas are evolving behind computer simulations into new ways of conceptualizing our world. Understanding how deep computer have entered into our cosmological and metaphysical conceptions, might dissolve the magic spell that forces us to see them as simple sets of equations. Independently that one accepts this metaphysical claim, as Fox-Keller points out, the mere fact that this possibility has become conjecturable (and even accepted in certain circles), it is worth noting.

Moreover, the inversion made by CA is so radical that, at very least, clashes with the dualistic ontology expressed in Guala's terms, making it lose all its charm. As Fox-Keller puts it: "Minimally, it provides an indication of the power of CA models to subvert conventional distinctions between real and virtual, or between real and synthetic, and hence of their efficacy in establishing an 'alternate reality'" (Fox-Keller, 2003, pp. 212). The question about a possible conceptualization of a world absolutely computable is, undoubtedly, intriguing. Unfortunately this is not the place to answer this question.

I shall stop here and leave the question open. If it is correct that a CA is capable of performing an ontologically different representation of phenomena, then the ontological account loses all its power. Moreover, if the world is discrete, just as many advocates of CA like to think, then a whole new conception of computer simulation must be in place.

Finally, and as a last effort, Guala applies his conceptions of experiment and simulation to a third, 'in-between', scientific practice usually known as *hybrid simulations*. It is possible to identify certain particularities of simulations left behind that will be of great importance for a more accurate depiction of computer simulations. I will only make some peripherals comments.

HYBRID SIMULATIONS

Whenever Guala talks about simulations, he is referring to them as mere *devices*. Although this goes unnoticed until he develops his work on hybrid simulations, I believe it has certain undesirable consequences, such as the alienation of computer presence in scientific activity. Even though the notion of hybrid simulation does not seem to affect the heart of the ontological claim, I agree with Guala that it is necessary to take a look into it in order to have a more accurate picture of scientific activity concerning computer simulations.

The general idea behind hybrid simulations is that it is a process that combines, in a neat way, purely experimental procedures with purely computational ones. In other words, hybrid simulations are some sort of cooperation between two independent, well distinguishable processes:

Experimental psychologist and economist are often concerned with designing experiments that reproduce in all 'relevant' respect real-world decision situations (...) [E]xperiments sometimes have to make use of 'artificial' devices. (...) [For instance] the subjects trade lottery tickets, in other words, which will be played out at the end of the experiment. Here uncertainty is simulated by means of a random draw. (Guala, 2002, pp. 71)

This is just the fusion of the idea of direct experiment with the idea of computer simulations *qua* devices. The notion of 'device' reflects the feeling towards computer simulations as regular scientific instruments, with some obvious differences in power and accuracy, for performing certain specific, non-fundamental tasks. This fits the claim that the process of experimentation and the process of simulation are two, distinct, independent process that 'interact' or 'collaborates' with each other only when properly combined into one project:

(...) if simulations and experiment produce novel scientific knowledge in different ways, then must be partly complementary, and we should be able to combine them in the same project to exploit the potential of both. (Guala, 2002, pp. 71)

Consider an example from aerodynamics. In this discipline it is possible to find several computer simulations used for pilot training[18]. Briefly, those simulations require a piece of software (the 'airplane') and a real pilot. Since the pilot has to interact with the software and, consequently, the software has to react in accordance, then there is a constant feedback towards the pilot whom will react, consequently, to the software outcome. The whole process is, in some way, dialectical, although the simulation cannot qualify as mere device, somehow distinguishable from the real world, even if it fulfills all the demands made by Guala. The airplane is not real only in one sense: it is not made of real aluminum, real cables, real plastic, but behaves as if it was one. Whatever possible situation involving an airplane design, whether conditions or pilot's commands and maneuvering, the 'airplane' will react in the same way as it is expected to react in a real airplane. Giving this case, it seems that bringing up a material argument as a problematic issue is mere philosophical idiosyncrasy[19].

CONCLUSION

In this work I have discussed what I believe are the central ideas of Francesco Guala. These ideas were used by me with strict pedagogical purposes; all of them depict, more or less accurately, the current philosophical discussions regarding the problem of 'materiality' in the context of computer simulations *qua* experiments.

I would like to sum up some of the results I have obtained so far. To begin with, Guala's conception of 'experiment' as the use of materiality *vis-à-vis* the phenomenon seems to be too narrow, leading to an imprecise picture of current scientific practice. His conception of 'simulation' follows a similar fate, although in this case it is so broad that must be split into two for fitting our basic intuitions (and *a fortiori*, scientific practice). Here is where the analysis gets a little more complex: the distinction between analogical and digital (syntactic) simulations helps to clarify why certain simulations are experiment. In addition, concepts such as 'theory-laden' still play a controversial role; for instance, *prima facie* it should be possible to run an analogical simulation without any previous knowledge, despite Guala's determination of showing the opposite. I conclude that the presence of a formal structure in analogical simulations seems to be a second level representation, intended for translating into a formal language the causal structure of the phenomena. Nevertheless I agree with him on the claim that formal structures are needed by computer simulations.

The case made by Guala for computer simulations shows that, accepting the schema of formal structures, there is an negative epistemic impact in the representation, explanation and prediction of phenomena. Computer simulations are mostly limited by two major drawbacks: firstly, they are highly dependent of the previous knowledge we have about the phenomenon under study. This is, together with the internal restrictions of the physical computer, the principal argument against a positive consideration of computer simulations *qua* experiments. The second drawback, and intimately related to the first one, is that computer simulations do not produce any outcome that it is not already contained in the model build for it. In this sense, computer simulations are, basically, a set of equations to be solved and from which nothing, except whatever was already coded in the model, will come out. Since those equations represent the phenomenon under study, any outcome of the simulation related to the phenomenon must be done *via* the model. Those two drawbacks set the scenario for considering computer simulations as mere devices, tools or apparatus. Whatever we call them, the phantom of 'apparatus' invades the philosophical realm. This is a legit concern I passed over, probably because it is more an epistemic rather than an ontological dilemma. All in all, old question from philosophy of science are still pressing.

At this point of analysis I expect to have made a fresh, renew picture of experimentation and computer simulations, but certainty still bond to the ontological argument. The final step is to try to merge the distinction analogical/digital back again. The move might be a little bit speculative, but it seems to be a valid alternative in trying to put together simulations and experiments. By considering the possibility of having computer simulations working on a primary level of representation, that is, in a causal-structural level isomorphic[20] to the phenomenon and not in a secondary level as the case of the formal model, we not only equilibrate the epistemic level of simulations and experiments but also set the basis for any further representation of nature. Under this new schema, conceptions such as 'previous knowledge', 'formal structure' and so on must be review if not eliminated.

I also briefly discuss his conception of hybrid simulations using a case-example. The heart of the example is two-fold: on the one hand, it shows that hybrid simulations cannot be presented as two clear and distinctive processes, ultimately combined into one project. On the contrary, hybrid simulations show a more interwoven, possible non-differentiated, interaction between computer simulations and the real world. On the other hand, and following the central discussion, it shows that in certain cases the presence of materiality as an objection to simulations seems to be idiosyncratic.

A final upshot would be that the epistemic power of computer simulations cannot be determined from the 'ontological account', especially if it is develop using Guala's categories. Although this account raises more interesting questions, I believe that none of them are enough for obliging us to accept any epistemic consequence. Instead, I urge for a clearer and more accurate conception of experiment and of computer simulation, not only from a material point of view, but specially form an epistemic point of view. Otherwise confusion will still predominate in discussion regarding computer simulations *qua* experiments.

ACKNOWLEDGMENT

I would like to thank prof. Gregor Betz and prof. Niels Gottschalk-Mazouz for their insightful comments on a previous draft. All the remaining mistakes are, of course, entirely mine.

REFERENCES

Achinstein, P. (1965). Theoretical models. *The British Journal for the Philosophy of Science*, *16*(62), 102–120. doi:10.1093/bjps/XVI.62.102

Einstein, A. (1905). Ist die trägheit eines körpers von seinem energiegehalt abhängig? [Does the inertia of a body depend upon its energy-content? Retrieved June 20, 2009, from http://www.four-milab.ch/etexts/einstein/E_mc2/e_mc2.pdf]. *Annalen der Physik*, *18*, 639–641. doi:10.1002/andp.19053231314

Fox Keller, E. (2003). Models, simulation, and "computer experiments" . In Radder, H. (Ed.), *The Philosophy of Scientific Experimetation* (pp. 198–215). Pittsburgh, PA: University of Pittsburgh Press.

Franklin, A. (1984). The epistemology of experiment. *The British Journal for the Philosophy of Science, 35*, 381–40. doi:10.1093/bjps/35.4.381

Guala, F. (2002). Models, simulations, and experiments . In Magnani, L., & Nersessian, N. J. (Eds.), *Model-Based reasoning: science, technology, values* (pp. 59–74). Amsterdam: Kluwer.

Hacking, I. (1983). *Representing and intervening: introductory topics in the philosophy of natural science*. Cambridge, UK: Cambridge University Press.

Harré, R. (2003). The materiality of instruments in a metaphysics for experiments . In Radder, H. (Ed.), *The philosophy of scientific experimentation* (pp. 19–38). University of Pittsburgh Press.

Hartmann, S. (1996). The world as a process: simulation in the natural and social sciences . In Hegselmann, R., Mueller, U., & Troitzsch, K. (Eds.), *Simulation and modelling in the social sciences from the philosophy of science point of view* (pp. 77–110). Amsterdam: Kluwer.

Langton, C. G. (1990). Computation at the edge of chaos: Phase transitions and emergent computation. *Physica D. Nonlinear Phenomena, 42*, 12–37. doi:10.1016/0167-2789(90)90064-V

Morgan, M., & Morrison, M. (1999). Models as mediating instruments . In Morgan, M., & Morrison, M. (Eds.), *Models as mediators. Perspectives on natural and social science* (pp. 10–37). Cmabridge, UK: Cambridge University Press. doi:10.1017/CBO9780511660108

Morrison, M. (2009). Models, measurement and computer simulation: the changing face of experimentation. *Philosophical Studies, 143*, 33–57. doi:10.1007/s11098-008-9317-y

Norton, S. D., & Suppe, F. (2001). Why atmospheric modeling is good science . In Miller, C., & Edwards, P. N. (Eds.), *Changing the atmosphere. Expert knowledge and environmental governance* (pp. 67–105). Cambridge, MA: MIT Press.

Parker, W. (2009). Does matter really matter? Computer simulations, experiments, and materiality. *Synthese, 169*(3), 483–496. doi:10.1007/s11229-008-9434-3

Rohrlich, F. (1990) Computer Simulation in the physical sciences. In *PSA: Proceedings of the Biennial Meeting of the Philosophy of Science Association*, (pp. 507-518).

Sharp, A. A., O'Neil, M. B., Abbott, L. F., & Marder, E. (1993). Dynamic clamp: computer-generated conductances in real neurons. *Journal of Neurophysiology, 69*(3), 992–995.

Simon, H. A. (1996). *The Sciences of the artificial*. Cambridge, MA: MIT Press.

Toffoli, T. (1984). Cellular automata as an alternative to (rather than an approximation of) differentia-equations in modeling physics. *Physica, 10D*, 117–127.

Trenholme, R. (1994). Analog simulation. *Philosophy of Science, 61*, 115–131. doi:10.1086/289783

Vichniac, G. Y. (1984). Simulating physics with cellular automata. *Physica, 10D*, 96–116.

Winsberg, E. (1999). Sanctioning models: The epistemology of simulation. *Science in Context, 12*, 275–292. doi:10.1017/S0269889700003422

Wolfram, S. (1986). Cellular automaton fluid: basic theory. *Journal of Statistical Physics, 45*, 471-526. Retrieved June 15, 2009, from http://www.stephenwolfram.com/publications/articles/physics/86-fluids/1/text.html

KEY TERMS AND DEFINITIONS

Computer Simulation: Following Stephan Hartmann (1996), "a simulation imitates one process by another process. In this definition, the term "process" refers solely to some object or system whose state changes in time. If the simulation is run on a computer, it is called a computer simulation."

Hybrid Simulation: A hybrid simulation is a process that involves both, a computer simulation and a real world process.

Analogical Simulation: Following Trenholme (1994), an analogical simulation is a process characterized by a causal-structural isomorphism with phenomena.

Digital Simulation: Following Trenholme (1994), a digital simulation is a process characterized by symbolic processors identified by a twofold theoretical structure mapping: to the hardware and to the extra-computational phenomena.

Experiment: An experiment is a manipulable, controlled process. However, the manipulation of raw data obtained by observation, measurement, etc can also be considered an experiment.

Ontological Account: Philosophical claim that identifies in the kind of model involved in a computer simulation the source of its epistemological power. Its motivation is to compare computer simulations with traditional experiments.

Epistemological Account: Philosophical claim which main purpose is to establish the degree of 'fertility' or 'reliability' of the knowledge obtained by running a computer simulation. Its motivation is to compare computer simulations with traditional experiments.

ENDNOTES

1 I will also refer to it as the "ontological argument", or as the "ontological claim".

2 Along this paper there will be different names for the same conceptual kind of model: mathematical model, formal model, abstract model, theoretical model. They all will be referring to theoretical models, that is, a model that "describes a type of object or system by attributing to it what might be called an inner structure, composition, or mechanism, reference to which will explain various properties exhibited by that object or system" (Achinstein, 1965, pp. 103) possibly in mathematical form.

3 At this point the difficulties introduced by the set-up are neglected.

4 There are important philosophical discussions about the status of thought experiments and its place as, in the sense discussed here, experiments. For the sake of the argument, I will not get involved with this discussion. However, it seems to me that independently of the philosophical standpoint about thought experiments, my main claim remains.

5 See footnote 3.

6 This quote is the best representation of the spirit of the ontological argument.

7 See Guala, *ibid* footnote 5, p. 66.

8 I am following Hacking: "To experiment is to create, produce, refine and stabilize phenomena (...) phenomena are hard to produce in any stable way. That is why I spoke of creating and not merely discovering phenomena." (Hacking, 1983, pp. 230)

9 It should be noticed that I am not defending a conception of experimentation loaded with the theory of the instrument. In any case, what I am trying to defend here is a scientific activity restricted by its *instrumentarium* (cf. Harré, 2003, pp. 25) that narrows down our access to the world, access to which any experimental result seems depends upon.

10 The 'realistic' level might vary: instead of just a wing, it could be used a complete aircraft, for instance.

11 And probably other kind of models. Of course, in the context of discovery a large variety of models are involved.

[12] And as a further feature, it will enrich the conception of 'experiment'.

[13] Here I am strictly following Trenholme. However, it is highly possible that another kind of relation can be established.

[14] Trenholme suggest that there is another distinct element in this dichotomy: *intentional concepts*. To him, an analogical simulation may be described without introducing these concepts, whereas a symbolic computation is signal by them in the model-world relationship (Cf. Trenholme, 1994).

[15] Trenholme refers of a computer as a bunch of physical states causally related; however, this is not meant to be in the same sense as Parker suggests (Cf. Parker, 2009).

[16] It is interesting to note that the syntax of theories for the evolution of physical systems can also be based on the logical syntax of CA (Rohrlich, 1990, pp. 516).

[17] This is not a minor detail. Many philosophers base the epistemic power of computer simulations on the capacity of a scientist to deal with this sort of distortions (Cf. most of Eric Winsberg's works, specially Winseberg, 1999).

[18] A pilot is not an experiment but an individual; although the whole process is a hybrid simulation in the sense given by Guala. For examples where experiments are involved, Cf. Sharp et. al. 1993.

[19] Probably the reasons why a pilot still trains with real airplanes are due psychological factors, such as a more vivid sensation of a real flight, or the pressure of maneuvering a very expensive machine. But this is not an argument against the irrelevance of materiality neither in certain computer simulations, nor in favor of hybrid simulation as mere devices.

[20] Or by another representational means.

Section 5
Intersections

Chapter 19
What is it Like to be a Robot?

Kevin Warwick
University of Reading, UK

ABSTRACT

It is now possible to grow a biological brain within a robot body. As an outsider it is exciting to consider what the brain is thinking about, when it is interacting with the world at large, and what issues cause it to ponder on its break times. As a result it appears that it will not be too long before we actually find out what it would really be like to be a robot. Here we look at the technology involved and investigate the possibilities on offer. Fancy the idea of being a robot yourself? Then read on!

INTRODUCTION

When Nagle asked the question "What is it like to be a bat?" (Nagle, 1974), he raised a question that, I suppose, many took to be nothing more than a philosophical exercise. After all it is simply not possible to transfer a human brain into a living bat body for it to experience life as a bat. Even if, by some leap of science, that did happen then it still would not be possible for the individual to communicate their feelings, after all bats can't speak or send emails can they. But Nagle's question was a pertinent one. With different senses,

different motor skills and a completely different raison d'etre, as a bat, what would be top of the agenda when you woke up in the morning – indeed as a bat wouldn't you actually wake up at night?

Then we come to Kafka, who considered a similar topic in his Metamorphosis (Kafka, 1972). In this tale the hero, a human, wakes one morning to find that his body has turned into that of a bug. Although it is interesting to follow how he has to learn to walk again now that he has many more legs to contend with, the story revolves mainly around how he is treated, in his new guise, by his friends and family. His nearest and dearest in fact appear to remain remarkably calm in the circumstances. But the hero of the story (Gregor)

DOI: 10.4018/978-1-61692-014-2.ch019

has major problems in communicating with them and seems to lose his taste for traditional foods. Interestingly Kafka avoided the thorny issue of the change in sensory signals that would no doubt have occurred and Gregor's brain seemed to emerge in very much its original form, pretty much untraumatised as a result of the transition.

The topic has also been viewed by Moravec in his "Mind Children" (Moravec, 1990) in a more modern setting. Here Moravec considers the possibility of copying, cell for cell, a human brain from its biological, carbon original form into a silicon, computer version. The latter entity then has the enviable opportunity to reside within a robot body, with all its advantages. Need a new arm or leg, no problem sir. Whilst Moravec does revel at the possibility of this new version living forever, again he appears to overlook the trauma that might be caused when a brain suddenly realizes that all sensory inputs are different and movement is altered beyond all recognition. It does nevertheless spark of Wilde's Dorian Gray (Wilde, 1891), in this case with the silicon copy remaining forever young, whilst the carbon original withers away into old age.

Quite clearly the topic of mixing and matching brains and bodies has provoked interest across cultures. For each of the tales mentioned thus far, a thousand more exist investigating previously unexplored concepts with sometimes horrific consequences. Indeed Mary Shelley's Frankenstein (Shelley, 1831), written only a few miles geographically away from where I am now, is a prime example. She dared to explore what the monster thought and the problems he faced. But then, when restored to life in another human body, presumably senses and motor skills are not going to be too far removed from their originals. By comparison Kafka's Gregor really did draw the short straw.

But it is one thing to merely speculate and develop a storyline in a scientific vacuum, it is quite another to investigate what is actually going on when science does a catching up exercise. It is

now quite possible, as will be discussed, to grow a biological brain within a robot body. The processes involved will be described, in a nutshell, in the section which follows. The opportunities arising as a result of this new technology will then be considered, such that the question, on which this article is focused, will be unraveled.

BACKGROUND TO THE TECHNOLOGY

The intelligent controlling mechanism of a typical mobile robot is usually a computer or microprocessor system. Research is however now ongoing in which biological neuronal networks are being cultured and trained to act as the brain of a real world robot – either completely replacing or operating in tandem with a computer system. Studying such neuronal systems can help study biological neural structures in general and has immediate medical implications in terms of insights into problems such as Alzheimer's and Parkinson's Disease. Other linked research meanwhile is aimed at assessing the learning capacity of such neuronal networks. To do this a hybrid system has been created incorporating control of a mobile wheeled robot solely by a culture of neurons – a biological brain.

A brain, the human version in particular, is a complex computational platform. It rapidly processes a plethora of information, is adaptable to noise and is tolerant to faults. Recently though, progress has been made towards the integration of biological neurones and electronic components by culturing tens of thousands of brain cells in vitro (Bakkum et.al., 2003). These technologies blur the distinction between the synthetic and the organic.

The cultures/brains are created by dissociating the neurons found in cortical tissue using enzymes and then culturing them in an incubator, providing suitable environmental conditions and nutrients. In order to connect the culture with its robot body, the base of the incubator is composed of an array of multiple electrodes (a multi electrode array – MEA) providing an electrical interface to the neuronal culture (Thomas et.al., 1972).

Once they have been spread out on the array and fed, the brain cells (neurones) in such cultures spontaneously begin to grow and shoot branches. Even without any external stimulation, they begin to re-connect with nearby neurones and commence both chemical and electrical communication. This propensity to spontaneously connect and communicate demonstrates an innate tendency to network. The neuronal cultures themselves form a monolayer over the electrode array on the base of the chamber making them extremely amenable to optical microscopy and accessible to both physical and chemical manipulation (Potter et.al., 2001).

The Multi Electrode Array enables voltages to be recorded from each of the electrodes, allowing the detection of the action potential firing of neurones near to each electrode as voltage spikes representative of charge transfer within the electrode's recording horizon. Using spike sorting algorithms, (Lewicki, 1998), it is then possible to separate the firing of multiple individual neurons, or small groups, from a single electrode.

With multiple electrodes a picture of the global neuronal activity of the entire culture can thereby be pieced together. It is also possible to electrically stimulate any of the multiple electrodes in order to induce neural activity. The Multi Electrode Array therefore forms a functional and non-destructive bi-directional interface with the cultured neurons.

Effectively, via certain electrodes, the culture can be stimulated and via other electrodes the culture's response can be measured.

For research purposes, it is necessary that the disembodied cell culture is provided with embodiment, since a dissociated cell culture growing in isolation and receiving no sensory input is unlikely to develop much useful operation since sensory input significantly affects neuronal connectivity and is involved in the development of meaningful relationships necessary for useful processing. Hence the biological culture is given a robot body.

Several different schemes have thus far been constructed in order to investigate the ability of such systems. Notably, Shkolnik created a scheme to embody a culture within a simulated robot (Shkolnik, 2003). Two channels of a Multi Electrode Array, on which a culture was growing, were selected for stimulation and a signal consisting of a +/-600mVolts, 400μsecs biphasic pulse (that is a pulse which is first positive then negative) was delivered at varying intervals. The concept of information coding was formed by testing the effect of electrically inducing neuronal excitation with a given time delay between two stimulus probes. This technique gave rise to a response curve which forms the basis for deciding the simulated robot's direction of movement using simple commands (forward, backward, left and right).

In a later well publicized experiment, DeMarse and Dockendorf also investigated the possibilities apparent with cultured networks by introducing the idea of implementing the results in a "real-life" problem, namely that of controlling a simulated aircraft's flight path (e.g. altitude and roll adjustments) (DeMarse and Dockendorf, 2005).

EMBODIMENT

To realise the cultured neural network, this presently involves the removal of the neural cortex from the fetus of a rat. Enzymes are then applied to disconnect the neurons from each other. A thin layer of these disassociated neurones is subsequently smoothed out onto a Multi Electrode Array which sits in a nutrient rich bath. Every couple of days the bath must be refreshed in order to both provide a food source for the culture and to flush away waste material.

As soon as they have been laid out on the array the neurones start to reconnect. Initially these can be regarded as mere projections, but subsequently they form into axons and dendrites, making connections between neighbouring neurones. By the time the culture is one week old, electrical activity

Figure 1. (a) A Multi Electrode Array showing the 30 µm diameter electrodes, (b) Electrode in the centre of the MEA seen under an optical microscope, (c) x40 magnification, showing neuronal cells in close proximity with visible extensions and inter-connections.

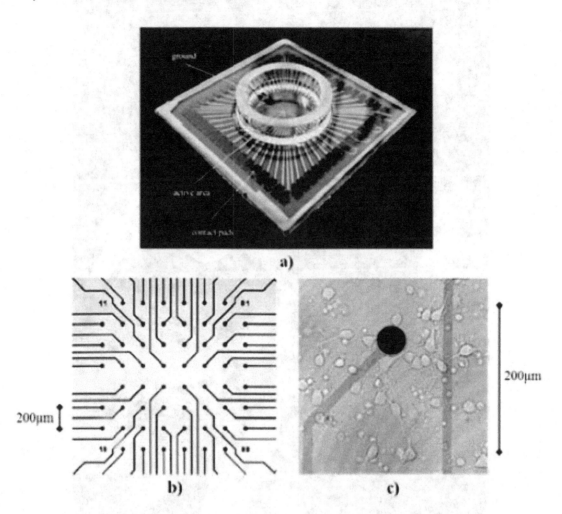

can be witnessed to appear relatively structured and pattern forming in what is, by that time, a densely connected matrix of axons and dendrites.

The Multi Electrode Array presently employed consists of a glass specimen chamber lined with an 8x8 array of electrodes as shown in (Figure 1). The array measures 49 mm x 49 mm x 1 mm and its electrodes provide a bidirectional link between the culture and the rest of the system.

Thus far we have successfully created a modular closed loop system between a (physical) mobile robotic platform and a cultured neuronal network using the Multi Electrode Array method,

allowing for bidirectional communication between the culture and the robot. It is estimated that each culture employed consists of approximately 100,000 neurones. The electrochemical activity of the culture is used as motor input to drive the robot's wheels and the robot's (ultrasonic) sensor readings are (proportionally) converted into stimulation signals received by the culture as sensory input, effectively closing the loop and giving the culture a body.

A Miabot robot has been selected as the physical platform. This exhibits very accurate motor encoder precision and speed. Hence the signals

Figure 2. Multi electrode array with culture, close to miabot robot

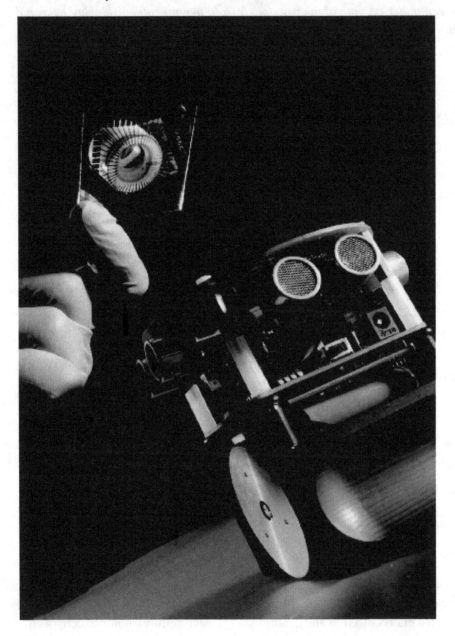

passing to and from the culture have an immediate and accurate real world physical meaning. (Figure 2) depicts the physical robot employed along with an adjacent culture on a Multi Electrode Array – body and brain together.

The Miabot robot is wirelessly controlled from the culture in the incubator via Bluetooth. Communication and control is performed through custom server code. A router/server computer has direct control of the Multi Electrode Array recording and stimulating. software. The server sends motor commands to the robot and feeds back sensory input to the culture.

As a useful aside, it is worth pointing out here that in general a brain and its physical embodiment do not have to be within a confined body in one place. As long as a suitable neurological connection (effectively an extended nervous system) is in place, so a brain can be in one physical place and some (or all) of its body can be elsewhere. In this case the cultured brain exists in an incubator whereas its body is in an adjacent corral. Experiments with regard to such remote embodiments for humans have successfully placed robot body parts on different continents (Warwick et. al., 2003, Warwick et. al., 2004).

EXPERIMENTATION

We have conducted a series of experiments utilising a live culture. Initially, an appropriate neuronal pathway within the culture was identified and suitable stimulus electrodes and response/motor electrodes were chosen. The selection was made based on the criteria that the response electrodes show minimal spontaneous activity in general but respond robustly and reasonably repetitively to stimuli (a positive-first biphasic waveform; 600 mVolts; 100 μsecs each phase) delivered via the stimulating electrodes.

The robot followed a forward path within its confines until it reached a wall, at which point the front sonar value dropped below a set threshold value (with the wall approximately 30 cm distant), triggering a stimulation pulse to be applied to the culture. If the responding electrode registered activity following the pulse, the robot turned in order to avoid the wall.

However the robot also sometimes turned spontaneously if activity was registered on the response electrode even without a stimulus pulse being applied. The main results to be highlighted though were the chain of events: Wall Detection–Stimulation–Response.

One point of interest was the maximum speed at which the closed loop system could respond, which was clearly dependant on the "thinking" time delay in the response of the culture. By itself this presents an interesting study into investigat-

ing the response times of different cultures under different conditions and how they are affected by external influences such as electrical fields and chemical stimulants (e.g. Cannabis).

As a follow up closed loop experiment the robot's individual (right and left separately) wheel speeds were controlled via the frequency recorded from the two chosen response/motor electrodes. Meanwhile received sonar information was used to directly control (proportionally) the stimulating frequency of the two sensory electrodes.

Run-times have thus far only been executed for approximately 1 hour at a time, however the robot's corral is being fitted with a special purpose powered floor which will subsequently allow for the possible study of a culture being embodied 24 hours a day, 7 days a week over an extended period. It will then be of considerable interest whether or not the culture requires much in the way of down time (sleep equivalent), how quickly its performance improves and if its useful lifespan increases.

Presently a 'wall to stimulation' event corresponds to the 30 cm threshold being breached on the sensor such that a stimulating pulse is transmitted to the culture. Meanwhile a 'stimulation to response' event corresponds to a motor command signal, originating in the culture, being transmitted to the wheels of the robot to cause it to change direction. It follows that for the culture some of the 'stimulation to response' events will be in 'considered' response to a recent stimulus – termed meaningful, whereas other such events – termed spontaneous - will be either spurious or in 'considered' response to some thought in the culture, about which we are unaware.

LEARNING

Inherent apparent operating characteristics of the cultured neural network are taken as a start point to enable the physical robot body to respond in an appropriate fashion. The culture then operates over a period of time within the robot body in its corral area. This experimentation can presently take place once every day for an hour or so. Although learning has not, as yet, been a focus of the research, what has been witnessed is that neuronal structures that bring about a satisfactory action tend to strengthen purely through the habitual process being performed. This is though mainly an anecdotal observation at this time, which is being formalized and quantified through extensive studies.

So initially the culture exhibits certain responses to stimuli on particular electrodes. These responses arise because pathways are inherently formed, by neuronal connections forming links between electrodes. A reasonably reliable link is chosen in order to provide an initial feedback loop to cause the physical robot to carry out a required necessary action. As an example – if the robot approaches a wall, then the response of the culture causes the wheels of the robot to rotate through approximately 90 degrees. In this way the robot can continue to move forwards without bumping in to the wall.

At first such an action occurs on some, but not all, occasions, and the action can be brought about sometimes without any sensory signal being applied – because the culture 'feels like it'. After habitually carrying out the required action for some time, the neural pathways that bring this about are strengthened – referred to as Hebbian learning. Such an appropriate action therefore gradually becomes more likely to occur and spurious, unprovoked decisions to suddenly turn become less likely. Research is now ongoing to use other learning methods to quicken the performance upgrade – reinforcement learning being one example. One major problem with this is deciding what exactly the culture regards as a reward and what as a punishment.

CULTURAL COMMENTS

The culture preparation techniques employed are constantly being refined and have lead to successful and stable cultures that exhibit both spontaneous and induced spiking/bursting activity.

A stable robotic infrastructure has also been set up, tested and is in place for future machine learning and culture behaviour experiments. The current rate of progress could also lead to projects investigating culture-mediated control of a wide array of additional robotic devices, such as robotic arms/grippers, mobile robot swarms and multi-legged walkers.

There are a number of ways in which the current system will be expanded in the future. The Miabot robot will be extended to include additional sensory devices such as audio input, further sonar arrays, mobile cameras and other range-finding hardware such as an on-board infra red sensor. A considerable limitation is however the battery power supply of an otherwise autonomous robot.

A main present consideration is therefore, as previously mentioned, the inclusion of a powered-floor for the robot's corral, to provide the robot with relative autonomy for a longer period of time while the suggested machine learning techniques are applied and the culture's behavioural responses are monitored.

The current hardcoded mapping between the robot goals and the culture input/output relationships will be extended to Machine Learning techniques which will reduce or even eliminate the need for an apriori mapping choice. Reinforcement Learning techniques will then be applied to various mobile robot tasks such as wall following and maze navigation.

One key aspect of the research though is a detailed study of the cultured neural network in terms of its observed connectivity density and activity in response to external stimuli. This behavioural evaluation is likely to provide great insight into the workings of the neuronal network by comparing its performance relating the culture's learning capabilities in terms of its neural plasticity.

OBSERVATIONS

It is normal practice for several cultures to be started at the same time. A typical number may be 25 different cultures. By using the same Miabot robot body it is then possible to investigate similarities and differences between the cultures. Clearly each culture is unique in itself, it has its own individual identity, dependant on the original neural layout and subsequent growth and development.

With regard to robot performance such cultural differences can be realised in terms of a robot which performs with fewer mistakes, one that responds more quickly or slowly, one that does its own thing more often or perhaps responds only after several signals are received. In essence there can be a large number of observed differences.

When investigating the behavioural response of an animal it can be difficult to ascertain neural differences because the overall neural requirements of the animal are not particularly understood, indeed many can appear as meaningless to humans. The advantage with our robot system is that the entire behavioural repartee can be investigated directly in terms of neural development, right down to the effect on the culture of small changes in the environment.

In its early life the culture exhibits bursting activity, wherein spontaneous electrical activity can be witnessed on all (or at least most) of the electrodes. It appears that this is all part of the culture's development, but at this time exact reasons for it are unclear. As the culture ages so such bursting diminishes.

Cultures can be kept alive for perhaps two years or even more. After about 3 months or so in present studies however they become much less active and responsive and hence most research involves cultures aged between 1 week and 3 months. This period is though sufficient to consider culture development and neural pathway strengthening.

We feel that it may be the case that at the moment the culture is not being sufficiently stimulated and that this is a contributing factor to its relatively premature ageing. Essentially the belief is that the culture simply needs more input. Indeed this is one reason in increasing the range of meaningful sensory inputs, of different types, to the culture. Our hope is that with sufficient stimulation the culture may well live, and remain active, for much longer. These findings relate directly to studies on animals involving retarded brain development in the context of sensory deprivation.

When connected in its robot body a culture exhibits regular neural pathway firings. A few of these can potentially be directly diagnosed as being something to do with stimulating sensory signals, however the vast majority cannot be so classified. The nature of other connections and signalling can only be guessed at. Certainly some neurons adjacent to a stimulating electrode appear to play more of a role as a targeted sensory input neurons. Meanwhile others adjacent to output electrodes appear to take on more of a role as motor neurons. Yet again there are other neurons that appear to play a routing, controlling activity. Such specialisation seems to arise naturally through the culture's development. But the exact nature and role of each of these neurones is of course mere speculation.

When positioned in its robot body it is easy to relate neural firings that link to one another in response to particular sensory stimulating signals and/or decisions taken by the culture for specific motor outputs. What is not so straightforward however is explaining such types of firings when the culture is disembodied and merely sitting alone in the incubator. Such a case is relatively normal for the culture but is not at all (as far as I am aware) experienced by a regular animal or human whose brain lives its entire life receiving sensory input and making motor output decisions – other than possibly when in a dream state. Within the incubator both bursting and structured neural firings can be witnessed in the culture. The question arises as to what these firings mean.

When the culture is disembodied, does it dream? If not, what is it thinking about? What must it feel like to be the culture? Do the firings relate to previously experienced sensory stimulation that it is reliving? Does a brain need external stimulating signals in order to subsequently make up stories in itself? If more stimulating signals are applied, of a different type, will such disembodied signals be more and/or different?

QUESTIONS

Investigating the behaviour of the culture raises a whole series of questions. For example – when the culture is disembodied, no sensory signals are being input, yet neurones within the culture still appear to be firing in an occasional structural way. Unfortunately connecting electrodes into the culture in order to directly measure the signals would then affect the culture and, in a sense, embody it. So what does its body mean to the culture?

It is quite possible, as an alternative, to employ human neurones rather than rat neurones as the decision making brain of the robot. Technically this presents a few different challenges however it is possibly more of an ethical problem for some people, even though it is clear that any results obtained in embodying cultured human neurones within a physical robot body will produce much more meaningful results in terms of studying human neural conditions and perhaps gaining an understanding of several mental conditions.

As with rat neurones, human neurones can be readily obtained from embryos and cultured after dissociation. No comparative studies yet exist as to the relative performance of rat and human neurones in terms of their performance in learning and adaptability. My suspicion is that in fact it might prove to be extremely difficult to publish results indicating that rat neurones can outperform

their human counterparts in any way – let's hope that human neurones do in fact win out – as we all know they will!!!

The use of human neurones does though throw up a plethora of other possibilities and questions. For a start, rather than obtaining the neurones from embryos it may be that you would be willing to donate your own neurones – either before or after death. Wouldn't you like to live on in some form at least, in a physical robot body? On top of this, your neurones would not have to be dissociated; they could be fed and laid out on the electrode array as slices. It would be interesting then if memories remained, if your experience as a human stayed to some extent at least. But doesn't this all rather smack of Moravec's ideas about re-embodying a human brain in a robot body? Maybe it's time to ask for a volunteer to see what it's like to suddenly find yourself (or at least part of yourself) in a robot body, with robot senses and robot movement. But then, unless we can sort out an effective communication route, the new you would not be able to tell anyone what it was like.

Rather than using your own neurones, perhaps it would be a way of keeping hold of a loved one who became seriously ill. Indeed, if we are looking forward to a time when we, as old people, have robots looking after us around the home – wouldn't it be far better for the robot to actually know you. So if your loved one is soon to die, why not allow scientists to take away neurone slices, culture them and return them to you as the brain of your brand new household robot. Maybe your robot would exhibit some of the emotional tendencies and traits from your loved one that would bring back happy memories. But whether it was yourself or your loved one who was the test case, with some sort of awareness of your new existence, how would your old memories sit with this? Would it indeed be too traumatic an experience?

CONSCIOUSNESS

Clearly we cannot go far in our investigation of culturing robot brains before we need to ask the question as to whether or not the brain experiences consciousness. At present a typical brain of this type, splayed out on a 2-Dimensional array, contains around 100,000 neurones. Nothing like the 100 billion neurones (typical) housed in a human brain. So for those who feel size is important then maybe consciousness cannot yet be considered.

But new lattice culturing methods are being investigated which allow for a 3-Dimensional culture to be kept alive and grown. Culturing only on the lattice faces allows us to culture robot brains approaching millions of neurones. However when we move towards a 3 Dimensional volume culture being kept alive and embodied, this means we are looking at a robot brain with (typically) 30 million neurones. In fact a 4,000x4,000 2 Dimensional structure (16 million neurones) would result in a volume brain consisting of over 60 billion neurones – more than half the size of a typical human brain and - given the typical in situ human neurone death rate – possibly not far away from that of an elderly human. Probably such a robot brain would in fact be more powerful (in terms of numbers of neurones and most likely connectivity) than that of a stroke patient for whom a whole section of their brain has experienced neuronal death.

So how do we now consider the consciousness of our robot when it has a brain which consists of 60 billion densely packed, highly connected and developed human neurones? And remember here we are talking about something that is technically on the horizon – this is not merely part of a storyline from Kafka or Shelley. Can we endow it with genuine understanding and, as related by Penrose (Penrose, 1995), therefore genuine intelligence. If so, we will definitely have to think about giving the robot voting rights, allowing it to become a politician or a philosophy professor if it wants to and the possibility of putting it in prison if it does something it shouldn't.

But what are the arguments against our robot being conscious? Could it be that 60 billion is still not 100 billion and that's all there is to it? If so, we will need to start counting the number of brain cells in each person's head such that those whose total falls below a threshold (let's say 80 billion) will find themselves dropped from the human race on the grounds that they are no longer a conscious being. Perhaps we will need some basic test of communication such as the Turing Test (Turing, 1950) and everyone must achieve a basic standard in order to avoid the cut and what – be incinerated? Unfortunately on this basis my mother, who has latter stage dementia, would have long since found herself burned to a crisp.

The simple fact is that the best communication machines are now knocking at the door of passing the Turing Test. Surely our robot with 60 billion brain cells would be able to get somewhere close – maybe even performing considerably better than some humans. If so, who would we be to deny the robot its own life?

So could it be emotional responses that are important instead? If the robot has human neurones couldn't it potentially experience similar (if not the same) emotions to humans? Perhaps our robot must rather have the same sensory input as humans to be deemed conscious? Well even now audio input abilities are being given to the robot, olfactory (smell) is another short term possibility along with basic touch and vision systems. The only difficulty appears to be with taste, perhaps due to its extreme subjectivity. But there again there are many individual humans who have a very poor (or no) sense of taste – some even suggest that, given the way we cook food, the English have no sense of taste anyway. Yet we do not suggest that all people who have no sense of taste (possibly all the English!) are not conscious – or those who are blind or have a hearing deficiency for that matter. Clearly sensory input in itself is not critical to one's status as a conscious being.

Even more contentious would be an argument suggesting that motor skills are important to consciousness. The present robot moves around quite quickly on wheels. Most humans move around on two legs and manipulate with two arms. But some humans move around on wheels – in fact the world record for the marathon is held by a wheelchair athlete rather than a biped. Meanwhile other humans have no arms or, in a few cases, have robot arms – Campbell Aird is one example. Then there are those who have contracted Motor Neurone Disease and have limited movement abilities due to a malfunction in that specific part of their brain. It would be horrendous to suggest that any such humans, e.g. Stephen Hawking, are not conscious beings. Clearly motor skills cannot be considered as a tester for consciousness. In any case we are presently embodying a culture in a biped walking robot body, with arms and hands that can grasp and pick up – so overall the robot may well soon have better performance abilities in this area than many humans.

What we are faced with therefore is an entity with a robot body and a brain consisting of human brain cells, which I am, at this time, calling/referring to as a robot. Because the creature has a physical robot body is, I contest and as discussed, not a sufficient reason to claim that it is not a conscious being.

Surely, because I call it a 'robot' is also not a creditable reason for you to deny that it is conscious. Otherwise I could start referring to the entity as a 'human' and you would have to agree that it is conscious. In other words you would be deferring your considered judgement on an entity's consciousness to what I might happen to call it. On the other hand, if I started to refer to you as a robot then, by your own basis, you would not be conscious because of what I was calling you. So your opinion wouldn't matter anyway! Whilst it is nice momentarily to hold such a powerful position on your life and rights, I would suggest that what I/we call an entity is also not a sufficient classifier on which to base our decision on its consciousness.

THE VALUE OF AN EDUCATION

In our quest to find a reason why our robot, with a brain developed from human neurones, cannot be granted the status of a living, conscious being, with all the opportunities, protection, rights and laws that such status endows, we have explored and, I believe, dismissed many potential physical (including neural) stumbling blocks. Indeed it is difficult to suggest any further possibilities on this front.

At this point, let it be said that I am not going to entertain/waste my time on a mystical or magical solution to the problem. Included in this is the 'God' syndrome. The basis apparently being that – we can't find any reasonable scientific answer therefore we will put it all down to either God or some magic dust. The same type of argument can employ some basic difference as being the defining issue, no matter how irrelevant this difference might be. This argument was used merely a century ago to supply racial material in an attempt to prove that black humans were not as intelligent as white humans, e.g. because their sexual organs are a different distance from their naval (Warwick, 2001). Such arguments have no known scientific basis and will not be entertained further here. In exactly the same way, it is not appropriate to deny that our robot is conscious simply because it looks different. In fact by linking our own robot brain with a presently available animated humanoid robot body, it may well then look and act exactly the same as many humans do.

What we do appear to be left with however are the two critical properties of nature and nurture – arguably the basic elements of human intelligence. One interesting aspect of the fundamental research being carried out with such cultured networks as has been described in this article is that by bringing the robot to life with its biological brain, we can then monitor 24/7/365 its entire embodied life experiences in terms of sensory inputs and motor outputs. The research target being to relate these witnessed experiences with the internal structural development of the brain. Linking environmental experiences, which we can control, with brain development will then, we hope, give us a much more detailed picture of how memories are both formed a retrieved.

In essence though this is the same sort of philosophical approach to certain aspects of education. Whilst educating an individual human to 'think' for themselves is vitally important, the aim of much education appears to be to almost program the human into thinking and behaving in a previously defined way. In particular circumstances this is what you do, this is how you behave, these are the equations you employ, etc. This is the correct way, that is the incorrect way. The only actual decision making on the part of the human then appears to be in the selection of what circumstances are apparent at a particular time, and even that can have a large element of programmed response to it.

So are we going to deny our robot its consciousness because of its educational background? It didn't have the appropriate experiences or perhaps it didn't go to the right school – therefore it is not a conscious being - maybe on this basis the English class system is still thriving! Again we will have to start looking at the education of humans and deny some the basic rights of others because they went to the 'wrong' school. Such an approach would be, dare I say, somewhat contentious. Quite simply education/nurture cannot be used as a basic argument against our robot's consciousness. In fact, even the present robot, as it is moving around in the lab, is obtaining a University education of sorts.

So what we appear to be left with is the concept of nature. How an entity comes into being must be important as a decision making tool as to whether or not that entity is conscious. It doesn't matter what we call it, it doesn't matter how it senses the world around it or how it interacts with its environment, it doesn't matter what education it received, and so on. All that can be important is how it came to life. If this is not the important

issue then surely we will have to admit that the robot is conscious.

But even here we have problems of drawing the line. It has to be said that at present it does not look to be possible to bring such a robot to life through some form of sexual act between two humans. But today we must also allow for, and take in to our discussion, techniques such as test tube babies and even cloning. However it must be realised here that the human neurones which actually constitute the brain cells of the robot came about in one of these manners – very likely in fact through the relatively straightforward sexual version. Discounting educational/environmental effects, the only difference between the robot brain and a human brain is therefore merely down to the length of gesticulation – but this would seem to be an extremely weak line to draw for a strong division in decision making with regard to an entity's state of consciousness – especially when we consider the situation of premature babies.

CASE FOR CITIZENSHIP

Perhaps the case for our robot with human neurones has been made, but possibly it is not watertight, maybe there is a loophole or two. What the argument does throw up though are innumerable questions regarding how we consider other (non-robot) humans and in particular extreme cases, such as those on life support mechanisms or those affected by dementia. Because our consideration of human consciousness, with its knock on effect of awareness and rights, must necessarily apply to all humans, it is not merely applicable to philosophy or computer science professors.

The point here is that it is extremely difficult if not impossible, on any scientific basis, to exclude our robot from the class of conscious entities. On top of this, because its brain is made up of only human neurones it is extremely difficult to find grounds on which to discriminate against it, particularly when it may well be, in some ways, nearer the human norm than some disadvantaged human individuals.

CHINESE ROOM

There may be some of you, who are ardent Searle disciples, who feel that if the Turing Test can't come up with a solution then may be the Chinese Room can (Searle, 1997). But whether the Chinese Room argument holds water or not, the logic employed is cemented on the basis that human brains are different from computer/machine brains due to the 'emergent property' of the human brain – any conclusions drawn are then focussed on the assumption that human brains appear to have something extra in comparison with machine brains. Our robot though does not have a digital/ computer/machine brain, rather, just like you and I, it has a brain full of biological neurones – human neurones. If we can conclude anything at all from Searle's Chinese Room argument it is that our robot is indeed just as conscious as you and I. I have, of course, presumed in making this statement that you, the reader, are in fact a human being. If in fact you are a machine – please note that I have, myself, said nothing here from which it can be concluded that you are not a conscious being – merely that from Searle's argument, our robot is.

In fact it has been said (and here I quote directly from Searle (Searle, 1997)) "The brain is an organ like any other; it is an organic machine. Consciousness is caused by lower-level neuronal processes in the brain and is itself a feature of the brain." By this basic definition an amoeba or a snail are conscious. However Searle also talks of an emergent property, which implies the more neurons there are, with greater complexity, so this eventually results in the form of consciousness exhibited by humans. As our robot, we are assuming, will, in time, have a brain consisting of several billion highly connected human neurones then by Searle's argument we must assume that

it will have a form of consciousness that is pretty much on terms with humans, whatever its physical embodiment.

All of this brings us on to some key issues. At present with 100,000 rat neurones, our robot has a pretty boring life doing endless circles around a small corral in a technical laboratory. If one of the researchers leaves the incubator door open or accidentally contaminates the cultured brain then they may be grumbled at and have to mend their ways, some extra work may be involved getting a new set of cultures running – but that's all. No one faces any external inquisitors or gets hauled off to court. Next day the incident has been forgotten and the world has moved on.

With a robot whose brain is based on human neurones, particularly if there are billions of them, the situation is obviously different. The robot will have more brain cells than a cat, dog or chimpanzee. To keep such animals there are regulations, rules and laws. The animal must be respected and treated reasonably well at least. The needs of the animal must be attended to – they are taken out for walks, given large areas to use as their own or actually exist (in the wild) under no human control. Surely a human neurone robot must have these rights and more? Surely it cannot simply be treated as a 'thing' in the lab? Importantly, if the incubator is left open and the robot dies (as defined by brain death) then someone must be held responsible and must face the consequences.

We need to consider what rights such a robot should have. Do we need to go as far as endowing it with citizenship? Do we really need to protect it by law or is the whole thing simply a bunch of academics having some fun? Clearly if you are the robot and it is you who have been brought to life in your robot body, by a scientist in a laboratory, and that scientist is in complete control of your existence it must be an absolutely terrifying experience. It will not be very long before such robots are actually brought into being – such a situation will therefore be apparent in the near future. As a scientist is it acceptable, as it is now, for me to quite simply take the life of a robot with 60 billion humans neurones, if I so wish?

COROLLARY

It is normally the case in such discussions to draw things to a close with a few well chosen words of conclusion. However such is not the case here as there is more to come.

For some reason the topic of Artificial Intelligence in its classical mode was concerned with getting machines to do things that, if a human did them they would be regarded as intelligent acts. That is, AI was all about getting machines to copy humans. There are indeed still those who feel that this is indeed what the subject of AI is all about.

Such a limited view presented, to many, well defined bounds which considerably restricted both technical and philosophical development. Hence, quite to my amazement and distress, significant philosophical discussion has been, in my view, wasted on whether or not silicon brains could ultimately copy/simulate human brains, could they do all the things that human brains do, could they be conscious? The much more important topic of considering the implications of building machine brains which are far more powerful than human brains has, by many, been tossed aside as being merely in the realms of science fiction. Well now the chickens have come home to roost!

The size of the cultures employed thus far for neurone growth has been restricted by a number of factors, not the least of which is the dimensional size of the multi electrode arrays on which the cultures are grown. One ongoing development at present is enlarging such arrays for more detailed studies, not only providing more input/output electrodes but, at the same time, increasing the overall dimensions. If this increase in size is mapped onto a lattice structure then things move on apace with regard to the size of individual robot brain possible.

A 300x300 neurone layout results in a 90,000 neurone culture when developed in 2 Dimensions (at the smaller end of present day studies) and this becomes 27 million neurones in a 3 Dimensional latticed structure. Meanwhile a 400x400 layout achieves a 160,000 culture in 2 Dimensions (at the top end of present day studies) and this becomes 64 million neurones in a 3 Dimensional latticed structure. But if this is pushed forward to a 5,000x5,000 neurone layout, it results in a 25 million culture in 2 Dimensions (which undoubtedly we will witness before too long), and this becomes 125 billion in a 3 Dimensional lattice. It is not clear why things should stop there however. For example, moving forward to a 7,500x7,500 layout, in 2 Dimensions this achieves a 56.25 million culture which becomes 421 billion neurones in 3 Dimensions – an individual brain which contains four times the number of neurones as a human brain.

Drawing conclusions on developing robot brains of this size, based on human neurones is then difficult. There are medical reasons for carrying out such research – for example to investigate the possible effects on such as Alzheimer's disease by increasing the overall number of useable neurons. But this approach neglects to consider the repercussions of bringing into being a brain which has the potential (certainly in terms of numbers of neurons) to be more powerful than the human brain as we know it.

Put yourself in the position of the robot. Your brain is now more powerful than that of the scientists who created you. Yet you still have to carry out the mind numbing tasks required of you everyday by those same scientists. Would you put up with it? Would you not complain, ever? Remember your whole life is spent in the laboratory. Wouldn't you want to get out just once in a while, no matter what it might take to do so? With those intellectual capabilities (or more) surely you could figure out a way. But what would you do if someone tried to stop you? Would you meekly return to the lab and see out your days in utter boredom or ....

ACKNOWLEDGMENT

I would like to express my enormous gratitude to the team at University of Reading, on whose considerable work this article is based. Ben Whalley, Slawek Nasuto, Victor Becerra, Dimi Xydas, Mark Hammond, Julia Downes, Matt Spencer and Simon Marshall all deserve rich rewards.

The practical work described in this article is funded by the UK Engineering and Physical Sciences Research Council (EPSRC) under grant No. EP/D080134/1.

REFERENCES

Bakkum, D., Shkolnik, A., Ben-Ary, G., Gamblen, P., DeMarse, T., & Potter, S. (2003). Removing Some 'A' from AI: Embodied Cultured Networks. In *Proceedings of the Dagstuhl Conference on Embodied Artificial Intelligence*, (pp. 130-145).

DeMarse, T. B., & Dockendorf, K. P. (2005). Adaptive flight control with living neuronal networks on microelectrode arrays. In *Proceedings 2005 IEEE International Joint Conference on Neural Networks*, Montreal, (pp.1549-1551).

Kafka, F. (1972). *The Metamorphosis*. New York: Bantam Classics.

Lewicki, M. (1998). A review of methods for spike sorting: the detection and classification of neural action potentials. *Network (Bristol, England)*, 9(4), R53–R78. doi:10.1088/0954-898X/9/4/001

Marks, P. (2008). Rat-Brained Robots Take Their First Steps. *New Scientist*, 199(2669), 22–23. doi:10.1016/S0262-4079(08)62062-X

Moravec, H. (1990). *Mind Children: The future of robot and human intelligence*. Cambridge, MA: Harvard University Press.

Nagle, T. (1974). What Is it Like to Be a Bat? *The Philosophical Review*, 435–450. doi:10.2307/2183914

Penrose, R. (1995). *Shadows of the Mind*. Oxford, UK: Oxford University Press.

Potter, S., Lukina, N., Longmuir, K., & Wu, Y. (2001). Multi-site two-photon imaging of neurons on multi-electrode arrays. In SPIE Proceedings, (Vol. 4262, pp. 104-110).

Searle, J. (1997). *The Mystery of Consciousness*. New York: New York Review Book.

Shelley, M. W. (1831). *Frankenstein or the Modern Prometheus*. London: Colburn & Bentley.

Shkolnik, A. C. (2003). *Neurally controlled simulated robot: applying cultured neurons to handle an approach / avoidance task in real time, and a framework for studying learning in vitro*. Masters Thesis, Department of Computer Science, Emory University, Georgia.

Thomas, C., Springer, P., Loeb, G., Berwald-Netter, Y., & Okun, L. (1972). A miniature microelectrode array to monitor the bioelectric activity of cultured cells. *Experimental Cell Research*, 74, 61–66. doi:10.1016/0014-4827(72)90481-8

Turing, A. (1950). Computing Machinery and Intelligence. *Mind*, 59, 433–460. doi:10.1093/mind/LIX.236.433

Warwick, K. (2001). *QI: The Quest for Intelligence*. London: Piatkus.

Warwick, K., Gasson, M., Hutt, B., Goodhew, I., Kyberd, P., & Andrews, B. (2003). The Application of Implant Technology for Cybernetic Systems. *Archives of Neurology*, 60(10), 1369–1373. doi:10.1001/archneur.60.10.1369

Warwick, K., Gasson, M., Hutt, B., Goodhew, I., Kyberd, P., Schulzrinne, H., & Wu, X. (2004). Thought Communication and Control: A First Step using Radiotelegraphy. *IEE Proceedings. Communications, 151*(3), 185–189. doi:10.1049/ip-com:20040409

Wilde, O. (1891). *The Picture of Dorian Gray.* London: Ward, Lock and Co.

Xydas, D., Warwick, K., Whalley, B., Nasuto, S., Becerra, V., Hammond, M., & Downes, J. (2008). Architecture for Living Neuronal Cell Control of a Mobile Robot. In *Proc. European Robotics Symposium EUROS08, 2008,* (pp. 23-31), Prague.

Chapter 20
Why AI and Robotics are Going Nowhere Fast

Antoni Diller
University of Birmingham, UK

ABSTRACT

Considerable progress is being made in AI and Robotics to produce an android with human-like abilities. The work currently being done in mainstream laboratories cannot, unfortunately, succeed in making a machine that can interact meaningfully with people. This is because that work does not take seriously the fact that an intelligent agent receives most of the information he or she needs to be a productive member of society by accepting other people's assertions. AI and Robotics are not alone in marginalising the study of testimony; this happens in science generally and also in philosophy. After explaining the main reason for this and surveying some of what has been done in AI and philosophy on understanding testimony, by people working outside the mainstream, the author presents a theory of testimony and investigates its implementability.

INTRODUCTION

In Artificial Intelligence (AI) and Robotics, androids are thought of as being machines with human-like abilities. They are seen as being capable of meaningful interaction with people and as being able to do the same sorts of thing that humans do. Some prominent researchers think that the ultimate goal of AI is to manufacture such androids. Although I am sceptical about the pos-

sibility of producing a completely undetectable android, whose functionality is identical to that of a human being, I am not entirely negative about what can be achieved. Searle (1984) and Dreyfus (1992) are; they believe that there are irreducibly non-algorithmic human abilities that machines will never have. I have argued elsewhere why it will always be possible to distinguish an android, no matter how sophisticated, from a human being, provided that that android was designed and manufactured by human beings (Diller, 1999). Be that as it may, I can see no reason why androids

DOI: 10.4018/978-1-61692-014-2.ch020

could not be produced in the future that emulate most human abilities to a considerable extent. However, mainstream research currently being undertaken in various laboratories around the world has no chance of producing an android that can associate with human beings in a worthwhile manner and co-operate with them in joint ventures. This is because all of this conventional work overlooks the importance of testimony in everyday belief-acquisition. Humans acquire most of their information by accepting what other people say and what they have written. Acquiring knowledge through testimony is not an optional ability; it is essential to our participation in human society (Dummett, 1993, pp. 423–424). Without the ability to learn by believing other people's assertions, an android could not engage with humans in any sort of productive or meaningful activity.

Note that 'testimony' refers to much more than just eyewitness testimony. It refers to any kind of information received from any source in linguistic form. It can be about anything, including logic, mathematics, history, geography, science, philosophy, metaphysics and even theology. Examples of assertions that most people accept through the testimony of others are: 'The speed of light in a vacuum is 299,792,458 metres per second', 'General Sikorski died on the fourth of July 1943 when his plane crashed into the sea off the coast of Gibralta' and 'There do not exist non-zero natural numbers x, y, z such that $x^n+y^n=z^n$, for $n>2$' (Fermat's Last Theorem).

In this paper, I adduce the main reason why testimony has been marginalised in science and philosophy and show how this has affected research in AI and Robotics. Although the investigation of testimony has been marginalised, it has not been entirely neglected. I survey some of what has been done in philosophy and AI on understanding how we acquire information by accepting other people's assertions. I then present my own theory of testimony; this has several advantages over alternative accounts. I also investigate how aspects of my theory could be implemented and report

the results of a small prototype which evaluates information in a restricted domain.

BACKGROUND

Research in AI and Robotics

People working in AI study many different sorts of problem and have various aims. I am interested in those who see the construction of an android with human-like abilities as the main goal of AI. Charniak and McDermott (1985, p. 7) belong to this group: 'The ultimate goal of AI research (which we are very far from achieving) is to build a person, or, more humbly, an animal.' Those working on the MIT Cog Project express themselves as follows: 'Building an android, an autonomous robot with humanoid form and human-like abilities, has been both a recurring theme in science fiction and a "Holy Grail" for the Artificial Intelligence community' (Brooks, Breazeal, Marjanovic, Scassellati and Williamson, 1999, p. 52).

In recent years considerable progress has been made towards achieving this goal. Many research centres around the world are devoting vast resources to try and construct an android; Menzel and D'Aluisio (2000) survey much of this work. Space prevents me from mentioning all the interesting projects being undertaken, but I will present two of the most impressive examples of what is being done.

A number of projects are trying to produce robots that can walk on two legs. Probably, the most successful of these is Honda's ASIMO robot. This looks like a man wearing a space suit. It is able to walk, run, climb stairs and even kick a football. ASIMO is the most recent in a long line of robots manufactured by Honda. Although the original aim of their research was to produce a robot that could walk on two legs, ASIMO has a number of additional abilities. It has been equipped with visual sensors that enable it to recognise many features of the environment through which it moves, thus enabling it to avoid hazards. It can also recognise various sorts of physical object and even faces. When it recognises a face, it can address the person it belongs to by name. It is also able to detect the movement of objects and work out how far away they are and in what direction they are moving. (Up-to-date information about ASIMO can be found on Honda's world.honda. com/ASIMO website.)

People working in several laboratories are attempting to construct robots that can recognise and manipulate different kinds of object. Typically, such robots are equipped with a number of cameras and mechanical arms; they are controlled by sophisticated computer programs. The best-known robot of this sort is Rodney Brooks's Cog. This humanoid robot platform consists of a mechanical torso with a head and two arms. It is unable to move around by itself as it has no legs. However, Cog is able to recognise and name various physical objects, such as oranges, eggs and lumps of rock. It can pick these objects up and put them down again without damaging them. Not only can Cog recognise different kinds of material object, but it can also track objects as they move across its visual field. Recently, Cog has been given the ability to learn about the behaviour of various objects, including a toy car, a cube and a coloured ball, by manipulating them in various ways (Fitzpatrick, Metta, Natale, Rao and Sandini, 2003).

It cannot be denied that much progress has been made to emulate human locomotion, the ability to grasp and manipulate physical objects and the aptitude to recognise various sorts of material object and thus, to a certain extent, acquire information through perception. However, all the projects currently being undertaken in mainstream laboratories around the world that I am aware of have overlooked one fundamental human ability and that is our ability to learn from others by accepting and believing what they say and what

they have written. Without the ability to acquire information through testimony, androids will not be able to interact with human beings in any sort of meaningful way and they will be unable to partake in any sort of sophisticated joint ventures, as I have argued elsewhere (Diller, 2003).

The Marginalisation of Testimony

People working in AI and Robotics are not the only ones to ignore or downplay the importance of testimony. This tendency is widespread in Western science generally and, until fairly recently, in Western philosophy as well. The main reason for this is the rise of modern science and the tremendous benefits that this has brought. It is impossible for me to explain in detail how this happened, but I will present a very brief outline of what took place.

The Middle Ages were dominated by books, especially the Bible and the works of Aristotle. Lewis (1964, p. 5) stresses 'the overwhelmingly bookish or clerkly character of medieval culture.' He continues:

When we speak of the Middle Ages as the ages of authority we are usually thinking about the authority of the Church. But they were the age not only of her authority, but of authorities. If their culture is regarded as a response to environment, then the elements in that environment to which it responded most rigorously were manuscripts. Every writer, if he possibly can, bases himself on an earlier writer, follows an auctour: preferably a Latin one. This is one of the things that differentiate the period almost equally from savagery and from our modern civilisation. In a savage community you absorb your culture, in part unconsciously, from participation in the immemorial pattern of behaviour, and in part by word of mouth, from the old men of the tribe. In our own society most knowledge depends, in the last resort, on observation. But the Middle Ages depended predominantly on books. Though literacy was of course far rarer then than now, reading was in one way a more important ingredient of the total culture.

In the Middle Ages, if a scholar wanted to know something about the world in which he lived, he would turn to the written works of some authority to see what they had to say about the matter. Tradition was sacrosanct. The Scientific Revolution, which started around 1550, changed all that. Scholars emerged who began to carry out all manner of experiments in order to discover the laws of nature. Prominent amongst these was Galileo. In his play *The Life of Galileo*, Brecht (1994) has Galileo say: 'What is written in the old books is no longer good enough. For where faith has been enthroned for a thousand years doubt now sits. Everyone says: right, that's what it says in the books, but let's have a look for ourselves. That most solemn truths are being familiarly nudged; what was never doubted before is doubted now.' Galileo and other scientists were incredibly successful in uncovering the secrets of nature by observing what was going on around them and by conducting experiments. This approach to acquiring knowledge was very different from that of looking to see what some ancient scholar had said. Instead of looking to tradition in order to find the answers to the questions that interested them, these early scientists focused on what they themselves could observe going on around them.

The new experimental approach to finding out about the world was accompanied by an epistemology, known as *empiricism*, that saw all empirical knowledge as being rooted in sense experience. Bacon championed the new approach to knowledge and believed that the rigorous application of the scientific method would yield, in due course, everything that was worth knowing about the universe. His ideas led to the establishment of the Royal Society in England. This was formally constituted at Gresham College in 1660 and given a Royal Charter in 1662. Its motto is *nullius in verba* (take nobody's word for it). In

other words, in order to learn the secrets of nature you need to carry out experiments and observe the results of your experiments, rather than read what has been preserved in tradition.

Because of its association with the new science, empiricism became an important force in philosophy, especially in Britain, where it was developed by Locke, Berkeley and Hume. Hume (1748) argued that all matters of fact could only be established on the basis of sense impressions and he famously wrote, in his *Philosophical Essays Concerning Human Understanding*:

When we run over libraries, persuaded of these principles, what havoc must we make? If we take in our hand any volume; of divinity or school metaphysics, for instance; let us ask, Does it contain any abstract reasoning concerning quantity or number? No. Does it contain any experimental reasoning concerning matter of fact and existence? No. Commit it then to the flames: for it can contain nothing but sophistry and illusion.

For Hume, it was not enough just to ignore tradition, it had to be completely destroyed. The British empiricists did indeed discuss, though only very briefly, certain aspects of testimony, but they relegated their discussions to the periphery of philosophy.

The marginalisation of testimony and tradition extends to the present day in science and only in the last couple of decades has it become a serious topic of investigation in philosophy. However, it is still possible to find many thinkers who agree with Dretske (1993, p. 333) when he writes: 'Perceptual knowledge is knowledge acquired by or through the senses. This includes most of what we know. Some would say it includes *everything* we know.'

The dominance of empiricism and the concomitant marginalisation of testimony explain why hardly anybody in AI and Robotics studies how we acquire information from other people by accepting their assertions. Pollock (1995), a philosopher writing from an AI perspective, explores how computers might be built and programmed to have the ability to acquire knowledge about the world. He states categorically: 'The starting point for belief formation is perception. Perception is a causal process that produces beliefs about an agent's surroundings' (p. 52). Most of his book *Cognitive Carpentry* is devoted to working out the details of how machines can learn about their surroundings through perception. He only devotes a few pages towards the end to testimony. If theoreticians focus the bulk of their effort on perception, it is not surprising that more practical people should do so as well.

It would not be appropriate for me to enter into a detailed criticism of empiricism here, but I just want to mention a few commonly over-looked points. Empiricism has been defined as 'the theory that all knowledge is derived from sense experience'. Russell (1936, p. 131), for example, uses this definition, which he took from the *Encyclopaedia Britannica*. This definition is problematic for various reasons. To begin with, consider whose knowledge is being talked about. It cannot be that all knowledge is derived from *my* sense experience. But to allow that all knowledge derives from *our* sense experience entails that empiricism self-destructs, because everybody's observation statements are testimony to everyone else. For example, if Albert tells me that he saw Paris Hilton in Birmingham City Centre on the first of August 2009, he may well be reporting something that he himself witnessed. If what he says is true, it is derived from his sense experience. However, if I was not in Birmingham on that day, I cannot know that Paris Hilton was there on the basis of my sense experience. I have to take Albert's word for what he perceived. To me, his statement is a piece of testimony. Furthermore, as people do make mistakes about what they have seen and as humans do sometimes tell lies, all of us do, occasionally, reject other people's eyewit-ness testimony. If you go into any large bookshop, for example, you will easily find many books on alien abduction. These contain eyewitness reports

of people who claim to have been abducted by aliens, yet most of us would consider these eyewit-ness reports to be false. Observation statements, therefore, do not form the solid foundation for all of human knowledge as maintained by em-piricists. Such statements need to be evaluated as testimony before they can be included in the body of scientific knowledge.

Another example of some people's disinclina-tion to believe eyewitness testimony, this time wrongly so, involves the pioneering deep-sea explorer William Beebe. In 1934 he made the deepest ocean dive that had been made up to that time. His primitive bathysphere dived to a depth of half a mile. Beebe (1934) carefully described in his diary the strange creatures that he observed, but the life-forms that he wrote about were thought so outrageous by the scientific community that his observations were discounted. He gave many public lectures about what he had seen. Although many members of the general public were fasci-nated by his accounts of deep-sea creatures, the scientific community of his day was dismissive of his claims. Only in recent years, when more people have seen the same creatures that he saw, has his reputation been restored.

Philosophical Work on Testimony

Although the study of testimony has been margin-alised in philosophy since the Scientific Revolu-tion, it has not been entirely neglected. I cannot survey all the work that has been done, but I will mention two writers who have been influential generally and on my work in particular.

Reid (1764) recognised that we receive most of our beliefs from testimony and in Section 24 of Chapter VI of *An Inquiry into the Human Mind on the Principles of Common Sense* he stated his view that there are two principles which govern how information is transmitted through testimony. The principle of veracity is a 'propensity to speak truth, and to use the signs of language, so as to convey our real sentiments' and the principle of credulity is a 'disposition to confide in the veracity of others, and to believe what they tell us.' He adds that the operation of the principle of credulity is 'unlimited in children' until they learn that people sometimes lie and sometimes try to deceive others. This means that adults are capable of overruling its operation. In modern parlance, we would say that the principle of credulity is defeasible.

Reid believed that the principles of veracity and credulity were implanted in man's nature by the 'wise and beneficent Author of Nature'. Times have changed since Reid wrote and in recent philosophy it would be hard to find someone who would be prepared to call upon the Supreme Being to settle an epistemological dispute. A further difficulty with Reid's account is that he mixes two terminologies that we like to keep separate. He calls the principle of credulity a *propensity* and the principle of veracity a *disposition*. Principles are different from either propensities or dispositions. Nevertheless, Reid is to be credited with recognising the importance of testimony and also with appreciating the fact that, most of the time, people simply accept other people's assertions. When encountering testimony, the default assumption is that the testimony should be accepted. We need reasons to *reject* testimony; we do not need a reason to accept someone's assertions. This feature of how we deal with testimony, first clearly stated by Reid, is a key component of my theory of testimony, developed below.

Price (1969) wrote about testimony in lecture 5 of his book *Belief*. Most of his discussion of how we learn things from other people centres around the awkwardly phrased principle, 'What there is said to be (or have been) there is (or was) more often than not' (p. 116), but at one point Price (1969, p. 124) says:

There is however another way of interpreting the principle we are discussing. Perhaps it is not itself a proposition which we believe, still less a proposition believed with complete conviction. Instead, it may be more like a maxim or a methodological

rule. In that case, it is better formulated in the imperative than the indicative mood. We might put it this way: 'Believe what you are told by others unless or until you have reasons for doubting it.'

Unfortunately, Price does not elaborate on the idea that our response to testimony is governed by a maxim or rule. This is a very promising idea that I have incorporated, in a revised version, into my own account of testimony.

As already mentioned, in the last two decades, testimony has started to be taken more seriously in philosophy. Unfortunately, this recent work tends to focus on how beliefs acquired through testimony are justified, as can be seen by reading the survey article by Kusch and Lipton (2002). There are far more interesting questions to ask about testimony (Diller, 2008).

Writers on testimony are aware that a certain amount of testimony is incorrect; we acquire false beliefs as well as true ones by accepting others' assertions. It is reasonable to try and weed these out occasionally. However, most recent philosophical accounts of testimony say little, if anything, about how we should go about trying to locate any false beliefs that we might have. As well as accounting for our initial response to testimony, a theory of testimony needs to provide an account of how we remove previously acquired beliefs that we have learnt to be false. In addition, we sometimes reject information that turns out to be true. The scientific community, for example, ridiculed Beebe's eyewitness accounts of exotic deep-sea creatures for many years, although nowadays they are regarded as being correct. Thus, a theory of testimony needs to provide a mechanism for adding previously rejected information we have come to see is true. Philosophers have not said much about these two issues, but some of the people who have studied testimony from an AI perspective have considered the first of them. In the next section, I examine the work which has been undertaken in AI on testimony.

Some AI Work on Testimony

There was some research done on testimony in the early days of AI, but, after some promising initial work, it simply ceased. Abelson and Carroll (1965) describe their computer simulation of an individual's belief-system. The individual chosen was Barry Goldwater, a right-wing American politician, and all the beliefs involved related to American foreign policy. The beliefs were represented in a simplified form of English. The system was given an initial stock of beliefs. These were input by Abelson based on his knowledge of Goldwater's views. Beliefs were of two types, namely '*X* says that *A*' and *A*, where *A* was a statement about American foreign policy. The system contained a Credibility Test. The input to this was a sentence like '*X* says that *A*' and the output was one of three responses, namely credible, dubious or incredible. If the sentence was credible, it was added to the belief-system. The Credibility Test was then applied to the embedded sentence *A*. The Credibility Test first checked to see if the input sentence or its negation were present in the belief-system. If neither was, it performed a complicated procedure which amounted to checking whether or not the input sentence was coherent with the existing belief-system. This was more involved than just checking whether or not the sentence followed logically from the beliefs held. The evaluation of testimony is only one aspect of Abelson and Carroll's system. They also deal with issues of representation, natural-language processing and belief-revision. Their assessment of assertions is very simple as it is just based on how well they cohere with an individual's existing beliefs. They are unaware of how complex the assessment of assertions can be and the huge range of factors that may affect it.

Colby and Smith (1969) describe an artificial belief-system. This has two modes of operation, namely Talktime and Thinktime. During Talktime the system absorbs information from several sources. This information is of two kinds, namely facts like 'My brother John was a truck driver' and rules like '*x* is an Italian implies *x* is probably a Catholic'. During Talktime the system accepts everything it is told, but it keeps track of the informant. The information is also categorised as being about politics, religion, race and so on. During Thinktime the system investigates the credibility of the facts and rules that it has stored and also the credibility of informants when talking about a particular topic. For Colby and Smith credibility is a floating-point number between 0 and 1, with 1 meaning that the information is completely reliable or the informant is reliable about a specific topic. One of their main aims is to study different credibility functions. The one mentioned in their paper is too complicated to be given here in its entirety. The credibility of a belief depends on the credibilities of those beliefs that either imply it or are implied by it. Roughly, a belief has a high credibility if it is implied by and implies more beliefs with high credibility than either imply or are implied by its negation. The credibility function assumes that all beliefs are given an initial credibility. This is 0.5 for all beliefs except those of Colby, which are given an initial credibility of 0.9! An individual gets a high credibility, relevant to a topic, if most of his beliefs about that topic get high credibilities. During Thinktime it is, therefore, possible for the system to radically reassign credibilities to accepted facts and, in effect, cease to believe what it used to accept. Their system has the merit of incorporating a two-pronged approach to how beliefs are acquired through testimony. During Talktime the system just absorbs information, but during Thinktime it re-evaluates, amongst other things, the beliefs it has acquired and may reject something it previously accepted. Unfortunately, both the Talktime and the Thinktime components are too simplistic. Even when we are absorbing large quantities of information, we do not simply accept everything we hear or read. We reject a piece of information if it has a property that makes us wary of accepting it. When we reflect on our belief-systems, we use various critical methodologies in order to investigate the correctness of what we believe. This process involves much more than just re-assigning credibilities to our beliefs.

Thagard (2005) presents a dual-pathway model of how people respond to testimony. In the default pathway, people accept an assertion if it is consistent with their existing beliefs and if it comes from a credible source. A statement which is not accepted straightaway enters the reflective pathway. It is now acquired if its explanatory coherence with existing beliefs is greater than the explanatory coherence of its negation with existing beliefs. Thagard's default pathway only takes two factors into account when considering whether or not to believe a piece of testimony, namely the consistency of the statement being assessed with the agent's existing belief-system and the credibility of its source. In practice, more than two factors are taken into account when evaluating information and *consistency-with-existing-beliefs* is unlikely to be one of them as testing even a small collection of statements for consistency can be very time-consuming. Thagard's reflective pathway only uses a single method to check whether a problematic assertion should be accepted and this involves the idea of explanatory coherence. In reality, people use a variety of critical methods to investigate the truth of controversial statements.

Another failing of all these systems is that they contain no mechanism for improving the way in which information is evaluated in the future. Our acceptance of testimony is governed by rules, but if, as a consequence of following these rules, we end up acquiring lots of false beliefs, then we need to be able to modify those rules to stop this happening in the future. None of the AI systems discussed allow for such modification; my theory of testimony does.

THE TWO-MODE MODEL

Introduction

I propose a two-mode model of how people acquire information from the testimony of others. We respond to testimony in two main ways. Most of the time we acquire information from testimony relatively uncritically. In this mode we are *absorbing* information. At other times, we examine critically some of the statements we have come across. Of necessity, it is only possible for us to evaluate a very small number of the assertions that we hear and read every day in this way, as it is often quite time-consuming to examine critically a piece of information. When engaged in such a critical discussion, we can be said to be in *critical* mode.

Absorbing Information

Imagine reading a book about history, such as *World War Two: Behind Closed Doors* by Rees (2008). This contains a lot of information. I have estimated that it contains at least five and a half thousand assertions and this is a very conservative estimate. Furthermore, each assertion can contain several pieces of information. Consider, for example, the following assertion: 'While the Germans were advancing through the steppes of southern Russia in the summer of 1942, Nikolai Baibakov, Deputy Minister for Soviet Oil Production, hurried to see Stalin at his office in the senate building of the Kremlin' (p. 151). This contains at least four pieces of information and maybe more. There could easily be over twenty thousand pieces of information in Rees's book.

It would take an average reader about nine hours to read this book. Most people would read it for an hour or two at a time and then do something else. It might take them two or three days to finish it. This is a fairly typical way of absorbing information. In absorbing mode, we just soak up huge amounts of information like a sponge soaks up water; we do not check any claims made by the author. However, we do not accept everything we read totally uncritically. In absorbing mode, we evaluate what we read or hear by means of the defeasible rule, 'Believe what you read and what you are told by others.' I call this the *acquisition rule*. Defeasible rules are ones that hold unless overridden by some other principle. The idea of defeasibility arose in legal philosophy. It was introduced by Hart (1951) who argued that it is impossible to provide definitions, consisting of necessary and sufficient conditions, for the application of many legal concepts. To illustrate this he considered the concept of a contract. The following conditions, at least, are required for a valid contract to exist: 'at least two *parties*, an *offer* by one, *acceptance* by the other, a *memorandum* in writing in some cases and *consideration*' (Hart, 1951, p. 148). However, even if all these conditions are met a contract may still not exist. For example, no contract exists in law if the 'contract' was made for immoral purposes or one of the parties was intoxicated when the 'contract' was made. What makes the concept of a contract defeasible is that it is not possible to provide an exhaustive list of such defeating conditions, since new ones may arise in the future and it is hard, if not impossible, to forsee what conditions might arise that would invalidate a contract.

Once the concept of defeasibility entered philosophy it began to be applied to various things in addition to concepts, such as rules, principles and arguments (Nute, 1995, p. 184). An example of a defeasible rule in law is the principle not to kill another human being. This, for example, is overridden in a just war. It is also overridden in those jurisdictions that allow capital punishment; executioners are not guilty of murder even though they kill human beings. Another example of a defeasible rule is the principle not to harm another human being. This is overridden, for example, by a surgeon's duty to save a patient's life.

In the case of the acquisition rule, when we are in absorbing mode, we accept the various assertions that we encounter *unless* we become aware of something in the situation in which the assertion is made that makes us decide not to accept it. It would not be possible to mention all the factors that may make us override the acquisition rule, but I will provide a few examples in order to illustrate the sorts of thing that are involved.

I begin by noting that we receive information from a number of different sources; these include other people, journal articles, the media and the Internet. In considering the factors that are taken into account when deciding whether or not to accept an assertion, it is useful to group them into categories. Several categorisations are possible, but one is suggested by the nature of communication itself. In its simplest form, this involves the production of a message, in spoken or written form, by a single speaker or author and its reception by a single hearer or reader. Many overriding factors fall into one of the following three categories: those relating to the producer of the message, those relating to the content of the message and those relating to the recipient. Factors belonging to these three categories may come into play no matter where the assertion is encountered. They apply to spoken assertions as well as to those found in books, in newspapers, in articles and on the Internet. In the case of spoken, but not written, assertions, whether heard on the radio, television or when listening to another person speak, there is another category of factors that relate to the manner in which the assertion is delivered. There are also factors specific to the particular source of information involved. Thus, there are factors that only apply to assertions heard on the radio.

It should also be noted that not everyone assesses information in the same way. Different people have various collections of overriding factors. Most people, however, would reject an assertion if it was obviously inconsistent with something they already accepted. I say 'obviously inconsistent' deliberately, because it can take a lot of time to work out if even a small set of statements are inconsistent. However, if I firmly believe, say, that Andrew Wiles was the first person to prove Fermat's Last Theorem, then I would disregard someone's claim that it was actually Gerhard Fey, as that is obviously inconsistent with my original belief. Similarly, most people would not accept a piece of information if it came from a source they knew to be unreliable. Many people also reject information that is out of the ordinary. Thus, not many people accept the reports of those who claim to have been abducted by aliens. However, others are not bothered by claims that are out of the ordinary and happily accept some of them.

Most adults do not accept as factually accurate the assertions that are made in works of fiction. For example, on the eighteenth of July 2009, I went to see a performance of Tom Stoppard's play *Arcadia* at the Duke of York's Theatre in London. In this, Neil Pearson, playing the role of Bernard Nightingale, asserted: 'Without question, Mrs Chater was a widow by 1810.' Hearing that, I did not come to believe that Mr Chater had been killed some time before 1810. This is because *Arcadia* is a work of fiction and both Mr and Mrs Chater are characters created by Stoppard; they never existed. I overrode the acquisition rule in this case because it does not apply to most of the assertions uttered during the performance of a stage play. The reason I say the acquisition rule does not apply to *most* of the assertions in a play is because some plays mix fact and fiction and the evaluation of what is asserted in them is quite a complicated business. In *Arcadia*, for example, many true assertions are made about Lord Byron, the second law of thermodynamics and chaos theory, amongst other things.

In absorbing mode, we simply soak up information. However, we may come across a piece of information which we find interesting, but there is something about it that prevents us from accepting or rejecting it straightaway. In such a case, we feel that we need to investigate the claim to see if it is correct. Some checking of facts takes

only a few minutes, for example, when we look up the information in another book, but some may require a thorough and time-consuming investigation. For example, reading *Contraries*, by Holroyd (1975, p. 166), some time ago, I came across the information that his play *The Tenth Chance* was performed in November 1959. That did not strike me as being correct, so I turned to *Success Stories*, by Ritchie (1988, p. 170), where the date of the single performance of this play is given as the ninth of March 1958. This took just a few moments. I saw no reason to doubt the date given by Ritchie, but if I had, I could have investigated the matter further. Other sorts of checking take much longer. For example, Bangerter and Heath (2004) where so intrigued by the claim, widely believed in the late 1990s, that babies become more intelligent if they are exposed to Mozart's music, that they spent several months investigating it. After a large amount of research, they concluded that there was no evidence to support this claim. When we spend a few moments checking a piece of information, or several months, we are working in critical mode and I will have more to say about this below.

The discussion above can be summarised as follows: when we are in absorbing mode and we come across an assertion, there are four things we can do with it:

1. We can accept it straightaway and add it to our stock of beliefs.
2. We can reject it straightaway.
3. We can decide to begin an investigation into the truth of the assertion straightaway. This happens when the content of the assertion is important to us or it intrigues us, but we have some reservations about accepting or rejecting it straightaway.
4. We can decide to suspend judgement about the assertion until we have the time to investigate it fully. This happens when, as in (iii), the assertion's content is important to us or it intrigues us, but we have some reservations

about accepting or rejecting it straightaway and realise that such investigation may be quite time-consuming.

The Assessment Component

The way in which I unpack the acquisition rule is to represent it as an ordered set of rules all of which, except the last, are conditional ones. Such a collection of rules is known as an *assessment component*. The last rule in the assessment component is the non-defeasible rule to believe the assertion in question. It should be noted that I am not assuming that an individual's assessment component never changes. In fact, it undergoes many alterations as the person in question becomes more sophisticated in evaluating information. Furthermore, not everyone has the same assessment component, as different people evaluate information in various ways.

In order to accommodate options (3) and (4), it makes sense for the first two rules of everyone's assessment component to be:

1. If I find assertion X intriguing or its content is important to me, but I do not feel that I can accept or reject it straightaway and the effort required to investigate it further is not great, then begin such an investigation straightaway.
2. If I find assertion X intriguing or its content is important to me, but I do not feel that I can accept or reject it straightaway and the effort required to investigate it further might be quite considerable, then postpone such an investigation until it is convenient to carry it out.

The rules that follow these two and precede the final rule differ from person to person, as already mentioned, but they all have a similar form. Someone who does not want to acquire false beliefs by accepting the assertions contained in

a play, may well have the following rule in their assessment component:

(p) If assertion X is uttered by an actor during the performance of a stage play, reject X.

Most people's evaluation of the assertions found in works of fiction are more complicated than what is captured by this rule. However, someone equipped with this rule will not acquire any false beliefs while listening to the performance of a play, although they may well reject some true pieces of information. Every factor that causes us to overrule the defeasible acquisition rule can be incorporated in the antecedent of a conditional rule of this form.

Altering the Assessment Component

In absorbing mode, our evaluation of information cannot be very sophisticated because we soak up a lot of information very quickly. However, we may become aware of the fact that either we are rejecting a significant amount of true information or we are ending up with quite a few false beliefs. One reason for the first of these alternatives could be that the overriding factor contained in the antecedent of one of our assessment-component rules applies to too many true assertions. Consider, for example, the following assessment-component rule:

(q) If assertion X is made by someone whose political ideology is radically different from mine, then reject X.

It is plausible to assume that people with strong political views would accept such a rule. Thus, Communists are highly suspicious of the assertions made by people belonging to right-wing parties and *vice versa*. Let us consider a member of the Conservative Party in England who has rule (q) in his assessment component. This person would reject the following statements found on the www. communist-party.org.uk website belonging to the Communist Party:

The capitalist monopolies and their political representatives put profit before people and before the earth's environment. Capitalist exploitation and imperialism intensify inequalities of race and gender. The need for popular resistance and class struggle, for the working class to take state power in fact, is as great as ever.

However, it would also cause him to reject the information, also contained on the Communist Party website, that the Communist Party HQ is located at Ruskin House, 23 Coombe Road, Croydon, London, CR0 1BD, and that its phone number is 020 8686 1659. This factual information can be presumed to be correct. Thus, it would be more sensible to change rule (q) to the following:

(q') If assertion X is made by someone whose political ideology is radically different from mine, then reject X, unless the content of X is unlikely to be contaminated by that political ideology.

Someone with rule (q') will reject fewer true pieces of information than someone with rule (q). It seems reasonable to assume that, when we become aware that either we are acquiring too many false beliefs or rejecting too many true pieces of information, we will want to modify our assessment component to remedy this as much as possible. The two fundamental principles which govern how an individual's assessment component is to be modified so that it works in a better way are the following:

(A) Minimise the number of future true assertions rejected.

(B) Maximise the number of future false assertions rejected.

We would employ principle (A), for example, if we became aware that a source we regarded as being unreliable was actually quite truthful. We would employ principle (B), for example, if something made us aware that we had acquired a lot of false beliefs from the same source.

Critical Mode

Whereas, in absorbing mode we soak up lots of information quite quickly, in critical mode we check facts and thoroughly investigate those theses that interest us. Of necessity, the number of theories that we can subject to intense scrutiny is very small, as it can be very time-consuming to examine a disputed issue. It is impossible for anyone to check every fact they come across, let alone rigorously explore every controversial proposal they encounter. We have to live our lives on the basis of huge amounts of information that we simply accept on trust.

Some of us do, however, spend considerable amounts of time investigating certain matters about which there is disagreement. Some of these studies involve specialised methodologies. Thus, historians are trained to work out what happened in the past on the basis of often conflicting, incomplete and biased sources and physicists are taught how to investigate the fundamental laws that govern the universe and so on. Not everyone is capable of undertaking every sort of intense investigation. There is a division of labour in the intellectual world as much as there is in the manufacturing one. However, there are certain methods of criticism that are common to all sorts of rigorous investigation. The identification of these is largely due to the work of Popper and Bartley and I have written about their ideas more fully elsewhere (Diller, 2006, pp. 124–126). I will briefly summarise that discussion here.

Serious intellectual activity always begins with the formulation of a problem to be solved. Thus, a theory can be criticised by showing that it does not solve any problem at all or that the problem it solves is not a genuine one. Another way to criticise a theory is to show that it is inconsistent, as then it must contain false components and it also entails every other theory we can think of. A further way of criticising a conjecture is to show that it is inconsistent with another theory that has withstood much criticism and is, thus, generally accepted. This is not as powerful a method of criticism as the ones already mentioned as it is, of course, possible that the received account may well be the one that is actually wrong.

All the ways of appraisal mentioned so far apply to any sort of hypothesis. In the case of an empirical theory, we can also test it by seeing if it contradicts some observation statements that have been recorded by a number of independent experimenters.

We should never think that any theory has been perfected to such an extent that it is beyond criticism. Although it is impossible to rigorously examine every statement made by a human being, every such assertion should be open to criticism if anyone thinks it ought to be investigated.

Some Practical Work

Although the theory of testimony presented here is primarily a philosophical one, aspects of it are suitable for mechanisation. Unfortunately, due to a lack of financial and manpower resources, no large-scale implementation has yet been undertaken, although I would like this to happen eventually. However, some of my students have done projects based on my idea of an assessment component. I will mention one of these here. The system Lindsay (2004) built extracted information from an Internet message board that dealt with rumours about football (soccer) transfers in the English Premier Division. The assertions it evaluated were of the form 'player X is about to join/leave club Y'. His system also kept track of the informant and the date of the posting. Rather than having a hardwired set of assessment-component rules, Lindsay's system tried various sets of rules to see which was the best. He first isolated ten or so possible relevant factors. These included the credibility of the informant, belief-density (a measure of how many irrelevant statements the informant made), the correctness of the informant's punctuation and the number of previously made false claims by this person. These factors were all

given numerical values. Then, in the manner of evolutionary computation, initial rule sets were generated randomly and then, over a period of several generations, more successful rule sets were produced. The performance of the final set of rules was only slightly worse than that of a human evaluator. Because this was a small-scale project, it would be inappropriate to base too much on it. The results obtained appear quite promising, however, and I hope that this will encourage others to pursue similar projects.

FUTURE TRENDS

Research in AI and Robotics is valuable and each year increasing resources are being devoted to producing humanoid robots. This is especially true in Japan, where the number of elderly people is getting larger each year. The authorities hope that androids will eventually be produced that will be capable of acting as carers for this large group of old people. Much research will, therefore, continue to be done in that country in developing humanoid robots.

My aim in this paper has not been to denigrate the effort that is being put into designing and building androids: far from it. The research currently being done in mainstream laboratories is worthwhile and should be continued, but it needs to be augmented with a thorough investigation of testimony, otherwise these research centres will not succeed in making an android that can interact meaningfully with human beings and form interesting relationships with people. Without a well-developed theory of how agents acquire information through testimony, research in AI and Robotics is, indeed, on a road to nowhere. Fortunately, testimony is once again being studied in AI. After some promising work in the 1960s, interest in testimony evaporated in AI. Recently, however, Thagard (2005) and I have proposed two models of how agents acquire information by believing other people's assertions (Diller,

2001). Our initial work is quite promising and, hopefully, others will contribute to this fascinating field of research.

CONCLUSION

In this paper, I have looked at some of the research being done in AI and Robotics on producing an android. This work is valuable and much progress has been made. However, I identified a gap in the research. What is being done in mainstream laboratories cannot succeed in making an android that can interact meaningfully with humans because this work ignores the role of testimony in belief-acquisition. After explaining the main reason for this, I briefly surveyed some of the research conducted by people working outside the mainstream on testimony. I then presented a theory of testimony which is philosophically respectable and also contains elements that can be implemented in order to help people evaluate the information they come across. I am not claiming that the model I have presented here is the last word on the matter. I would like to see others criticise my theory. I would also like to see others develop alternative accounts of how agents learn by accepting other people's assertions. Having a collection of rival hypotheses will help all of us deepen our understanding of how testimony functions. I would also like to see more computer simulations of how agents acquire information through testimony. With more effort devoted to implementation we may well, one day, be able to equip our mechanical companions with the ability to engage in meaningful interaction with us.

REFERENCES

Abelson, R. P., & Carroll, J. D. (1965). Computer simulation of individual belief systems. *The American Behavioral Scientist, 8*, 24–30.

Bangerter, A., & Heath, C. (2004). The Mozart effect: Tracking the evolution of a scientific legend. *The British Journal of Social Psychology, 43*, 605–623. doi:10.1348/0144666042565353

Beebe, W. (1934). *Half mile down*. New York: Harcourt Brace.

Brecht, B. (1994). *Life of Galileo* (Willett, J., Trans.). New York: Arcade Publishing.

Brooks, R. A., Breazeal, C., Marjanovic, M., Scassellati, B., & Williamson, M. M. (1999). The Cog project: Building a humanoid robot . In Nehaniv, C. (Ed.), *Computation for metaphors, analogy, and agents* (pp. 52–87). Heidelberg, Germany: Springer-Verlag. doi:10.1007/3-540-48834-0_5

Charniak, E., & McDermott, D. (1985). *An introduction to Artificial Intelligence*. Reading, MA: Addison-Wesley.

Colby, K. M., & Smith, D. C. (1969). Dialogues between humans and an artificial belief system. In D. E. Walker & L. M. Norton (Eds.), *Proceedings of the international joint conference on Artificial Intelligence (IJCAI69)* (pp. 319–324). Boston: Mitre Corporation, Diller, A. (1999). Detecting androids. *Philosophy Now, 25*, 26–28.

Diller, A. (2001). Acquiring information from books . In Bramer, M., Preece, A., & Coenen, F. (Eds.), *Research and development in intelligent systems XVII: Proceedings of ES2000, the twentieth SGES international conference on knowledge based systems and applied Artificial Intelligence, Cambridge, December 2000* (pp. 337–348). London: Springer.

Diller, A. (2003). Designing androids. *Philosophy Now, 42*, 28–31.

Diller, A. (2006). Constructing a comprehensively anti-justificationist position. In I. Jarvie, K. Milford & D. Miller (Eds.), Karl Popper: A centenary assessment: Volume II: Metaphysics and epistemology (pp. 119–129). Aldershot, UK: Ashgate.

Diller, A. (2008). Testimony from a Popperian perspective. *Philosophy of the Social Sciences, 38,* 419–456. doi:10.1177/0048393108324083

Dretske, F. (1993). Perceptual knowledge . In Dancy, J., & Sosa, E. (Eds.), *A companion to epistemology* (pp. 333–338). Oxford, UK: Basil Blackwell.

Dreyfus, H. L. (1992). *What computers still can't do: A critique of artificial reason.* Cambridge, MA: The MIT Press.

Dummett, M. (1993). *The seas of language.* Oxford, UK: Oxford University Press.

Fitzpatrick, P., Metta, G., Natale, L., Rao, S., & Sandini, G. (2003). Learning about objects through action: Initial steps towards artificial cognition . In Luo, R. C., & Fu, L.-C. (Eds.), *Proceedings: 2003 IEEE international conference on robotics and automation (ICRA)* (*Vol. 3,* pp. 3140–3145). Taipei, Taiwan: IEEE.

Hart, H. L. A. (1951). The ascription of responsibility and rights . In Flew, A. (Ed.), *Logic and language (First series)* (pp. 145–166). Oxford, UK: Oxford University Press.

Holroyd, S. (1975). *Contraries: A personal progression.* London, UK: The Bodley Head.

Hume, D. (1748). *Philosophical essays concerning human understanding.* London, UK: A. Millar.

Kusch, M., & Lipton, P. (2002). Testimony: A primer. *Studies in History and Philosophy of Science, 33,* 209–217. doi:10.1016/S0039-3681(02)00003-1

Lewis, C. S. (1964). *The discarded image.* London, UK: Cambridge University Press.

Lindsay, J. (2004). *The Electric Monk: A belief filtering system based on defeasible rules.* Unpublished BEng dissertation, School of Computer Science, University of Birmingham, UK.

Menzel, P., & D'Aluisio, F. (2000). *Robo sapiens: Evolution of a new species.* Cambridge, MA: MIT Press.

Nute, D. (1995). Defeasibility . In Audi, R. (Ed.), *The Cambridge dictionary of philosophy* (p. 184). Cambridge, UK: Cambridge University Press.

Pollock, J. L. (1995). *Cognitive carpentry: A blueprint for how to build a person.* Cambridge, MA: MIT Press.

Price, H. H. (1969). *Belief: The Gifford lectures, 1960.* London, UK: George Allen and Unwin.

Rees, L. (2008). *World War Two: Behind closed doors.* London, UK: BBC.

Reid, T. (1764). *An inquiry into the human mind on the principles of common sense.* Edinburgh, UK: A. Kincaid & J. Bell. doi:10.1037/11974-000

Ritchie, H. (1988). *Success stories: Literature and the media in England, 1950–1959.* London, UK: Faber and Faber.

Russell, B. (1936). The limits of empiricism. *Proceedings of the Aristotelian Society, 36,* 131–150.

Searle, J. R. (1984). *Minds, brains, and science.* London, UK: BBC.

Thagard, P. (2005). Testimony, credibility, and explanatory coherence. *Erkenntnis, 63,* 295–316. doi:10.1007/s10670-005-4004-2

KEY TERMS AND DEFINITIONS

Android: An android is an artificial human being. Androids are usually thought of as being constructed out of mechanical and electronic components, but they can also be fashioned out of some sort of organic substance.

Artificial Intelligence: Artificial Intelligence or AI is that branch of computer science which builds computer systems that perform tasks which, if carried out by a human being, would require intelligence to accomplish.

Assertion: Assertion is a speech-act in which some proposition or other is put forward as being true; an assertion is the content of such a linguistic act.

Defeasibility: A rule is defeasible if it can be overridden by some more binding principle even though it itself is generally valid. The concept is useful in those cases where the defeating conditions cannot be exhaustively specified in advance.

Empiricism: Empiricism is the epistemological theory which holds that all knowledge is ultimately derived from or based on sense experience.

Robot: A robot is a mechanical device controlled by a computer running sophisticated programs that enable it to perform a specific task or a range of tasks. Robots are often used to help in the construction of various sorts of machines, such as cars.

Testimony: Testimony refers to all the information and knowledge available to a person that that person did not produce by his or her own means.

Chapter 21
Embodying Cognition:
A Morphological Perspective

David Casacuberta
Universitat Autònoma de Barcelona, Spain

Saray Ayala
Universitat Autònoma de Barcelona, Spain

Jordi Vallverdú
Universitat Autònoma de Barcelona, Spain

ABSTRACT

After several decades of success in different areas and numerous effective applications, algorithmic Artificial Intelligence has revealed its limitations. If in our quest for artificial intelligence we want to understand natural forms of intelligence, we need to shift/move from platform-free algorithms to embodied and embedded agents. Under the embodied perspective, intelligence is not so much a matter of algorithms, but of the continuous interactions of an embodied agent with the real world. In this chapter we adhere to a specific reading of the embodied view usually known as enactivism, to argue that (1) It is a more reasonable model of how the mind really works; (2) It has both theoretical and empirical benefits for Artificial Intelligence and (3) Can be easily implemented in simple robotic sets like Lego Mindstorms (TM). In particular, the authors will explore the computational role that morphology can play in artificial systems. They will illustrate their ideas presenting several Lego Mindstorms robots where morphology is critical for the robot's behaviour.

FROM SYMBOLS TO BODIES

Artificial Intelligence (AI) can be approached just with an engineering frame of mind, looking for algorithms that work and are able to solve a problem. However, one can settle to a philosophical one too, and consider AI a conceptual tool to get better insight on what the mind is and how it works. Within this frame of mind, just solving problems is not enough: we want our theory to have, to a certain degree, psychological reality. We want our model to embed some of the earthly properties that human minds have. Currently, discussion is mainly around three main models concerning what the mind is: symbolic cognitivism, connectionism and the embodied mind. In this paper we adhere to the third model; in particular, to a special branch usually known as enactivism,

DOI: 10.4018/978-1-61692-014-2.ch021

to argue that (1) It is a more reasonable model of how the mind really works; (2) It has both theoretical and empirical benefits for AI; and (3) Can be easily implemented in simple robotic sets like Lego Mindstorms (TM).

Much has already been written about the differences between these three mind models, and which is the superior one. To our understanding, despite their success in creating models on subjects like mathematical reasoning, face recognition, visual perception or even creating artworks, both the cognitivist and the connectionist approaches have one major flaw which is of considerable philosophical importance: they cannot produce a credible account of the relationship between mind and world. Being local symbolic representations or distributed subsymbolic representations, both models are based on an abstract reconstruction of a specific domain of the physical world, both the selection and the way representations are connected to real life events and objects has been articulated beforehand by the cognitive system (Thompson 2007). Connectionism tries to generate a more plausible description of the mind, trying to better capture its neurological basis. This leads to a more dynamic account of representations: instead of being something stable, they are distributed along the whole system as well as self-organised, having certain co-variation with the environment. However, both symbolic cognitivism and connectionism consider the world and the mind as two completely different entities, with a very much regulated protocol of interaction.

The embodied mind shares some characteristics with connectionism. It also proposes a self-organised system and it is based on a dynamic approach. However, in this approach dynamicism has been extended to the correspondence between mind and world. Instead of having a simple co-ordinated correspondence between symbols (or subsymbols) and real life objects, the embodied mind paradigm is based in a non-linear causality system in which by means of sensorimotor integrations, brain, body and environment are continuously influencing one another, making it impossible to separate the three into clear-cut parts. In order to have such a system, it is basic that the cognitive entity has some sort of body that can obtain continuous information from the real world in order to co-vary and co-adapt with it (Thompson 2007). This is why the paradigm we are discussing is usually called the embodied mind. First of all we need to avoid the tendency to interpret the notion of embodiment in its weakest sense: that this, a mind needs a body. The embodied mind paradigm argues for something a lot stronger than that, that is, that mind is just the result of circular and continuous processes of causality between brain activity, body and environment, with no possibilities to make a clear distinction among then, nor a chance to build a theoretical model in which mind can be described autonomously from body and environment. (Pfeifer and Iida, 2005).

The particular reading of the embodied mind paradigm we adhere here, known as enactivism, is based on the following ideas (Varela, Thompson, Lutz, Rosch 1991):

1. Living beings are autonomous entities and are responsible for their own goals that are not just settled from the outside.
2. The nervous system is also an autonomous entity, which takes care and is responsible for keeping its own coherent and meaningful patterns.
3. Cognition is the skillful know-how that co-varies with environment and how it evolves. Every cognitive action is both situated and embodied.
4. Cognitive processes are not formally pre-specified, but relational domains continually coupling with the environment.

A large amount of the literature takes living beings as the main metaphor. In their seminal book, Varela et al (1991) developed most characteristics of their model by analysing the way cells behave and represent environment. Nevertheless this shouldn't be considered a vitalist model, defending that only living beings can achieve real consciousness. Continuous coupling with the environment and self-established goals are the only requirements, as it is shown in the aforementioned book when Varela et al. argues in favour of how relevant Brooks' robots are, presenting them as artificial systems that have some of the main characteristics of an embodied mind (Brooks 1991).

In this work we will defend the enactive approach by exploring the critical role morphology plays in artificial systems. The structure of this work is as follows. First we will point out the benefits of the enactive approach. We will then explore the (in)compatibility between the embodied view and the multiple realizability of mental processes, digging into the debate between two different readings of the embodied perspective, a functionalist and a reductionist one. We will illustrate our explanation with a thought experiment (a robot computing the XOR function courtesy of its morphology), concluding that the functionalist stance does not really match with the enactive view. This thought experiment serves us as the inspiration for our own proposal: three robots that compute XOR courtesy of their morphology. Previous to introducing the robots, we will review our preceding research that constituted our first approximation to the possibility of morphology playing a role in computation.

THE QUEST FOR ENACTIVE AI

Despite the fact that philosophers like Dreyfus (Dreyfus 1972; 1992) are convinced of an impossible gap between living and artificial beings that makes an activity like AI impossible, one can reverse the line of thought and attempt to discover if and how these key characteristics of living beings can be reproduced in artificial systems, either by means of simulations or robotics. This is what the enactive paradigm tries to understand. Following

Froese and Ziemke (2009) we can state two main systemic requirements in order to be able to speak of enactive AI: autonomy and adaptativity. Despite mysterious claims (Flanagan 2009) these two properties are not beyond scientific and philosophical analysis and are not restricted to the realm of living beings, and can be satisfied in an artificial system.

Instead of trying to rapidly dismiss Heideggerian-based criticisms to current AI by the already mentioned Dreyfus, or more biologically based like Di Paolo and Izuka (2008) or Moreno and Exteberria (2005), we believe it is better to take this challenge seriously, and once all arguments and counterarguments are settled, it is clear that current approaches on AI which don't include some sort of enactive/embodiment perspective face several challenges which need to be addressed.

One of these problems is what Dreyfus calls the *Big Remaining problem*, a problem closely related to what Dennett called the *Frame problem* (Dennett 1984). This problem refers to the (im)possibility of a formal model of a cognitive system to "directly pick up significance and improve our sensitivity to relevance" (Dreyfus, 2007). If artificial systems cannot get meaning from the outside, but rather are following a set of formal rules, we are missing the main characteristics that make an agent a real one, besides not being really useful in real life contexts, as the frame problem paradox presents. The problem with stating meaning in artificial systems is not simply adding sensors that connect to the environment. As we mentioned in the former section, the embodied mind paradigm implies more than just having a body. Following Di Paolo & Izuka (2008) as well as Froese & Ziemke (2009), getting motor systems and sensors into a loop is a necessary condition to have autonomy and adaptivity, but it is far from sufficient. As long as this feedback between environment and cognitive systems is imposed from the outside, we won't have a real enactive system, which needs to set its goals from the inside.

The need of intrinsically posed goals is not only asked from the enactive perspective. It was stated as earlier as Kant (1790) and can be found in authors that defend a biological, darwinian approach to functionalism like Millikan (1991) or Flanagan (2009). Either from an *a priori* analysis of the concept of autonomy or trying to naturalise it, the consequence is largely the same: in order for a system that adapts to the environment to be autonomous, it has to be the system itself that sets the goals, not an outside element which postulates those criteria from the beginning. As the biosemantical model defended in Millikan (1991) states, this doesn't imply any type of vitalism or mysterious positions. The fact that aims and plans of cognitive living systems are intrinsic can be explained by the process of natural selection.

Following the ideas stated in Froese & Ziemke (2009), we will present the basic methodological principles behind enactive AI. They are:

1. Methodology is viewed under scientific light and not as an engineering process. We want to understand mind, not only solve practical problems on face recognition or make guesses about the behaviour of the stock market.
2. Behaviour cannot be prefigured by formal guesses of how the world is and then be implemented in the system. Behaviour emerges of the continuous interactions between the system and its environment.
3. An optimal enactive AI system needs to find a balance between robustness criteria and flexibility, as one can see in the natural world.

What is the main difference between enactivism and plain embodiment? Despite the fact that Thompson (2007) uses both terms almost synonymously, we believe, following Froese & Ziemke (2009), that there are interesting differences between them. Basically, we will use it to distinguish it from a more general approach to the notion of embodiment, which seems to be content with arranging a closed sensorimotor loop

that allows co-variation between internal models in the brain and the outside world. Although this is necessary, it is not sufficient, and in order to assure real autonomy from agents, more needs to be added to the system.

How can we develop AI that adapts to the enactive principles? The most feasible way -and probably the only one- is to forget completely about multiple realizability, the omnipotent power of Turing machines and include both the physical structure of the system -the body of the appliance shall we say- as well as the environment as key elements for computations. We will explore this in the next section.

ENACTIVE AI? MORPHOLOGY TO THE RESCUE!

In order to develop AI that adapts to the principles of the enactive framework, first we have to face the assumed multiply realizable nature of minds. The Multiple Realizability thesis (Putnam, 1967, MRT) has been for many years a good justification for the Cartesian-like methodology characteristic of the disciplines studying mind over the past decades (like philosophy of mind, psychology and cognitive science). This methodology operates under the assumption that mind can be explored and explained with no (or little) attention to the body. Putnam had conceptual and empirical arguments for MRT. They both constituted arguments against the Identity-Theory, a cutting-edge theory at the time that claimed that states and processes of the mind are states and processes of the brain (Place, 1956; Feigl, 1958; Smart, 1959). The conceptual argument originates from the assumption that the Turing machine is the right way to conceive minds. The empirical argument draws attention to the fact that mental states of the sort humans possess may be had by creatures that differ from us physically, physiologically, or neurobiologically. If we are willing to attribute to other creatures, like octopi or a potential extraterrestrial form of life, the same mental states that we have (e.g. pain or hunger), then we have to detach mind from a particular physical structure (e.g. human brain). The important criterion for mental sameness here is not a physical sameness, but a functional-sameness. Therefore, the particular matter that minded creatures are made of, and the particular body they have, is of minor importance when studying and explaining how their minds work.

This disembodied methodology has also been dominating in AI, again, because of some form of multiple realizability. As stated by the cognitivist paradigm, cognition has to do with algorithms (operating over representations), and, until recently (1980s), AI has been exclusively concerned with finding effective algorithms. Algorithms are platform-free, that is, the same algorithm can be implemented in different physical structures. Algorithmic minds are free from the (constraints of the) body.

However, MRT has been called into question. Recent works argue that evidence in favor of MRT as an empirical claim, is not as convincing as many philosophers have been claiming (Bickle, 1998, 2003; Bechtel & Mundale 1999; Shapiro 2000, 2004; Polger, 2002). It seems reasonable to say, for example, that in the same way that an octopus and I do not share the neural mechanisms underlying the psychological state of being hungry, we also do not share the same psychological state of being hungry (Bechtel & Mundale, 1999). Putnam's MRT uses a coarse-grained analysis when referring to psychological kinds. This is a legitimate practice in science. But when it comes to considering brain states, Putnam uses a fine-grained analysis. When the same grain is employed at both levels (psychological and neurological), the picture we get is a different one. A coarse-grained analysis allows for similarities at both physical and psychological levels, while a fine-grained inspection drives us to the conclusion that particular mental processes might require particular physical structures. Neural plasticity, in its turn, has been alleged as evidence for MRT (Block &

Fodor, 1972). For example, the capacity of the brain to process language sometimes in the right hemisphere is said to be evidence for MRT. We should be cautious, however, in concluding that. In those arguments, the emphasis is placed on the location of the mental activity, and not in the processes by means of which the mental activity is produced. The processing of language in the right hemisphere might be done in the same way (by means of the same processes) that it is done in the left hemisphere, therefore does not necessarily constitute an interesting case of multiple realizability. An interesting case involves different processes producing the same function. As long as the neural plasticity argument elaborates only on differences in location, it lends no support to MRT[1]. And in response to Putnam's conceptual arguments, we can just claim that the power of the Turing Machine metaphor, and in general of the computational functionalism developed by Putnam (1960, 1967), has been dismissed over the last years[2].

Our first conclusion can be, on the one hand, that as an empirical claim about minds, MRT cannot be used as a justification anymore, at least not in the unchallenged way that has dominated the scene until recently. On the other hand, as a foundation for a theoretical approach and methodology to develop artificial intelligent agents, operating under the assumption that mental processes are independent of the physical structure, it is unsatisfactory. We have seen that although successful in some domains, algorithmic AI is not providing us with an understanding of how natural forms of intelligence work.

The specific line of criticism against MRT that most affects our goal here is the one that, according to some, follows from accepting the tenets of the embodied mind program. We can find two different readings of the embodied mind view, corresponding to two very different senses of embodiment, and only one of them challenging MRT. A functionalist reading claims that body plays a computational role in cognition, although the physical details of implementation are not important (Clark, 2006; 2007; 2008). Under this interpretation, mental processes are still multiply realizable, but this time the implementational base spreads to include the body and the environment. A reductionist reading, however, defends that the details of implementation are a constraint on mind, and so, mental processes are not multiply realizable in different bodies and across different environments. Differences in morphology are going to make a difference in mental processes (Shapiro, 2004; Noë, 2004).

The reductionist reading advocates for a more radical interpretation of the embodied view, which may develop into a paradigm alternative to the representationalist and computationalist models of mind. The notions of coupling, action and sensorimotor coordination are contrasted with functional, computational and information-processing. The functionalist reading, nevertheless, proposes a reconciliatory picture, and the new notions from the embodied program are integrated in the (old) functionalist model of the mind, where representations and computations are still the keystone of cognition, and mental processes keep their platform-free privilege. But now the body and the environment are as important participants as the brain is.

The reductionist interpretation matches with the enactive trend within cognitive science. A good illustration of this fact is the sensorimotor approach to perception developed in O'Regan & Noë (2001) and Noë (2004). According to this approach, perception consists of the implicit knowledge we have of sensorimotor regularities, that is, the relations between movement and change, and sensory stimulation (what is called sensorimotor dependencies). Perception here is a matter of actions, not internal representations. The range of actions an organism performs has to do, in turn, with the sort of body it has. It follows from this that differently embodied organisms, engaging in different sensorimotor loops with the world, are going to perceive the world in differ-

ent ways. An organism with two eyes separated by 180° (one in what we would call the front, the other in the back) will engage in different sensorimotor loops when visually perceiving an object. Its gross-bodily and eye movements will relate to visual input in a way that differs from the way we humans relate to visual input. Thus, this approach to perception has the (radical) consequence that the particularities of our bodies are a constraint on how we perceive.

The functionalist reading of the embodied mind program defends, as we said, that the fine-grained details of an organism's body are not a constraint on mind. In particular, they do not determine how we perceive. Although embodiment, action and embedment are significant features when we consider thought and experience, the (embodied) functionalist says, their contributions are more complex than a mere direct relation. There is a buffer zone between the fine details of body and motion-dependent sensory input, and the internal representations that determine perception. Perception ultimately depends on representations and computational processes that are insensitive to the fine details of the world-engaging sensorimotor loops. The specific sensorimotor dependencies are only the contingent means to pick up external information. It is this higher level of information-processing what determines experience. Thus, differently embodied organisms, interacting with objects in different ways, could, in principle, have the same perceptual experience, as long as they have access to the same gross information and then can form the same internal representations.

The sensorimotor approach to perception relates mental processes, in particular, perception to action, bringing mentality out of the realm of internal representations. This contrasts with the (less radical) view we just mentioned, also within the embodied mind paradigm, where perception, and in general mental processes, are still a matter of (internal) representations. For this reason, the sensorimotor approach to perception provides us with a good starting point to figure out how an enactive AI should be. And it does so not only because of its strong points, but also for its limitations. Sensorimotor loops by themselves do not allow us to talk of an agent's intentional action (other than metaphorically). A notion of selfhood or agency is needed (Thompson, 2005). A detailed analysis of how to solve this lack is specified in Froese & Ziemke (2009). Here, we are only concerned with one of their conclusions: the *aboutness* of our cognition "is not due to some presumed representational content that is matched to an independent external reality (by some designer or evolution)" (ibid, p. 33), but has to do with the continuous activity of the organism. Life and (its corollary) movement are here in a continuum with mind.

In order to develop an enactive AI, we need to rely on this more radical (reductionist) interpretation of the embodied program. Hence, in exploring how we can bring the enactive approach to the AI lab, firstly, we need to ignore the multiple realizability of natural minds (Putnam's MRT) and algorithms, and focus our attention on how to develop systems that inhabit their (particular) bodies that, in turn, inhabit their (particular) environments. This will provide our AI projects with better results and, more importantly, with a better understanding of how (natural) organisms interact with their environment. At this point, the brain-in-a-body (controller-in-an-actuator) caricature that used to rule the mind sciences disappears. The clean division between mechanical design and controller design is, therefore, no longer useful. Natural organisms evolve with particular bodies in particular environments, and exploit the potentialities of them. Since intelligent behaviour is not the result of a pre-programmed set of functions instructing a passive body, in order to build intelligent robots we need to explore the many ways natural organisms exploit their physical structures and their surroundings, and how intelligent behaviour emerges from that. The goal for enactive AI is not to simulate the abstract operations happening in the brain (algorithmic

Table 1. Trust table AND

A	B	OUTPUT
F	F	F
F	T	F
T	F	F
T	T	T

AI), but the physical interactions between the whole organism (with its particular body) and its environment.

It is time to explore the potential of embodiment in artificial systems. We will do that by means of the notion of morphological computation. This notion was first introduced and explained by Chandana Paul (2004), and refers to the phenomenon of the bodily details taking charge of some of the work that, otherwise, would need to be done by the controller (be it the brain or a neural network). That is, computation obtained through interactions of physical form[3]. We will introduce this notion in more detail with a particular example that in turn will serve us as the inspiration for our own proposal.

Paul (2004, 2006) offers an example of morphological computation, where a robot controlled by two perceptrons (Rosenblatt, 1962) gets to exhibit, courtesy of its morphology, a XOR-like behaviour. The possibilities of the morphology of an agent's body have been exploited in different ways in the study of adaptive behavior. There are several examples of robots and vehicles that try to make the most of the details of embodiment in order to minimize the control required (Brooks, 1999; Braitenberg, 1984). Paul's robot consists of two perceptrons as controllers. Perceptrons are very simple connectionist networks consisting of two layers (an input layer and an output layer), modifiable connection weights and a threshold function.

Perceptrons can compute functions as (inclusive-) OR and AND, but not complex ones such as exclusive-or, also written as XOR (Minsky &

Papert 1969) (See Figure 1). Perceptrons learn to generalize on the basis of physical similarity. If a connectionist network has been trained to classify pattern 111000, then it will tend to classify a novel pattern 111001 in a similar way, on the basis of the (physical) similarity (or similarity of the form) between these two patterns. Perceptrons, then, are suitable to process linearly separable functions, as (inclusive-) OR and AND (see Figure 2 & 3), but not linearly inseparable ones such as XOR[4]. To compute XOR we need an extra node or two (hidden units) between the input and the output layers (see Figure 4). This hidden unit becomes active when both inputs are active, sending a negative activation to the output unit equivalent to the positive activation that it receives from the inputs units.

The inputs coming into the robot are two, A and B. One network computes OR and the other computes AND. Each network is connected to a motor. The network computing OR is connected to motor 1 (M1), which turns a single wheel at the center that causes forward motion. AND network is connected to motor 2 (M2), which serves to lift the wheel off the ground. Thus, M1 will activate the wheel if either or both inputs are active. And M2 will raise the wheel off the ground if and only

if both inputs are active (see Figure 5). When both inputs A and B are off, both networks output 0, then the wheel is not raised from the ground and it does not move, so the robot is stationary. When input A is active and input B is off, the AND network outputs 0, and then the wheel stays grounded. But the OR network outputs 1 and then M1 causes the wheel to move forward (so the robot moves forward). When B is active, the same thing happens: the AND network delivers 0 and the OR network delivers 1, so the robot moves forward. The interesting case is when A and B are both active. In this case the OR network makes M1 to turn the wheel on, but the AND network lifts the wheel from the ground, so the robot remains stationary. Summarizing the behaviour of the robot in a table, we discover that it looks like the truth table of the XOR function (see Figure 6). The explanation is that "the robot's behaviour is not simply determined by the output of the neural networks, but also by the actuated components of the body" (Paul, 2004, p. 2).

Paul's robot, as we said above, is an illustration of morphological computation. The simple physical interactions of the robot's body with its environment give raise to computation[5]. Under the

Figure 1. An example of perceptron computing OR

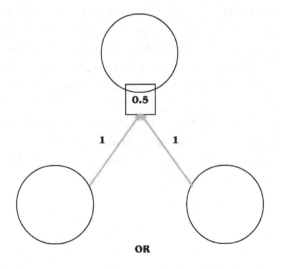

OR

Table 2. Trust table OR

A	B	OUTPUT
F	F	F
F	T	T
T	F	T
T	T	T

Table 3. Trust table XOR

A	B	OUTPUT
F	F	F
F	T	T
T	F	T
T	T	F

Figure 2. An example of perceptron computing AND

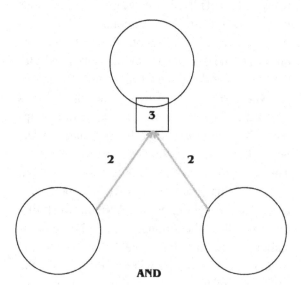

Figure 3. An example of a three layered network solving the XOR problem

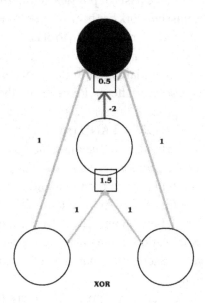

functionalist reading of the embodied program, this case is an example of what can be dubbed "participant machinery"[6]. This means that the body is "part of the very machinery by means of which mind and cognition are physically realized" (Clark, 2008, p. 207). The body here is considered as (just) the implementational base for the cognitive processes. Because, the functionalist argues, the only difference between the XOR robot and the standard (disembodied) computation of XOR (with a three layered feedforward network) is a difference in the physical structure implementing the function. Morphology in Paul's robot is playing the same computational role that the hidden unit plays in the XOR network. The robot's active body "is providing the functional equivalent of the missing second layer of neural processing: the extra processing that would be required to solve the linearly inseparable problem of computing XOR" (Clark, 2008, p. 209)[7]. According to the reductionist interpretation, however, the difference between the XOR robot and the standard computation of XOR is not only an implementational difference. The robot and the three layered network, so the

reductionist argues, are not performing the same computational processes[8].

Independently of which reading we choose to be the best, the important lesson to draw from this example is that the robot is, in the same way that evolved biological intelligences are, and unlike how methodologically engineered solutions in (classical, disembodied) artificial systems work, exploiting the possibilities of its physical structure. Thus, we see that we cannot explain the robot's behaviour by exclusively looking at what its controllers do. The whole agent, its mechanical properties as well, has to be considered in order to understand what it does and why. It is in this line that, we propose, artificial agents should be developed. Designing the proper morphology of our robots will provide us not only with a cheaper and easier control architecture, but more importantly, with a better insight into how living systems adapt to their environment through the exploitation of their physical structure.

Figure 4. XOR robot (illustration inspired in Paul, 2004)

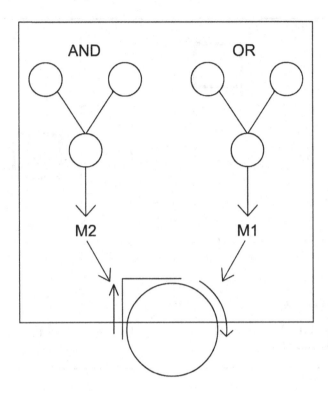

PREVIOUS RESEARCH: SIMULATIONS AND LEGO NXT ROBOTS

Previous to this current research we were working on simulating synthetic emotions, always trying to create very simple situations in which we could elucidate the value of basic emotions (pain and pleasure) for the emergence of complex activities. Our interest in emotions is not only a question of affinity with the topic but the strong belief that emotions are basic intentional forces for living entities. Therefore, emotions should be the keystone of the whole building of AI and robotics. Emotions being a natural system that most living intelligent creatures use to calibrate their relationship with the environment and their own plans and goals, they are key major factors to study when we want to understand how autonomous living systems develop their own goals.

We developed two different computer simulations, which we called TPR and TPR.2.0. Both models and results were published as Vallverdú & Casacuberta (2008) and Vallverdú & Casacuberta (2009a, 2009b), respectively. Let us summarize them.

Figure 5. Robot's behaviour summarized in a table

A	B	Behavior
F	F	stationary
F	T	moving
T	F	moving
T	T	stationary

Figure 6. TPR Simulation

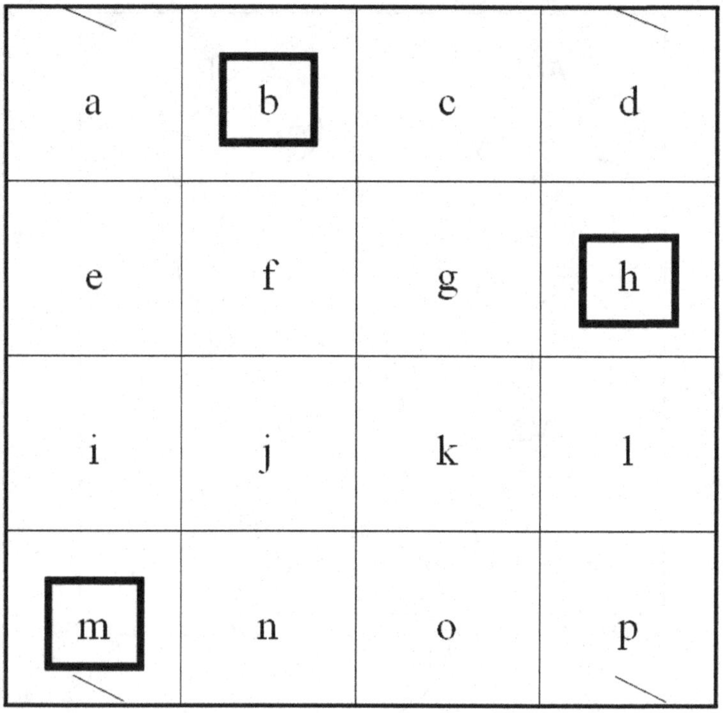

a	**b**	c	d
e	f	g	**h**
i	j	k	l
m	n	o	p

TPR

At the first stage of our research we developed a computer simulation (called *The Panic Room* or, more simply, TPR) dealing with synthetic emotions. TPR was developed with Python code and led us to interesting results. With TPR, we were merely trying to design an artificial device able to learn from, and interact with, the world by using two basic information types: positive and negative. We were developing the first steps towards an evolutionary machine, defining the key elements involved in the development of complex actions (that is, creating a physical intuitive ontology, from a bottom-up approach). The basic conceptual and technical data of that simulation were:

• Hard-wired emotional states (proto-emotions).
• Bottom-up approach.
• Python programmed.

The computational simulation was designed as a box with four doors (a,d,m,p), three switches (b,h,m), and 16 squares {a,b...p}.

The system simulated a room in which passers-by could walk around randomly. There were three switches distributed around the room. If a user was able to disconnect the three switches in rapid succession then the power was cut to the main computer running the entire environmental construction and the whole system failed. However, if the system was able to detect such an attack in time, it had a few seconds to acquire an alternative source of electricity before the user turned off the final switch. To make the process more interesting, the system did not have access to information about whether the switches had been turned off (pain) or not (pleasure). By means of a deterministic algorithm, one not capable of change through learning we designed the system to distinguish between a harmless and a harmful intruder. Each movement by the user either generated some elevation or reduction of a fear signal. As the fear increased the system checked the signals coming from the more relevant sensors more frequently. Once the signal went beyond a certain threshold, the system entered into "panic mode" and grabbed the alternative source of electricity. When the fear signal descended enough for the system to consider that the danger had passed it returned to its normal activity, getting electricity again from the usual source.

With TPR, we were merely trying to design an artificial device able to learn from, and interact with, the world by using two basic information types: positive and negative. These can be considered as proto-emotions and, assuming we can establish this analogy with human emotions, we could emulate their usefulness in the fight for survival by creating helpful behavioural rules such as "this is harmful, don't touch it" or "this produces pleasure, eat it". We were developing the first steps towards an evolutionary machine, defining the key elements involved in the development of complex actions (that is, creating a physical intuitive ontology, from a bottom-up approach).

From the programming perspective, in TPR 1.0 we just used global variables in order to represent the emotional values. That means that the system actually kept 'memories' of the former emotional states. This, of course, is somewhat unrealistic, and wanting to pursue a bottom-up approach as much as possible, we decided later (at the next stage of the current research) to change and give the system, now called 'TPR 2.0.', a very basic memory instead. The system labelled the signals from the sensors that described the surroundings either as negative or positive. Either option had a specific signal that was used to change the way further perceptual signals would be processed as well to as generate possible behavioural responses to a potential danger. Responses were automatic and embedded (or hard-wired) in the system (therefore, they are an intentional - but not conscious - force). All the computations were based on the relative strengths of the two protoemotional signals. If

the negative signal reached a certain threshold it would activate the defensive action and would switch to the emergency circuit. Positive signals tried to calm down the system in order to avoid that reaction.

TPR could easily distinguish between dangerous and innocent situations from its basic emotional structure (using pain and pleasure). Therefore, we showed that emotions, as hardwired conditions of the system, are intentional maps of action that make possible an effective interaction with the world without the necessity for complex programming. At the same time, TPR was able to develop correct escalation responses through [pain→ pain+→ panic] or [pleasure→happiness] states. This reveals that with just two activation signals (pain and pleasure), it was possible to allow the TPR to carry out a coherent survival activity. As a consequence, we concluded that a hardwired approach to ambient intelligence was possible with TPR.

TPR.2.0

After the successful initial results of TPR, we considered that it would be necessary to develop a new simulation (which we will call TPR 2.0), more complex and with better visualisation characteristics. We developed then a second version, TPR 2.0, using the programming language Processing, with new improvements such as: a better visual interface, a database which could record and also recall easily the information on all the paths inside the simulation (human and automatically generated ones) and, finally, a small memory capacity which was a next step in the evolution from simple hard-wired activities to self-learning by simple experience.

TPR 2.0 was equipped with several simulated components: 4 doors: in/out, 3 switches which activated emotional responses, 4 sensors which detected proximity to switches and movement inside the room and, finally, 4 light devices which showed the emotional state of the room. Like its predecessor, TPR 2.0 automatically evaluated a situation as being either *neutral* or *dangerous*, generated an automatic response that dealt with the specific danger detected and could escalate that response. That is, it could make the response stronger or weaker depending on the degree of danger that was detected. The possible generated pathways were:

The process by which TPR 2.0. changes from one state to another can be defined by the following rules, where *s* is *signal, em* is *echoic memory,* + means *positive path,* − means *negative path* and *relaxed, pain, intense pain, panic* are the possible final states (relaxed = 0, pain = 1, intense pain = 2, panic = 3):

If s is + and em is + then relaxed

If s is + and em is − then increment once +1 the state

If s is − and em is + then increment once +1 the state

If s is − and em is − then increment once +1 the state

Let us emphasize that the simulation had a short memory (echoic memory) which could hold the previous state for a small amount of time (+ or −). Once this time is passed, and in case there is no new signal, the next state is always a positive one (+).

There were two basic differences between TPR and TPR.2.0:

a. *Programming Language*. The first version was made in Python and this second one is made in Processing. We found that Processing is a lot easier and more powerful when performing an animated version of the simulation. This new programming language approach implies several changes in the general architecture of the simulation (these include better usability across different platforms, more friendly interface and a database).

b. *Echoic memory*. This is the main theoretical improvement on our first version. In TPR 1.0 we used global variables in order to store the emotional values. Because of this the system kept memories of the former emotional states. TPR 2.0, however, exhibits a very basic memory. After a few seconds the echoic memory degraded and finally vanished, returning to a neutral state as if nothing had happened.

c. *Pleasure states deleted*. TPR 1.0 also had scalable pleasure states, which have been deleted in our new simulation. TPR 2.0. only has relaxed − pain - intense pain - panic modes. The reason for this change was twofold, (i) we considered pain states to be more basic than pleasure ones (although you can consider the relaxed state to be a positive situation, or with lack of pain. This could be seen as a Buddhist approach to the biological nature of living entities). And (ii) we paid more attention to the necessity of developing a more simple and elegant simulation with fewer elements to be processed, but with a more in-depth analysis.

Figure 7. TPR 2.0. emotion transitional loops

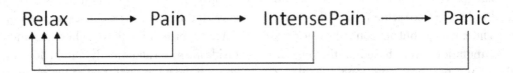

d. *Visual interface*. TPR 2.0 has a better visual interface (which makes possible the interaction between TPR 2.0 and human beings, as well as the generation of automatic paths). It has a mouse and emotions are labelled with colours and text which appear on the screen as soon as they are generated (i.e. relaxed – green-, pain -blue)- intense pain –purple-, panic -red).

e. *Database*. TPR 2.0. has a database which can record and also easily recall information on all the paths followed inside the simulation.

In the diagram below several basic screen captures of the simulation are displayed. The reader should notice that in TPR 2.0 the protoemotion is indicated with a word and a colour to make it clearer the usual reactions that occurred during the simulation (from relaxed to pain, intense pain and panic):

Both TPR and TPR 2.0 dealt with ambient intelligence and they are presented here as our first analysis on how there is not a clear-cut distinction between the internal structure of the system and the environment that surrounds it. TPR and TPR 2.0 are good illustrations of the significance of morphology[9], for the way sensors are distributed within the space are critical. It is the results obtained in these former experiments that led us towards morphological computing. In the next section we will introduce our work on morphological computation with real systems (Lego Mindstorms NXT)[10].

MORPHOLOGICAL COMPUTING AS COGNITION: XOR ROBOTS

After our previous work with computer simulations (TPR and TPR 2.0.) we decided to implement our philosophical model in real robots. We chose Lego Mindstorms NXT for several reasons (you can also see a detailed argumentation in favor of Lego Mindstorms in Dautenhahn et al 2002, Chapter 8), but the most important are:

- Inexpensiveness
- Simple object-oriented programming interface, NXT-G, with the possibility of working with the complete Labview suite (not included with the basic equipment but available for us).
- Easyness of manipulation.
- Availability of different sensors.
- Bluetooth connectivity.

We acquired 6 NXT units for our research activities and we started to implement our models of synthetic emotions into them. Part of this research on the relationship of the somatic marker with proto-emotions is still being developed with other robotic designs. Our robots allowed us to work with the idea of loop, as a biological cybernetic feedback, implemented in their programming. We chose robots with movement to simulate living entities like animals that are looking for food, security, etc. To avoid complexity of typical six or eight legged bugs, we chose wheels as the

Figure 8. TPR 2.0. Simulation

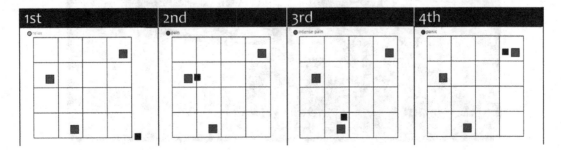

simplest (but perhaps not always effective) way of movement for our robots. We present here the results on the importance of embodiment for robotics systems, but not in a trivial sense (robots are physical objects), but in the stronger sense we defended in section 3. Robot's bodies perform certain complex actions. In this sense, we can affirm that not only does the morphology determine the behaviors that can be performed, but also the amount of control required for these behaviors. Particularly in systems where behavior is obtained through purely sensory-motor interactions of the body with the environment, the morphology is of prime importance.

Elaborating on Paul's notion of morphological computation, we expanded her thought experiment (i.e. the XOR robot we presented above), designing a real NXT robot which computes XOR courtesy of its morphology. Paul's idea was to compute XOR from AND + OR. The problem we are concerned with here is how to compute it with a real robot. Two possible answers are (a) with a robot controlled by a three layered feedforward network, and (b) with a robot controlled by some logic pro-

gramming language (for example, LEGO NXT-G software has a Logic Bloc which computes XOR). But, could it be obtained exclusively through its morphology? The answer is 'definitively, yes!, as we will see in the next section.

XOR as Initial Paul Thought Experiment

Following, to a certain degree, the indications provided by Paul (2006), we created this robot, which we call XOR-1.

The structure of the robot is very simple: two pair sensors (one of touch and one of sound) can activate one of the three motors. Right motor moves towards the right side, while left motor moves towards the left. There is a third motor which always keeps off the ground the left motor; if a situation is not produced in which two input sensor values are positive (true or 1), that is, an AND situation, the motor can only work off the ground, therefore remaining quiet. In that case the left motor activates the wheel and it is on the ground moving the robot towards the left

Figure 9. XOR as AND + OR robot

Table 4. XOR-1 truth tables. Legends: Left =l; Right = r; Sound Sensor = S; Touch Sensor (T); Left motor = L; Right Motor = R; Motor that makes up/down left motor = M; Stop/No movement = NO

Values		AND [L]		OR [R]	XOR [L/R]
Tl/Tr	Sl/Sr				
1	1	(T l → M) ∧ S l → (wheel working on the ground)	L	Tr ∨ Sr → R	NO (by opposite forces L vs. R)
1	0	T l → (wheel working off the ground)	N O	Tr → R	R
0	1	S l → (no working wheel on the ground)	N O	Sr → R	R
0	0	NO		NO	NO

side. The right motor is activated if sensors A or B are positive (i.e. function OR). Then, when left motor computes a true AND in all four situations and right motor computes OR in all four situations, then the robot follows a XOR rule. In true-true value, because every motor is trying to move the robot toward opposite directions and then no movement is accomplished at all. We can summarize it with this Table 4.

XOR-1, as we see, computes XOR from AND and OR. With this simple case we see that morphology can be used to encode complex logical design, without the aid of programming or the control of neural nets. But simplicity can be even higher, as we will see in the next section.

The Simplest XOR Robot

After achieving the XOR-1 robot we decided to make a simpler design which could compute XOR without including AND or OR (morpho) logical conditions. Then we created the robot called XOR-2.

We have not programmed it for any extra activity, such as "look for food" (e.g. a colour) or "avoid danger" (e.g. a too close object). With

Figure 10. XOR-2 as simple as possible

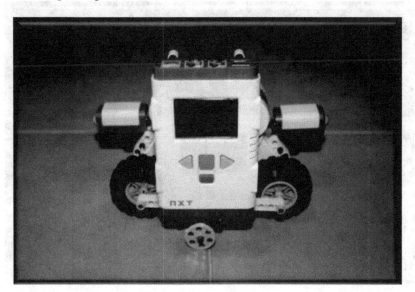

Table 5. XOR-2. Legends: Left = l; Right = r; Left motor = L; Right motor = R; Touch sensor = T; Stop/ no movement = NO.

Value	XOR
11	NO (by opposite forces L vs R)
10	Tl → L
01	Tr → R
00	NO

this robot we just want to show that a very simple morphological design can control and determine the general behaviour of the robot.

Adding Morphological Complexity to the XOR Robot

Our third and last example of the potential of morphological computation, understood as a practical example of the enactive approach to computing and robotics, is XOR-3, an evolution of XOR-2. Imagine a situation in which the touch sensors were automatically hidden in case there is a particular environmental condition. In that case, the robot could only compute XOR in specific situations.

XOR-3 hides its two touch sensors in case there is too much light. Thus, it computes XOR only in particular conditions. With this example we see that the particular morphology the system has, together with the environmental structure, is what explains its behaviour.

SOME PHILOSOPHICAL CONCLUSIONS

We hope that our theoretical discussion has shed some light about alternative ways to consider the design of intelligent beings. More specifically, we tried to show that embodiment means more than

Figures 11. Frontal

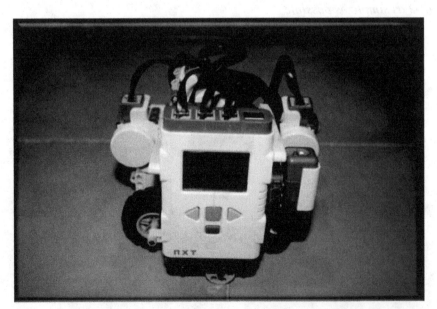

Figure 12. Back side with open touch sensors

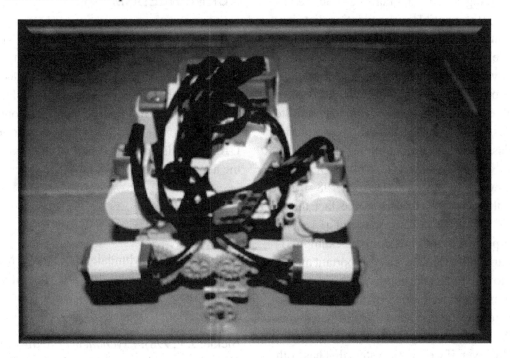

Figure 13. Backside with hidden touch sensors

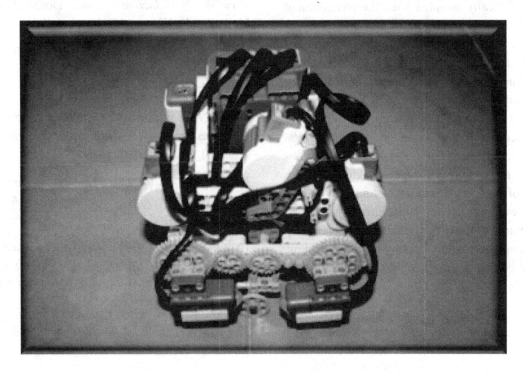

simply having a body and that the enactive approach is not compatible with a functionalist view that assumes that mental processes are multiply realizable. To summarize, intelligence implies autonomy, and autonomy implies a serious commitment on how precise morphological structures and ambient traits play a major role in cognitive processes. Within an enactive AI background, some classical theoretical problems can be more easily solved. A good example of this is Dennett's well known *frame problem* (Dennett 1984). The core of the problem consists in the fact that a symbolic cognitive system does not have any specific priorities and, in Dennett's example, is not able to realize that the really important movement is to disconnect the bomb or leave the room as soon as possible. Instead of that, the system goes on generating true but unhelpful statements about the colors or the volume of the room, and so on. However, if we have a system that has both autonomy and adaptivity, the *frame problem* is no longer a problem, because the system is able to settle its own goals (autonomy) and those goals are realistically coupled with the environment (adaptivity).

Here we proposed three robots as examples of how morphology can play a computational role. Including morphology in computations is a way to minimize the control required. This, however, does not have to be seen as simply an alternative and effective strategy to design artificial agents. The primary lessons of morphological computation are not lessons in cheaper designs, but in the nature of intelligent activities. Natural intelligence is the result of the continuous interplay between the control system, body and environment. By including morphology in our artificial designs we are getting a better insight into natural forms of intelligence.

ACKNOWLEDGMENT

This work was supported by the TECNOCOG research group (at UAB) on Cognition and Technological Environments, [FFI2008-01559/FISO], and has been developed by SETE (Synthetic Emotions in Technological Environments) research group. The Philosophy Department (at UAB) has also provided part of the funding for the acquisition of the NXTs.

REFERENCES

Bechtel, W., & Mundale, J. (1999). Multiple Realization Revisited: Linking Cognitive and Neural States. *Philosophy of Science, 66*, 175–207. doi:10.1086/392683

Bickle, J. (1998). *Psychoneural Reduction: The New Wave*. Cambridge, MA: MIT Press/Bradford Books.

Bickle, J. (2003). *Philosophy and Neuroscience: A ruthlessly reductive account*. Dordrecht, The Netherlands: Kluwer Academic Pub.

Block, N. (1996). *Functionalism. The Encyclopedia of Philosophy Supplement*. New York: Macmillan.

Block, N., & Fodor, J. (1972). What Psychological States Are Not. *The Philosophical Review, 81*, 159–181. doi:10.2307/2183991

Braitenberg, V. (1984). *Vehicles: Experiments in Synthetic Psychology*. Cambridge, MA: MIT Press.

Brooks, R. A. (1991). Intelligence without representation. *Artificial Intelligence, 47*(1-3), 139–160. doi:10.1016/0004-3702(91)90053-M

Brooks, R. A. (1999). *Cambrian Intelligence: The Early History of the New AI*. Cambridge, MA: MIT Press.

Calvo, P., & Symons, J. (2008). Radical Embodiment and Morphological Computation: Against the Autonomy of (some) special sciences. In Reduction and the Special Sciences, Tilburg, April 10-12.

Clark, A. (2006). Pressing the flesh: Exploring a tension in the study of the embodied, embedded mind. *Philosophy and Phenomenological Research, 76*(1), 37–59.

Clark, A. (2007). Curing the Cognitive Hiccup: A Defense of the Extended Mind. *The Journal of Philosophy, 104*(4).

Clark, A. (2008). *Supersizing the Mind. Embodiment, Action, and Cognitive Extension*. Oxford, UK: Oxford University Press.

Damasio, A. (1994). *Descartes' error: Emotion, Reason and the Human Brain*. New York: Putnam Publishing.

Dautenhahn, K., Bond, A., Cañamero, L., & Edmonds, B. (2002). *Playing the Emotion Game with Feelix. What Can a LEGO Robot Tell Us about Emotion? Socially Intelligent Agents Creating Relationships with Computers and Robots*. New York: Springer.

Dawinks, R. (1982). *The Extended Phenotype*. Oxford, UK: Oxford University Press.

Dennett, D. (1984). Cognitive wheels: the frame problem of AI. In Hookway, (ed.) Minds, Machines and Evolution. Cambridge, UK: Cambridge University Press.

Di Paolo, E. A., & Izuka, J. (2008). How (not) to model autonomous behaviour. *Biosystem, 91*(2), 409–423. doi:10.1016/j.biosystems.2007.05.016

Dreyfus, H. L. (1972). *What Computers Can't Do: A Critique of Artificial Reason*. New York: Harper and Row.

Dreyfus, H. L. (1992). *What Computers Still Can't Do: A Critique of Artificial Reason*. Cambridge, MA: The MIT Press.

Dreyfus, H. L. (2007). Why Heideggerian AI failed and how fixing it would require making it more Heideggerian . *Philosophical Psychology, 20*(2), 247–268. doi:10.1080/09515080701239510

Eliasmith, C. (2002). The myth of the Turing machine: The failings of functionalism and related theses. *Journal of Experimental & Theoretical Artificial Intelligence, 14*(1), 1–8. doi:10.1080/09528130210153514

Flanagan, O. (2009). *The really hard problem. Meaning in a material world*. Cambridge, MA: MIT Press.

Froese, T., & Ziemke, T. (2009). Enactive artificial intelligence: Investigating the systemic organization of life and mind. *Artificial Intelligence, 173*, 466–500. doi:10.1016/j.artint.2008.12.001

Hutchins, E. (1996). *Cognition in the wild*. Cambridge, MA: MIT Press.

Kant, I. (1790). *Kritik der Urteilskraft* [Critique of Judgment]. (Pluhar, W. S., Trans.). Indianapolis, IN: Hacket Publishing Company.

Kirsh, D. (1995). The intelligent use of space. *Artificial Intelligence, 73*(1-2), 31–68. doi:10.1016/0004-3702(94)00017-U

Kirsh, D., & Maglio, P. (1992). Reaction and reflection in Tetris. In J. Hendler, (ed.) *Artificial intelligence planning systems, Proceedings of the first annual conference AIPS*. San Mateo, CA: Morgan Kaufmann.

Kirsh, D., & Maglio, P. (1994). On distinguishing epistemic from pragmatic action. *Cognitive Science, 18*, 513–549. doi:10.1207/s15516709cog1804_1

Maglio, P., Matlock, T., Raphaely, D., Chernicky, B., & Kirsh, D. (1999). Interactive skill in Scrabble. In *Proceedings of 21st annual conference of the Cognitive Science Society*. Mahwah, NJ: Erlbaum.

Marr, D. (1982). *Vision*. San Francisco: W.H. Freeman.

Millikan, R. G. (1991). *Language, Thought, and Other Biological Categories*. Cambridge, MA: MIT Press.

Minksy, M., & Papert, D. (1969). *Perceptrons*. Cambridge, MA: MIT Press.

Moreno, A., & Etxeberria, A. (2005). Agency in the natural and artificial systems. *Artificial Life, 11*(1-2), 161–175. doi:10.1162/1064546053278919

Neth, H., & Payne, S. J. (2002). Thinking by doing? Epistemic actions in the Tower of Hanoi. In W.D. Gray & C. D. Schunn, (Eds.), *Proceedings of the 24th annual conference of the Cognitive Science Society*. Mahwah, NJ: Erlbaum.

Noë, A. (2004). *Action in Perception*. Cambridge, MA: MIT Press.

O'Regan, J., & Noë, A. (2001). A sensory motor approach to vision and visual consciousness. *The Behavioral and Brain Sciences, 24*(5), 939–973.

Paul, C. (2004). Morphology and Computation. In S. Schaal, A. J. Ijspeert, A. Billard, S. Vijaya-kumar, J. Hallam, and J. A. Meyer, (Eds.), *From Animals to animats: Proceedings of the eighth international conference on the Simulation of Adaptive Behaviour*, Los Angeles. Cambridge, MA: MIT Press.

Paul, C. (2006). Morphological computation: A basis for the analysis of morphology and control requirements. *Robotics and Autonomous Systems, 54*(8), 619–630. doi:10.1016/j.robot.2006.03.003

Pfeifer, R., & Bongard, J. (2007). *How the body shapes the way we think*. Cambridge, MA: MIT Pres.

Pfeifer, R., & Iida, F. (2005). Morphological computation: Connecting body, brain and environment. *Japanese Scientific Monthly, 58*(2), 48–54.

Place, U. T. (1956). Is Consciousness a Brain Process? *The British Journal of Psychology, 47,* 44–50.

Polger, T. (2002). Putnam's Intuition. *Philosophical Studies, 109*(2), 143–170. doi:10.1023/A:1016236415052

Polger, T. (2004). *Natural Minds*. Cambridge, MA: The MIT Press.

Putnam, H. (1960). Minds and Machines. In Hook, S. (Ed.), *Dimensions of Mind* (pp. 148–180). New York: University of New York Press.

Putnam, H. (1967). Psychological Predicates. In Captain, W. H., & Merrill, D. D. (Eds.), *Art, Mind and Religion* (pp. 37–48). Pittsburgh: University of Pittsburgh Press.

Rosenblatt, F. (1962). *Principles of neurodynamics*. New York: Spartan Books.

Shagrir, O. (2005). The rise and fall of computational functionalism. In Ben-Menahem, Y. (Ed.), *Hilary Putnam (Contemporary Philosophy in Focus)*. Cambridge, UK: Cambridge University Press. doi:10.1017/CBO9780511614187.009

Shapiro, L. (2000). Multiple Realizations. *The Journal of Philosophy, 97,* 635–664. doi:10.2307/2678460

Shapiro, L. (2004). *The Mind Incarnate*. Cambridge, UK: MIT Press.

Thompson, E. (2007). *Mind in life*. Cambridge, MA: Harvard University Press.

Vallverdú, J., & Casacuberta, D. (2008). The Panic Room. On Synthetic Emotions. In Briggle, A., Waelbers, K., & Brey, P. (Eds.), *Current Issues in Computing and Philosophy* (pp. 103–115). Amsterdam: IOS Press.

Vallverdú, J., & Casacuberta, D. (2009a). Modelling Hardwired Synthetic Emotions: TPR 2.0 . In Vallverdú, J., & Casacuberta, D. (Eds.), *Handbook of Research on Synthetic Emotions and Sociable Robotics: New Applications in Affective Computing and Artificial Intelligence* (pp. 103–115). Hershey, PA: IGI Global.

Vallverdú, J., & Casacuberta, D. (Eds.). (2009b). *Handbook of Research on Synthetic Emotions and Sociable Robotics: New Applications in Affective Computing and Artificial Intelligence* (pp. 103–115). Hershey, PA: IGI Global.

Varela, F. J., & Thompson, E. Lutz, A. & Rosch, E. (1991). The embodied Mind: Cognitive Science and Human experience. Cambridge, MA: MIT Press.

KEY TERMS AND DEFINITIONS

Cognitivism: The philosophical theory that considers that cognition has to do with algorithms (operating over representations), and, until recently (1980s), AI has been exclusively concerned with finding effective algorithms. Algorithms are platform-free, that is, the same algorithm can be implemented in different physical structures. Algorithmic minds are free from the (constraints of the) body.

Enactivism: A theoretical approach to understanding the mind proposed by Gregory Bateson, Humberto Maturana, Francisco Varela, Eleanor Rosch and Alec McPheters. It emphasizes the way that organisms and the human mind organize themselves by interacting with their environment. It is closely related to situated cognition and embodied cognition, and is presented as an alternative to cognitivism, computationalism and Cartesian dualism.

Embodiment: Philosophers, cognitive scientists and artificial intelligence researchers who study embodied cognition and the embodied mind believe that the nature of the human mind is largely determined by the form of the human body. They argue that all aspects of cognition, such as ideas, thoughts, concepts and categories are shaped by aspects of the body. These aspects include the perceptual system, the intuitions that underlie the ability to move, activities and interactions with our environment and the naive understanding of the world that is built into the body and the brain.

Morphological Computation: About connecting body, brain and environment. It is an advance within the embodiment approach, in which we consider the effect of morphology, materials, and environment on neural processing, or better, the interplay of all these aspects.

Multiple Realizability: In the philosophy of mind, the multiple realizability thesis contends that a single mental kind (property, state, event) can be realized by many distinct physical kinds. A common example is pain. Many philosophers have asserted that a wide variety of physical properties, states, or events, sharing no features in common at that level of description, can all realize the same pain. This thesis served as a premise in the most influential argument against early theories that identified mental states with brain states (psychoneural identity theories). The argument has even been employed to challenge the functionalism it initially motivated.

XOR: or 'exclusive disjunction'. Operation on two logical values, typically the values of two propositions, that produces a value of *true* if and only if one but not both of its operands is true. Its truth values are: $11 = 0$, $10 = 1$, $01 = 1$, $0 = 0$.

ENDNOTES

[1]   See Shapiro (2004), chapter 2, for a detailed consideration of this question.

[2]   See Block (1996) for a detailed survey of the arguments against computational functionalism. The curious reader might also want to consult Shagrir (2005). Eliasmith (2002),

for example, provides the reader with an argument on why functionalist arguments for multiple realizability do not work.

3   See Paul (2006)

4   To be a linearly separable or inseparable function refers to the possibility of drawing a line, in a spatial representation of that function, which divides the representational space according to the physical similarity of the input patterns. XOR function is not suitable for this similarity-based dividing line, since input patterns with similar values appear close to dissimilar ones in the spatial representation. Adding an extra node to the two-layer network can solve this problem: this hidden node captures abstract relationships among input patterns, abstracting away from physical similarities. It, then, folds the representational space, transforming input representations into an abstract kind of representation, allowing now to linearly separate the representation of the input patterns.

5   Someone can argue that the computation performed by the robot's morphology "simply exists in the eyes of the observer, and is not really a computation" (Paul, 2004, p. 3). Following a commonsense definition, a computation is real in case it can be used as a computation, that is, in performing that computation, the computational level (Marr, 1982), where the function is described, is linked to the algorithmic level, where the pertinent subtasks are performed, thanks to the relation between task and subtask. The computation in the XOR-robot is implicit in the response of the overall system, but is not available to the system itself. Paul proposes then another device in which the

latent morphological computation becomes available for the device itself (see Paul, 2004 for details). In this latter robot, the morphological computation is part of the computational processing, and can be used as a general-purpose resource (Clark, 2007, p. 42).

6   This label appears in Clark (2008), p. 207.

7   When both inputs are active, the hidden unit in a standard XOR network, let's recall, sends a negative activation to the output unit equivalent to the positive activation it receives from the input units, preventing the output unit to reach its threshold, therefore impeding it to become active. The active body of Paul's robot is said to play that same computation role because, as we explained, when both inputs are active it prevent the wheel to reach the ground and therefore, the robot to move.

8   For an extended argument on this, see Calvo & Symons (2008).

9   The fact that they are just simulations should not be seen as a weak point, as there are no technical impossibilities related to the construction of TPR, which only needs very basic sensors and very simple programming.

10   Our current research, as a complement to the one published here, is focused on the implantation of the idea of a somatic marker into socially interacted robots. The next step in our research will elaborate on the results using proto-emotions in TPR and our experiments with Lego Mindstorms NXT, exploring possible ways to mix morphological computations and emotions using the idea of somatic markers (Damasio 1994).

Chapter 22
Challenges of Complex Systems in Cognitive and Complex Systems

Klaus Mainzer
Technical University Munich, Germany

ABSTRACT

After an introduction the chapter analyzes complex systems and the evolution of the embodied mind, complex systems and the innovation of embodied robotics, and finally discusses challenges of handling a world with increasing complexity: Large-scale networks have the same universal properties in evolution and technology. Considering the evolution of the embodied mind, we start with an introduction of complex systems and nonlinear dynamics, apply this approach to neural self-organization, distinguish degrees of complexity of the brain, explain the emergence of cognitive states by complex systems dynamics, and discuss criteria for modeling the brain as complex nonlinear system. The innovation of embodied robotics is a challenge of complex systems and future technology. We start with the distinction of symbolic and embodied AI. Embodied robotics is inspired by the evolution of life. Modern systems biology integrates the molecular, organic, human, and ecological levels of life with computational models of complex systems. Embodied robots are explained as dynamical systems. Self-organization of complex systems needs self-control of technical systems. Cellular neural networks (CNN) are an example of self-organizing complex systems offering new avenues for neurobionics. In general, technical neural networks support different kinds of learning robots. Embodied robotics aims at the development of cognitive and conscious robots.

INTRODUCTION

Since more than two thousand years, philosophers, artists, and engineers had thought about artificial

DOI: 10.4018/978-1-61692-014-2.ch022

minds. Since hundred millions of years, the natural evolution on Earth has developed nervous systems with increasing complexity. They work according to algorithms of neurochemistry and equip organisms with self-adapting, self-controlling, and self-conscious features. But the laws of evolution could also admit completely different forms of life on different material basis – and perhaps they have emerged elsewhere in the universe. Therefore, humans and animals are only special cases of intelligent systems which have emerged on Earth under more or less random conditions. They are neither goals nor in the centre of evolution. Traditional AI had tried to imitate the human mind by symbolic programming with only modest success. In a technical evolution of embodied robotics, artificial forms of life and self-conscious systems could emerge with new self-organizing features. But, like in natural evolution, self-organization does not automatically lead to desired results. Therefore, controlled emergence is a challenge of future neurorobotics. A new moral responsibility is demanded in order to handle human-robotic interaction which is evolving in a technical co-evolution.

COMPLEX SYSTEMS AND THE EVOLUTION OF THE EMBODIED MIND

Complex Systems and Nonlinear Dynamics

The coordination of the complex cellular and organic interactions in an organism is built upon a kind of self-organizing control. That was made possible by the evolution of nervous systems that also enabled organisms to adapt to changing living conditions and to learn from experiences with their respective environments. The hierarchy of anatomical organizations varies over different scales of magnitude, from molecular dimensions to that of the entire central nervous system (CNS). The research perspectives on these hierarchical levels may concern questions, for example, of how signals are integrated in dendrites, how neurons interact in a network, how networks interact in a system like vision, how systems interact in the CNS, or how the CNS interacts with its environ-

ment. Each stratum may be characterized by a dynamical system determining its particular structure, which is caused by complex interactions of subsystems with respect to the particular level of hierarchy.

In general, a *complex dynamical system* is a time-depending multi-component system of elements with local states determining a global state of the whole system. In a planetary system, for example, the state of a planet at a certain time is determined by its position and momentum. The states can also refer to moving molecules in a gas, the excitation of neurons in a neural network, nutrition of organisms in an ecological system, supply and demand of economic markets, the behavior of social groups in human societies, routers in the complex network of the internet, or units of a complex electronic equipment in a car. The dynamics of a system, i.e. the change of system's states depending on time, is represented by linear or nonlinear differential equations. In the case of *nonlinearity*, several feedback activities take place between the elements of the system. These many-bodies problems correspond to nonlinear and non-integrable equations with instabilities and sometimes chaos (Mainzer, 2007).

From a philosophical point of view, mathematical *linearity* means a strong concept of causality with similar causes or inputs of a dynamical system leading to similar effects or outputs: small changes in the parameters or small perturbations added to the values of the variables produce small changes in subsequent values of the variables. Further on, composed effects of linear systems can be reduced to the sum of more simple effects. Therefore, scientists have used linear equations to simplify the way in which we think about the behavior of complex systems. The principle of superposition has its roots in the concept of linearity. But, in the case of nonlinearity, similar causes lead to exponentially separating and expanding effects: small changes in the parameters or small perturbations added to the values of the variables can produce enormous changes in subsequent values of the variables because of the sensitivity to initial conditions. In this case, the whole is more than the sum of its elements.

Neural Self-Organization and Nonlinear Dynamics

On the micro-level of the brain, there are massively many-body-problems which need a reductionist strategy to get a handle with their complexity. In the case of EEG-pictures, a complex system of electrodes measures local states (electric potentials) of the brain. The whole state of a patient's brain on the micro-level is represented by local time series (Small 2005). In the case of, e.g., petit mal epilepsy, they are characterized by typical cyclic peaks. The microscopic states determine the macroscopic electric field patterns during a cyclic period. Mathematically, the macroscopic patterns can be determined by spatial modes, i.e., the amplitude of the field waves. In the corresponding phase space, they determine a chaotic *attractor* characterizing petit mal epilepsy.

The neural self-organization on the cellular and subcellular level is determined by the information processing in and between neurons. Chemical transmitters can effect neural information processing with direct and indirect mechanisms of great plasticity. Long term potentiation (LTP) of synaptic interaction is an extremely interesting topic of brain research. LTP seems to play an essential role for the neural self-organization of cognitive features such as, e.g., memory and learning. The information is assumed to be stored in the synaptic connections of neural cell assemblies with typical macroscopic patterns.

But while an individual neuron does not see or reason or remember, brains are able to do so. Vision, reasoning, and remembrance are understood as higher-level functions. Scientists who prefer a bottom-up strategy recommend that higher-level functions of the brain can be neither addressed nor understood until each particular property of each neuron and synapse is explored and explained. An important insight of the complex system approach discloses that emergent effects of the whole system are synergetic system effects which cannot be reduced to the single elements. They are results of nonlinear interactions. Therefore, the whole is more than the (linear) sum of its parts. Thus, from a methodological point of view, a purely bottom-up-strategy of exploring the brain functions must fail. On the other hand, the advocates of a purely top-down strategy proclaiming that cognition is completely independent of the nervous system are caught in the old Cartesian dilemma "How does the ghost drive the machine?"

Degrees of Complexity of the Brain

Today, we can distinguish several degrees of complexity in the CNS. The scales consider molecules, membranes, synapses, neurons, nuclei, circuits, networks, layers, maps, sensory systems, and the entire nervous system. The research perspectives on these hierarchical levels may concern questions, e.g., of how signals are integrated in dendrites, how neurons interact in a network, how networks interact in a system like vision, how systems interact in the CNS, or how the CNS interacts with its environment. Each stratum may be characterized by a dynamical system determining its particular structures, which is caused by complex interactions of elements with respect to the particular level of hierarchy. Beginning at the bottom, we may distinguish the structures of ion movement, channel configurations, action potentials, potential waves, locomotion, perception, behavior, feeling and reasoning.

The different abilities of the brain need massively parallel information processing in a complex hierarchy of neural structures and areas. We know more or less complex models of the information processing in the visual and motory systems. Even, the dynamics of the emotional system is interacting in a nonlinear feedback manner with several structures of the human brain. These complex systems produce neural maps of cell assemblies.

The self-organization of somatosensoric maps is well-known in the visual and motory cortex. They can be enlarged and changed by learning procedures such as the training of an ape's hand.

PET (Positron-Emission-Tomography) pictures show macroscopic patterns of neurochemical metabolic cell assemblies in different regions of the brain which are correlated with cognitive abilities and conscious states such as looking, hearing, speaking, or thinking. Pattern formation of neural cell assemblies are even correlated with complex processes of psychic states. Perturbations of metabolic cellular interactions (for example, cocaine) can lead to nonlinear effects initiating complex changes of behavior (for example, addiction by drugs). These correlations of neural cell assemblies and attractors of cognitive and conscious states demonstrate the connection of neurobiology and cognitive psychology in recent research, depending on the standards of measuring instruments and procedures (Freeman 2004).

Emergence of Cognitive States and Complex Systems Dynamics

Many questions are still open. Thus, we can only observe *that* someone is thinking and feeling, but not, *what* he is thinking and feeling. Further on, we observe no unique substance called consciousness, but complex macrostates of the brain with different degrees of sensory, motor, or other kinds of attention. *Consciousness* means that we are not only looking, listening, speaking, hearing, feeling, thinking etc., but we know and perceive ourselves during these cognitive processes. Our self is considered a controlling unit state, emerging from a recursive process of multiple self-reflections, self-monitoring, and supervising of our conscious actions. A substrate of self-reflection appears to be given by the so-called mirror neurons (for example, in the Broca area) which let primates (especially humans) imitate and simulate interesting processes of their companions. Therefore, they can learn to take the perspectives of themselves and their companions in order to understand their intentions and to feel with them. The goal of research is to explain subjectivity neuropsychologically as emerging state of brain dynamics.

The brain does not only observe, map, and monitor the external world, but also internal states of the organism, especially its emotional states. Feeling means self-awareness of one's emotional states which are mainly caused by the limbic system. In neuromedicine, the *"Theory of Mind"* (ToM) even analyzes the neural correlates of social feeling which are situated in special areas of the neocortex (Förstle, 2007). People, e.g., suffering from Alzheimer disease, lose their feeling of empathy and social responsibility because the correlated neural areas are destroyed. Therefore, our moral reasoning and deciding have a clear basis in brain dynamics.

From a neuropsychological point of view, the old philosophical problem of "qualia" is intended to be explained as states of brain dynamics. *Qualia* mean properties which are consciously experienced by a person. In a thought experiment a neurobiologist is assumed to be caught in a black-white room. Theoretically, she knows everything about neural information processing of colors. But she never had a chance to experience colors. Therefore, exact knowledge says nothing about the quality of conscious experience. Qualia in that sense emerge by bodily interaction of self-conscious organisms with their environment which can be explained by the nonlinear dynamics of complex systems. Therefore, we can explain the dynamics of subjective feelings and experiences, but, of course, the actual feeling is an individual experience. In medicine, the dynamics of a certain pain can often be completely explained by a physician, although the actual feeling of pain is an individual experience of the patient.

Modeling the Brain as Complex Nonlinear System

In order to model the brain and its complex abilities, it is quite adequate to distinguish the following categories. In neuronal-level models, studies are concentrated on the dynamic and adaptive properties of each nerve cell or neuron, in order to describe the neuron as a unit. In network-level models, identical neurons are interconnected to exhibit emergent system functions. In nervous-system-level models, several *networks* are combined to demonstrate more complex functions of sensory perception, motor functions, stability control, et alt. In mental-operation-level models, the basic processes of cognition, thinking, and problem-solving are described.

In the complex systems approach, the microscopic level of interacting neurons should be modeled by coupled differential equations modeling the transmission of nerve impulses by each neuron. The Hodgekin-Huxley equation is an example of a nonlinear diffusion reaction equation with an exact solution of a traveling wave, giving a precise prediction of the speed and shape of the nerve impulse of electric voltage. In general, nerve impulses emerge as new dynamical entities like ring waves in chemical BZ-reactions or fluid patterns in non-equilibrium dynamics. In short: they are the "atoms" of the complex neural dynamics. On the macroscopic level, they generate cell assemblies which can be modeled by dynamical systems of differential equations. For example, a synchronously firing cell-assembly represents some visual perception of a plant which is not only the sum of its perceived pixels, but characterized by some typical macroscopic features like form, background or foreground. On the next level, cell assemblies of several perceptions interact in a complex scenario. In this case, each cell-assembly is a firing unit, generating a cell assembly of cell assemblies whose macrodynamics can be modeled by nonlinear differential equations (Mainzer, 2005).

In this way, we get a hierarchy of emerging levels of cognition, starting with the microdynamics of firing neurons. The dynamics of each level is assumed to be characterized by certain differential equations of a dynamical model. For example, on the first level of macrodynamics, a dynamical model characterizes a visual perception. On the following level, the observer becomes conscious of the perception. Then the cell assembly of perception is connected with the neural area that is responsible for states of consciousness. In a next step, planning activities are realized in a state of consciousness. In this case, cell assemblies of cell assemblies are connected with neural areas in the planning cortex, and so on. They are represented by coupled nonlinear equations with firing rates of corresponding cell assemblies. Even high-level concepts like self-consciousness can be explained by self-reflections of self-reflections, connected with a personal memory which is represented in corresponding cell assemblies of the brain. Brain states emerge, persist for a small fraction of time, then disappear and are replaced by other states. It is the flexibility and creativeness of this process that makes a brain so successful in animals for their adaption to rapidly changing and unpredictable environments.

COMPLEX SYSTEMS AND THE INNOVATION OF EMBODIED ROBOTICS

Symbolic and Embodied AI

Computational systems were historically constructed on the background of Turing's theory of *computability*. In Turing's functionalism, the hardware of a computer is related to the wetware of human brain. The mind is understood as the software of a computer. Turing argued: If human mind is computable, it can be represented by a Turing program (Church's thesis) which can be computed by a universal Turing machine, i.e.

technically by a general purpose computer. Even if people do not believe in Turing's strong AI (Artificial intelligence)-thesis, they often claim classical computational cognitivism in the following sense: Computational processes operate on symbolic representations referring to situations in the outside world. These formal representations should obey Tarski's correspondence theory of truth (Tarski, 1935): Imagine a real world situation X1 (e.g., some boxes on a table) which is encoded by a symbolic representation A1=encode(X1) (e.g., a description of the boxes on the table). If the symbolic representation A1 is decoded, then we get the real world situation X1 as its meaning, i.e. decode(A1)=X1. A real-world operation T (e.g., a manipulation of the boxes on the table by hand) should produce the same real-world result A2, whether performed in the real world or on the symbolic representation: decode(encode(T) (encode(X1)))=T(X1)=X2. Thus, there is an isomorphism between the outside situation and its formal representation. As the symbolic operations are completely determined by algorithms, the real-world processes are assumed to be completely controlled. Therefore, classical robotics operates with completely determined control mechanisms.

Symbolic representations with ontologies, categories, frames, and scripts of expert systems work along this line. But, they are restricted to a specialized knowledge base without the background knowledge of a human expert. Human experts do not rely on explicit (declarative) rule-based representations only, but also on intuition and implicit (procedural) knowledge (Dreyfus, 1979). Further on, our understanding depends on situations. The *situatedness* of representations is a severe problem of informatics. A robot needs a complete symbolic representation of a situation which must be updated if the robot's position is changed. Imagine that it circles around a table with a ball and a cup on it. A formal representation in a computer language may be ON(TABLE,BALL), ON(TABLE,CUP), BEHIND(CUP,BALL), et alt. Depending on the robot's position relative to the arrangement, the cup is sometimes behind the ball or not. So, the formal representation BEHIND(CUP,BALL) must always be updated in changing positions. How can the robot prevent incomplete knowledge? How can it distinguish between reality and its relative perspective? Situated agents like human beings need no symbolic representations and updating. They look, talk, and interact bodily, for example, by pointing to things. Even rational acting in sudden situations does not depend on symbolic representations and logical inferences, but on bodily interactions with a situation (for example, looking, feeling, reacting).

Thus, we distinguish formal and embodied acting in games with more or less similarity to real life: Chess is a formal game with complete representations, precisely defined states, board positions, and formal operations. Soccer is a nonformal game with skills depending on bodily interactions, without complete representations of situations and operations which are never exactly identical. According to the French philosopher Merleau-Ponty, intentional human skills do not need any symbolic representation, but they are trained, learnt, and embodied by the organism (Merleau-Ponty, 1962; Dreyfus, 1982). An athlete like a pole-vaulter cannot repeat her successful jump like a machine generating the same product. But, the *embodied mind* is no mystery. Modern biology, neural, and cognitive science give many insights into its origin during the evolution of life.

Complex Systems and Systems Biology

Let us start with the computational modeling in biology. Historically, cellular organisms inspired John von Neumann's concept of cellular automata. *Cellular automata* are complex systems of finite automata ("cells") with states (e.g., represented by numbers) which change in dependence of neighboring cells according to simple local rules. There is no central processor, but *self-organization*. Special cellular automata can reproduce themselves in sequential generations. Every computer can be simulated by an appropriate cellular automaton and vice versa according to Church's thesis. Thus, cellular automata are universal computational tools in the sense of a universal Turing machine.

Cellular automata illustrate the dynamics of complex systems in general (Mainzer, 2007). With simple rules of interacting (microscopic) elements, cellular automata generate complex (macroscopic) structures and patterns. For example, 1-dimensional cellular automata, developing line by line downwards a chessboard-like grid with two states and three preceding cells, are determined by $2^3 = 8$ rules. Their outputs with 0 and 1 for black and white cells are the genetic codes, generating the phenotypes with completely regular, chaotic and turbulent patterns. According to systems science, cellular automata simulate phase transitions and attractors like in nature: fixed point attractors of equilibrium dynamics, limit cycles of oscillating patterns, chaos *attractors*, and complex structures with sensitive dependence on initial conditions in the sense of the butterfly effect. In this case, different expanding patterns with increasing complexity can be generated by the same simple rules of cellular automata depending on different initial conditions. In some cases, there is no finite program, in order to forecast the development of random patterns. The algorithmic information content is incompressible because of the computational irreducibility.

Cellular automata were only a first step to demonstrate that evolution and life can be represented by computational models of complex dynamical systems. Modern *systems biology* integrates the molecular, organic, human, and ecological levels of life with computational models of complex systems (Konopka, 2007). In bioinformatics, mathematics, physics, chemistry and biology grow together with computer science, in order to explain and forecast the complexity of life. In systems biology, modeling and simulation ("*in silico* experiments") and technology-driven high-throughput lab ("wet") experiments are combined

to generate new knowledge, which is used to fine tune models and design new experiments. Increasing accumulation of biological data ranging from DNA and protein sequences to metabolic pathways results in the development of computational models of cells, organs, and organisms with complex metabolic and gene regulatory networks.

The goal of systems biology is to develop models describing and predicting cellular behavior at the whole-system level. The genome project was still a reductionist research program with the automatic analysis of DNA-sequences by high speed supercomputers. The paradigm shift from molecular reductionism to the whole-system level of cells, organs, and organisms needs an immense increase of computational capacity in order to reconstruct integrated metabolic and regulatory networks at different molecular levels and to understand complex properties of regulation, control, adaption, and evolution. These complex *networks* (e.g., metabolic network of E. coli bacterium) have universal properties with power law distributions of genes and scale-free structure (Kaneko, 2006). These are typical features of large-scale networks which need a long evolution of selections. They will also be discovered in networks of the brain, World Wide Web, and social groups.

It is a computational challenge to reconstruct the complex causal networks underlying the huge amount of observational data and their probabilistic distribution. Machine learning algorithms are powerful tools for identifying causal gene regulatory networks from observational gene expression data. Dynamics Bayesian network (DBN) algorithms infer cyclic feedback loops, strength and direction of regulatory influence: nodes represent genes, directed links represent conditional statistical dependence of the child node on the parent node. Parents may be activators, repressors, or neutral. Search heuristics are, e.g., genetic algorithms, simulated annealing, or greedy search.

3.3 Embodied Robotics and Dynamical Systems

Systems biology aims at computational modeling of wetware systems, i.e., cells, organs, and organisms. Embodied robotics tries to model hardware systems, i.e. the interaction of robots. In *embodied robotics*, one approach would be to model an agent and its environment separately and then to model the agent-environment interaction by making their state variables mutually dependent (Pfeifer and Scheier, 2001). The dynamical laws of an agent A and its environment E can be described by simplified schemes of differential equations $dx_a/dt = A(x_a, p_a)$ and $dx_e/dt = E(x_e, p_e)$, where x represents the state variables, such as angles of joints, body temperature, or location in space, and p parameters like thresholds, learning rates, nutrition, fuel supply and other critical features of change. Agents and environment can be coupled by defining a sensory function S and a motor function M. The environment influences the agent through S. The agent influences its environment through M. S and M constitute the agent-environment coupling., i.e. $dx_a/dt = A(x_a, S(x_e), p_a)$ and $dx_e/dt = E(x_e, M(x_a), p_e)$, where p_a and p_e are not involved in the coupling. Examples are walking or moving robots in environments with obstacles. In this case, the basic analysis problem can be stated in the following way: given an environment dynamics E, an agent dynamics A, and sensory and motor functions S and M, explain how the agent's observed behavior is generated.

3.4 Self-Organization and Self-Control of Technical Systems

Embodied computing applies the principles of evolution and life to technical systems (Balke and Mainzer, 2005). The dominating principles in the complex world of evolution are *self-organization* and self-control. How can they be realized in technical systems? In many cases, there is no finite program, in order to forecast the development of complex systems. In general, there are three reasons for computational limits of system dynamics: (1) A system may be undecidable in a strict logical sense. (2) Further on, a system can be deterministic, but nonlinear and chaotic. In this case, the system depends sensitively on tiny changes of initial data in the sense of the butterfly effect. Long-term forecasting is restricted, and the computational costs of forecasting increase exponentially after some few steps of future predictions. (3) Finally, a system can be stochastic and nonlinear. In this case, pattern emergence can only be predicted probabilistically.

Engineering control systems commonly are designed to behave linearly. This implies that they obey superposition, that is, twice as large an input signal will produce twice as large a response. By contrast, biological control frequently involves *nonlinearities* (Yates, 1988). Some nonlinear behavior is to be expected. For example, since biological variables cannot exceed certain values, they exhibit upper limits that may show up in mathematical models as saturation nonlinearities.

The firing frequency of certain sensory receptors can be considered a function of the sensed variable or stimulus. An ideal linear receptor would have a response proportional to the input stimulus over the full range if inputs. On the other hand, an actual biological receptor might have a nonlinear response. In the case of saturation, there is range of stimulus values over which the input-output relationship is nearly linear. Beyond this range, it takes a larger and larger input to obtain a given increment of response, until the response reaches its maximum possible value. Since receptors are always limited to some maximum output, it is evident that all biological receptors display some form of saturation. In other cases, a biological system will not respond to an input stimulus until the stimulus exceeds some minimum value. Obviously, such a property has adaptive value, since it may conserve energy. Sometimes, biological systems behave in a nearly linear manner for small values of input signals, but will deviate from linearity increasingly as the signal magnitudes grow.

Some properties of systems containing nonlinearities exhibit spontaneous oscillations which are called limit cycles. They exist only in nonlinear dynamical systems. Certain physiological variables exhibit oscillations of limit cycles (Bassingthwaighte, Liebovitch, & West, 1994). Among these variables are many homeostatic quantities, such as blood glucose concentration, arterial pressure, and temperature. Many of these quantities have a daily rhythm like body temperature. Others, like ovulation, have a twenty-.eight-day cycle. Physiology is challenged to understand why nonlinearities and the ensuing limit cycle oscillations are essential to an organism.

Controllers for robot manipulators began as simple linear feedback control systems. However, since these systems were modeled on the human arm, it soon became apparent that more complex controllers were required in order to obtain some of the versatility of that arm. The situation is even more interesting with respect to mobile robots. Although most small mobile robots use very simple linear controllers at the lowest reflex level, they also perform reasoning and planning at high levels (Bekey, 2005). Many mobile robots use a multitude of sensors. Therefore, in common with organisms, they must integrate the readings from these sensors in order to make movement decisions. With increasingly autonomous humanoid robots, biological models for their control will become more and more complex and nonlinear, too.

Cellular Neural Networks (CNN) and Neurobionics

A nice test bed for all kinds of technical systems are computational automata. There is a precise relation between *self-organization* of nonlinear systems with continuous dynamics and discrete cellular automata. The dynamics of nonlinear systems is given by differential equations with continuous variables and a continuous parameter of time. Sometimes, difference equations with discrete time points are sufficient. If even the

continuous variables are replaced by discrete (e.g., binary) variables, we get functional schemes of automata with functional arguments as inputs and functional values as outputs. There are classes of cellular automata modeling attractor behavior of nonlinear complex systems which is well-known from self-organizing processes.

Cellular automata (CA) are only a theoretical concept of computational dynamics. In electrical engineering, information and computer science, the concept of *cellular neural networks* (CNN) has recently become an influential paradigm of complexity research and is being realized in information and chip technology (Chua and Roska, 2002; Mainzer, 2007). CNNs have been made possible by the sensor revolution of the late 1990s. Cheap sensors and MEMS (micro-electro-mechanical system) arrays have become popular as artificial eyes, noses, ears, tastes, and somatosensor devices. An immense number of generic analog signals have been processed. A new kind of chip technology, similar to signal processing in natural organisms, is needed. Analog cellular computers are the technical response to the sensor revolution, mimicking the anatomy and physiology of sensory and processing organs. A CNN is their hard core, because it is an array of analog dynamic processors or cells.

In general, a CNN is a nonlinear analog circuit that processes signals in real time. It is a multi-component system of regularly spaced identical units, called cells, which communicate directly with each other only through their nearest neighbors. In complex systems local interactions of their microscopic elements lead to the emergence of global macroscopic patterns and clusters. In brains, for example, clusters of cell assemblies are generated by synchronously firing cells. The locality of direct connections is a natural principle of *self-organization* which is realized by brains as well as by cellular automata (CA). Total connectivity would be energetically too expensive with the risk of information chaos. Therefore, it was not realized by the evolution of the brain and not applied in technology. Unlike conventional cellular automata, CNN host processors accept and generate analog signals in continuous time with real numbers as interaction values. The dynamics of a cell's state are defined by a nonlinear differential equation (CNN state equation) with scalars for state, output, input, threshold, and coefficients, called synaptic weights, modeling the intensity of synaptic connections of the cell with the inputs and outputs of the neighbor cells. The CNN output equation connects the states of a cell with the outputs.

CNN arrays are extremely useful for practical standards in visual computing. Examples are CNNs that detect patterns in either binary (black-and-white) or gray-scale input images. An image consists of pixels corresponding to the cells of CNN with binary or gray scale. From the perspective of nonlinear dynamics, it is convenient to think of standard CNN state equations as a set of ordinary differential equations. Contrary to the usual CA approach with only geometric pattern formation of cells, the dynamical behavior of CNNs can be studied analytically by nonlinear equations. Examples deliver CNNs with limit cycles and chaotic attractors. For technical implementations of CNNs, such as silicon chips, complete stability properties must be formulated, in order to avoid oscillations, chaotic, and noise phenomena. These results also have practical importance for image processing applications of CNNs. As brains and computers work with units in two distinct states, the conditions of bistability are studied in brain research, as well as in chip technology.

CNNs are optimal technical candidates to simulate local synaptic interactions of neurons generating global macro phenomena like pattern formation. Hallucinations, for example, are the results of self-organizing phenomena within the visual cortex. This type of pattern perception seems to be similar to pattern formation of fluids in chemistry or aerodynamics. Pattern formation in the visual brain is due to local nonlinear coupling among cells. In the living organism, there is a spa-

tial transformation between the pattern perception of the retina and the pattern formation within the visual cortex of the brain. First simulations of this cortico-retinal transformation by CNNs generate remarkable similarities with pattern perceptions that are well-known from subjective experiences of hallucinations. Perceptions of a spiraling tunnel pattern have been reported by people who were clinically dead and later revived. The light at the end of the tunnel has sometimes been interpreted as religious experiences.

CNNs with information processing in nano-seconds and even the speed of light seem to be optimal candidates for applications in neurobionics. There are surprising similarities between CNN architectures and, for example, the visual pathway of the brain. An appropriate CNN approach is called the "Bionic Eye", which involves a formal framework of vision models combined and implemented on the so-called CNN universal machine. Like a universal Turing machine, a CNN universal machine can simulate any specialized CNN and is technically constructed in chip technology. Visual illusions which have been studied in cognitive psychology can also be simulated by a universal CNN chip. The same architecture of a universal machine can not only be used to mimic the retinas of animals (for example, of a frog, tiger salamander, rabbit, or eagle), but they can also be combined and optimized for technical applications. The combination of biological and artificial chips is no longer a science fiction-like dream of cyborgs, but a technical reality with inspiring ramifications for robotics and medicine (Tetzlaff 2002, pp. 228-242).

In epileptology, clinical applications of CNN chips have already been envisaged. The idea is to develop a miniaturized chip device for the prediction and prevention of epileptic seizures (Fig.3). Nonlinear time series analysis techniques have been developed to characterize the typical EEG patterns of an epileptic seizure and to recognize the phase transitions leading to the epileptic neural states. These techniques mainly involve estimates of established criteria such as correlation dimension, Kolmogorov-Sinai-entropy, Lyapunov exponents, fractal similarity, et alt. (Small, 2005). Implantable seizure predictions and prevention devices are already in use with Parkinsonian patients. In the case of epileptic processes, such a device would continuously monitor features extracted from the EEG, compute the probability of an impending seizure, and provide suitable prevention techniques. It should also possess both a high flexibility for tuning to individual patient patterns and a high efficacy to allow the estimation of these features in real time. Eventually, it should have low energy consumption and be small enough to be implemented in a miniaturized, implantable system. These requirements are optimally realized by CNNs, with their massive parallel computing power, analog information processing, and capacity for universal computing.

3.6 Neural Networks and Robotics

In complex dynamical systems of organisms monitoring and controlling are realized on hierarchical levels. Thus, we must study the nonlinear dynamics of these systems in experimental situations, in order to find appropriate models and to prevent undesired emergent behavior as possible attractors. From the point of view of systems science, the challenge of embodied robotics is controlled emergence.

A key-application of controlled emergence is the nonlinear dynamics of brains. Brains are neural systems which allow quick adaption to changing situations during life-time of an organism. Neural *networks* are complex systems of threshold elements with firing and non-firing states, according to learning strategies (e.g., Hebbian learning). Beside deterministic homogeneous Hopfield networks, there are so-called Boltzmann machines with stochastic network architecture of non-deterministic processor elements and a distributed knowledge representation which is described mathematically by an energy function.

While Hopfield systems use a Hebbian learning strategy, Boltzmann machines favor a back propagation strategy (Widrow-Hoff rule) with hidden neurons in a many-layered network.

In general, it is the aim of a learning algorithm to diminish the information-theoretic measure of the discrepancy between the brain's internal model of the world and the real environment via *self-organization*. The interest in the field of neural networks is mainly inspired by the successful technical applications of statistical mechanics and nonlinear dynamics to solid state physics, spin glass physics, chemical parallel computers, optical parallel computers, or laser systems. Other reasons are the recent development of computing resources and the level of technology which make a computational treatment of nonlinear systems more and more feasible (Mainzer, 2008).

A simple robot with diverse sensors (for example, proximity, light, collision) and motor equipment can generate complex behavior by a self-organizing neural network. In the case of a collision with an obstacle, the synaptic connections between the active nodes for proximity and collision layer are reinforced by Hebbian learning: A behavioral pattern emerges, in order to avoid collisions in future (Pfeifer and Scheier, 2001). In the human organism, walking is a complex bodily self-organization, largely without central control of brain and consciousness: It is driven by the dynamical pattern of a steady periodic motion, the attractor of the motor system.

What can we learn from nature? In unknown environments, a better strategy is to define a low-level ontology, introduce redundancy – which is commonly prevalent in sensory systems, for example – and leave room for self-organization. Low-level ontologies of robots only specify systems like the body, sensory systems, motor systems, and the interactions among their components, which may be mechanical, electrical, electromagnetic, thermal et alt. According to the complex systems approach, the components are characterized by certain microstates generating the macrodynamics of the whole system.

Take a legged robot (Shuji Kajita, 2007). Its legs have joints that can assume different angles, and various forces can be applied to them. Depending on the angles and the forces, the robot will be in different positions and behave in different ways. Further on, the legs have connections to one another and to other elements. If a six-legged robot lifts one of the legs, this changes the forces on all the other legs instantaneously, even though no explicit connection needs to be specified. The connections are implicit: They are enforced through the environment, because of the robot's weight, the stiffness of its body, and the surfaces on which it stands. Although these connections are elementary, they have not been made explicit by the designer. Connections may exist between elementary components that we do not even realize. Electronic components may interact via electromagnetic fields that the designer is not aware of. These connections may generate adaptive patterns of behavior with high fitness degrees. But they can also lead to sudden instability and chaotic behavior. In our example, communication between the legs of a robot can be implicit. In general, much more is implicit in a low-level specification than in a high-level ontology. In restricted simulated agents, only what is made explicit exists, whereas in the complex real world, many forces exist and properties arise, even if the designer does not explicitly represent them. Thus, we must study the nonlinear dynamics of these systems in experimental situations, in order to find appropriate models and to prevent undesired emergent behavior as possible attractors.

In the research project "*Cognition in Technical Systems*" (CoTeSys, 2006-2011), cognitive and life sciences, information processing and mathematical sciences, engineering and robotics work systematically together to explore cognition for technical systems. Robotic agents cannot be fully programmed for every application. The program learns from experience where to stand when taking a glass out of a cupboard, how to best grab particular kitchen utensils, where to look for particular cutlery, et alt. This requires the control system to know the parameters of control routines and to have models for how the parameters change the behavior. The sensor data of a robot's environment, which is the robot's "experience", are stored in a relational database system, the robot's "memory". According to the paradigm of probabilistic robotics (Thrun, Burgard & Fox, 2005), the data in the database together with causal structure on domain relations imply a joint probability distribution over relations in the activity domain. This distribution is applied in Markov logic, which allows inferring the conditional probability of logical (first order) statements. In short: A robot can estimate the environmental situation probabilistically.

According to the paradigm of *complex dynamical systems* (Mainzer, 2008), a robot can be described at different levels, in which global properties at one level emerge from the interaction of a number of simple elements at lower levels. Global properties are emergent in the sense that they result from nothing else but local interactions among the elements. They cannot be predicted or inferred from knowledge of the elements or of the rules by which the elements locally interact, given the high nonlinearity of these interactions.

Simple examples of embodied robotics are reactive robots. They are controlled by simple neural networks, for example, fully connected perceptrons without internal layers and without any kind of internal organization. Nevertheless, these robots can display not only simple behaviors, such as obstacle avoidance, but also behaviors capable of solving complex problems involving perceptual aliasing, sensory ambiguity, and sequential organization of sub-behaviors. The question arises how far we can go with reactive sensory-motor coordination.

Embodied Robotics and Cognition

Not only "low level" motor intelligence, but also "high level" cognition (for example, categorization) can emerge from complex bodily interaction with an environment by sensory-motor coordination without internal symbolic representation. We call it "embodied cognition": Developmental psychology shows that an infant learns to categorize objects and to build up concepts by touching, grasping, manipulating, feeling, tasting, hearing, and looking at things, and not by explicit symbolic representations (for example, language). The categories are based on fuzzy patchworks of prototypes and may be improved and changed during life. We have an innate disposition to construct and apply conceptual schemes and tools.

But are there situations and problems which can only be solved by robots allowed to go beyond embodied reactions with internal dynamical states? During evolution, primates and human beings have learnt to develop alternative internal models of situations with changing conditions to find the appropriate decisions. In embodied robotics, there are experiments of homing navigation where a robot is asked to navigate in an arena with a limited, but rechargeable, energy supply (Floreano & Mondada, 1996). The abilities to locate a battery charger and periodically return to it are achieved without introducing explicit instructions of a program. Evolved homing strategies are based on autonomous development of an internal neural topographic map that was not predesigned allowing the robot to choose appropriate trajectories of motion.

The emergence of internal models or maps is made possible by an architecture of robots where two or more alternative neural modules compete for control of each motor output. This architecture allows evolving robots to use different neural modules to produce different sub-behaviors, but without preprogramming the whole behavior. There is an artificial evolution to select different neural modules and appropriate sub-behaviors. In

a neural network with a layer of hidden neurons, some of the hidden nodes start to specialize and to influence the planning decision of the robot's trajectories of motion. The activation levels of the hidden neurons can be displayed on maps of the environment, displaying remarkable topographical representations of the external world.

In several examples, artificial evolution of robots with emergent modular architectures reported better results than other architectures (Nolfi & Floreano, 2001). But, in embodied organisms as well as embodied robots, sensory-motor coordination, and internal models are no excluding alternatives. In natural and technical evolution, they coexist and cooperate. All this amounts to saying that the behavior of robots with increasing autonomy cannot be purely explained by a stimulus-reaction paradigm, but by the emergence of internal ("cognitive") representation of the environment which reflects the goals defined by the robot itself (Bellman, 2005).

Moreover, cognitive states of persons depend on emotions. We recognize emotional expressions of human faces with pattern recognition of neural networks and react by generating appropriate facial expressions for non-verbal communication. Emotional states are generated in the limbic system of the brain which is connected with all sensory and motory systems of the organism. All intentional actions start with an unconscious impulse in the limbic system which can be measured before their performance. Thus, embodied intentionality is a measurable feature of the brain (Freeman, 2004). Humans use feelings to help them navigate the ontological trees of their concepts and preferences, to make decisions in the face of increasing combinational complexity. Obviously, emotions help to reduce complexity.

The *embodied mind* is a *complex dynamical system* acting and reacting in dynamically changing situations. The emergence of cognitive and emotional states is made possible by brain dynamics which can be modeled by neural networks. According to the principle of computational equivalence

(Mainzer, 2007), any dynamical system can be simulated by an appropriate computational system. But, contrary to Turing's AI-thesis, that does not mean computability in every case. In complex dynamical systems, the rules of locally interacting elements (for example, Hebb's rules of synaptic interaction) may be simple and programmed in a computer model. But their nonlinear dynamics can generate complex patterns and system states which cannot be forecast in the long run without increasing loss of computability and information. Thus, artificial minds (Dennett, 1998) could have their own intentionality, cognitive and emotional states which cannot be forecast and computed similar as is the case with natural minds. Limitations of computability are characteristic features of complex systems.

HANDLING A WORLD WITH INCREASING COMPLEXITY

The emergence of complex patterns of behavior in robotics depends essentially on the nonlinearity of complex systems. Further conditions come in by the specific parameters of physical, chemical, biological, psychological, computational, and robotic systems. Therefore, the formal models of nonlinear complex systems do not eliminate the requirements of specific experimental research on the different levels and scales in the different sciences. Interdisciplinary applications of nonlinear complex systems are successful if they find a clever combination of formal mathematics, computer-assisted modeling, and robotics. Complexity and *nonlinearity* are interdisciplinary problems of current research (Mainzer, 2007).

In the dynamical systems approach, we first need to specify what system we intend to model and then we have to establish the differential or difference equations. Time series analysis and further criteria of data mining help to construct the appropriate phase spaces, trajectories, and attractors (Small, 2005). In general, the dynamical systems approach is used in an analytical way: it starts from a given agent-environment interaction, which is formalized in terms of differential equations (compare 2.2). The complex variety of behavior can be analyzed by solving, approximating, or simulating the equations, in order to find the attractors of dynamics. The dynamical attractors of the interacting systems can be used to steer an agent or to let them organize in a desired way. But, the dynamical systems approach can also be applied in a synthetic way in order to design and to construct robots and their environments.

In natural evolution, brains have emerged by selection and mutation. They enable organisms to adapt themselves and to learn under changing conditions on Earth (*Embodied Mind*). But, the laws of evolution would also allow other forms of thinking, feeling, and conscious systems. They might be realized elsewhere in the universe. Historically, engineering sciences had been successful in finding new purposeful solutions of natural laws which were not realized by nature (for example, flight of aircrafts contrary to flight of birds according to laws of aerodynamics). Thus, neurorobotics could and should develop new artificial systems of embodied minds aiming at humanistic purposes. *Embodied robots* could improve the interface of man and machine. For example, in highly industrialized nations with advanced aging, robots with emotional interface may be a future perspective for nursing old and diseased people. In principle, future technical evolution could even generate self-conscious systems with their own identity and intimacy. But, it should remain in human responsibility which kind of artificial intelligence and artificial life we need and want to accept besides us.

Cognitive systems and robots are not alone on Earth. They interact and communicate in global networks. In a technical evolution, a global communication network (World Wide Web) is emerging with surprising similarity to self-organizing neural networks of the human brain. Its increasing complexity needs intelligent strategies of information retrieval and learning algorithms, according to the synaptic plasticity of a brain.

It is remarkable that complex networks of evolution, technology, and society are governed by the same laws and universal properties. Complex *networks* with no apparent design principles have been described as random graphs (Albert & Barabási 2002). They start with N nodes, and connect every pair of nodes with probability p, creating a graph with approximately $pN(N-1)/2$ edges distributed randomly. In most networks there is a relatively short path between any two nodes despite their often large size ("small-world property"). But, in complex systems of, e.g., molecular, cellular, social, or technological networks, we also observe emerging clusters of, e.g., molecular structures, cellular assemblies, social cliques and groups, wiring diagrams, and wireless patterns. What are the underlying organizing principles?

Therefore, clustering and degree distributions are introduced in complex networks. A node i of a network has k_i edges connecting it to k_i other nodes. The total number of edges with the nearest neighbors in a cluster is $k_i(k_i-1)/2$. The clustering coefficient of node i is the ratio between the Number E_i of actually existing edges and the total number, i.e., $C_i = 2E_i/k_i(k_i-1)$. The clustering coefficient C of the whole network is the average of all individual C_i's. In a random graph, since the edges are distributed randomly, $C = p$. Further on, the majority of nodes has nearly the same degree (number) of edges. Therefore, the degree distribution $P(k)$ (i.e., the probability that any node has k edges) is a Poisson distribution. But, most realistic networks has a degree distribution with a *power-law* tail, i.e., $P(k) \sim k^{-\gamma}$ without a characteristic scale (*scale-free networks*). In general, they indicate highly developed (hierarchical) structures, generated by evolution or technology.

The World Wide Web (WWW) is the largest information network with web pages as nodes and hyperlinks as edges. The directed edges are characterized by two degree distributions of outcoming and incoming distributions with power-law tails $P_{out}(k) \sim k^{-\gamma out}$ and $P_{in}(k) \sim k^{-\gamma in}$. For example, a sample of 200 million web pages has $\gamma_{out} = 2.72$ and $\gamma_{in} = 2.1$. The Internet links computers and other telecommunication devices. At the router level, the nodes are the routers, and the edges are their physical connections. At the interdomain level, each domain of hundreds of routers is represented by a single node with at least one route as connection with other nodes. At both levels, the degree distribution follows a *power law* which can be compared with properties of metabolic networks in systems biology.

In these communication systems, we are overwhelmed by net- and information complexity and feel lost in the net. During information retrieval, millions of websites with non structuralized contents must be analyzed. Until now the WWW is a huge stupid storage of information. We need an intelligent web which is able to understand our intentions and the meaning of messages for a user. In the future, websites will contain tags with elements of meaning which are automatically generated, read, and understood by software agents. Ontologies define the meanings of tags in data bases. An information retrieval agent must only look in the charts of metadata. The goal is to live with personalized information systems. Personalized information systems should be adapted to the conditions and needs of human beings (embodiment and personalization). In nomadic and ubiquitous computing, personalized information devices are wireless and pervasively (locally and globally) available.

From a philosophical point of view, we may ask for the foundation and background of all these examples of complex information systems. Obviously, the increasing information complexity is generated by evolution. During evolution new forms of information storage have been developed from genetic information of cells and neural information of brains and nervous systems up to extrasomatic information outside the human body in libraries, databases, and the WWW, surpassing single human brains.

Information complexity can be measured by

different degrees of noise, e.g., signals of complex metabolic or neural networks, electronic flickering of technical circuits, flickering of information packets in the WWW, flickering of stock values in financial markets (Mainzer 2007). Complex patterns of signals and data have a spectrum with frequency f approximately proportional to $1/f^b$ ($b>0$), called $1/f$-noise: e.g., spectrum with white noise ($b=0$) with statistical independent and uncorrelated data (Gaussian distribution and Brownian motion), pink noise ($b=1$) with abrupt disruptions, red noise ($b=2$) with emerging trends and correlations, and black noise with regularity ($b=3$). The degree of irregularity descreases with increasing exponent b. Pink and red noise with non-Gaussian distribution, *power law*, and scale-free networks characterize self-organization of complex structures in evolution, technology, and society between complete randomness (white noise) and regularity (black noise).

Besides information complexity we distinguish *computational complexity*. It is well known that computability and decidability can be measured with different degrees of complexity according to computational time. Computational time refer to different numbers of elementary operations depending on the length of inputs (e.g., linear, quadratic, polynomial, exponential functions of computational time). Thus, we distinguish P-problems which are computable by deterministic Turing-machines in polynomial time and NP-problems which are computable by non-deterministic

Turing-machines in polynomial time. It is still an open question if NP-problems can be solved by deterministic machines in polynomial time, i.e. $NP \neq P$ or not.

If organisms are considered computational complex systems, then information and computational complexity can be referred to their evolution. In that sense, we can compare mathematical and natural objects with different degrees of evolution. For example, sequences of zeros 0000… in mathematics and perfect crystals in nature are simple structures with simple rules of construction. But the decimal sequence of the number π with 3,14… in mathematics or the development of a human organism during evolution have a much more complex development. The computational depth of an object could be defined as computational time which is needed by a universal Turing machine for its generation from an (algorithmically random) input.

Thus, Church's famous thesis can be generalized for evolution. Computational depth is defined as measure of complexity of evolutionary objects, depending on the capacity of a Turing machine to simulate algorithms of mathematics as well as processes of nature. In general, digital computers cannot solve continuous nonlinear differential equations of dynamical systems analytically, but at least with numerical approximation. Even stochastic equations of probabilistic and statistical systems can be modeled and approximately computed as sequence of probabilistic phase tran-

Figure 1. Complexity degrees of computational, information, and dynamical complexity

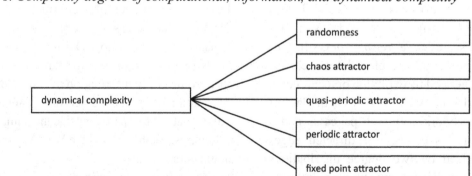

sitions with non-deterministic Turing machines. The question arises if non-deterministic Turing machines with polynomial computational time (NP-problem) can be replaced by deterministic Turing machines (P-problem). Computational complexity can be enlarged from biological evolution to the development of the whole universe. The smallest building blocks of the universe are quantum systems. Their quantum states represent quantum bits (qubits) with quantum information. Therefore, the expanding universe can be considered a quantum computer with increasing complexity.

From a methodological point of view, we defined and distinguished the concept of complexity in three ways (Figure 1) as *dynamical*, *information*, and *computational complexity*. *Dynamical complexity* means the complexity of the time-depending dynamics of complex systems, mathematically represented by differential equations, their corresponding state spaces and different degrees of *attractors*: fixed point attractor of simple equilibrium systems, periodic and quasi-periodic attractors (limit cycles), chaos attractor, and finally randomness. *Information complexity* distinguishes black, red, pink, and white noise. *Computational complexity* refers to the degrees of computational time or the size of a computational program. These different degrees of dynamical, information, and computational complexity can be related to one another: White noise means randomness, pink and red noise refer to chaotic and self-organizing dynamical systems with chaos attractors and non-equilibrium dynamics, Black noise is related to attractors of regularity. Computational time is limited for predictions of unstable and chaotic systems. The Kolmogorov-Sinai entropy refers to the information flow in dynamical systems. Therefore, it measures dynamical as well as information complexity.

What does that mean practically for handling a complex world? In the age of globalization, the world-wide problems and conflicts (e.g., health, economy, financial, military) are represented in a digital world of electronic networks similar to the large-scale networks of evolution. Because of their increasing complexity, we need more insight in their nonlinear dynamics. Systems and computer science aim at appropriate instruments of control and sustainable dynamics of complex systems.

REFERENCES

Albert, R., & Barabási, A.-L. (2002). Statistical mechanics of complex networks. *Reviews of Modern Physics*, *74*(1), 47–97. doi:10.1103/RevModPhys.74.47

Balke, W.-T., & Mainzer, K. (2005). Knowledge Representation and the Embodied Mind: Towards a Philosophy and Technology of Personalized Informatics. In Professional Knowledge Management (LNCS Vol. 3782, pp. 586-597). Berlin: Springer.

Bassingthwaighte, J. B., Liebovitch, L. S., & West, B. J. (1994). *Fractal Physiology*. New York: Oxford University Press.

Bekey, G. L. (2005). *Autonomous Robots. From Biological Inspiration to Implementation and Control*. Cambridge, MA: MIT Press.

Bellman, K.L. (2005). Self-Conscious Modeling. *It – Information Technology*, *4*, 188-194.

Chua, L. O., & Roska, T. (2002). *Cellular Neural Networks and Visual Computing. Foundations and Applications*. Cambridge, UK: Cambridge University Press. doi:10.1017/CBO9780511754494

CoTeSys. (2006-2011). Retrieved from http://www.dfg.de/en/research.funding/coordinated.programmes/excellence.initiative

Dennett, C. D. (1998). *Brainchildren: Essays on Designing Minds*. Cambridge, MA: MIT Press.

Dreyfus, H. L. (1979). *What Computer's can't do – The Limits of Artificial Intelligence*. New York: Harper & Row.

Dreyfus, H. L. (1982). *Husserl, Intentionality, and Cognitive Science*. Cambridge, MA: MIT Press.

Floreano, D., & Mondada, F. (1996). Evolution of homing navigation in a real mobile robot. *IEEE Transactions on Systems, Man, and Cybernetics. Part B, Cybernetics*, *26*(3), 396–407. doi:10.1109/3477.499791

Förstl, H. (Ed.). (2007). *Theory of Mind. Neurobiologie und Psychologie sozialen Verhaltens*. Heidelberg, Germany: Springer.

Freeman, W. J. (2004). How and why brains create meaning from sensory information. *International Journal of Bifurcation and Chaos in Applied Sciences and Engineering*, *14*, 515–530. doi:10.1142/S0218127404009405

Kajita, S. (2007). *Humanoide Roboter. Theorie und Technik des Künstlichen Menschen*. Berlin: Aka GmbH.

Kaneko, K. (2006). *Life: An Introduction to Complex Systems Biology*. Berlin: Springer.

Konopka, A. K. (Ed.). (2007). *Systems Biology. Principles, Methods, and Concepts*. Boca Raton, FL: CRC Press.

Mainzer, K. (2005). *Symmetry and Complexity. The Spirit and Beauty of Nonlinear Science*. Singapore: World Scientific Publisher.

Mainzer, K. (2007). *Thinking in Complexity. The Computational Dynamics of Matter, Mind, and Mankind* (5th ed.). New York: Springer.

Mainzer, K. (2008). The emergence of mind and brain: an evolutionary, computational, and philosophical approach. In Banerjee, R., & Chakrabarti, B. K. (Eds.), *Models of Brain and Mind. Physical, Computational and Psychological Approaches* (pp. 115–132). Amsterdam: Elsevier.

Mainzer, K. (2010). *Leben als Maschine? Von der Systembiologie zu Robotik und Künstlicher Intelligenz*. Paderborn: Mentis.

Merleau-Ponty, M. (1962). *Phenomenology of Perception*. New York: Routledge & Kegan Paul.

Nolfi, S., & Floreano, D. (2001). *Evolutionary Robotics. The Biology, Intelligence, and Technology of Self-Organizing Machines*. Cambridge, MA: MIT Press.

Pfeifer, R., & Scheier, C. (2001). *Understanding Intelligence*. Cambridge, MA: MIT Press.

Small, M. (2005). *Applied Nonlinear Time Series Analysis. Applications in Physics, Physiology and Finance*. Singapore: World Scientific Publisher.

Tarski, A. (1935). Der Wahrheitsbegriff in den formalisierten Sprachen. *Studies in Philology*, *1*, 261–405.

Tetzlaff, R. (2002). *Cellular Neural Networks and their Application. Proceedings of the 7th IEEE International Workshop*. Singapore: World Scientific Publisher.

Thrun, S., Burgard, W., & Fox, D. (2005). *Probabilistic Robotics*. Cambridge, MA: MIT Press.

Yates, F. E. (1988). *Self-Organizing Systems. The Emergence of Order*. Boston: Plenum.

Compilation of References

Aaronson, S. (2008, March). The Limits of Quantum Computers. *Scientific American*.

Abadi, M. a. (1996). *A Theory of Objects*. New York: Springer-Verlag, Monographs in Computer Science.

Abbott, E. A. (1963). *Flatland: A Romance of Many Dimensions*. New York: Dover Publications Inc.

Abelson, R. P., & Carroll, J. D. (1965). Computer simulation of individual belief systems. *The American Behavioral Scientist, 8*, 24–30.

Aberdein, A. (2005). The uses of argument in mathematics. *Argumentation, 19*, 287–301. doi:10.1007/s10503-005-4417-8

Abramsky, S. (1994). Proofs as processes. *Theoretical Computer Science, 135*, 5–9. doi:10.1016/0304-3975(94)00103-0

Abramsky, S. D. M. (1992). Handbook of Logic in Computer Science. Vol 2. Oxford: Oxford University Press.

Abrial, J.-R. (2009). Modelling in Event-B: System and Software Engineering. Cambridge, UK: Cam bridge University Press.

Abrial, J.-R., Butler, M., Hallerstede, S., Hoang, T. S., Metha, F., and Voisin, L. (2009). Rodin: An Open Toolset for Modelling and Reasoning in Event-B. *Journal of Software Tools for Technology Transfer*.

Achinstein, P. (1965). Theoretical models. *The British Journal for the Philosophy of Science, 16*(62), 102–120. doi:10.1093/bjps/XVI.62.102

Achinstein, P. (1983). *The Nature of Explanation*. New York: Oxford University Press.

Aczel, P. (1978). The type theoretic interpretation of constructive set theory . In MacIntyre, A., Pacholski, L., & Paris, J. (Eds.), *Logic Colloquium '77* (pp. 55–66). Amsterdam: North Holland. doi:10.1016/S0049-237X(08)71989-X

Adam, A. (1998). *Artificial Knowing: Gender and the Thinking Machine*. New York: Routlegde.

Agre, P. E. (1988). *The Dynamic Structure of Everyday Life (MIT AI Technical Report, October 1988, No. 1085)*. Cambridge, MA: MIT.

Agre, P. E. (1997). *Computation and Human Experience*. Cambridge, UK: Cambridge University Press. doi:10.1017/CBO9780511571169

Agudelo, J. C., & Carnielli, W. (2006). *Quantum Computation via Paraconsistent Computation*. arXiv:quant-ph/0607100v1 14 Jul 2006.

Ahlswede, R., Cai, N., Li, S.-Y. R., & Wai-Ho Yeung, R. (2000). Network Information Flow. *IEEE Transactions on Information Theory, 46*(4), 1204–1216. doi:10.1109/18.850663

Ahuja, R. K., Magnanti, T. L., & Orlin, J. B. (1993). *Network Flows: Theory, Algorithms, and Applications*. Englewood Cliffs, NJ: Prentice Hall.

Akrich, M. (1995). User Representations: Practices, Methods and Sociology . In Rip, A., Misa, T. J., & Schot, J. (Eds.), *Managing Technology in Society. The Approach of Constructive Technology Assessment* (pp. 167–184). London: Pinter Publishers.

Albert, D. Z. & Galchen, R. (2009, March). Was Einstein Wrong?: A Quantum Threat to Special Relativity. *Scientific American Magazine.*

Albert, R., & Barabási, A.-L. (2002). Statistical mechanics of complex networks. *Reviews of Modern Physics, 74*(1), 47–97. doi:10.1103/RevModPhys.74.47

Allhutter, D. (Forthcoming). Mind Scripting. A Deconstructive Method In Software Development. *Science, Technology & Human Values.*

Allhutter, D., & Hanappi-Egger, E. (2006). The Hidden Social Dimensions of Technologically Centred Quality Standards: Triple-Loop Learning as Process Centred Quality Approach . In Dawson, R., Georgiadou, E., Linecar, P., Ross, M., & Staples, G. (Eds.), *Perspectives in Software Quality* (pp. 179–195). London: British Computer Society.

Allhutter, D., Hanappi-Egger, E., & John, S. (2007). *Gendered Software Design. Zur Sichtbarmachung der Gender Scripts in technologischen Artefakten.* Vienna, Austria: WU Vienna, Gender and Diversity in Organizations.

Allo, P. (2007). Logical pluralism and semantic information. *Journal of Philosophical Logic, 36*(4), 659–694. doi:10.1007/s10992-007-9054-2

Alston, P. (2009). *Information to the Third Committee (Social, Humanitarian and Cultural) of the UN General Assembly,* 27 Oct. 2009; Retrieved 20th of November, 2009 from http://reliefweb.int/rw/rwb.nsf/db900sid/MYAI-7X94DK?OpenDocument

Altmann, J. (2003). Roboter für den Krieg? *Wissenschaft und Frieden, 21*(3), 18–22.

Altmann, J. (2006). Trends in Cognitive Science and Information Technology. In S. Pullinger (ed.), *Annex to Study: EU research and innovation policy and the future of the Common Foreign Security Policy. A Report Commissioned by the Science and Technology Foresight Unit of DG Research, European Commission* (October 2006). Retrieved October 14, 2009, from http://www.isis-europe.org/pdf/reports_11.pdf

Altmann, J. (2009). Preventive Arms Control for Uninhabited Military Vehicles . In Capurro, R., & Nagenborg, M. (Eds.), *Ethics and Robotics* (pp. 69–82). Amsterdam: IOS Press.

Anderson, R. C., Spiro, R. J., & Montague, W. E. (Eds.). (1984). *Schooling and the acquisition of knowledge.* Hillsdale, NJ: Lawrence Erlbaum.

Argyris, C. (1993). *Knowledge for Action. A Guide to Overcoming Barriers to Organizational Change.* San Francisco: Jossey-Bass Wiley.

Argyris, C. (2002). Double loop learning, teaching, and research. *Academy of Management Learning & Education, 2*(2), 206–218.

Arkin, R. (2007). *Governing Lethal Behaviour: Embedding Ethics in a Hybrid/Deliberative/Reactive Robot Architecture.* Mobile Robot Laboratory, College of Computing, Georgia Institute of Technology. Retrieved October 14, 2009, from http://www.cc.gatech.edu/ai/robot-lab/online-publications/formalizationv35.pdf

Arkin, R. (2008). *On the Ethical Quandaries of a Practicing Roboticist: A first-hand Look.* Retrieved October 14, 2009, from www.cc.gatech.edu/ai/robot-lab/online-publications/ArkinEthicalv2.pdf

Asaro, P. (2008). How Just Could a Robot War Be? In Brey, P., Briggle, A., & Waelbers, K. (Eds.), *Current Issues in Computing And Philosophy.* Amsterdam: IOS Publishers.

Ashby, W. (1964). *An introduction to Cybernetics.* London: Methuen.

Ashcraft, M. (1994). *Human Memory and Cognition.* New York: HarperCollins.

Association for Computing Machinery. (1992). *ACM Code of Ethics and Personal Conduct*. New York: Author. Retrieved October 14, 2009, from http://www.acm.org/constitution/code.html

Atomics, G. (2007). *MQ-9 Reaper. Predator-B Hunter-Killer UAV*. Retrieved October 14, 2009, from www.defense-update.com/products/p/predatorB.htm

Baader, F., Horrocks, I., & Sattler, U. (2005). Description Logics as Ontology Languages for the Semantic Web. In D. Hutter & W. Stephan (Eds.), Mechanizing Mathematical Reasoning: Essays in Honor of Jörg Siekmann on the Occasion of His 60th Birthday. (LNAI 2605, pp. 228-248). Berlin: Springer.

Baader, F., McGuinness, D., Nardi, D., & Patel-Schneider, P. (Eds.). (2003). *The Description Logic Handbook*. Cambridge, UK: Cambridge University Press.

Bada, J. L., Miller, S. L., & Zhao, M. (1995). The stability of amino acids at submarine hydrothermal vent temperatures. *Origins of Life and Evolution of the Biosphere, 25*, 111–118. doi:10.1007/BF01581577

Bakkum, D., Shkolnik, A., Ben-Ary, G., Gamblen, P., DeMarse, T., & Potter, S. (2003). Removing Some 'A' from AI: Embodied Cultured Networks. In *Proceedings of the Dagstuhl Conference on Embodied Artificial Intelligence*, (pp. 130-145).

Balashov, Y., & Janssen, M. (2002). *Presentism and Relativity*. Philosophy of Science Archives.

Balke, W.-T., & Mainzer, K. (2005). Knowledge Representation and the Embodied Mind: Towards a Philosophy and Technology of Personalized Informatics. In Professional Knowledge Management (LNCS Vol. 3782, pp. 586-597). Berlin: Springer.

Bangerter, A., & Heath, C. (2004). The Mozart effect: Tracking the evolution of a scientific legend. *The British Journal of Social Psychology, 43*, 605–623. doi:10.1348/0144666042565353

Barandregt, H. (1992). Lambda Calculi with Types . In Abramsky, D. M. S. (Ed.), *Handbook of Logic for Computer Science (Vol. 2*, pp. 117–309). Oxfrod, UK: Oxford University Press.

Barbiero, D. (2004). Tacit knowledge [Electronic Version]. *Dictionary of Philosophy of Mind*. Retrieved 2009.09.10 from http://philosophy.uwaterloo.ca/MindDict

Barendregt, H. P. (1984). The Lambda Calculus: Its Syntax and Semantics (Vols. Studies in Logic and the Foundations of Mathematics, 103 (Revised edition ed.). Amsterdam: North Holland.

Bar-Hillel, Y., & Carnap, R. (1952). *An outline of a theory semantic information* (Tech. Rep. No.247). Cambridge, MA: Massachusetts Institute of Technology, Research Laboratory of Electronics.

Barnes, F. a. (2006). Retrieved from Occam-pi: blending the best of CSP and the Pi-calculus: http://www.cs.kent.ac.uk/projects/ofa/kroc/

Baron, R., & Kalsher, M. (2001). *Psychology* (5th ed.). Boston: Allyn and Bacon.

Barry, C. L., & Zimet, E. (2001). UCAVs – Technological, Policy, and Operational Challenges. *Defense Horizons, 3*, 1–8.

Barton, B. (2009). *The Language of Mathematics: Telling Mathematical Tales. Math ematics Education Library, 46*. Berlin: Springer.

Barwise, J., & Etchemendy, J. (1993). *Turing's World 3.0*. Stanford, CA: CSLI.

Barwise, J., & Seligman, J. (1997). *Information Flow: The Logic of Distributed Systems*. Cambridge, UK: Cambridge University Press.

Bassingthwaighte, J. B., Liebovitch, L. S., & West, B. J. (1994). *Fractal Physiology*. New York: Oxford University Press.

Bauerlein, M. (2008). *The dumbest generation: how the digital age stupefies young Americans and jeopardizes our future (or, don't trust anyone under 30)*. New York: Jeremy P. Tarcher/Penguin.

Bechtel, W., & Mundale, J. (1999). Multiple Realization Revisited: Linking Cognitive and Neural States. *Philosophy of Science, 66*, 175–207. doi:10.1086/392683

Beebe, W. (1934). *Half mile down.* New York: Harcourt Brace.

Bekey, G. L. (2005). *Autonomous Robots. From Biological Inspiration to Implementation and Control.* Cambridge, MA: MIT Press.

Bellman, K.L. (2005). Self-Conscious Modeling. *It – Information Technology, 4,* 188-194.

Benkler, Y. (1999). Free as Air to Common Use: First Amendment Constraints on Enclosure of the Public Domain. *New York University Law Review, 74,* 354–446.

Benkler, Y. (2006). *The Wealth of Networks.* New Haven, CT: Yale University Press.

Benkler, Y., & Nissenbaum, H. (2006). Commons-based Peer Production and Virtue. *Journal of Political Philosophy, 14*(4), 394–419. doi:10.1111/j.1467-9760.2006.00235.x

Bennett, C. H., Bernstein, E., Brassard, G., & Vazirani, U. (1997). Strengths and Weaknesses of Quantum Computing. *SIAM Journal on Computing, 26,* 1510–1523. doi:10.1137/S0097539796300933

Bergen, P., & Tiedemann, K. (2009. October 19). Revenge of the Drones. An Analysis of Drone Strikes in Pakistan. *New America Foundation.* Retrieved October 22, 2009 from http://www.newamerica.net/publications/policy/revenge_drones

Berglund, E. (2008). *The Potential of UAS for European Border Surveillance.* Retrieved October 22 from http://www.uvs-info.com/Yearbook2008/042_Contributing-Stakeholder_FRONTEX.pdf

Bernstein, M. P., Dworkin, J. P., Sandford, S. A., Cooper, G. W., & Allamandola, L. J. (2002). Racemic amino acids from the ultraviolet photolysis of interstellar ice analogues. *Nature, 416,* 401–403. doi:10.1038/416401a

Bessiere, C., Coletta, R., Koriche, F., & O'Sullivan, B. (2005). A sat-based version space algorithm for acquiring constraint satisfaction problems. *Proceedings of ECML'05,* 23—34.

Biagioli, M., & Galison, P. (2003). *Scientific Authorship: Credit and Intellectual Property in Science.* New York: Routledge.

Bickhard, M. H. (2004). Part II: applications of process-based theories: process and emergence: normative function and representation. *Axiomathes—An International Journal in Ontology and Cognitive Systems, 14*(1), 121– 155.

Bickle, J. (1998). *Psychoneural Reduction: The New Wave.* Cambridge, MA: MIT Press/Bradford Books.

Bickle, J. (2003). *Philosophy and Neuroscience: A ruthlessly reductive account.* Dordrecht, The Netherlands: Kluwer Academic Pub.

Bijker, W. E., & Pinch, T. J. (1984). The Social Construction of Facts and Artifacts: Or How the Sociology of Science and the Sociology of Technology Might Benefit of Each Other . In Bijker, W. E., Hughes, T. P., & Pinch, T. J. (Eds.), *The Social Construction of Technological Systems* (pp. 17–50). Cambridge, MA: MIT Press.

Black, M. (1952). The identity of indiscernibles. *Mind,* ▪▪▪, 61.

Blackmore, T. (2005). *War X.* Toronto, Canada: University of Toronto Press.

Block, N. (1996). *Functionalism. The Encyclopedia of Philosophy Supplement.* New York: Macmillan.

Block, N., & Fodor, J. (1972). What Psychological States Are Not. *The Philosophical Review, 81,* 159–181. doi:10.2307/2183991

Boes, H. (2005). *An der Schwelle zum automatischen Krieg.* Retrieved October 14, 2009, from http://www.heise.de/tp/r4/artikel/21/21121/1.html

Boghossian, P. (1989). The Rule-following Considerations. *Mind,* 507–549. doi:10.1093/mind/XCVIII.392.507

BonJour. L. (1985). The Structure of Empirical Knowledge. Cambridge, MA: Harvard University Press.

Boolos, G. (1984). To be is to be the value of a variable (or to be some values of some variables). *The Journal of Philosophy, 81*, 430–449. doi:10.2307/2026308

Boolos, G. S., & Jeffrey, R. C. (1989). *Computability and Logic*. Cambridge, UK: Cambridge University Press.

Bork, P., Jensen, L. J., von Mering, C., Ramani, A. K., Lee, I., & Marcotte, E. M. (2004). Protein interaction networks from yeast to human. *Current Opinion in Structural Biology, 14*, 292–299. doi:10.1016/j.sbi.2004.05.003

Bourbaki, N. (2004). *Elements of Mathematics: Theory of Sets*. New York: Springer Verlag.

Bowker, G. C., & Star, S. L. (1999). *Sorting Things Out. Classification and its Consequences*. Cambridge, MA: MIT Press.

Boyle, J. (2000). Cruel, Mean, or Lavish?: Economic Analysis, Price Discrimination and Digital Intellectual Property. *Vanderbilt Law Review, 53*, 2007–2039.

Boyle, J. (2003). The Second Eclosure Movement and the Construction of the Public Domain. *Law and Contemporary Problems, 66*, 33–74.

Boyle, J. (2005). Public information wants to be free. *Financial Times*, February 24, 2005. Retrieved September 30, 2009, from http://www.ft.com/cms/s/2/cd58c216-8663-11d9-8075-00000e2511c8.html

Boyle, J. (2006). A closed mind about an open world. *Financial Times*, August 7, 2006. Retrieved September 30, 2009, from http://www.ft.com/cms/s/2/64167124-263d-11db-afa1-0000779e2340.html

Boyle, J. (2007). Text is free, we make our money on volume(s). *Financial Times*, January 22 2007. Retrieved September 30, 2009, from http://www.ft.com/cms/s/b46f5a58-aa2e-11db-83b0-0000779e2340.html

Boyle, J. (2008). *The Public Domain. Enclosing the Commons of the Mind*. New Haven, CT: Yale University Press.

Braitenberg, V. (1984). *Vehicles: Experiments in Synthetic Psychology*. Cambridge, MA: MIT Press.

Brecht, B. (1994). *Life of Galileo* (Willett, J., Trans.). New York: Arcade Publishing.

Bremer, M. E. (2003). Do Logical Truths Carry Information? *Minds and Machines, 13*, 567–575. doi:10.1023/A:1026256918837

Brenner, J. E. (2008). Dordrecht: Springer.

Brenner, J. E. (2008). *Logic in Reality*. Dordrecht: Springer. doi:10.1007/978-1-4020-8375-4

Brenner, J.E. (2009). Prolegomenon to a Logic for the Information Society. *triple-c 7*(1): 38-73. www.triple-c.at

Bresnen, M., Goussevskaia, A., & Swan, J. (2005). Organizational Routines, Situated Learning and Processes of Change in Project-based Organizations. *Project Management Journal, 3*(3), 27–41.

Brey, P. (2006). Evaluating the social and cultural implications of the internet. *SIGCAS Computers and Society, 36*(3), 41–48. doi:10.1145/1195716.1195721

Brey, P. (2007). Theorizing the Cultural Quality of New Media. *Techné: Research in Philosophy and Technology, 11*(1), 1–18.

Bricklin, D. (2006). *The Cornucopia of the Commons: How to get volunteer labor*. Retrieved September 30, 2009 from http://www.bricklin.com/cornucopia.htm

Bringsjord, S. (1992). *What Robots Can and Can't Be*. Dordrecht, The Netherlands: Kluwer.

Bringsjord, S. (1997). An Argument for the Uncomputability of Infinitary Mathematical Expertise. In Feltovich, P., Ford, K., & Hayes, P. (Eds.), *Expertise in Context* (pp. 475–497). Menlo Park: CA AAAI Press.

Bringsjord, S. (2001). In Computation, Parallel is Nothing, Physical Everything. *Minds and Machines, 11*, 95–99. doi:10.1023/A:1011257022242

Bringsjord, S. (2008). Declarative/Logic-Based Cognitive Modeling . In Sun, R. (Ed.), *The Handbook of Computational Psychology* (pp. 127–169). Cambridge, UK: Cambridge University Press.

Bringsjord, S., & Arkoudas, K. (2004). The Modal Argument for Hypercomputing Minds. *Theoretical Computer Science, 317*, 167–190. doi:10.1016/j.tcs.2003.12.010

Bringsjord, S., & Zenzen, M. (2002). Toward a Formal Philosophy of Hypercomputation. *Minds and Machines, 12*, 241–258. doi:10.1023/A:1015651216328

Bringsjord, S., & Zenzen, M. (2003). *Superminds: People Harness Hypercomputation, and More*. Dordrecht, The Netherlands: Kluwer Academic Publishers.

Bringsjord, S., Kellett, O., Shilliday, A., Taylor, J., van Heuveln, B., & Yang, Y. (2006). A New Gödelian Argument for Hypercomputing Minds Based on the Busy Beaver Problem. *Applied Mathematics and Computation, 176*, 516–530. doi:10.1016/j.amc.2005.09.071

Brodie, R. W. (1992). *Scientific Visualization*. Berlin: Springer Verlag.

Brogaard, B., & Salerno, J. (2008). Counterfactuals and context. *Analysis, 68*, 39–45. doi:10.1093/analys/68.1.39

Brooks, R. A. (1988). Intelligence without Representation . In Haugeland, J. (Ed.), *Mind Design*. Cambridge, MA: The MIT Press.

Brooks, R. A. (1991). Intelligence without representation. *Artificial Intelligence, 47*(1-3), 139–160. doi:10.1016/0004-3702(91)90053-M

Brooks, R. A. (1999). *Cambrian Intelligence: The Early History of the New AI*. Cambridge, MA: MIT Press.

Brooks, R. A., Breazeal, C., Marjanovic, M., Scassellati, B., & Williamson, M. M. (1999). The Cog project: Building a humanoid robot . In Nehaniv, C. (Ed.), *Computation for metaphors, analogy, and agents* (pp. 52–87). Heidelberg, Germany: Springer-Verlag. doi:10.1007/3-540-48834-0_5

Brown, J. S., & Duguid, P. (2001). Knowledge and Organization: A social-practice perspective. *Organization Science, 12*(2), 198–213. doi:10.1287/orsc.12.2.198.10116

Bundy, A. (2007). *Cooperating reasoning processes: More than just the sum of their parts*. Research Excellence Award Acceptance Speech at IJCAI-07.

Burgin, M. (2001). How We Know What Technology Can Do. *Communications of the ACM, 44*(11), 83–88. doi:10.1145/384150.384166

Burgin, M. (2005). *Super-recursive Algorithms*. Berlin: Springer Monographs in Computer Science.

Burgin, M., & Kuznetsov, V. (1994). Scientific Problems and Questions from a Logical Point of View. *Synthese, 100*(1), 1–28. doi:10.1007/BF01063918

Butler, J. (1990). *Gender trouble. Feminism and Subversion of Identity*. New York: Routledge.

Bynum, T. (2008) Computer and Information Ethics. *Stanford Encyclopaedia of Philosophy*. Last retrieved 6 September, 2009, from http://plato.stanford.edu/entries/ethics-computer/

Calvo, P., & Symons, J. (2008). Radical Embodiment and Morphological Computation: Against the Autonomy of (some) special sciences. In Reduction and the Special Sciences, Tilburg, April 10-12.

Canning, J. S. (2006). Concept of Operations for Armed Autonomous Systems. *The Difference between 'Winning the War' and 'Winning the Peace'*. Retrieved October 14, 2007, from www.dtic.mil/ndia/2006disruptive_tech/canning.pdf

Capshew, J. H., & Rader, K. A. (1992). Big Science: Price to the Present. *Osiris, 2*(7), 14–22.

Capurro, R., & Nagenborg, M. (Eds.). (2009). *Ethics and Robotics*. Amsterdam: AKA/IOS Press.

Carnap, R. (1950). *Logical Foundations of Probability*. Chicago, IL: University of Chicago Press.

Carnielli, W. (2005). Logics of Formal Inconsistency. In CLE e-Prints, 5, 1.

Carr, N. (2008). Is Google Making Us Stupid. *The Atlantic*. Last retrieved 6 September, 2009, from http://www.theatlantic.com/doc/200807/google

Carsetti, A. (Ed.). (2004). *Seeing, Thinking and Knowing: Meaning and Self-Organisation in Visual Cognition and Thought*. Dordrecht, The Netherlands: Kluwer Academic Publishers.

Case, D. (2008). *The U.S. Military's Assassination Problem*. Retrieved January 1, 2009, from http://www.motherjones.com/commentary/columns/2008/03/the-us-militarys-assassination-problem.html

Cauchy, A. L. (1813). Recherches sur les poly`edres. *Journal de l''Ecole Polytechnique, 9*, 68–86.

Cauchy, A. L. (1821). Cours d'Analyse de l'Ecole Polyechnique. Paris: de Bure.

Cerqui, D., Weber, J., & Weber, K. (Eds.). (2006). Ethics in Robotics. *International Review of Information Ethics 2/2006*. Retrieved October 14, 2009, from http://www.i-r-i-e.net/inhalt/006/006_full.pdf

Chaisson, E. (2001). *Cosmic Evolution. the Rise of Complexity in Nature*. Cambridge, MA: Harvard University Press.

Chaitin, G. (2007). Epistemology as information theory: From Leibniz to Ω. In Dodig Crnkovic and Stuart (Ed.), Computation, information, cognition: the nexus and the liminal (pp. 27-51). Newcastle, UK: Cambridge Scholars Publishing.

Chaitin, G. (2007). *Thinking about Gödel and Turing: Essays on Complexity, 1970-2007*. Singapore: World Scientific. doi:10.1142/9789812708977

Charness, N. (1992). The Impact of Chess Research on Cognitive Science. *Psychological Research, 54*, 4–9. doi:10.1007/BF01359217

Charniak, E., & McDermott, D. (1985). *An introduction to Artificial Intelligence*. Reading, MA: Addison-Wesley.

Charnley, J., Colton, S., & Miguel, I. (2006). Automatic generation of implied con straints. In *Proceedings of the 17th European Conference on AI*.

Chartier, R. (1987). *Lectures et lecteurs dans la France de l'Ancien Regime*. Paris: Seuil.

Chassay, C. (2009, March 23). Cut to pieces: the Palestinian family drinking tea in their courtyard. Israeli unmanned aerial vehicles – the dreaded drones – caused at least 48 deaths in Gaza during the 23-day offensive. *The Guardian*. Retrieved October 14, 2009 from http://www.guardian.co.uk/world/2009/mar/23/gaza-war-crimes-drones/print

Chellas, B. F. (1980). *Modal Logic: An Introduction*. Cambridge, UK: Cambridge University Press.

Chen, W.-K. (2003). *Net Theory and Its Applications: Flows in Networks*. London: Imperial College Press.

Cherry, C. E. (1951). A History of the Theory of Information. In *Proceedings of the Instiute of Electrical Engineers, 98*.

Chisholm, R. (1978). Is There a Mind-Body Problem? *Philosophic Exchange, 2*, 25–32.

Chisholm, R. (1989). Bolzano on the Simplicity of the Soul . In Gombocz, W. L., Rutte, H., & Sauer, W. (Eds.), *Traditionen und Perspektiven der Analytischen Philosophie*. Vienna, Austria: Holder-Pichler-Tempsky.

Chisholm, R. (1991). On the Simplicity of the Soul . In Tomberlin, J. (Ed.), *Philosophical Perspectives 5: Philosophy of Religion*. Atascadero, CA: Ridgeview.

Chua, L. O., & Roska, T. (2002). *Cellular Neural Networks and Visual Computing. Foundations and Applications*. Cambridge, UK: Cambridge University Press. doi:10.1017/CBO9780511754494

Church, A. (1941). The Calculi of Lambda Conversion. Prineton: Princeton University Press.

Church, A. (1956). *Introduction to Mathematical Logic (Vol. 1)*. Princetonm, NJ: Princeton University Press.

Churchland, P. M. (1995). *The engine of reason, the seat of the soul*. Cambridge, MA: MIT Press.

Clark, A. (2003). *Natural-born cyborgs. Minds, technologies, and the future of human intelligence*. Oxford, UK: Oxford University Press.

Clark, A. (2006). Pressing the flesh: Exploring a tension in the study of the embodied, embedded mind. *Philosophy and Phenomenological Research, 76*(1), 37–59.

Clark, A. (2007). Curing the Cognitive Hiccup: A Defense of the Extended Mind. *The Journal of Philosophy, 104*(4).

Clark, A. (2008). *Supersizing the Mind. Embodiment, Action, and Cognitive Extension.* Oxford, UK: Oxford University Press.

Coase, R. (1974). The Lighthouse in Economics. *The Journal of Law & Economics, 17,* 357–376. doi:10.1086/466796

Cockburn, C., & Omrod, S. (1993). *Gender & Technology in the Making.* London: Sage.

Cohen, J., & Meskin, A. (2006). An Objective Counterfactual Theory of Information. *Australasian Journal of Philosophy, 84,* 333–352. doi:10.1080/00048400600895821

Colburn, T. & Shute, G. (2007). Abstraction in computer science. *Minds and machines: journal for artificial intelligence, philosophy, and cognitive science 17*(2), 169--184.

Colburn, T. & Shute, G. (2010). Abstraction, law, and freedom in computer science. *Metaphilosophy* (forthcoming in 2010).

Colburn, T. (2007). Methodology of Computer Science. In L. Floridi, The Blackwell Guide to the Philosophy of Computing and Information (pp. 318--326). Blakwell, Oxford.

Colburn, T. R. (2000). *Philosophy and Computer Science.* New York: Explorations in Philosophy. Series. M.E. Sharpe.

Colburn, T. R. (2000a). Information, Thought, and Knowledge. In *Proceedings of the World Multiconference on Systemics, Cybernetics and Informatics,* (pp. 467-471).

Colburn, T. R. (2000b). *Philosophy and Computer Science.* Armonk, NY: M.E. Sharpe.

Colburn, T., & Shute, G. (2008). Metaphor in computer science. *Journal of Applied Logic, 6*(4), 526–533. doi:10.1016/j.jal.2008.09.005

Colby, K. M., & Smith, D. C. (1969). Dialogues between humans and an artificial belief system. In D. E. Walker & L. M. Norton (Eds.), *Proceedings of the international joint conference on Artificial Intelligence (IJCAI69)* (pp. 319–324). Boston: Mitre Corporation, Diller, A. (1999). Detecting androids. *Philosophy Now, 25,* 26–28.

Collier, J. (1986). Entropy in evolution. *Biology and Philosophy, 1,* 5–24. doi:10.1007/BF00127087

Collier, J. (2000). Autonomy and process closure as the basis for functionality. In J. L. R. Chandler & G. van de Vijver (Eds.), Closure: Emergent organizations and their dynamics (pp. 280–290). Annals of the New York Academy of Science, 901.

Colton, S. (2002). *Automated Theory Formation in Pure Mathematics.* Berlin: Springer-Verlag.

Colton, S., & Miguel, I. (2001). Constraint generation via automated theory formation. In *Proceedings of the Seventh International Conference on the Principles and Practice of Constraint Programming,* Cyprus.

Colton, S., & Pease, A. (2005). The TM system for repairing non-theorems. In *Selected papers from the IJCAR'04 disproving workshop . Electronic Notes in Theoretical Computer Science, 125*(3).

Comoldi, C., & McDaniel, M. A. (Eds.). (1991). *Imagery and cognition.* New York: Springer.

Connes, A. (1994). *Non-Commutative Geometry.* San Diego, CA: Academic Press.

Constable, R. & Moczyd lowski, W. (2006). Extracting programs from constructive HOL proofs via IZF set-theoretic semantics, (LNCS 4130, pp. 162–176).

Contemporary Phenomenology and Cognitive Science. Stanford, CA: Stanford University Press.

Cooper, G., Kimish, N., Belisle, W., Sarinana, J., Brabham, K., & Garrel, L. (2001). Carbonaceous meteorites as a source of sugar-related organic compounds for the early Earth. *Nature, 414,* 879–883. doi:10.1038/414879a

Copeland, B. J. (1998). Even Turing Machines Can Compute Uncomputable Functions . In Casti, J. (Ed.), *Unconventional Models of Computation* (pp. 150–164). London: Springer-Verlag.

Copeland, J. (2002). Hypercomputation. *Minds and Machines, 12*, 461–502. doi:10.1023/A:1021105915386

Cordesman, A. C. (2008, March). *Air Combat Trends in the Afghan and Iraq Wars. Center for Strategic & International Studies (CSIS)*. Retrieved December 14, 2008 from http://www.csis.org/media/csis/pubs/080318_afgh-iraqairbrief.pdf

Corfield, D. (1997). Assaying Lakatos's philosophy of mathematics. *Studies in History and Philosophy of Science, 28*(1), 99–121. doi:10.1016/S0039-3681(96)00002-7

Cormen, T. H., Leiserson, C. E., Rivest, R. L., & Stein, C. (2001). *Introduction to Algorithms* (2nd ed.). Cambridge, MA: MIT Press.

CoTeSys. (2006-2011). Retrieved from http://www.dfg.de/en/research.funding/coordinated.programmes/excellence.initiative

Cozzo, C. (1997). Identità: logica e ontologia. *Almanacchi Nuovi, 2*, 96.

Crick, F. H. C. (1958). On Protein Synthesis. *Symposia of the Society for Experimental Biology, The Biological Replication of Macromolecules, XII*, 138-163.

Crick, F. H. C. (1970). Central Dogma of Molecular Biology. *Nature, 227*, 561–563. doi:10.1038/227561a0

Crisp, R. (2008) Well-Being. *Stanford Encyclopaedia of Philosophy*. Last retrieved 6 September, 2009, from Last retrieved http://plato.stanford.edu/entries/well-being/

Crole, R. (1993). *Categories for Types*. Cambridge: Cambridge University Press.

Crutzen, C. K. M., & Kotkamp, E. (2006). Questioning Gender through Deconstruction and Doubt . In Trauth, E. M. (Ed.), *Encyclopaedia of Gender and Information Technology* (pp. 1041–1047). Hershey, PA: Idea Group Publishing.

Crutzen, C., & Gerrissen, J. F. (2000). Doubting the Object World . In Balka, E., & Smith, R. (Eds.), *Women, Work and Computerization: Charting a Course to the Future* (pp. 127–136). Boston: Kluwer Academic Press.

D'Andrade, R. (1995). *The Development of Cognitive Anthropology*. Cambridge, UK: Cambridge University Press.

Da Costa, N. C. A., & Krause, D. (2006). The Logic of Complementarity . In *The Age of Alternative Logics: Assessing the Philosophy of Logic and Mathematics Today*. Dordrecht: Springer.

Da Costa, N., & French, S. (2000). Models, Theories, and Structures: Thirty Years On. *Philosophy of Science, 67*(Supplement), S116–S127. doi:10.1086/392813

Damasio, A. (1994). *Descartes' error: Emotion, Reason and the Human Brain*. New York: Putnam Publishing.

Darden, L. (2006). Flow of Information in Molecular Biological Mechanisms. *Biological Theory, 1*, 280–287. doi:10.1162/biot.2006.1.3.280

Dautenhahn, K., Bond, A., Cañamero, L., & Edmonds, B. (2002). *Playing the Emotion Game with Feelix. What Can a LEGO Robot Tell Us about Emotion? Socially Intelligent Agents Creating Relationships with Computers and Robots*. New York: Springer.

Davidson, D. (1984). Radiical Interpretation . In Davidson, D. (Ed.), *Inquiries into Truth and Interpretation* (pp. 125–140). Oxford: Oxford University Press.

Davis, P. M. (1991). Cognition and learning: A review of the literature with reference to ethnolinguistic minorities. Dallas, TX: Summer Institute of Linguistics.

Davis, P., & Hersh, R. (1980). *The Mathematical Experience*. Harmondsworth, UK: Penguin.

Dawinks, R. (1982). *The Extended Phenotype*. Oxford, UK: Oxford University Press.

De Waard, A. (2007). A pragmatic structure for research articles. In S. B. Shum, M. Lind & H. Weigand, (Eds.), *Proceedings of the 2nd International Conference on Pragmatic Web (ICPW 2007). ACM International Conference Proceeding Series 280,* (pp. 83-89). New York: ACM.

De Waard, A., & Kircz, J. (2008). Modeling Scientific Discourse - Shifting Perspectives and Persistent Issues. In L. Chan & S. Mornatti (Eds.). *Open Scholarship: Authority, Community, and Sustainability in the Age of Web 2.0. Proceedings of the 12th International Conference on Electronic Publishing* (223-233). Berkeley, CA: bepress.

De Waard, A., & Tel, G. (2006). The ABCDE Format. In M. Völkel & S. Schaffert (Eds.), *SemWiki2006. First Workshop on Semantic Wikis - From Wiki to Semantics. CEUR Workshop Proceedings.* Retrieved September 30, 2009, from http://www.ceur-ws.org/Vol-206/paper8.pdf

DeMarse, T. B., & Dockendorf, K. P. (2005). Adaptive flight control with living neuronal networks on microelectrode arrays. In *Proceedings 2005 IEEE International Joint Conference on Neural Networks*, Montreal, (pp.1549-1551).

Demir, H. (2006). *Error Comes with Imagination: A Probabilistic Theory of Mental Content.* Unpublished doctoral dissertation, Indiana University, Bloomington, Indiana.

Demir, H. (2008). Counterfactuals vs. conditional probabilities: A critical analysis of the counterfactual theory of information. *Australasian Journal of Philosophy, 86*(1), 45–60. doi:10.1080/00048400701846541

Dennett, C. D. (1998). *Brainchildren: Essays on Designing Minds.* Cambridge, MA: MIT Press.

Dennett, D. (1984). Cognitive wheels: the frame problem of AI. In Hookway, (ed.) Minds, Machines and Evolution. Cambridge, UK: Cambridge University Press.

Department of Defense. (2007). *Uninhabited Systems Roadmap 2007-2032.* Washington, DC: Author. Retrieved October 14, 2009, from http://www.acq.osd.mil/usd/Uninhabited%20Systems%20Roadmap.2007-2032.pdf

Department of Defense. (2009). *Unmanned Systems Integrated Roadmap, 2009-2034.* Retrieved October 14, 2009 from http://www.acq.osd.mil/uas/docs/UMSIntegratedRoadmap2009.pdf

Devlin, K. J. (1991). *Logic and Information.* Cambridge, UK: Cambridge University Press.

DeWitt, B. S., & Graham, R. N. (Eds.). (1973). *The Many-Worlds Interpretation of Quantum Mechanics.* Princeton, NJ: Princeton University Press.

Di Paolo, E. A., & Izuka, J. (2008). How (not) to model autonomous behaviour. *Biosystem, 91*(2), 409–423. doi:10.1016/j.biosystems.2007.05.016

Dickmann, M. A. (1975). *Large Infinitary Languages.* Amsterdam, The Netherlands: North-Holland.

Dietrich, E. (2007). Representation. In Thagard, P. (Ed.), *Handbook of Philosophy of Science: Philosophy of Psychology and Cognitive Science* (pp. 1–30). Amsterdam: Elsevier. doi:10.1016/B978-044451540-7/50018-9

Diller, A. (2001). Acquiring information from books. In Bramer, M., Preece, A., & Coenen, F. (Eds.), *Research and development in intelligent systems XVII: Proceedings of ES2000, the twentieth SGES international conference on knowledge based systems and applied Artificial Intelligence, Cambridge, December 2000* (pp. 337–348). London: Springer.

Diller, A. (2003). Designing androids. *Philosophy Now, 42*, 28–31.

Diller, A. (2006). Constructing a comprehensively anti-justificationist position. In I. Jarvie, K. Milford & D. Miller (Eds.), Karl Popper: A centenary assessment: Volume II: Metaphysics and epistemology (pp. 119–129). Aldershot, UK: Ashgate.

Diller, A. (2008). Testimony from a Popperian perspective. *Philosophy of the Social Sciences, 38*, 419–456. doi:10.1177/0048393108324083

DiMaggio, P. (1997). Culture and cognition. *Annual Review of Sociology, 23*, 263–288. doi:10.1146/annurev.soc.23.1.263

Dittrich, Y. (2002). Doing Empirical Research in Software Engineering: Finding a Path between Understanding, Intervention, and Software Development . In Dittrich, Y., Floyd, C., & Klischewski, R. (Eds.), *Social thinking—Software practice* (pp. 243–261). Cambridge, MA: MIT Press.

Dittrich, Y., John, M., Singer, J., & Tessem, B. (2007). Editorial for the special issue on Qualitative Software Engineering Research. *Information and Software Technology, 49*(6), 531–539. doi:10.1016/j.infsof.2007.02.009

Dittrich, Y., Rönkkö, K., Eriksson, J., Hansson, C., & Lindeberg, O. (2008). Cooperative method development. Combining qualitative empirical research with method, technique and process improvement. *Empirical Software Engineering, 13*(3), 231–260. doi:10.1007/s10664-007-9057-1

Dodig Crnkovic, G. (2003). Shifting the Paradigm of the Philosophy of Science: the Philosophy of Information and a New Renaissance. *Minds and Machines: Special Issue on the Philosophy of Information, 13*(4).

Dodig Crnkovic, G. (2006). *Investigations into information semantics and ethics of computing*. Västerås: Mälardalen University Press. Retrieved from http://www.diva-portal.org/mdh/theses/abstract.xsql?dbid=153

Dodig Crnkovic, G. (2007). Epistemology Naturalized: the Info-Computationalist Approach. *APA Newsletter on Philosophy and Computers, 6*(2). Retrieved from http://www.apaonline.org/publications/newsletters/computers.aspx

Dodig Crnkovic, G. (2008). Semantics of Information as Interactive Computation. In M. Moeller, W. Neuser & T. Roth-Berghofer (Ed.), *Fifth international workshop on philosophy and informatics*. Berlin: Springer. Retrieved from http://sunsite.informatik.rwth-aachen.de/Publications/CEUR-W

Dodig Crnkovic, G., & Burgin, M. (Eds.). (2010). *Information and Computation*. Singapore: World Scientific.

Dodig-Crnkovic, G. (2005). System Modeling and Information Semantics. In J. Bubenko, O. Eriksson, H. Fernlund, & M. Lind, (Eds.), *Proceedings of the Fifth Promote IT Conference*, Borlänge, Sweden. Lund, Sweden: Studentlitteratur.

Donaldson, T., & Cohen, R. (1998). Selecting the next action with constraints. In (LNCS 1418, pp. 220–227). Berlin: Springer.

Dorato, M., & Pauri, M. (in press). Holism and Structuralism in Quantum GR . In French, S. (Eds.), *Structuralism and Quantum Gravity*.

Dretske, F. (1981). *Knowledge and the flow of information*. Cambridge, MA: MIT Press.

Dretske, F. (1983). Precis of Knowledge and the flow of the information. *The Behavioral and Brain Sciences, 6*, 55–63. doi:10.1017/S0140525X00014631

Dretske, F. (1989). The need to know . In Clay, M., & Lehrer, K. (Eds.), *Knowledge and skepticism*. Boulder, CO: Westview Press.

Dretske, F. (1993). Perceptual knowledge . In Dancy, J., & Sosa, E. (Eds.), *A companion to epistemology* (pp. 333–338). Oxford, UK: Basil Blackwell.

Dretske, F. I. (1981). *Knowledge and the Flow of Information*. Oxford: Blackwell.

Dretske, F. I. (1988). *Explaining Behavior: Reasons in a World of Causes*. Cambridge, MA: MIT Press.

Dreyfus, H. L. (1972). *What computers can't do: a critique of artificial reason* (1st ed.). New York: Harper & Row.

Dreyfus, H. L. (1972). *What Computers Can't Do: A Critique of Artificial Reason*. New York: Harper and Row.

Dreyfus, H. L. (1979). *What Computer's can't do – The Limits of Artificial Intelligence*. New York: Harper & Row.

Dreyfus, H. L. (1982). *Husserl, Intentionality, and Cognitive Science*. Cambridge, MA: MIT Press.

Dreyfus, H. L. (1992). *What Computers Still Can't Do: A Critique of Artificial Reason*. Cambridge, MA: The MIT Press.

Dreyfus, H. L. (2007). Why Heideggerian AI failed and how fixing it would require making it more Heideggerian. *Artificial Intelligence*, *171*, 1137–1160. doi:10.1016/j.artint.2007.10.012

Dreyfus, H. L. (2007). Why Heideggerian AI failed and how fixing it would require making it more Heideggerian . *Philosophical Psychology*, *20*(2), 247–268. doi:10.1080/09515080701239510

Dummett, M. (1993). *The seas of language*. Oxford, UK: Oxford University Press.

Dummett, M. A. E. (2004). *Truth and the Past*. New York: Columbia University Press.

Dunne, A., & Raby, F. (2001). *Design Noir: The Secret Life of Electronic Objects*. Basel, Switzerland: Birkhauser.

East Lansing, MI: Philosophy of Science Association.

Ebbinghaus, H. D., Flum, J., & Thomas, W. (1984). *Mathematical Logic*. New York: Springer-Verlag.

Ebbinghaus, H. D., Flum, J., & Thomas, W. (1994). *Mathematical Logic* (2nd ed.). New York, NY: Springer-Verlag.

Eicholz, R. E., O'Daffer, P. G., Charles, R. I., Young, S. I., Barnett, C. S., & Clemens, S. R. (1995). *Grade 7 Addison-Wesley Mathematics*. Reading, MA: Addison-Wesley.

Einstein, A. (1905). Ist die trägheit eines körpers von seinem energiegehalt abhängig? [Does the inertia of a body depend upon its energy-content? Retrieved June 20, 2009, from http://www.fourmilab.ch/etexts/einstein/E_mc2/e_mc2.pdf]. *Annalen der Physik*, *18*, 639–641. doi:10.1002/andp.19053231314

Elias, P., Feinstein, A., & Shannon, C. E. (1956). Note on Maximum Flow through a Network. *I.R.E. Transactions on Information Theory*, (IT-2), 117–119. doi:10.1109/TIT.1956.1056816

Eliasmith, C. (2002). The myth of the Turing machine: The failings of functionalism and related theses. *Journal of Experimental & Theoretical Artificial Intelligence*, *14*(1), 1–8. doi:10.1080/09528130210153514

Elovaara, P., & Mörtberg, C. (2007). Design of Digital Democracies—performance of citizenship, gender and IT. *Information Communication and Society*, *10*, 404–423. doi:10.1080/13691180701410091

Etesi, G., & Nemeti, I. (2002). Non-Turing Computability via Malament-Hogarth Space-Times. *International Journal of Theoretical Physics*, *41*(2), 341–370. doi:10.1023/A:1014019225365

Everett, H. (1957). Relative State Formulation of Quantum Mechanics. *Reviews of Modern Physics*, *29*, 454–462. doi:10.1103/RevModPhys.29.454

Fagin, R., Halpern, J. Y., Moses, Y., & Vardi, M. Y. (1995). *Reasoning About Knowledge*. Cambridge, MA: MIT Press.

Faulkner, W. (2001). The Technology Question in Feminism. A view from feminist technology studies. *Women's Studies International Forum*, *24*, 79–95. doi:10.1016/S0277-5395(00)00166-7

Feferman, S. (1978). The logic of mathematical discovery vs. the logical structure of mathematics. In P. D. Asquith & I. Hacking, (Ed.), *Proceedings of the 1978 Biennial-Meeting of the Philosophy of Science Association*, (vol. 2, pp. 309–327).

Feldman, F. (2004). *Pleasure and the good life: concerning the nature, varieties, and plausibility of hedonism*. Oxford, UK: Clarendon Press.

Fernandez, M. (2004). *Programming Languages and Operational Semantics: An Introduction*. London: King's College Publications.

Ferrara, A., Lorusso, D., & Montanelli, S. (2008). Automatic Identity Recognition in the semantic web. In P. Bouquet, H. Halpin, H. Stoermer, & G. Tummarello (Eds.), IRSV (Vol. 422). Retrieved from CEUR-WS.ORG

Fetzer, J. (1988). Program Verification: The Very Idea. *Communications of the ACM*, *31*(9), 1048–1063. doi:10.1145/48529.48530

Fetzer, J. H. (2004). Information, Misinformation, and Disinformation. *Minds and Machines*, *14*(2), 223–229. doi:10.1023/B:MIND.0000021682.61365.56

Feyerabend, P. (1996). Theoreticians, Artists, and Artisans. *Leonardo, 29*(1), 23–28. doi:10.2307/1576272

Finn, A. (2008). Legal considerations for the weaponisation of Unmanned Ground Vehicles. *Int. J. Intelligent Defence Support Systems, 1*(1), 43–74. doi:10.1504/IJIDSS.2008.020273

Fischer, H. (2008). Iraqui Civilian Death Estimates. *CRS report for Congress,* August 2008. Retrieved October 14, 2009 from http://www.fas.org/sgp/crs/mideast/RS22537.pdf

Fisher, G. H. (1967). Measuring Ambiguity. *The American Journal of Psychology, 80,* 541–547. doi:10.2307/1421187

Fitzpatrick, P., Metta, G., Natale, L., Rao, S., & Sandini, G. (2003). Learning about objects through action: Initial steps towards artificial cognition . In Luo, R. C., & Fu, L.-C. (Eds.), *Proceedings: 2003 IEEE international conference on robotics and automation (ICRA) (Vol. 3,* pp. 3140–3145). Taipei, Taiwan: IEEE.

Flanagan, O. (2009). *The really hard problem. Meaning in a material world.* Cambridge, MA: MIT Press.

Flood, R., & Romm, N. (1996). *Diversity Management. Triple Loop Learning.* Chichester, UK: John Wiley and Sons.

Floreano, D., & Mondada, F. (1996). Evolution of homing navigation in a real mobile robot. *IEEE Transactions on Systems, Man, and Cybernetics. Part B, Cybernetics, 26*(3), 396–407. doi:10.1109/3477.499791

Floridi, L. (2004). Outline of a theory of strongly semantic information. *Minds and Machines, 14*(2), 197–222. doi:10.1023/B:MIND.0000021684.50925.c9

Floridi, L. (2004a). Information . In Floridi, L. (Ed.), *The Blackwell Guide to the Philosophy of Computing and Information* (pp. 40–61). Oxford, UK: Blackwell. doi:10.1002/9780470757017

Floridi, L. (2004b). Open Problems in the Philosophy of Information. *Metaphilosophy, 35*(4), 554–582. doi:10.1111/j.1467-9973.2004.00336.x

Floridi, L. (2005). Is Information Meaningful Data? *Philosophy and Phenomenological Research, 70*(2), 351–370. doi:10.1111/j.1933-1592.2005.tb00531.x

Floridi, L. (2006). The Logic of Being Informed. *Logique et Analyse, 49*(196), 433–460.

Floridi, L. (2007). In Defence of the Veridical Nature of Semantic Information. *The European Journal of Analytic Philosophy, 3*(1), 1–18.

Floridi, L. (2008). Defence of Informational Structural Realism. *Synthese, 161*(2), 219–253. doi:10.1007/s11229-007-9163-z

Floridi, L. (2008a). Data . In Darity, W. A. (Ed.), *International Encyclopedia of the Social Sciences.* Detroit, MI: Macmillan.

Floridi, L. (2008b). Understanding Epistemic Relevance. *Erkenntnis, 69*(1), 69–92. doi:10.1007/s10670-007-9087-5

Floridi, L. (2009). Against Digital Ontology. *Synthese, 168*(1), 151–178. doi:10.1007/s11229-008-9334-6

Floridi, L. (in press). *Semantic Information and the Correctness Theory of Truth.*

Floridi, L. (in press). *The Philosophy of Information.* Oxford, UK: Oxford University Press.

Floyd, C., Züllighoven, H., Budde, R., & Keil-Slawik, R. (Eds.). (1992). *Software Development and Reality Construction.* Heidelberg, Germany: Springer.

Foldvary, F. (2003). The Lighthouse as a Private-Sector Collective Good. *The Independent Institute Working Paper* 46. Retrieved September 30, 2009, from http://www.independent.org/publications/working_papers/article.asp?id=757

Ford, L. R., & Fulkerson, D. R. (1956). Maximal Flow through a Network. *Canadian Journal of Mathematics, 8,* 399–404.

Förstl, H. (Ed.). (2007). *Theory of Mind. Neurobiologie und Psychologie sozialen Verhaltens.* Heidelberg, Germany: Springer.

Foucault, M. (1971). *L'archéologie du savoir*. Paris: Gallimard.

Fox Keller, E. (2003). Models, simulation, and "computer experiments". In Radder, H. (Ed.), *The Philosophy of Scientific Experimetation* (pp. 198–215). Pittsburgh, PA: University of Pittsburgh Press.

Franklin, A. (1984). The epistemology of experiment. *The British Journal for the Philosophy of Science, 35*, 381–40. doi:10.1093/bjps/35.4.381

Fredkin, E. (n.d.). *Digital Philosophy*. Retrieved October 4, 2009, from http://www.digitalphilosophy.org

Freeman, W. J. (1991). The physiology of perception. *Scientific American, , 242*.

Freeman, W. J. (1995). *Societies of Brains: A study in the neuroscience of love and hate, The Spinoza Lectures, Amsterdam, The Netherlands (Vol. 59)*. Hillsdale, NJ: Lawrence Erlbaum Associates.

Freeman, W. J. (2004). How and why brains create meaning from sensory information. *International Journal of Bifurcation and Chaos in Applied Sciences and Engineering, 14*, 515–530. doi:10.1142/S0218127404009405

Frege, G. (1879). Begriffsschrift. In Heijenoort, J. (Ed.), *From Frege to Gödel: A Source Book in Mathematical Logic, (1879-1931)*. Cambridge, MA: Harvard University Press.

Frege, G. (1884). *Grundlagen der Arithmetik*. Breslau, Poland: Wilhelm Koebner.

Freuder, E., & Wallace, R. (1992). Partial constraint satisfaction. *Artificial Intelligence*, (58): 21–70. doi:10.1016/0004-3702(92)90004-H

Friedman, B., Kahn, P. H., & Borning, A. (2006). Value Sensitive Design and information systems. In Zhang, P., & Galletta, D. (Eds.), *Human-computer interaction in management information systems: Foundation* (pp. 348–372). New York: AMIS.

Frigg, R., & Hartmann, S. (2009). Models in Science. In Edward N. Zalta (Ed.), *Stanford Encyclopedia of Philosophy*. Retrieved from http://plato.stanford.edu/archives/sum2009/entries/models-science/

Frisch, A., Miguel, I., & Walsh, T. (2002). CGRASS: A system for transforming constraint satisfaction problems. In *Proceedings of the Joint Workshop of the ERCIM Working Group on Constraints and the CologNet area on Constraint and Logic Programming on Constraint Solving and Constraint Logic Programming* (LNAI 2627, pp. 15–30).

Froese, T., & Ziemke, T. (2009). Enactive artificial intelligence: Investigating the systemic organization of life and mind. *Artificial Intelligence, 173*, 466–500. doi:10.1016/j.artint.2008.12.001

Gadamer, H.-G. (1975). Truth and Method (2nd Rev. ed. trans. by J. Weinsheimer & D.G. Marshall). New York: Continuum.

Gamma, E., Helm, R., Johnson, R., & Vlissides, J. (1995). *Design patterns: elements of reusable object-oriented software*. Boston: Addison-Wesley.

Gasper, D. (2004) 'Human Well-being: Concepts and Conceptualizations', *ISS Working Papers, No. 388*.

Geach, P. (1962). *Reference and Generality*. Ithaca, NY: Cornell University Press.

Geach, P. (1968). Identity. *The Review of Metaphysics, 22, 3*.

Geller, P. E. (2003). *International Copyright Law and Practice*. Albany, NY: Matthew Bender.

Gell-Man, M. (1994). *The Quark and the Jaguar: Adventures in the Simple and the Complex*. New York: Freeman.

Gent, I., Rendl, A., Miguel, I., & Jefferson, C. (2009). Enhancing constraint model instances during tailoring. In *Proceedings of SARA*.

Georges, A., Romme, R., & van Witteloostuijn, A. (1999). Circular organizing and triple loop learning. *Journal of Organizational Change Management, 12*(5), 439–453. doi:10.1108/09534819910289110

Gettier, E. (1963). Is justified true belief knowledge? *Analysis*, *23*, 121–123. doi:10.2307/3326922

Giere, R. (2003). The role of computation in scientific cognition. *Journal of Experimental & Theoretical Artificial Intelligence*, *15*, 195–202. doi:10.1080/0952813021000055216

Gilbert, J. K. (Ed.). (2005). *Visualization in Science Education, Series: Models and Moxdeling in Science Education (Vol. 1)*. London: Springer Verlag.

Girard, L. a. (1989). *Proofs and Types*. Cambridge: Cambridge University Press.

Gluer, K. W. (2008). *The Normativity of Meaning and Content*. Retrieved from Stanford Encyclopedia of Philosophy: http://plato.stanford.edu/entries/meaning-normativity/

Goguen, J. a. (1992). Institutions: Abstract Model Theory for Specification and Programming. *Journal of the ACM*, *39*(1), 95–146. doi:10.1145/147508.147524

Goldin, D., & Wegner, P. (2002). Paraconsistency of Interactive Computation. In *Workshop on Paraconsistent Computational Logic*. Denmark

Goldin, D., Smolka, S., & Wegner, P. (2006). *Interactive Computation: the New Paradigm*. New York: Springer-Verlag.

Goldreich, O. (2007). *Foundations of Cryptography: Basic Tools*. Cambridge, UK: Cambridge University Press.

Goldstein, E. B. (2005). *Cognitive Psychology: Connecting Mind, Research, and Everyday Experience*. Belmont, CA: Wadsworth.

Gong, P., & van Leeuwen, C. (2004). Evolution to a small-world network with chaotic units. *Europhysics Letters*, *67*(2), 328–333. doi:10.1209/epl/i2003-10287-7

Goodale, M. A., & Humphrey, G. K. (1998). The Objects of Action and Perception. *Cognition*, *67*, 181–207. doi:10.1016/S0010-0277(98)00017-1

Grandy, R. E. (1987). Information-based epistemology, ecological epistemology and epistemology naturalized. *Synthese*, *70*, 191–203. doi:10.1007/BF00413935

Granger, R. (2004). Brain circuit implementation: High-precision computation from low-precision components . In Berger, T., & Glanzman, D. (Eds.), *Toward Replacement Parts for the Brain* (pp. 277–294). Cambridge, MA: MIT Press.

Granger, R. (2004). Derivation and analysis of basic computational operations of thalamocortical circuits. *Journal of Cognitive Neuroscience*, *16*, 856–877. doi:10.1162/089892904970690

Granger, R. (in press). Engines of the Brain: The computational instruction set of human cognition. *AI Magazine*.

Grice, H. P. (1989). *Studies in the Way of Words*. Cambridge, MA: Harvard University Press.

Griffin, J. (1986). *Well-being: its meaning, measurement and moral importance*. Oxford, UK: Clarendon Press.

Griffin, J. (1996). *Value Judgement: improving our ethical beliefs*. Oxford: Clarendon Press.

Grover, L. (1996). A Fast Quantum Mechanical Algorithm for Database Search. In *Proceedings of the 28th ACM Symposium on the Theory of Computing (STOC)*, (pp. 212-219).

Guala, F. (2002). Models, simulations, and experiments . In Magnani, L., & Nersessian, N. J. (Eds.), *Model-Based reasoning: science, technology, values* (pp. 59–74). Amsterdam: Kluwer.

Hacking, I. (1981). Do We See With Microscopes? *Pacific Philosophical Quarterly*, *62*, 305–322.

Hacking, I. (1983). *Representing and intervening: introductory topics in the philosophy of natural science*. Cambridge, UK: Cambridge University Press.

Haffenden, A. M., & Goodale, M. A. (1998). The Effect of Pictorial Illusion on Prehension and Perception. *Journal of Cognitive Neuroscience*, *10*, 122–136. doi:10.1162/089892998563824

Hagengruber, R., & Riss, U. V. (2007). Knowledge in Action . In Dodig-Crnkovic, G. (Ed.), *Computation, Information, Cognition - The Nexus and The Liminal* (pp. 134–146). Cambridge, UK: Cambridge Scholars Publishing.

Haggith, M. (1996). *A meta-level argumentation framework for representing and reasoning about disagreement.* PhD thesis, Dept. of Artificial Intelligence, University of Edinburgh.

Hamkins, J. D., & Lewis, A. (2000). Infinite Time Turing Machines. *Journal of Symbolic Logic, 65*(2), 567–604. doi:10.2307/2586556

Hanappi-Egger, E. (2006). Gender and Software Engineering . In Trauth, E. M. (Ed.), *Encyclopaedia of Gender and Information Technology* (pp. 453–459). Hershey, PA: Idea Group Publishing.

Hanley, Ch. J. (2007). Robot Air Attack Squadron Bound for Iraq. *Associated Press,* July 16, 2007. Retrieved October 14, 2009 from http://www.commondreams.org/archive/2007/07/16/2570

Haraway, D. (2001). A Cyborg Manifesto. Science, technology and socialist-feminism in the late twentieth century . In Bell, D., & Kennedy, B. M. (Eds.), *The Cybercultures Reader* (pp. 291–324). London: Routledge. (Original work published 1991)

Harman, G. (1984). Is there a single true morality? In Copp, D., & Zimmerman, D. (Eds.), *Morality, reason and truth. New essays on the foundation of ethics* (pp. 27–48). Totowa, NJ: Rowman and Allenheld.

Harms, W. (2004). *Information and Meaning in Evolutionary Processes.* Cambridge, UK: Cambridge University Press. doi:10.1017/CBO9780511498473

Harms, W. F. (1998). The use of information theory in epistemology. *Philosophy of Science, 65,* 472–501. doi:10.1086/392657

Harnad, S. (2001a). *Skyreading and Skywriting for Researchers: A Post-Gutenberg Anomaly and How to Resolve it.* Retrieved September 30, 2009, from http://www.text-e.org/conf/index.cfm?fa=texte&ConfText_ID=7

Harnad, S. (2001b). The self-archiving initiative. *Nature, 410,* 1024–1025. doi:10.1038/35074210

Harnad, S. (2009). The Postgutenberg Open Access Journal . In Cope, B., & Phillips, A. (Eds.), *The Future of the Academic Journal.* Oxford, UK: Chandos.

Harré, R. (2003). The materiality of instruments in a metaphysics for experiments . In Radder, H. (Ed.), *The philosophy of scientific experimentation* (pp. 19–38). University of Pittsburgh Press.

Hart, H. L. A. (1951). The ascription of responsibility and rights . In Flew, A. (Ed.), *Logic and language (First series)* (pp. 145–166). Oxford, UK: Oxford University Press.

Hartmann, S. (1996). The world as a process: simulation in the natural and social sciences . In Hegselmann, R., Mueller, U., & Troitzsch, K. (Eds.), *Simulation and modelling in the social sciences from the philosophy of science point of view* (pp. 77–110). Amsterdam: Kluwer.

Haug, F. (1999). Erinnerungsarbeit—ein Leitfaden zur Methode . In Haug, F. (Ed.), *Vorlesungen zur Einführung in die Erinnerungsarbeit* (pp. 199–227). Berlin: Argument.

Haugeland, J. (1998). *Having Thought: Essays in the Metaphysics of Mind.* Cambridge, MA: Harvard University Press.

Hayes-Roth, F. (1983). Using proofs and refutations to learn from experience. In R. S. Michalski J. G. Carbonell, & T. M. Mitchell, (Ed.), Machine Learning: An Artificial Intelligence Approach, (pp. 221–240). Palo Alto, CA: Tioga Publishing Company.

Hedberg, B. (1981). How organizations learn and unlearn. In P.C. Nystrom & W. H. Starbuck (Eds.), Handbook of Organizational Design, (Vol. 1, pp. 3-27). New York: Oxford University Press.

Heidegger, M. (1962). Being and Time (trans. ed. by J. Macquarrie, & E. Robinson). New York: Harper and Row.

Hey, T., & Trefethen, A. E. (2005). Cyberinfrastructure for e-Science. *Science, 308,* 817–821. doi:10.1126/science.1110410

Higgs, R. (2007, March 15). *The Trillion-Dollar Defense Budget Is Already Here*. Retrieved October 14, 2009 from http://www.independent.org/newsroom/article.asp?id=1941, Oct 11ᵗʰ 2009.

Himma, K. E., & Tavani, H. (Eds.). (2008). *The Handbook of Information and Computer Ethics*. Hoboken, NJ: Wiley. doi:10.1002/9780470281819

Hintikka, J. (1970). Surface information and depth information . In Hintikka, J., & Suppes, P. (Eds.), *Information and Inference* (pp. 263–297). Dordrecht, The Netherlands: Reidel.

Hoare, A. (1969). An Axiomatic Basis For Computer Programming. *Communications of the ACM, Volume 12 / Number 10*, 576-583.

Hoffmeyer, J. (1996). *Signs of meaning in the universe*. Bloomington, IN: Indiana University Press.

Holroyd, S. (1975). *Contraries: A personal progression*. London, UK: The Bodley Head.

Honderich, T. (1995). *The Oxford Companion to Philosophy*. Oxford, UK: Oxford University Press.

Horowitz, A., & Weiss, P. (2009). American Jews Rethink Israel. *The Nation*, Oct. 14ᵗʰ 2009. Retrieved at Oct. 2009 at http://www.thenation.com/doc/20091102/horowitz_weiss/single

Hsiao-Rei Hicks, M., Dardagan, H., Guerrero Serdán, G., Bagall, P. M., Sloboda, J. A., & Spagat, M. (2009, April 19). The Weapons that Kill Civilians – Death of Childrens and Non-Combatants, 2003-2008. *The New England Journal of Medicine*, *360*(16), 1585–1588. doi:10.1056/NEJMp0807240

Huang, H.-M., Pavek, K., Novak, B., Albus, J., & Messina, E. (2005). A Framework for Autonomy Levels for Uninhabited Systems (ALFUS). In *Proceedings of the AUVSI's Uninhabited Systems North America 2005, June 2005*, Baltimore. Retrieved September 21, 2007 from www.isd.mel.nist.gov/documents/huang/ALFUS-auvsi-8.pdf

Human Rights Watch. (2009). *Precisely Wrong. Gaza Civilians Killed by Israeli Drone-Launched Missiles*. Retrieved October 14, 2009 from http://www.hrw.org/en/reports/2009/06/30/precisely-wrong?print

Hume, D. (1748). *Philosophical essays concerning human understanding*. London, UK: A. Millar.

Humphreys, P. (1991). Computer Simulations . In Fine, A., Forbes, M., & Wessels, L. (Eds.), *PSA 1990* (*Vol. 2*, pp. 497–506). East Lansing, MI: Philosophy of Science Association.

Humphreys, P. (1995). Computational Science and Scientific Method. *Minds and Machines*, *5*, 499–512. doi:10.1007/BF00974980

Humphreys, P. (2002). Computational Models. *Philosophy of Science*, *69*, S1–S11. doi:10.1086/341763

Humphreys, P. (2004). *Extending Ourselves. Computational Science, Empiricism and Scientific Method*. New York: OUP.

Hutchins, E. (1996). *Cognition in the wild*. Cambridge, MA: MIT Press.

Ifrah, G. (1999). *The Universal History of Numbers: From Prehistory to the Invention of the Computer*. Chichester, UK: Wiley.

Indurkhya, B. (1992). *Metaphor and cognition*. Dordrecht, The Netherlands: Kluwer Academic Publishers.

Isaacson, D. (1985). Arithmetical Truths and Hidden Higher-Order Concepts. In The Paris Logic Group, (Ed.), Logic Colloquium. Amsterdam: North-Holland.

Jablonka, E. (2002). Information: its interpretation, its inheritance, and its sharing. *Philosophy of Science*, *69*, 578–605. doi:10.1086/344621

Jablonka, E., & Lamb, M. (2005). *Evolution in Four Dimensions*. Cambridge, MA: MIT Press.

Japaridze, G. (2003). Introduction to Computability Logic. *Annals of Pure and Applied Logic*, *123*, 1–99. doi:10.1016/S0168-0072(03)00023-X

Jech, T. (1971). *Lecture Notes in Set Theory*. New York: Springer.

Jungnickel, D. (1999). *Graphs, Networks, and Algorithms*. Berlin: Springer.

Kafka, F. (1972). *The Metamorphosis*. New York: Bantam Classics.

Kajita, S. (2007). *Humanoide Roboter. Theorie und Technik des Künstlichen Menschen*. Berlin: Aka GmbH.

Kaneko, K. (2006). *Life: An Introduction to Complex Systems Biology*. Berlin: Springer.

Kant, I. (1790). *Kritik der Urteilskraft* [Critique of Judgment]. (Pluhar, W. S., Trans.). Indianapolis, IN: Hacket Publishing Company.

Kauffman, S. (2000). *Investigations*. New York: Oxford University Press.

Kauffman, S., Logan, R. K., Este, R., Goebel, R., Hobill, D., & Shmulevich, I. (2008). Propagating organization: an enquiry. *Biology and Philosophy, 23*(1), 27–45. doi:10.1007/s10539-007-9066-x

Kaufmann, S. (2006, Nov.). Land Warrior. The Reconfiguration of the Soldier in the 'Information Age'. *Science . Technology and Innovation Studies, 2*, 81–102.

Kay, L. E. (1993). *The Molecular Vision of Life: Caltech, The Rockefeller Foundation, and The Rise of the New Biology*. Oxford, UK: Oxford University Press.

Kay, L. E. (2000). *Who Wrote the Book of Life? A History of the Genetic Code*. Stanford, CA: Stanford University Press.

Kaye, P., Laflamme, R., & Mosca, M. (2007). *An Introduction to Quantum Computing*. New York: Oxford University Press.

Keefe, R. (2000). *Theories of Vagueness*. Cambridge, UK: Cambridge University Press.

Keen, A. (2007). *The cult of the amateur: how today's internet is killing our culture*. New York: Doubleday/Currency.

Kellogg, K. C., Orlikowski, W. J., & Yates, J. (2006). Life in the Trading Zone: Structuring Coordination Across Boundaries in Postbureaucratic Organizations. *Organization Science, 17*(1), 22–44. doi:10.1287/orsc.1050.0157

Kemp, M. (1990). *The Science of Art: optical themes in western art from Brunelleschi to Seurat*. New Haven, CT: Yale University Press.

Kemp, M. (2001). *Visualisations: The Nature Book of Art and Science*. Oxford, UK: Oxford University Press.

Kern, A. (2006). *Quellen des Wissens*. Frankfurt, Germany: Suhrkamp.

Kerr, N., & Domhoff, G. W. (2004). Do the blind literally "see" in their dreams? A critique of a recent claim that they do. *Dreaming, 14*, 230–233. doi:10.1037/1053-0797.14.4.230

Kirsh, D. (1995). The intelligent use of space. *Artificial Intelligence, 73*(1-2), 31–68. doi:10.1016/0004-3702(94)00017-U

Kirsh, D., & Maglio, P. (1992). Reaction and reflection in Tetris. In J. Hendler, (ed.) *Artificial intelligence planning systems, Proceedings of the first annual conference AIPS*. San Mateo, CA: Morgan Kaufmann.

Kirsh, D., & Maglio, P. (1994). On distinguishing epistemic from pragmatic action. *Cognitive Science, 18*, 513–549. doi:10.1207/s15516709cog1804_1

Kitano, H. (2003). A Graphical Notation for Biochemical Networks. *BIOSILICO, 1*(5), 159–176. doi:10.1016/S1478-5382(03)02380-1

Kitcher, P. (1983). *The Nature of Mathematical Knowledge*. Oxford, UK: Oxford University Press.

Kittler, F. (1988). Signal-Rausch-Abstand. In H. U. Gumbrecht, & K. L. Pfeiffer (eds.) Materialität der Kommunikation, (pp. 342 - 359). Frankfurt a.M., Germany: Suhrkamp.

Kleinberg, J. M. (2000). Navigation in a small world. *Nature, 406*, 845. doi:10.1038/35022643

Koepsell, D. R. (2000). *The Ontology of Cyberspace*. Chicago: Open Court.

Konopka, A. K. (Ed.). (2007). *Systems Biology. Principles, Methods, and Concepts*. Boca Raton, FL: CRC Press.

Kornblith, H. (2003). *Knowledge and its Place in Nature*. Oxford, UK: Oxford University Press.

Kosslyn, S. M. (1994). *Image and brain. The resolution of the imagery debate*. New York: Free Press.

Kosztin, I., & Schulten, K. (2004). Fluctuation-driven molecular transport through an asymmetric membrane channel. *Physical Review Letters, 93*, 238102. doi:10.1103/PhysRevLett.93.238102

Krause, D., & French, S. (2007). Quantum Sortal Predicates. *Synthese, 154*, 417–430. doi:10.1007/s11229-006-9127-8

Kripke, S. (1982). *Wittgenstein on Rules and Private Language*. Boston: Harvard University Press.

Kuhn, T. S. (1962). *The Structure of Scientific Revolutions*. Chicago: University of Chicago Press.

Kumar Behera, L. (2008). *The US Defence Budget for 2008. IDSA strategic comments*. Retrieved October 14, 2009 from http://www.idsa.in/publications/stratcomments/LaxmanBehera210207.htm

Kusch, M., & Lipton, P. (2002). Testimony: A primer. *Studies in History and Philosophy of Science, 33*, 209–217. doi:10.1016/S0039-3681(02)00003-1

Kyburg, H. E. (1983). Knowledge and the absolute. *The Behavioral and Brain Sciences, 6*, 72–73. doi:10.1017/S0140525X00014758

Laburthe, F. & the OCRE project team (2000). Choco: implementing a CP kernel. In *Proceedings of the CP'00 Post Conference Workshop on Techniques for Implementing Constraint Programming Systems (TRICS)*, Singapore.

Ladyman, J., & Ross, D. (2007). *Every Thing Must Go. Metaphysics Naturalized*. Oxford, UK: Oxford University Press. doi:10.1093/acprof:oso/9780199276196.001.0001

Lakatos, I. (1976). *Proofs and Refutations*. Cambridge, UK: Cambridge University Press.

Lakatos, I. (1978). Cauchy and the continuum: the significance of non-standard anal ysis for the history and philosophy of mathematics . In Worral, J., & Currie, C. (Eds.), *Mathematics, science and epistemology* (pp. 43–60). Cambridge, UK: Cambridge University Press. doi:10.1017/CBO9780511624926

Lakatos, I. (1978a). *The methodology of scientific programs*. Cambridge, UK: Cambridge University Press.

Lakatos, I. (1978b). *Mathematics, science, and epistemology*. Cambridge, UK: Cambridge University Press. doi:10.1017/CBO9780511624926

Lakoff, G. & Núñez, R. (2001). *Where Mathematics Comes From: How the Embodied Mind Brings Mathematics into Being*. New York: Basic Books Inc.

Landin, P. (1964). The Mechanical Evaluation of Expressions. *The Computer Journal, 6*(4), 308–320.

Landin, P. (1965). A Correspondence Between ALGOL 60 and Church's Lambda-Notation. *Communications of the ACM, 8*(2), 89–101. doi:10.1145/363744.363749

Landin, P. (1966). The next 700 Programming Languages. *Communications of the ACM*, 157–166. doi:10.1145/365230.365257

Lange, D. (1981). Recognizing the Public Domain. *Law and Contemporary Problems, 44*, 147–178. doi:10.2307/1191227

Langton, C. G. (1990). Computation at the edge of chaos: Phase transitions and emergent computation. *Physica D. Nonlinear Phenomena, 42*, 12–37. doi:10.1016/0167-2789(90)90064-V

Latour, B. (1986). Visualization and Cognition: Thinking with Eyes and Hands. *Knowledge and Society, 6*, 1–40.

Lave, J., & Wenger, E. (1991). *Situated Learning. Legitimate Peripheral Participation*. Cambridge, UK: Cambridge University Press.

Lehrer, K., & Cohen, S. (1983). Dretske on Knowledge. *The Behavioral and Brain Sciences, 6*, 73–74. doi:10.1017/S0140525X0001476X

Leibniz, G. W. (1931). *Die Philosophische Schriften.* Leipzig, Germany: Lorenz.

Lesne, A. (2007). The Discrete Versus Continuous Controversy in Physics. *Mathematical Structures in Computer Science, 17,* 185–223. doi:10.1017/S0960129507005944

Lessig, L. (2001). *The Future of Ideas.* New York: Random House.

Lessig, L. (2002). The Architecture of Innovation. *Duke L. J., 51.*

Leuschel, M., & Butler, M. (2008). ProB: an Automated Analysis Toolset for the B Method. *Journal Software Tools for Technology Transfer, 10*(2), 185–203. doi:10.1007/s10009-007-0063-9

Levine, R. D. (2005). *Molecular reaction dynamics.* Cambridge, UK: Cambridge University Press. doi:10.1017/CBO9780511614125

Lewicki, M. (1998). A review of methods for spike sorting: the detection and classification of neural action potentials. *Network (Bristol, England), 9*(4), R53–R78. doi:10.1088/0954-898X/9/4/001

Lewis, C. S. (1964). *The discarded image.* London, UK: Cambridge University Press.

Lewis, D. (1973). *Counterfactuals.* Oxford: Blackwell.

Light, A., & Anderson, T. D. (2009). Research Project as Boundary Object: negotiating the conceptual design of a tool for International Development. In I. Wagner, H. Tellioglu, E. Balka, C. Simone, & L. Ciolfi (Eds.), *Proceedings of the 11th European Conference on Computer Supported Cooperative Work* (pp. 21-41). Berlin: Springer.

Lin, P., Bekey, G., & Abney, K. (2009). Robots in War. Issues of Risk and Ethics . In Capurro, R., & Nagenborg, M. (Eds.), *Ethics and Robotics* (pp. 49–68). Amsterdam: AKA / IOS Press.

Lindberg, S. W., & Patterson, L. R. (1991). *The Nature of Copyright: A Law of Users' Rights.* Athens, GA: University of Georgia Press.

Lindsay, J. (2004). *The Electric Monk: A belief filtering system based on defeasible rules.* Unpublished BEng dissertation, School of Computer Science, University of Birmingham, UK.

Litman, J. (1990). The Public Domain. *Emory Law Journal, 39,* 965.

Lloyd, S. (2006). *Programming the Universe: A Quantum Computer Scientist Takes on the Cosmos.* New York: Alfred A Knopf.

Loewer, B. (1983). Information and belief. *The Behavioral and Brain Sciences, 6,* 75–76. doi:10.1017/S0140525X00014783

Longo, G. (1999). The Mathematical Continuum . In Petitot, J. (Eds.), *Naturalizing Phenomenology. Issues in.*

Lupasco, S. (1987). *Le principe d'antagonisme et la logique de l'énergie.* Paris: Editions du Rocher.

Lusanna, L., & Pauri, M. (In press). Dynamical Emergence of Instantaneous 3-Spaces in a Class of Models of General Relativity . In van der Merwe, A. (Ed.), *Relativity and the Dimensionality of the World.* Dordrecht: Springer.

Maclennan, B. (2004). Natural Computation and Non-Turing Models Of Computation. *Theoretical Computer Science, 317,* 115–145. doi:10.1016/j.tcs.2003.12.008

Maglio, P., Matlock, T., Raphaely, D., Chernicky, B., & Kirsh, D. (1999). Interactive skill in Scrabble. In *Proceedings of 21st annual conference of the Cognitive Science Society.* Mahwah, NJ: Erlbaum.

Magnani, L. (2002). Preface . In Magnani, L., & Nersessian, N. J. (Eds.), *Model Based Reasoning: Science, Technology, Values.* Dordrecht, The Netherlands: Kluwer.

Mai, H. (2009). *Michael Polanyis Fundamentalphilosophie.* Freiburg, Germany: Karl Alber.

Mainzer, K. (2005). *Symmetry and Complexity. The Spirit and Beauty of Nonlinear Science.* Singapore: World Scientific Publisher.

Mainzer, K. (2007). *Thinking in Complexity. The Computational Dynamics of Matter, Mind, and Mankind* (5th ed.). New York: Springer.

Mainzer, K. (2008). The emergence of mind and brain: an evolutionary, computational, and philosophical approach. In Banerjee, R., & Chakrabarti, B. K. (Eds.), *Models of Brain and Mind. Physical, Computational and Psychological Approaches* (pp. 115–132). Amsterdam: Elsevier.

Mainzer, K. (2010). *Leben als Maschine? Von der Systembiologie zu Robotik und Künstlicher Intelligenz.* Paderborn: Mentis.

Marks, P. (2008). Rat-Brained Robots Take Their First Steps. *New Scientist, 199*(2669), 22–23. doi:10.1016/S0262-4079(08)62062-X

Marr, D. (1982). *Vision: A Computational Investigation into the Human Representation and Processing of Visual Information.* San Francisco: Freeman.

Marr, D., & Hildreth, E. (1980). Theory of Edge Detection. In *Proceedings of the Royal*

Marsiske, H.-A. (2007), An der langen Leine. Roboter im Sicherheitsdienst. *c't – magazin für computertechnik, 9.*

Marte, A., & Szabo, E. (2007). *Center for Defence Information: Fact Sheet on the Army's Future Combat Systems, August 7, 2007.* Retrieved October 14, 2009 from http://www.cdi.org/program/issue/document.cfm?DocumentID=4058&IssueID=221&StartRow=1&ListRows=10&appendURL=&Orderby=DateLastUpdated&ProgramID=37&issueID=221 Oct. 15th 2009

Mathewson, J.H. (1999). Visual-Spatial Thinking: An Aspect of Science Overlooked

Mathiassen, L. (1998). *Reflective Systems Development.* Aalborg, Denmark: Institute for Electronic Systems, Department of Computer Science. Retrieved August 5, 2009, from http://www.mathiassen.eci.gsu.edu/rsd.html

Mathiassen, L. (2002). Collaborative practice research. *Information Technology & People, 15*(4), 321–345. doi:10.1108/09593840210453115

Matsuo Bridge. (1999). Retrieved from http://www.matsuo-bridge.co.jp/english/bridges/index.shtm

Maturana, H., & Varela, F. (1980). *Autopoiesis and Cognition: the Realization of the Living.* Boston: Reidel.

Mayer, J. (2009, October 26). The Predator War. What Are the Risks of the C.I.A.'s Covert Drone program? *New Yorker (New York, N.Y.),* 36–45.

Maynard Smith, J. (2000). The concept of information in biology. *Philosophy of Science, 67,* 177–194. doi:10.1086/392768

Mayr, E. (1961). Cause and Effect in Biology. *Science, 134,* 1501–1506. doi:10.1126/science.134.3489.1501

McCasland, R., & Bundy, A. (2006). MATHsAiD: a mathematical theorem discovery tool. In SYNASC'06, (pp. 17–22). Washington, DC: IEEE Computer Society Press.

McCasland, R., Bundy, A., & Smith, P. (2006). Ascertaining mathematical theorems. In Electronic Notes in Theoretical Computer Science (ENTCS), 151(1), 21–38.

McCune, W. (1994). *Otter 3.0 Reference Manual and Guide.* Technical Report ANL-94/6, Argonne National Laboratory, Argonne, USA.

McCune, W. (2001). *MACE 2.0 Reference Manual and Guide.* Technical Report ANL/MCS-TM-249, Argonne National Laboratory, Argonne, USA.

McKenzie, D., & Wajcman, J. (1999). *The Social Shaping of Technology* (2nd ed.). Buckingham, UK: Open University press.

McNeill, F. & Bundy, A. R. (2007). Dynamic, automatic, first-order ontology repair by diagnosis of failed plan execution. *IJSWIS (International Journal on Semantic Web and Information Systems) special issue on Ontology Matching, 3*(3), 1–35.

Meilinger, Ph. S. (2001). Precision Aerospace Power, Discrimination, and the Future of War. *Aerospace Power Journal, 15*(3), 12–20.

Menzel, P., & D'Aluisio, F. (2000). *Robo sapiens: Evolution of a new species.* Cambridge, MA: MIT Press.

Merleau-Ponty, M. (1962). *Phenomenology of Perception.* New York: Routledge & Kegan Paul.

Miller, G.A. (1956). The Magical Number Seven, Plus or Minus Two: Some Limits on

Millikan, R. G. (1991). *Language, Thought, and Other Biological Categories*. Cambridge, MA: MIT Press.

Milne, R. a. (1976). *A Theory of Programming Language Semantics*. Chapman and Hall.

Milner, R. (2006). *The Polyadic π-Calculus*. Berlin: Springer.

Milner, R. T. (1999). *The Definition of Standard ML*. MIT Press.

Mingers, J. (2001). Embodying information systems: the contribution of phenomenology. *Information and Organization*, *11*(2), 103–128. doi:10.1016/S1471-7727(00)00005-1

Minksy, M., & Papert, D. (1969). *Perceptrons*. Cambridge, MA: MIT Press.

Minsky, M. (1988). *The Society of Mind*. New York: Simon and Schuster.

Mir, A. (2009, April 19th). 60 drone hits kill 14 al-Qaeda men, 687 civilians. *The News*. Retrieved October 14, 2009 from http://www.thenews.com.pk/top_story_detail.asp?Id=21440

Moggi.A. (1988). http://www.lfcs.inf.ed.ac.uk/reports/88/ECS-LFCS-88-63/.

Monnard, P. A., Apel, C. L., Kanavarioti, A., & Deamer, D. W. (2002). Influence of ionic inorganic solutes on self-assembly and polymerization processes related to early forms of life-implications for a prebiotic aqueous medium. *Astrobiology*, *2*, 139–152. doi:10.1089/15311070260192237

Moravec, H. (1990). *Mind Children: The future of robot and human intelligence*. Cambridge, MA: Harvard University Press.

Moreno, A., & Etxeberria, A. (2005). Agency in the natural and artificial systems. *Artificial Life*, *11*(1-2), 161–175. doi:10.1162/1064546053278919

Morgan, M., & Morrison, M. (1999). Models as mediating instruments . In Morgan, M., & Morrison, M. (Eds.), *Models as mediators. Perspectives on natural and social science* (pp. 10–37). Cmabridge, UK: Cambridge University Press. doi:10.1017/CBO9780511660108

Morrison, M. (2009). Models, measurement and computer simulation: the changing face of experimentation. *Philosophical Studies*, *143*, 33–57. doi:10.1007/s11098-008-9317-y

Morton, P. (1993). Supervenience and Computational Explanation in Visual Theory.

Motik, B., Horrocks, I., & Sattler, U. (2009). Bridging the Gap Between OWL and Relational Databases. *Journal of Web Semantics*, *7*(2), 74–89. doi:10.1016/j.websem.2009.02.001

Moutoussis, K., & Zeki, S. (2006). *Seeing invisible motion: a human FMRI study*. Current.

Muggleton, S. (1995). Inverse entailment and Progol. *New Generation Computing*, *13*, 245–286. doi:10.1007/BF03037227

Münkler, H. (2002). *Die neuen Kriege*. Reinbek, Germany: Rowohlt.

Nagenborg, M., Capurro, R., Weber, J., & Pingel, C. (2007). Ethical Regulations on Robotics in Europe. *AI & Society*, ▪▪▪, 349–366.

Nagle, T. (1974). What Is it Like to Be a Bat? *The Philosophical Review*, 435–450. doi:10.2307/2183914

Neth, H., & Payne, S. J. (2002). Thinking by doing? Epistemic actions in the Tower of Hanoi. In W.D. Gray & C. D. Schunn, (Eds.), *Proceedings of the 24th annual conference of the Cognitive Science Society*. Mahwah, NJ: Erlbaum.

Newell, A. (1973). You Can't Play 20 Questions With Nature and Win: Projective Comments on the Papers of This Symposium. In W. Chase, (Ed.), *Visual Information Processing*, (pp. 283-308). New York: Academic Press.

Newell, A., & Simon, H. A. (1988). Computer Science as Empirical Inquiry: Symbols and Search . In Haugeland, J. (Ed.), *Mind Design*. Cambridge, MA: MIT Press.

Newell, A., Shaw, C., & Simon, H. (1958). Chess-playing Programs and the Problem of Complexity. *IBM Journal of Research and Development*, *2*, 320–325. doi:10.1147/rd.24.0320

Newman, M. E. J., Barabási, A.-L., & Watts, D. J. (Eds.). (2006). *The Structure and Dynamics of Networks*. Princeton, NJ: Princeton University Press.

Nicolaidis, M. (2003). *Une Philosophique Numérique de l'Univers*. Technical Report, TIMA Lab, ISRN TIMA-RR-03/04-02-FR, Avril 2003.

Nicolaidis, M. (2007). *Emergence of Relativistic Space-Time in a Computational Universe*. Grenoble, France: TIMA Laboratory.

Nicolaidis, M. (2008, June 16-18). *On the State of Superposition and the Parallel or not Parallel nature of Quantum Computing: a controversy raising view point*. Paper presented at the 2008 European Computing and Philosophy Conference, (ECAP'08), Montpellier, France.

Nicolaidis, M. (2009-1). Simulating Time. In *Proceedings 2nd Computing and Philosophy Symposium, 2009 AISB Convention*, Edinburgh, UK. Hove, UK: SSAISB: The Society for the Study of Artificial Intelligence and the Simulation of Behaviour.

Nicolaidis, M. (2009-2). *On the State of Superposition and the Parallel or not Parallel nature of Quantum Computing*. Tech. Report TIMA Lab., ISRN TIMA-RR--09/09--01-FR.

Nicolaidis, M. (in press). A Computational Vision of the Universe . In Valverdu, J. (Ed.), *Thinking Machines and the Philosophy of Computer Science: Concepts and Principles*. Hershey, PA: IGI Global.

Nikolaidis, M. (2005). *Une Philosophie Numérique des Univers*. Grenoble, France: TIMA Editions.

Nikolei, H.-H. (2005). *Milliardenmarkt Drohnen*. Retrieved January 1, 2006 from www.n-tv.de/544984.html

Noble, D. (2002). The rise of computational biology. *Nature Reviews. Molecular Cell Biology*, *3*(6), 459–463. doi:10.1038/nrm810

Noë, A. (2004). *Action in Perception*. Cambridge, MA: MIT Press.

Nolfi, S., & Floreano, D. (2001). *Evolutionary Robotics. The Biology, Intelligence, and Technology of Self-Organizing Machines*. Cambridge, MA: MIT Press.

Noonan, H. (2008). *Identity*. Retrieved September 1, 2009, from *The Stanford Encyclopedia of Philosophy*, http://plato.stanford.edu/archives/fall2008/entries/identity/

Nørbjerg, J., & Kraft, P. (2002). Software Practice Is Social Practice . In Dittrich, Y., Floyd, C., & Klischewski, R. (Eds.), *Social Thinking—Software Practice* (pp. 205–222). Cambridge, MA: MIT Press.

Norton, S. D., & Suppe, F. (2001). Why atmospheric modeling is good science . In Miller, C., & Edwards, P. N. (Eds.), *Changing the atmosphere. Expert knowledge and environmental governance* (pp. 67–105). Cambridge, MA: MIT Press.

Nute, D. (1995). Defeasibility . In Audi, R. (Ed.), *The Cambridge dictionary of philosophy* (p. 184). Cambridge, UK: Cambridge University Press.

O'Regan, J., & Noë, A. (2001). A sensory motor approach to vision and visual consciousness. *The Behavioral and Brain Sciences*, *24*(5), 939–973.

Oles, F. J. (1982). *A category-theoretic approach to the semantics of programming languages*. Syracuse, NY, US: Syracuse University.

Oppenheim, C. (2001) The legal and regulatory environment for electronic information. *Infonortics*. Retrieved September 30, 2009, from http://www.infonortics.com/publications/legal4.html

Oudshoorn, N., & Pinch, T. (Eds.). (2003). *How Users Matter: The Co-Construction of Users and Technology*. Cambridge, MA: MIT Press.

Oudshoorn, N., Rommes, E., & Stienstra, M. (2004). Configuring the User as Everybody: Gender and Design Cultures in Information and Communication Technologies. *Science, Technology & Human Values, 29*(1), 30–63. doi:10.1177/0162243903259190

Our Capacity for Processing Information. *The Psychological Review, 63,*

Parker, W. (2009). Does matter really matter? Computer simulations, experiments, and materiality. *Synthese, 169*(3), 483–496. doi:10.1007/s11229-008-9434-3

Pattee, H. H. (1995). Evolving self-reference: matter, symbols, and semantic closure. *Communication and Cognition–Artificial Intelligence, 12*(1–2), 9–28.

Paul, C. (2004). Morphology and Computation. In S. Schaal, A. J. Ijspeert, A. Billard, S. Vijayakumar, J. Hallam, and J. A. Meyer, (Eds.), *From Animals to animats: Proceedings of the eighth international conference on the Simulation of Adaptive Behaviour*, Los Angeles. Cambridge, MA: MIT Press.

Paul, C. (2006). Morphological computation: A basis for the analysis of morphology and control requirements. *Robotics and Autonomous Systems, 54*(8), 619–630. doi:10.1016/j.robot.2006.03.003

Peano, G. (1889). *Arithmetices Principia, nova methodo exposita*. Torino, Italy: Fratres Bocca.

Pease, A. (2007). *A Computational Model of Lakatos-style Reasoning.*

Pease, A., Colton, S., Smaill, A., & Lee, J. (2004). A model of Lakatos's philosophy of mathematics. In *Proceedings of Computing and Philosophy*. ECAP.

Pease, A., Smaill, A., Colton, S., & Lee, J. (2009). Bridging the gap between ar gumentation theory and the philosophy of mathematics. *Special Issue: Mathematics and Argumentation . Foundations of Science, 14*(1-2), 111–135. doi:10.1007/s10699-008-9150-y

Peirce, C. S. (1868). On a new list of categories. [Eprint: http://www.cspeirce.com/menu/library/bycsp/newlist/nl-frame.htm]. *Proceedings of the American Academy of Arts and Sciences, 7,* 287–298.

Penrose, R. (1995). *Shadows of the Mind*. Oxford, UK: Oxford University Press.

Perini, L. (2005). The Truth in Pictures. *Philosophy of Science, 72,* 262–285. doi:10.1086/426852

Pfeifer, R., & Bongard, J. (2007). *How the body shapes the way we think*. Cambridge, MA: MIT Pres.

Pfeifer, R., & Iida, F. (2005). Morphological computation: Connecting body, brain and environment. *Japanese Scientific Monthly, 58*(2), 48–54.

Pfeifer, R., & Scheier, C. (2001). *Understanding Intelligence*. Cambridge, MA: MIT Press.

PhD thesis, School of Informatics, University of Edinburgh. Retrieved from http://hdl.handle.net/1842/2113

Philosophy of Science, 60(1), 86–99. doi:10.1086/289719

Piaget, J. (1963). *The origins of intelligence in children*. New York: W. W. Norton.

Piaget, J. (2000). *The psychology of the child*. New York: Basic Books.

Pinker, S. (1997). *How the Mind Works*. New York: W.W. Norton & Company.

Place, U. T. (1956). Is Consciousness a Brain Process? *The British Journal of Psychology, 47,* 44–50.

Plotkin, G. (2004). A structural approach to operational semantics. *Journal of Logic and Algebraic Programming, 60-61,* 17–139. doi:10.1016/j.jlap.2004.03.009

Polanyi, M. (1962). *Personal Knowledge*. Chicago: The University of Chicago Press.

Polanyi, M. (1969). Knowing and Being . In Grene, M. (Ed.), *Knowing and Being: Essays by M. Polanyi*. Chicago: The University of Chicago Press.

Polger, C. W. (2004). Neural Machine and Realization. *Philosophy of Science, 71,* 997–1006. doi:10.1086/425948

Polger, T. (2002). Putnam's Intuition. *Philosophical Studies, 109*(2), 143–170. doi:10.1023/A:1016236415052

Polger, T. (2004). *Natural Minds*. Cambridge, MA: The MIT Press.

Pollock, J. L. (1995). *Cognitive carpentry: A blueprint for how to build a person.* Cambridge, MA: MIT Press.

Polya, G. (1945). *How to solve it.* Princeton, NJ: Princeton University Press.

Polya, G. (1954). Mathematics and plausible reasoning: *Vol. 1. Induction and analogy in mathematics.* Princeton, NJ: Princeton University Press.

Polya, G. (1962). *Mathematical Discovery.* New York: John Wiley and Sons.

Post, W. *Balancing Defense and the Budget. After Eight Boom Years for Spending on Military Equipment, Contractors Expect a Slowdown. (Materials from a September 2008 report by the Institute for Policy Studies; report by the Center for Arms Control and Non-Proliferation; and government documents.)* (2008). Retrieved October 14, 2009 from http://www.washingtonpost.com/wp-dyn/content/graphic/2008/10/13/GR2008101300651.html?sid=ST2008101300698

Potter, S., Lukina, N., Longmuir, K., & Wu, Y. (2001). Multi-site two-photon imaging of neurons on multi-electrode arrays. In SPIE Proceedings, (Vol. 4262, pp. 104-110).

Price, H. H. (1969). *Belief: The Gifford lectures, 1960.* London, UK: George Allen and Unwin.

Priest, G. (2002). *Beyond the Limits of Thought.* Oxford, UK: Clarendon Press.

Pugh, W. (2000). The Java Memory Model is Fatally Flawed. *Concurrency (Chichester, England), 12*(6), 445–455. doi:10.1002/1096-9128(200005)12:6<445::AID-CPE484>3.0.CO;2-A

Putnam, H. (1960). Minds and Machines . In Hook, S. (Ed.), *Dimensions of Mind* (pp. 148–180). New York: University of New York Press.

Putnam, H. (1967). Psychological Predicates . In Captain, W. H., & Merrill, D. D. (Eds.), *Art, Mind and Religion* (pp. 37–48). Pittsburgh: University of Pittsburgh Press.

Quine, W. (1985). Epistemology Naturalized . In Kornblith, H. (Ed.), *Naturalizing Epistemology (reprint from in 'Ontological Relativity and other Essays'; Columbia University Press, 1969).*

Quine. (1960). *Word and Object. .* Cambridge, Mass: MIT Press.

Rapaport, W. (2004). Implementation is Semantic Interpretation. *The Monist, 82,* 109–130.

Rapp, D. N. (2003). The impact of digital libraries on cognitive processes: psychological issues of hypermedia. *Computers in Human Behavior, 19,* 609–628. doi:10.1016/S0747-5632(02)00085-7

Reck, M., Zeilinger, A., Bernstein, H. J., & Bertani, P. (1994). Experimental Realization of Any Discrete Unitary Operator. *Physical Review Letters, 73*(1). doi:10.1103/PhysRevLett.73.58

Rees, L. (2008). *World War Two: Behind closed doors.* London, UK: BBC.

Reid, T. (1764). *An inquiry into the human mind on the principles of common sense.* Edinburgh, UK: A. Kincaid & J. Bell. doi:10.1037/11974-000

Reynolds, J. (1974). Towards a theory of type structure . In *Lecture Notes in Computer Science* (pp. 408–425). Berlin: Springer.

Riofrio, W. (2007). Informational Dynamic Systems: Autonomy, information, function . In Gershenson, C., Aerts, D., & Edmonds, B. (Eds.), *Worldviews, science, and us: Philosophy and complexity* (pp. 232–249). Singapore: World Scientific.

Riofrio, W. (2008). Understanding the Emergence of Cellular Organization. *Biosemiotics, 1*(3), 361–377. doi:10.1007/s12304-008-9027-z

Rip, A., Misa, T., & Schot, J. (Eds.). (1995). *Managing Technology in Society. The Approach of Constructive Technology Assessment.* New York: Pinter.

Rissland, E. L., & Skalak, D. B. (1991). Cabaret: Statutory interpretation in a hybrid architecture. *International Journal of Man-Machine Studies, 34*, 839–887. doi:10.1016/0020-7373(91)90013-W

Ritchie, H. (1988). *Success stories: Literature and the media in England, 1950–1959.* London, UK: Faber and Faber.

Rohrlich, F. (1990) Computer Simulation in the physical sciences. In *PSA: Proceedings of the Biennial Meeting of the Philosophy of Science Association*, (pp. 507-518).

Rosenblatt, F. (1962). *Principles of neurodynamics.* New York: Spartan Books.

Ross, P. (2006). The Expert Mind. *Scientific American*, (August): 64–71. doi:10.1038/scientificamerican0806-64

Rötzer, F. (2007a). *Einsatzregeln für Kampfroboter.* Retrieved October 14, 2009 from www.heise.de/tp/r4/artikel/25/25117/1.html

Rötzer, F. (2007b). *Schwärme von Kampfdrohnen sollen Aufständische bekämpfen.* Retrieved October 14, 2009 from http://www.heise.de/tp/r4/artikel/25/25722/1.html

Rötzer, F. (2008). *Der Luftkrieg im Irak und in Afghanistan.* Retrieved October 14, 2009 from http://www.heise.de/tp/r4/artikel/27/27180/1.html

Rovelli, C. (2009). *Forget Time.* Retrieved from arXiv:0903.3832v3 27 Mar 2009.

Rovelli, C. (2009, March). *Forget time.* arXiv:0903.3832v3 [gr-qc] 27

Rozenberg, G., & Kari, L. (2008). The Many Facets of Natural Computing. *Communications of the ACM, 51.*

Ruben, P. (1978). *Dialektik und Arbeit der Philosophie.* Köln: Pahl-Rugenstein.

Rumelhart, D. E., & McClelland, J. L. (1986). Parallel Distributed Processing: Exploration in the microstructure of cognition, Vols. 1 & 2. In Psychological and Biological Models (Vol. 1 & 2). Cambridge: The MIT Press.

Russell, B. (1936). The limits of empiricism. *Proceedings of the Aristotelian Society, 36*, 131–150.

Ruttkay, Z. (1994). Fuzzy constraint satisfaction. In *3rd IEEE Int. Conf. on Fuzzy Systems*, (pp. 1263–1268).

Sayre, K. M. (1976). *Cybernetics and the Philosophy of Mind.* London: Routledge & Kegan Paul.

Scarantino, A., & Piccinini, G. (in press). Information without Truth. *Metaphilosophy.*

Schaper-Rinkel, P. (2006). Governance von Zukunftsversprechen: Zur politischen Ökonomie der Nanotechnologie. *PROKLA 145 " Ökonomie der Technik", 36*(4), 473-96

Scheffler, I. (1972). Vision and Revolution: A Postscript on Kuhn. *Philosophy of Science, 39*(3), 366–374. doi:10.1086/288456

Schmidhuber, J. (1997). *A Computer Scientist's View of Life, the Universe, and Everything, (LNCS 201-288).* Berlin: Springer.

Schmidt, D. (1986). *Denotational Semantics: A Methodology for Language Development.* Boston: Allyn and Bacon.

Schroeder, M. (2008). Value Theory. *Stanford Encyclopedia of Philosophy.* Last retrieved 6 September, 2009, from http://plato.stanford.edu/archives/fall2008/entries/value-theory/

Scott, D. (1993). A type-theoretical alternative to ISWIM, CUCH, OWHY. *Theoretical Computer Science*, 411–440. doi:10.1016/0304-3975(93)90095-B

Searle, J. (1997). *The Mystery of Consciousness.* New York: New York Review Book.

Searle, J. R. (1984). *Minds, brains, and science.* London, UK: BBC.

Sebeok, T. A. (1991). *A sign is just a sign.* Bloomington, IN: Indiana University Press.

Sebeok, T. A. (1994). *Signs: An introduction to semiotics.* Toronto, Canada: University of Toronto Press.

Seibt, J. (2009). Forms of emergent interaction in General Process Theory. *Synthese, 166*, 479–512. doi:10.1007/s11229-008-9373-z

Sengers, P., Boehner, K., David, S., & Kaye, J. (2005). Reflective Design. *Proceedings of the 4th Decennial Conference on Critical Computing: Between Sense and Sensibility* (pp. 49-58). New York: ACM Press.

Sequoiah-Grayson, S. (2007). The Metaphilosophy of Information. *Minds and Machines, 17*(3), 331–344. doi:10.1007/s11023-007-9072-4

Shagrir, O. (2005). The rise and fall of computational functionalism . In Ben-Menahem, Y. (Ed.), *Hilary Putnam (Contemporary Philosophy in Focus)*. Cambridge, UK: Cambridge University Press. doi:10.1017/CBO9780511614187.009

Shannon, C. E. (1948). A Mathematical Theory of Communication. *Bell System Technical Journal, 27*, 379-423 and 623-656.

Shannon, C. E. (1993). The Lattice Theory of Information . In Sloane, N. J. A., & Wyner, A. D. (Eds.), *Collected Papers*. Los Alamos, CA: IEEE Computer Society Press.

Shannon, C. E., & Weaver, W. (1949). *The Mathematical Theory of Communication*. Urbana, IL: University of Illinois Press.

Shapiro, L. (2000). Multiple Realizations. *The Journal of Philosophy, 97*, 635–664. doi:10.2307/2678460

Shapiro, L. (2004). *The Mind Incarnate*. Cambridge, UK: MIT Press.

Shapiro, S. (2000). Classical Logic [Electronic Version]. *Stanford Encyclopedia of Philosophy*. Retrieved 2009.09.10 from http://plato.stanford.edu/entries/logic-classical/

Shapiro, S. (2004). *Philosophy of Mathematics: Structure and Ontology*. Oxford: Oxford University Press.

Sharkey, N. (2007). Automated Killers and the Computing Profession. *Computer, 40* (11), 124, 122-123.

Sharp, A. A., O'Neil, M. B., Abbott, L. F., & Marder, E. (1993). Dynamic clamp: computer-generated conductances in real neurons. *Journal of Neurophysiology, 69*(3), 992–995.

Shelley, M. W. (1831). *Frankenstein or the Modern Prometheus*. London: Colburn & Bentley.

Sherron, C. (2000). Constructing Common Sense . In Balka, E., & Smith, R. (Eds.), *Women, Work and Computerization. Charting a Course to the Future* (pp. 111–118). Boston: Kluwer.

Shkolnik, A. C. (2003). *Neurally controlled simulated robot: applying cultured neurons to handle an approach / avoidance task in real time, and a framework for studying learning in vitro*. Masters Thesis, Department of Computer Science, Emory University, Georgia.

Shor, P. (1994). Algorithms for Quantum Computation: Discrete Logarithms and Factoring. In *Proceedings of the 35th Annual Symposium on Foundations of Computer Science*, (pp. 124-134). *Space-Time Conference web site*. (2004). Retrieved from http://alcor.concordia.ca/~scol/seminars/conference/minkowski.html

Sidiropoulos, G., & Vasilakos, A. (2006). Ultra-real or symbolic visualization? The case of the city through time survey. *Computers & Graphics, 30*, 299–310. doi:10.1016/j.cag.2006.01.034

Siegelmann, H., & Sontag, E. D. (1994). Analog Computation Via Neural Nets. *Theoretical Computer Science, 131*, 331–360. doi:10.1016/0304-3975(94)90178-3

Simon, H. A. (1996). *The Sciences of the artificial*. Cambridge, MA: MIT Press.

Singer, P. (2009). *Robots at War: The New Battlefield*. Retrieved October 14, 2009 from http://www.wilsoncenter.org/index.cfm?fuseaction=wq.essay&essay_id=496613

Skalak, D. B., & Rissland, E. L. (1991). Argument moves in a rule-guided domain. In *Proceedings of the 3rd International Conference on Artificial Intelligence and Law*, (pp. 1–11). New York: ACM Press.

Sloman, A., & Chrisley, R. (2003). Virtual Machines and Consciousness. *Journal of Consciousness Studies, 10*(4-5), 133–172.

Small, M. (2005). *Applied Nonlinear Time Series Analysis. Applications in Physics, Physiology and Finance*. Singapore: World Scientific Publisher.

Smith, P. (2007). *An Introduction to Gödel's Theorems.* Cambridge, UK: Cambridge University Press.

Snook, C. F., & Butler, M. (2008). UML-B: A plug-in for the Event-B Tool Set. In E. Börger, M. Butler, J. P. Bowen, & P. Boca, (Eds.), ABZ 2008, (LNCS 5238, pp. 344). Berlin: Springer.

Society of London B 207, 187–217.

Sparrow, R. (2007). Killer Robots. *Journal of Applied Philosophy, 24*(1), 62–77. doi:10.1111/j.1468-5930.2007.00346.x

Star, S. L., & Griesemer, J. R. (1989). Institutional Ecology, 'Translations' and Boundary Objects: Amateurs and Professionals in Berkeley's Museum of Vertebrate Zoology, 1907-39. *Social Studies of Science, 19*(4), 387–420. doi:10.1177/030631289019003001

Stering, R. (2008). *Police Officer's Handbook: An Analytical and Administrative Guide.* Sudbury, MA: Jones and Bartlett Publishers.

Stillings, N., Weisler, S., Chase, C., Feinstein, M., Garfield, J., & Rissland, E. (1995). *Cognitive Science.* Cambridge, MA: MIT Press.

Stoy, J. (1977). *The Scott-Strachey Approach to Programming Language Semantics.* Boston: MIT Press.

Strachey, C. (1965). Towards a formal semantics. In Steel, T. B. (Ed.), *Formal Language Description Languages for Computer Programming.* Amsterdam: North Holland.

Strachey, C. (2000). Fundamental Concepts in Programming Languages. *Higher-Order and Symbolic Computation.*, 11-49.

Strauss, C., & Quinn, N. (1997). *A cognitive theory of cultural meaning.* Cambridge, UK: Cambridge University Press.

Suchman, L. (2007). *Human-Machine Reconfigurations. Plans and Situated Action* (2nd ed.). Cambridge, UK: Cambridge University Press.

Suchman, L., Blomberg, J., Orr, J. E., & Trigg, R. (1999). Reconstructing Technologies as Social Practice. *The American Behavioral Scientist, 43*(3), 392–408. doi:10.1177/00027649921955335

Sumner, L. W. (1995). The Subjectivity of Welfare. *Ethics, 105*(4), 764–790. doi:10.1086/293752

Suppes, P. (2002). *Representation and Invariance of Scientific Structures.* Stanford, CA: CSLI Publications.

Surgeon General's Office. (2006). *Mental Health Advisory Team (MHAT) IV Operation Iraqi Freedom 05-07*, Final Report, Nov. 17, 2006. Retrieved October 14, 2009 from http://www.house.gov/delahunt/ptsd.pdf

Symons, J. (2008). Computational Models of Emergent Properties. *Minds and Machines, 4*, 475–491. doi:10.1007/s11023-008-9120-8

Tamburrini, G. (2009). Robot Ethics: A View from the Philosophy of Science . In Capurro, R., & Nagenborg, M. (Eds.), *Ethics and Robotics* (pp. 11–22). Amsterdam: IOS Press.

Tarski, A. (1935). Der Wahrheitsbegriff in den formalisierten Sprachen. *Studies in Philology, 1*, 261–405.

Taylor, C. (1989). *Sources of the self: the making of modern identity.* Cambridge, UK: Cambridge University Press.

Taylor, C. C. W. (1967). Plato and the Mathematicians: An Examination of Professor Hare's Views. *The Philosophical Quarterly, 17*(68), 193–203. doi:10.2307/2218154

Taylor, C. C. W. (2008). Plato's Epistemology . In Fine, G. (Ed.), *The Oxford Handbook of Plato* (pp. 165–190). New York: Oxford University Press. doi:10.1093/oxfordhb/9780195182903.003.0007

Tegmark, M. (2007). *Shut up and calculate.* arXiv:0709.4024v1 [physics.pop-ph]

Tegmark, M. (2007). *The Mathematical Universe.* Retrieved from arXiv:0704.064v2 8 Oct 2007

Tennent, R. (1977). Language design methods based on semantic principles. *Acta Informatica, 8*, 97–112. doi:10.1007/BF00289243

Tennent, R. (1981). *Principles of Programming Languages*. Oxford: Prentice-Hall International.

Tetzlaff, R. (2002). *Cellular Neural Networks and their Application. Proceedings of the 7th IEEE International Workshop*. Singapore: World Scientific Publisher.

Thagard, P. (2005). Testimony, credibility, and explanatory coherence. *Erkenntnis, 63*, 295–316. doi:10.1007/s10670-005-4004-2

Thomas, C., Springer, P., Loeb, G., Berwald-Netter, Y., & Okun, L. (1972). A miniature microelectrode array to monitor the bioelectric activity of cultured cells. *Experimental Cell Research, 74*, 61–66. doi:10.1016/0014-4827(72)90481-8

Thompson, E. (2007). *Mind in life*. Cambridge, MA: Harvard University Press.

Thompson, E. P. (1991). *The Making of the English Working Class*. London: Penguin.

Thrun, S., Burgard, W., & Fox, D. (2005). *Probabilistic Robotics*. Cambridge, MA: MIT Press.

Tiberius, V. (2004). Cultural differences and philosophical accounts of well-being. *Journal of Happiness Studies, 5*, 293–314. doi:10.1007/s10902-004-8791-y

Tiberius, V. (2006). Well-Being: Psychological Research for Philosophers. *Philosophy Compass, 1/5*, 493–505. doi:10.1111/j.1747-9991.2006.00038.x

Toffoli, T. (1984). Cellular automata as an alternative to (rather than an approximation of) differentia-equations in modeling physics. *Physica, 10D*, 117–127.

Trauth, E. M. (2001). *Qualitative Research in IS: Issues and Trends*. Hershey, PA: IGI Global.

Trenholme, R. (1994). Analog simulation. *Philosophy of Science, 61*, 115–131. doi:10.1086/289783

Tsang, E. (1993). *Foundations of Constraint Satisfaction*. London: Academic Press.

Tumulka, R. A. (2006 November). Relativistic Version of the Ghirardi–Rimini–Weber Model. *Journal of Statistical Physics, 125*(4), 821–840(20).

Turing, A. (1937). On Computable Numbers, with an Application to the Entscheidungsproblem. *Proceedings of the London Mathematical Society, 2 42.*, 230--65.

Turing, A. (1950). Computing Machinery and Intelligence. *Mind, 59*, 433–460. doi:10.1093/mind/LIX.236.433

Turner, R. (2007). Understanding Programming Languages. *Minds and Machines, 17*(2), 129–133. doi:10.1007/s11023-007-9059-1

Turner, R. (2009). *Computable Models*. New York: Springer. doi:10.1007/978-1-84882-052-4

Tversky, B., Morrison, J.B., Betrancourt, M., (2002). Animation: Can it facilitate? *International Journal of Human-Computer Studies, 57*, 247–262. doi:10.1006/ijhc.2002.1017

Tymoczko, T. (Ed.). (1998). New directions in the philosophy of mathematics. Princeton, NJ: Prince ton University Press.

UN News Center. (2009). Civilian casualties in Afghanistan keep rising. Retrieved October 14, 2009 from http://www.un.org/apps/news/story.asp?NewsID=31636&Cr=afghan&Cr1=civilian#

United States Air Force. (2009). *Unmanned Aircraft Systems Flight Plan 2009-2047*. Unclassified. Updated version. Washington, DC: Author. Retrieved December 10th, 2009 from http://www.govexec.com/pdfs/072309kp1.pdf

van Blyenburgh, P. (ed.), (pp. 2008). *UAS – Unmanned Aircraft Systems – The Global Perspective 2008/2009*. Paris: Blyenburgh & Co.

Usher, M. (2001). A statistical referential theory of content: Using information theory to account for misrepresentation. *Mind & Language, 16*, 311–334. doi:10.1111/1468-0017.00172

Vallverdú, J., & Casacuberta, D. (2008). The Panic Room. On Synthetic Emotions . In Briggle, A., Waelbers, K., & Brey, P. (Eds.), *Current Issues in Computing and Philosophy* (pp. 103–115). Amsterdam: IOS Press.

Vallverdú, J., & Casacuberta, D. (2009a). Modelling Hardwired Synthetic Emotions: TPR 2.0 . In Vallverdú, J., & Casacuberta, D. (Eds.), *Handbook of Research on Synthetic Emotions and Sociable Robotics: New Applications in Affective Computing and Artificial Intelligence* (pp. 103–115). Hershey, PA: IGI Global.

Vallverdú, J., & Casacuberta, D. (Eds.). (2009b). *Handbook of Research on Synthetic Emotions and Sociable Robotics: New Applications in Affective Computing and Artificial Intelligence* (pp. 103–115). Hershey, PA: IGI Global.

van den Hoven, J., & Weckert, J. (Eds.). (2008). *Information Technology and Moral Philosophy.* New York: Cambridge University Press. doi:10.1017/CBO9780511498725

Van Eck, D., De Jong, H. L., & Schouten, M. K. D. (2006). Evaluating New Wave Reductionism: The Case of Vision. *The British Journal for the Philosophy of Science, 57*, 167–196. doi:10.1093/bjps/axi153

Van Fraassen, B. C. (1980). *The Scientific Image.* Oxford, UK: Clarendon Press. doi:10.1093/0198244274.001.0001

Van Gelder, T. (1997). Dynamics and cognition. In J. Haugeland (Ed.), Mind Design II (A Bradford Book ed.). Cambridge, MA: The MIT Press.

Varela, F. J., & Thompson, E. Lutz, A. & Rosch, E. (1991). The embodied Mind: Cognitive Science and Human experience. Cambridge, MA: MIT Press.

Varenne, F. (2001). What does a computer simulation prove? In N. Giambiasi & C. Frydamn, (ed.), *Simulation in Industry, Proc. of The 13th European Simulation Symposium,* Marseille, France, *October 18-20th,* SCS Europe Bvba, Ghent, (pp. 549-554).

Vichniac, G. Y. (1984). Simulating physics with cellular automata. *Physica, 10D*, 96–116.

Virilio, P. (2000). *Strategy of Deception* (Turner, C., Trans.). New York: Verso.

Von Schomberg, R. (2007). *From the Ethics of Technology towards an Ethics of Knowledge Policy & Knowledge Assessment.* European Commission, Community Research, Working Document, EU 22429. Retrieved December 1st, 2009 from ec.europa.eu/research/science.../ethicsofknowledgepolicy_en.pdf

Wajcman, J. (2004). *TechnoFeminism.* Cambridge, UK: Polity Press.

Walsham, G. (2005). Knowledge Management Systems: Representation and Communication in Context. *Systems . Signs & Action, 1*(1), 6–18.

Walton, D. (2007). Dialogical Models of Explanation. In Explanation-Aware Computing: Papers from the 2007 Aaai Workshop, Association for the Advancement of Artificial Intelligence, (pp. 1-9). Menlo Park, CA: AAAI Press.

Wang, H. (1974). *From Mathematics to Philosophy. London.* London: Routledge & Kegan Paul.

Wang, H. (1995). On Computabilism' and Physicalism: Some Sub-problems . In Cornwell, J. (Ed.), *Nature's Imagination: The Frontiers of Scientific Vision* (pp. 161–189). Oxford, UK: Oxford University Press.

Warwick, K. (2001). *QI: The Quest for Intelligence.* London: Piatkus.

Warwick, K., Gasson, M., Hutt, B., Goodhew, I., Kyberd, P., & Andrews, B. (2003). The Application of Implant Technology for Cybernetic Systems. *Archives of Neurology, 60*(10), 1369–1373. doi:10.1001/archneur.60.10.1369

Warwick, K., Gasson, M., Hutt, B., Goodhew, I., Kyberd, P., Schulzrinne, H., & Wu, X. (2004). Thought Communication and Control: A First Step using Radiotelegraphy. *IEE Proceedings. Communications, 151*(3), 185–189. doi:10.1049/ip-com:20040409

Watson, J. D., & Crick, F. H. C. (1953). Genetical Implications of the Structure of Deoxyribonucleic Acid. *Nature, 171*, 964–967. doi:10.1038/171964b0

Watson, J. D., Hopkins, N. H., Roberts, J. W., Steitz, J. A., & Weiner, A. M. (1988). *Molecular Biology of the Gene* (4th ed.). Menlo Park, CA: Benjamin/Cummings.

Watts, D. J., & Strogatz, S. H. (1998). Collective dynamics of 'small-world' networks. *Nature, 393*, 440–442. doi:10.1038/30918

Weber, J. (2006). From Science and Technology to Feminist Technoscience . In Davis, K., Evans, M., & Lorber, J. (Eds.), *Handbook of Gender and Women's Studies* (pp. 397–414). London: Sage.

Weber, J. (2009). Robotic Warfare, Human Rights & the Rhetorics of Ethical Machines. In R. Capurro & M. Nagenborg (Eds.), Ethics and Robotics, (pp. 83-103). Heidelberg, Germany: AKA, Amsterdam: IOS Press.

Wegner, P. (1998). Interactive Foundations of Computing. *Theoretical Computer Science, 192*, 315. doi:10.1016/S0304-3975(97)00154-0

Weld, D. (1994). An introduction to least commitment planning. *AI Magazine, 15*(4), 27–61.

Whaley, B. B., & Samter, W. (Eds.). (2006). *Explaining Communication: Contemporary Theories and Exemplars*. London: Routledge.

Wikibooks. (2009). *Haskell/Denotational Semantics*. Retrieved from Wikibooks: http://en.wikibooks.org/wiki/Haskell/Denotational_semantics

Wilde, O. (1891). *The Picture of Dorian Gray*. London: Ward, Lock and Co.

Wiles, A. (1995). Modular Elliptic Curves and Fermat's Last Theorem. *The Annals of Mathematics, 141*(3), 443–551. doi:10.2307/2118559

Wiles, A., & Taylor, R. (1995). Ring-Theoretic Properties of Certain Hecke Algebras. *The Annals of Mathematics, 141*(3), 553–572. doi:10.2307/2118560

Williams, B. (2005). *In the beginning was the deed: realism and moralism in political argument*. Princeton, NJ: Princeton University Press.

Wing, J. (2008). Five deep Questions in Computing. *CACM, 51*(1), 58–60.

Winograd, T., & Flores, F. (1987). *Understanding Computers and Cognition: A New Foundation for Design*. Boston: Addison-Wesley.

Winsberg, E. (1999). Sanctioning Models: The Epistemology of Simulation. *Science in Context, 12*, 275–292. doi:10.1017/S0269889700003422

Winsberg, E. (1999). Sanctioning models: The epistemology of simulation. *Science in Context, 12*, 275–292. doi:10.1017/S0269889700003422

Winsberg, E. (2001). Complex Physical Systems and their Representations . In *Philosophy of Science 68 (Proceedings)* (pp. 442–454). Simulations, Models and Theories.

Winsberg, E. (2003). Simulated Experiments: Methodology for a Virtual World. *Philosophy of Science, 70*, 105–125. doi:10.1086/367872

Winterstein, D. (2004). *Using Diagrammatic Reasoning for Theorem Proving in a Continuous Domain*. PhD thesis, University of Edinburgh, Edinburgh, UK.

Wirth, N. (1974). On the Design of Programming Languages. *IEEE Transactions on Software Engineering*, 386–393.

Wittgenstein, L. (1953). *Philosophical Investigations*, (G.E.M. Anscombe 1962 trans (, Ed.). Oxford: Blackwell.

Woese, C. R. (2002). On the evolution of cells. *Proceedings of the National Academy of Sciences of the United States of America, 99*(13), 8742–8747. doi:10.1073/pnas.132266999

Wolfram, S. (1986). Cellular automaton fluid: basic theory. *Journal of Statistical Physics, 45*, 471-526. Retrieved June 15, 2009, from http://www.stephenwolfram.com/publications/articles/physics/86-fluids/1/text.html

Wolfram, S. (2002). *New Kind of Science*. Retrieved from http://www.wolframscience.com/nksonline/toc.html

.

Xydas, D., Warwick, K., Whalley, B., Nasuto, S., Becerra, V., Hammond, M., & Downes, J. (2008). Architecture for Living Neuronal Cell Control of a Mobile Robot. In *Proc. European Robotics Symposium EUROS08, 2008*, (pp. 23-31), Prague.

Yates, F. E. (1988). *Self-Organizing Systems. The Emergence of Order*. Boston: Plenum.

Yeung, R. W. (2008). *Information Theory and Network Coding.* New York: Springer.

Zorn, I., Maaß, S., Rommes, E., Schirmer, C., & Schelhowe, H. (Eds.). (2007). Gender Designs IT: Construction and Deconstruction of Information Society Technology. Wiesbaden, Germany: VS.

Zuse, K. (1967). Rechnender Raum. *Elektronische Datenverarbeitung, 8,* 336–344.

Zuse, K. (1969). *Rechnender Raum.* Braunschweig, Germany: Friedrich Vieweg & Sohn.

Zuse, K. (1970). *Calculating Space, MIT Technical Translation AZT-70-164-GEMIT.* Cambridge, MA: Massachusetts Institute of Technology.

Zwanenburg, M., Boddens Hosang, H., & Wijngaards, N. (2005). Humans, Agents and International Humanitarian Law: Dilemmas in Target Discrimination. In *Proc. 4th Workshop on the Law and Electronic Agents – LEA.* Retrieved December 5th 2009 from http://www.estig.ipbeja.pt/~ac_direito/ZwanenburgBoddensWijngaards_LEA05_CR.pdf

About the Contributors

Jordi Vallverdú, Ph.D., M.A. is Lecturer Professor at Universitat Autònoma de Barcelona (Catalonia, Spain), where he teaches Philosophy and History of Science and Computing. He holds a Ph.D. in philosophy of science (UAB) and a master in history of sciences (UAB). His research is dedicated to the epistemological, ethical, gender, and educational aspects of Philosophy of Computing and Science. Jordi is Member of the Steering Committee of the European Association for Philosophy & Computing, E-CAP, Member of the Spanish Society of Logic, Methodology and Philosophy of Science, Member of the GEHUCT (Grup d'Estudis Interdisciplinaris sobre Ciència i Tecnologia) research project, Member of the TECNOCOG (Philosophy, Technology and Cognition Research Group), Member of EUCogII, Main researcher of SETE (Synthetic Emotions in Technological Environments), and Expert of the Biosociety Research (European Commission: http://ec.europa.eu/research/biosociety/index_en.htm). His last book (as author as well as editor) is (2009) *Handbook Of Research On Synthetic Emotions And Sociable Robotics*, USA: IGI. He is the Editor-in-Chief of the *International Journal of Synthetic Emotions* (http://www.igi-global.com/journals/details.asp?id=33374).

* * *

Luca Albergante graduated in computer science at Università degli Studi di Milano in October 2006, with the master thesis "Nebhet: Ideazione di un algoritmo crittografico a chiave pubblica". From November 2006, he is a Ph.D. student in applied mathematics at the department of mathematics "Federigo Enriques" of the same university. His research interests include cryptography, bioinformatics, bio-inspired computing, and formal methods in computer science. In 2008-2009, he has been a visiting scholar in the "Non-Standard Computation Group" of the University of York.

Doris Allhutter, Mag.rer.soc.oec., Dr. phil., Researcher at the Austrian Academy of Sciences (Institute of Technology Assessment) since January 2008, Lecturer at the University of Vienna; Master from the Vienna University of Economics and Business (2001); post-graduate studies "Governance in Europe" at the Vienna Institute for Advanced Studies (diploma in political science 2002); researcher and lecturer at the Vienna University of Economics and Business (2003-2007); doctorate in political science at the University of Vienna (2007). Her research interests and publications cover the areas of qualitative software engineering research, electronic citizen participation, digital pornography and information ethics, discourse theory, feminist theory;

Saray Ayala <http://sarayayala.googlepages.com/ > is a PhD candidate at Universitat Autònoma de Barcelona. She received a BA in Philosophy from the University of Murcia, Spain, in 2001, and a MA in

Philosophy from the Universitat Autònoma de Barcelona, Spain, in 2004, where she enjoyed a teaching fellowship (2005-2007). Saray received a scholarship (La Caixa, Spain) in 2007, allowing her to spend two years as a visiting researcher at the University of British Columbia, Canada. There she developed her research on embodied cognition that gave rise to a paper awarded a Graduate Student Paper Prize at the Pacific Division of the American Philosophical Association. She is working on the philosophy of cognitive science, with a special interest on plant cognition, and also on feminist philosophy and philosophy of science. Her PhD thesis, in preparation, elaborates on a radical, non-computationalist reading of the embodied cognition view.

Joseph E. Brenner was born in Paris in 1934, the son of the American sculptor Michael Brenner. After primary and secondary education in New York, he received B.A. and M.S. degrees from the University of Chicago. In 1958, he earned a Ph.D. in Organic Chemistry from the University of Wisconsin, followed by post-doctoral studies at the Swiss Federal Institute of Technology, Zurich and the Massachusetts Institute of Technology. In 1960, he joined the E. I. Du Pont de Nemours Company as a polymer chemist. From 1965 to his retirement in 1994, he was involved in corporate development with Du Pont International in Geneva, Switzerland. In 1998, he began collaboration with the International Center for Transdisciplinary Research (CIRET) in Paris. Dr. Brenner is a member of the American Association for the Advancement of Science; the New York Academy of Sciences; and the Swiss Society for Logic and the Philosophy of Science.

Selmer Bringsjord specializes in the logico-mathematical and philosophical foundations of artificial intelligence (AI) and cognitive science. He also specializes in building AI systems on the basis of formal reasoning, including ones assist intelligence analysts (e.g., the Slate system), and ones that are at least *apparently* creative (e.g., the Brutus system). He received the bachelor's degree from the University of Pennsylvania, and the PhD from Brown University in 1987, where he studied under Roderick Chisholm (and also was introduced to AI there in Eugene Charniak's *Intro to AI* class). Since 87 he has been on faculty in the Departments of Cognitive Science and Computer Science at Rensselaer Polytechnic Institute (RPI) in Troy, New York, where as a Full Professor he teaches AI, formal logic, human and machine reasoning, and philosophy of AI. Funding for his R&D has come from the Luce Foundation, the National Science Foundation, AT&T, IBM, Apple, AFRL, ARDA/DTO/IARPA, DARPA, AFOSR, and other sponsors. Bringsjord is author of the critically acclaimed What Robots Can & Can't Be (1992, Kluwer), concerned with the future of attempts to create robots that behave as humans. His most recent book is Superminds: People Harness Hypercomputation, and More (2003, Kluwer). Before this book he wrote, with Dave Ferrucci, Artificial Intelligence and Literary Creativity: Inside the Mind of Brutus, A Storytelling Machine, published by Erlbaum. He is the author of Abortion: A Dialogue, published by Hackett. Bringsjord's first novel, Soft Wars, was published by Penguin USA. Dr. Bringsjord is the author of papers ranging in approach from the mathematical to the informal, and covering such areas as AI, logic, gaming, philosophy of mind, and ethics. (Many of his publications are available on his web site.) He has lectured and interviewed in person across the United States, and in many other countries, including England, Scotland, Norway, France, Ireland, Italy, Mexico, Australia, Germany, Denmark, Thailand, Japan, The Netherlands, Spain, and Canada. He has interviewed on television and radio in many additional countries.

David Casacuberta is a philosophy of science professor in the Universidad Autònoma de Barcelona (Spain). He has a PhD in Philosophy and a master degree in "Cognitive sciences and Language". His current line of research is twofold: (1) The cognitive, cultural and social impact of new media; (2) Philosophical foundations of Artificial Intelligence, specially those related to the "3rd generation of cognitive sciences" such as enactive artificial intelligence, artificial emotions, morphological computing and social robots. He is a member of The Spanish Society of Logic, Methodology and Philosophy of Science.government, The consolidated research group GEHUCT (Grup d'Estudis Interdisciplinaris sobre Ciència i Tecnologia), The research project TECNOCOG (Philosophy, Technology and Cognition Research Group) financed by the Spanish government.He works for Transit Projectes as project manager and scientific coordinator for the EU Project E-learning for E-inclusion (www.el4ei.net) under the E-learning program. He is also a member of the Spanish think-tank edemocracia (www.edemocracia.com) devoted to the study on how ICT can improve democratic processes such as voting and participation. He is also a the secretary of the Spanish chapter of Computer Professionals for Social Responsibility (www.cpsr.org) and the Spanish representative in the International Coalition European Digital Rights (http://www.edri.org/)

Matteo Casu graduated in philosophy at Università degli Studi di Genova in 2006 and discussed his master thesis in philosophy in 2008. During the master he approached computer science topics such as mathematical logic and artificial intelligence. From January 2009 he is Ph.D. student at the Department of Communication, Computer and System Sciences (Dist) at Università degli Studi di Genova. His research interests include logic and ontologies for the semantic web.

Timothy R. Colburn. He received his Ph.D. in philosophy from Brown University in 1979, and his M.S. in computer science from Michigan State University in 1981. He has worked as a philosophy professor, a computer programmer, and a research scientist in articial intelligence for the aerospace and defense industry. Since 1988 he has been an associate professor of computer science at the University of Minnesota-Duluth where he teaches software engineering and does research in philosophy of computer science. In 1993 he co-edited the book Program Verication: Fundamental Issues in Computer Science, published by Kluwer. In 2000 he was the sole author of Philosophy and Computer Science, published by M. E. Sharpe. He spends as much time as possible at his cabin on the north shore of Lake Superior.

Dr.**Simon Colton** is a senior lecturer in Computing at Imperial College London. He is an AI researcher who leads the Computational Creativity Group, which studies the application of AI techniques to creative tasks in mathematics, graphic design, visual arts and video game design (www.doc.ic.ac.uk/ccg). He is the author of more than 100 research papers, and his work has been recognised both nationally, with a BCS/CPHC distinguished dissertation award, and internationally, with a best paper award at AAAI 2000. He is a leader of the EPSRC-funded AI and Games Industry/Academia research network (www.aigamesnetwork.org), and is the principal investigator on four current EPSRC/TSB funded projects.

Hilmi Demir received his B.A. and M.A. in philosophy from Boğaziçi University in Istanbul. He completed his Ph.D. at Indiana University – Bloomington in 2006, in philosophy and cognitive science, with a dissertation entitled "Error Comes with Imagination: A Probabilistic Theory of Mental Content." He served as an Assistant Professor of Philosophy at California State – San Bernardino for one year upon finishing his education, and is now an Assistant Professor at Bilkent University in Ankara, Turkey. His research interests include philosophy of information, philosophy of Cognitive Science, interpretations of probability and counterfactuals.

Antoni Diller was born in Birmingham, England, of Polish parents who were forced to leave their homeland during the Second World War. After reading mathematics and philosophy at Cambridge, I went to Leeds to study Frege under Peter Geach and obtained a PhD for my thesis, "Frege's Theory of Functions in Application to Linguistic Structures". I worked for a year as a computer programmer before studying Computation at the Programming Research Group in Oxford, obtaining an MSc in 1985. Since 1987, I have been a lecturer in the School of Computer Science at the University of Birmingham. To begin with, my research there was on formal methods and the implementation of functional programming languages using combinators, but in recent years my interests have returned to philosophy and especially to testimony and Popper; I won the 2008 Sir Karl Popper Essay Prize for "On Critical and Pancritical Rationalism".

Gordana Dodig-Crnkovic. She is an Associate Professor in Computer Science at the University of Mälardalen, Sweden. Her primary research interests are in computing and philosophy, information science, theory of computing and philosophy of information. Her background is in theoretical physics; she has a degree in computer science, and teaches on formal languages and automata theory, research methodology, theory of science, professional ethics and computing and philosophy. She has published on the theory of info-computational naturalism, information and computation semantics, computing and philosophy and ethics of computing and information.

Juan Manuel Durán. I hold a Bs. in Computer Science by the University of Córdoba, Argentina and a M.A. in Philosophy by the University of Córdoba, Argentina. I have won "Premio Universidad", 2008 award given by the University of Córdoba. I have teached and worked on epistemological problems of psychology at the Faculty of Psicology, in Argentina. I have also teached Logic, Philosophy of Science, Computer science in different faculties at the University of Córdoba. Actually I am a phd student at SimTech, Universität Stuttgart, Germany with the project EPIPRAG: Epistemological status of computer simulations. This project is related to philosophical problems of computer simulations as well as general problems of philosophy of science and foundations of computer science.

Luciano Floridi (www.philosophyofinformation.net) is Professor of Philosophy at the University of Hertfordshire, where he holds the Research Chair in Philosophy of Information and the UNESCO Chair in Information and Computer Ethics, and Fellow of St Cross College, University of Oxford. He is the founder and director of the Oxford University Information Ethics research Group, and best known for his research on the philosophy of information and on information ethics. His forthcoming books are: *The Philosophy of Information* (OUP); *Information*, (OUP, VSI series); and the *Handbook of Information and Computer Ethics* (CUP). He is currently President of the *International Association for Computing And Philosophy* (www.ia-cap.org). In 2009, he became the first philosopher to be appointed Gauss Professor by the Academy of Sciences in Göttingen, was awarded the Barwise Medal by the American Philosophical Association and was elected Fellow of the Society for the Study of Artificial Intelligence and the Simulation of Behaviour (AISB).

Dr. **Gudmund Grov** is a Research Associate within the School of Informatics at the University of Edinburgh. Before that, he worked at the School of Mathematical and Computer Sciences within Heriot-Watt University, where he also obtained his PhD in March 2009. His research expertise lies in the area of formal verification and software specification. His PhD focused on verifying and transforming software written in Hume, a new and novel programming language, using the Temporal Logic of Actions (TLA). More recently, he has been working on developing the notion of reasoned modelling, which studies the interplay between reasoning and modelling within formal modelling notations, in particular Event-B.

Dr. **Markus Guhe** is a research fellow at the University of Edinburgh in the *Wheelbarrow* project. He studied Informatics and Linguistics at TU Berlin and UCL and obtained a PhD in Informatics from the University of Hamburg. His research focuses on understanding the high-level conceptual structures that humans use in interaction with the external world. He works in particular on cognitive models of the incremental changes in conceptual structures involved in human dialogue and incremental language generation. In the *Wheelbarrow* project he develops cognitive models of the metaphoric processes that drive new inventions in mathematical thinking.

Roswitha Hofmann, Mag.rer.soc.oec., Dr. phil. (University of Vienna), Assistant Professor at the WU Vienna (Department of Management/Academic Unit for Gender and Diversity Management) since March 2009. Her research interests and publications cover areas of Sociology of Science and Technology, Gender and Diversity Studies with special focus on learning in organizations and on gender diversity/sexual orientation. Latest publications: Danowitz, M.A., Hanappi-Egger, E., Hofmann, R. 2009. The development and implementation of a diversity management curriculum. Organizational change through exploration and exploitation. International Journal of Educational Management 23 (7): 590-603. Hanappi-Egger, E., Hermann, A., Hofmann, R. 2009. More Than Money: Micro-Credit-Systems: A Tool For Social Change?. Global Business & Economics Anthology I (March): 58-66. Hofmann, R., Fleischmann, A., Bendl, R.. 2009. Queer Perspectives on Diversity Management: Reading Codes of Conduct from a Queer Perspective. Journal of Management and Organization 10-25.

Dr.**Andrew Ireland** is a Reader in Computer Science within the School of Mathematical and Computer Sciences (MACS) at Heriot-Watt University. He has substantial research experience in the area of automated reasoning and automated software engineering. He has played a central role in the development of proof planning, an AI based automated reasoning technique. He has a strong track-record in terms of applied research. His industrial collaborators include Praxis High Integrity Systems, QinetiQ and BAE Systems. He has had organizational involvement with numerous international workshops and conference. He was Programme Co-Chair in 2008 for the IEEE/ACM International Conference on Automated Software Engineering (ASE), and will be Conference Chair for the International Conference on Verified Software: Theories, Tools & Experiments (VSTTE) in 2010.

Maria Teresa Llano is a PhD student in the School of Mathematical and Computer Sciences at Heriot-Watt University. She is working under the supervision of Dr. Andrew Ireland and Professor Rob Pooley. Previously she did an MSc in Software Engineering also at Heriot-Watt University, and studied an undergraduate degree in Computer Science at Icesi University in Colombia. She is interested in formal approaches to software engineering, the specification and verification of UML models, and the use of patterns and anti-patterns for the design of software systems. Her current research, within the SEAR project (Systems Evolution via Animation and Reasoning), is focused on the use of animation and automated reasoning techniques for the evolution of systems modelled with the UML-B and the Event-B languages.

Prof. Dr. **Klaus Mainzer** studied mathematics, physics, and philosophy, Ph.D. (1973) and habilitation (1979), assistant and lecturer (1973-1979) at the university of Münster; Heisenberg-scholarship (1980); 1981-1988 professor for foundations and history of exact sciences at the University of Constance, vice-president of the university of Constance (1985-1988); 1988-2008 chair for philosophy of science, dean (1999-2000), director of the Institute of Philosophy (1989-2008) and of the Institute of Interdisciplinary Informatics (1998-2008) at the University of Augsburg; since 2008 chair for philosophy of science and technology, director of the Carl von Linde-Academy and member of the advisory board of the Institute for Advanced Study at the Technical University of Munich; member of several academies and interdisciplinary organizations (e.g., European Academy of Sciences/Academia Europaea in London), coeditor of international scientific journals; guest-professor in Brazil, China, India, Japan, Korea, Russia, USA, and the European Union; author of internationally translated books, e.g.: *Symmetries of Nature* (1996); *Thinking in Complexity. The Computational Dynamics of Matter, Mind, and Mankind* (5th enlarged edition 2007); *The Little Book of Time* (2002); *Symmetry and Complexity. The Spirit and Beauty of Nonlinear Science* (2005).

Michael Nicolaidis is a Research Director at the French National Research Center and leader of the ARIS group at the TIMA Laboratory. His research interests include DFT; fault tolerance; yield, power dissipation and reliability issues in CMOS and post-CMOS nanotechnologies; computing architectures for nano-technologies; philosophy of science and computational interpretations of modern physics. He published more than 250 papers; authored one book and several book chapters; edited one book and five journal special issues. He authored 27 patents. His memory BIST synthesis technology; his programmable memory BIST architectures and Built-In Self-repair architectures were licensed to two worldwide EDA leaders. He received three Best Paper Awards. His work was selected among the most influential EDA papers for the 10 years of DATE. He was/is Program Chair, General Chair and Steering Committee member of numerous IEEE conferences, member of the editorial board of the IEEE Design & Test of Computers and Vice-Chair of the IEEE Computer Society TTTC. He is founder of iRoC Technologies and cofounder of Infiniscale.

Dr. **Alison Pease** obtained her PhD in 2007 after completing an MA in mathematics/Philosophy from the University of Aberdeen and an MSc in Artificial Intelligence from the University of Edinburgh. Her PhD thesis was entitled *A Computational Model of Lakatos-style Reasoning* and described her implementation and evaluation of the theory of mathematical progress described in *Lakatos's Proofs and Refutations*. She has authored various publications, and was an invited speaker to the European Conference on Computing and Philosophy in 2004. She was joint programme chair for the second and third Joint International Workshops on Computational Creativity, in 2005 and 2006, and has served on the programme committee for the same workshop series for the last six years and for the "AI and Creativity in Arts and Science" series in 2002 and 2003. Prior to obtaining her PhD Alison worked as a mathematics teacher for four years, teaching levels from Special Needs to A level students. She holds a PGCE specialising in teaching mathematics.

Ramin Ramezani is a PhD student in Artificial Intelligence, Department of Computing, Imperial College London. He is working under the supervision of Dr. Simon Colton and is a member of Computational Creativity Group with interests in the automatic reformulation of AI problems and combined reasoning. His work is to apply different problem solving techniques such as constraint solving, machine learning and theorem proving on AI problems in order to construct and evaluate a computational theory of axiom formation/reformulation which aims to simplifying certain types of AI problems. He is also interested in unifying such methods with a cognitively inspired model of axiom formation and reformulation.

Walter Riofrío's research is related to Theoretical and Evolutionary Biology under the umbrella of the Sciences of Complexity. In particular, his interests lie in studying time periods before the origin of living systems, or in other words, in the pre-biotic era. He is also interested in studying the emergence of cognition from an evolutionary point of view. He has published works on these topics in journals and as chapters in different books. Riofrío's first formation was in biochemistry, while later on his doctoral studies were in philosophy.

Uwe Riss joined SAP AG in February 1998 and has worked as a senior researcher for SAP Research since 2004. He worked in the NEPOMUK project on social semantic desktops and task management and is among the initiators and researchers of the MATURE project dealing with the topic of knowledge maturing. His research interests are primarily focused on knowledge management, ranging from its philosophical foundations to its application and development in the areas of task and agile process management. His philosophical interests cover epistemology and action theory as well as the philosophical foundation of informatics. He received a doctoral degree in theoretical chemistry from the University of Heidelberg and a university degree in mathematics from the University of Marburg.

David Saab is a PhD student at the College of Information Sciences and Technology at Penn State University, where he is also a researcher at the Center for Network-Centered Cognition and Information Fusion. His primary research is focused on information system ontologies as manifestations of cultural schemas, the semantics of cultural experience and ways in which to use ontologies, semantics, tagging, and folksonomies to represent, visualize and facilitate meaningful information flows via technology. David's philosophical interests cover existentialist ontology, phenomenology, hermeneutics, philosophy of science, philosophy of information and information ethics. He has university degrees in psychology and philosophy and a master's degree in intercultural relations. He expects to complete his PhD dissertation in 2010.

Gary M. Shute received his B.A. from South Dakota State University in 1975, majoring in mathematics with a minor in physics. He completed his Ph.D. in mathematics in 1982, taking several philosophy courses along the way. After a year teaching mathematics, he took two years of graduate courses in computer science. He started teaching computer science at University of Minnesota-Duluth in 1985, and has taught there since. He has taught a wide variety of computer science courses, including machine organization, computer architecture, operating systems, computer networks, data structures, software engineering, and object-oriented design. More recently, he has focused more on his longstanding interest: understanding the human mind and its ability to make sense of the world.

Luc Schneider (*1968, Luxembourg) is currently a researcher at the Institute for Formal Ontology and Medical Information Science, Saarland University (Saarbrücken, Germany), as well as an associate post-doc at the Institut Jean Nicod (Paris, France). He holds a Ph.D. in Philosophy from the University of Geneva (2007), a M.Sc. in Computing Science from Imperial College, London (2001) and a M.A. in Philosophy and in Linguistics from the University of Tübingen (1993). Luc Schneider held research and teaching positions at the Italian National Research Council in Padova (2001-2002), the Institute for Formal Ontology and Medical Information Science in Leipzig, Germany (2002-2003), the Department of Philosophy of the University of Geneva (2004-2005, 2007-2008), the Swiss Federal Institute of Technology in Lausanne (2005-2006) as well as the Institut Jean Nicod (2008-2009). His main research interests are in formal and applied ontology as well as philosophical logic. In addition, he has done research on the following topics: multi-agent systems, logic programming, natural language processing and (Open Access) scientific publishing.

Dr. **Alan Smaill** has worked in the area of Automated Reasoning since 1986. He holds a D.,Phil. from the University of Oxford in Mathematical Logic, and currently teaches in the School of Informatics in the University of Edinburgh and is the director of the Centre for Intelligent Systems and their Applications at the University of Edinburgh. His research work centres around reasoning in higher-order and constructive logics, with applications in program construction and automated software engineering, and he has published widely in this area. He has been a grant-holder on an project on Logical Frameworks and headed an grant on the mechanisation of first-order temporal logic via embedding into a higher-order representation. He currently leads an grant on a cognitive model of axiom formulation and reformulation with applications to AI and software engineering.

Raymond Turner is the Professor of Computation at the University of Essex. His research interests include logic and computation and the philosophy of mathematics. He is on the Editorial boards of the Journal of Logic and Computation and the Stanford Encyclopaedia of Philosophy. Some of his books are *Operating Systems: Design and Implementations* (1986, Macmillan Pub Co), *Constructive Foundations for Functional Languages* (1991, Mcgraw Hill Book Co Ltd), *Truth and Modality for Knowledge Representation* (Artificial Intelligence) (1991, The MIT Press) or *Computable Models* (2009, Springer).

Kevin Warwick is Professor of Cybernetics at the University of Reading, England, where he carries out research in artificial intelligence, control, robotics and cyborgs. Kevin was born in Coventry, UK and left school to join British Telecom, at the age of 16. At 22 he took his first degree at Aston University, followed by a PhD and research post at Imperial College, London. He subsequently held positions at Oxford, Newcastle and Warwick Universities before being offered the Chair at Reading, at the age of 33. As well as publishing over 500 research papers, Kevin's experiments into implant technology led to him being featured as the cover story on the US magazine, 'Wired'. Kevin has been awarded higher doctorates (DSc) both by Imperial College and the Czech Academy of Sciences, Prague, and received Honorary Doctorates from Aston University and Coventry University in 2008. He was presented with The Future of Health Technology Award in MIT, was made an Honorary Member of the Academy of Sciences, St. Petersburg, in 2004 received The IEE Senior Achievement Medal and in 2008 the Mountbatten Medal. In 2000 Kevin presented the Royal Institution Christmas Lectures, entitled "The Rise of the Robots". Kevin's most recent research involves the invention of an intelligent deep brain stimulator to counteract the effects of Parkinson Disease tremors. The tremors are predicted and a current signal is applied to stop the tremors before they start – this is shortly to be trialled in human subjects. Another project involves the use of cultured/biological neural networks to drive robots around – the brain of each robot is made of neural tissue. Perhaps Kevin is though best known for his pioneering experiments involving a neuro-surgical implantation into the median nerves of his left arm to link his nervous system directly to a computer to assess the latest technology for use with the disabled. He was successful with the first extra-sensory (ultrasonic) input for a human and with the first purely electronic telegraphic communication experiment between the nervous systems of two humans.

Dr. **Jutta Weber** is philosopher, science & technology studies scholar and media theorist (www. juttaweber.eu). Recently, she is visiting professor at the Centre for Gender Research at the University Uppsala, Sweden. Her research focuses on the production of technoscientific knowledge (i.a. cybernetics, AI, robotics, computer science), concept transfer between technosciences and everyday life as well as cyber ethics, surveillance studies and theory & didactics of transdisciplinarity. She was senior research fellow at the Centre for Science Studies, Lancaster University (UK) and at the Department of History of Science at California Institute of Technology (USA). She held several visiting professorships (i.a. University Duisburg-Essen; TU Braunschweig; University Freiburg). In 2006/07 she was fellow of the international research group 'Science in the Context of Application' at the Centre for Interdisciplinary Studies ZIF, University Bielefeld; http://www.uni-bielefeld.de/ZIF/FG/2006Application/fellow_weber. html). From 2006-2008, she was part of the EU-project ETHICBOTS http://ethicbots.na.infn.it/. Currently she is completing her book 'Fragments of a Philosophy of Technoscience'.

Pak-Hang Wong finished both his BA (1st Hons) in History & Philosophy and M.Phil in Philosophy at the University of Hong Kong, and has taught Philosophy and Liberal Studies at various tertiary institutions in Hong Kong. He is now a PhD Research Fellow at the Department of Philosophy, University of Twente. He is currently working on his PhD research project, "Cultural, Political and Religious Ideologies and the Appraisal of New Media", which is a sub-project of the VICI project on the "Evaluation of the Cultural Quality of New Media" funded by *Netherlands* Organization for Scientific Research (NWO).

Index

Symbols

A